www.wadsworth.com

wadsworth.com is the World Wide Web site for Wadsworth Publishing Company and is your direct source to dozens of online resources.

At *wadsworth.com* you can find out about supplements, demonstration software, and student resources. You can also send e-mail to many of our authors and preview new publications and exciting new technologies.

wadsworth.com
Changing the way the world learns®

Introduction to Physical Anthropology

Eighth Edition

Robert Jurmain
San Jose State University

Harry Nelson
Emeritus, Foothill College

Lynn Kilgore
Colorado State University

Wenda Trevathan
New Mexico State University

Wadsworth
Thomson Learning™

Australia • Canada • Denmark • Japan • Mexico • New Zealand • Philippines • Puerto Rico
Singapore • South Africa • Spain • United Kingdom • United States

Publisher: Eve Howard
Development Editor: Robert Jucha
Assistant Editor: Ari Levenfeld
Editorial Assistant: Jennifer Jones
Marketing Assistant: Kelli Goslin
Project Editor: Jerilyn Emori
Print Buyer: Karen Hunt
Permissions Editor: Susan Walters
Production: Hespenheide Design

Interior and Cover Designer: Hespenheide Design
Copyeditor: Janet Greenblatt
Illustrators: Alexander Productions, Paragon 3,
    Sue Sellars, Cyndie Wooley
Cover Image: Reconstructed cranium of *Australopithecus garhi*
    from Bouri, Ethiopia. Approximate age 2.5 million years.
    © 1999 David L. Brill/Atlanta
Compositor: Hespenheide Design
Printer: World Color Book Services/Versailles

Library of Congress Cataloging-in-Publication Data
Introduction to physical anthropology / Robert Jurmain . . .
    [et al.]. — 8th ed.
        p.   cm.
    Includes bibliographical references and index.
    ISBN 0-534-51444-8 (pbk.)
    1. Physical anthropology.   I. Jurmain, Robert.
GN60.I57   1999
599.9—dc21
99-32906

Wadsworth/Thomson Learning
10 Davis Drive
Belmont, CA 94002-3098
USA
www.wadsworth.com

International Headquarters
Thomson Learning
290 Harbor Drive, 2nd Floor
Stamford, CT 06902-7477
USA

UK/Europe/Middle East
Thomson Learning
Berkshire House
168-173 High Holborn
London WC1V 7AA
United Kingdom

Asia
Thomson Learning
60 Albert Street #15-01
Albert Complex
Singapore 189969

Canada
Nelson/Thomson Learning
1120 Birchmount Road
Scarborough, Ontario M1K 5G4
Canada

Contents

The Biological Basis of Life

Heredity and Evolution

An Overview of the Living Primates

Fundamentals of Primate Behavior

Models for Human Evolution

Processes of Macroevolution: Mammalian/Primate Evolutionary History

Paleoanthropology: Reconstructing Early Hominid Behavior and Ecology

Hominid Origins

Homo erectus and Contemporaries

Neandertals and Other Archaic *Homo sapiens*

Homo sapiens sapiens

Microevolution in Modern Human Populations

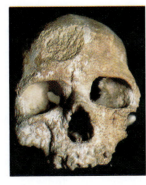

15

Human Variation and Adaptation

16

The Anthropological Perspective on the Human Life Course

Preface

The history of our textbooks has always been characterized by a continual process of revision as we have attempted to provide a current and accessible synthesis of the ever-changing field of physical anthropology. Consequently, readers who are familiar with earlier editions will find numerous alterations in both the organization and content of this 8th edition of *Introduction to Physical Anthropology*.

Organization of the Eighth Edition

Two immediately obvious major organizational changes are a reduction in the number of chapters (from 18 in the 7th edition to 16 in the current edition) and an alteration in chapter sequence. First, the reduction in number of chapters was accomplished by combining (and somewhat condensing) materials on mammalian and primate evolution (formerly Chapters 8 and 12, now found in Chapter 8) and on Plio-Pleistocene hominids (formerly Chapters 14 and 15, now Chapter 10). We believe this organization is more efficient and pedagogically more succinct.

Second, the materials on human variation, microevolution, adaptation, growth, and development have been moved from the earlier sections of the book (in the 7th and most earlier editions) to their current position as the concluding three chapters. Again, we feel that pedagogically this more chronological sequence is clearer then the prior arrangement. Further, we conclude from reviewer comments and surveys that many instructors prefer this ordering of topics. Finally, by placing Chapter 16 at the end of the book, with its comprehensive anthropological discussion of the human life course, we are able to draw upon much of the material presented in the rest of the text. Consequently, Chapter 16 now serves as a more appropriate concluding chapter (as reflected in its new title, The Anthropological Perspective on the Human Life Course).

However, we are also aware that a substantial number of instructors prefer to deal with the materials on human variation and adaptation in their former chapter sequence. Accordingly, as in all our previous editions, we have made a concerted effort to allow chapters to be assigned in variable order. Thus, for those more comfortable with the chapter sequence in the last several editions of the text, Chapters 14, 15, and 16 still can be readily accommodated following Chapter 4.

We also have significantly reorganized some of the topical materials in Chapters 6 and 7. This reorganization better divides these primate materials so that the basic aspects of primate social behavior and ecology are covered in Chapter 6, while the interpretation of such data for reconstructing human origins is emphasized in Chapter 7.

What's New in the Eighth Edition?

Physical anthropology is a challenging and dynamic field, and many updates are contained in this edition. In Chapter 3, there is a new discussion of mitochondrial DNA; the section that concerns gene function has been expanded to include coverage of regulatory genes, and coding and noncoding DNA sequences (exons and introns). Also, in Chapter 3, there is a new section on genetic technologies that includes such topics as the Human Genome Project, polymerase chain reaction (PCR), and cloning. New to Chapter 4 are discussions of pleiotropy and commonly held misconceptions of dominant and recessive alleles.

In Chapter 8 there is greatly expanded coverage of the basic interpretive perspective used today in paleontology, i.e., phylogenetic systematics ("cladistics") as it compares with more traditional approaches (i.e., evolutionary systematics). We feel that, at the beginning of the materials dealing with fossils (Chapters 8-13), it is important for students to understand how the current approach is used. There is also considerable change of focus in Chapter 9, where we now concentrate much more on environmental and behavioral reconstructions of early hominids (as reflected in the new chapter title, Paleoanthropology: Reconstructing the Environments and Behavior of Early Hominids).

New fossil discoveries from both South and East Africa (e.g., *Ardipithecus; Australopithecus garhi*) are covered in Chapter 10, and interpretations are ventured, as far as current evidence permits. We have also revised, wherever appropriate, the dating estimates for fossil hominid finds, including the surprisingly late dates for the Ngandong *Homo erectus* evidence from Java (Chapter 11). In addition, fascinating new materials and interpretations of discoveries from Ceprano, Dmanisi, and Atapuerca are also discussed in Chapter 11; the exciting results of attempts to extract and sequence Neandertal DNA are covered in Chapter 12. Contemporary (and sometimes controversial) perspectives relating to the latter stages of human evolution are also greatly expanded in this edition, especially those views relating to species diversity within *Homo* (*Homo rudolfensis, Homo ergaster,* and *Homo heidelbergensis*). A comprehensive discussion of these issues is incorporated into Chapter 12 as a major new section.

Chapter 15, *Human Variation and Adaptation,* includes an expanded treatment of infectious disease and its role as a selective agent. Particular emphasis is placed on HIV/AIDS, its evolutionary history and recent studies of population variation with regard to HIV resistance. This discussion of infectious disease also concerns itself with the role of cultural factors such as population growth, climate change, and overuse of antibiotics in the reemergence of some infectious diseases. In addition, Chapter 16 now more clearly emphasizes the *biocultural* approach to understanding how humans grow and develop in the context of culture. Further, the material concerning nutritional and hormonal influences on growth has been simplified/reduced, while material on genetic effects has been expanded. A new section on aging (separate from the section on adulthood) has also been added. One final minor (but frequent) change is our adoption of the traditional spelling for "archaeology." In the U.S. either spelling is accepted, but most professionals over the last two decades have returned to the more traditional usage.

Features

Introduction to Physical Anthropology contains a number of special features that will heighten student interest and learning. A final organizational change is found in the

Issues. In the 7th edition Issues were found interspersed with Guest Essays in each chapter. Following the suggestions of our reviewers, we have returned to using only Issues, and they are now placed in alternating, odd-numbered chapters. As in the last edition, the Issues are placed at the end of chapters, in order to better emphasize their critical thinking perspective. In this regard, we also continue to include specific critical thinking questions with each of these short, nontechnical compositions.

Of the eight issues, three are new to this edition: Are the Sites at Olduvai Really "Sites"? (Chapter 9); Man the Hunter, Woman the Gatherer (Chapter 11); and The Evolution of Language (Chapter 13). These Issues, as well as the new and expanded focus of Chapter 9, all reflect the greater *behavioral* emphasis of this edition.

Finally, we have continued to incorporate a variety of pedagogical aids which have become popular in earlier editions. These include a running glossary, a glossary at the end of the text, boxes, tables, anatomical charts, maps, and time lines. We should also note that as in all our texts, we provide systematic citation in the text and a full bibliography at the back.

Multimedia Learning Aids

This edition is also designed to allow students easier access to multimedia learning aids. A major new addition is the systematic integration of links with the Virtual Laboratories for Introductory Physical Anthropology CD-ROM, prepared by John Kappelman of the University of Texas at Austin. Throughout the text, in the margins, there are icons [**show example here**] linking the concepts discussed in the book with specific sections of the CD-ROM.

Another new addition to the 8th edition is a greatly expanded Internet Resource section at the end of each chapter. Included in this section are Internet exercises, incorporating specific sites on the Internet, designed to help students become more competent in using the Internet. Also included in the Internet Resources Section are further exercises utilizing InfoTrac College Edition, an on-line library. Tracey O'Rourke of San Jose State University prepared both the Internet and InfoTrac College Edition exercises.

Acknowledgments

Over the more than 20 years we have worked on editions of this text we have been greatly assisted by many colleagues, students, and friends. For this edition we are especially indebted to the following reviewers:

Diane E. Barbolla
San Diego Mesa College

Innui Choi
California Polytechnic State University–San Luis Obispo

Hilton Pereira da Silva
Ohio State University

Philip de Barros
Palomar College

Charles B. Eastman
Moorpark College

Suzanne K. Engler
Los Angeles Valley College

Rosanne L. Higgins
State University of New York, College at Potsdam

Ann L. Magennis
Colorado State University

Jonathan Marks
University of California–Berkeley

Mark G. Plew
Boise State University

Craig B. Stanford
University of Southern California

Andrea Wiley
James Madison University

Sloan R. Williams
University of Illinois at Chicago

We would like to thank the following individuals who took the time to respond to our survey that provided useful insights into the teaching of physical anthropology:

Leon H. Albert
Los Angeles Valley College

Robert L. Anemone
Western Michigan University

Lauren J. Arenson
Pasadena City College

Debra Bolter
Modesto Junior College

John Boyer
Union College

Doug Broadfield
City University of New York, Herbert H. Lehman College

Margaret R. Clarke
Tulane University

Linda S. Curran
University of Colorado at Denver

Glen H. Doran
Florida State University

Faith L. Duncan
Red Rocks Community College

Elizabeth Goerke
College of Marin

Jere D. Haas
Cornell University

Lorena M. Havill
Indiana University

Jane Hoff
University of South Alabama

Barry D. Kass
Orange County (NY) Community College

Kenneth A. R. Kennedy
Cornell University

Peer H. Moore-Jansen
Wichita State University

Wes Niewoehner
University of New Mexico

Anne Pike-Tay
Vassar College

Elizabeth Salter
University of Texas at Dallas

Dennis Satterlee
Northeast Louisiana University

David R. Schwimmer
Columbus State University

In addition, we thank the reviewers of the previous edition:

David R. Begun
University of Toronto

Susan Cachel
Rutgers University

Steven Churchill
Duke University

Barbara J. King
College of William and Mary

Mary H. Manhein
Louisiana State University

Sam D. Stout
University of Missouri, Columbia

Linda L. Taylor
University of Miami

William Wihr
Portland Community College

Marcus Young Owl
California State University–Long Beach

We also wish to express our enduring gratitude to our friend, Denise Simon, former editor at Wadsworth Publishing Company. Our deep appreciation for their support and professionalism also goes to former editor, Halee Dinsey; Robert Jucha, Senior Developmental Editor; Ari Levenfeld, Assistant Editor; and to Jennifer Jones, Editorial Assistant. We wish to extend our thanks to Eve Howard, Publisher; and Susan Badger, President and CEO; for the interest they have shown in our books. For overseeing the book through the many stages of its production, we wish to thank Jerilyn Emori, Senior Project Editor. Moreover, for their unwavering expertise and patience we are indebted to our copyeditor Janet Greenblatt and our production coordinator Gary Hespenheide.

To the many friends and colleagues who have generously provided photographs we are greatly appreciative: C. K. Brain, Günter Bräuer, Desmond Clark, Raymond Dart, Jean deRousseau, Denis Etler, Diane France, David Frayer, Kathleen Galvin, David Haring, Ellen Ingmanson, Fred Jacobs, Peter Jones, Arlene Kruse, Richard Leakey, Carol Lofton, Lorna Moore, John Oates, Bonnie Pedersen, Lorna Pierce, David Pilbeam, William Pratt, Judith Regensteiner, Sastrohamijoyo Sartono, Wayne Savage, Eugenie Scott, Rose Sevick, Elwyn Simons, Meredith Small, Fred Smith, Judy Suchey, Li Tianyuan, Philip Tobias, Alan Walker, Milford Wolpoff, and Xinzhi Wu.

Robert Jurmain   Harry Nelson
Lynn Kilgore   Wenda Trevathan

Robert Jurmain and Lynn Kilgore dedicate this eighth edition to Brighton, a much loved and greatly missed friend.

1986–1998

Supplements

Supplements for Instructors

Instructor's Manual with Test Bank   Written by the text authors, the manual includes concept outlines, chapter overviews, learning objectives, and a Video/Film/Internet Resource Guide. The Test Bank provides 40 to 50 questions per chapter.

Computerized Testing   Thomson Learning Testing Tools is available for both Macintosh and Windows.

Transparency Acetates   Over 50 transparencies of the great artwork from the text are available.

Slides   Color slides of art found in the text are available.

AnthroLink CD-ROM   With this classroom presentation tool, instructors can easily assemble art and database files with lecture notes to create fluid lectures that may help stimulate and engage their students. It includes illustrations found in the book, art from other Wadsworth textbooks, and video. Upon its creation, a file or lecture with AnthroLink can be posted to the Web where students can access it for study needs.

Wadsworth Anthropology Video Library   Completely updated, qualified instructors can select from over 20 cultural and physical anthropology videos made available from such great series as *NOVA, Films for the Humanities and Sciences, The Disappearing World, and In Search of Human Origins*.

CNN Today Video Series: Physical Anthropology, Vol. 1 and 2   Instructors may choose between two 45-minute videotapes comprised of short clips from recent CNN broadcasts. Both videos illuminate the principles of physical anthropology and archaeology and their impact on today's world.

Web-Based Resources

Anthropology Online: Wadsworth Anthropology Resource Center   *http:///anthropology.wadsworth.com* At Anthropology Online: Wadsworth's Anthropology Resource Center, you can find surfing lessons (tips to find information on the Web), anthropology surfing, a career center, links to great anthropology Web sites and many other selections.

You will also find a text-specific Web page for *Introduction to Physical Anthropology,* Eighth Edition, by Jurmain, et al. You will have access to text-specific quizzes, flashcards, Internet projects, hyper-contents, and much more.

InfoTrac College Edition   There's no better reason to use the Internet than with Wadsworth's exclusive offer of InfoTrac College Edition. Give your students access to the over 900 scholarly and popular publications available on InfoTrac College Edition. Ask your Wadsworth representative how to get the four-month "account ID" for your students.

Let's Go Anthropology, Joan Ferrante, Northern Kentucky University

This is a URL directory specifically designed for anthropology that contains detailed descriptions of each Web site listed. This handy guide can be used as a resource for additional classroom assignments and exercises. This guide can be packaged with your text at a discount price, please see your Wadsworth sales representative for more details.

🌿 Supplements for Students

Virtual Laboratories for Physical Anthropology CD-ROM, Second Edition, John Kappelman

The new version of this Interactive CD-ROM provides students with a hands-on computer component for doing lab assignments at school or at home. It encourages students to actively participate in their physical anthropology lab or course through the taking of measurements and the plotting of data, as well as giving them a format for testing their knowledge of important concepts. Contains full-color images, video clips, 3-D animations, sound, and more. In addition, students can link between this CD and the Web page to access additional tutorial quizzes.

Study Guide, prepared by Marcus Young Owl and Denise Cucurny, California State University–Long Beach

Chapter-by-chapter resources for the student, including learning objective outlines, fill-in-the-blank chapter outlines, key terms, and extensive opportunities for self-quizzing.

Lab Manual and Workbook for Physical Anthropology, Diane L. France, Colorado State University

By emphasizing human osteology, forensic anthropology, anthropometry, primates, human evolution, and genetics, this lab manual provides students with hands-on lab assignments to help make the concepts of physical anthropology more clear. It contains short-answer questions, identification problems, and observation exercises.

Introduction

Introduction

See Virtual Lab 1, section II, part D, for a discussion of the place of hominids within the mammalian order of primates.*

■ **Hominidae**
The taxonomic family to which humans belong; also includes other, now extinct, bipedal relatives.

■ **Hominids**
Members of the family Hominidae.

FIGURE 1–1

Early hominid footprints at Laetoli. The tracks to the left were made by one individual, while those to the right appear to have been formed by two individuals, the second stepping in the tracks of the first.

One day, perhaps at the beginning of the rainy season some 3.7 million years ago, two or three individuals walked across a grassland savanna in what is now northern Tanzania in East Africa. These individuals were early members of the taxonomic family **Hominidae**, the family that also includes ourselves, modern *Homo sapiens*. Fortunately for us (the living descendants of those distant travelers), a record of their passage on that long-forgotten day remains in the form of fossilized footprints, preserved in hardened volcanic deposits.

As chance would have it, shortly after heels and toes were pressed into the dampened soil and volcanic ash of the area, a volcano, some 12 miles distant, erupted. The ensuing ashfall blanketed everything on the ground surface, including the footprints of the **hominids** and those of numerous other species as well. In time, the ash layer hardened into a deposit, which preserved a quite remarkable assortment of tracks and other materials that lay beneath it (Fig. 1–1).

These now-famous Laetoli prints indicate that two hominids, one smaller than the other, perhaps walked side by side, leaving parallel sets of tracks. But because the prints of the larger individual are obscured, possibly by those of a

*This CD-ROM icon indicates additional material that can be found on the *Virtual Laboratories for Physical Anthropology* CD-ROM, which is further described in the preface to this book.

third, it is unclear how many actually made that journey so long ago. What is clear from the prints is that they were left by an animal that habitually walked **bipedally** (on two feet). It is this critical feature that has led scientists to consider these ancient passersby as hominids.

In addition to the preserved footprints, scientists at Laetoli and elsewhere have discovered numerous fossilized skeletal remains of what we now call *Australopithecus afarensis*. These fossils and prints have volumes to say about the beings they represent, provided we can learn to interpret them.

What, then, have we actually gleaned from the meager evidence we possess of those creatures who beckon to us from an incomprehensibly distant past? Where did their journey take them that far-gone day, and why were they walking in that particular place? Were they foraging for food within the boundaries of their territory, or were they going to a nearby water source? Did the two (or three) indeed travel together at all, or did they simply use the same route within a short period of time?

We could ask myriad questions about these individuals, but we will never be able to answer them all. They walked down a path into what became their future, and their immediate journey has long since ended. It remains for us to sort out what little we can know about them and the **species** they represent. In this sense, their greater journey continues.

From the footprints and from fossilized fragmentary skeletons, we know that these hominids walked in an upright posture. Thus, they were, in many respects, anatomically similar to ourselves, but their brains were only about one-third the size of ours. Although they may have used stones and sticks as tools, much as modern chimpanzees do, there is no current evidence to suggest they manufactured stone tools. In short, these early hominids were very much at the mercy of nature's whims. They certainly could not outrun most predators, and their lack of large canine teeth rendered them relatively defenseless.

Chimpanzees often serve as living models for our early ancestors, but in fact, the earliest hominids occupied a different habitat, exploited different resources, and probably had more to fear from predators than do chimpanzees. However much we may be tempted to compare early hominids to living species, we must constantly remind ourselves that there is no living form that adequately represents them. Just like every other living thing, they were unique.

On July 20, 1969, a television audience numbering in the hundreds of millions watched as two human beings stepped out of a spacecraft and onto the surface of the moon. To anyone born after that date, this event is taken more or less for granted, even though it has not been repeated often. But the significance of that first moonwalk cannot be overstated, for it represents humankind's presumed mastery over the natural forces that govern our presence on earth. For the first time ever, people actually walked upon the surface of a celestial body that (as far as we know) has never given birth to biological life.

As the astronauts gathered geological specimens and frolicked in near weightlessness, they left traces of their fleeting presence in the form of footprints in the lunar dust (Fig. 1–2). On the atmosphereless surface of the moon, where no rain falls and no wind blows, the footprints remain undisturbed to this day. They survive as mute testimony to a brief visit by a medium-sized, big-brained creature who presumed to challenge the very forces that had created it.

We humans uncovered the Laetoli footprints, and we question the nature of the animal who made them. Perhaps one day, creatures as yet unimagined will ponder the essence of the being that made the lunar footprints. What do you suppose they will think?

▌ Bipedally
On two feet. Walking habitually on two legs is the single most distinctive feature of the Hominidae.

Discussions of fossil hominids and the record for human evolution are found in Virtual Labs 8–12.

▌ Species
A group of organisms that can interbreed to produce fertile offspring. Members of one species are reproductively isolated from members of all other species (i.e., they cannot mate with them to produce fertile offspring).

FIGURE 1–2

Human footprints left on the lunar surface during the Apollo mission.

Primate
A member of the order of mammals Primates (pronounced "pry-may´-tees"), which includes prosimians, monkeys, apes, and humans.

Many examples of evolution and human adaptation are given in Virtual Lab 2.

Culture
All aspects of human adaptation, including technology, traditions, language, and social roles. Culture is learned and transmitted from one generation to the next by nonbiological means.

We humans, who can barely comprehend a century, can only grasp at the enormity of 3.7 million years. We want to understand those creatures who traveled that day across the savanna. By what route did an insignificant but clever bipedal **primate** give rise to a species that would, in time, walk on the surface of a moon some 230,000 miles from earth? How did it come to be that in the relatively short (geologically speaking) span of fewer than 4 million years, an inconsequential savanna dweller evolved into the species that has developed the ability to dominate and destroy much (if not all) of life on the planet?

How did it happen that *Homo sapiens,* a result of the same evolutionary forces that produced all other life on this planet, gained the power to control the flow of rivers and alter the very climate in which we live? As tropical animals, how were we able to leave the tropics and disperse over most of the earth's land surfaces, and how did we adjust to local environmental conditions as we so expanded? How could our species, which numbered fewer than 1 billion individuals until the mid-nineteenth century, come to number nearly 6 billion worldwide today and, as we now do, add another billion every 11 years?

These are some of the many questions that physical or biological anthropologists attempt to answer, and these questions are largely the focus of the study of human evolution, variation, and adaptation. These issues, and many more, are the topics covered directly or indirectly in this text, for physical anthropology is, in part, human biology seen from an evolutionary perspective. However, physical anthropologists are not exclusively involved in the study of physiological systems and biological phenomena. When such topics are placed within the broader context of human evolution, another factor must also be considered: the role of **culture**.

Culture is an extremely important concept, not only as it pertains to modern human beings, but also in terms of its critical role in human evolution. It has been said that there are as many definitions of culture as there are people who attempt to define it. Quite simply, culture can be said to be the strategy by which humans adapt to the natural environment. In this sense, culture includes technologies that range from stone tools to computers; subsistence patterns ranging from hunting and gathering to agribusiness on a global scale; housing types, from thatched huts to skyscrapers; and clothing, from animal skins to high-tech synthetic fibers (Fig. 1–3). Because religion, values, social organization, language, kinship, marriage rules, gender roles, inheritance of property, and so on, are all aspects of culture, each culture shapes people's perceptions of the external environment, or world view, in particular ways that distinguish that culture from all others.

One fundamental point to remember is that culture is *learned* and not biologically determined. Culture is transmitted from generation to generation independently of biological factors (i.e., genes). For example, if a young girl of Vietnamese ancestry is raised in the United States by English-speaking parents, she will acquire English as her native language. She will eat Western foods with Western utensils and will wear Western clothes. In short, she will be a product of Western culture, because that is the culture she will have learned. We are all products of the culture in which we are socialized, and since most human behavior is learned, it clearly is also culturally patterned.

But as biological organisms, humans are subject to the same evolutionary forces as all other species. On hearing the term *evolution,* most people think of the appearance of new species. Certainly, new species formation is one consequence of evolution; however, biologists see evolution as an ongoing biological process with a precise genetic meaning. Quite simply, evolution is a change in the genetic makeup of a population from one generation to the next. It is the accumulation

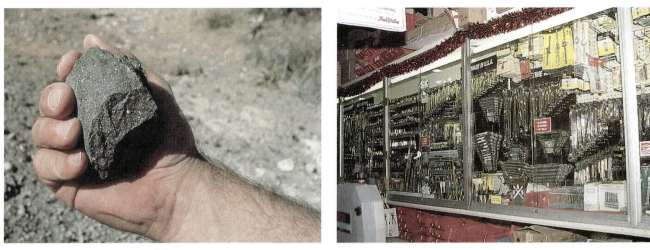

(a)

(b)

(c)

(d)

of such changes, over considerable periods of time, that can result in the appearance of a new species. Thus, evolution can be defined and studied at two different levels. At one level there are genetic alterations *within* populations. Although this type of change may not lead to the development of new species, it frequently results in variation between populations with regard to the frequency of certain traits. Evolution at this level is referred to as *microevolution*. At the other level is genetic change sufficient to result in the appearance of a new species, a process termed *macroevolution* or speciation. Evolution as it occurs at both these levels will be addressed in this text.

One critical point to remember is that the human predisposition to assimilate culture and to function within it is influenced by biological factors. In the course

FIGURE 1–3

(a) An early stone tool from East Africa. This artifact represents the oldest type of stone tools found anywhere. (b) Assortment of implements available today in a modern hardware store. (c) A Samburu woman building a simple, traditional dwelling of stems, plant fibers, and mud. (d) A modern high-rise apartment complex, typical of industrialized cities.

■ Biocultural evolution
The mutual, interactive evolution of human biology and culture; the concept that biology makes culture possible and that developing culture further influences the direction of biological evolution; a basic concept in understanding the unique components of human evolution.

■ Adaptation
Functional response of organisms or populations to the environment. Adaptation results from evolutionary change (specifically, as a result of natural selection).

■ Anthropology
The field of inquiry that studies human culture and evolutionary aspects of human biology; includes cultural anthropology, archaeology, linguistics, and physical anthropology.

The place of physical anthropology within the discipline of anthropology is discussed in Virtual Lab 1, section I.

of human evolution, as you will see, the role of culture increasingly assumed an added importance. Over time, culture and biology interacted in such a way that humans are said to be the result of **biocultural evolution.** In this respect, humans are unique among biological organisms.

Biocultural interactions have resulted in such anatomical, biological, and behavioral changes as increased brain size, reorganization of neurological structures, decreased tooth size, and development of language in humans, to list a few, and they continue to be critical in changing disease patterns as well. As a contemporary example, rapid culture change (particularly in Africa) and changing social and sexual mores may have influenced evolutionary rates of HIV, the virus that causes AIDS. Certainly, these cultural factors influenced the spread of HIV throughout populations in both the developed and developing worlds.

The study of many of the biological aspects of humankind, including **adaptation** and evolution, could certainly be the purview of human biologists, and it frequently is. However, particularly in the United States, when such research also considers the role of cultural factors, it is placed within the discipline of **anthropology.**

What Is Anthropology?

Stated ambitiously but simply, anthropology is the study of humankind. (The term *anthropology* is derived from the Greek words *anthropos,* meaning "human," and *logos,* meaning "word" or "study of.") Anthropologists are not the only scientists who study humans, and the goals of anthropology are shared by other disciplines within the social, behavioral, and biological sciences. For example, psychologists and psychiatrists investigate various aspects of human motivation and behavior while developing theories that have clinical significance. Historians focus on recorded events in the past, but since their research concerns documented occurrences, it is limited to, at most, a few thousand years. The main difference between anthropology and such related fields is that anthropology integrates the findings of many disciplines, including sociology, economics, history, psychology, and biology.

The focus of anthropology is very broad indeed. Like other disciplines, anthropology is divided into numerous specialized subfields, but fundamentally its concentration is on human biological and cultural evolution. In short, anthropologists explore all aspects of what it means to be human.

In the United States, anthropology comprises three main subfields: cultural, or social, anthropology; archaeology; and physical, or biological, anthropology. Additionally, some universities include linguistic anthropology as a fourth area. Each of these subdisciplines, in turn, is divided into more specialized areas of interest. Following is a brief discussion of the main subdisciplines of anthropology.

Cultural Anthropology

Cultural anthropology is the study of all aspects of human behavior. It could reasonably be argued that cultural anthropology began with the fourth-century B.C. Greek philosopher Aristotle, or even earlier. But for practical purposes, the beginnings of cultural anthropology are found in the nineteenth century, when

Europeans became increasingly aware of what they termed "primitive societies" in Africa and Asia. Likewise, in the New World, there was much interest in the vanishing cultures of Native Americans.

The interest in traditional societies led numerous early anthropologists to study and record lifeways that unfortunately are now mostly extinct. These studies produced many descriptive **ethnographies** that became the basis for subsequent comparisons between groups. Early ethnographies emphasized various phenomena, such as religion, ritual, myth, use of symbols, subsistence strategies, technology, gender roles, child-rearing practices, dietary preferences, taboos, medical practices, and how kinship was reckoned.

Ethnographic accounts, in turn, formed the basis for comparative studies of numerous cultures. Such *cross-cultural* studies, termed *ethnologies,* broadened the context within which cultural anthropologists studied human behavior. By examining the similarities and differences between diverse cultures, anthropologists have been able to formulate many theories about the fundamental aspects of human behavior.

The focus of cultural anthropology has shifted over the course of the twentieth century. But traditional ethnographic techniques, wherein anthropologists spend months or years living in and studying various societies, are still employed, although the nature of the study groups may have changed. For example, in recent decades, ethnographic techniques have been applied to the study of diverse subcultures and their interactions with one another in contemporary metropolitan areas. The subfield of cultural anthropology that deals with issues of inner cities is appropriately called *urban anthropology.* Among the many issues addressed by urban anthropologists are the relationships between ethnic groups, those aspects of traditional cultures maintained by immigrant populations, poverty, labor relations, homelessness, access to health care, and problems facing the elderly.

Medical anthropology is the subfield of cultural anthropology that explores the relationship between various cultural attributes and health and disease. One area of interest is how different groups view disease processes and how these views affect treatment or the willingness to accept treatment. When a medical anthropologist focuses on the social dimensions of disease, physicians and physical anthropologists may also collaborate. Indeed, many medical anthropologists have received much of their training in physical anthropology.

Economic anthropologists are concerned with factors that influence the distribution of goods and resources within and between cultures. Areas of interest include such topics as division of labor (by gender and age), factors that influence who controls resources and wealth, and trade practices and regulations.

Many cultural anthropologists are involved in gender studies. Such studies may focus on gender norms, how such norms are learned, and the specific cultural factors that lead to individual development of gender identity. It is also valuable to explore the social consequences if gender norms are violated.

There is also increasing interest in the social aspects of development and aging. This field is particularly relevant in industrialized nations, where the proportion of elderly individuals is higher than ever before. As populations age, the needs of the elderly, particularly in the area of health care, become social issues that require more and more attention.

Another relevant area for cultural anthropologists today is in the resettlement of refugees in many parts of the world. To develop plans that properly accommodate the needs of displaced peoples, governments may find the special talents of cultural anthropologists of considerable benefit.

▌ Ethnographies
Detailed descriptive studies of human societies. In cultural anthropology, an ethnography is traditionally the study of a non-Western society.

Many of the subfields of cultural anthropology (e.g., medical anthropology) have practical applications and are pursued by anthropologists working outside the university setting. This approach is aptly termed *applied anthropology*. While most applied anthropologists regard themselves as cultural anthropologists, the designation is also sometimes used to describe the activities of archaeologists and physical anthropologists. Indeed, the various fields of anthropology, as they are practiced in the United States, overlap to a considerable degree, which, after all, was the rationale for combining them under the umbrella of anthropology in the first place.

Archaeology

Archaeology is the study of earlier cultures and lifeways by anthropologists who specialize in the scientific recovery, analysis, and interpretation of the material remains of past societies. Although archaeology often deals with cultures that existed before the invention of writing (the period commonly known as *prehistory*), *historical archaeologists* also examine the evidence of later, complex civilizations that produced written records.

Archaeologists are concerned with culture, but they differ from cultural anthropologists in that their sources of information are not living people but rather the **artifacts** and other **material culture** left behind by earlier societies. Obviously, no one has ever excavated such aspects of culture as religious belief, spoken language, or a political system. However, archaeologists assume that the surviving evidence of human occupation reflects some of those important but less tangible features of the culture that created them. Therefore, the material remains of a given ancient society may serve to inform us about the nature of that society.

The roots of modern archaeology are found in the fascination of nineteenth-century Europeans with the classical world (particularly Greece and Egypt). This interest was primarily manifested in the excavation (sometimes controlled, sometimes not) and removal of thousands of treasures and artifacts, destined for the museums and private collections of wealthy Europeans.

New World archaeology has long focused on the pre-Columbian civilizations of Mexico and Central and South America (the Aztecs, Maya, and Inca). In North America, archaeological interest was sparked particularly by the large earthen burial mounds found throughout much of the southeast. In fact, Thomas Jefferson conducted one of the first controlled excavations of a burial mound on his Virginia plantation in 1784. Importantly, his goal was not simply the recovery of artifacts; he specifically wished to address the question of how the mound was constructed.

Today, archaeology is aimed at answering specific questions pertaining to human behavior. Sites are not excavated simply because they exist or for the artifacts they may yield; excavation is conducted for the explicit purpose of gaining information about human behavior. Patterns of behavior are reflected in the dispersal of human settlements across a landscape and in the distribution of cultural remains within them. Through the identification of these patterns, archaeologists can elucidate the commonalities shared by many or all populations as well as those features that differ between groups. Research questions may focus on specific localities or peoples and attempt to identify, for example, various aspects of social organization, subsistence techniques, or the factors that led to the collapse of a civilization. Alternatively, inquiry may reflect an interest

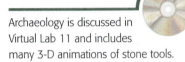

Archaeology is discussed in Virtual Lab 11 and includes many 3-D animations of stone tools.

▌Artifacts
Objects or materials made or modified for use by hominids. The earliest artifacts tend to be tools made of stone or, occasionally, bone.

▌Material culture
The physical manifestations of human activities; includes tools, art, and structures. As the most durable aspects of culture, material remains make up the majority of archaeological evidence of past societies.

in broader issues relating to human culture in general, such as the development of agriculture or the rise of cities. But the design of most archaeological projects centers around a number of questions that address a wide range of interests, both specific and broad.

Archaeology is a discipline that requires precise measurement, description, and excavation techniques, for it must be remembered that when a site is dug, it is also destroyed. Errors in excavation or recording result in the permanent loss or misinterpretation of valuable information. Therefore, contrary to what many people think, the science of archaeology is much more than simply digging up artifacts. Rather, archaeology is a multidisciplinary approach to the study of human behavior as evidenced by cultural remains.

For many projects, the specialized expertise of many disciplines is needed. Chemists, geologists, physicists, paleontologists, and physical anthropologists may all be called on. Even the sophisticated satellite technologies of NASA have been called on to locate archaeological sites.

In the United States, the greatest expansion in archaeology in recent years has been in the important area of *cultural resource management (CRM)*. This applied approach arose from environmental legislation requiring the archaeological evaluation and even excavation of sites that may be threatened by construction and other forms of development. Many contract archaeologists (so called because their services are contracted out to developers, government agencies, and municipalities) are affiliated with private archaeological consulting firms, state or federal agencies, or educational institutions. In fact, an estimated 40 percent of all archaeologists in the United States now fill such positions.

Archaeological techniques are used to identify and excavate not only remains of human cities and settlements, but also paleontological sites containing remains of extinct species, including everything from dinosaurs to early hominids. Together, prehistoric archaeology and physical anthropology form the core of a joint science called *paleoanthropology,* described below.

Linguistic Anthropology

Linguistic anthropology is the study of human speech and language, including the origins of language in general as well as of specific languages. By examining similarities between contemporary languages, linguists have been able to trace historical ties between languages and groups of languages, thus facilitating the identification of language families and perhaps past relationships between human populations.

There is also much interest in the relationship between language and culture: how language reflects the way members of a society perceive phenomena and how the use of language shapes perceptions in different cultures. For instance, vocabulary provides important clues as to the importance of certain items and concepts in particular cultures. The most famous example is the use of some 50 terms for snow among the Inuit (Eskimos), reflecting their need to convey specific information about the properties of this form of frozen precipitation. (For that matter, skiers also employ many more increasingly precise terms for snow than do nonskiers.)

Because the spontaneous acquisition and use of language is a uniquely human characteristic, it is a topic that holds considerable interest for linguistic anthropologists, who, along with specialists in other fields, study the process of language acquisition in infants. Since insights into the process may well have implications for the development of language skills in human evolution, as well as in growing children, it is also an important subject to physical anthropologists.

Physical Anthropology

Physical anthropology, as has already been stated, is the study of human biology within the framework of evolution, with an emphasis on the interaction between biology and culture. Physical anthropology is composed of several subdisciplines, or areas of specialization, the most significant of which are briefly described in the following paragraphs.

The origins of physical anthropology are to be found in two principal areas of interest among nineteenth-century scholars. First, there was increasing concern among many scientists (at the time called *natural historians*) regarding the mechanisms by which modern species had come to be. In other words, increasing numbers of intellectuals were beginning to doubt the literal, biblical interpretation of creation. This does not mean that all natural historians had abandoned all religious explanations of natural occurrences. But scientific explanations emphasizing natural, rather than supernatural, phenomena were becoming increasingly popular in scientific and intellectual circles. Although few were actually prepared to believe that humans had evolved from earlier forms, discoveries of several Neandertal fossils in the 1800s began to raise questions regarding the origins and antiquity of the human species.

The sparks of interest in biological change over time were fueled into flames by the publication of Charles Darwin's *Origin of Species* in 1859. Today, **paleoanthropology**, or the study of human evolution, particularly as evidenced in the fossil record, is one of the major subfields of physical anthropology (Fig. 1–4). There are now thousands of specimens of human ancestors housed in museum and research collections. Taken together, these fossils cover a span of at least 4 million years of human prehistory, and although incomplete, they provide us with significantly more knowledge than was available even 15 years ago. It is the ultimate goal of paleoanthropological research to identify the various early hominid species, establish a chronological sequence of relationships among them, and gain insights into their adaptation and behavior. Only then will there emerge a clear picture of how and when humankind came into being.

A second nineteenth-century interest that had direct relevance to anthropology was observable physical variation, particularly as seen in skin color. Enormous effort was aimed at describing and explaining the biological differences among various human populations. Although some endeavors were misguided, they gave birth to literally thousands of body measurements that could be used to compare people. Physical anthropologists use many of the techniques of **anthropometry** today, not only to study living groups, but also to study skeletal remains from archaeological sites (Fig. 1–5). Moreover, anthropometric techniques have considerable application in the design of everything from airplane cockpits to office furniture.

Anthropologists today are concerned with human variation primarily because of its *adaptive significance.* In other words, many traits that typify certain populations are seen as having evolved as biological adaptations, or adjustments, to local environmental conditions. Examining biological variation between populations of any species provides valuable information as to the mechanisms of

Paleoanthropology
The interdisciplinary approach to the study of earlier hominids—their chronology, physical structure, archaeological remains, habitats, etc.

Anthropometry
Measurement of human body parts. When osteologists measure skeletal elements, the term *osteometry* is often used.

FIGURE 1–4
Paleoanthropological research at Hadar, Ethiopia, during a field season in 1993.

genetic change in groups over time, which is precisely what the evolutionary process is all about.

Modern population studies also examine other important aspects of human variation, including how various groups respond physiologically to different kinds of environmentally induced stress (Fig. 1–6). Such stresses may include high altitude, cold, or heat.

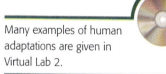

Many examples of human adaptations are given in Virtual Lab 2.

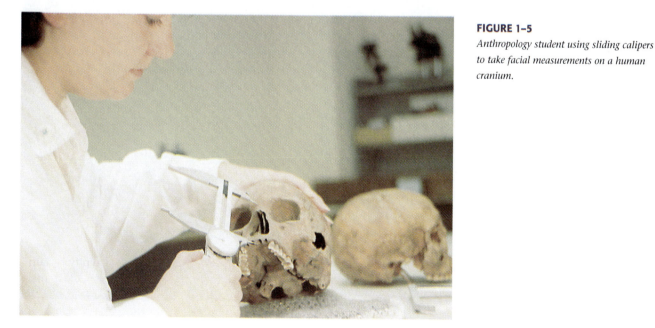

FIGURE 1–5
Anthropology student using sliding calipers to take facial measurements on a human cranium.

FIGURE 1–6

Researcher using a treadmill test to assess a subject's heart rate, blood pressure, and oxygen consumption.

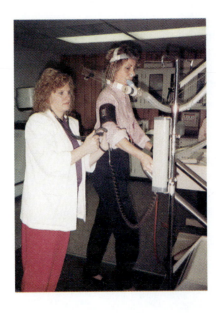

▪ Genetics

The study of gene structure and action and the patterns of inheritance of traits from parent to offspring. Genetic mechanisms are the underlying foundation for evolutionary change.

▪ Primatology

The study of the biology and behavior of nonhuman primates (prosimians, monkeys, and apes).

FIGURE 1–7

(a) Yahaya Alamasi, a member of the senior field staff at Gombe National Park, Tanzania. Alamasi is recording behaviors in free-ranging chimpanzees. (b) Oakland Zoo docent uses a laptop computer to record behaviors of a captive chimpanzee.

Other physical anthropologists conduct nutritional studies, investigating the relationships between various dietary components, cultural practices, physiology, and certain aspects of health and disease. Closely related to the topic of nutrition are investigations of human fertility, growth, and development. These fields of inquiry are fundamental to studies of adaptation in modern human populations, and they can provide insights into hominid evolution as well.

It would be impossible to study evolutionary processes, and therefore adaptation, without a knowledge of genetic principles. For this reason and others, **genetics** is a crucial field for physical anthropologists. Modern physical anthropology would not exist as an evolutionary science were it not for advances in the understanding of genetic principles.

Not only does genetics allow us to explain how evolutionary processes work, but today's anthropologists use recently developed genetic technologies to investigate evolutionary distances between living primate species (including humans). Moreover, genetic theories have been used (with much debate) to explain, among other things, the origins of modern *Homo sapiens.*

Primatology, the study of nonhuman primates, has become increasingly important since the late 1950s for several reasons (Fig. 1–7). Behavioral studies,

(a)

(b)

especially those conducted on groups in natural environments, have implications for numerous scientific disciplines. Perhaps more importantly, studies of nonhuman animal behavior have assumed a greater urgency in recent decades owing to concern over declining numbers of many species.

The behavioral study of any species provides a wealth of data pertaining to adaptation. Because nonhuman primates are our closest living relatives, the identification of underlying factors related to social behavior, communication, infant care, reproductive behavior, and so on, aids in developing a better understanding of the natural forces that have shaped so many aspects of modern human behavior.

Moreover, nonhuman primates are important to study in their own right (particularly true today because the majority of species are threatened or seriously endangered). Only through study will scientists be able to recommend policies that can better ensure the survival of many nonhuman primates and thousands of other species as well.

Primate paleontology, the study of the primate fossil record, has implications not only for nonhuman primates but also for hominids. Virtually every year, fossil-bearing beds in North America, Africa, Asia, and Europe yield important new discoveries. Through the study of fossil primates, we are able to learn much about factors such as diet or locomotion in earlier forms. By comparisons with anatomically similar living species, primate paleontologists can make reasoned inferences regarding behavior in earlier groups as well. Moreover, we hope to be able to clarify what we know about evolutionary relationships between extinct and modern species, including ourselves.

Osteology, the study of the skeleton, is central to physical anthropology. Indeed, it is so important that when many people think of physical anthropology, the first thing that comes to mind is bones. The emphasis on osteology exists in part because of the concern with the analysis of fossil material. Certainly, a thorough knowledge of the structure and function of the skeleton is critical to the interpretation of fossil material.

Bone biology and physiology are of major importance to many other aspects of physical anthropology (in addition to paleontology). Many osteologists specialize in studies that emphasize various measurements of skeletal elements. This type of research is essential, for example, to the identification of stature and growth patterns in archaeological populations.

One subdiscipline of osteology is the study of disease and trauma in archaeologically derived skeletal populations. **Paleopathology** is a prominent subfield that investigates the incidence of trauma, certain infectious diseases (including syphilis and tuberculosis), nutritional deficiencies, and numerous other conditions that leave evidence in bone (Fig. 1–8). In this area of research, a precise knowledge of bone physiology and response to insult is required.

A field directly related to osteology and paleopathology is **forensic anthropology.** Technically, this approach is the application of anthropological (usually osteological and sometimes archaeological) techniques to the law (Fig. 1–9). Forensic anthropologists are commonly called on to help identify skeletal remains in cases of disaster or other situations where a human body has been found.

Forensic anthropologists have been involved in a number of cases having important legal and historical consequences. They assisted medical examiners in 1993 with the identification of human remains at the Branch Davidian compound in Waco, Texas. They have also been prominent in the identification of remains of missing American soldiers in Southeast Asia and the skeletons of most of the Russian imperial family, executed in 1918.

Virtual Lab 6 introduces you to the methods of observing and quantifying primate behavior.

■ Osteology
The study of skeletal material. Human osteology focuses on the interpretation of the skeletal remains of past groups. The same techniques are used in paleoanthropology to study early hominids.

■ Paleopathology
The branch of osteology that studies the traces of disease and injury in human skeletal (or, occasionally, mummified) remains.

■ Forensic anthropology
An applied anthropological approach dealing with legal matters. Physical anthropologists work with coroners and others in the analysis and identification of human remains.

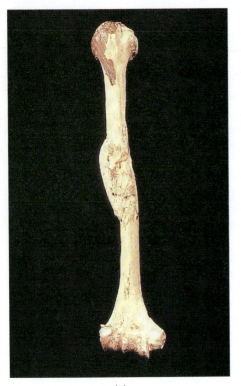

(a)

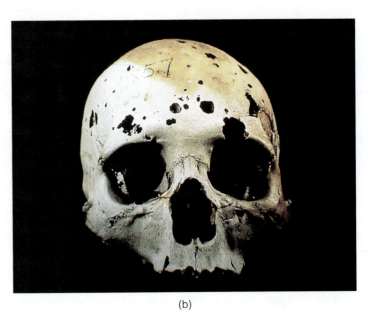

(b)

FIGURE 1–8

*(a) Healing fracture of a humerus (upper arm bone) in a skeleton from Nubia
(North Africa). (b) Cranial lesions, probably resulting from metastasized cancer.*

Anatomical studies constitute another important area of interest for physical anthropologists. In the living organism, bone and dental structures are intimately linked to the soft tissues that surround and act on them. Thus, a thorough knowledge of soft tissue anatomy is essential to the understanding of biomechanical relationships involved in movement. Such relationships are

FIGURE 1–9

Physical anthropologists Lorna Pierce (to left) and Judy Suchey (to right) working as forensic consultants. The dog has just located a concealed human cranium during a training session.

important to the accurate assessment of the structure and function of limbs and other components in fossilized remains. For these reasons, and others, many physical anthropologists specialize in anatomical studies. In fact, several physical anthropologists hold professorships in anatomy departments at universities and medical schools.

From this brief overview, it can be seen that physical anthropology is the subdiscipline of anthropology that focuses on many varied aspects of the biological and behavioral nature of *Homo sapiens*. Humans are a product of the same forces that produced all life on earth. As such, we represent one contemporary component of a vast biological **continuum** at one point in time, and in this regard, we are not particularly unique. Stating that humans are part of a continuum does not imply that we are at the peak of development on that continuum. Depending on which criteria one uses, humans can be seen to exist at one end of the continuum or the other, or somewhere in between. But humans do not necessarily occupy a position of inherent superiority over other species.

There is, however, one dimension in which human beings are truly unique, and that is intellect. After all, humans are the only species, born of earth, to stir the lunar dust. Humans are the only species to develop language and complex culture as a means of buffering the challenges posed by nature and by so doing eventually gain the power to shape the very destiny of the planet.

It has been said that humans created culture and that culture created humans. This statement is true to the extent that the increased brain size and reorganization of neurological structures that typify much of the course of human evolution would never have occurred if not for the complex interactions between biological and behavioral factors (i.e., biocultural evolution). In this sense, then, it is neither unreasonable nor presumptuous to say that we have created ourselves.

Physical Anthropology and the Scientific Method

Science is a process of understanding phenomena through observation, generalization, and verification. By this we mean that there is an **empirical** approach to gaining information through the use of systematic and explicit techniques. Because physical anthropologists are engaged in scientific pursuits, they adhere to the principles of the **scientific method,** whereby a research problem is identified and information subsequently gathered to solve it.

The gathering of information is referred to as **data** collection, and when researchers use a rigorously controlled approach, they are able to describe precisely their techniques and results in a manner that facilitates comparisons with the work of others. For example, when scientists collect data on tooth size in hominid fossils, they must specify precisely which teeth are being measured, how they are being measured, and what the results of the measurements are (expressed numerically, or **quantitatively**). Subsequently, it is up to the investigators to draw conclusions as to the meaning and significance of their measurements. This body of information then becomes the basis of future studies, perhaps by other researchers, who can compare their own results with those already obtained. The eventual outcome of this type of inquiry may be the acceptance or rejection of certain proposed facts and explanations.

Once facts have been established, scientists attempt to explain them. First, a **hypothesis,** or provisional explanation of phenomena, is developed. But before a

■ Continuum
A set of relationships in which all components fall along a single integrated spectrum. All life reflects a single *biological* continuum.

■ Science
A body of knowledge gained through observation and experimentation; from the Latin *scientia,* meaning "knowledge."

■ Empirical
Relying on experiment or observation; from the Latin *empiricus,* meaning "experienced."

■ Scientific method
A research method whereby a problem is identified, a hypothesis (or hypothetical explanation) is stated, and that hypothesis is tested through the collection and analysis of data. If the hypothesis is verified, it becomes a theory.

■ Data
(*sing.,* datum)
Facts from which conclusions can be drawn; scientific information.

■ Quantitatively
In a manner involving measurements of quantity and including such properties as size, number, and capacity. When data are quantified, they are expressed numerically and are capable of being tested statistically.

■ Hypothesis
(*pl.,* hypotheses)
A provisional explanation of a phenomenon. Hypotheses require verification.

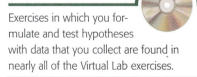

Exercises in which you formulate and test hypotheses with data that you collect are found in nearly all of the Virtual Lab exercises.

hypothesis can be accepted, it must be tested by means of data collection and analysis. Indeed, the testing of hypotheses with the possibility of proving them false is the very basis of the scientific method.

> **■ Scientific testing**
> The precise repetition of an experiment or expansion of observed data to provide verification; the procedure by which hypotheses and theories are verified, modified, or discarded.

Scientific testing of hypotheses may take several years (or longer) and may involve researchers who were not involved with the original work. In subsequent studies, other investigators may attempt to obtain the original results, but such repetition may not occur. For example, repeated failures to duplicate the results of highly publicized cold fusion experiments led most scientists to question and ultimately reject the claims made in the original research. While it is easier to duplicate original studies conducted in laboratory settings, it is equally important to verify data collected outside tightly controlled situations. In the latter circumstance, results are tested relative to other, often larger, samples. The predicted patterns will either be confirmed through such further research or be viewed as limited or even incorrect.

If a hypothesis cannot be falsified, it is accepted as a **theory.** A theory, then, is a statement of relationships that has a firm basis as demonstrated through testing and the accumulation of evidence. As such, it not only helps organize current knowledge, but should also predict how new facts may fit into the established pattern.

> **■ Theory**
> A broad statement of scientific relationships or underlying principles that has been at least partially verified.

Use of the scientific method not only allows for the development and testing of hypotheses, but also permits various types of *bias* to be addressed and controlled. It is important to realize that bias occurs in all studies. Sources of bias include how the investigator was trained and by whom; what particular questions interest the researcher; what specific skills and talents he or she possesses; what earlier results (if any) have been established in this realm of study and by whom (e.g., the researcher, close colleagues, or those with rival approaches or even rival personalities); and what sources of data are available (e.g., accessible countries or museums) and thus what samples can be collected (at all or at least conveniently).

Application of the scientific method thus requires constant vigilance by all those who practice it. The goal is not to establish "truth" in any absolute sense, but rather to generate ever more accurate and consistent depictions and explanations of phenomena in our universe. At its very heart, scientific methodology is an exercise in rational thought and critical thinking (see Issue, pp. 21–22).

The Anthropological Perspective

Perhaps the most important benefit you will receive from this textbook—and this course—is a wider appreciation of the human experience. To understand human beings and how our species came to be, it is necessary to broaden our viewpoint, both through time and over space. All branches of anthropology fundamentally seek to do this in what we call the *anthropological perspective.*

Physical anthropologists, for example, are keenly interested in how humans differ from and are similar to other animals, especially nonhuman primates. For example, we have defined *hominids* as bipedal primates, but what are the major components of bipedal locomotion, and how do they differ from, say, those in a quadrupedal ape? To answer these questions, we would need to study human locomotion and compare it with the locomotion seen in various nonhuman primates. Moreover, in addition to observing how humans walk while wearing shoes, we also would be interested in their pattern of locomotion while walking barefoot. Indeed, it would probably be useful to look at the locomotion of people

Locomotion is investigated in detail in Virtual Labs 3, 4, and 9. For a video clip of human bipedalism, see Virtual Lab 1, section IV, part D, under positional behaviors.

who have never worn shoes, and to obtain these data, we would probably have to leave our own culture and study other quite geographically distant groups.

Through such a wider perspective, we can begin to grasp the contemporary diversity of the human experience and, in so doing, understand more fully both human potentialities and human constraints. And, by extending our breadth of knowledge, it is easier to avoid the **ethnocentric** pitfalls inherent in a more limited view of humanity.

In addition to broadening perspectives over space (i.e., encompassing many cultures and ecological circumstances as well as nonhuman species), an anthropological perspective also extends our horizons *through time*. For example, in Chapter 16 we will discuss human nutrition. However, the vast majority of the kinds of foods currently eaten (coming from domesticated plants and animals) were unavailable prior to 10,000 years ago. Human physiological mechanisms for chewing and digesting foods nevertheless were already well established long before that date. These adaptive complexes go back many hundreds of thousands—perhaps even millions—of years. In addition to the obviously different diets prior to the development of agriculture (approximately 10,000 years ago), earlier hominids might well have differed from humans today in average body size, metabolism, and activity patterns. How, then, does the basic evolutionary "equipment" (i.e., physiology) inherited from our hominid forebears accommodate our modern diets? Clearly, the way to understand such processes is not just by looking at contemporary human responses, but also by placing them in the perspective of evolutionary development through time.

Indeed, most of the topics covered in this book—as most topics considered by all types of anthropologists—are addressed by using a broad application of the anthropological perspective. For physical anthropologists, such an approach usually means extending the perspective both over space as well as through considerable periods of time.

We hope that the ensuing pages will help you develop an increased understanding of the similarities we share with other biological organisms and also of the processes that have shaped the traits that make us unique. We live in what may well be the most crucial period for our planet in the last 65 million years. We are members of the one species that, through the very agency of culture, has wrought such devastating changes in ecological systems that we must now alter our technologies or face potentially unspeakable consequences. In such a time, it is vital that we attempt to gain the best possible understanding of what it means to be human. We believe that the study of physical anthropology is one endeavor that aids in this attempt, and that is indeed the goal of this text.

■ Ethnocentric
Viewing other cultures from the inherently biased perspective of one's own culture. Ethnocentrism often results in cultures being seen as inferior to one's own.

Summary

In this chapter, we have introduced the field of physical anthropology and have placed it within the overall context of anthropological studies. As a major academic area within the social sciences, anthropology also includes archaeology, cultural anthropology, and linguistic anthropology as its major subfields.

Physical anthropology itself includes aspects of human biology (emphasizing evolutionary perspectives), the study of nonhuman primates, and the hominid fossil record. Especially as applied to the study of early hominids (as incorporated within the interdisciplinary field of paleoanthropology), physical anthropologists work in close collaboration with many other scientists from the fields of archaeology, geology, chemistry, and so forth.

Additional self-test questions about the concepts discussed in this chapter can be found in the Self-Quiz in Virtual Lab 1 (1.V).

Questions for Review

1. What is anthropology? What are the major subfields of anthropology?
2. How does physical anthropology differ from other disciplines interested in human biology?
3. What is meant by biocultural evolution, and why is it important in understanding human evolution?
4. What are some of the primary areas of research within physical anthropology? Give two or three examples of the types of research pursued by physical anthropologists.
5. What is meant by the term *hominid?* Be specific.
6. What fields, in addition to physical anthropology, contribute to paleo-anthropology?

Suggested Further Reading

Ferraro, Gary, Wenda Trevathan, and Janet Levy. 1994. *Anthropology, an Applied Perspective.* St. Paul: West.

Spencer, Frank, ed. 1982. *A History of Physical Anthropology.* New York: Academic Press.

Stiebing, William H., Jr. 1993. *Uncovering the Past: A History of Archaeology.* New York: Oxford University Press.

Additional Resources

Multimedia Tools

■ **Virtual Laboratories for Physical Anthropology CD-ROM**
The following concepts in this chapter are covered on the physical anthropology CD-ROM:
hominids, primates, mammals (Virtual Lab 1.II.D)
Australopithecus, Homo, human evolution (Virtual Labs 8, 9, 10, 11, 12)
evolution, adaptation, genetics (Virtual Lab 2)
physical anthropology, anthropology (Virtual Lab 1.I)
archaeology, stone tools, technology (Virtual Lab 11)
adaptation, human variation (Virtual Lab 2)
primate behavior, ethogram, primatology (Virtual Lab 6)
scientific method, hypothesis, predictions, theory (Virtual Labs 3.III; 6.I)
bipedalism, locomotion (Virtual Labs 1.IV.D; 3; 4; 9)
Additional self-test questions about the concepts discussed in this chapter can be found in the Self-Quiz in Virtual Lab 1 (1.V).

■ **Wadsworth Anthropology Resource Center**
http://anthropology.wadsworth.com
Visit Anthropology Online to obtain current updates in the field, surfing tips, career information and more. In addition, enrich your study efforts with text-specific study aids arranged by chapter.

InfoTrac College Edition
http://www.infotrac-college.com/wadsworth

1. Anthropology is a very broad discipline. Search InfroTrac College Edition for the subject *anthropology*. How many different topics can be found? How many of these topics are related to biological or physical anthropology? Choose one topic not introduced in the text and read or skim some of the articles about this topic. What makes this topic anthropological?

2. Now, choose *forensic anthropology* and go to the periodical articles. Read "'Let the bones talk' is the watchword for scientist-sleuths" (forensic anthropology at the Smithsonian Institution) by Elizabeth Royte, *Smithsonian,* May 1996, v27 n2 p82(7). What does a forensic anthropologist do? What sort of training is needed? Go through your college catalog and make a list of courses that you might take if you were interested in becoming a forensic anthropologist.

3. The anthropological perspective is central to the entire discipline. Go to InfoTrac College Edition and search for key words *anthropological perspective*. Read "Helping students deal with cultural differences" by Jane J. White, *The Social Studies,* May–June 1998, v89 n3 p107(5). After reading this, write a paper about how a course you took last year or last semester might have been improved if it had taken an anthropological perspective. Why would this perspective have improved that course? Finally, go through the *How do you do space* exercise. What differences did you find amongst your friends in how they feel about space?

Internet Exercises

1. You should begin by becoming familiar with the scope of anthropology on the Internet. Visit one of the many Internet search engines or indexes, such as Excite (**www.excite.com**) or Yahoo! (**www.yahoo. com**) and search for *anthropology*. How many sites did you find? Do these sites cover the range of anthropological subdisciplines? Visit a couple of these sites. What do they have in common?

2. Now, restrict your search to *anthropology organizations*. How many anthropology groups have Internet sites? Visit a couple of these. Are these professional organizations? Are there any which you, as a student, might be interested in joining? Which associations would you guess an anthropologist interested in human evolution might join? Which ones might a physical anthropologist join?

3. Visit the major association of anthropologists in the United States, the American Anthropological Association. (If your search did not provide the link, try **http://www.ameranthassn.org.**) The American Anthropological Association represents anthropologists in all subdisciplines and this site serves as a good indicator of the breadth of anthropology. Take time to explore this site thoroughly. Visit About AAA to learn more about the field and the association. Read "Careers in Anthropology." What could YOU do with a major in anthropology, even without going to graduate school?

4. Because anthropology is about being human, it is of great interest to many people, and thus anthropological stories often make the news. Visit several news sources, such as Nando (**www.nando.net**), Excite News (**nt.excite.com**), CNN (**www.cnn.com**), the New York Times

(**www.nytimes.com**), the Washington Post (**www.washingtonpost. com**) or MSNBC (**www.msnbc.com**) and search for recent news articles about anthropology. Some search terms you might use include *anthropology, archaeology, biology, human evolution, paleoanthropology* or any other term you might think of. Try to find at least five recent articles on anthropology. Write a page about the topics these articles discuss and what the articles have in common. What makes all these articles anthropological?

Evaluation in Science: Lessons in Critical Thinking

At the end of various chapters throughout this book, you will find a brief discussion of a contemporary topic. Some of these subjects, such as the use of nonhuman primates in biomedical research, are not usually covered in textbooks. However, we feel that it is important to address such issues, because scientists should not simply dismiss those views or ideas of which they are skeptical. Similarly, you should be reluctant to *accept* a view based solely on its personal appeal. Accepting or rejecting an idea based on personal feelings is as good a definition of "bias" as one could devise. Science is an approach—indeed, a *tool*—used to eliminate (or at least minimize) bias.

Scientific approaches of evaluation are, in fact, a part of a broader framework of intellectual rigor that is termed *critical thinking*. The development of critical thinking skills is an important and lasting benefit of a college education. Such skills enable people to evaluate, compare, analyze, critique, and synthesize information so that they will not accept all they hear and read at face value but will be able to reach their own conclusions. Critical thinkers are able to assess the evidence supporting their own beliefs (in a sense, to step outside themselves) and to identify the weaknesses in their own positions. They recognize that knowledge is not merely a collection of facts but an ongoing process of examining information to expand our understanding of the world.

In scientific inquiry, individual "facts" (or better put, *observations*)

must be presented clearly, with appropriate documentation. That is the purpose of bibliographical citation, as exemplified throughout this textbook. Once "facts" are established, scientists attempt to develop explanations concerning their relationships. In this way, initial hypotheses can be broadened into more general and better-supported theories.

A crucial aspect of scientific statements is that they are *falsifiable;* that is, there must be a means of evaluating the validity of hypotheses and theories to demonstrate that the statements may be incorrect. In this way, scientific conclusions are constantly *tested.* Statements such as "Heaven exists" may well be "true" (i.e., describe some actual state), but there is no rational, *empirical* means (based on experience or experiment) by which to test it. Acceptance of such a view is thus based on faith rather than on scientific verification.

We should emphasize that perceived phenomena understood through faith do not necessarily conflict with empirical demonstration. In fact, precisely because there may be areas of knowledge beyond the reach of scientific inquiry, faith-based beliefs provide a powerful influence for many people. Furthermore, these beliefs need not (and for many individuals, scientist and nonscientist alike, do not) conflict with the demonstrable values of scientific thought.

One of the most appealing aspects of perspectives based in faith is that such beliefs are widely and comfortably accepted as true. In sci-

ence, statements can be tested and falsified (indeed, this is a central component of the scientific method), but they can never completely be proved "true." Theories can simply be better substantiated and are thus more fully established. However, new evidence can also require modification of hypotheses and theories; and some theories might prove so inadequate as to be rejected altogether. Thus, Newton's theory of gravitation was substantially altered by Einstein's theory of relativity. The old theory of a "missing link" (a kind of halfway compromise between modern humans and modern apes) preceded modern evolutionary thinking and is now seen as simplistic, misleading, and, at a practical level, of no value.

This inherent aspect of scientific inquiry in which theories are always subject to ongoing evaluation is widely misunderstood, frequently with disturbing consequences. For example, as we will note in Chapter 2, claims are often made that evolution is "just a theory." Pronouncements like these, as related to the teaching of evolution in public schools, have found their way into court decisions in California and recent policy statements by the Alabama State Board of Education. In science, knowledge is always proposed, organized, and tested in the form of hypotheses and, more generally, as theories. Our understanding of the action of gravity is just a theory, and so is the sun-centered depiction of the solar system. These two theories have, of course, been supported by an overwhelming amount

Evaluation in Science:
Lessons in Critical Thinking (continued)

of highly consistent evidence—but *so has evolutionary theory.* The constraint that science can never establish absolute "truth" should not be confused with an inability to understand the world around us. The human brain is a product of 4 billion years of evolution on this planet, and by using this neurological structure, *Homo sapiens* has the ability to apply rational thought. In the last few hundred years, the scientific method has developed into the most powerful tool invented by our species to utilize these rational capabilities and, in so doing, to come to grips with the universe and how we fit into it.

Throughout this text, you will be presented with the results of numerous studies that utilize numerical data. For example, it might be stated that female chimpanzees eat more insects than male chimpanzees or that Neandertal males were bigger than females or that the gene for cystic fibrosis is more common in European populations than in other groups. First of all, you should always be cautious of generalizations. What is the specific nature of the argument? What data support it? Can these data be quantified? If so, how is this information presented? (*Note:* Always read the tables in textbooks or articles.)

Regardless of the discipline you ultimately study, at some point in your academic career you should take a course in statistics. Many universities now make statistics a gen-

eral education requirement (sometimes under the category "quantitative reasoning"). Whether you are required to take such an offering or elect to do so, we strongly encourage it. Statistics often seems a very dry subject, and many students are intimidated by the math it requires. Nevertheless, perhaps more than any other skill you will acquire in your college years, quantitative critical reasoning is a tool you will be able to use every day of your life.

The topics chosen for the chapter-closing issues are those that intrigue the authors, and we hope that you also will find them stimulating. Some subjects are of historical interest. In addition, we address several topics that relate to recent advances in science, as exemplified by recombinant DNA research (Chapter 3). Here, in addition to challenging you to grasp the basic scientific principles involved, we also ask you to consider the *social implications* of scientific/technological advances.

A responsibility of an educated society is to be both informed and vigilant. The knowledge we possess and attempt to build on is neither "good" nor "bad"; however, the uses to which knowledge may be put have highly charged moral and ethical implications. Thus, a goal of the chapter-closing issues is to stimulate your interest and provide you with a basis to reach your own conclusions. Here are some useful questions to ask in making critical evaluations

about these issues or any other controversial scientific topic:

1. What data are presented?
2. What conclusions are presented, and how are they organized (as tentative hypotheses or as more dogmatic assertions)?
3. Are these views the individual opinions of the authors, or are they supported by a larger body of research?
4. What are the research findings? Are they adequately documented?
5. Is the information consistent with information that you already possess? If not, can the inconsistencies be explained?
6. Are the conclusions (hypotheses) testable? How might one go about testing the various hypotheses that are presented?
7. If presentation of new research findings is at odds with previous hypotheses (or theories), must these hypotheses now be modified (or completely rejected)?
8. How do your own personal views bias you in interpreting the results?
9. Once you have identified your own biases, are you able to set them aside so as to evaluate the information objectively?
10. Are you able to discuss both the pros and cons of a scientific topic in an evenhanded manner?

2

The Development of Evolutionary Theory

Introduction

The term **evolution** is sometimes charged with emotion. The concept is often controversial, particularly in the United States, because some religious views hold that evolutionary statements run counter to biblical teachings. Indeed, as you are probably aware, there continues to be much opposition to the teaching of evolution in public schools.

Those who wish to denigrate evolution frequently insist that it is "only a theory"—an attempt, perhaps, to reduce its status to supposition. Actually, to refer to a concept as "theory" is to lend it support. As we noted in Chapter 1, theories are general hypotheses that have been tested and subjected to verification through accumulated evidence. Evolution *is* a theory, one that has increasingly been supported by a mounting body of genetic evidence. It is a theory that has stood the test of time, and today it stands as the most fundamental unifying force in biological science.

Because physical anthropology is concerned with all aspects of how humans came to be and how we adapt physiologically to the external environment, the details of the evolutionary process are crucial to the field. Moreover, given the central importance of evolution to physical anthropology, it is valuable to know how the mechanics of the process came to be discovered. Additionally, to appreciate the nature of the controversy that continues to surround the issue today, it is important to examine the basic evolutionary principles within the social and political context in which the theory emerged.

A Brief History of Evolutionary Thought

The individual most responsible for the elucidation of the evolutionary process was Charles Darwin. But while Darwin was formulating his theory of **natural selection**, his ideas were being duplicated by another English naturalist, Alfred Russel Wallace.

That natural selection, the single most important mechanism of evolutionary change, should be proposed at more or less the same time by two British men in the mid-nineteenth century may seen highly improbable. But actually, it is not all that surprising. Indeed, if Darwin and Wallace had not made their simultaneous discoveries, someone else would have done so in short order. That is to say, the groundwork had already been laid, and many within the scientific community were prepared to accept explanations of biological change that would have been unacceptable even 25 years before.

Like other human endeavors, scientific knowledge is usually gained through a series of small steps rather than giant leaps. Just as technological innovation is based on past achievements, scientific knowledge builds on previously developed theories. (One does not build a space shuttle without first having invented the airplane.) Given this stepwise aspect of scientific discovery, it is informative to examine the development of ideas that led Darwin and Wallace independently to develop the theory of evolution by natural selection.

Throughout the Middle Ages, one predominant component of the European **world view** was *stasis*. That is, all aspects of nature, including all forms of life and their relationships to one another, were seen as fixed and unchanging. This view of natural phenomena was shaped in part by a feudal society that was very much

Evolution
A change in the genetic structure of a population. The term is also frequently used to refer to the appearance of a new species.

Natural selection
The mechanism of evolutionary change first articulated by Charles Darwin; refers to genetic change or changes in the frequencies of certain traits in populations due to differential reproductive success between individuals.

World view
General cultural orientation or perspective shared by members of a society.

a hierarchical arrangement supporting a rigid class system that had changed little for several centuries.

The world view of Europeans during the Middle Ages was also shaped by a powerful religious system. The teachings of Christianity were taken quite literally, and it was generally accepted that all life on earth had been created by God exactly as it existed in the present. Indeed, alterations in plants and animals were seen to be impossible because they would have run counter to God's plan. This belief that life forms could not change eventually came to be known in European intellectual circles as **fixity of species.**

Accompanying the notion of fixity of species was the belief that all God's creations were arranged in a hierarchy that progressed from the simplest organisms to the most complex. At the top of this linear sequence were humans. This concept of a ranked order of living things is termed the *Great Chain of Being* and was first proposed in the fourth century B.C. by the Greek philosopher Aristotle. Although position within the chain was based on physical similarities between species, no evolutionary or biological relationships were implied. Nor did "lower" forms move up the scale to become "superior" ones.

In addition, there was the common notion that the earth was "full" and that nothing new (such as species) could be added. Thus, it was believed that since the creation, no new species had appeared and none had disappeared, or become extinct. And since all of nature and the Great Chain of Being were created by God in a fixed state, change was inconceivable. Questioning the assumptions of fixity was ultimately seen as a challenge to God's perfection and could be considered heresy.

The plan of the entire universe was seen as the Grand Design—that is, God's design. In what is called the "argument from design," anatomical structures were viewed as planned to meet the purpose for which they were required. Wings, arms, eyes—all these structures were interpreted as neatly fitting the functions they performed, and nature was considered to be a deliberate plan of the Grand Designer.

The date the Grand Designer had completed his works was relatively recent—4004 B.C., according to Archbishop James Ussher (1581–1656), an Irish scholar who worked out the date of creation by analyzing the "begat" chapter of Genesis. Archbishop Ussher was not the first person to propose a recent origin of the earth, but he was responsible for providing a precise date for it.

The prevailing notion of the earth's brief existence, together with fixity of species, provided a formidable obstacle to the development of evolutionary theory because evolution requires time. Thus, in addition to overcoming the notion of fixity of species, scientists needed a theory of immense geological time in order to formulate evolutionary principles. In fact, until these prior concepts of fixity and time were fundamentally altered, it would have been unlikely that the idea of natural selection could even have been conceived.

The Scientific Revolution

What, then, upset the medieval belief in a rigid universe of planets, stars, plants, and animals? How did the scientific method as we know it today develop and, with the help of Newton and Galileo in the seventeenth century, demonstrate a moving, not static, universe?

The discovery of the New World and circumnavigation of the globe in the fifteenth century overturned some very fundamental ideas about the planet. For one

■ Fixity of species
The notion that species, once created, can never change; an idea diametrically opposed to theories of biological evolution.

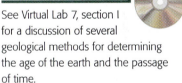
See Virtual Lab 7, section I for a discussion of several geological methods for determining the age of the earth and the passage of time.

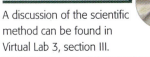
A discussion of the scientific method can be found in Virtual Lab 3, section III.

thing, the earth could no longer be perceived as flat. Also, as Europeans began to explore the New World, their awareness of biological diversity was greatly expanded through exposure to plants and animals previously unknown to them.

There were other attacks on the complacency of traditional beliefs. In 1514, a Polish mathematician named Copernicus challenged Aristotle's long-believed assertion that the earth, circled by the sun, moon, and stars, was the center of the universe. Copernicus removed the earth as the center of all things by proposing a *heliocentric* (sun-centered) solar system.

Copernicus' theory did not attract widespread attention at the time, but in the early 1600s, it was restated and further substantiated by an Italian mathematics professor, Galileo Galilei. Galileo came into direct confrontation with the Catholic Church over his publications, to the extent that he spent the last nine years of his life under house arrest. Even so, in intellectual circles, the universe had changed from one of fixity to one of motion, although most scholars still believed that change was impossible for living forms.

Scholars of the sixteenth and seventeenth centuries developed methods and theories that revolutionized scientific thought. The seventeenth century, in particular, was a beehive of scientific activity. The works of such individuals as Keppler, Descartes, and Newton established the laws of physics, motion, and gravity. Other achievements included the discovery of the circulation of blood and the development of numerous scientific instruments, including the telescope, barometer, and microscope. These technological advances permitted investigations of natural phenomena and opened up entire worlds for discoveries such as had never before been imagined.

The species concept is presented in Virtual Lab 1, section II.

Scientific achievement increasingly came to direct as well as reflect the changing views of Europeans. Investigations of stars, planets, animals, and plants came to be conducted without significant reference to the supernatural. In other words, nature was seen as a mechanism, functioning according to certain universal physical laws, and it was these laws that scientists were seeking. Yet, most scientists still insisted that a First Cause initiated the entire system. The argument from design was still defended, and support for it continued well into the nineteenth century and persists even today.

The Path to Natural Selection

Before early naturalists could begin to understand the forms of organic life, it was necessary to list and describe those forms. As attempts in this direction were made, scholars became increasingly impressed with the amount of biological diversity that confronted them.

John Ray By the sixteenth century, a keen interest in nature's variation had developed, and by the mid-1500s, there were a few descriptive works on plants, birds, fish, and mammals. But it was not until the seventeenth century that the concept of species was clearly defined by Englishman John Ray (1627–1705), an ordained minister trained at Cambridge University.

Ray was the first to recognize that groups of plants and animals could be distinguished from other groups by their ability to reproduce with one another and produce offspring. Such groups of reproductively isolated organisms were placed into a single category he called *species* (*pl.,* species). Thus, by the late 1600s, the biological criterion of reproduction was used to define species much as it is today (Young, 1992), and upon its publication, the concept was enthusiastically received by the scientific community.

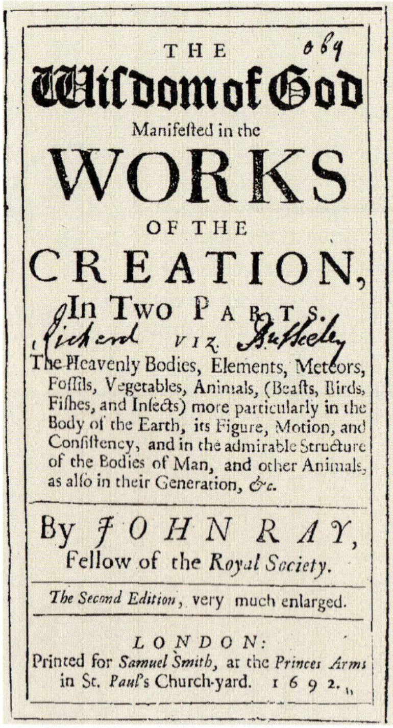
THE
Wiſdom of God
Manifeſted in the
WORKS
OF THE
CREATION,
In Two Parts.
VIZ.
The Heavenly Bodies, Elements, Meteors, Foſſils, Vegetables, Animals, (Beaſts, Birds, Fiſhes, and Inſects) more particularly in the Body of the Earth, its Figure, Motion, and Conſiſtency, and in the admirable Structure of the Bodies of Man, and other Animals; as alſo in their Generation, &c.

By JOHN RAY,
Fellow of the Royal Society.

The Second Edition, very much enlarged.

LONDON:
Printed for Samuel Smith, at the Princes Arms in St. Paul's Church-yard. 1692.

FIGURE 2–1

Title page from John Ray's publication showing God's plan in nature.

Ray also recognized that species frequently shared similarities with other species, and these he grouped together in a second level of classification he called the *genus* (*pl.,* genera). Ray was the first to use the labels *genus* and *species* in this manner, and they are the terms still in use today. But Ray was very much an adherent of fixity of species. His 1691 publication, *The Wisdom of God Manifested in the Works of Creation* (Fig. 2–1), was intended to demonstrate God's plan in nature, and in this work Ray stressed that nature was a deliberate outcome of a Grand Design.

Carolus Linnaeus   One of the leading naturalists of the eighteenth century was Carolus Linnaeus (1707–1778), of Sweden (Fig. 2–2). He is best known for developing a classification of plants and animals, the *Systema Naturae* (Systems of Nature), first published in 1735.

Linnaeus standardized Ray's more sporadic use of two names (genus and species) for organisms, thus firmly establishing the use of **binomial nomenclature.** Moreover, he added two more categories: class and order. Linnaeus' four-level system of classification became the basis for **taxonomy,** the system of classification still used today.

Another of Linnaeus' innovations was to include humans in his classification of animals, placing them in the genus *Homo* and species *sapiens.* The inclusion of humans in this scheme was controversial because it defied contemporary thought that humans, made in God's image, should be considered separately and outside the animal kingdom.

Linnaeus was also a believer in fixity of species, although in later years, faced with mounting evidence to the contrary, he came to question this long-held assumption. Indeed, fixity of species was being challenged on many fronts, especially in France, where voices were being raised in favor of a universe based on change and, more to the point, in favor of the relationship between similar forms based on descent from a common ancestor.

Comte de Buffon   Georges-Louis Leclerc (1707–1788), who was raised to the rank of count under the name Buffon, was Keeper of the King's Gardens in Paris (Fig. 2–3). He believed neither in the perfection of nature nor in the idea that nature had a purpose, as declared by the argument from design, but he did recognize the dynamic relationship between the external environment and living forms. In his *Natural History,* first published in 1749, he stressed again and again the importance of change in the universe, and he underlined the changing nature of species.

Buffon believed that when groups migrated to new areas of the world, each group would subsequently be influenced by local climatic conditions and would gradually change as a result of adaptation to the environment. Buffon's recognition of the external environment as an agent of change in species was an important innovation. However, he rejected the idea that one species could give rise to another.

Erasmus Darwin   Erasmus Darwin (1731–1802) is today best known as Charles Darwin's grandfather (Fig. 2–4). However, during his life, this freethinking, high-living physician was well known in literary circles for his poetry and other writings. Chief among the latter was his *Zoonomia,* in which evolutionary concepts were expressed in verse.

More than 50 years before his grandson was to startle the world with his views on natural selection, Erasmus Darwin had expressed similar ideas and had even commented on *human* evolution. From letters and other sources, it is known that Charles Darwin had read and was fond of his grandfather's writings. But the degree to which the grandson's theories were influenced by the grandfather is not known.

FIGURE 2–2

Linnaeus developed a classification system for plants and animals.

■ **Binomial nomenclature**
(*binomial,* meaning "two names") In taxonomy, the convention established by Carolus Linnaeus whereby genus and species names are used to refer to species. For example, *Homo sapiens* refers to human beings.

■ **Taxonomy**
The branch of science concerned with the rules of classifying organisms on the basis of evolutionary relationships.

The Linnaean system of binomial nomenclature for classifying animals and plants is discussed in Virtual Lab 1, section II.

FIGURE 2–3

Buffon recognized the influence of the environment on life forms.

FIGURE 2–4

Erasmus Darwin, grandfather of Charles Darwin, believed in species change.

FIGURE 2–5

Lamarck believed that species change was influenced by environmental change. He is known for his theory of the inheritance of acquired characteristics.

❚ Catastrophism

The view that the earth's geological landscape is the result of violent cataclysmic events. This view was promoted by Cuvier, especially in opposition to Lamarck.

Jean-Baptiste Lamarck   Neither Buffon nor Erasmus Darwin codified his beliefs into a comprehensive system that attempted to *explain* the evolutionary process. The first European scientist to do so was the French scholar Jean-Baptiste Pierre Antoine de Monet Chevalier de Lamarck (1744–1829). (Thankfully, most references to Lamarck use only his surname.)

Expanding beyond the views of Buffon, Lamarck (Fig. 2–5) attempted to *explain* evolution. He postulated a dynamic interaction between organic forms and the environment, such that organic forms could become altered in the face of changing environmental circumstances. Thus, as the environment changed, an animal's activity patterns would also change, resulting in increased or decreased use of certain body parts. As a result of this use or disuse, body parts became altered.

Physical alteration occurred as a function of perceived bodily "needs." If a particular part of the body felt a certain need, "fluids and forces" would be directed toward that point and the structure would be modified to satisfy the need. Because the modification would render the animal better suited to its habitat, the new trait would be passed on to offspring. This theory is known as the *inheritance of acquired characteristics,* or the *use-disuse* theory.

One of the most frequently given examples of Lamarck's theory is the giraffe, who, having stripped all the leaves from the lower branches of a tree (environmental change), strives to reach those leaves on upper branches. As vital forces progress to tissues of the neck, the neck increases slightly in length, thus enabling the giraffe to obtain more food. The longer neck is subsequently transmitted to offspring, with the eventual result that all giraffes have longer necks than did their predecessors (Fig. 2–6a). Thus, according to the theory of acquired characteristics, *a trait acquired by an animal during its lifetime can be passed on to offspring.* Today we know this explanation to be inaccurate, for only those traits coded for by genetic information contained within sex cells (eggs and sperm) can be inherited (see Chapters 3 and 4).

Because Lamarck's explanation of species change was not genetically correct, his theories are frequently derided. Actually, Lamarck deserves much credit. He was the first to recognize and stress the importance of interactions between organisms and the environment in the evolutionary process. Moreover, Lamarck was one of the first to acknowledge the need for a distinct branch of science that dealt solely with living things (i.e., separate from geology). For this new science, Lamarck coined the term *biology,* and a central feature of this new science was the notion of evolutionary change.

Georges Cuvier   The most vehement opponent of Lamarck was a young colleague, Georges Cuvier (1769–1832). Cuvier (Fig. 2–7) specialized in vertebrate paleontology, and it was he who introduced the concept of extinction to explain the disappearance of animals represented by fossils. Although a brilliant anatomist, Cuvier never grasped the dynamic concept of nature, and he adamantly insisted on the fixity of species. Just as the abundance of fossils in geological strata was becoming increasingly apparent, it also became more important to explain what they were. But rather than assume that similarities between certain fossil forms and living species indicated evolutionary relationships, Cuvier proposed a variation of a theory known as **catastrophism.**

Catastrophism held that the earth's geological features were the results of sudden, worldwide cataclysmic events, such as the Noah flood. Cuvier's version of catastrophism also postulated a series of regional disasters that destroyed most or all of the local plant and animal life. These areas of destruction were subsequently restocked with new forms that migrated in from neighboring, unaffected regions.

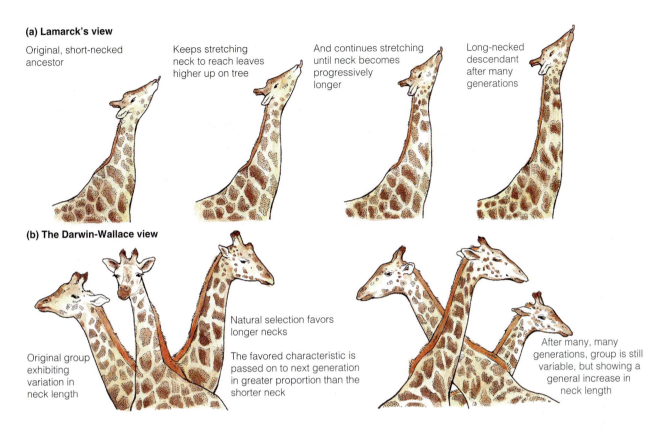

(a) Lamarck's view

Original, short-necked ancestor

Keeps stretching neck to reach leaves higher up on tree

And continues stretching until neck becomes progressively longer

Long-necked descendant after many generations

(b) The Darwin-Wallace view

Original group exhibiting variation in neck length

Natural selection favors longer necks

The favored characteristic is passed on to next generation in greater proportion than the shorter neck

After many, many generations, group is still variable, but showing a general increase in neck length

FIGURE 2–6

Contrasting ideas about the mechanism of evolution. (a) According to Lamarck's theory, acquired characteristics can be passed to subsequent generations. Thus, short-necked giraffes stretched their necks to reach higher into trees for food, and, according to Lamarck, this acquired trait was passed on to offspring, who were born with longer necks. (b) According to the Darwin-Wallace theory of natural selection, among giraffes there is variation in neck length. If having a longer neck provides an advantage for feeding, this trait will be passed on to a greater number of offspring, leading to an increase in the length of giraffe necks over many generations.

To be consistent with the fossil evidence, Cuvier also proposed that destroyed regions were repopulated by new organisms of a more modern appearance and that these forms were the results of more recent creation events. (The last of these creations is the one depicted in Genesis.) Thus, Cuvier's explanation of increased complexity over time avoided any notion of evolution, while still being able to account for the evidence of change as preserved in the fossil record.

Charles Lyell   Charles Lyell (1797–1875), the son of Scottish landowners, is considered the founder of modern geology (Fig. 2–8). He was a barrister by training, a geologist by avocation, and for many years Charles Darwin's friend and mentor. Before he met Darwin in 1836, Lyell had earned wide popular acclaim as well as acceptance in Europe's most prestigious scientific circles, thanks to his highly praised *Principles of Geology*, first published in three volumes in 1830–1833.

In this immensely important work, Lyell argued that the geological processes observed in the present are the same as those that occurred in the past. This

FIGURE 2–7

Cuvier explained the fossil record as the result of a succession of catastrophes followed by new creation events.

■ **Uniformitarianism**
The theory that the earth's features are the result of long-term processes that continue to operate in the present as they did in the past. Elaborated on by Lyell, this theory opposed catastrophism and provided for immense geological time.

FIGURE 2–8

Lyell, the father of geology, stated the theory of uniformitarianism in his Principles of Geology.

FIGURE 2–9

Thomas Malthus' Essay on the Principle of Population *led both Darwin and Wallace to the principle of natural selection.*

theory, which has come to be known as **uniformitarianism**, did not originate entirely with Lyell, but had been proposed by James Hutton in the late 1700s. Nevertheless, it was Lyell who demonstrated that such forces as wind, water erosion, local flooding, frost, the decomposition of vegetable matter, volcanoes, earthquakes, and glacial movements all had contributed in the past to produce the geological landscape that exists in the present. Moreover, the fact that these processes could still be observed in operation indicated that geological change continued to occur and that the forces that drove such change were consistent, or *uniform,* over time. In other words, although various aspects of the earth's surface (e.g., climate, flora, fauna, and land surfaces) are variable through time, the *underlying processes* that influence them are constant.

The theory of uniformitarianism flew in the face of Cuvier's catastrophism and did not go unopposed. Additionally, and every bit as controversially, Lyell emphasized the obvious: namely, that for such slow-acting forces to produce momentous change, the earth must indeed be far older than anyone had previously suspected.

By providing an immense time scale and thereby altering perceptions of earth's history from a few thousand to many millions of years, Lyell changed the framework within which scientists viewed the geological past. Thus, the concept of "deep time" (Gould, 1987) remains one of Lyell's most significant contributions to the discovery of evolutionary principles. The immensity of geological time permitted the necessary time depth for the inherently slow process of evolutionary change.

Thomas Malthus   In 1798, Thomas Robert Malthus (1766–1834), an English clergyman and economist, wrote *An Essay on the Principle of Population,* which inspired both Charles Darwin and Alfred Wallace in their separate discoveries of the principle of natural selection (Fig. 2–9). In his essay, Malthus pointed out that if not kept in check by limited food supplies, human populations could double in size every 25 years. That is, population size increases exponentially while food supplies remain relatively stable.

Malthus focused on humans because the ability to increase food supplies artificially reduces constraints on population growth, and he was arguing for population control. However, the same logic could be applied to nonhuman organisms. In nature, the tendency for populations to increase is continuously checked by resource availability. Thus, there is constant competition for food and other resources. In time, the extension of Malthus' principles to all organisms would be made by both Darwin and Wallace.

Charles Darwin   Charles Darwin (1809–1882) was one of six children of Dr. Robert and Susanna Darwin (Fig. 2–10). Being the grandson of wealthy Josiah Wedgwood (of Wedgwood pottery fame) as well as Erasmus Darwin, he grew up enjoying the lifestyle of the landed gentry in rural England.

As a boy, Darwin displayed a keen interest in nature and spent his days fishing and collecting shells, birds' eggs, and rocks. However, this developing interest in natural history did not dispel the generally held view of family and friends that he was not in any way remarkable. In fact, his performance at school was no more than ordinary.

After the death of his mother when he was eight, Darwin's upbringing was guided by his rather stern father and his older sisters. Because he showed little interest in, or aptitude for, anything except hunting, shooting, and perhaps science, his father, fearing Charles would sink into dissipation, sent him to

Edinburgh University to study medicine. It was in Edinburgh that Darwin first became acquainted with the evolutionary theories of Lamarck and others.

During this time (the 1820s), notions of evolution were becoming much feared in England and elsewhere. Certainly, anything identifiable with post-revolutionary France was viewed with grave suspicion by the established order in England. Lamarck, especially, was vilified by most English academicians, the majority of whom were also members of the Anglican clergy.

This was also a time of growing political unrest in Britain. The Reform Movement, which sought to undo many of the wrongs of the class system, was under way, and as with most social movements, this one contained a radical faction. Because many of the radicals were atheists and socialists who also supported Lamarck's evolutionary theory, evolution came to be associated, in the minds of many, with atheism and political subversion. Such was the growing fear of evolutionary ideas that many believed that if it were generally accepted that nature evolved unaided by God, "the Church would crash, the moral fabric of society would be torn apart, and civilized man would return to savagery" (Desmond and Moore, 1991, p. 34). It is unfortunate that some of the most outspoken early proponents of **transmutation** were so vehemently anti-Christian, because their rhetoric helped establish the entrenched suspicion and misunderstanding of evolutionary theory that persists even today.

While at Edinburgh, the young Darwin spent endless hours studying with professors who were outspoken supporters of Lamarck. Darwin's second year in Edinburgh saw him examining museum collections and attending natural history lectures. Therefore, although he hated medicine and left Edinburgh after two years, his experience there was a formative period in his intellectual development.

Subsequently, Darwin took up residence at Christ's College, Cambridge, to study theology. (Although he was rather indifferent to religion, theology was often seen as a last resort by parents who viewed their sons as having no discernible academic leanings.) It was during his Cambridge years that Darwin seriously cultivated his interests in natural science, and he often joined the field excursions of botany classes. He also was immersed in geology and was a frequent and serious participant in geological expeditions.

It was no wonder that following his graduation in 1831 at age 22, he was recommended to accompany a scientific expedition that would circle the globe. Thus it was, after overcoming his father's objections, that Darwin set sail aboard the HMS *Beagle* on December 17, 1831 (Fig. 2–11). The famous voyage of the *Beagle* was to last for almost five years and would forever change not only the course of Darwin's life, but also the history of biological science.

Darwin went aboard the *Beagle* believing in fixity of species. But during the voyage, he privately began to have doubts. As early as 1832, for example, he noted in his diary that a snake with rudimentary hind limbs marked "the passage by which Nature joins the lizards to the snakes." He came across fossils of ancient giant animals that looked, except for size, very much like living forms in the same vicinity, and he wondered whether the fossils were the ancestors of those living forms.

During the famous stopover at the Galápagos Islands (see Fig. 2–11), Darwin noted that the flora and fauna of South America showed striking similarities to those of the Galápagos, as well as intriguing differences. Even more surprising, the inhabitants of the various islands differed slightly from one another.

For example, Darwin collected 13 different varieties of Galápagos finches. These varieties shared many structural similarities, and clearly they represented a closely affiliated group. But at the same time, they differed with regard to certain

FIGURE 2–10

Charles Darwin as a young man.

▌**Transmutation**

The change of one species to another. The term *evolution* did not assume its current meaning until the late nineteenth century.

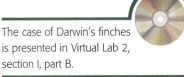

The case of Darwin's finches is presented in Virtual Lab 2, section I, part B.

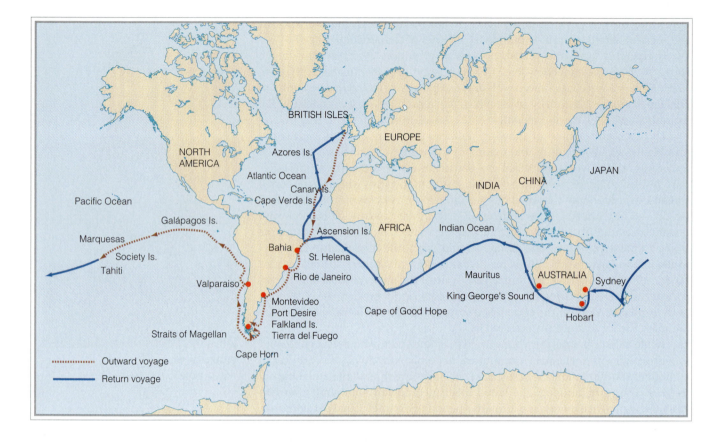

FIGURE 2–11

The route of the HMS Beagle.

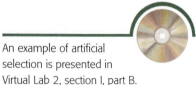

An example of artificial selection is presented in Virtual Lab 2, section I, part B.

physical traits, particularly in the shape and size of their beaks (Fig. 2–12). Darwin also collected finches from the South American mainland, and these appeared to represent only one group, or species.

The insight that Darwin gained from the finches is legendary. He recognized that the various Galápagos finches had all descended from a common, mainland ancestor and had become modified in response to the varying island habitats and to altered dietary preferences. But actually, it was not until *after* he had returned to England that Darwin recognized the significance of the variation in beak structure. In fact, during the voyage, Darwin had paid little attention to his finches. It was only in retrospect that he considered the factors that could lead to the modification of 1 species into 13 (Gould, 1985; Desmond and Moore, 1991).

Darwin returned to England in October 1836 and almost immediately was accepted into the most eminent of scientific circles. He married his cousin Emma Wedgwood and moved to the village of Down, near London, where he spent the rest of his life writing on topics ranging from fossils to orchids (Fig. 2–13). But his overriding concern was the question of species change.

At Down, Darwin began developing his views on what he termed *natural selection*. This concept was borrowed from animal breeders, who "select" as breeding stock those animals that exhibit specific traits they hope to emphasize in offspring. Animals with undesirable traits are "selected against," or prevented from breeding.

Darwin was keenly interested in domestic animals—pigeons, in particular—and how breeders could develop distinctive varieties in just a few generations. (The variations seen in domestic dog breeds may be the best example of the effects of selective breeding.) He applied his knowledge of domesticated species to naturally occurring ones, recognizing that in undomesticated organisms, the selective agent was nature, not humans.

By the late 1830s, Darwin recognized that biological variation within a species was critically important. Furthermore, he acknowledged the importance of sexual reproduction in increasing variation. Then, in 1838, Darwin read Malthus' essay, and in it he found the answer to his question of how new species came to be. He accepted from Malthus that populations increase at a faster rate than do resources, and he inferred that in nonhuman animals, increase in population size is continuously checked by limited food supplies. He also accepted Lyell's observation that in nature there is a constant "struggle for existence." The idea that in each generation more offspring are born than survive to adulthood coupled with the notions of competition for resources and biological diversity were all Darwin needed to develop his theory of natural selection. He wrote: "It at once struck me that under these circumstances favourable variations would tend to be preserved, and unfavourable ones to be destroyed. The result of this would be the formation of a new species" (F. Darwin, 1950, pp. 53–54). Basically, this quotation summarizes the whole of natural selection theory.

Darwin wrote a short summary of his views on natural selection in 1842 and revised it in 1844. The 1844 sketch is similar to the argument he presented 15 years later in *On the Origin of Species,* but in 1844 he did not feel he had sufficient data to support his views, so he continued his research without publishing.

Darwin had another reason for not publishing what he knew would be, to say the least, a highly controversial work. As a member of the established order, Darwin knew that many of his friends and associates were concerned with threats to the status quo, and evolutionary theory was viewed as a serious threat indeed. In addition, Darwin was a man to whom reputation was of paramount importance, and he was tormented by fears of bringing dishonor and public criticism to those he loved. Thus, he hesitated.

(a) Ground finch
   Main food: seeds
   Beak: heavy

(b) Tree finch
   Main food: leaves, buds,
   blossoms, fruits
   Beak: thick, short

(c) Tree finch (called
   woodpecker finch)
   Main food: insects
   Beak: stout, straight

(d) Ground finch (known as
   warbler finch)
   Main food: insects
   Beak: slender

FIGURE 2–12

Beak variation in Darwin's Galápagos finches.

FIGURE 2–13

The Darwin home, Down House, in the village of Down, as seen from the rear garden. On the Origin of Species was written here.

FIGURE 2–14

Alfred Russel Wallace independently uncovered the key to the evolutionary process.

Virtual Lab 2, section I, provides a discussion of the concept of natural selection.

Alfred Russel Wallace   Unlike Darwin, Alfred Russel Wallace (1823–1913) was born into a family of modest means (Fig. 2–14). He went to work at 14, and without any special talent and little formal education, he moved from one job to the next. He became interested in collecting plants and animals, and in 1848 he joined an expedition to the Amazon, where he acquired firsthand knowledge of natural phenomena. Then, in 1854, he sailed for Southeast Asia and the Malay Peninsula to continue his study and to collect bird and insect specimens.

In 1855, Wallace published a paper suggesting that species were descended from other species and that the appearance of new species was influenced by environmental factors (Trinkaus and Shipman, 1992). The Wallace paper spurred Lyell and others to urge Darwin to publish, but still he hesitated. Wallace and Darwin even corresponded briefly.

Then, in 1858, Wallace sent Darwin another paper titled *On the Tendency of Varieties to Depart Indefinitely from the Original Type*. In this paper, Wallace described evolution as a process driven by competition and natural selection. Upon receipt of Wallace's paper, Darwin despaired. He feared that Wallace might be credited for a theory (natural selection) that he himself had formulated. He quickly wrote a paper presenting his ideas, and both the paper by Darwin and the one by Wallace were read before the Linnean Society of London in 1858. Neither author was present. Wallace was not in the country, and Darwin was mourning the very recent death of his young son.

The papers received little notice at the time, but at the urging of Lyell and others, Darwin completed and published his greatest work, *On the Origin of Species,** in December 1859. Upon publication, the storm broke, and it has not abated even to this day. While there was much praise for the book, the gist of opinion was negative. Scientific opinion gradually came to Darwin's support, assisted by Darwin's able friend, Thomas Huxley, who for years wrote and spoke in favor of natural selection. The riddle of species was now explained: Species were mutable, not fixed; and they evolved from other species through the mechanism of natural selection.

Natural Selection

Early in his research, Darwin had realized that selection was the key to evolution. With the help of Malthus' ideas, he saw *how* selection in nature could be explained. In the struggle for existence, those *individuals* with favorable variations would survive and reproduce; those with unfavorable variations would not.

For Darwin, the explanation of evolution was simple. The basic processes, as he understood them, are as follows:

1. All species are capable of producing offspring at a faster rate than food supplies increase.
2. There is biological variation within all species; except for identical twins, no two individuals are exactly alike.
3. Because in each generation more individuals are produced than can survive, owing to limited resources, there is competition between individuals. (*Note:* This statement does not imply that there is constant fierce fighting.)
4. Those individuals who possess favorable variations or traits (e.g., speed, disease resistance, protective coloration) have an advantage over individuals

---

*The full title is *On the Origin of Species by Means of Natural Selection, or the Preservation of Favoured Races in the Struggle for Life*.

that do not possess them. By virtue of the favorable trait, these individuals are more likely to survive to produce offspring than are others.

5. The environmental context determines whether or not a trait is beneficial. That is, what is favorable in one setting may be a liability in another. In this way, which traits become most advantageous is the result of a natural process.

6. Traits are inherited and are passed on to the next generation. Because individuals who possess favorable traits contribute more offspring to the next generation than do others, over time, such traits become more common in the population; less favorable traits are not passed on as frequently and become less common. Those individuals who produce more offspring, compared to others, are said to have greater **reproductive success.**

7. Over long periods of geological time, successful variations accumulate in a population, so that later generations may be distinct from ancestral ones. Thus, in time, a new species may appear.

8. Geographical isolation may also lead to the formation of new species. As populations of a species become geographically isolated from one another, for whatever reasons, they begin to adapt to different environments. Over time, as populations continue to respond to different **selective pressures** (i.e., different ecological circumstances), they may become distinct species, descended from a common ancestor. The 13 species of Galápagos finches, presumably all descended from a common ancestor on the South American mainland, provide an example of the role of geographical isolation.

Before Darwin, scientists thought of species as entities that could not change. Because individuals within the species did not appear to be significant, they were not the object of study; therefore, it was difficult for many scientists to imagine how change could occur. Darwin, as we have pointed out, saw that variation among individuals could explain how selection occurred. Favorable variations were selected for survival by nature; unfavorable ones were eliminated.

This emphasis on the uniqueness of the individual led Darwin to natural selection as the mechanism that made evolution work. *Natural selection operates on individuals,* favorably or unfavorably, but *it is the population that evolves.* The unit of natural selection is the individual; the unit of evolution is the population.

Natural Selection in Action

A well-documented case of natural selection acting in modern populations concerns changes in pigmentation among peppered moths near Manchester, England (Fig. 2–15). Before the nineteenth century, the common variety of moth was a mottled gray color. This light, mottled coloration provided extremely effective camouflage against lichen-covered tree trunks. Also present, though less common, was a dark variety of the same species. While resting on light, lichen-covered trees, the dark, uncamouflaged moths were more visible to birds and were therefore eaten more often. (In this example, birds are the *selective agent.*) Thus, in the end, the dark moths produced fewer offspring than the light, camouflaged moths. Yet, by the end of the nineteenth century, the common gray form had been almost completely replaced by the black variety.

What had brought about this rapid change? The answer lies in the rapidly changing environment of industrialized nineteenth-century England. Coal dust in the area settled on trees, killing the lichen and turning the bark a dark color. Moths continued to rest on trees, but the gray (light) variety was increasingly

■ **Reproductive success**
The number of offspring an individual produces and rears to reproductive age; an individual's genetic contribution to the next generation, as compared to the contributions of other individuals.

■ **Selective pressures**
Forces in the environment that influence reproductive success in individuals. In the example of the peppered moth, birds applied the selective pressure.

An example of natural selection acting on human populations is given in Virtual Lab 2, section III, part B.

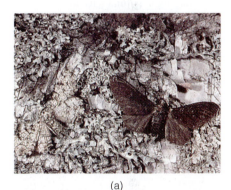

(a)

(b)

FIGURE 2–15

Variation in the peppered moth. (a) The dark form is more visible on the light, lichen-covered tree. (b) On trees darkened by pollution, the lighter form is more visible.

conspicuous as the trees became darker. Consequently, they began to be preyed on more frequently by birds and contributed fewer genes to the next generation. In the late twentieth century, increasing control of pollutants allowed trees to return to their lighter, lichen-covered, preindustrial condition. As would be expected, the black variety of moth is now being supplanted by the gray.

The substance that produces coloration is a pigment called *melanin,* and the evolutionary shift in the peppered moth, as well as in many other moth species, is termed *industrial melanism.* Such an evolutionary shift in response to environmental change is called *adaptation.*

This example of the peppered moths provides numerous insights into the mechanism of evolutionary change by natural selection:

1. *A trait must be inherited to have importance in natural selection.* A characteristic that is not hereditary (such as a temporary change in hair pigmentation brought about by dye) will not be passed on to succeeding generations. In moths, pigmentation is a demonstrated hereditary trait.

2. *Natural selection cannot occur without variation in inherited characteristics.* If all the moths had initially been gray (you will recall that some dark forms were present) and the trees had become darker, the survival and reproduction of all moths could have been so low that the population might have become extinct. Such an event is not unusual and without variation would nearly always occur. *Selection can work only with variation that already exists.*

3. **Fitness** *is a relative measure that will change as the environment changes.* Fitness is simply differential reproductive success. In the initial stage, the gray moth was the more fit variety because gray moths produced more offspring. But as the environment changed, the black moths became more fit, and a further change reversed the adaptive pattern. It should be obvious that statements regarding the "most fit" life form mean nothing without reference to specific environments.

The example of the peppered moths shows how different death rates influence natural selection, since moths that die early tend to leave fewer offspring. But mortality is not the entire picture. Another important aspect of natural selection is fertility, for an animal that gives birth to more young would pass its genes on at a faster rate than one that bears fewer offspring. However, fertility is not the entire picture either, for the crucial element is the number of young raised successfully to the point at which they themselves reproduce. We may state this simply as *differential net reproductive success.* The way this mechanism works can be demonstrated through another example.

In a common variety of small birds called swifts, data show that giving birth to more offspring does not necessarily guarantee that more young will be successfully raised. The number of eggs hatched in a breeding season is a measure of fertility. The number of birds that mature and are eventually able to leave the nest is a measure of net reproductive success, or offspring successfully raised. The following tabulation shows the correlation between the number of eggs hatched (fertility) and the number of young that leave the nest (reproductive success) averaged over four breeding seasons (Lack, 1966):

Number of eggs hatched (fertility)	2 eggs	3 eggs	4 eggs
Average number of young raised (reproductive success)	1.92	2.54	1.76
Sample size (number of nests)	72	20	16

❚ Fitness

Pertaining to natural selection, a measure of *relative* reproductive success of individuals. Fitness can be measured by an individual's genetic contribution to the next generation compared to that of other individuals.

As the tabulation shows, the most efficient fertility number is three eggs, since that number yields the highest reproductive success. Raising two is less beneficial to the parents, since the end result is not as successful as with three eggs. Trying to raise more than three young is actually detrimental, since the parents may not be able to provide adequate nourishment for any of the offspring. An offspring that dies before reaching reproductive age is, in evolutionary terms, equivalent to never having been born in the first place. Actually, such a result may be an evolutionary minus to the parents, for this offspring will drain their resources and may inhibit their ability to raise other offspring, thereby lowering their reproductive success even further. Selection will favor those genetic traits that yield the maximum net reproductive success. If the number of eggs laid* is a genetic trait in birds (and it seems to be), natural selection in swifts should act to favor the laying of three eggs as opposed to two or four.

Constraints on Nineteenth-Century Evolutionary Theory

Darwin argued eloquently for the notion of evolution in general and the role of natural selection in particular, but he did not entirely comprehend the exact mechanisms of evolutionary change.

As we have seen, natural selection acts on *variation* within species. Neither Darwin nor anyone else in the nineteenth century understood the source of all this variation. Consequently, Darwin speculated about variation arising from "use"—an idea similar to Lamarck's. Darwin, however, was not as dogmatic in his views as Lamarck and most emphatically argued against inner "needs" or "effort." Darwin had to confess that when it came to explaining variation, he simply did not know: "Our ignorance of the laws of variation is profound. Not in one case out of a hundred can we pretend to assign any reason why this or that part differs, more or less, from the same part in the parents" (Darwin, 1859, pp. 167–168).

In addition to his inability to explain the origins of variation, Darwin also did not completely understand the mechanism by which parents transmitted traits to offspring. Almost without exception, nineteenth-century scholars were confused about the laws of heredity, and the popular consensus was that inheritance was *blending* by nature. In other words, offspring were expected to express intermediate traits as a result of a blending of their parents' contributions. Given this view, we can see why the actual nature of genes was unimaginable. Without any viable alternatives, Darwin accepted this popular misconception. As it turned out, a contemporary of Darwin's had systematically worked out the rules of heredity. However, the work of this Augustinian monk, Gregor Mendel (whom you will meet in Chapter 4), was not recognized until the beginning of the twentieth century.

See Virtual Lab 2, section II, for a discussion of the genetic basis for inheritance.

Opposition to Evolution

The publication of *On the Origin of Species* fanned the flames of controversy over evolution into an inferno, but the question had already been debated in intellectual

---

*The number of eggs hatched is directly related to the number of eggs laid.

circles for some years, with most people vehemently opposed to evolutionary theory. The very idea that species could give rise to other species was particularly offensive to many Christians because it appeared to be in direct conflict to the special creation event depicted in Genesis. People were horrified at the notion that humans might be biologically related to other animals and especially that they might share a common ancestor with the great apes. Even to make such a claim was degrading, for it denied humanity its unique and exalted place in the universe; in the minds of many, it denied the very existence of God.

The debate has not ended even now, some 140 years later. For the majority of scientists today, evolution is fact. Indeed, the genetic evidence for it is indisputable, and anyone who appreciates and understands genetic mechanisms cannot avoid the conclusion that populations and species evolve. Moreover, the majority of Christians do not believe that biblical depictions are to be taken literally. But at the same time, surveys show that almost half of all Americans believe that evolution does not occur. There a number of reasons for this.

The mechanisms of evolution are complex and do not lend themselves to simple explanations. To understand these mechanisms requires some familiarity with genetics and biology, a familiarity that most people do not possess. Moreover, people who have not been exposed to scientific training, want definitive answers to complicated questions. But as you learned in Chapter 1, science does not prove truths, and it frequently does not provide definitive answers.

Another fact to consider is that while all religions offer explanations for natural phenomena, and some even feature the transformation of individuals from one form to another, none really proposes biological change over time. Most people, regardless of their culture, are raised in belief systems that do not emphasize biological continuity between species or offer scientific explanations for natural phenomena.

The relationship between science and religion has never been easy. While both serve, in their own ways, to explain phenomena, scientific explanations are based in data analysis and interpretation. Religion, meanwhile, is a system of beliefs not amenable to scientific testing and falsification; it is based in faith. Religion and science concern different aspects of the human experience, and although they use different approaches in areas where they overlap, they are not inherently mutually exclusive. In fact, many people see them as two sides of the same coin. Moreover, evolutionary theories are not considered anathema by all religions (or even by all forms of Christianity). Some years ago, the Vatican hosted an international conference on human evolution, and in 1996, Pope John Paul II issued a statement to the Pontifical Academy of Sciences acknowledging that "fresh knowledge leads to recognition of the theory of evolution as more than just a hypothesis." Today, the official position of the Catholic Church is that evolutionary processes do occur but that the human soul is of divine creation and not subject to evolutionary processes. Likewise, mainstream Protestants do not generally see a conflict. Unfortunately, those who believe in a literal interpretation of the Bible (termed fundamentalists) do not accept any form of compromise.

Reacting to rapid cultural changes after World War I, conservative Christians in the United States sought a revival of what they considered traditional values. In their view, one way to do this was to prevent any mention of Darwinism in public schools. The Butler Act, passed in Tennessee in 1925, was one result of this effort, and it banned the teaching of evolution in public schools in that state. To test the validity of the law, the American Civil Liberties Union persuaded John Scopes, a high school teacher, to be arrested and ultimately tried for teaching evolution.

The subsequent trial was the famous Scopes Monkey Trial, in which the well-known orator William Jennings Bryan was the prosecuting attorney. The lawyer for the defense was Clarence Darrow, a nationally known labor and criminal lawyer. The trial ended with the conviction of Scopes, who was fined $100. The case was appealed to the Tennessee Supreme Court, which upheld the law, and the teaching of evolution remained illegal in Tennessee. Eventually, several other states, mostly in the South, passed similar laws, and it was not until 1967 that the last two states (Tennessee and Arkansas) ceased to prohibit the teaching of evolution.

But the story does not end there. In the more than 70 years since the Scopes trial, religious fundamentalists have persisted in their attempts to remove evolution from public school curricula. Known as creationists because they explain the existence of the universe as a result of a sudden creation, they are determined either to eliminate the teaching of evolution or to introduce antievolutionary material into public school classes. In the past 20 years, creationists have insisted that creation "science" is just as valid a scientific endeavor as is the study of evolution. They argue that in the interest of fairness, a balanced view should be offered: If evolution is taught as science, then creationism should also be taught as science. But creation "science" is, by definition, not science at all. Creationists assert that their view is absolute and infallible. Consequently, creationism is not a hypothesis that can be tested, nor is it amenable to falsification. Because such testing is the basis of all science, creationism, by its very nature, cannot be considered science. It is religion.

Still, creationists have been active in state legislatures, promoting the passage of laws mandating the inclusion of creationism in school curricula. To this effect, the Arkansas state legislature passed Act 590 in 1981. But this law was challenged and overturned in 1982. Judge William Ray Overton, in his ruling against the state, found that "a theory that is by its own terms dogmatic, absolutist and never subject to revision is not a scientific theory." And he added: "Since creation is not science, the conclusion is inescapable that the only real effect of Act 590 is the advancement of religion." In 1987, the United States Supreme Court struck down a similar law in Louisiana.

So far, these and related laws have been overturned because they violate the provision for separation of church and state in the First Amendment to the Constitution. But this has not stopped the creationists, who have encouraged teachers to claim "academic freedom" to teach creationism. Also, they have dropped the term *creationism* in favor of less religious sounding terms, such as *intelligent design theory*.

Although the courts have consistently ruled against the creationists, these religious fundamentalists have nevertheless had an impact on the teaching of evolution. Many public school teachers, seeking to avoid controversy, simply do not cover evolution, or they refer to it as "just a theory" (see p. 16). Thus, students may not be exposed to theories of evolution until they go to college—and only then if they take related courses. This consequence is ultimately to the detriment of the biological sciences (and education in general) in the United States.

Summary

Our current understanding of evolutionary processes is directly traceable to developments in intellectual thought in western Europe over the last 300 years. In particular, the contributions of Linnaeus, Lamarck, Buffon, Lyell, and Malthus all had

Be sure to complete the exercise at the end of Virtual Lab 2, section IV.

a significant impact on Darwin. The year 1859 marks a watershed in evolutionary theory, for in that year, the publication of Darwin's *On the Origin of Species* crystallized the understanding of the evolutionary process (particularly the crucial role of natural selection) and for the first time thrust evolutionary theory into the consciousness of the general public. Debates both inside and outside the sciences continued for several decades (and in some quarters persist today), but the theory of evolution irrevocably changed the tide of intellectual thought. Gradually, Darwin's formulation of the evolutionary process became accepted almost universally by scientists as the very foundation of all the biological sciences, physical anthropology included. As we approach the twenty-first century, contributions from genetics allow us to demonstrate the mechanics of evolution in a way unknown to Darwin and his contemporaries.

Natural selection is the central determining factor influencing the long-term direction of evolutionary change. How natural selection works can best be explained as differential reproductive success—in other words, how successful individuals are in leaving offspring to succeeding generations.

Questions for Review

1. Trace the history of intellectual thought immediately leading to Darwin's theory.
2. What is fixity of species? Why did it pose a problem for the development of evolutionary thinking?
3. What was John Ray's major contribution to biology and the development of evolutionary theories?
4. In what ways did Linnaeus and Buffon differ in their approach to the concept of evolution?
5. What are the bases of Lamarck's theory of acquired characteristics? Why is this theory incorrect?
6. What was Lamarck's contribution to nineteenth-century evolutionary ideas?
7. Explain Cuvier's notion of catastrophism.
8. What did Malthus and Lyell contribute to Darwin's thinking on evolution?
9. Darwin approached the subject of species change by emphasizing individuals within populations. Why was this significant to the development of the concept of natural selection?
10. What evidence did Darwin use to strengthen his argument concerning evolution?
11. How did Darwin's explanation of evolution differ from Lamarck's?
12. What is meant by adaptation? Illustrate through the example of industrial melanism.
13. Define natural selection. What is a selective agent? Give an example.
14. Explain why the changes in coloration in populations of peppered moths serve as a good example of natural selection.
15. Explain why some people are opposed to the teaching of evolutionary principles.

Suggested Further Reading

Burke, James. 1985. *The Day the Universe Changed.* Boston: Little, Brown.
Desmond, Adrian, and James Moore. 1991. *Darwin.* New York: Warner Books.

Gould, Stephen Jay. 1987. *Time's Arrow, Time's Cycle*. Cambridge, MA: Harvard University Press.

Ridley, Mark. 1993. *Evolution*. Boston: Blackwell Scientific Publications.

Trinkaus, Eric, and Pat Shipman. 1993. *The Neandertals*. New York: Knopf.

Young, David. 1992. *The Discovery of Evolution*. London: Natural History Museum Publications, Cambridge University Press.

Additional Resources

Multimedia Tools

Virtual Laboratories for Physical Anthropology CD-ROM
The following concepts in this chapter are covered on the physical anthropology CD-ROM:
geology, dating methods (Virtual Lab 7.I)
scientific method, hypothesis, predictions, theory (Virtual Lab 3.III)
species, classification (Virtual Lab 1.II)
Linnaeus, binomial nomenclature (Virtual Lab 1.II)
Darwin's finches, variation (Virtual Lab 2.I.B)
artificial selection, domestication (Virtual Lab 2.I.B)
natural selection, individual variation (Virtual Lab 2.I)
natural selection, individual variation (Virtual Lab 2.III.B)
genetics, inheritance (Virtual Lab 2.II)
natural selection, evolution (Virtual Lab 2.IV)

Wadsworth Anthropology Resource Center
http://anthropology.wadsworth.com
Visit Anthropology Online to obtain current updates in the field, surfing tips, career information and more. In addition, enrich your study efforts with text-specific study aids arranged by chapter.

InfoTrac College Edition
http://www.infotrac-college.com/wadsworth
1. Darwin's theory of evolution by natural selection is a straightforward explanation of evolutionary change. Yet, many people find it hard to understand how complicated features like the human brain or eye could evolve solely by means of natural selection. An interesting investigation of this can be found in an article by Stephen J. Gould, entitled "Creating the creators: if creation demands a visionary creator, then how does blind evolution manage to build such splendid new things as ourselves?" from *Discover Magazine*. Find this article on InfoTrac College Edition. What is Gould's explanation for how complex structures evolve? How does this differ from or add to Darwin's explanation of evolution by natural selection?
2. This chapter contains a great deal of information about Darwin and the theory of evolution through natural selection, yet there is a great deal of information that could not be discussed in these pages. What more can you learn about Darwin and the theory of evolution by natural selection on InfoTrac College Edition? After reading two or three articles, take the Charles Darwin Birthday Quiz from *American Scientist*, March–April 1997, v85 n2 p104(4). It should have come up

during your search. How did you do? Try to find the answers to those questions you answered incorrectly either in InfoTrac or on the Web.

■ ⊕ **Internet Exercises**

1. As you learned in this chapter, Charles Darwin's theory of natural selection was influenced by the writings of numerous other naturalists. You can either use your search engine or go to **www.ucmp. berkeley.edu/history/evolution.html** to read more about these influential people and the development of evolutionary thought. Under "Preludes to Evolution" click on the name of someone discussed in this chapter (perhaps Lamarck). What additional facts did you learn? Than choose someone not discussed in the textbook and write one or two paragraphs describing that person's contributions.

2. Using the same Web site or another you have discovered, read about Thomas Huxley. (In the above-mentioned Web site he is listed under "Natural Selection and Beyond".) Although this chapter does not discuss Huxley, he was instrumental in the acceptance of Darwin's theories. Write a few paragraphs summarizing Huxley's defense of evolutionary theory. On what points was he critical?

3. Search for *Origin of Species* or go to **www.literature.org/Works/ CharlesDarwin** to find full text versions of *Origin* and *The Voyage of the Beagle*. Read Chapter 4 of *Origin* on natural selection and write a summary of what Darwin said. What did he mean by "favourable variations"? Can you think of an example? Also, in anticipation of things to come in this textbook, read his discussion of sexual selection also included under *natural selection*.

4. You may also wish to read a chapter or two of *The Voyage of the Beagle* for insights into how Darwin collected specimens and formulated his theory. Pay particular attention to his descriptions of the natural environment, animal anatomy and behavior, and local people.

The Biological Basis of Life

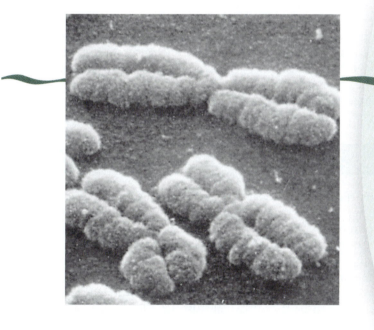

Introduction

This text is about human evolution and adaptation, both of which are intimately linked to life processes that involve cells, the replication and decoding of genetic information, and the transmission of this information between generations. Thus, to present human evolution and adaptation in the broad sense, we must first examine how life is organized at the cellular and molecular levels, and this, in turn, necessitates a brief discussion of the fundamental principles of genetics.

Genetics is the study of how traits are transmitted from one generation to the next. Because physical anthropologists are concerned with human evolution, adaptation, and variation, they must have a thorough understanding of the factors that lie at the very root of these phenomena. Indeed, although many physical anthropologists do not actually specialize in genetics, it is genetics that ultimately links or influences many of the various subdisciplines of biological anthropology.

The discipline of genetics is largely a twentieth-century development, and much of our present knowledge has been acquired within the last 50 years. Today, insights into the numerous aspects of inheritance are increasing at an exponential rate, with new discoveries being made virtually every day. Moreover, as genetic technologies develop and increasingly come into use, they assume an ever greater role in the lives of us all.

It is therefore more important than ever that, as people living at the beginning of the twenty-first century, we achieve a basic understanding of the factors that influence our lives. Also, from an anthropological perspective, it is only through the further elucidation of genetic principles that we can hope to understand fully the evolutionary mechanisms that have permitted humans to become the species we are today.

The Cell

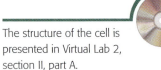

The structure of the cell is presented in Virtual Lab 2, section II, part A.

To discuss genetic and evolutionary principles, we must first have a fundamental understanding of cell function. Cells are the basic units of life in all living organisms. In some forms, such as bacteria, a single cell constitutes the entire organism. However, more complex *multicellular* forms, such as plants, insects, birds, and mammals, are composed of billions of cells. Indeed, an adult human is made up of perhaps as many as 1,000 billion (1,000,000,000,000) cells, all functioning in complex ways that ultimately promote the survival of the individual.

Life on earth can be traced back at least 3.7 billion years, in the form of *prokaryotic* cells. Prokaryotes are single-celled organisms, represented today by bacteria and blue-green algae. Structurally more complex cells appeared approximately 1.2 billion years ago, and these are referred to as *eukaryotic* cells. Because eukaryotic cells are found in all multicellular organisms, they are the focus of the remainder of this discussion. In spite of the numerous differences between various life forms and the cells that constitute them, it is important to understand that the cells of all living organisms share many similarities as a result of their common evolutionary past.

In general, a eukaryotic cell is a three-dimensional entity composed of *carbohydrates, lipids, nucleic acids,* and *proteins.* It contains a variety of structures called *organelles* within the *cell membrane* (Fig. 3–1). One of these organelles is the **nucleus** (*pl.,* nuclei), a discrete unit surrounded by a thin membrane. Within the nucleus are two nucleic acids that contain the genetic information that controls

■ **Nucleus**
A structure (organelle) found in all eukaryotic cells. The nucleus contains chromosomes (nuclear DNA).

the cell's functions. These two critically important **molecules** are **deoxyribonu-cleic acid (DNA)** and **ribonucleic acid (RNA)**. (In prokaryotic cells, genetic information is not contained within a walled nucleus.) Surrounding the nucleus is the **cytoplasm**, which contains numerous other types of organelles involved in various activities, such as breaking down nutrients and converting them to other substances (*metabolism*), storing and releasing energy, eliminating waste, and manufacturing **proteins (protein synthesis)**.

Two of these organelles—**mitochondria** and **ribosomes**—require further mention. The mitochondria (*sing.*, mitochondrion) are responsible for energy production in the cell and are thus the "engines" that drive the cell. Mitochondria are round or oval structures enclosed within a folded membrane, and they contain their own distinct DNA, called mitochondrial DNA (mtDNA), which directs mitochondrial activities. Mitochondrial DNA has the same molecular structure and function as nuclear DNA, but it is organized somewhat differently. In recent years, mtDNA has attracted much attention because of particular traits it influences and because it has significance for studies of certain evolutionary processes. For these reasons, mitochondrial inheritance will be discussed in more detail in Chapters 4 and 13. Ribosomes are roughly spherical in shape and are the most common type of cytoplasmic organelle. They are made up partly of RNA and are essential to the synthesis of proteins (see p. 50).

There are basically two types of cells: **somatic cells** and **gametes**. Somatic cells are the cellular components of body tissues, such as muscle, bone, skin, nerve, heart, and brain. Gametes, or sex cells, are specifically involved in reproduction and are not important as structural components of the body. There are two types of gametes: *ova*, or egg cells, produced in the ovaries in females; and *sperm*, which develop in male testes. The sole function of a sex cell is to unite with a gamete from another individual to form a **zygote**, which has the potential of developing into a new individual. By so doing, gametes transmit genetic information from parent to offspring.

■ Molecules
Structures made up of two or more atoms. Molecules can combine with other molecules to form more complex structures.

■ Deoxyribonucleic acid (DNA)
The double-stranded molecule that contains the genetic code. DNA is a main component of chromosomes.

■ Ribonucleic acid (RNA)
A single-stranded molecule, similar in structure to DNA. The three forms of RNA are essential to protein synthesis.

■ Cytoplasm
The portion of the cell contained within the cell membrane, excluding the nucleus. The cytoplasm consists of a semifluid material and contains numerous structures involved with cell function.

■ Proteins
Three-dimensional molecules that serve a wide variety of functions through their ability to bind to other molecules.

■ Protein synthesis
The assembly of chains of amino acids into functional protein molecules. The process is directed by DNA.

■ Mitochondria
(*sing.*, mitochondrion) Organelles found in the cytoplasm of cells that are responsible for producing energy for cellular functions.

■ Ribosomes
Structures found in the cytoplasm that are essential to the manufacture of proteins.

■ Somatic cells
Basically, all the cells in the body except those involved with reproduction.

■ Gametes
Reproductive cells (eggs and sperm in animals) developed from precursor cells in ovaries and testes.

■ Zygote
A cell formed by the union of an egg and a sperm cell. It contains the full complement of chromosomes (in humans, 46) and has the potential of developing into an entire organism.

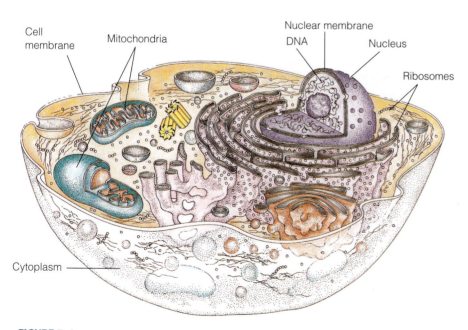

Cell membrane
Mitochondria
Nuclear membrane
DNA
Nucleus
Ribosomes
Cytoplasm

FIGURE 3–1

Structure of a generalized eukaryotic cell, illustrating the cell's three-dimensional nature. Although various organelles are shown, for the sake of simplicity only those we discuss are labeled.

Virtual Lab 2, section II, parts A and E, discusses the importance of gametes in sexual reproduction and inheritance.

■ **Nucleotides**
Basic units of the DNA molecule, composed of a sugar, a phosphate, and one of four DNA bases.

■ **Complementary**
Referring to the fact that DNA bases form base pairs in a precise manner. For example, adenine can bond only to thymine. Thus, these two bases are said to be *complementary* because one requires the other to form a complete DNA base pair.

■ **Replicate**
To duplicate. The DNA molecule is able to make copies of itself.

Discussions of DNA structure and the process of replication are presented in Virtual Lab 2, section II, parts B and C.

■ **Enzymes**
Specialized proteins that initiate and direct chemical reactions in the body.

DNA Structure

As already mentioned, cellular functions are directed by DNA. If we are to understand these functions and how characteristics are inherited, we must first know something about the structure and function of DNA.

In 1944, the results of a 10-year study demonstrated that the DNA molecule was the material responsible for the transmission of inherited traits, at least in some bacteria (Avery, MacLeod, and McCarty, 1944). However, the exact physical and chemical properties of DNA were at that time still unknown. Subsequently, in 1953, James Watson and Francis Crick developed a structural and functional model of DNA (Watson and Crick, 1953a, 1953b). The importance of their achievement cannot be overstated, for it completely revolutionized the fields of biology and medicine and forever altered our understanding of biological and evolutionary mechanisms.

The DNA molecule is composed of two chains of even smaller molecules called **nucleotides.** A nucleotide, in turn, is made up of three components: a sugar molecule (deoxyribose), a phosphate unit, and one of four nitrogenous bases (Fig. 3–2). In DNA, nucleotides are stacked upon one another to form a chain that is bonded along its bases to another **complementary** nucleotide chain. Together the two twist to form a spiral, or helical, shape. The resulting DNA molecule, then, is two-stranded and is described as forming a *double helix* that resembles a twisted ladder. If we follow the twisted ladder analogy, the sugars and phosphates represent the two sides, while the bases and the bonds that join them form the rungs.

The secret of how DNA functions lies within the four bases. These bases are *adenine, guanine, thymine,* and *cytosine,* and they are frequently referred to by their initial letters, A, G, T, and C. In the formation of the double helix, it is possible for one type of base to pair, or bond, with only one other type. Thus, base pairs can form *only* between adenine and thymine and between guanine and cytosine (see Fig. 3–2). This specificity is essential to the DNA molecule's ability to **replicate,** or make an exact copy of itself, and DNA is the only molecule known to have this capacity.

DNA Replication

Growth and development of organisms and tissue repair following injury or disease are among the crucial processes made possible by cell division. Cells multiply by dividing in such a way that each new cell receives a full complement of genetic material. This is a crucial point, since a cell cannot function properly without the appropriate amount of DNA. For new cells to receive the essential amount of DNA, it is first necessary for the DNA to replicate.

Prior to cell division, specialized **enzymes** break the bonds between bases in the DNA molecule, leaving the two previously joined strands of nucleotides with their bases exposed (Fig. 3–3). The exposed bases then attract unattached DNA nucleotides, which are free-floating in the cell nucleus.

Because one base can be joined to only one other, the attraction between bases occurs in a complementary fashion. Thus, the two previously joined parental nucleotide chains serve as models, or *templates,* for the formation of new strands of nucleotides. As each new strand is formed, its bases are joined to the bases of an original strand. When the process is completed, there are two double-

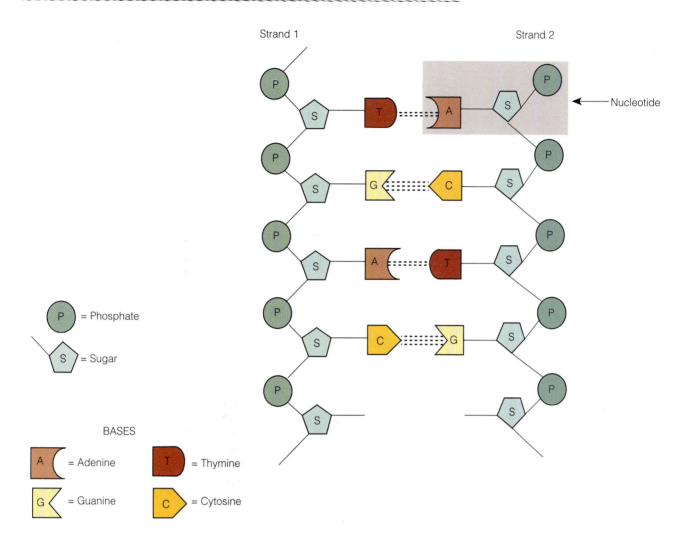

Strand 1   Strand 2

Nucleotide

P = Phosphate

S = Sugar

BASES

A = Adenine   T = Thymine

G = Guanine   C = Cytosine

stranded DNA molecules exactly like the original one, and each newly formed molecule consists of one original nucleotide chain joined to a newly formed chain (see Fig. 3–3).

Protein Synthesis

One of the most important functions of DNA is that it directs protein synthesis within the cell. Proteins are complex, three-dimensional molecules that function through their ability to bind to other molecules. For example, the protein **hemoglobin,** found in red blood cells, is able to bind to oxygen and serves to transport oxygen to cells throughout the body.

Proteins function in myriad ways. Some are structural components of tissues. Collagen, for example, is the most common protein in the body and is a major component of all connective tissues. Aside from mineral components, it is the most abundant structural material in bone. Enzymes are also proteins, and their function is to initiate and enhance chemical reactions. An example of a digestive enzyme is *lactase,* which breaks down *lactose,* or milk sugar, into two simpler

FIGURE 3–2

Part of a DNA molecule. The illustration shows the two DNA strands with the sugar and phosphate backbone and the bases extending toward the center.

Virtual Lab 2, section II, part C, presents an example of protein synthesis.

▮ **Hemoglobin**

A protein molecule that occurs in red blood cells and binds to oxygen molecules.

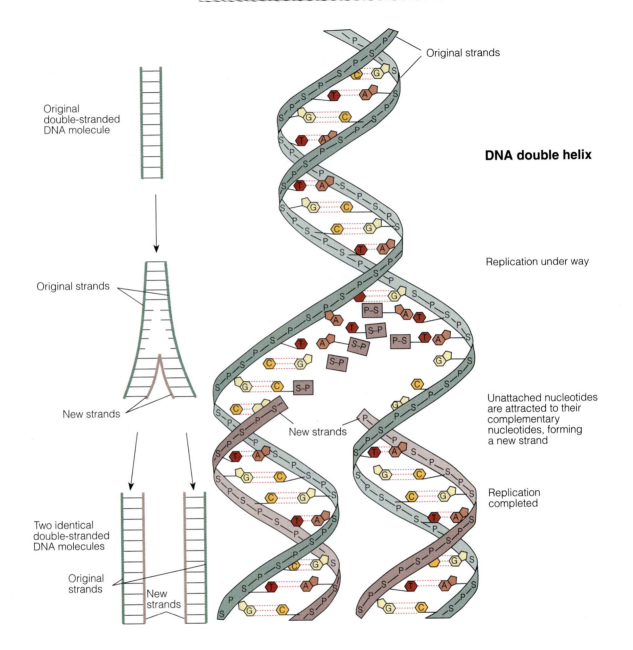

Original double-stranded DNA molecule

Original strands

New strands

Two identical double-stranded DNA molecules

Original strands

New strands

Original strands

DNA double helix

Replication under way

Unattached nucleotides are attracted to their complementary nucleotides, forming a new strand

New strands

Replication completed

FIGURE 3–3

DNA replication. During DNA replication, the two strands of the DNA molecule are separated, and each strand serves as a template for the formation of a new strand. When replication is complete, there are two DNA molecules. Each molecule consists of one new and one original DNA strand.

■ **Hormones**
Substances (usually proteins) that are produced by specialized cells and that travel to other parts of the body, where they influence chemical reactions and regulate various cellular functions.

sugars. Another class of proteins includes many types of **hormones.** Specialized cells produce and release hormones into the bloodstream to circulate to other areas of the body, where they produce specific effects in tissues and organs. A good example of this type of protein is *insulin,* produced by cells in the pancreas. Insulin causes cells in the liver and certain types of muscle tissue to absorb glucose (sugar) from the blood. (Enzymes and hormones will be discussed in more detail in Chapter 16.)

As you can see, proteins make us what we are. Not only are they the major constituents of all body tissues, but they also direct and perform physiological and cellular functions. It is therefore critical that protein synthesis occur accurately, for if it does not, physiological development and activities can be disrupted or even prevented.

Proteins are composed of linear chains of smaller molecules called **amino acids.** In all, there are 20 amino acids, 8 of which must be obtained from dietary sources (see Chapter 16). The remaining 12 are produced in cells. These 20 amino acids are combined in different amounts and sequences to produce potentially millions of proteins. What makes proteins different from one another is the number of amino acids involved and the *sequence* in which they are arranged. For a protein to function properly, its amino acids must be arranged in the proper sequence.

DNA serves as a recipe for making a protein, for it is the sequence of DNA bases that ultimately determines the order of amino acids in a protein molecule. In the DNA instructions, a *triplet,* or group of three bases, specifies a particular amino acid. For example, if a triplet consists of the base sequence cytosine, guanine, and adenine (CGA), it specifies the amino acid *alanine.* If the next triplet in the chain consists of the sequence guanine, thymine, and cytosine (GTC), it refers to another amino acid—*glutamine.* Therefore, a DNA recipe might look like this: AGA CGA ACA ACC TAC TTT TTC CTT AAG GTC and so on (Table 3–1).

▌ Amino acids

Small molecules that are the components of proteins.

TABLE 3–1 The Genetic Code

Amino Acid Symbol	Amino Acid	mRNA Codon	DNA Triplet
Ala	Alanine	GCU, GCC, GCA, GCG	CGA, CGG, CGT, CGC
Arg	Arginine	CGU, CGC, CGA, CGG, AGA, AGG	GCA, GCG, GCT, GCC, TCT, TCC
Asn	Asparagine	AAU, AAC	TTA, TTG
Asp	Aspartic acid	GAU, GAC	CTA, CTG
Cys	Cysteine	UGU, UGC	ACA, ACG
Gln	Glutamine	CAA, CAG	GTT, GTC
Glu	Glutamic acid	GAA, GAG	CTT, CTC
Gly	Glycine	GGU, GGC, GGA, GGG	CCA, CCG, CCT, CCC
His	Histidine	CAU, CAC	GTA, GTG
Ile	Isoleucine	AUU, AUC, AUA	TAA, TAG, TAT
Leu	Leucine	UUA, UUG, CUU, CUC, CUA, CUG	AAT, AAC, GAA, GAG, GAT, GAC
Lys	Lysine	AAA, AAG	TTT, TTC
Met	Methionine	AUG	TAC
Phe	Phenylalanine	UUU, UUC	AAA, AAG
Pro	Proline	CCU, CCC, CCA, CCG	GGA, GGG, GGT, GGC
Ser	Serine	UCU, UCC, UCA, UCG, AGU, AGC	AGA, AGG, AGT, AGC, TCA, TCG
Thr	Threonine	ACU, ACC, ACA, ACG	TGA, TGG, TGT, TGC
Trp	Tryptophan	UGG	ACC
Tyr	Tyrosine	UAU, UAC	ATA, ATG
Val	Valine	GUU, GUC, GUA, GUG	CAA, CAG, CAT, CAC
Terminating triplets		UAA, UAG, UGA	ATT, ATC, ACT

■ Messenger RNA (mRNA)

A form of RNA that is assembled on a sequence of DNA bases. It carries the DNA code to the ribosome during protein synthesis.

■ Codon

A triplet of messenger RNA bases that refers to a specific amino acid during protein synthesis.

■ Transfer RNA (tRNA)

The type of RNA that binds to specific amino acids and transports them to the ribosome during protein synthesis.

Protein synthesis is a little more complicated than the preceding few sentences would imply. For one thing, protein synthesis occurs outside the nucleus at specialized structures in the cytoplasm called *ribosomes* (see p. 45). A logistics problem arises because the DNA molecule is not capable of traveling outside the cell's nucleus. Thus, the first step in protein synthesis is to copy the DNA message into a form that can pass through the nuclear membrane into the cytoplasm. This process is accomplished through the formation of a molecule similar to DNA called ribonucleic acid, or RNA. RNA is different from DNA in three important ways:

1. It is single-stranded.
2. It contains a different type of sugar.
3. It contains the base uracil as a substitute for the DNA base thymine. (Uracil is attracted to adenine, just as thymine is.)

The RNA molecule forms on the DNA template in much the same manner as new DNA molecules are assembled. As in DNA replication, the two DNA strands separate, but only partially, and one of these strands attracts free-floating RNA nucleotides, which are joined together on the DNA template. This new RNA nucleotide chain is called **messenger RNA (mRNA)** and its formation is called *transcription* because, in fact, it is transcribing, or copying, the DNA code (Fig. 3–4). But the resulting mRNA segment is actually a complement, rather than an identical copy, of the DNA strand on which it is formed. If, for example, the DNA triplet reads CTA, then the corresponding mRNA triplet, or **codon**, will be GAU. (Remember that in RNA, the base uracil replaces thymine; see Table 3–1.) The process continues until a section of DNA called a terminator region (composed of one of three DNA triplets) is reached and transcription stops (see Table 3–1). At this point, the mRNA strand, comprising anywhere from 5,000 to perhaps as many as 200,000 nucleotides, peels away from the DNA model and a portion of it travels through the nuclear membrane to the ribosome. Meanwhile, the bonds between the DNA bases are reestablished, and the DNA molecule is once more intact.

As the mRNA strand arrives at the ribosome, the message it contains is translated. (This stage of the process is called *translation* because at this point, the genetic instructions are actually being decoded and implemented.) Just as each DNA triplet specifies one amino acid, mRNA codons also serve this function. Therefore, the mRNA strand is "read" in codons, or groups of three bases taken together (see Table 3–1).

One other form of RNA—**transfer RNA (tRNA)**—is essential to the actual assembly of a protein. Each molecule of tRNA has the ability to bind to one specific amino acid. A particular tRNA molecule carrying the amino acid matching the mRNA codon being translated arrives at the ribosome and deposits its amino acid (Fig. 3–5). As a sec-

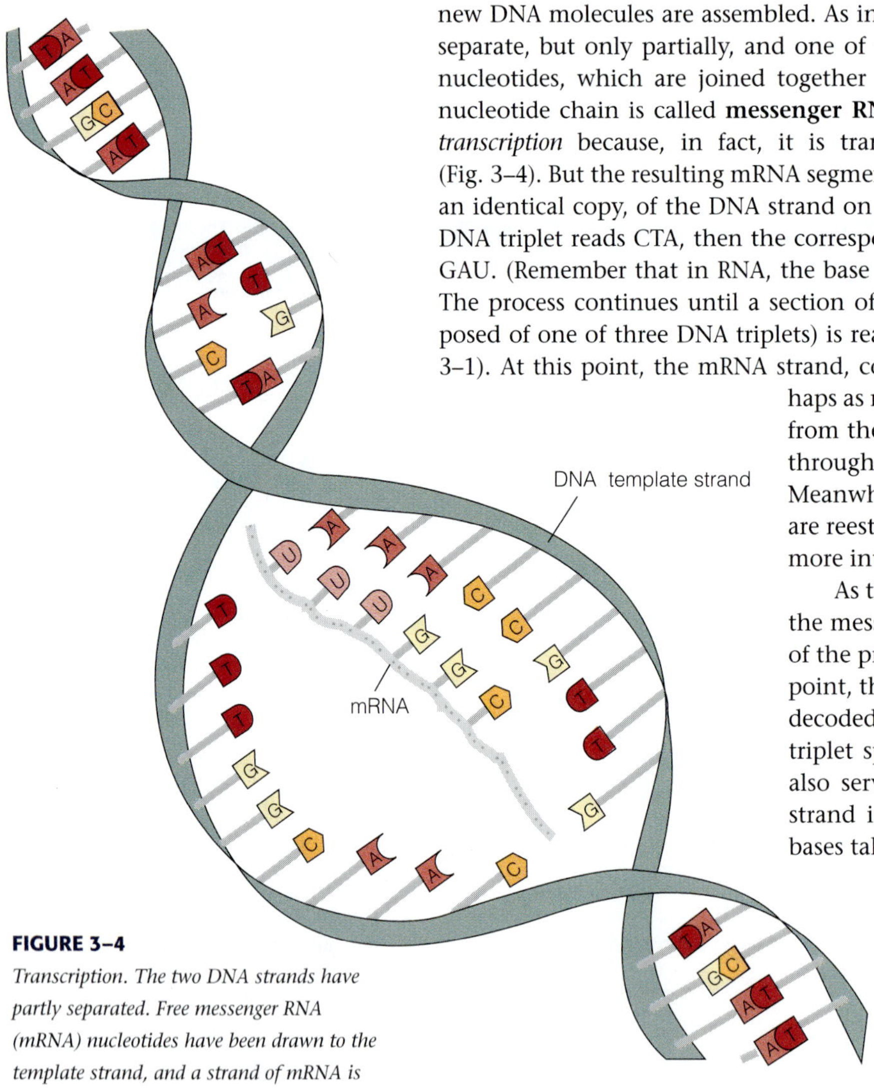

DNA template strand

mRNA

FIGURE 3–4

Transcription. The two DNA strands have partly separated. Free messenger RNA (mRNA) nucleotides have been drawn to the template strand, and a strand of mRNA is being made. Note that the mRNA strand will exactly complement the DNA template strand, except that uracil (U) replaces thymine (T).

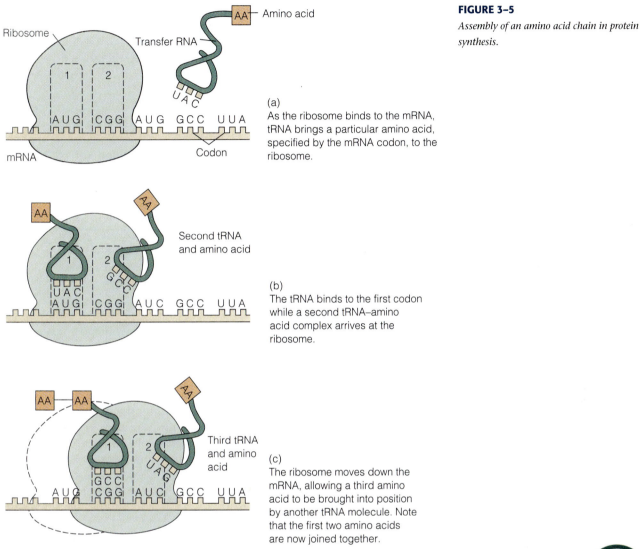

(a)
As the ribosome binds to the mRNA, tRNA brings a particular amino acid, specified by the mRNA codon, to the ribosome.

(b)
The tRNA binds to the first codon while a second tRNA–amino acid complex arrives at the ribosome.

(c)
The ribosome moves down the mRNA, allowing a third amino acid to be brought into position by another tRNA molecule. Note that the first two amino acids are now joined together.

FIGURE 3–5

Assembly of an amino acid chain in protein synthesis.

ond amino acid is deposited, the two are joined in the order dictated by the sequence of mRNA codons. In this way, series of amino acids are linked together to form a structure that will eventually function as a protein.

What Is a Gene?

The entire sequence of DNA bases responsible for the synthesis (or manufacture) of a protein or, in some cases, a portion of a protein is referred to as a **gene.** Or, put another way, a gene is a segment of DNA that specifies the sequence of amino acids in a particular protein. Even more precisely, a gene codes for the production of a **polypeptide chain.** Those proteins composed of only a single polypeptide chain are produced through the action of a single gene. However, some proteins (collagen and hemoglobin, for example) are made up of two or more polypeptide chains, each of which results from the action of a different gene. Thus, while

The concept of the gene is discussed in Virtual Lab 2, section II, part B.

■ **Gene**

A sequence of DNA bases that specifies the order of amino acids in an entire protein or, in some cases, a portion of a protein. A gene may be made up of hundreds or thousands of DNA bases.

■ **Polypeptide chain**

A sequence of amino acids that may act alone or in combination as a functional protein.

■ Mutation
A change in DNA. Technically, mutation refers to changes in DNA bases as well as changes in chromosome number and/or structure.

some proteins result from the action of only one gene, others are produced by two or more.

A gene may comprise only a few hundred bases, or it may be composed of thousands. If the sequence of DNA bases is altered through **mutation** (a change in the DNA), the manufacture of some proteins may not occur, and the cell (or indeed the organism) may not function properly (if it functions at all).

This definition of a gene is a functional one and it is technically correct. But it is important to understand that gene action is an incredibly complex phenomenon that is only partly understood. For example, the DNA segments that are transcribed into mRNA and therefore code for specific amino acids are termed *exons.* But not all nucleotide sequences in a gene are actually expressed during protein synthesis. In fact, some sequences, called *introns,* are initially transcribed but subsequently eliminated. Thus, introns are not represented in the newly formed mRNA segment and they are not translated into amino acid sequences. But while introns are not instrumental in protein synthesis, they are indeed a part of the DNA molecule, and it is the combination of introns and exons, interspersed along a strand of DNA, that comprises the unit we call a gene.

While we usually think of genes as coding for the production of structural proteins, some genes function primarily to control the expression of other genes. Basically, these *regulatory genes* produce enzymes and other proteins that either switch on or turn off other segments of DNA. Consequently, this mechanism is critical for individual organisms and also has important evolutionary implications.

All somatic cells contain the same genetic information, but in any given cell, only a fraction of the DNA is actually involved in protein synthesis. For example, bone cells carry the same DNA that codes for the production of digestive enzymes, as do the cells of the stomach lining. But bone cells do not produce digestive enzymes. Instead, they manufacture collagen, the major organic component of bone. Bone cells produce collagen and not digestive enzymes because of the differentiation of cell lines early in embryonic development. During this process, cells undergo changes in form, their functions become specialized, and most of their DNA is permanently deactivated through the action of regulatory genes.

Gene regulation also means that cells express some genes only at certain times during the life cycle. An example of this type of control is the production of hemoglobin in human development. As mentioned, hemoglobin is the protein molecule contained in red blood cells that is responsible for transporting oxygen molecules to body cells and tissues. But humans produce three different varieties of hemoglobin at different developmental stages, depending on the availability of oxygen. Consequently, the hemoglobin produced in an early embryo differs from that in a 6-month fetus, which is again different from the hemoglobin of a 6-month-old infant. The existence of embryonic, fetal, and adult hemoglobin results from genes being turned off and on at various developmental stages by regulatory genes.

On a larger scale, alterations in the behavior of regulatory genes that influence the activities of the structural genes involved in growth and development may be responsible for some of the physical differences between closely related species. For example, some of the anatomical differences between humans and chimpanzees, who share 98 percent of their DNA, may be the results of evolutionary changes in regulatory genes in one or both lineages.

A final point is that the genetic code is *universal* (Box 3–1); that is, DNA is the genetic material in all forms of life (at least on earth). This means that the DNA of all organisms, from bacteria to oak trees to human beings, is composed of the

BOX 3-1

Characteristics of the DNA Code

1. **The Code is universal.** In other words, the same basic messages apply to all life forms on the planet, from bacteria to humans. The same triplet code, specifying each amino acid, thus applies to all life on earth. This commonality is the basis for the methods used in recombinant DNA technology.
2. **The Code is triplet.** Each amino acid is specified by a sequence of three bases in the mRNA (the codon), which in turn is coded for by three bases in the DNA.
3. **The Code is continuous—without pauses.** There are no pauses or other delimiters separating one codon from another. Thus, if a base should be deleted, the entire frame would be moved, drastically altering the message downstream for successive codons. Such a gross alteration is termed a *frame-shift mutation.* Note that although the code lacks "commas," it does contain "periods"; that is, three specific codons act to stop translation.

4. **The Code is redundant.** While there are 20 amino acids, there are 4 DNA bases and 64 possible codons. Even considering the three "stop" messages, that still leaves 61 codons specifying the 20 amino acids. Thus, many amino acids are specified by more than one codon (see Table 3–1). For example, leucine and serine are each coded for by six different codons. In fact, only two amino acids (methionine and tryptophan) are coded for by a single codon. Redundancy is useful. For one thing, it serves as a safety net of sorts by helping to reduce the likelihood of severe consequences if there is a change, or *mutation,* in a DNA base. For example, four different DNA triplets—CGA, CGG, CGT, and CGC—code for the amino acid alanine. If, in the codon CGA, A mutates to G, the resulting triplet, CGG, will still specify alanine; thus, there will be no functional change.

same molecules using the same kinds of instructions. These similarities imply biological relationships among, and ultimately a common ancestry for, all forms of life. What makes oak trees distinct from humans is not differences in the basic DNA material, but differences in how that material is arranged.

Mutation: When a Gene Changes

Probably the best way to envision how genetic material is organized and functions is to see what happens when it changes, or mutates. The first clearly elucidated example of a molecular mutation in humans concerned a portion of the hemoglobin molecule. Normal adult hemoglobin is made up of four polypeptide chains (two *alpha* chains and two *beta* chains) that are direct products of gene action. Each beta chain is in turn composed of 146 amino acids.

There are several hemoglobin disorders with genetic origins, and perhaps the best known of these is **sickle-cell anemia,** which results from a defect in the beta chain. Individuals with sickle-cell anemia inherit a variant of a gene from *both* parents that contains the substitution of one amino acid (*valine*) for the normally occurring *glutamic acid.* This single amino acid substitution at the sixth position of the beta chain results in the production of an altered and less efficient form of hemoglobin called hemoglobin S (Hb^S). The normal form is called hemoglobin A (Hb^A). In situations where the availability of oxygen is reduced, such as high altitude, or when oxygen requirements are increased through

Virtual Lab 2, section III, part B, presents the example of sickle-cell anemia in human populations.

■ Sickle-cell anemia
A severe inherited hemoglobin disorder that results from inheriting two copies of a mutant allele. This allele results from a single base substitution at the DNA level.

exercise, red cells bearing Hb^S collapse, roughly assuming a sickle shape. What follows is a cascade of events, all of which result in severe anemia and its consequences. Briefly, these events include impaired circulation from blocked capillaries, red blood cell destruction, oxygen deprivation to vital organs (including the brain), and, without treatment, death.

Individuals who inherit the altered form of the gene from only one parent have what is termed *sickle-cell trait;* because only about 40 percent of their hemoglobin is abnormal, they are much less severely affected and usually have a normal life span.

The cause of all the serious problems associated with sickle-cell anemia is a minute change in the Hb gene. Remember that both normal hemoglobin and the sickle-cell variety have 146 amino acids, 145 of which are identical. Moreover, to emphasize further the importance of a seemingly minimal alteration, consider that triplets of DNA bases are required to specify amino acids. Therefore, it takes 438 bases (146 × 3) to produce the chain of 146 amino acids forming the adult hemoglobin beta chain. But a change in only one of these 438 bases produces the cascade of life-threatening complications seen in sickle-cell anemia.

Figure 3–6 shows a possible DNA base sequence and the resulting amino acid products for both normal and sickling hemoglobin. As can be seen, a single base substitution (from CTC to CAC) can result in an altered amino acid sequence, from

FIGURE 3–6

Substitution of one base at position #6 produces sickling hemoglobin.

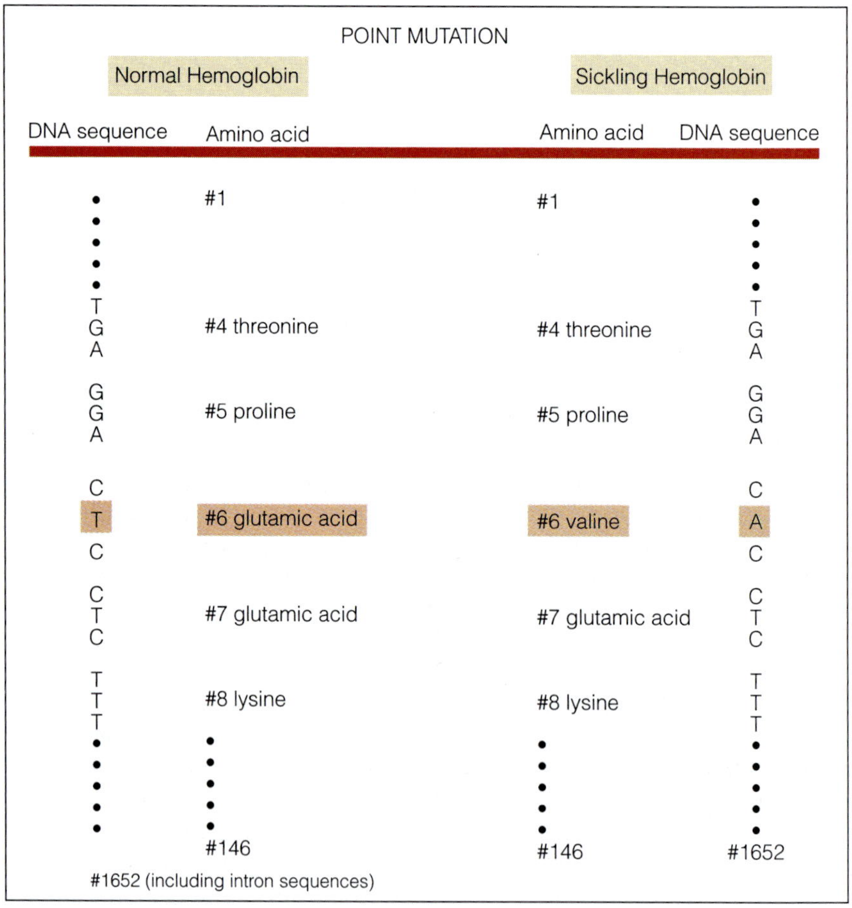

. . . proline—*glutamic acid*—glutamic acid . . .
to
. . . proline—*valine*—glutamic acid . . .

Such a change in the genetic code is referred to as a **point mutation**, and in evolution, it is the most common and most important source of new genetic variation in populations. Point mutations, like that for the Hb gene, probably occur relatively frequently during cell division. But a new mutation will have evolutionary significance only if it is passed on to offspring through the gametes. Once such a mutation has occurred, its fate in the population will depend on the other evolutionary forces, especially natural selection. In fact, sickle-cell anemia is the best-demonstrated example of natural selection acting on human beings, a point that will be considered in more detail in Chapter 4.

Chromosomes

Much of a cell's existence is spent in **interphase**, the portion of its life cycle during which the cell is involved with metabolic processes and other activities. During interphase, the cell's DNA exists as an uncoiled, granular substance called **chromatin.** (Incredibly, there are an estimated 6 feet of DNA in the nucleus of every one of your somatic cells!) However, at various times in the life of most types of cells, interphase is interrupted, activities cease, and the cell divides.

Cell division is the process that results in the production of new cells, and it is during this process that the chromatin becomes tightly coiled and is visible under a light microscope as a set of discrete structures called **chromosomes** (Fig. 3–7). A chromosome is composed of a DNA molecule and associated proteins (Fig. 3–8). During normal cell function, if chromosomes were visible, they would appear as single-stranded structures. However, during the early stages of cell

◾ Point mutation
A chemical change in a single base of a DNA sequence.

◾ Interphase
The portion of a cell's cycle during which metabolic processes and other cellular activities occur. Chromosomes are not visible as discrete structures at this time. DNA replication occurs during interphase.

◾ Chromatin
The loose, diffuse form of DNA seen during interphase. When condensed, chromatin forms into chromosomes.

◾ Chromosomes
Discrete structures composed of DNA and protein found only in the nuclei of cells. Chromosomes are only visible under magnification during certain phases of cell division.

FIGURE 3–7
Scanning electron micrograph of human chromosomes during cell division. Note that these chromosomes are composed of two strands, or two DNA molecules.

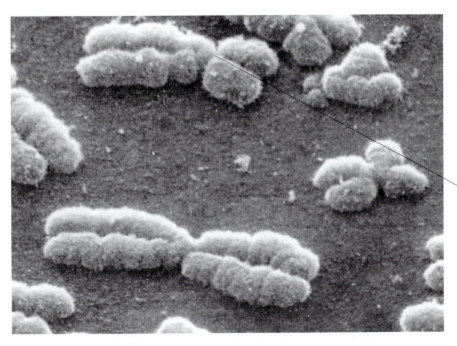

Centromere

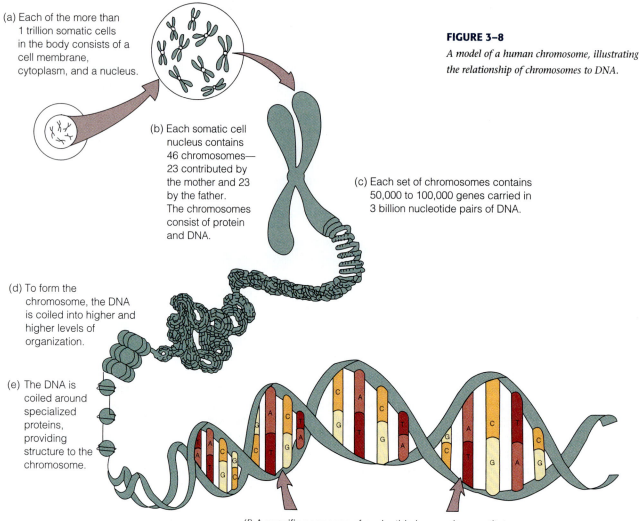

(a) Each of the more than 1 trillion somatic cells in the body consists of a cell membrane, cytoplasm, and a nucleus.

(b) Each somatic cell nucleus contains 46 chromosomes— 23 contributed by the mother and 23 by the father. The chromosomes consist of protein and DNA.

(c) Each set of chromosomes contains 50,000 to 100,000 genes carried in 3 billion nucleotide pairs of DNA.

(d) To form the chromosome, the DNA is coiled into higher and higher levels of organization.

(e) The DNA is coiled around specialized proteins, providing structure to the chromosome.

(f) A specific sequence of nucleotide base pairs constitutes a gene.

■ **Centromere**
The constricted portion of a chromosome. After replication, the two strands of a double-stranded chromosome are joined at the centromere.

■ **Homologous**
Referring to members of chromosome pairs. Homologous chromosomes carry loci that govern the same traits. During meiosis, homologous chromosomes pair and exchange segments of DNA. They are alike with regard to size, position of centromere, and banding pattern.

division, they are made up of two strands, or two DNA molecules, joined together at a constricted area called the **centromere**. There are two strands simply because the DNA molecules have *replicated* during interphase, and one strand of a chromosome is an exact copy of the other.

Every species is characterized by a specific number of chromosomes in somatic cells (Table 3–2). In humans, there are 46. Chimpanzees and gorillas possess 48. This difference in chromosome number does not necessarily indicate that humans possess less DNA than chimpanzees and gorillas. The DNA is simply packaged differently in the three species.

In eukaryotic species, chromosomes generally occur in pairs. Thus, human somatic cells contain 23 pairs. One member of each pair is inherited from the father (paternal), while the other member is inherited from the mother (maternal).

Members of chromosomal pairs are said to be **homologous** in that they are alike in size and position of the centromere and they carry genetic information influencing the same *traits*. This does not imply that homologous chromosomes

TABLE 3–2 Standard Chromosomal Complement in Various Organisms

Organism	Chromosome Number in Somatic Cells	Chromosome Number in Gametes
Human (Homo sapiens)	46	23
Chimpanzee (Pan troglodytes)	48	24
Gorilla (Gorilla gorilla)	48	24
Dog (Canis familiaris)	78	39
Chicken (Gallus domesticus)	78	39
Frog (Rana pipiens)	26	13
Housefly (Musca domestica)	12	6
Onion (Allium cepa)	16	8
Corn (Zea mays)	20	10
Tobacco (Nicotiana tabacum)	48	24

Source: Cummings, 1991, p. 16.

are genetically identical. It simply means that the characteristics they govern are the same. For example, on both of a person's ninth chromosomes, there is a **locus,** or gene position, that determines which of the four ABO blood types (A, B, AB, or O) he or she will have. However, the two ninth chromosomes might not have identical DNA segments at the ABO locus. In other words, at numerous genetic loci, there may be more than one possible form of a gene, and these molecularly different forms are called **alleles.** Thus, alleles are alternate forms of a gene that can direct the cell to produce slightly different forms of the same protein and, ultimately, different expressions of traits. At the ABO locus, there are three possible alleles: *A, B,* and *O.* (However, since individuals only possess two ninth chromosomes, only two alleles are present in any one person.) It is the allelic variation at the ABO locus that is responsible for the variation among humans in ABO blood type. Moreover, the potential variation that exists at specific loci in homologous chromosomes (as illustrated by the ABO example) explains how members of a chromosome pair may influence the same traits and yet not be genetically identical. (This point is covered in more detail in Chapter 4.)

There are two basic types of chromosomes: **autosomes** and **sex chromosomes.** Autosomes carry genetic information that governs all physical characteristics except primary sex determination. The two sex chromosomes are the X and Y chromosomes. In mammals, the Y chromosome carries genetic information directly involved with determining maleness. The X chromosome, although termed a "sex chromosome," is larger and functions more like an autosome in that it is not actually involved in primary sex determination but does influence a number of other traits.

Among mammals, all genetically normal females have two X chromosomes (XX); they are female simply because the Y chromosome is not present. All genetically normal males have one X and one Y chromosome (XY). In other classes of animals, such as birds or insects, primary sex determination is governed by differing chromosomal mechanisms.

It is extremely important to note that *all* autosomes occur in pairs. Normal human somatic cells have 22 pairs of autosomes and one pair of sex chromosomes.

Locus

(*pl.,* loci) (pronounced lo´-kus and lo-sigh´) The position on a chromosome where a given gene occurs. The term is sometimes used interchangeably with *gene,* but this usage is technically incorrect.

Alleles

Alternate forms of a gene. Alleles occur at the same locus on homologous chromosomes and thus govern the same trait. However, because they are different, their action may result in different expressions of that trait. The term is often used synonymously with *gene.*

Autosomes

All chromosomes except the sex chromosomes.

Sex chromosomes

In mammals, the X and Y chromosomes.

It should also be noted that abnormal numbers of autosomes are almost always fatal to the individual, usually soon after conception. Although abnormal numbers of sex chromosomes are not usually fatal, they may result in sterility and frequently have other consequences as well (see p. 64 for further discussion). Therefore, to function normally, it is essential for a human cell to possess both members of each chromosomal pair, or a total of 46 chromosomes.

Karyotyping Chromosomes

One method frequently used to examine chromosomes in an individual is to produce what is termed a **karyotype**. (An example of a human karyotype is shown in Fig. 3–9.) Chromosomes used in karyotypes are obtained from dividing cells. (You will remember that chromosomes are visible as discrete entities only during cell division.) For example, white blood cells, because they are easily obtained, may be cultured, chemically treated, and microscopically examined to identify those that are dividing. These cells are then photographed through a microscope to produce *photomicrographs* of intact, double-stranded chromosomes. Homologous chromosomes are then matched up, and the entire set is arranged in descending order by size so that the largest (number 1) appears first.

In addition to overall size, position of the centromere also aids in identification of individual chromosomes, since the position of the centromere is characteristic of each chromosome. Moreover, with the development of special techniques to highlight DNA segments that differentially take up various colored stains, it is now possible to identify every chromosome on the basis of specific *banding patterns*.

Karyotyping has numerous practical applications. Physicians and genetic counselors routinely use karyotypes to aid in the diagnosis of chromosomal disorders in patients. Moreover, karyotypes are often employed in the prenatal diagnosis of chromosomal abnormalities in developing fetuses.

Karyotype
The chromosomal complement of an individual or that which is typical for a species. Usually displayed in a photomicrograph, the chromosomes are arranged in pairs and according to size and position of the centromere.

FIGURE 3–9

A karyotype of a male, with the chromosomes arranged by size and position of the centromere, as well as by the banding patterns.

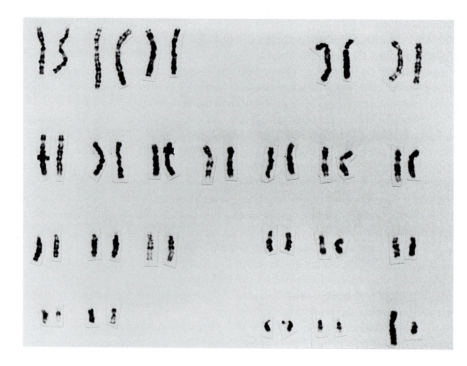

Karyotypes have also proved extremely useful in comparing the chromosomes of different species. Indeed, karyotype analysis has revealed marked chromosomal similarities shared by different primate species, including humans. The similarities in overall karyotype, as well as the marked biochemical and DNA similarities indicated by banding patterns (discussed in Chapter 5), point to close *genetic* relationships especially between humans and the African great apes.

Cell Division

Mitosis

Cell division in somatic cells is called **mitosis.** Mitosis occurs during growth of the individual. It also acts to promote healing of injured tissues and to replace older cells with newer ones. In short, it is the way somatic cells reproduce.

In the early stages of mitosis, a human somatic cell possesses 46 double-stranded chromosomes. As the cell begins to divide, the chromosomes line up in random order along the center of the cell (Fig. 3–10c). The chromosomes then split apart at the centromere, so that the strands are separated. Once the two strands are apart, they pull away from each other and move to opposite ends of the dividing cell (Fig. 3–10d). At this point, each strand is now a distinct chromosome, *composed of one DNA molecule.* Following the separation of chromosome strands, the cell membrane pinches in and becomes sealed, so that two new cells are formed, each with a full complement of DNA, or 46 chromosomes. Most biology textbooks subdivide the continuous process of mitotic cell division into four phases: *prophase, metaphase, anaphase,* and *telophase.*

Mitosis is referred to as "simple cell division" because a somatic cell divides one time to produce two daughter cells that are genetically identical to each other and to the original cell. In mitosis, the original cell possesses 46 chromosomes, and each new daughter cell inherits an exact copy of all 46. This arrangement is made possible by the ability of the DNA molecule to replicate. Thus, it is DNA replication that ensures that the quantity and quality of the genetic material remain constant from one generation of cells to the next.

Meiosis

While mitosis produces new cells, **meiosis** may lead to the development of new individuals, since it produces reproductive cells, or gametes. Although meiosis is another form of cell division and is in some ways similar to mitosis, it is a more complicated process.

During meiosis, specialized cells in male testes and female ovaries divide and develop, eventually to become sperm or egg cells. Initially, these cells contain the full complement of chromosomes (46 in humans) and are referred to as **diploid** cells. (The number of chromosomes forming a complete set in a somatic cell is called the diploid number.) Meiosis is characterized by two divisions that result in four daughter cells, each of which contains 23 chromosomes, or half the original number. Because each of these newly formed cells receives only one member of each chromosomal pair, they are said to be **haploid** cells containing a haploid number of chromosomes.

Mitosis
Simple cell division; the process by which somatic cells divide to produce two identical daughter cells.

Meiosis
Cell division in specialized cells in ovaries and testes. Meiosis involves two divisions and results in four daughter cells, each containing only half the original number of chromosomes. These cells can develop into gametes.

Diploid
Referring to the full complement of chromosomes in a somatic cell—two of each pair.

Haploid
Referring to a half set of chromosomes, one member of each pair. Haploid sets are found in gametes.

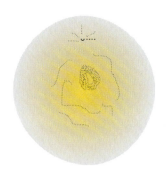

(a) The cell is involved in metabolic activities. DNA replication occurs, but chromosomes are not visible.

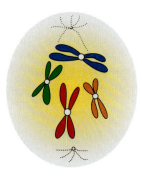

(b) The nuclear membrane disappears, and double-stranded chromosomes are visible.

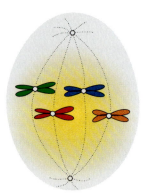

(c) The chromosomes align themselves at the center of the cell.

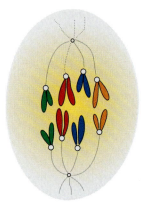

(d) The chromosomes split at the centromere, and the strands separate and move to opposite ends of the dividing cell.

(e) The cell membrane pinches in as the cell continues to divide. The chromosomes begin to uncoil (not shown here).

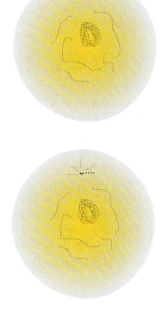

(f) After mitosis is complete, there are two identical daughter cells. The nuclear membrane is present, and chromosomes are no longer visible.

FIGURE 3–10

Mitosis.

Reduction of chromosome number is a critical feature of meiosis, for the resulting gamete, with its 23 chromosomes, may ultimately unite with another gamete, which also carries 23 chromosomes. The product of this union, the *zygote,* or fertilized egg, reestablishes the diploid number of chromosomes (46). In other words, the zygote inherits the full complement of DNA it needs (half from each parent) to develop and function normally. If it were not for *reduction division* (the first division) in meiosis, it would not be possible to maintain the correct number of chromosomes from one generation to the next.

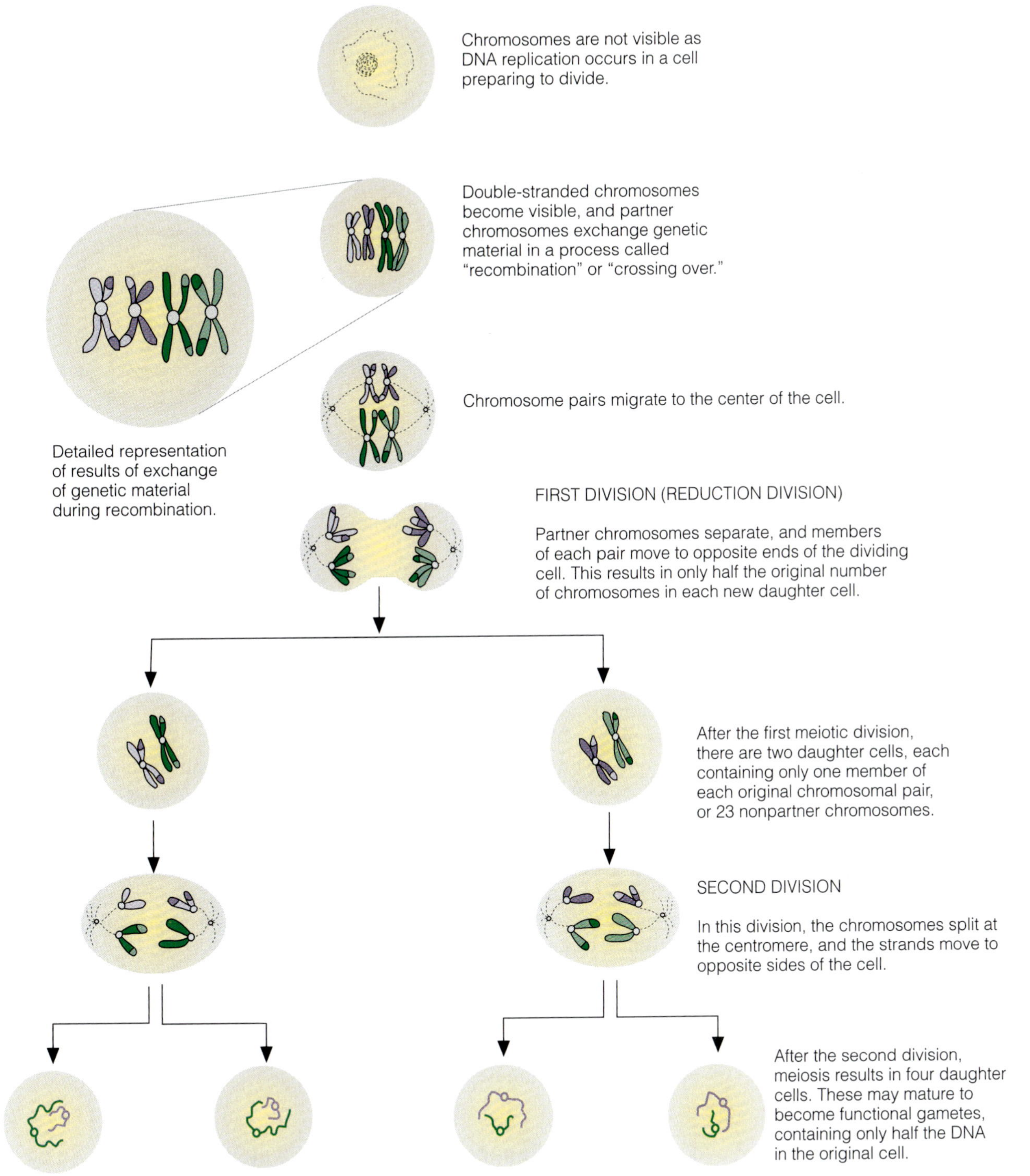

Chromosomes are not visible as DNA replication occurs in a cell preparing to divide.

Double-stranded chromosomes become visible, and partner chromosomes exchange genetic material in a process called "recombination" or "crossing over."

Detailed representation of results of exchange of genetic material during recombination.

Chromosome pairs migrate to the center of the cell.

FIRST DIVISION (REDUCTION DIVISION)

Partner chromosomes separate, and members of each pair move to opposite ends of the dividing cell. This results in only half the original number of chromosomes in each new daughter cell.

After the first meiotic division, there are two daughter cells, each containing only one member of each original chromosomal pair, or 23 nonpartner chromosomes.

SECOND DIVISION

In this division, the chromosomes split at the centromere, and the strands move to opposite sides of the cell.

After the second division, meiosis results in four daughter cells. These may mature to become functional gametes, containing only half the DNA in the original cell.

FIGURE 3–11

Meiosis.

During the first division of meiosis, partner chromosomes come together, forming pairs of double-stranded chromosomes. In this way, pairs of chromosomes line up along the cell's center (see Fig. 3–11). Pairing of homologous chromosomes is highly significant, for while they are together, members of pairs exchange genetic information in a process called **recombination**, or **crossing over**. Pairing is also important because it facilitates the accurate reduction of

■ **Recombination (crossing over)**
The exchange of genetic material between homologous chromosomes during meiosis.

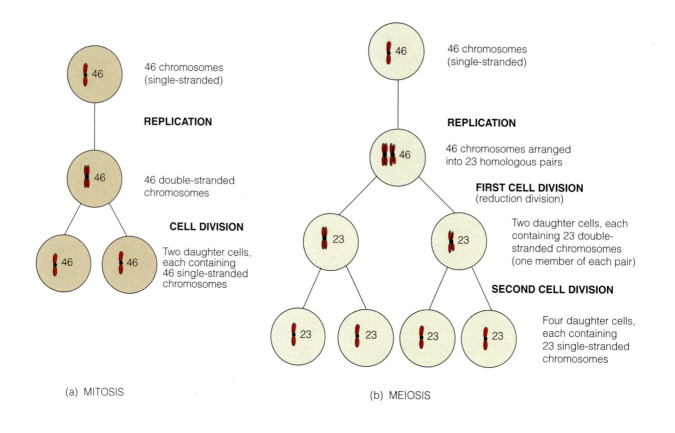

(a) MITOSIS   (b) MEIOSIS

FIGURE 3–12

Mitosis and meiosis compared. In mitosis, one division produces two daughter cells, each of which contains 46 chromosomes. Meiosis is characterized by two divisions. After the first, there are two cells, each containing only 23 chromosomes (one member of each original chromosome pair). Each daughter cell divides again, so that the final result is four cells, each with only half the original number of chromosomes.

chromosome number by ensuring that each new daughter cell will receive only one member of each pair.

As the cell begins to divide, the chromosomes themselves remain intact (i.e., double-stranded), but *members of pairs* separate and migrate to opposite ends of the cell. After the first division, there are two new daughter cells, but they are not identical to each other or to the parental cell because each contains only one member of each chromosome pair and therefore only 23 chromosomes, each of which still has two strands (see Fig. 3–11). Moreover, because of crossing over, each chromosome now contains some genetic variations it did not have previously.

The second meiotic division proceeds in much the same way as in mitosis (Fig. 3–12). In the two newly formed cells, the 23 double-stranded chromosomes align themselves at the cell's center, and as in mitosis, the strands of each chromosome separate at the centromere and move apart. Once this second division is completed, there are four daughter cells, each with 23 single-stranded chromosomes (i.e., 23 DNA molecules).

The Evolutionary Significance of Meiosis

Meiosis occurs in all sexually reproducing organisms and is a highly important evolutionary innovation, since it increases genetic variation in populations at a faster rate than mutation alone can do in asexually reproducing species. Individual members of sexually reproducing species are not genetically identical clones of other individuals. Rather, they result from the contribution of genetic information from two parents. From any one human mating, an enormous number of possible offspring can result. From just the random arrangements of chromosome pairs lining up along the center of the cell during the first division of meiosis, each parent can produce 8 million genetically different gametes. And given the joint probability accounting for both parents, the total number of possible genetic combinations for any human mating is about 70 trillion. It should be noted that this staggering number is the result solely of the paired arrangements (called **random assortment**) and does not even take into account the many more combinations resulting from crossing over.

The genetic uniqueness of individuals is further enhanced by recombination between homologous chromosomes during meiosis, for recombination ensures that chromosomes are not passed on unaltered from one generation to the next. Instead, in every generation, parental contributions are reshuffled in an almost infinite number of combinations, thus altering the genetic composition of chromosomes even before they are passed on. Some estimates suggest that recombination (i.e., crossing over) adds to the number of genetic possibilities by a factor of up to 10 billion (i.e., $10,000,000,000 \times 70,000,000,000,000$), which produces a number really beyond comprehension. Suffice it to say, with the exception of identical twins, no human being is genetically identical to any other who has ever lived or who ever will live.

Natural selection acts on genetic variation in populations (you will recall that Charles Darwin emphasized this point). In all species, *mutation* is the only source of *new* genetic variation. But in sexually reproducing species, recombination produces new *arrangements* of genetic information, which potentially provide additional material for natural selection to act on.

Genetic variation is essential if species are to adapt to changing selective pressures. If all individuals were genetically identical, natural selection would have nothing to act on and evolution could not occur. It has been argued that this influence on variation is the principal adaptive advantage of sexual reproduction. Therefore, although reproduction has been strictly asexual for most of the time life has existed on this planet, sexual reproduction and meiosis are of major evolutionary importance because they contribute to the role of natural selection in populations.

■ **Random assortment**
The chance distribution of chromosomes to daughter cells during meiosis; along with recombination, the source of variation resulting from meiosis.

Meiosis in Males and Females

As discussed, meiosis involves two divisions that ultimately produce four daughter cells. However, human females and males differ in the distribution of materials to these cells as well as in the *timing* of the process. In females, the process is called oogenesis, and it occurs in the ovaries. The first meiotic division yields one quite large cell, called the *secondary oocyte,* and it contains about 95 percent of the cytoplasm. The other, much smaller cell is called a **polar body.** In the second division, there is again a markedly disproportionate distribution of the cytoplasm, so that one large functional gamete, called the *ovum,* is produced. The other three cells—the polar bodies—receive almost no cytoplasm and cannot function as gametes.

In males, the meiotic process is called *spermatogenesis,* and it occurs in the testes, where primary sex cells divide to produce four haploid cells called *spermatids*. These, in turn, differentiate to yield mature sperm. It should be noted that each haploid sperm cell contains 22 autosomes and either an X *or* Y chromosome. Ova, by contrast, also contain 22 autosomes, but *always* with an X chromosome. Thus, it is the presence of either the X or Y chromosome in the sperm cell that determines the sex of the offspring.

■ **Polar body**
A small nonviable cell that is a product of meiosis in females.

There is also a notable difference in the timing of meiosis in human females and males. In females, meiosis begins in fetal life and is "arrested" before birth early in meiosis. Years later, with sexual maturation, meiosis resumes, producing just one gamete per cycle (about every 28 days). Even then, meiosis does not reach finality to produce a mature ovum unless the gamete is fertilized by a sperm cell. Thus, an ovum that is fertilized when a female is, say, 35 years old actually began meiosis somewhat more than 35 years before. This long-term period of suspended development has been suggested as a reason for a greater number of meiotic problems accumulating with advanced maternal age (see the following section).

Problems with Meiosis

For meiosis to ensure a reasonably good opportunity for normal fetal development, the process must be quite exact. The two-stage division must produce a viable gamete with exactly 23 chromosomes—that is, with only one member of each chromosome pair present. Superficially, it appears that the process works quite well, since more than 98 percent of newborns have the correct number of chromosomes. However, this statistic is misleading. It has been estimated that as many as one of every two pregnancies naturally terminates early as a spontaneous abortion (miscarriage). An estimated 70 percent of these miscarriages are caused by an improper number of chromosomes (Cummings, 1997). Thus, it appears that during meiosis, there are frequent errors with quite serious consequences.

If chromosomes or chromosome strands fail to separate during either of the two meiotic divisions, serious problems can arise. This failure to separate is called **nondisjunction.** The result of nondisjunction is that one of the daughter cells receives two copies of the affected chromosome. The other daughter cell receives none. If such an affected gamete unites with a normal gamete containing 23 chromosomes, the resulting zygote will have either 45 or 47 chromosomes. Having only one member of a chromosome pair is referred to as *monosomy.* The term *trisomy* refers to the presence of three copies of a particular chromosome.

The far-reaching effects of an abnormal number of chromosomes can be appreciated only by remembering that the zygote will faithfully reproduce itself through mitosis. Thus, every cell in the developing body will also have the abnormal chromosomal complement. Most situations of this type involving autosomes are lethal, and the embryo is spontaneously aborted, frequently before the pregnancy is even recognized.

One example of a result of an abnormal number of autosomes is *Down syndrome,* more properly called *trisomy 21,* where there are three copies of the twenty-first chromosome. This is the only example of an abnormal number of autosomes being compatible with life beyond the first few months after birth. Trisomy 21, which occurs in approximately 1 out of every 1,000 live births, is associated with a number of developmental and health problems. These problems include congenital heart defects (seen in about 40 percent of affected newborns), increased susceptibility to respiratory infections, and leukemia. However, the most widely recognized effect of trisomy 21 is mental retardation, which is variably expressed and ranges from mild to severe.

Trisomy 21 is partly associated with advanced maternal age. For example, the risk of a 20-year-old woman giving birth to an affected infant is just 0.05 percent (5 in 10,000). However, 3 percent of babies born to mothers 45 and older are affected (a 60-fold increase). Actually, most affected infants are born to women

Nondisjunction
The failure of homologous chromosomes or chromosome strands to separate during cell division.

TABLE 3–3 Examples of Nondisjunction in Sex Chromosomes

Chromosomal Complement	Condition	Estimated Incidence	Manifestations
XXX	Trisomy X	1 per 1,000 female births	Affected women are usually clinically normal, but there is a slight increase in sterility and mental retardation compared to the general population. In cases with more than three X chromosomes, mental retardation can be severe.
XYY	XYY syndrome	1 per 1,000 male births	Affected males are fertile and tend to be taller than average.
XO	Turner syndrome	1 per 10,000 female births	Affected females are short-statured, have broad chests and webbed necks, and are sterile. There is usually no mental retardation, but concepts relating to spatial relationships, including mathematics, can pose difficulties. Between 95 and 99 percent of affected fetuses die before birth.
XXY	Klinefelter syndrome	1 per 1,000 male births	Symptoms are noticeable by puberty: reduced testicular development, reduced facial and body hair, some breast development in about half of all cases, and reduced fertility or sterility. Some individuals exhibit lowered intelligence. Additional X chromosomes (XXXY) are associated with mental retardation.

under the age of 35, but this statistic is due to the fact that the majority of babies are born to women in this age category. The increase in incidence with maternal age is thought to be related to the early initiation of meiosis in females and the presumed age changes in the gametic cell lines, resulting in increased risk of nondisjunction. Indeed, a number of conditions related to nondisjunction of chromosomes are thought to be influenced, in part, by increased maternal age.

Nondisjunctions may also occur in sex chromosomes, producing individuals who, for example, are XXY (47 chromosomes), XO (45 chromosomes), XXX (47 chromosomes), or XYY (47 chromosomes). While these conditions do not always result in death or mental retardation, some are associated with impaired mental function and/or sterility (Table 3–3). Moreover, still greater numbers of X chromosomes, such as XXXX or XXXY, result in marked mental retardation. And some nondisjunctions of sex chromosomes are lethal. While it is possible to survive without a Y chromosome (roughly half of all humans do), it is not possible to live without an X chromosome. Indeed, the evidence suggests that embryos that possess only a Y chromosome are spontaneously aborted before a pregnancy is even recognized.

Clearly, the importance of accuracy during meiosis cannot be overstated. If normal development is to occur, it is essential that the correct number of both autosomes and sex chromosomes be present.

New Frontiers

Since the discovery of DNA structure and function in the 1950s, the field of genetics has revolutionized biological science and reshaped our understanding of inheritance, genetic disease, and evolutionary processes. For example, it is now possible to ascertain the exact sequence of nucleotides in a DNA sample, and in

■ **Human Genome Project**

An international effort aimed at sequencing and mapping the entire human genome.

■ **Genome**

The entire genetic makeup of an individual or of a species. In humans, it is estimated that each individual possesses approximately 3 billion DNA nucleotides.

■ **Polymerase chain reaction (PCR)**

A method of producing thousands of copies of a DNA segment using the enzyme DNA polymerase.

■ **Clone**

An organism that is genetically identical to another organism. The term may also be used to refer to genetically identical DNA segments and molecules.

The context and phylogenetic significance of the Neanderthal sequence is discussed in Virtual Lab 12, section I, part A.

fact, the goal of the **Human Genome Project** is to sequence the entire human **genome.**

A technique developed in 1986 called **polymerase chain reaction (PCR)** enables scientists to produce multiple copies of DNA, and consequently it has made it possible to analyze segments of DNA as small as one molecule. This ability is important because samples of DNA, such as those obtained at crime scenes or from fossils, are often too small to permit reliable analysis of DNA sequences.

In PCR, the two strands of a DNA sample are separated, and the enzyme *DNA polymerase* synthesizes complementary strands on the exposed bases, as in DNA replication. Because this process can be repeated many times, it is possible to produce over a million copies of the original DNA material! Thus, scientists have been able to identify nucleotide sequences in, for example, fossils (including Neandertals), Egyptian mummies, and members of the Russian royal family murdered in 1918. As you can imagine, PCR has limitless potential for many disciplines, including forensic science, medicine, and evolutionary biology.

Regardless of how exciting and important new techniques such as PCR may be, nothing has generated as much attention and controversy as the birth of Dolly, a **clone** of a female sheep, in 1997 (Wilmut et al., 1997). Actually, cloning is not as new as you might think. Anyone who has ever taken a cutting from a plant and rooted it to grow a new plant has produced a clone. In the 1950s, plant biologists developed methods of cloning carrots by culturing cells taken from mature plants. In the 1960s, an African toad became the first animal to be cloned, but for a number of reasons, cloning a mammal remained an elusive goal. Then, in 1981, a Swiss team of geneticists successfully produced cloned mice, and these experiments were followed by cloned cattle and sheep. So, you might ask, why was Dolly such a big deal? The furor was partly due to the fact that earlier cloning results had not been well publicized. But in the scientific community, the enthusiasm was due to the techniques that were used.

Animal cloning can be done in two ways. Traditionally, nuclei from fertilized eggs are removed and replaced with nuclei taken from cells derived from an embryo. (Embryonic cells have been used because they have not yet become specialized.) The altered egg is then implanted into the uterus of a surrogate (substitute) mother, where it develops into an individual that is genetically identical to the embryo donor.

The Dolly project was unique because the donor nucleus was said to be derived from a somatic cell of a *mature* sheep. Until now, this ability has been questioned because any cell taken from an adult animal would be a specialized cell in which much of the DNA would be switched off. This DNA would therefore be incapable of directing embryonic and fetal development.

Since the original reports of the Dolly experiment were published, it has emerged that the donor cell for Dolly may inadvertently have been a fetal cell and not one taken from an adult sheep after all. But since the birth of Dolly, teams of Japanese scientists have reported cloning cattle and mice using donor cells from adult animals (Wakayama et. al, 1998). Thus, while it is possible (but not certain) that Dolly was not derived from an adult somatic cell, other animals have been. These experiments have demonstrated that DNA derived from a specialized somatic cell is capable of being "turned back on" so that it can orchestrate the development of an entire organism.

This brief discussion really only hints at the possibilities that lie in the future of genetic technology (see Issue, pp. 71–72). While humans certainly have much to gain from genetic research, the emerging technologies are highly controversial, and the number of ethical and moral questions will only increase. Indeed, it is an exciting time for genetic discovery, and it is to be hoped that an informed public will be able to evaluate the issues that will increasingly become the concerns of the scientific community, the legal experts, and, ultimately, the politicians.

Summary

This chapter has dealt with several concepts that are fundamental to understanding the processes of biological evolution, especially as related to human adaptation and variation. These are topics that will be discussed in succeeding chapters.

It has been shown that cells are the fundamental units of life and that there are basically two types of cells. Somatic cells make up body tissues, while gametes (eggs and sperm) are reproductive cells that transmit genetic information from parent to offspring.

Genetic information is contained in the DNA molecule, found in the nuclei of cells. The DNA molecule is capable of replication, or making copies of itself, and it is the only molecule known to have this ability. Replication makes it possible for daughter cells to receive a full complement of DNA (contained in chromosomes).

DNA also controls protein synthesis by directing the cell to arrange amino acids in the proper sequence for each particular type of protein. Also involved in the process of protein synthesis is another, similar molecule called RNA. Not all the DNA in a gene codes for the production of a protein. Segments called introns are deleted after the formation of messenger RNA, and it is the remaining segments called exons that actually direct protein synthesis. There are also genes that control the function of other genes. These regulatory genes are crucial to growth and development, and they have evolutionary significance as well. The DNA code for all life is universal and triplet, the latter meaning that amino acids are coded for by DNA bases occurring in groups of three.

Cells multiply by dividing, and during cell division, DNA is visible under a microscope in the form of chromosomes. In humans, there are 46 chromosomes (23 pairs). If the complement is not precisely distributed to succeeding generations of cells, severe consequences will follow.

Somatic cells divide during growth or tissue repair or to replace old, worn-out cells. Somatic cell division is called mitosis. A cell divides one time to produce two daughter cells, each possessing a full and identical (diploid) set of chromosomes.

Sex cells are produced when specialized cells in the ovaries and testes divide in meiosis. Unlike mitosis, meiosis is characterized by two divisions, which produce four nonidentical daughter cells, each containing only half (haploid) the amount of DNA (23 chromosomes) as that carried by the original cell.

Questions for Review

1. Genetics is the study of what?
2. What components of a eukaryotic cell are discussed in this chapter?
3. What are the two basic types of cells in individuals? Give an example of each.
4. What are nucleotides?
5. Name the four DNA bases. Which pairs with which?
6. What is DNA replication, and why is it important?

7. What are proteins? Give two examples.
8. What are enzymes?
9. What are the building blocks of protein? How many different kinds are there?
10. What is the function of DNA in protein synthesis?
11. What is the function of mRNA?

12. What is the function of tRNA?
13. Does the entire DNA molecule code for the manufacture of proteins? Explain.
14. What is the role of regulatory genes? Give an example.
15. Define gene, allele, and locus.
16. Define chromosome.
17. What are homologous chromosomes?
18. What is polymerase chain reaction (PCR), and why is it important?
19. How many cell divisions occur in mitosis? In humans, how many chromosomes does each new cell have?
20. How many cell divisions occur in meiosis? How many daughter cells are produced when meiosis is complete? In humans, how many chromosomes does each new cell contain?
21. Why is reduction division important?
22. What is recombination, and why is it important? When does it occur?
23. Why is the genetic code said to be universal? Why is it said to be redundant?
24. What are the two sex chromosomes? Which two do males have? Which two do females have?
25. Why is meiosis important to the process of natural selection?
26. How does meiosis in females differ from meiosis in males?
27. Why is the study of genetics important to physical anthropology?

Suggested Further Reading

Brennan, James R. 1985. *Patterns of Human Heredity.* Englewood Cliffs, NJ: Prentice Hall.

Cummings, Michael R. 2000. *Human Heredity, Principles and Issues.* 5th ed. Pacific Grove: Brooks/Cole.

Gribbin, John. 1987. *In Search of the Double Helix.* New York: Bantam Books.

See entire issue of *Scientific American,* vol. 253(4), October 1985, for numerous articles pertaining to molecular genetics and evolution.

Additional Resources

Multimedia Tools

- **Virtual Laboratories for Physical Anthropology CD-ROM**
  The following concepts in this chapter are covered on the physical anthropology CD-ROM:
  cell, nucleus, organelles (Virtual Lab 2.II.A)
  gametes, sexual reproduction (Virtual Lab 2.II.A, E)

DNA, base, replication (Virtual Lab 2.II.B, C)
protein synthesis, amino acid, mRNA (Virtual Lab 2.II.C)
gene, exon, intron (Virtual Lab 2.II.B)
sickle-cell anemia, hemoglobin (Virtual Lab 2.III.B)
meiosis, random assortment (Virtual Lab 2.II.E)
DNA sequencing, Neandertal (Virtual Lab 12.I.A)

■ **Wadsworth Anthropology Resource Center**
http://anthropology.wadsworth.com
Visit Anthropology Online to obtain current updates in the field, surfing tips, career information and more. In addition, enrich your study
efforts with text-specific study aids arranged by chapter.

■   **InfoTrac College Edition**
       http://www.infotrac-college.com/wadsworth

1. What exactly is a *gene?* How many human genes have been identified to date? Use InfoTrac College Edition to help answer these two
   questions. Depending on the key words you select, you will probably
   get a great many citations. What are ways you can narrow down
   your search to find only those articles relevant to answering the two
   questions?

2. Just to complicate things, some researchers think that DNA is not as
   simple as previously thought. Read "Decoding 'coding'—information
   and DNA" by Sahotra Sarkar, *BioScience,* Dec 1996, v46 n11 p857(8).
   This article can be found on InfoTrac College Edition. How does this
   article change your understanding of how traits are inherited and of
   what DNA does?

3. How is it that meiosis works so well so much of the time? Read "How
   cells get the right chromosomes" by R. Bruce Nicklas, *Science,* Jan 31,
   1997, v275 n5300 p632(6) on InfoTrac College Edition. Write a short
   paper on how errors in meiosis and mitosis are prevented.

4. The Human Genome Project is an international effort aimed at
   sequencing the human genome. The first five years of this project
   were completed in 1998, and goals were set for the next five years.
   "New Goals for the U.S. Human Genome Project: 1998–2003" by
   Francis S. Collins, Ari Patrinos, Elke Jordan, Aravinda Chakravarti,
   Raymond Gesteland, and LeRoy Walters, *Science,* Oct 23, 1998, v282
   i5389 p682(1), available on InfoTrac College Edition, outlines these
   goals. What parts of this chapter do you think will be rewritten if
   these goals are met?

■   **Internet Exercises**

1. Molecular biology and cell biology provide the basic concepts for
   much of the material in this chapter. The Beginners Guide to
   Molecular Biology online (**http://www.res.bbsrc.ac.uk/molbio/
   guide/**) can supply much information to help you understand these
   concepts. Start with *cell biology* to learn more about the cell and continue through this guide, paying special attention to the concepts
   you find difficult.

2. Having problems with the topic of *meiosis?* The Internet offers several meiosis tutorials and explanations. Visit one of these sites. Two
   examples can be found at **http://www.biology.arizona.edu/
   cell_bio/tutorials/meiosis/main.html** or **http://gened.emc.**

maricopa.edu/bio/bio181/BIOBK/BioBookmeiosis.html. If these do not work, just go to one of the search engines and search for *meiosis* or *meiosis* tutorial and help will be at your fingertips.

3. Genetics is not an easy topic to master. Thankfully, there is plenty of help available. Either search for *genetics* at any of the search engines, or visit one of the sites below.

Principles of Genetics: **http://www.rtt.ab.ca/rtt/tmills/pg.html**

Primer on Molecular Genetics: **http://www.bis.med.jhmi.edu/ Dan/DOE/intro.html**

Access Excellence, from Genentech: **http://www.gene.com/ae/**

ISSUE

Genetic Technologies: A Revolution in Science

The basic premise of Michael Crichton's *Jurassic Park* is as follows: A Silicon Valley biotechnology firm develops a method of extracting 150-million-year-old dinosaur DNA from mosquitoes preserved in amber, or fossilized tree sap. Prior to being trapped in tree sap, the mosquitoes had ingested minute quantities of dinosaur blood, a few cells of which remained in the insects' digestive tracts. From the dinosaur DNA, embryos are produced, inserted in genetically engineered plastic eggs. and incubated. The resulting animals, resurrections of several dinosaur species, become the central attraction of an island theme park—*Jurassic Park*.

Far-fetched? Probably. Or is it just possible that someday, science will develop the technology to accomplish at least some of the *Jurassic Park* achievements? Consider that in 1992, a group of scientists at California Polytechnic State University and the University of California at Berkeley used PCR techniques to clone DNA fragments obtained from a bee trapped in amber 25 million years ago. Does this feat mean that scientists will soon be able to produce a bee that has been extinct for 25 million years? Certainly not with today's technology. For one thing, the ancient DNA extracted from fossil species represents only a minute sample of the entire genome of an organism. But by cloning DNA sequences from extinct species and comparing them to the DNA of their presumed descendants, scientists are able to estimate *rates* of genetic change within lineages. This achievement in itself is remarkable; the rest may well remain the stuff of fantasy.

Beginning with research in the 1950s, the possibility of using cloning procedures to increase the frequency of desirable traits in domesticated species has approached reality. Cells from a single plant can be cultured to produce masses of cells, which are then induced to develop roots and shoots, resulting in large numbers of plants, all identical to the original. Variations of these techniques have been applied to the loblolly pine, with the goal of producing forests of genetically identical fast-growing trees with high wood content. The result has obvious benefits for the lumber industry and could perhaps also allow for the setting aside of natural forests for preservation.

However, it is important to consider that such cloned forests would not be natural. For one thing, they could possess an unforeseen susceptibility to certain infectious organisms and parasites. Additionally, because they would lack many other types of plants, they would not provide the necessary habitat for most animal species provided by natural forests. These high-tech solutions could be acceptable as long as such tree stands are seen simply as tree farms and providing that sufficient primary and secondary forests are left standing in the interest of species preservation. But these solutions do challenge traditional views of what constitutes a forest. And we must bear in mind that in terms of biodiversity, such forests of the future run the risk of being little more than sterile wastelands.

Likewise, the cloning of cattle and sheep has enormous implications for the livestock industry. Theoretically, breeders will be able to produce quantities of animals all possessing—to the same degree—whatever traits are deemed desirable. This capability could mean that cattle with uniformly higher milk yield or increased muscle mass and sheep that produce more and better quality wool may be on the horizon. But, again, such genetic homogeneity could certainly render such strains of livestock highly susceptible to the introduction of disease organisms, and with no genetic variation to offer resistance, entire herds could potentially be lost.

Because of the universality of the genetic code, it is possible to transfer DNA from one species to another. For example, recombinant DNA technology permits the insertion of human genes into bacterial cells, which subsequently possess an altered genetic makeup.

Insertion of foreign DNA into bacteria or other organisms was made possible by the discovery of *restriction enzymes* in the mid-1970s. These enzymes (over 300 are currently known) are used to snip out base pair sequences that are then spliced into circular strands of bacterial DNA called *plasmids*. The introduced strand of DNA is sealed into place by other enzymes. The recombinant plasmid then serves as a vector, or carrier, for transferring the foreign DNA into cultured bacterial

Genetic Technologies:
A Revolution in Science (continued)

cells. As these cells divide, the plasmid, including its introduced segment, replicates with the rest of the cell's DNA. Thus, entire colonies of altered cells serve as manufacturing plants for the gene products (insulin, clotting factor, growth hormone, etc.) specified by the human genes inserted into the plasmid vector.

Genetic engineering has enormous potential for the treatment of disease. Because bacterial cells divide rapidly, ever-increasing numbers are capable of producing commercial quantities of beneficial gene products. For example, insulin for use by patients with insulin-dependent diabetes was formerly derived from nonhuman animals. But since 1982, insulin produced by genetically altered bacteria has helped lower the cost of therapy for the over 2 million Americans who suffer from insulin-dependent diabetes.

In the same manner, numerous other products, such as blood clotting factors (for hemophiliacs), growth hormone, and various other hormones, can now be produced. Previously, these products were derived through blood donations and tissues from human cadavers. Unfortunately, as we are all aware, recipients of products derived in these ways can be exposed to several infectious agents. Therefore, the use of artificially produced substances not only lowers the cost to the patient in many cases, but also greatly reduces the threat of contamination.

By changing the genetic structure of other organisms, we are indeed creating new life forms and potential new species. (It would certainly seem that such capabilities would put to rest any doubts about the reality of biological evolution.) Following are a few examples of how humans are now capable of manipulating biological processes in other organisms:

- Pig embryos have received, and incorporated into their own DNA, genes for human growth hormone in attempts to produce faster-maturing pigs.
- Researchers at Harvard University have developed a genetically engineered mouse that carries a gene rendering it highly susceptible to several types of cancer. The resultant strain of mice is now being used in laboratories to test cancer-resistant compounds and also the possible carcinogenic effects of various substances.
- Genes conferring resistance to insect pests are now being experimentally introduced into numerous food crops.
- Plant geneticists are developing methods of increasing the amino acid content of vegetables and grains normally low in protein.
- The gene that causes tomatoes to soften when ripe has been manipulated so that this fruit can be allowed to ripen on the vine before being picked and shipped to market.
- Genetically altered bacteria, sprayed on strawberries and other crops, can protect such crops from devastating frost buildup even at temperatures some 10–12° F below freezing.

The field of genetic engineering is in its infancy, and we are tempted to believe that these new technologies will offer solutions to many contemporary medical and nutritional problems. Moreover, as we discussed, these genetic technologies can help reveal the mechanisms of biological evolution. With such promise and such tools at our disposal, it is also to be hoped that we use these powerful new techniques wisely.

Critical Thinking Questions

1. What is a clone? How can cloning potentially benefit the agriculture industry? What are some possible problems that might arise from cloning?
2. Do you have doubts or concerns about any of the new genetic technologies? If so, what is the basis for your concern? What kinds of information would you require (and from whom) to alleviate these doubts?
3. Do emerging genetic technologies challenge your personal views of life, nature, science, and the role that humans will play in the future? If so, how?

Sources

Crichton, Michael. 1990. *Jurassic Park.* New York: Ballantine Books.

Cummings, Michael R. 2000. *Human Heredity, Principles and Issues.* 5th ed. Pacific Grove: Brooks/Cole.

Ross, Philip E. 1992. "Eloquent Remains." *Scientific American* 266(5): 114–125.

Heredity and Evolution

Introduction

This chapter is roughly divided into two parts. In the first, we continue with the discussion of genetic principles we began in Chapter 3. That chapter dealt with the structure and function of DNA within the cell. In this chapter, we shift to a somewhat broader perspective and focus on the principles that guide the transmission of traits from parent to offspring. These principles, first elucidated by Gregor Mendel, form much of the basis of modern genetics, and we cover them in some detail because of their relevance to the evolutionary process. The second part of this chapter integrates these basics of DNA function and Mendelian patterns of inheritance into a comprehensive theory of the forces that guide biological evolution.

For at least 10,000 years, beginning with the domestication of plants and animals, people have attempted to explain how traits are passed from parents to offspring. Although most theories have been far from accurate, farmers and herders have known for millennia that they could enhance the frequency and expression of desirable attributes through selective breeding. However, exactly why desirable traits were often seen in the offspring of carefully chosen breeding stock remained a mystery. It was equally curious when offspring did not show the traits their human owners had hoped for.

From the time ancient Greek philosophers considered the problem until well into the nineteenth century, one predominant belief was that characteristics of offspring resulted from the *blending* of parental traits. Blending was supposedly accomplished by means of particles that existed in every part of the body. These so-called *pangenes* contained miniatures of the body part (limbs, organs, etc.) from which the particles derived, and they traveled through the blood to the reproductive organs and blended with particles of another individual during reproduction. There were variations on the theme of *pangenesis,* and numerous scholars, including Charles Darwin, adhered to some aspects of the theory.

The importance of sexual reproduction is discussed in Virtual Lab 2, section II, part E.

FIGURE 4–1
Gregor Mendel.

■ **Hybrids**
Offspring of mixed ancestry; heterozygotes.

The Genetic Principles Discovered by Mendel

It was not until Gregor Mendel (1822–1884) addressed the question of heredity that it began to be resolved (Fig. 4–1). Mendel was a monk living in an Augustinian abbey at Brno in what is now the Czech Republic. At the time he began his research, he had already acquired scientific expertise in botany, physics, and mathematics at the University of Vienna and had conducted various experiments in the monastery gardens. These experiments led him to explore the various ways in which physical traits, such as color or height, could be expressed in plant **hybrids.** He hoped that by making crosses between two strains of *purebred* plants and examining their progeny, he could determine (and predict) how many different forms of hybrids there were, arrange the forms according to generation, and evaluate the proportion of each type in each generation.

Mendel chose to work with common garden peas, and unlike previous researchers, he chose to consider only one trait at a time. In all, he focused on seven traits, each of which could be expressed in two different ways (Table 4–1). Because the genetic principles Mendel discovered apply to humans as well as to peas (and all other biological organisms), we discuss his work in some detail to illustrate the basic rules of inheritance.

TABLE 4-1	The Seven Garden Pea Characteristics Studied by Mendel	
Characteristic	Dominant Trait	Recessive Trait
1. Form of ripe seed	Smooth	Wrinkled
2. Color of seed albumen	Yellow	Green
3. Color of seed coat	Gray	White
4. Form of ripe pods	Inflated	Constricted
5. Color of unripe pods	Green	Yellow
6. Position of flowers on stem	Axial	Terminal
7. Length of stem	Tall	Short

Segregation

Mendel began by crossing different varieties of purebred plants that differed with regard to a specific trait. For example, if he was interested in stem length, he crossed varieties that produced only tall plants with varieties that produced only short plants.

The plants used in the first cross were designated the *parental,* or *P,* generation, and all were either tall or short. The hybrid offspring of the P generation were designated the F_1 (first filial) generation. As they matured, the F_1 plants were not intermediate in height, as blending theories of inheritance would have predicted. To the contrary, they were all tall (Fig. 4–2).

Next, Mendel allowed the F_1 plants to self-fertilize and produce a second generation of plants (the F_2 generation). But this time, only approximately $3/4$ of the offspring plants were tall, and the remaining $1/4$ were short. Regardless of the trait he examined, every time he performed the experiment, he obtained almost the same results. One expression of the trait completely disappeared in the F_1 generation and reappeared in the F_2 generation. Moreover, the expression that was present in the F_1 generation was more common in the F_2 plants, occurring in a ratio of approximately 3:1.

These results suggested an important fact. It appeared that different expressions of a trait were controlled by discrete *units,* which occurred in pairs, and that offspring inherited one unit from each parent. Mendel correctly concluded that the members of a pair of units controlling a trait somehow separated into different sex cells and were again united with another member during fertilization of the egg. This is Mendel's *first principle of inheritance,* known as the **principle of segregation.**

Today we know that meiosis explains Mendel's principle of segregation. You will remember that during meiosis, paired chromosomes (and the genes they carry) separate from one another and are distributed to different gametes. However, in the zygote, the full complement of chromosomes is restored, and both members of each chromosome pair are present in the offspring.

Dominance and Recessiveness

Mendel also recognized that the expression that was absent in the F_1 plants had not actually disappeared at all. It had remained present, but somehow it was

The results of these experiments are similar to the goals that are pursued by breeders during animal and plant domestication. See Virtual Lab 2, section I, part B.

■ Principle of segregation

Genes (alleles) occur in pairs (because chromosomes occur in pairs). During gamete production, the members of each gene pair separate, so that each gamete contains one member of each pair. During fertilization, the full number of chromosomes is restored, and members of gene or allele pairs are reunited.

FIGURE 4–2

Results of crosses when only one trait at a time is considered.

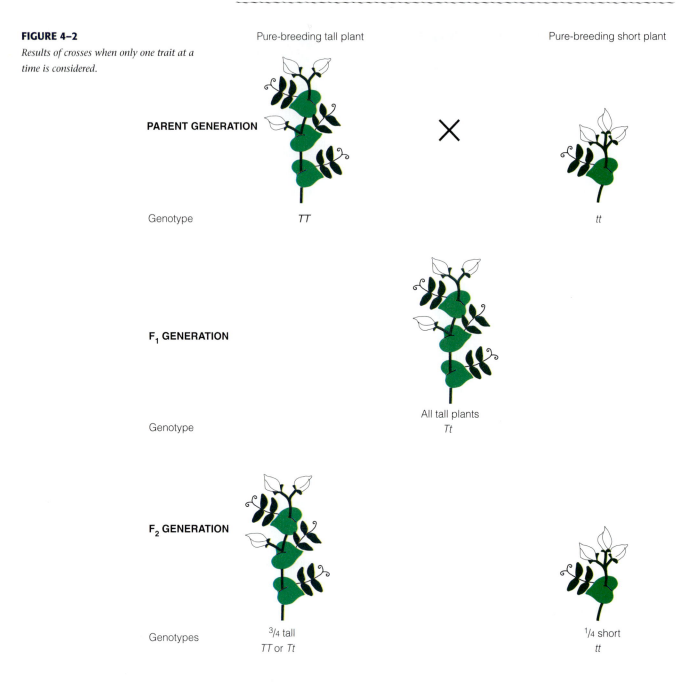

Pure-breeding tall plant   Pure-breeding short plant

PARENT GENERATION   X

Genotype   *TT*   *tt*

F₁ GENERATION

Genotype

All tall plants
Tt

F₂ GENERATION

Genotypes   ³/₄ tall   ¹/₄ short
                     TT or *Tt*   *tt*

■ Recessive

Describing a trait that is not expressed in heterozygotes; also refers to the allele that governs the trait. For a recessive allele to be expressed, there must be two copies of the allele (i.e., the individual must be homozygous).

masked and could not be expressed. To describe the trait that seemed to be lost, Mendel used the term **recessive;** the trait that was expressed was said to be **dominant.** Thus, the important principles of *dominance* and *recessiveness* were formulated, and they remain today as important concepts in the field of genetics.

You will recall that a *gene* is a segment of DNA that directs the production of a specific protein or part of a protein. Furthermore, the location of a gene on a chromosome is its *locus* (*pl.,* loci). At numerous genetic loci, however, there is more than one possible form of the gene, and these variations of genes at specific loci are called *alleles*. Therefore, alleles are alternate forms of a gene that can direct the cell to produce slightly different forms of the same protein and, ultimately, different expressions of traits.

As it turns out, plant height in garden peas is controlled by two different alleles at one genetic locus. The allele that determines that a plant will be tall is dominant to the allele for short. (It is worth mentioning that height is not governed in this manner in all plants.)

In Mendel's experiments, all the parent (P) plants had two copies of the same allele, either dominant or recessive, depending on whether they were tall or short. When two copies of the same allele are present, the individual is said to be **homozygous.** Thus, all the tall P plants were homozygous for the dominant allele, and all the short P plants were homozygous for the recessive allele. (This homozygosity explains why tall plants crossed with tall plants produced only tall offspring, and short plants crossed with short plants produced all short offspring; i.e., they were "pure lines" and lacked genetic variation at this locus.) However, all the F_1 plants (hybrids) had inherited one allele from each parent plant; therefore, they all possessed two different alleles at specific loci. Individuals that possess two different alleles at a locus are **heterozygous.**

Figure 4–2 illustrates the crosses that Mendel initially performed. Geneticists use standard symbols to refer to alleles. Uppercase letters refer to dominant alleles (or dominant traits), and lowercase letters refer to recessive alleles (or recessive traits). Therefore,

T = the allele for tallness
t = the allele for shortness (dwarfism)

The same symbols are combined to describe an individual's actual genetic makeup, or **genotype.** The term *genotype* can be used to refer to an organism's entire genetic makeup or to the alleles at a specific genetic locus. Thus, the genotypes of the plants in Mendel's experiments were

TT = homozygous tall plants
$T t$ = heterozygous tall plants
$t t$ = homozygous short plants

Figure 4–3 is a *Punnett square.* It represents the different ways the alleles can be combined when the F_1 plants are self-fertilized to produce an F_2 generation. In this way, the figure shows the *genotypes* that are possible in the F_2 generation, and it also demonstrates that approximately $1/4$ of the F_2 plants are homozygous dominant (TT); $1/2$ are heterozygous (Tt); and the remaining $1/4$ are homozygous recessive (tt).

■ Dominant
Describing a trait governed by an allele that can be expressed in the presence of another, different allele (i.e., in heterozygotes). Dominant alleles prevent the expression of recessive alleles in heterozygotes. (This is the definition of *complete* dominance.)

■ Homozygous
Having the same allele at the same locus on both members of a chromosome pair.

■ Heterozygous
Having different alleles at the same locus on members of a chromosome pair.

■ Genotype
The genetic makeup of an individual. Genotype can refer to an organism's entire genetic makeup or to the alleles at a particular locus.

Virtual Lab 2, section II, part E, provides a Punnett square exercise for you to complete.

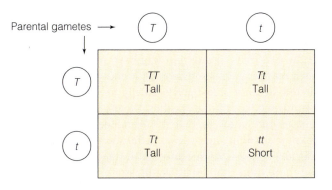

FIGURE 4–3
Punnett square representing possible genotypes and phenotypes and their proportions in the F_2 generation. The circles across the top and at the left of the Punnett square represent the gametes of the F_1 parents. The four squares illustrate that $1/4$ of the F_2 plants will be homozygous tall (TT); another $1/2$ also will be tall but will be heterozygous (Tt); and the remaining $1/4$ will be short (tt). Thus, $3/4$ can be expected to be tall and $1/4$ will be short.

■ Phenotypes

The observable or detectable physical characteristics of an organism; the detectable expressions of genotypes.

■ Phenotypic ratio

The proportion of one phenotype to other phenotypes in a group of organisms. For example, Mendel observed that there were approximately three tall plants for every short plant in the F_2 generation. This is expressed as a phenotypic ratio of 3:1.

■ Mendelian traits

Characteristics that are influenced by alleles at only one genetic locus. Examples include many blood types, such as ABO. Many genetic disorders, including sickle-cell anemia and Tay-Sachs disease, are also Mendelian traits.

■ Principle of independent assortment

The distribution of one pair of alleles into gametes does not influence the distribution of another pair. The genes controlling different traits are inherited independently of one another.

■ Linked

Describing genetic loci or genes located on the same chromosome.

The Punnett square can also be used to show (and predict) the proportions of F_2 **phenotypes**, or the observed physical manifestations of genes. Moreover, the Punnett square illustrates why Mendel observed three tall plants for every short plant in the F_2 generation. By examining the Punnett square, you can see that $1/4$ of the F_2 plants are tall because they have the *TT* genotype. Furthermore, an additional $1/2$, which are heterozygous (*Tt*), will also be tall because *T* is dominant to *t* and will therefore be expressed in the phenotype. The remaining $1/4$ are homozygous recessive (*tt*), and they will be short because no dominant allele is present. It is important to note that the *only* way a recessive allele can be expressed is if it occurs with another recessive allele, that is, if the individual is homozygous recessive at the particular locus in question.

In conclusion, $3/4$ of the F_2 generation will express the dominant phenotype, and $1/4$ will show the recessive phenotype. This relationship is expressed as a **phenotypic ratio** of 3:1 and typifies all **Mendelian traits** (characteristics governed by only one genetic locus) when only two alleles are involved, one of which is completely dominant to the other.

Independent Assortment

Mendel also made crosses in which two characteristics were considered simultaneously to determine whether there was a relationship between them. Two such characteristics were plant height and seed (pea) color. Mendel's peas came in two colors: yellow (dominant) and green (recessive).

In the P generation, crosses were made between pure-breeding tall plants with yellow seeds and short plants with green seeds. As expected, the recessive expression of each trait was not seen in the F_1 generation; all these plants were tall and produced yellow seeds. However, in the next (F_2) generation, both recessive traits reappeared in a small proportion of plants (Fig. 4–4). The phenotypic ratio for this type of cross is 9:3:3:1, meaning that $9/16$ will be tall with yellow seeds, $3/16$ will be tall with green seeds, $3/16$ will be short with yellow seeds, and $1/16$ will show both recessive traits and be short with green seeds. Although this may seem confusing, it illustrates that there is no relationship between the two traits; that is, there is nothing to dictate that a tall plant must have yellow (or green) seeds. The expression of one trait is not influenced by the expression of the other trait. The allele for tallness *(T)* has the same chance (50-50) of ending up in a zygote with either *Y* or *y*.

Mendel stated this relationship as the **principle of independent assortment**, which says that the genes that code for different traits assort independently of each other during gamete formation. Today, we know that this occurs because the genetic loci controlling these two characteristics are located on different chromosomes, and during meiosis, chromosomes travel to newly forming cells independently of one another. But if Mendel had used just *any* two traits, the phenotypic ratios might not have conformed to those expected by independent assortment. For example, if the two traits in question had been influenced by **linked** genes (i.e., genes located on the same chromosome), Mendel's results would have been considerably altered. Because linked genes usually remain together during meiosis, they are not independent of one another; therefore, the traits they influence do not conform to the ratios predicted by independent assortment. While Mendel did not know about linkage, he was certainly aware that all characteristics did not sort out independently of one another in the F_2 generation. He therefore reported only on those traits that did in fact illustrate independent assortment.

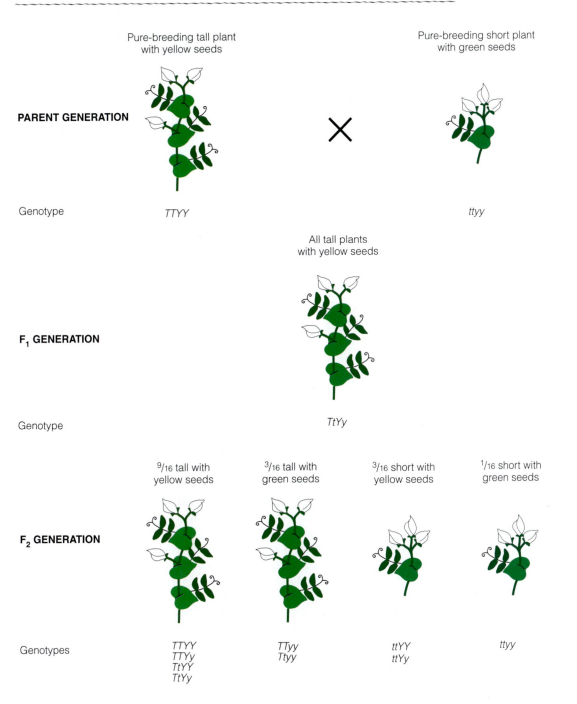

PARENT GENERATION

Pure-breeding tall plant
with yellow seeds

Pure-breeding short plant
with green seeds

Genotype   *TTYY*   *ttyy*

F₁ GENERATION

All tall plants
with yellow seeds

Genotype   *TtYy*

F₂ GENERATION

⁹/₁₆ tall with
yellow seeds

³/₁₆ tall with
green seeds

³/₁₆ short with
yellow seeds

¹/₁₆ short with
green seeds

Genotypes   *TTYY*   *TTyy*   *ttYY*   *ttyy*
             TTYy   *Ttyy*   *ttYy*
             TtYY
             TtYy

In 1866, Mendel's results were published, but the methodology and statistical nature of the research were beyond the thinking of the time, and their significance was overlooked and unappreciated. However, by the end of the nineteenth century, several investigators had made important contributions to the understanding of chromosomes and cell division. These discoveries paved the way for the acceptance of Mendel's work by 1900, when three different groups of scientists, conducting similar breeding experiments, came across his paper. Regrettably, Mendel had died 16 years earlier and thus never saw his work vindicated.

FIGURE 4–4

Results of crosses when two traits are considered simultaneously. Stem length and seed color are independent of each other. Also shown are the genotypes associated with each phenotype. Note that the ratio of tall plants to short plants is ³/₄ to ¹/₄, or 3:1, the same as in Figure 4–2. The ratio of yellow to green seeds is also 3:1.

An example of human
blood groups is given in
Virtual Lab 2, section II, part E.

■ Antigens
Large molecules found on the surface
of cells. Several different loci governing
antigens on red and white blood cells
are known. Foreign antigens provoke
an immune response in individuals.

■ Codominance
The expression of two alleles in heterozygotes. In this situation, neither
allele is dominant or recessive, so that
both influence the phenotype.

Mendelian Inheritance in Humans

Mendelian traits (also referred to as *discrete traits* or *traits of simple inheritance*) are
controlled by alleles at *one* genetic locus. Currently, more than 4,000 human traits
are known to be inherited according to simple Mendelian principles. Examples
include several blood group systems, such as ABO.

The ABO system is governed by three alleles, *A, B,* and *O,* found at the ABO
locus on the ninth chromosome. These alleles determine which ABO blood type
an individual has by coding for the production of special substances called **antigens** on the surface of red blood cells. If only antigen A is present, the blood type
(phenotype) is A; if only B is present, the blood type is B; if both are present, the
blood type is AB; and when neither is present, the blood type is O.

Dominance and recessiveness are clearly illustrated by the ABO system. The *O*
allele is recessive to both *A* and *B;* therefore, if a person has type O blood, he or
she must be homozygous for (have two copies of) the *O* allele. However, since
both *A* and *B* are dominant to *O,* an individual with blood type A can actually
have one of two genotypes: *AA* or *AO.* The same is true of type B, which results
from the genotypes *BB* and *BO* (Table 4–2). However, type AB presents a slightly
different situation and is an example of **codominance.**

Codominance is seen when two different alleles occur in heterozygous condition, but instead of one having the ability to mask the expression of the other, the
products of *both* are expressed in the phenotype. Therefore, when both *A* and *B*
alleles are present, both A and B antigens can be detected on the surface of red
blood cells.

A number of genetic disorders are inherited as dominant traits (Table 4–3).
This means that if a person inherits only one copy of a harmful, dominant allele,
the condition it causes will be present, regardless of the existence of a different,
recessive allele on the corresponding chromosome.

Recessive conditions are commonly associated with the lack of a substance,
usually an enzyme (see Table 4–3). For a person actually to have a recessive disorder, he or she must have *two* copies of the recessive allele that causes it.
Heterozygotes who have only one copy of a harmful recessive allele are unaffected. Such individuals are frequently called *carriers.*

Although carriers do not actually show full-blown manifestations of the
recessive allele they carry, they can pass the allele on to their children.
(Remember, half their gametes will carry the recessive allele.) If their mate is also

TABLE 4–2 ABO Genotypes and Associated Phenotypes		
Genotype	Antigens on Red Blood Cells	ABO Blood Type (Phenotype)
AA, AO	A	A
BB, BO	B	B
AB	A and B	AB
OO	None	O

TABLE 4–3 Some Mendelian Disorders in Humans

Dominant Traits		Recessive Traits	
Condition	Manifestations	Condition	Manifestations
Achondroplasia	Dwarfism due to growth defects involving the long bones of the arms and legs; trunk and head size usually normal.	Cystic fibrosis	Among the most common genetic (Mendelian) disorders among whites in the United States; abnormal secretions of the exocrine glands, with pronounced involvement of the pancreas; most patients develop obstructive lung disease. Until the recent development of new treatments, only about half of all patients survived to early adulthood.
Brachydactyly	Shortened fingers and toes.		
Familial hyper-cholesterolemia	Elevated cholesterol levels and cholesterol plaque deposition; a leading cause of heart disease, with death frequently occurring by middle age.		
		Tay-Sachs disease	Most common among Ashkenazi Jews; degeneration of the nervous system beginning at about 6 months of age; lethal by age 2 or 3 years.
Neurofibromatosis	Symptoms range from the appearance of abnormal skin pigmentation to large tumors resulting in gross deformities; this so-called Elephant Man disease can, in extreme cases, lead to paralysis, blindness, and death.	Phenylketonuria (PKU)	Inability to metabolize the amino acid phenylalanine; results in mental retardation if left untreated during childhood; treatment involves strict dietary management and some supplementation.
Marfan syndrome	The eyes and cardiovascular and skeletal systems are affected; symptoms include greater than average height, long arms and legs, eye problems, and enlargement of the aorta; death due to rupture of the aorta is common. Abraham Lincoln may have had Marfan syndrome.	Albinism	Inability to produce normal amounts of the pigment melanin; results in very fair, untannable skin, light blond hair, and light eyes; may also be associated with vision problems.

a carrier, then it is possible for them to have a child who will be homozygous for the allele, and that child will be affected. In fact, in a mating between two carriers, the risk of having an affected child is 25 percent (refer back to Fig. 4–3).

Misconceptions Regarding Dominance and Recessiveness

Traditional methods of teaching genetics have led to some misunderstanding of dominance and recessiveness. Thus, virtually all introductory students (and most people in general) have the impression that these phenomena are all-or-nothing situations. This misconception especially pertains to recessive alleles, and the general view is that when these alleles occur in heterozygotes (i.e., carriers), they have absolutely no effect on the phenotype—that is, they are completely inactivated by the presence of another (dominant) allele. Certainly, this is how it appeared to Gregor Mendel and, until the last two or three decades, to most geneticists.

However, various biochemical techniques, unavailable in the past but in wide use today, have demonstrated that recessive alleles do indeed exert some influence on phenotype, although these effects are not usually detectable through simple observation. Indeed, it is now clear that our *perception* of recessive alleles greatly depends on one important factor: whether we examine them at the directly observable phenotypic level or the biochemical level.

Scientists now know of several recessive alleles that do produce detectable phenotypic effects in heterozygotes. Consider Tay-Sachs disease, a lethal condition that results from the inability to produce the enzyme hexosaminidase A (see Table 4–3). This inability, seen in people who are homozygous for a recessive allele (*ts*) on chromosome 15, invariably results in death by early childhood. Carriers do not have the disease, and practically speaking, they are unaffected. However, in 1979, it was shown that Tay-Sachs carriers, although functionally normal, have only about 40 to 60 percent of the amount of the enzyme seen in normal people. In fact, there are now voluntary tests to screen carriers in populations at risk for Tay-Sachs disease.

Similar misconceptions also relate to dominant alleles. The majority of people see dominant alleles as somehow "stronger" or "better," and there is always the mistaken notion that dominant alleles are more common in populations. These misconceptions undoubtedly stem partly from the label "dominant" and the connotations that the term carries. But in genetic usage, those connotations are somewhat misleading. If dominant alleles were always more common, then a majority of people would be affected by such conditions as achondroplasia and Marfan syndrome (see Table 4–3).

Clearly, the relationship between recessive and dominant alleles and their functions are more complicated than they would appear at first glance. (Indeed, most things are.) Previously held views of dominance and recessiveness were guided by available technologies; as genetic technologies continue to change, new theories may emerge, and if so, our perceptions will be further altered.

Patterns of Inheritance

It is of obvious importance to be able to establish the pattern of inheritance of genetic traits, especially those that result in serious disease. Equally important is the ability to determine an individual's risk of inheriting deleterious alleles, or expressing symptoms, in families with a history of inherited disorders. But because humans cannot be used in experimental breeding programs, as were Mendel's peas, a more indirect approach must be used to demonstrate patterns of inheritance. The principal technique traditionally used in human genetic studies has been the construction of a **pedigree chart**, a diagram of matings and offspring in a family over the span of a few generations.

Pedigree analysis helps determine if a trait is indeed Mendelian in nature. It also helps establish the mode of inheritance. From considerations of whether the locus that influences a particular trait is located on an autosome or sex chromosome and whether it is dominant or recessive, six different modes of Mendelian inheritance have been recognized in humans: *autosomal dominant, autosomal recessive, X-linked recessive, X-linked dominant, Y-linked,* and *mitochondrial.* We shall discuss the first three of these in some detail.

Standardized symbols are used in the construction of pedigree charts. Squares and circles represent males and females, respectively. Horizontal lines connecting individuals indicate matings, and offspring are connected to horizontal mating lines by vertical lines. Siblings are joined to one another by a horizontal line to which they are connected by vertical lines (Fig. 4–5).

Autosomal Dominant Traits   As the term implies, autosomal dominant traits are governed by loci on autosomes (i.e., any chromosomes except X or Y). One example of an autosomal dominant trait is brachydactyly, a condition characterized by malformed hands and shortened fingers.

■ **Pedigree chart**
A diagram showing family relationships in order to trace the hereditary pattern of particular genetic (usually Mendelian) traits.

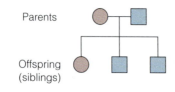

FIGURE 4–5
Typical symbols used in pedigree charts.

Because brachydactyly is caused by a dominant allele, anyone who inherits just one copy will express the trait. (For purposes of this discussion, we will use the symbol *B* to refer to the dominant allele that causes the condition, and *b* for the recessive, normal allele.) Since the allele is rare, virtually everyone who has brachydactyly is a heterozygote (*Bb*). (Generally speaking, individuals who are homozygous dominant

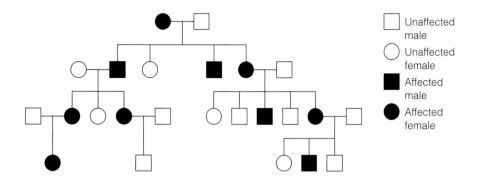

for rare, deleterious alleles are uncommon. Mutant alleles that produce abnormalities in heterozygotes cause such extreme defects in homozygotes that affected fetuses frequently abort prior to reaching full term.) Unaffected individuals are homozygous recessive (*bb*).

Figure 4–6 is a partial pedigree for brachydactyly. It is apparent from this pedigree that all affected members have at least one affected parent; thus, the abnormality does not skip generations. This pattern is true of all autosomal dominant traits. Another characteristic of autosomal dominant traits is that there is no sex bias, and males and females are more or less equally affected.

One other fact illustrated by Figure 4–6 is that approximately half the offspring of affected parents are also affected. This proportion is what we would predict for an autosomal dominant trait where only one parent is affected, and it is explained by events in meiosis as well as by Mendel's principle of segregation (see Fig. 4–7).

Autosomal Recessive Traits   Autosomal recessive traits are also influenced by loci on autosomes but show a different pattern of inheritance. A good example of such a trait is shown in Fig. 4–8, a pedigree for albinism, a metabolic disorder causing deficient production of a skin pigment called melanin (see Chapter 15). This disorder is phenotypically expressed as very light skin, hair, and iris of the eyes.

Actually, albinism is a group of genetic disorders, each influenced by different loci. Some forms affect only the eyes, while others also involve skin and hair. The most widely known variety of albinism does influence eye, skin, and hair pigmentation and is caused by an autosomal recessive allele. The frequency of this particular form of albinism varies widely among populations, with an incidence of about 1 in 37,000 in American whites but a much higher frequency, approaching 1 in 200, among Hopi Indians. How populations have come to be so different in the frequencies of various alleles (such as those for albinism) will be a major focus of Chapter 14.

Pedigrees for autosomal recessive traits show obvious differences from those for autosomal dominant

FIGURE 4–6

Inheritance of an autosomal dominant trait: a human pedigree for brachydactyly.

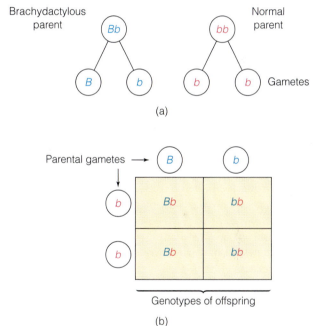

FIGURE 4–7

The pattern of inheritance of autosomal dominant traits is the direct result of the distribution of chromosomes, and the alleles they carry, into gametes during meiosis. (a) Diagrammatic representation of possible gametes produced by two parents: one with brachydactyly and another with normal hands and fingers. The brachydactylous individual can produce two types of gametes: half with the dominant allele (B), and half with the recessive allele (b). All the gametes produced by the normal parent will carry the recessive allele. (b) A Punnett square depicting the possible genotypes in the offspring of one parent with brachydactyly (Bb) and one with normal hands and fingers (bb). Statistically speaking, half the offspring would be expected to have the Bb genotype and thus brachydactyly. The other half would be homozygous recessive (bb) and would be normal.

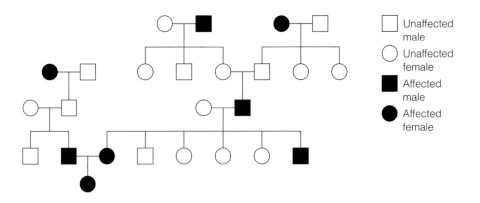

FIGURE 4-8

Partial pedigree for albinism, an autosomal recessive trait.

Unaffected
male

Unaffected
female

Affected
male

Affected
female

characteristics. For one thing, recessive traits often appear to skip generations, so that an affected offspring is produced by two phenotypically normal parents. In fact, most affected individuals have unaffected parents. In addition, the proportion of affected offspring from most matings is less than the 50 percent so frequently seen in pedigrees for autosomal dominant traits. As in the pattern for autosomal dominant traits, males and females are equally affected. However, when both parents have the trait, all the offspring will be affected.

As Figure 4-9 illustrates, the Mendelian principle of segregation explains the pattern of inheritance of autosomal recessive traits. In fact, this pattern is the very one first elucidated by Mendel in his pea experiments (refer back to Fig. 4-3). Unaffected parents who produce an albino child *must* both be carriers, and their child is homozygous for the recessive allele that causes the abnormality. The Punnett square in Figure 4-9 shows how such a mating produces both affected and unaffected offspring in predictable proportions—the typical phenotypic ratio of 3:1.

FIGURE 4-9

A cross between two phenotypically normal parents, both of whom are carriers of the albinism allele. From a mating such as this between two carriers, we would expect the following possible proportions of genotypes and phenotypes in the offspring; homozygous dominants (AA) with normal phenotype, 25 percent; heterozygotes, or carriers (Aa), with normal phenotype, 50 percent; and homozygous recessives (aa) with albinism, 25 percent. This yields the phenotypic ratio of three normal to one albino.

Sex-Linked Traits   Sex-linked traits are controlled by loci on sex chromosomes; the term *sex-linked* simply refers to the fact that these loci are located on the X or Y chromosome. (Almost all such loci have no role in primary sex determination.) Of the more than 240 traits suspected to result from this form of inheritance, almost all are controlled by loci on the X chromosome (Table 4-4). Only recently have any traits been traced to regions on the Y chromosome, where at least four loci have been identified. One is involved in determining maleness (the TDF locus), and one other may be involved with sperm production (the H-Y locus). Because of the scarcity of known Y-linked traits, they are not dealt with here.

The best known of the sex-linked traits is hemophilia, caused by a recessive allele at a locus on the X chromosome. This type of condition is thus said to be *X-linked recessive*. Hemophilia results from the lack of a clotting factor in the blood (factor VIII), and affected individuals suffer bleeding episodes and may hemorrhage to death from incidents that most of us would consider trivial.

The most famous pedigree documenting this malady is that of Queen Victoria and her descendants (shown in Fig. 4-10). The most striking feature shown by this pattern of inheritance is that usually only males are affected. To understand this pattern, once again we must refer to the principle of segregation, but with one additional stipulation: We are now dealing with *sex chromosomes*.

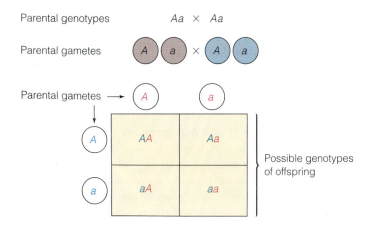

Parental genotypes   Aa × Aa

Parental gametes   A   a × A   a

Parental gametes →   A   a

	A	a
A	AA	Aa
a	aA	aa

Possible genotypes of offspring

TABLE 4–4 Some Mendelian Disorders Inherited as X-Linked Recessive Traits in Humans	
Condition	**Manifestations**
G6PD (glucose-6-phosphate dehydrogenase) deficiency	Lack of an enzyme (G6PD) in red blood cells; produces severe, sometimes fatal anemia in the presence of certain foods (e.g., fava beans) and/or drugs (e.g., the antimalarial drug primaquin). (See p. 97 for further discussion relating to a possible link with malaria as a selective agent.)
Muscular dystrophy	One form; other forms can be inherited as autosomal recessives. Progressive weakness and atrophy of muscles beginning in early childhood; continues to progress throughout life; some female carriers may develop heart problems.
Red-green color blindness	Actually, there are two separate forms, one involving the perception of red and the other affecting only the perception of green. About 8 percent of European males have an impaired ability to distinguish green.
Lesch-Nyhan disease	Impaired motor development noticeable by 5 months; progressive motor impairment, diminished kidney function, self-mutilation, and early death.
Hemophilia	There are three forms; two (hemophilia A and B) are X-linked. In hemophilia A, a clotting factor is missing; hemophilia B is caused by a defective clotting factor. Both produce abnormal internal and external bleeding from minor injuries; severe pain is a frequent accompaniment; without treatment, death usually occurs before adulthood.
Ichthyosis	There are several forms; one is X-linked. A skin condition due to lack of an enzyme; characterized by scaly, brown lesions on the extremities and trunk. In the past, people with this condition sometimes were exhibited in circuses and sideshows as "the alligator man."

Because they possess two X chromosomes, females show the same pattern of expression of X-linked traits as for autosomal traits. That is, the only way an X-linked recessive allele can be phenotypically expressed in a female is when she is homozygous for it. Therefore, heterozygous females are unaffected. In cases where female heterozygotes express an X-linked trait, it is an X-linked dominant.

On the other hand, since males are XY and have only one X chromosome, they possess only one copy of an X-linked gene. With only one X chromosome, males can never be homozygous or heterozygous for X-linked loci and are thus referred to as **hemizygous.** Moreover, males do not exhibit dominance or recessiveness for X-linked traits because *any* allele located on their X chromosome, even a recessive one, will be expressed. In fact, any time a recessive allele occurs in a hemizygous state, it is expressed.

The difference between males and females in number of X chromosomes is directly related to the incidence of hemophilia seen in Figure 4–10. Females who have one copy of the hemophilia allele are carriers for the trait. Although they may have some tendency toward bleeding, they are not severely affected. On the other hand, males who have the allele in single dose (on their *only* X chromosome) are severely afflicted, and prior to the availability of recent therapy, they faced short and painful lives.

▌ Hemizygous
(*hemi,* meaning "half") Having only one member of a pair of alleles. Because males have only one X chromosome, all their X-linked alleles are hemizygous. All recessive alleles on a male's X chromosome are expressed in the phenotype.

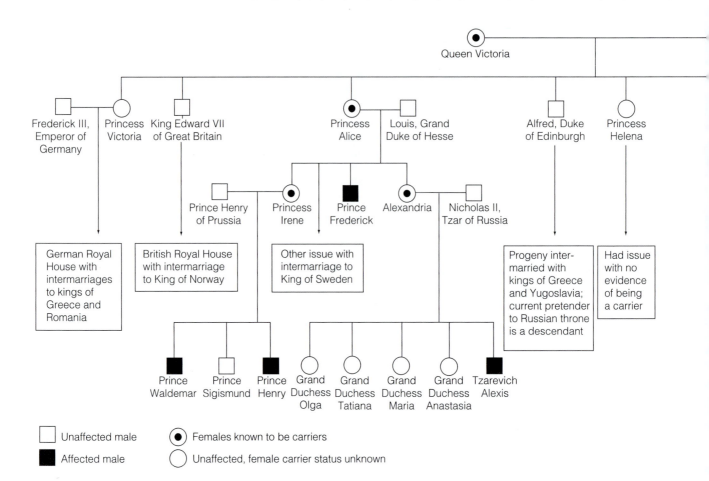

Unaffected male

Affected male

Females known to be carriers

Unaffected, female carrier status unknown

FIGURE 4–10

Pedigree for Queen Victoria and some of her descendants, showing inheritance of hemophilia, an X-linked recessive trait in humans.

See the exercise in Virtual Lab 2, section IV, for a discussion of skin color in humans.

■ **Polygenic**

Referring to traits that are influenced by genes at two or more loci. Examples of such traits are stature, skin color, and eye color. Many polygenic traits are also influenced by environmental factors.

Non-Mendelian Patterns of Inheritance

Polygenic Inheritance

Mendelian traits are said to be *discrete,* or *discontinuous,* because their phenotypic expressions do not overlap; rather, they fall into clearly defined categories. For example, Mendel's pea plants were either short or tall, but none was intermediate in height. In the ABO system, the four phenotypes are completely distinct from one another; that is, there is no intermediate form between type A and type B to represent a gradation between the two. In other words, Mendelian traits do not show *continuous* variation.

However, many traits do have a wide range of phenotypic expressions that form a graded series. These are called **polygenic**, or *continuous,* traits. While Mendelian traits are governed by only one genetic locus, polygenic characteristics are influenced by alleles at *several* loci, with each locus making a contribution to the phenotype. For example, one of the most frequently cited instances of polygenic inheritance in humans is skin color. The single most important factor influencing skin color is the amount of the pigment melanin present.

Melanin production is believed to be influenced by between three and six genetic loci, with each locus having at least two alleles, neither of which is domi-

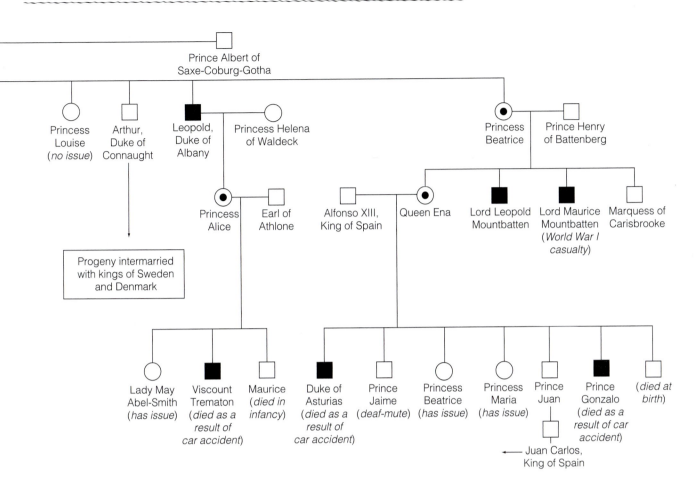

nant. Individuals having only alleles for more melanin production (i.e., they are homozygous at all loci) have the darkest skin. Those having only alleles that code for reduced melanin production have very fair skin.

As there are perhaps six loci and at least 12 alleles, there are numerous ways in which these alleles can combine in individuals. If an individual inherits 11 alleles coding for maximum pigmentation and only one for reduced melanin production, skin color will be very dark. As the proportion of reduced pigmentation alleles increases, skin color becomes lighter. In this system, as in some other polygenic systems, there is an *additive effect*. This means that each allele that codes for melanin production makes a contribution to increased melanization (although for some characteristics the contributions of the alleles are not all equal). Likewise, each allele coding for reduced melanin production contributes to reduced pigmentation. Therefore, the effect of multiple alleles at several loci, each making a contribution to individual phenotypes, is to produce continuous variation from very dark to very fair skin within the species. (Skin color is also discussed in Chapter 15.)

Polygenic traits actually account for most of the readily observable phenotypic variation seen in humans, and they have traditionally served as a basis for "racial" classification (see Chapter 15). In addition to skin color, polygenic inheritance in humans is seen in hair color, weight, stature, eye color, shape of face, shape of nose, and fingerprint pattern. Because they exhibit continuous variation, most polygenic traits can be measured on a scale composed of equal increments.

For example, height (stature) is measured in feet and inches (or meters and centimeters). If one were to measure height in a large number of individuals, the distribution of measurements would continue uninterrupted from the shortest extreme to the tallest. That is what is meant by *continuous traits*.

Because polygenic traits usually lend themselves to metric analysis, biologists, geneticists, and physical anthropologists treat them statistically. Although statistical analysis can be complicated, the use of simple summary statistics, such as the *mean* (average) or *standard deviation* (a measure of within-group variation), permits basic descriptions of, and comparisons between, populations. For example, one might be interested in average height in two different populations and whether or not differences between the two are significant, and if so, why. Or a researcher might determine that in the same geographical area, one group shows significantly more variation in skin color than another, and it would be useful to explain this variability. (You should also note that *all* physical traits measured and statistically treated in fossils are polygenic in nature.)

However, these particular statistical manipulations are not possible with Mendelian traits simply because those traits cannot be measured in the same manner. They are either present or they are not; they are expressed one way or another and can be described in terms of frequencies. But just because Mendelian traits are not amenable to the same types of statistical tests as polygenic traits does not mean that Mendelian traits are less worthy of study or less informative of genetic processes. It simply means that scientists must approach the study of these two types of inheritance from different perspectives.

Mendelian characteristics can be described in terms of frequency within populations, yielding between-group comparisons regarding incidence. Moreover, these characteristics can also be analyzed for mode of inheritance (dominant or recessive) from pedigree data. Finally, for many Mendelian traits, the approximate or exact position of genetic loci has been identified, making it possible to examine the mechanisms and patterns of inheritance at these loci. Because polygenic characters are influenced by several loci, they cannot as yet be traced to specific genes on specific chromosomes; therefore, such analysis is currently not possible.

Genetic and Environmental Factors

From the preceding discussion, it might appear that phenotype is solely the expression of the genotype, but this is not true. (Here we use the terms *genotype* and *phenotype* in a broader sense to refer to an individual's *entire* genetic makeup and *all* observable or detectable characteristics.) The genotype sets limits and potentials for development, but it also interacts with the environment, and many aspects of phenotype are influenced by this genetic-environmental interaction. For many traits, scientists have developed statistical methods for calculating what proportion of phenotypic variation is due to genetic or environmental components. However, it is usually not possible to identify the *specific* environmental factors affecting the phenotype.

Many polygenic traits are quite obviously influenced by environmental conditions. Adult stature is strongly affected by the individual's nutritional status during growth and development. One study showed that children of Japanese immigrants to Hawaii were, on average, 3 to 4 inches taller than their parents. This dramatic difference, seen in one generation, was attributed to environmental alteration—specifically to a change in diet (Froelich, 1970).

Other important environmental factors include exposure to sunlight, altitude, temperature, and, unfortunately, increasing levels of exposure to toxic waste and airborne pollutants. All these and many more contribute in complex ways to the continuous phenotypic variation seen in characteristics governed by multiple loci.

Mendelian traits are less likely to be influenced by environmental factors. For example, ABO blood type is determined at fertilization and remains fixed throughout the individual's lifetime, regardless of diet, exposure to ultraviolet radiation, temperature, and so forth.

Mendelian and polygenic inheritance produce different kinds of phenotypic variation. In the former, variation occurs in discrete categories, while in the latter, it is continuous. However, it is important to understand that even for polygenic characteristics, Mendelian principles still apply at individual loci. In other words, if a trait is influenced by seven loci, each one of those loci may have two or more alleles, with one perhaps being dominant to the other or with the alleles being codominant. It is the combined action of the alleles at all seven loci, interacting with the environment, that results in observable phenotypic expression.

Pleiotropy

Whereas polygenic traits are governed by the actions of several genes, **pleiotropy** is a situation where a single gene influences more than one phenotypic expression. Although this might seem unusual, in fact, pleiotropic effects are probably the rule rather than the exception.

The autosomal recessive disorder phenylketonuria (PKU) provides one example of pleiotropy (see Table 4–3). Individuals who are homozygous for the PKU allele do not produce phenylketonurase, the enzyme involved in the initial conversion of the amino acid phenylalanine to another amino acid, tyrosine. Because of this block in the metabolic pathway, phenylalanine breaks down into substances that accumulate in the central nervous system, and without dietary management, they lead to mental retardation. And there are several additional consequences. Because tyrosine is ultimately converted into several other substances, including the pigment melanin, numerous other systems can also be affected. Consequently, one additional manifestation of PKU, owing to a diminished ability to produce melanin, is that affected people usually have blue eyes, fair skin, and light hair.

There are many known examples of pleiotropic genes, including the allele that causes sickle-cell anemia. Although is is not necessary to include a detailed discussion here, it is clear that gene action may exert an influence over a number of seemingly unrelated phenotypic expressions.

Pleiotropy
A situation whereby several seemingly unrelated phenotypic effects are influenced by the action of a single gene.

Modern Evolutionary Theory

By the beginning of the twentieth century, the essential foundations for evolutionary theory had already been developed. Darwin and Wallace had articulated the key principle of natural selection 40 years earlier, and the rediscovery of Mendelian genetics in 1900 contributed the other major component—a mechanism for inheritance. We might expect that these two basic contributions would have been joined rather quickly into a consistent theory of evolution. However, such was not the case. For the first 30 years of the twentieth century, rival explanations emphasized mutation *or* natural selection as the prime mover of evolutionary change. A *synthesis* of these two views was not achieved until the

BOX 4–1

Development of Modern Evolutionary Theory

Our understanding of the evolutionary process came about through contributions of biologists in the United States, Great Britain, and Russia.

While "mutationists" were arguing with "selectionists" about the single primary mechanism in evolution, several population geneticists began to realize that both small genetic changes and natural selection were necessary ingredients in the evolutionary formula.

These population geneticists were largely concerned with mathematical reconstructions of evolution—in particular, measuring those small accumulations of genetic changes in populations over just a few generations. Central figures in these early theoretical developments included Ronald Fisher and J.B.S. Haldane in Great Britain, Sewall Wright in the United States, and Sergei Chetverikov in Russia.

While the work of these scientists often produced brilliant insights (see particularly Fisher's *The Genetical Theory of Natural Selection,* 1930), their conclusions were largely unknown to most evolutionary biologists, especially in North America. It remained, therefore, for someone to

transcend these two worlds: the mathematical jargon of the population geneticists and the general constructs of theoretical evolutionary biologists. The scientist who performed this task (and who is credited as the first true synthesizer) was Theodosius Dobzhansky. In his *Genetics and the Origin of Species* (1937), Dobzhansky skillfully integrated the mathematics of population genetics with overall evolutionary theory. His insights then became the basis for a period of tremendous activity in evolutionary thinking that directly led to major contributions by George Gaylord Simpson (who brought paleontology into the synthesis), Ernst Mayr,* and others. In fact, the "modern synthesis" produced by these scientists stood basically unchallenged for an entire generation as *the* explanation of the evolutionary process. In recent years, however, some aspects of this theory have been brought under serious question (see Chapter 8).

---

*For an interesting discussion of the intellectual developments concerning the formulation of modern evolutionary theory, see Ernst Mayr and William B. Provine (eds.), *The Evolutionary Synthesis* (Cambridge, MA.: Harvard University Press, 1980).

mid-1930s, and we owe much of our current view of the evolutionary process to this intellectual development (see Box 4–1).

The Modern Synthesis

Biologists working on mathematical models of evolutionary change in the late 1920s and early 1930s came to realize that mutational and selective processes were not opposing themes, but that a comprehensive explanation of organic evolution required *both.* Small new changes in the genetic material—transmitted from parent to offspring are, in fact, the fuel for natural selection. The two major foundations of the biological sciences had thus been brought together in what Julian Huxley termed the "modern synthesis."

From such a "modern" (i.e., the middle of the twentieth century onward) perspective, we define evolution as a two-stage process. These two stages are:

1. The production and redistribution of **variation** (inherited differences between individuals)

■ **Variation (genetic)**
Inherited differences between individuals; the basis of all evolutionary change.

2. *Natural selection* acting on this variation (whereby inherited differences, or variation, among individuals differentially affect their ability to reproduce successfully)

Definition of Evolution

As discussed in Chapter 2, Darwin saw evolution as the gradual unfolding of new varieties of life from previous forms over long periods of time. This depiction is what most of us think of as evolution, and it is indeed the end result of the evolutionary process. But these long-term effects can come about only by the accumulation of many small genetic changes occurring every generation. To understand how the process of evolution works, we must study these short-term events. Today, we study evolutionary changes occurring between generations in various organisms (including humans) and are able to demonstrate how evolution works. From such a modern genetic perspective, we define **evolution** as *a change in **allele frequency** from one generation to the next.*

Allele frequencies are indicators of the genetic makeup of an interbreeding group of individuals known as a **population.** (We will return to this topic in more detail in Chapter 14.) Let us illustrate the way allele frequencies change (i.e., how evolution occurs) through a simplified example. First of all, we must look at a physical trait that is inherited—in this case, human blood type (discussed on p. 80). The best known of the human blood types is ABO. There are, however, many similar blood type systems controlled by different loci that determine genetically transmitted properties of the red blood cells.

Let us assume that your present class of students represents a population, an interbreeding group of individuals, and that we have ascertained the ABO blood type of each member. (To comprise a population, individuals must choose mates more often from *within* the group than from outside it. Of course, the individuals in your class will not meet this requirement, but for the sake of our example, we will overlook this stipulation.) The proportions of the *A, B,* and *O* alleles are the allele frequencies for this trait. For example, suppose we find that 50 percent of all the ABO alleles in your class are *A,* 40 percent are *B,* and 10 percent are *O.* Then the frequencies of these alleles are *A* = .50, *B* = .40, and *O* = .10.*

Since the frequencies for these genes represent only proportions of a total, it is obvious that allele frequencies can refer only to groups of individuals, that is, populations. Individuals do not have an allele frequency; they have either *A, B,* or *O* (or a combination of these). Nor can individuals change alleles. From conception onward, the genetic composition of an individual is fixed. If you start out with blood type A, you will remain type A. Therefore, an individual cannot evolve: Only a group of individuals—a population—can evolve over time.

What happens when a population evolves? Evolution is not an unusual or mysterious process. In fact, it is incredibly commonplace and may occur between every generation for every group of organisms in the world, including humans. Assume that 25 years from now, we calculate the frequencies of the ABO alleles for the children (offspring) of our classroom population and find the following: *A* = .30, *B* = .40, and *O* = .30.

Evolution
(modern genetic definition) A change in the frequency of alleles from one generation to the next.

Allele frequency
In a population, the percentage of all the alleles at a locus accounted for by one specific allele.

Population
Within a species, a community of individuals where mates are usually found.

---

*This is a simplified example. Because the ABO system is governed by three alleles, calculating allele frequencies is more complicated than for a two-allele system. The way allele frequencies are calculated for a simple two-allele locus will be shown in Chapter 14.

We can see that the relative proportions have changed: *A* has decreased, *O* has increased, and *B* has remained the same. Such a simple, apparently minor change is what we call evolution. Over the short run of just a few generations, such changes in inherited traits may be only very small, but if further continued and elaborated, the results can and do produce spectacular kinds of adaptation and whole new varieties of life.

Whether we are talking about the short-term effects (as in our classroom population) from one generation to the next, which is sometimes called **microevolution**, or the long-term effects through fossil history, sometimes called **macroevolution**, the basic evolutionary mechanisms are similar. As we will discuss in Chapter 8, however, they are not identical.

The question may be asked, How do allele frequencies change? Or, to put it another way, what causes evolution? The modern theory of evolution isolates general factors that can produce alterations in allele frequencies. As we have noted, evolution is a two-stage process. Genetic variation must first be produced and distributed before it can be acted on by natural selection.

Factors that Produce and Redistribute Variation

Mutation

You have already learned that a molecular alteration in genetic material is called a mutation. A genetic locus may take one of several alternative forms, which we have defined as alleles (*A*, *B*, or *O* for example). If one allele changes to another—that is, if the gene itself is altered—a mutation has occurred. (In fact, alleles are the results of mutation.) For such changes to have evolutionary significance, they must occur in the sex cells, which are passed between generations. Evolution is a change in allele frequencies *between* generations. If mutations do not occur in gametes (either the egg or sperm), they will not be transmitted to the next generation, and no evolutionary change can result. If, however, a genetic change does occur in the sperm or egg of one of the individuals in our classroom (*A* mutates to *B*, for instance), the offspring's blood type also will be altered, causing a minute shift in allele frequencies of that generation. In Chapter 3, we showed how a change in a single DNA base, a *point mutation,* could cause a change in hemoglobin structure (from normal to sickle-cell). Other mutations that produce phenotypic effects (as discussed earlier in this chapter) include the albinism allele, the allele producing brachydactyly, and the alteration causing Tay-Sachs disease.

Actually, it would be rare to see evolution occurring by mutation alone. Mutation rates for any given trait are quite low; thus, mutations would rarely be seen in such a small population as our class. In larger populations, mutations might be observed (1 individual in 10,000, say), but would by themselves have very little impact on shifting allele frequencies. However, when mutation is coupled with natural selection, evolutionary changes not only can occur, but can occur more rapidly.

It is important to remember that mutation is the basic creative force in evolution because it is the *only* way to produce new variation. Its key role in the production of variation represents the first stage of the evolutionary process. Darwin was not aware of the nature of mutation. Only in the twentieth century, with the

Microevolution
Small changes occurring within species, such as a change in allele frequencies.

Macroevolution
Changes produced only after many generations, such as the appearance of a new species.

Mutation, gene flow, genetic drift, and recombination are discussed in Virtual Lab 2, section III, part A.

spectacular development of molecular biology, have the secrets of genetic structure been revealed.

Gene Flow

The exchange of genes between populations is called **gene flow**. The term *migration* is frequently used instead, but strictly speaking, migration means movement of people, whereas gene flow refers to the exchange of *genes,* which can occur only if the migrants interbreed. Moreover, it should be remembered that even if individuals move temporarily and interbreed within the new population (thus leaving a genetic contribution), they need not remain as part of the population. For example, the offspring of U.S. soldiers and Vietnamese women are the result of gene flow, even though their fathers may have returned to their native population. Even more exotic avenues for gene flow are possible with the advent of new genetic technologies. For generations, frozen sperm (and more recently, frozen eggs) have been routinely transported long distances in commercial farming (e.g., dairy cattle). The same technologies could be used to further disseminate human genes, although this potential hardly seems necessary.

In humans, social rules more than any other factor determine mating patterns, and cultural anthropologists must work closely with physical anthropologists to isolate and measure this aspect of evolutionary change. Population movements (particularly in the last 500 years) have reached enormous proportions, and few breeding isolates remain. It should not, however, be assumed that significant population movements did not occur prior to modern times. Our hunting and gathering ancestors probably lived in small groups that were both mobile and flexible in membership. Early farmers also were probably mobile, expanding into new areas as land wore out and human population size increased. Intensive, highly sedentary agricultural communities came later, but even then, significant migration was still possible. From the Near East, one of the early farming centers, populations spread very gradually in a "creeping occupation of Europe, India, and northern and eastern Africa" (Bodmer and Cavalli-Sforza, 1976, p. 563).

Migration between populations has been a consistent feature of hominid evolution since the first dispersal of our genus and helps explain why in the last million years, speciation has been rare. Of course, migration patterns are a manifestation of human cultural behavior, once again emphasizing the essential biocultural nature of human evolution.

An interesting example of how gene flow influences microevolutionary changes in modern human populations is seen in African Americans. African Americans in the United States are largely of West African descent, but there has also been considerable genetic admixture with Europeans. By measuring allele frequencies for specific genetic loci (e.g., Rh and Duffy blood groups, discussed in Chapter 14), we can estimate the amount of migration of European alleles into the African American gene pool. Data from northern and western U.S. cities (including New York, Detroit, and Oakland) have shown the migration rate (i.e., the proportion of *non*-African genes in the African American gene pool) at 20 to 25 percent (Cummings, 1997). However, more restricted data from the southern United States (Charleston and rural Georgia) have suggested a lower degree of gene flow (4 to 11 percent). The most consistent of these studies employ new genetic techniques, especially those involving direct DNA comparisons (discussed in Chapter 14).

■ **Gene flow**

Exchange of genes between populations.

It would be a misconception to think that gene flow can occur only through such large-scale movements of whole groups. In fact, significant alterations in allele frequencies can come about through long-term patterns of mate selection whereby members of a group obtain mates from one or more other groups. If exchange of mates consistently moved in one direction over a long period of time, allele frequencies would ultimately be altered.

Transportation plays a crucial role in determining the potential radius for finding mates. Today, highly efficient mechanized forms of transportation make the potential radius of mate choice worldwide, but actual patterns are obviously somewhat more restricted. For example, data from Ann Arbor, Michigan, indicate a mean marital distance (the average distance between birthplaces of partners) of about 160 miles, which obviously includes a tremendous number of potential marriage partners.

Genetic Drift

Genetic drift

Evolutionary changes—that is, changes in allele frequencies—produced by random factors. Genetic drift is a result of small population size.

The random factor in evolution is called **genetic drift** and is due primarily to sampling phenomena (i.e., the size of the population). Since evolution occurs in populations, it is directly tied not only to the nature of the initial allele freqencies of the population, but to the size of the group as well. If, in a population of 100 individuals, five type O individuals had been killed in an auto accident before they reproduced, they would not have made a genetic contribution to the next generation. The frequency of the O allele would have been reduced in the next generation, and evolution would have occurred. In this case, with only 100 individuals in the population, the change due to the accident would have altered the O frequency in a noticeable way. If, however, our initial population had been very large (10,000 people), then the evolutionary effect of removing a few individuals would be very small indeed. In fact, in a population of large size, random effects, such as traffic accidents, would be balanced out by the likelihood of such events also affecting individuals with different genetic combinations (i.e., different genotypes). As you can see, evolutionary change due to genetic drift is directly and inversely related to population size. To put it simply, the smaller the population, the larger the effect of genetic drift.

When considering genetic drift, we must remember that the genetic makeup of individuals is in no way related to the chance happenings that affect their lives. In our example, the genetic makeup of individuals has absolutely nothing to do with their being involved in automobile accidents. The accidents are random events, which is why this factor is usually called *random genetic drift.* If, however, a person dies in an auto accident caused by hereditary poor eyesight, such an event would not be genetic drift. If this individual, because of a hereditary trait, dies early and produces fewer offspring than other individuals, this is an example of natural selection.

Founder effect

Also called the *Sewall Wright effect,* a type of genetic drift in which allele frequencies are altered in small populations that are taken from, or are remnants of, larger populations.

A particular kind of drift seen in modern human populations is called **founder effect**, or, after its formulator, the *Sewall Wright effect.* Founder effect operates when an exceedingly small group of individuals contributes exclusively to the gene pool of the next generation. This situation leads to what is termed a *genetic bottleneck,* since the "founding" group and its descendants carry only a small proportion of all the alleles (and of the variation) that were present in the original population. This phenomenon can occur when a small migrant band of "founders" colonizes a new and separate area away from the parent group. Small founding populations may also be left as remnants when famine, plague, or war

ravage a normally larger group. Actually, each generation is the founder of all succeeding generations in any population.

The cases of founder effect producing noticeable microevolutionary changes
are necessarily in small groups. For example, the Hopi Indians of Arizona have
unusually high frequencies of albinism, and an island in the South Atlantic,
Tristan da Cunha, has unusually high frequencies of a hereditary eye disorder.
First settled in 1817 by one Scottish family, this isolated island's native inhabitants include only descendants of this one family and a few other individuals,
such as shipwrecked sailors. All in all, only about two dozen individuals constituted the founding population of this island. In 1961, the 294 inhabitants were
evacuated because of an impending volcanic eruption and removed to England.
Extensive medical tests were performed, which revealed four individuals with the
very rare recessive disease retinitis pigmentosa. The frequency for the allele causing this disease was abnormally high in this population, and a considerable portion of the group were no doubt carriers.

How did this circumstance come about? Apparently, just by chance, one of
the initial founders was heterozygous for the gene and later passed it on to offspring who, through inbreeding, occasionally produced affected individuals.
The fact that so few people founded the Tristan da Cunha population made it
possible for one person (who carried the allele for this disease) to make a disproportionate genetic contribution to succeeding generations (Bodmer and Cavalli-
Sforza, 1976).

Genetic drift has probably played an important role in human evolution,
influencing genetic changes in small isolated groups. From studies of recent
hunter-gatherers in Australia, we know that the range of potential mates is limited to the linguistic tribe usually consisting of around 500 members. Given this
small population size, drift could act significantly, particularly if drought or disease should reduce the population even further.

Much insight concerning the evolutionary factors that have acted in the past
can be gained by understanding how such mechanisms continue to operate on
human populations today. In small populations like Tristan da Cunha, drift plays
a major evolutionary role. Fairly sudden fluctuations in allele frequency can and
do occur owing to the small population size. Likewise, throughout a good deal of
human evolution (at least the last 4–5 m.y.*), hominids probably lived in small
groups, and drift would have had significant impact.

Joseph Birdsell, a physical anthropologist who has worked extensively in
Australia, has postulated general models for human evolution from his Australian
data. He suggests that population size during most of the Pleistocene was comparable to the 500 figure seen in Australia. Moreover, when people adopted agriculture and became sedentary and isolated in small villages, the effects of drift may
have been even greater. Indications of such a phenomenon are still operative in
Melanesia, where individuals often spend their entire lives within just a few miles
of their birthplace.

While drift has been a factor producing evolutionary change in certain circumstances, the effects have been irregular and nondirectional (for drift is *random*
in nature). Certainly, the pace of evolutionary change could have been accelerated
if many small populations were isolated and thus subject to drift. By modifying
such populations, drift can provide significantly greater opportunities for the truly
directional force in evolution—natural selection.

---

*The abbreviation m.y. stands for "million years."

It is important to emphasize that natural selection need not be the inevitable and *only* prime mover of evolutionary change. As we have seen, both gene flow and genetic drift can produce some evolutionary changes by themselves. However, these changes are usually *microevolutionary* ones; that is, they produce changes within species over the short term. To yield the kind of evolutionary changes that ultimately result in entire new groups (e.g., the diversification of the first primates, the appearance of the hominids), natural selection most likely would play the major role. Remember, however, that natural selection does not and cannot operate independently of the other evolutionary factors—mutation, gene flow, and genetic drift. All four factors (sometimes called the "four forces of evolution") work interactively.

Additional insight concerning the relative influences of the different evolutionary factors has emerged in recent studies of the early dispersal of modern *Homo sapiens* (discussed in Chapter 13). New evidence suggests that in the last 100,000 to 200,000 years, our species experienced a genetic bottleneck, which considerably influenced the pattern of genetic variation seen in all human populations today. In this sense, modern humans can ben seen as the fairly recent product of a form of genetic drift (founder effect) acting on a somewhat grand scale. Such evolutionary changes could be potentially significant over tens of thousands of years and could cause substantial genetic shifts within species.

Recombination

Since in any sexually reproducing species both parents contribute genes to offspring, the genetic information is inevitably reshuffled every generation. Such recombination does not in itself change allele frequencies (i.e., cause evolution). However, it does produce the whole array of genetic combinations, which natural selection can then act upon. In fact, we have shown how the reshuffling of chromosomes during meiosis can produce literally trillions of gene combinations, making every human being genetically unique.

Natural Selection Acts on Variation

The evolutionary factors just discussed—mutation, gene flow, genetic drift, and recombination—interact to produce variation and to distribute genes within and between populations. But there is no long-term *direction* to any of these factors. How, then, do populations adapt? The answer is natural selection. Natural selection provides directional change in allele frequency relative to *specific environmental factors*. If the environment changes, then the selection pressures change as well. Such a functional shift in allele frequencies is what we mean by *adaptation*. If there are long-term environmental changes in a consistent direction, then allele frequencies should also shift gradually each generation. If sustained for many generations, the results may be quite dramatic.

In Chapter 2, we discussed the general principles underlying natural selection and gave two examples in nonhuman animals (peppered moths and swifts). Physical anthropology is, of course, centrally concerned with human evolution, and it is thus most relevant to show how natural selection operates in *human* populations. However, demonstrating clear-cut examples in our species is not an easy task. In fact, the best documented example of natural selection in humans

The importance of meiosis to random assortment and inheritance is discussed in Virtual Lab 2, section II, part E.

Virtual Lab 2, section I, part B, provides an example of how selection operates on variation within populations.

involves hemoglobin S, an altered form of hemoglobin that results from a point mutation in the gene that produces the hemoglobin beta chain (see p. 53). As you have already learned, if an individual inherits this allele (Hb^S) from both parents, he or she will suffer the severe manifestations of sickle-cell anemia. Even with aggressive medical treatment, life expectancy in the United States today is less than 45 years for patients with sickle-cell anemia. Worldwide, sickle-cell anemia causes an estimated 100,000 deaths each year, and in the United States, approximately 40,000 to 50,000 individuals, mostly of African descent, suffer from this disease.

Apparently Hb^S is a mutation that occurs occasionally in all human populations, but the allele usually remains relatively rare. In some populations, however, Hb^S is more common, and this is especially true in western and central Africa, where its frequency approaches 20 percent. The frequency of the allele is also moderately high in parts of Greece and

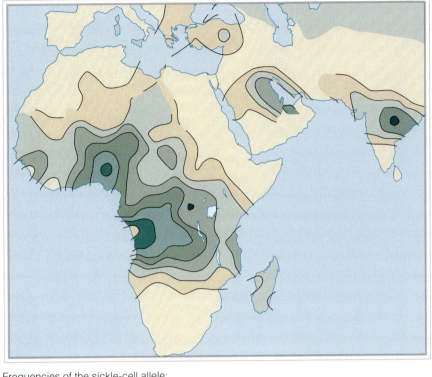

Frequencies of the sickle-cell allele:

Greater than .14	.08–.10	.02–.04
.12–.14	.06–.08	.00–.02
.10–.12	.04–.06	

FIGURE 4–11

A frequency map of the sickle-cell distribution in the Old World.

India (Fig. 4-11). Given the devastating effects of Hb^S in homozygotes, how do we explain its higher prevalence in some populations? The answer to this question lies in malaria, a serious infectious disease that has exerted enormous selective pressures in the past and continues to do so today. Malaria currently kills an estimated 1 to 3 million people worldwide annually. It is caused by one of several protozoan parasites belonging to the genus *Plasmodium*. These parasites are in turn transmitted to humans by mosquitoes.

Very briefly, after an infected mosquito bite, plasmodial parasites invade red blood cells, where they obtain the oxygen they need for reproduction. The consequences of this infection to the human host include fever, chills, headache, nausea, vomiting, and, frequently, death. In parts of western and central Africa, where malaria is always present, the burden of the disease is borne by children, with as many as 50 to 75 percent of 2- to 9-year-olds being afflicted.

The geographical correlation between malaria and the distribution of the sickle-cell allele is indirect evidence of a biological relationship (Fig. 4–12). Further confirmation was provided by British biologist A. C. Allison in the 1950s. Volunteers from the Luo tribe of East Africa with known hemoglobin phenotypes and genotypes were injected with the malarial parasite. It goes without saying that the ethics concerning human subjects would, and should, preclude such experimentation today. The results of this study showed that those subjects with one Hb^S allele (i.e., those with sickle-cell trait) and thus some

Virtual Lab 2, section III, part B presents the relationship between malaria and sickle-cell anemia in human populations.

FIGURE 4–12

Malaria distribution in the Old World.

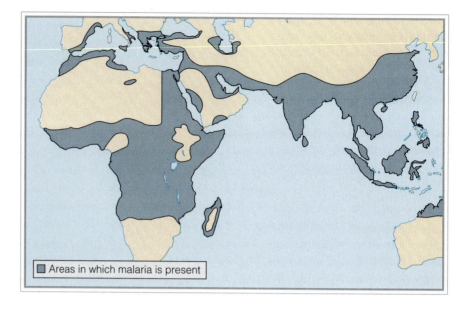

Areas in which malaria is present

hemoglobin S had greater resistance to malaria than the homozygous "normals." It was subsequently demonstrated that heterozygotes resist infection because their red blood cells provide a less conducive environment for the parasite to reproduce. Thus, in environments where the prevalence of malaria is always high, individuals with sickle-cell trait have higher reproductive success than those with normal hemoglobin. Those afflicted with sickle-cell anemia, of course, have the lowest reproductive success, since without treatment, most die before reaching adulthood.

The relationship between malaria and hemoglobin S provides the best example we have of natural selection in contemporary humans. In this case, natural selection has favored the heterozygous phenotype, thus increasing the frequency of Hb^S, an allele that in homozygotes causes severe disease and early death.

Review of Genetics and Evolutionary Factors

Starting in Chapter 3 with a discussion of the molecular and cellular bases of heredity, we proceeded in this chapter to show how such genetic information is passed from individuals in one generation to those in the next. In this chapter, we also have reviewed evolutionary theory and its current applications, emphasizing the crucial role of natural selection. These different levels—molecular, cellular, individual, and populational—are different aspects of evolution, and they are all related and highly integrated in a way that can eventually produce evolutionary change. A step-by-step example will make this clear.

We begin with a situation in which everyone in the population has the same hemoglobin type; therefore, initially no variation for this trait exists, and without some source of new variation, evolution is not possible. How does this gene change? We have seen that a substitution of a single base in the DNA sequence can alter the code significantly enough to alter the protein product and ultimately the whole phenotype of the individual. Consider that in each generation such an incident occurs in one or a few individuals. For a mutated allele to be passed on to succeeding offspring, the gametes must carry the alteration. Any new mutation, therefore, must be transmitted during sex cell formation.

Once the mutation has occurred in the DNA, it will be packaged into chromosomes, and these chromosomes in turn will assort during meiosis to be passed to offspring. The results of this process are seen by looking at phenotypes (traits) in individuals, and the mode of inheritance is described simply by Mendel's principle of segregation. In other words, if our initial individual has a mutation in only one paired allele on a set of homologous chromosomes, there will be a 50 percent chance of passing this chromosome (with the new mutation) to an offspring.

But what does all this activity have to do with *evolution*? To repeat an earlier definition, evolution is a change in allele frequency in a *population* from one generation to the next. The key point here is that we are now looking at a whole group of individuals, a population, and it is the population that will or will not change over time.

We know whether allele frequencies have changed in a population where sickle-cell hemoglobin is found by ascertaining the percentage of individuals with the sickling allele (Hb^S) versus those with the normal allele (Hb^A). If the relative proportions of these alleles alter with time, evolution has occurred. In addition to discovering that evolution has occurred, it is important to know why. Several possibilities arise. First, we know that the only way the new allele Hb^S could have arisen is by mutation, and we have shown how this process can happen in a single individual. This change, however, is not yet really an evolutionary one, for in a relatively large population, the alteration of one individual's genes will not significantly alter allele frequencies of the entire population. Somehow, this new allele must *spread* in the population.

One way this could happen is in a small population, where mutations in one or just a few individuals and their offspring may indeed alter the overall frequency quite quickly. This case would be representative of genetic drift. As discussed, drift acts in small populations where random factors may cause significant changes in allele frequency. With a small population size, there is not likely to be a balance of factors affecting individual survival or reproduction. Consequently, some alleles may be completely removed from the population, while others may become established as the only allele present at that particular locus (and are said to be "fixed" in the population).

In the course of human evolution, drift may have played a significant role at times, and it is important to remember that at this microevolutionary level, drift and/or gene flow can (and will) produce evolutionary change, even in the absence of natural selection. However, directional evolutionary trends could only have been sustained by *natural selection*. The way this has worked in the past and still operates today (as in sickle-cell) is through differential reproduction. That is, individuals who carry a particular allele or combination of alleles produce more offspring. By producing more offspring than other individuals with alternative alleles, such individuals cause the frequency of the new allele in the population to increase slowly from generation to generation. When this process is compounded over hundreds of generations for numerous loci, the result is significant evolutionary change. The levels of organization in the evolutionary process are summarized in Table 4–5.

TABLE 4–5   Levels of Organization in the Evolutionary Process

Evolutionary Factor	Level	Evolutionary Process	Technique of Study
Mutation	DNA	Storage of genetic information; ability to replicate; influences phenotype by production of proteins	Biochemistry, electron microscope, recombinant DNA
Mutation	Chromosomes	A vehicle for packaging and transmitting genetic material (DNA)	Light or electron microscope
Recombination (sex cells only)	Cell	The basic unit of life that contains the chromosomes and divides for growth and for production of sex cells	Light or electron microscope
Natural selection	Organism	The unit, composed of cells, that reproduces and which we observe for phenotypic traits	Visual study, biochemistry
Drift, gene flow	Population	A group of interbreeding organisms; changes in allele frequencies between generations; it is the population that evolves	Statistical study

Summary

We have seen how Gregor Mendel discovered the principles of segregation, independent assortment, and dominance and recessiveness by conducting experiments on garden peas. Although the field of genetics has progressed dramatically in the twentieth century, the concepts first put forth by Gregor Mendel remain the basis of our current knowledge on how traits are inherited.

Basic Mendelian principles are applied to the study of the various modes of inheritance we are familiar with today. We have presented three of these in some detail: autosomal dominants, autosomal recessives, and X-linked recessives. The most important factor in all the Mendelian modes of inheritance is the role of segregation of chromosomes, and the alleles they carry, during meiosis. Although our understanding of human inheritance has virtually exploded in the last 50 years, the very foundation of our knowledge rests in the basic rules as set forth by Gregor Mendel almost 150 years ago.

Building on fundamental nineteenth-century contributions by Charles Darwin and his contemporaries and the rediscovery in 1900 of Mendel's work, further refinements later in the twentieth century added to contemporary evolutionary thought. In particular, the combination of natural selection with Mendel's principles of inheritance and experimental evidence concerning the nature of mutation have all been synthesized into a modern understanding of evolutionary change, appropriately termed the *modern synthesis*. In this, the central contemporary theory of evolution, evolutionary change is seen as a two-stage process. The first stage is the production and redistribution of variation. The second stage is the process whereby natural selection acts on the accumulated genetic variation.

Crucial to all evolutionary change is mutation, the only source of completely new genetic variation. In addition, the factors of gene flow, genetic drift, and recombination function to redistribute variation within individuals (recombination), within populations (genetic drift), and between populations (gene flow).

Natural selection is the central determining factor influencing the long-term direction of evolutionary change. How natural selection works can best be explained as differential reproductive success—in other words, how successful individuals are in leaving offspring to succeeding generations. To more fully illustrate the mechanics of evolutionary change through natural selection, comprehensive and well-understood examples from other organisms are most helpful. The detailed history of the evolutionary spread of the sickle-cell allele provides the best-documented example of natural selection among recent human populations. It must be remembered that evolution is an integrated process, and this chapter concludes with a discussion of how the various evolutionary factors can be integrated into a single, comprehensive view of evolutionary change.

Questions for Review

1. What is Mendel's principle of segregation?
2. How does meiosis explain the principle of segregation?
3. What is Mendel's principle of independent assortment?
4. Explain dominance and recessiveness.
5. Define allele.
6. What is a phenotype, and what is its relationship to a genotype?
7. Why were all of Mendel's F_1 pea plants phenotypically the same?
8. Explain what is meant by a phenotypic ratio of 3:1 in the F_2 generation.
9. What is codominance? Give an example.
10. If two people who have blood type A (both with the *AO* genotype) have children, what proportion of their children would be expected to have the O blood type? Why?
11. Can the two parents in question 10 have a child with AB blood? Why or why not?
12. Explain why X-linked recessive traits are more common in males than in females.
13. In a cross between two carriers for a recessive trait, why would 3/4 of the offspring be expected *not* to show the recessive characteristic?
14. Explain how natural selection works. Illustrate through an example in humans.
15. What is polygenic inheritance? How does it differ from Mendelian inheritance?
16. What is pleiotropy? Give an example.
17. Explain why natural selection has acted to increase the frequency of Hb^S, the allele that causes sickle-cell anemia, in heterozygotes in some populations.
18. What is the modern synthesis? Explain how the major components of this theory explain evolutionary change.
19. What is genetic drift? Illustrate through an example for human populations.
20. Define gene flow. Give an example in human populations.
21. What role does variation play in the evolutionary process? Where does variation come from? (*Hint:* You may wish to discuss the source of variation as completely new to a species or as it is introduced into a population *within* a species.)
22. Discuss how evolutionary change occurs as an integrated process. Illustrate through an example.

Suggested Further Reading

Cummings, Michael R. 1997. *Human Heredity.* 4th ed. Belmont: West/Wadsworth.
Heim, Werner G. 1991. "What is a Recessive Allele?" *The American Biology Teacher* 53(2): 94–97.
Ridley, Mark. 1993. *Evolution.* Cambridge, MA: Blackwell Scientific.

Additional Resources

Multimedia Tools

- **Virtual Laboratories for Physical Anthropology CD-ROM**
  The following concepts in this chapter are covered on the physical anthropology CD-ROM:
  sexual reproduction, inheritance (Virtual Lab 2.II.E)
  artificial selection, domestication (Virtual Lab 2.I.B)
  Punnett square, dominant, recessive (Virtual Lab 2.II.E)
  human blood groups, discrete traits (Virtual Lab 2.II.E)
  skin color, polygenic traits (Virtual Lab 2.IV)
  mutation, gene flow, genetic drift, recombination (Virtual Lab 2.III.A)
  natural selection, variation (Virtual Lab 2.I.B)
  sickle-cell anemia, hemoglobin, malaria (Virtual Lab 2.III.B)

- **Wadsworth Anthropology Resource Center**
  http://anthropology.wadsworth.com
  Visit Anthropology Online to obtain current updates in the field, surfing tips, career information and more. In addition, enrich your study efforts with text-specific study aids arranged by chapter.

- **InfoTrac College Edition**
  http://www.infotrac-college.com/wadsworth

1. Use InfoTrac College Edition and search for *human genetics.* Is there any information in recent articles about dominant and recessive traits in humans? Read one of the articles and write half a page to a page summarizing the research in the article and indicating how this article relates to anthropological questions regarding human evolution and behavior.
2. The ABO blood system is one often cited example of Mendelian inheritance. In fact, our blood provides some of the best examples of Mendelian inheritance known. Of course, however, our blood types are not the only features that are passed on in a simple Mendelian fashion. Use the Internet to compile a list of other traits that are inherited in this fashion and to determine whether they are carried as dominant or recessive traits. We suggest you start this search at InfoTrac College Edition.
3. What do genes do? On InfoTrac College Edition, find and read "A Gene for Nothing" by Robert Sapolsky, *Discover,* Oct 1997, v18 n10

p40(6). After reading this article, write one page about how behaviors can be passed on genetically. How do genes and the environment work together to determine a behavioral phenotype?

4. On every can of diet soda there is a warning to phenylketonuriacs that the product contains phenalalynine. As you learned in this chapter, phenylketonuria (PKU) is an autosomal recessive condition. Go to InfoTrac College Edition to learn more about this disorder. Finally write a paragraph or more describing *why* the can of diet soda carries such a warning.

5. Mutations are the ultimate source of all genetic variation, but how often do they occur? Apparently, they occur in humans less often than in other animals. Read "When it comes to evolution, humans are in the slow class" by Ann Gibbons, *Science,* March 31, 1995, v267 n5206 p1907(2), on InfoTrac College Edition. What do these results imply for human evolution?

6. "Gene frequency clines produced by kin-structured founder effects" by Alan G. Fix, *Human Biology,* Oct 1997, v69 n5 p663(11) on InfoTrac College Edition examines the effects of the various forces of evolution on human populations in Europe. Read this article and then write a few paragraphs discussing how this article explains human variation in Europe.

7. This chapter illustrates how the sickle cell allele (Hb^S) exemplifies the role of natural selection in modern humans. Supplement the information regarding Hb^S in this chapter using InfoTrac College Edition. Did you find any information that was not covered in the chapter?

Internet Exercises

1. Our understanding of inheritance originated with the research of Gregor Mendel. Visit MendelWeb (**http://www-hpcc.astro. washington.edu/mirrors/MendelWeb/**) to learn more about Mendel, his research, and the implications of his research. Also on MendelWeb is the text of his original paper. Click on Mendel's paper. Read the first four sections. What are your overall impressions of Mendel's research? Was he thorough? What criteria did Mendel use when choosing which plants to work with? Do you think these criteria are valid today? Why? In the section entitled, "The Forms of the Hybrids," Mendel introduces and defines the terms *dominant* and *recessive*. Having read the cautionary statements regarding dominant and recessive alleles in the textbook, what do you think Mendel would say today?

2. While the terminology used at this site is very technical, online Mendelian Inheritance in Man (OMIM) is the most comprehensive Web site dealing with Mendelian and many non-Mendelian traits. To appreciate the complexity of such characteristics, go to **http://www.ncbi.nlm.nih.gov/OMIM**, click on "search the OMIM database," and enter the name of one of the conditions listed in Table 4.5 in the search field. (We suggest albinism.) Then click on #203100, the catalog number for albinism; then click on "description." Read this entry and make a list of three facts not included in the chapter. What kinds of information have you found that you think would be useful to your classmates?

3. Pedigrees and karyotypes are two tools often used in genetic research. This Genetic Analysis site (**http://hyperion.advanced.org/18258/ped-karyo.htm**) provides more explanation about how to use these tools. It also offers the Pedigree Quiz (**http://hyperion.advanced.org/18258/quiz/quiz3.htm**). Visit and take the quiz. How well can you read your pedigrees?

4. One well-known sex-linked trait is red-green color blindness. This is not the only form of color blindness that is inherited, however. Visit The Genetic Occurrence of Colour Vision Deficiencies (**http://www.biol.napier.ac.uk/BWS/courses/projects98/colourblindness/annie/pilotam/private/genetic.htm**) to learn more about this form of color blindness and the forms that are inherited in other ways. Compare the inheritance of the different forms of color blindness and make up a potential pedigree for each.

An Overview of the Living Primates

Introduction

Thus far, we have presented the basic biological background for understanding human evolution. The remainder of this textbook is devoted to the very formidable task of explaining what it is to be human.

Evolution has produced a continuum of life forms, as demonstrated genetically, anatomically, and behaviorally. To gain an understanding of any organism, it is necessary, whenever possible, to compare its anatomy and behavior with those of other closely related forms. This comparative approach helps elucidate the significance of physiological and behavioral systems as adaptive responses to various selective pressures throughout the course of evolution. This statement applies to *Homo sapiens* just as surely as to any other species, and if we are to identify the components that have shaped hominid evolution, the starting point must be a systematic comparison between humans and our closest living relatives, the approximately 190 species of nonhuman **primates** (prosimians, monkeys, and apes). This chapter describes the physical characteristics that define the order Primates, gives a brief overview of the major groups of living nonhuman primates, and introduces some methods of comparing living primates through genetic data. (For a detailed comparison of human and nonhuman skeletons, see Appendix A.) The following two chapters concentrate on various behavioral features that characterize nonhuman primates.

Before proceeding further, we once again must call attention to a few common misunderstandings about evolutionary processes. As we have previously emphasized, evolution is not a goal-directed process. The fact that **prosimians** evolved before **anthropoids** does not mean that prosimians "progressed" or "advanced," to become anthropoids. Extant primate species are in no way "superior" to their evolutionary predecessors or to one another. Consequently, in discussions of major groupings of contemporary nonhuman primates, there is no implied superiority or inferiority of any of these groups. Each grouping (lineage, or species) has come to possess unique qualities that make it better suited than others to a particular habitat and lifestyle. Given that all contemporary organisms are "successful" results of the evolutionary process, it is best to avoid altogether the use of such loaded terms as "superior" and "inferior."

Finally, you should not make the mistake of thinking that contemporary primates (including humans) necessarily represent the final stage or apex of a primate lineage. Remember, the only species that represent final evolutionary stages of particular lineages are those that become extinct.

Primates as Mammals

The order Primates is a subgroup of a larger group of organisms, the mammals (technically, the class **Mammalia**). There are today over 4,000 species of mammals, which can be further subdivided into three major subgroups: (1) the egg-laying mammals, (2) the pouched mammals (i.e., marsupials), and (3) the placental mammals. We will discuss mammalian evolution in more detail in Chapter 8. For the moment, you should recognize that primates are members of the placental subgroup, by far the most common of living mammals (and including other common orders such as rodents and carnivores). Placental mammals today are distributed over most of the world in a wide variety of forms, including flying, swimming, and burrowing varieties and a host of other adaptations as

---

■ Primates

Members of the mammalian order Primates (pronounced "pry-may´-tees"), which includes prosimians, monkeys, apes, and humans. When the term is used colloquially, it is pronounced "pry´-mates."

■ Prosimians

Members of a suborder of Primates, the *Prosimii* (pronounced "pro-sim´-ee-eye"). Traditionally, the suborder includes lemurs, lorises, and tarsiers.

■ Anthropoids

Members of the suborder of Primates, the *Anthropoidea* (pronounced "ann-throw-poid´-ee-uh"). Traditionally, the suborder includes monkeys, apes, and humans.

■ Mammalia

The technical term for the formal grouping (class) of mammals.

well. Sizes range from the tiny dwarf shrews (just a few grams) to the whales (over 100 tons), the largest animals ever to inhabit the earth.

All primates possess numerous characteristics they share in common with other placental mammals. Such traits include body hair; a relatively long gestation period followed by live birth; mammary glands (thus the term *mammal*); different types of teeth (incisors, canines, premolars, and molars); the ability to maintain a constant internal body temperature through physiological means (*homeothermy*); increased brain size; and a considerable capacity for learning and behavioral flexibility. Therefore, to differentiate primates, as a group, from other mammals, we must describe those characteristics that define the primate order.

The placement of the Order Primates within the class Mammalia is discussed in Virtual Lab 1, section II.

Characteristics of Primates

Identifying single traits that define the primate order is not a simple task, because among mammals, primates have remained quite *generalized*. That is, primates have retained many **primitive** mammalian traits that other mammalian species have lost over time. In response to particular selective pressures, many mammalian groups have become increasingly **specialized**. For example, through the course of evolution, horses and cattle have undergone a reduction of the number of digits (fingers and toes) from the ancestral pattern of five to one and two, respectively. Moreover, these species have developed hard, protective coverings over their feet in the form of hooves. While this type of limb structure is adaptive in prey species, whose survival depends on speed and stability, it restricts the animal to only one type of locomotion. Moreover, limb function is limited entirely to support and locomotion, while the ability to manipulate objects is completely lost.

Primates, precisely because they are *not* so specialized, cannot be simply defined by one or even two common traits. As a result, biologists (Napier and Napier, 1967; Clark, 1971) have pointed to a group of **evolutionary trends** that, to a greater or lesser degree, characterize the entire order. Keep in mind that these are a set of *general* tendencies and are not all equally expressed in all primates. Indeed, this is the situation we would expect in a group of related but diverse animals. Moreover, while some of the trends are unique features found in primates, many others are retained primitive mammalian characteristics. These latter are useful in contrasting the generalized primates with the more specialized varieties of other placental mammals.

Thus, the following list is intended to give an overall structural and behavioral picture of that kind of animal we call "primate," focusing on those characteristics that tend to set primates apart from other mammals. Using certain retained (ancestral) mammalian traits along with more specific ones to accomplish this task has been the traditional approach of **primatologists**. Some contemporary primatologists (Fleagle, 1988) feel that it is highly useful to enumerate all these features to better illustrate primate adaptations. Thus, a common evolutionary history with adaptations to similar environmental challenges is seen to be reflected in the limbs and locomotion, teeth and diet, senses, brain, and behaviors of those animals that make up the primate order.

A. *Limbs and locomotion*
    1. *A tendency toward erect posture (especially in the upper body).* Shown to some degree in all primates, this tendency is variously associated with sitting, leaping, standing, and, occasionally, bipedal walking.

Virtual Lab 1, section II, part A, presents a discussion of the characteristics that are typically used to define primates, while section IV, part A, provides a contrast of mammalian life history variables.

▪ Primitive
Referring to a trait or combination of traits present in an ancestral form.

▪ Specialized
Evolved for a particular function; usually refers to a specific trait (e.g., incisor teeth), but may also refer to the whole way of life of an organism.

▪ Evolutionary trends
Overall characteristics of an evolving lineage, such as the primates. Such trends are useful in helping categorize the lineage as compared to other lineages (i.e., other placental mammals).

▪ Primatologists
Scientists who study the evolution, anatomy, and behavior of nonhuman primates. Those who study primate behavior in noncaptive animals are usually trained as anthropologists.

Detailed discussions of primate locomotion are provided in Virtual Labs 3 and 4.

■ Morphology

The form (shape, size) of anatomical structures; can also refer to the entire organism.

■ Prehensility

Grasping, as by the hands and feet of primates.

FIGURE 5–1

Primate (macaque) hand.

Virtual Lab 5 provides in-depth discussions of primate diets and dental adaptations.

■ Diurnal

Active during the day.

■ Nocturnal

Active during the night.

■ Stereoscopic vision

The condition whereby visual images are, to varying degrees, superimposed on one another. This provides for depth perception, or the perception of the external environment in three dimensions. Stereoscopic vision is partly a function of structures in the brain.

■ Binocular vision

Vision characterized by overlapping visual fields provided by forward-facing eyes; essential to depth perception.

2. *A flexible, generalized limb structure, permitting most primates to engage in a number of locomotor behaviors.* Primates have retained some bones (e.g., the clavicle, or collarbone) and certain abilities, (e.g., rotation of the forearm) that have been lost in some more specialized mammals. Various aspects of hip and shoulder **morphology** also provide primates with a wide range of limb movement and function. Thus, by maintaining a generalized locomotor anatomy, primates are not restricted to one form of movement, as are many other mammals. Primate limbs are also used for activities other than locomotion.

3. *Hands and feet with a high degree of **prehensility** (grasping ability).* All primates use the hands, and frequently the feet, to grasp and manipulate objects (Fig. 5–1). This capability is variably expressed and is enhanced by a number of characteristics, including:

   a. *Retention of five digits on hands and feet.* This varies somewhat throughout the order, with some species showing marked reduction of the thumb or of the second digit.

   b. *An opposable thumb and, in most species, a divergent and partially opposable big toe.* Most primates are capable of moving the thumb so that it comes in contact (in some fashion) with the second digit or the palm of the hand.

   c. *Nails instead of claws.* This characteristic is seen in all primates except some New World monkeys. All prosimians also possess a claw on one digit.

   d. *Tactile pads enriched with sensory nerve fibers at the ends of digits.* This characteristic serves to enhance the sense of touch.

B. *Diet and teeth*

   1. *Lack of dietary specialization.* This is typical of most primates, who tend to eat a wide assortment of food items.

   2. *A generalized dentition.* The teeth are not specialized for processing only one type of food, a pattern correlated with the lack of dietary specialization.

C. *The senses and the brain*

   All primates (**diurnal** ones in particular) rely heavily on the visual sense and less so on the sense of smell, especially compared to many other mammals. This emphasis is reflected in evolutionary changes in the skull, eyes, and brain.

   1. *Color vision.* This is characteristic of all diurnal primates. **Nocturnal** primates lack color vision.

   2. *Depth perception.* **Stereoscopic vision**, or the ability to perceive objects in three dimensions, is made possible through a variety of mechanisms, including:

   a. *Eyes positioned toward the front of the face (not to the sides).* This configuration provides for overlapping visual fields, or **binocular vision** (Fig. 5–2).

   b. *Visual information from each eye transmitted to visual centers in both hemispheres of the brain.* In nonprimate mammals, most optic nerve fibers cross to the opposite hemisphere through a structure at the base of the brain. In primates, about 40 percent of the fibers remain on the same side (see Fig. 5–2).

   c. *Visual information organized into three-dimensional images by specialized structures in the brain itself.* The capacity for stereoscopic vision is dependent on each hemisphere of the brain having received visual information from both eyes and from overlapping visual fields.

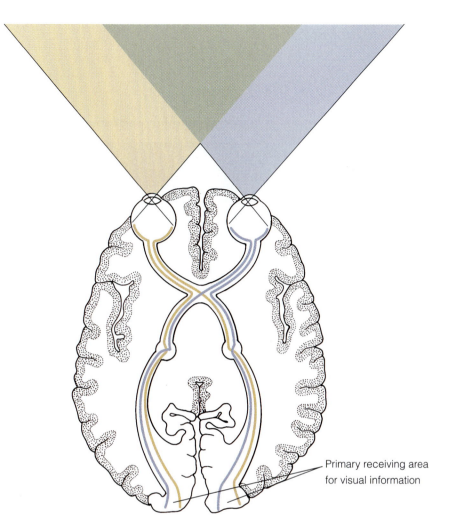

Primary receiving area
for visual information

FIGURE 5–2

Simplified diagram showing overlapping visual fields (binocular vision) in primates (and some predators) with eyes positioned at the front of the face. (The green shaded area represents the area of overlap.) Stereoscopic vision (three-dimensional vision) is provided in part by binocular vision and in part by the transmission of visual stimuli from each eye to both hemispheres of the brain. (In non-primate mammals, all visual information crosses over to the hemisphere opposite the eye in which it was initially received.)

3. *Decreased reliance on the sense of smell (olfaction).* This trend is seen in an overall reduction in the size of olfactory structures in the brain. Corresponding reduction of the entire olfactory apparatus has also resulted in decreased size of the snout. (In some species, such as baboons, the large muzzle is not related to olfaction, but to the presence of large teeth, especially the canines; see Box 5–1).

4. *Expansion and increased complexity of the brain.* This is a general trend among placental mammals, but it is especially true of primates. In primates, this expansion is most evident in the visual and association areas (portions of the brain where information from different sensory modalities is integrated) of the neocortex. Expansion in regions involved with the hand (both sensory and motor) is seen in many species, particularly humans.

D. *Maturation, learning, and behavior*

1. *A more efficient means of fetal nourishment, longer periods of gestation, reduced numbers of offspring (with single births the norm), delayed maturation, and extension of the entire life span.*

2. *A greater dependence on flexible, learned behavior.* This trend is correlated with delayed maturation and consequently longer periods of dependency

BOX 5–1

Primate Cranial Anatomy

Several significant anatomical features of the primate cranium help us distinguish primates from other mammals. The mammalian trend toward increased brain development has been further emphasized in primates, as shown by a relatively enlarged braincase. In addition, the primate emphasis on vision is reflected in generally large eye sockets; and the decreased dependence on olfaction is indicated by reduction of the snout and corresponding flattening of the face (Fig. 1).

Here are some of the specific anatomical details seen in modern and most fossil primate crania:

1. The primate face is shortened, and the size of the braincase, relative to that of the face, is enlarged compared to other mammals (Fig. 1).
2. Eye sockets are enclosed at the sides by a ring of bone called the *postorbital bar* (Fig. 1). In most other mammals, there is no postorbital bar. In addition, in anthropoids and tarsiers, there is a plate of bone at the back of the eye orbit called the *postorbital plate.* The postorbital plate is not present in prosimians. The functional significance of these structures has not been thoroughly explained, but it may be related to stresses on the eye orbits imposed by chewing (Fleagle, 1988).
3. The region of the skull that contains the structures of the middle ear is completely encircled by a bony structure called the *auditory bulla.* In primates, the floor of the auditory bulla is derived from a segment of the temporal bone (Fig. 2). Of the skeletal structures, most primate paleontologists consider the postorbital bar and the derivation of the auditory bulla to be the two best diagnostic traits of the primate order.

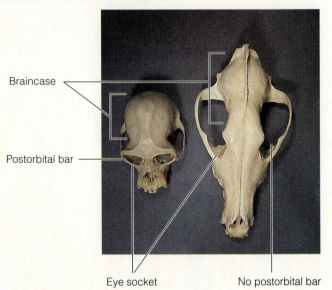

Braincase

Postorbital bar

Eye socket   No postorbital bar

FIGURE 1

The skull of a gibbon (left) compared to that of a red wolf (right). Note that the absolute size of the braincase in the gibbon is slightly larger than that of the wolf, even though the wolf (at about 60 to 80 pounds) is four times the size of the gibbon (about 15 pounds).

4. The base of the skull in primates is somewhat flexed, so that the muzzle (mouth and nose) is positioned lower relative to the braincase (Fig. 3). This arrangement provides for the exertion of greater force during chewing, particularly as needed for the crushing and grinding of tough vegetable fibers, seeds, and hard-shelled fruits.

on the parent. As a result of both these trends, parental investment in each offspring is increased, so that although fewer offspring are born, they receive more intense and efficient rearing.

3. *The tendency to live in social groups and the permanent association of adult males with the group.* Except for some nocturnal forms, primates tend to associate with others, at least with offspring. The permanent association of adult males with the group is uncommon in mammals but widespread in primates.
4. *The tendency to diurnal activity patterns.* This is seen in most primates; only one monkey species and some prosimians are nocturnal.

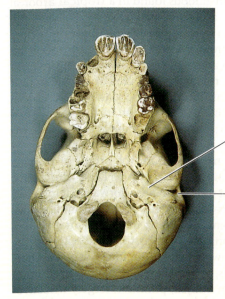

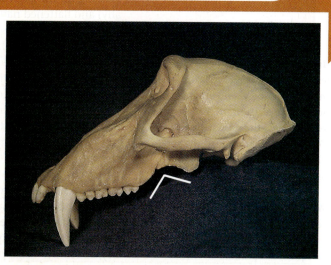

Portion of temporal
bone enclosing
auditory bulla

External opening to
ear (external audi-
tory meatus)

(a)

FIGURE 2

*The base of an adolescent chimpanzee skull. Note that in an adult ani-
mal, the bones of the skull would be fused together and would not
appear as separate elements as shown here.*

FIGURE 3

*The skull of a male baboon (a) compared to that of a red wolf (b). The
angle at the base of the baboon skull is due to flexion. The corresponding
area of the wolf skull is flat. Note the forward-facing position of the eye
orbits above the snout in the baboon. Also, be aware that in the baboon,
the enlarged muzzle does not reflect a heavy reliance on the sense of
smell. Rather, it serves to support very large canine teeth, the roots of
which curve back through the bone for as much as 1½ inches.*

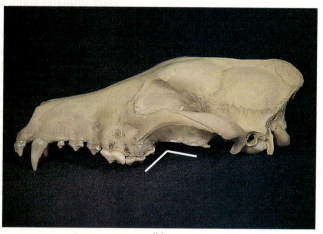

(b)

The Arboreal Adaptation

The single most important factor influencing the evolutionary divergence of primates was the adaptation to **arboreal** living. While other mammals were adapting to grasslands or to subterranean or even marine environments, primates
found their **adaptive niche** in the trees. Indeed, some other mammals also were
adapting to arboreal living, but this environment—with its myriad challenges
and opportunities—was the one in which our ancestors established themselves as
a unique kind of animal.

▮ **Arboreal**
Tree-living; adapted to life in the trees.

▮ **Adaptive niche**
The entire way of life of an organism:
where it lives, what it eats, how it gets
food, etc.

FIGURE 5–26

White-handed gibbon.

specialized locomotor adaptations may be related to feeding behavior while hanging beneath branches. The diet of these species is largely composed of fruit. Both (especially the siamang) also eat a variety of leaves, flowers, and insects.

The basic social unit of gibbons and siamangs is the monogamous pair with dependent offspring. As in marmosets and tamarins, male gibbons and siamangs are very much involved in rearing their young. Both males and females are highly territorial and protect their territories with elaborate whoops and sirenlike "songs."

Orangutans   Orangutans (*Pongo pygmaeus*) (Fig. 5–27) are represented by two subspecies found today only in heavily forested areas on the Indonesian islands of Borneo and Sumatra (see Fig. 5–25). Due to poaching by humans and continuing habitat loss on both islands, orangutans face imminent extinction in the wild.

Orangutans are slow, cautious climbers whose locomotor behavior can best be described as "four-handed," referring to the tendency to use all four limbs for grasping and support. Although they are almost completely arboreal, orangutans do sometimes travel quadrupedally on the ground. Orangutans are very large animals with pronounced sexual dimorphism (males may weigh 200 pounds or more and females less than 100 pounds).

FIGURE 5–27

Female orangutan.

In the wild, orangutans lead largely solitary lives, although adult females are usually accompanied by one or two dependent offspring. They are primarily **frugivorous**, but bark, leaves, insects, and meat (on rare occasions) may also be eaten.

Gorillas   The largest of all living primates, gorillas (*Gorilla gorilla*) are today confined to forested areas of western and eastern equatorial Africa (Fig. 5–28). There are three generally recognized subspecies, although molecular data suggest that the western lowland gorilla is perhaps sufficiently genetically distinct to warrant designation as a separate species (Ruvolo et al., 1994; Garner and Ryder, 1996). The western lowland gorilla is found in several countries of western central Africa and is the most numerous of the three subspecies, with a population size of perhaps 110,000 (Doran and McNeilage, 1998). The eastern lowland gorilla is found near the eastern border of the Democratic Republic of the Congo (formerly Zaire) and numbers about 12,000. Mountain gorillas (Fig. 5–29), the most extensively studied of the three, are found in the mountainous areas of central Africa in Rwanda, Democratic Republic of the Congo, and Uganda. Mountain gorillas have probably never been very numerous, and today they are among the more endangered primates, numbering only about 600.

Gorillas exhibit marked sexual dimorphism, with males weighing up to 400 pounds and females around 150 to 200 pounds. Because of their weight, adult gorillas, especially males, are primarily terrestrial and adopt a semiquadrupedal (knuckle-walking) posture on the ground (see Fig. 5-29).

Gorillas live in groups consisting of one (or sometimes two) large *silverback* males, a few adult females, and their subadult offspring. The term *silverback* refers to the saddle of white hair across the back of full adult (at least 12 or 13 years of age) male gorillas. Additionally, the silverback male may tolerate the presence of one or more young adult *blackback* males, probably his sons. Typically, but not always, both females and males leave their natal group as young adults. Females join other groups, and males, who appear to be less likely to emigrate, may live alone for a while, or they may join an all-male group before eventually forming their own group.

Gorillas are almost exclusively vegetarian. Mountain gorillas concentrate primarily on leaves, pith, and stalks. These foods are also important for lowland

❚ Frugivorous
(fru-give´-or-us)
Having a diet composed primarily of fruit.

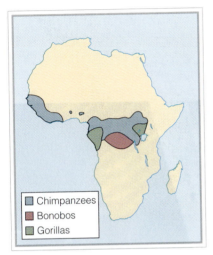

FIGURE 5–28
Geographical distribution of modern African apes.

FIGURE 5–29
Mountain gorillas. (a) Male. (b) Female.

(a)

(b)

slip away unnoticed. Tragically, this will occur, in most cases, before we have even had the opportunity to get to know them.

Each species on earth is the current result of a unique set of evolutionary events that, over millions of years, has produced a finely adapted component of a diverse ecosystem. When it becomes extinct, that adaptation and that part of biodiversity is lost forever. What a tragedy it will be if, through our own mismanagement and greed, we awaken to a world without chimpanzees, mountain gorillas, or the tiny, exquisite lion tamarin. If and when this day comes, we truly will have lost a part of ourselves, and we will be the poorer for it.

Summary

In this chapter, we have introduced you to the primates, the mammalian order that includes prosimians, monkeys, apes, and humans. As a group, the primates are generalized in terms of diet and locomotor patterns, and these behavioral generalizations are reflected in the morphology of the teeth and limbs.

We have also discussed some of the anatomical similarities and differences between the major groupings of primates: prosimians, monkeys (New and Old World), and hominoids. In the next two chapters, we will turn our attention to primate social behavior and cognitive abilities. These are extremely important topics, for it is through better understanding of nonhuman primate behavior that we can make more accurate statements regarding the evolution of human behavior. Moreover, increasing our knowledge is essential if we are to prevent many of these uniquely adapted and marvelous relatives of ours from being lost forever.

Questions for Review

1. Discuss why primates are said to be "generalized mammals."
2. Summarize the major evolutionary trends that characterize the primate order.
3. How does adaptation to an arboreal environment help explain primate evolution?
4. What is the geographical distribution of the nonhuman primates?
5. What are the two major subdivisions of the order Primates?
6. Which major groups of primates are included within the anthropoids?
7. What is a dental formula? What is the dental formula of all the Old World anthropoids?
8. What are quadrupedalism, vertical clinging and leaping, and brachiation? Name at least one primate species that is characterized by each of these.
9. What are the major differences between prosimians and anthropoids?
10. What are at least three anatomical differences between monkeys and apes?
11. Name the two major categories (subfamilies) of Old World monkeys. In general, what is the geographical distribution of each?
12. Explain how a taxonomic classification scheme reflects biological relationships. Discuss the taxonomic questions related to tarsiers.
13. Where are lemurs and lorises found today?

14. In which taxonomic family are the great apes placed?
15. Define estrus.
16. Describe the type of social organization seen in chimpanzees (*Pan troglodytes*) and gorillas.
17. In what ways are humans anatomically like other primates? What are some ways in which humans are different from other primates?

Suggested Further Reading

Fleagle, John. 1998. *Primate Adaptation and Evolution* New York: Academic Press.

Jolly, Alison. 1985. *The Evolution of Primate Behavior*. 2nd ed. New York: Macmillan.

Napier, J. R., and P. H. Napier. 1985. *The Natural History of the Primates*. Cambridge, MA: MIT Press.

Mittermeier, Russell A., Ian Tattersall, William R. Konstant, David M. Meyers, and Roderick B. Mast. 1994. *Lemurs of Madagascar*. Washington, DC: Conservation International.

Wright, Patricia C. 1992. "Primate Ecology, Rainforest Conservation, and Economic Development: Building a National Park in Madagascar." *Evolutionary Anthropology* 1(1): 25–32.

Additional Resources

Multimedia Tools

- **Virtual Laboratories for Physical Anthropology CD-ROM**
  The following concepts in this chapter are covered on the physical anthropology CD-ROM:
  Primates, Mammalia (Virtual Lab 1.II)
  primates, characteristics, life history variables (Virtual Lab 1.II.A; IV.A)
  locomotion (Virtual Labs 3 and 4)
  diet, teeth (Virtual Lab 5)
  habitats, distribution (Virtual Lab 1.III.A, B)
  teeth, dental formula (Virtual Lab 5.II.A)
  anatomical terms, intermembral index (Virtual Labs 3; 4.I and II)
  quadrupedalism, brachiation, bipedalism (Virtual Lab 4.I.D)
  primate taxonomy, classification (Virtual Lab 1.II.D)
  hominoid, human, ape, classification (Virtual Lab 1.II.D)
  anthropoid, monkey, human, ape (Virtual Lab 1.II.D)
  brachiation, spider monkey (Virtual Lab 4.I.D)
  sexual dimorphism (Virtual Lab 1.IV.B)
  New World Monkeys, Old World Monkeys (Virtual Lab 7.III.C)
  Pronunciations (Virtual Lab 1.II, glossary)
  geographical range (Virtual Lab 1.III.A)

■ **Wadsworth Anthropology Resource Center**
http://anthropology.wadsworth.com
Visit Anthropology Online to obtain current updates in the field, surfing tips, career information and more. In addition, enrich your study efforts with text-specific study aids arranged by chapter.

■ **InfoTrac College Edition**
http://www.infotrac-college.com/wadsworth

1. Primatologists study a wide range of different topics. Go to InfoTrac College Edition and search for the key word *primate*. Make a list of the different topics the articles discuss. What sort of training would you need to be a primatologist?

2. Choose one form of primate and search InfoTrac College Edition for any information you can find on this primate. Write a short paper about this primate, its biology, ecology, and behavior.

3. Apes are humans' closest relatives, but not everyone is comfortable with this relationship. Read "Brothers under the hair: the uneasy kinship between human and ape" by Stephen Jay Gould, *The Sciences,* Jan–Feb 1996, v36 n1 p32(2). How do you feel about having apes as distant relatives? What do you think of Gould's argument?

4. Human and chimpanzee DNA is at least 98% identical. For a comparison, go to InfoTrac College Edition and read "Which of our genes make us human" by Ann Gibbons, *Science,* Sept 4, 1998, v281 n5382 p1432. What are some differences between chimpanzee and human DNA?

5. Primate populations around the world are declining in numbers. Go to InfoTrac College Edition and read "The global decline of primates" by John Tuxill, *World Watch,* Sept–Oct 1997, v10 n5 p16. What can we do to lessen or stop this decline?

■ **Internet Exercises**

1. Visit The Primate Gallery (**http://www.selu.com/~bio/PrimateGallery/main.html**) and go to the section on the *primate of the week*. After reading this description, and looking at the pictures, make a list of the primate characteristics and adaptations this primate displays. Are there any typical primate features that it does not display? Next, identify this primate's place in the taxonomic classification of primates. To which suborder, infraorder, superfamily, and family does this primate belong?

2. Once you have read about this primate at the Primate Gallery, what else can you find out about this animal on the Internet? Go to one of the search engines and search for this primate. Can you gain more information about this animal's habitat, diet, ecological niche, life history, or behavior on the Internet?

3. Many primate species are endangered and, therefore, conservation is a major topic. To learn more about conservation visit Primate Infonet (**www.primate.wisc.edu/pin**). Follow the link to Information Resources, to Conservation, and then choose one of the conservation

links. Read the link and write a short summary. What animal, together with its habitat, is discussed at the link? What can we do, or what can you do, to improve the chances for this species?

4. How many primate species are endangered? Visit the World Conservation Monitoring Centre (**http://www.wcmc.org.uk/data/ database/rl_anml_combo.html**) and search their threatened animals list. Make lists of the primate species that are threatened, and the degree to which they are threatened. About what is the percentage of all primate species that are endangered?

Can the Mountain Gorilla Be Saved?

The threatened habitat of the mountain gorilla is today largely restricted to a series of mostly extinct volcanoes known as the Virungas. These tropical, densely forested mountains, some of which soar to over 14,000 feet, straddle the shared borders of Rwanda, the Democratic Republic of the Congo (formerly Zaire), and Uganda in central Africa (Fig. 1).

Probably never as numerous as the two subspecies of lowland gorilla, the mountain gorilla currently numbers only about 620 in the wild, and there are no captive mountain gorillas. The single most serious threat to their continued existence is habitat loss resulting from forest clearing by a rapidly expanding human population. Illegal hunting of other species, which indirectly affects gorillas, also continues to be a factor; however, until 1994, protection was afforded by governmental jurisdiction of the national park that was established to protect gorillas.

The mountain gorilla was first recognized and described as a distinct subspecies in 1902, but no behavioral studies were conducted until George Shaller's pioneering work in the Democratic Republic of the Congo in 1959–1960. Following in Schaller's footsteps, Dian Fossey in 1967 established Karisoke, a research station located in the forest between Mt. Karisimbi and Mt. Visoke. In time, she was to become world-famous, not only for her field studies, detailed in her popular book, *Gorillas in the Mist,* but also for her efforts to eliminate poaching and restrict human access to park areas. Indeed, her dedication to preserving the mountain gorilla led to much conflict and probably contributed to her still unsolved murder on December 26, 1985.

Rwanda, a small country of approximately 10,000 square miles (a bit smaller than the state of Maryland), has faced the same problems seen in most of the world's developing nations (unchecked population growth, poverty, and lack of access to goods and services, to name a few). With a population density of over 700 people per square mile, Rwanda is the most densely inhabited country in Africa. In the spring of 1994, Rwanda's population numbered almost 8 million and was increasing at an annual rate of 3.4 percent. On average, a Rwandan woman gives birth to 8.6 children, and efforts to control population increase have not met with success. To make matters even worse, between October 1990 and the summer of 1994, Rwanda suffered from a devastating civil war that largely destroyed tourism. This conflict between the majority tribal group, the Hutu, and the minority Tutsi culminated in the slaughter of between 500,000 and 1 million Tutsi and Tutsi sympathizers. Moreover, as many as 1 million Rwandans, fled the country for refugee camps in neighboring countries.

Prior to the war, the Rwandan countryside was one of the most intensively cultivated regions in the world; indeed, terraced fields and grazing lands extended right up to national park boundaries (Fig. 2).

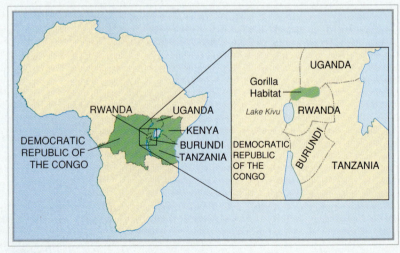

FIGURE 1

Map of central Africa showing Rwanda, Democratic Republic of the Congo, and Uganda with location of mountain gorilla habitat.

FIGURE 2

Cultivated fields and grazing land encroach upon national park boundaries. Forested slopes are part of the Parc National des Volcans.

Furthermore, poachers constituted an extremely serious threat to wildlife, a threat that has dramatically increased (Fig. 3). The target species of poachers' snares are primarily small antelopes, but more than a few gorillas have also been caught. All too often, this results in the loss of a limb, if not death from infection.

As catastrophic as continued forest clearing, cattle grazing, and poaching are for wildlife in Rwanda, it is important to remember the very real problems faced by an increasingly hard-pressed human population. In 1991, before the most devastating effects of the war had come about, Rwanda's annual gross national product was a mere $310 per capita, compared to $21,000 in the United States. Only 48 percent of Rwandans living in rural areas had access to safe drinking water, and just 55 percent had sanitation facilities.

These few statistics represent the desperate conditions faced by real people. Translated to the local level, where people are attempting simply to "get by," the needs of gorillas are of little practical concern.

The war ended in a Tutsi victory, and the new government pledged to continue to protect the park and the gorillas. But, given the magnitude of human suffering and the necessity of restoring the government and the country's infrastructure, these goals

have not been reached. Researchers did return to Karisoke; they rebuilt their facilities there, and they and the Rwandan staff were able to reestablish contact with the gorilla study groups. Tourism even resumed for a while. But sadly, ex-members of the former Hutu army have formed militia groups and they continue to terrorize the inhabitants of the region. Even a few Rwandan gorilla trackers, some of whom had worked at Karisoke since Dian Fossey established her project, have been murdered. Research at Karisoke was again suspended in 1997, but fortunately Rwandan trackers resumed monitoring the gorilla groups in September, 1998.

Because currently there is no official protection of the forest, refugees and local inhabitants have continued to cut down literally millions of trees. Moreover, cattle grazing and hunting and trapping have resumed. Although it is not possible to know how all the gorilla groups have fared, it has been ascertained that those under study have managed to thrive. Indeed several infants have been born! Tragically, a few have been killed and there have been sightings of gorillas with snares wrapped around their limbs.

In early 1999, the world was again tragically reminded of the tensions that continue to exist in Central Africa when eight British and American tourists, on their way to see mountain gorillas, were murdered in Uganda by Hutu militia members. The stated purpose of this appallingly brutal act was to punish

Can the Mountain Gorilla Be Saved? (continued)

FIGURE 3

Tour guides dismantle a poacher's snare.

Britain and the United States for their support for the Tutsi-led Rwandan government. But, another outcome is that it raised fears for the safety of tourists hoping to see mountain gorillas in any of the countries in which they reside.

It is important to note that before the war, tourism was the third largest source of foreign revenue for Rwanda, and most of Rwanda's allure for foreign tourists was embodied in the mountain gorillas. It goes without saying that if tourism ceases, the economic importance of the mountain gorillas will also disappear.

If mountain gorillas are to be saved, it must be done by means that also help the Rwandan people. The salvation of the gorillas, if indeed it occurs, is likely to be won through their exploitation as economic assets to those countries fortunate enough to have them as residents. We can only hope that the humans who share their world with these extraordinary animals find their association mutually beneficial. Otherwise, it is all too likely that in the not too distant future, the mists that shroud the Virunga volcanoes will conceal neither the breathtakingly beautiful forests nor the magnificent mountain gorilla.

Critical Thinking Questions

1. Do you think it important to protect an endangered species such as the mountain gorilla? Why or why not? At what point would you consider it no longer important?

2. How does one weigh the needs of seriously endangered species, such as the mountain gorilla, against the needs of people? Your answer can refer to situations other than those in Rwanda, but various aspects of the Rwandan situation (e.g., overpopulation, war, and the Rwandan attempt to protect gorillas as tourist attractions) should influence your answer.

3. What do you think will be the situation in Rwanda in 30 years? In 75 years? Why?

Sources

Fossey, Dian. 1983. *Gorillas in the Mist.* Boston: Houghton Mifflin.

Schaller, George B. 1963. *The Mountain Gorilla.* Chicago: University of Chicago Press.

Vedder, Amy. 1989. "In the Hall of the Mountain Gorilla." *Animal Kingdom* 92(3):30-43.

World Resources Institute. 1992. *The 1992 Information Please Environmental Almanac.* Boston: Houghton Mifflin.

Special appreciation goes to Dieter Steklis, Executive Director, and to Path McGrath, President Emeritus, The Dian Fossey Gorilla Fund, for providing valuable historical details and up-to-date information for this Issue.

Fundamentals of Primate Behavior

Introduction

In the preceding chapter, you were introduced to the primate order. In that chapter, we discussed primate anatomical characteristics and primate taxonomy, and we provided a brief overview of the major primate groups to acquaint you with those species most closely related to ourselves.

In this chapter, discussion shifts to various aspects of nonhuman primate behavior. These are extremely important topics for anthropologists because one method of gaining a fuller understanding of human and early hominid behavior is to become more familiar with the behavior and intellectual capacities of nonhuman primates. As a group, primates exhibit a wide array of behavioral responses to environmental challenges. Because these responses have been shaped, in part, by natural selection, understanding them can help elucidate general principles that pertain to the interactions between behavior and ecology. This approach can ultimately help us understand the behavioral and environmental components that may have shaped the evolution of our own lineage (a topic we will address more fully in Chapter 7).

In addition to studying nonhuman primates to learn more about ourselves, it is just as important to learn more about them in their own right. Only within the past four decades have they been systematically studied, and we still have much to learn. Indeed, many species, especially arboreal monkeys, have scarcely been studied at all. The beginning of the twenty-first century is an especially critical time for much of life on our planet. If we hope to save even some of the many threatened and endangered species from extinction, we must understand their needs (space, diet, group organization, etc.) in the wild. Without this knowledge, we can neither preserve sufficient natural habitat for their survival in the wild nor re-create it in captivity.

Primate behavior is discussed in Virtual Lab 6.

Primate Field Studies

Virtual Lab 6, section I, presents a discussion of field methods and the scientific method.

While other disciplines, such as psychology and zoology, have long been concerned with nonhuman primates, the study of these animals in their *natural habitats* has primarily become a focus of anthropology. Early work—that done before World War II—was especially stimulated through the influence of the American psychologist Robert Yerkes, who in the late 1920s and 1930s sent students out to the field to study gorillas, chimpanzees, and howler monkeys. It was the last of these studies by Clarence Ray Carpenter (along with his work on gibbons) that stands out particularly as a hallmark of early primate field investigations. Other such studies followed. Japanese scientists began their pioneering work with Japanese macaques in 1948 (Sugiyama, 1965). In 1960, Jane Goodall began her now-famous field study of chimpanzees at Gombe National Park, Tanzania. This project continues today and, along with several others, has provided us with a wealth of information regarding the natural behavior of these remarkable animals. By the early 1960s, field research was in full swing, and since that time, researchers have studied savanna baboons (DeVore and Washburn, 1963; Altmann and Altmann, 1970; Smuts, 1985; Strum 1987), langurs (Dolhinow, 1977; Hrdy, 1977), vervets (Cheney and Seyfarth, 1990), orangutans (Rodman, 1973; Horr, 1975; Galdikas, 1979, 1981, 1985), mountain gorillas (Schaller, 1963; Goodall, 1977; Fossey, 1983), chimpanzees (Nishida, 1968, 1979; Wrangham, 1977, 1986; Goodall, 1986, 1990; McGrew, 1992), and bonobos (Kano, 1980, 1992; Susman, 1984).

The key aspect of these field studies is that researchers attempt to collect information on **free-ranging** animals. Free-ranging animals are not necessarily uninfluenced by human activities. With the exception of populations in a recently explored forest in the Democratic Republic of the Congo, it is highly unlikely that there is a single group of nonhuman primates in the world that has not experienced some human interference. Nevertheless, if we are to understand the adaptations and behavior of nonhuman primates, it is necessary to study them in their natural habitats, where human disturbance is reduced and where they feed, travel, mate, and so forth, with minimal human constraints.

Because of the problems inherent to the study of arboreal primates that move swiftly through dense vegetation (Fig 6–1), the most systematic information thus far collected on free-ranging animals comes from species that spend considerable time on the ground (including langurs, gorillas, and chimpanzees) and most especially those species that travel and feed frequently in open country (e.g., macaques, baboons, vervets, and patas monkeys). Fortunately, more data are now being collected on many arboreal species, including colobus, some guenons, howlers, and capuchins.

Another approach taken by some anthropologists involves studying primates in large provisioned colonies, where at least some movement, group dynamics, and so on, are possible. Probably the best example of this type of research is the long-term study of rhesus macaques (Fig 6–2) conducted on Cayo Santiago Island off the coast of Puerto Rico. First established in 1938, the island population now totals close to 1,000 individuals (Richard, 1985).

Despite significant gaps in our knowledge about many aspects of primate behavior, we presently have field data on more than 100 nonhuman primate species. The information from this fascinating and rapidly advancing discipline of primatology forms the remainder of this chapter.

Primate Socioecology

As is true of all animals, primates spend their lives solving the very basic problems of finding food, avoiding predators, finding mates, and (especially for females) rearing offspring. Just as anatomical features have evolved in response to selective pressures imposed by the environment, behaviors have also evolved to meet these demands. Thus, behaviors can be seen as adaptive responses that provide the most fundamental necessities of life, and their evolution has been the result of the complex interactions of numerous factors.

FIGURE 6–1

Black-and-white colobus monkeys high up in the forest canopy. Can you spot the animals? Imagine trying to recognize them as individuals!

Free-ranging

Pertaining to noncaptive animals living in their natural habitat, largely free from constraints imposed by humans.

FIGURE 6–2

Rhesus macaques, part of the large colony on Cayo Santiago Island.

■ **Ecological**
Pertaining to the relationship between organisms and all aspects of their environment.

■ **Socioecology**
The study of animals and their habitats; specifically, attempts to find patterns of relationship between the environment and social behavior.

■ **Social structure**
The composition, size, and sex ratio of a group of animals. Social structures, in part, are the result of natural selection in specific habitats, and they function to guide individual interactions and social relationships.

These ecological factors are discussed in Lab 5, section I.

Scientists who study behavior in free-ranging primates do so within an **ecological** framework, focusing on the relationship between aspects of social behavior and the natural environment, an approach called **socioecology**. One underlying assumption of this approach is that the various components of ecological systems have evolved together. Therefore, to understand the functioning of one particular component, such as the **social structure** of a given species, it is necessary to determine its relationships with numerous environmental factors, including:

1. Diet: quantity and quality of different kinds of foods (caloric value, digestive energy required, net value to the animal)
2. Distribution of food resources (dense, scattered, clumps, or seasonal availability)
3. Body size
4. Distribution of water
5. Distribution and types of predators
6. Distribution of sleeping sites
7. Activity patterns (nocturnal, diurnal)
8. Relationships with other (nonpredator) species, both primate and nonprimate
9. Impact of human activities (a more recent phenomenon)

Primatologists view ecology, behavior, and biology as complexly interdependent (McKenna, 1982a, 1982b). They must consider an animal's relative brain size, metabolism, and reproductive physiology in addition to such ecological factors as the distribution of food resources and the nutritional value of foods and how they are selected and processed. (See Fleagle, 1999, for a good discussion of these factors.) Moreover, the variability exhibited between closely related species (and even *within* the same species) in ecological adaptations must be understood. Also, the way primates relate to surrounding biological communities, especially to other species of primates, must be described. Indeed, it is a common phenomenon for many prosimian and monkey species to travel and interact with other primate species. (It is important to determine if they eat different foods or how efficiently they divide their habitat.) Lastly, it is of interest to study why primates select certain foods and avoid others. (What is the nutritional value of insects, fruits, leaves, nuts, gums, small mammals, etc., that are available to them? What toxins exist in certain plant foods that could cause harm?)

Unfortunately, the relationships among ecological variables, social organization, and behavior have not yet been thoroughly worked out; but numerous factors certainly suggest a relationship between, for example, group size and problems of obtaining food and avoiding predators. Indeed, average group size and group composition can be viewed as adaptive responses to these problems (Pulliam and Caraco, 1984).

For example, groups composed of several adult males and females (multimale and multifemale groups) have traditionally been viewed as advantageous in areas where predation pressure is high, particularly in mixed woodlands and on open savannas where there are a number of large predators (e.g., hyenas, leopards, and lions). Where members of prey species occur in larger groups, there is increased likelihood of early predator detection and thus predator avoidance. Moreover, large-bodied males in such groups are capable of joining forces to chase and even attack predators.

These principles are supported by a recent report that groups of red colobus monkeys and Diana monkeys (a guenon species) form interspecific aggregations in response to predation by chimpanzees in the Tai National Park in the Ivory Coast (see Chapter 7). Normally, these two species do not form close associations with each other. However, when chimpanzee predation increases, new groupings develop and preexisting ones remain intact for longer than normal durations. This reaction was also seen to occur when human observers played recordings of chimpanzee vocalizations (Noe and Bshary, 1997).

Savanna baboons have long been used as an example of these principles. They are found in semiarid grassland and broken woodland habitats throughout sub-Saharan Africa. To avoid nocturnal predators, savanna baboons sleep in trees; however, they spend much of the day on the ground foraging for food. In the presence of nonhuman predators, baboons flee to the safety of trees. (Frequently, they abandon trees at the approach of humans, for they have learned that humans shoot them from the ground.) However, if they are at some distance from safety, or if a predator is nearby, adult males may join forces to chase an intruder away. The effectiveness of male baboons in this regard should not be underestimated, for baboons have been known to kill domestic dogs and even to attack leopards and lions (Altmann and Altmann, 1970).

But as you have already learned, not all primates are found in large groups. Solitary foraging is seen in both small- and (one) large-bodied species, and it is probably related to diet and distribution of resources. In the case of the small, slow-moving, insectivorous loris, for example, solitary feeding reduces competition, which allows for less distance traveled (and thus less expenditure of energy) in the search for prey. Moreover, because insects usually do not appear in dense patches but are scattered, they are more efficiently exploited by widely dispersed individuals rather than by groups. Solitary foraging may also be related to predator avoidance in species that rely chiefly on concealment for protection, rather than on escape. Again, the loris serves as a good example.

Foraging alone or with offspring is also seen in females of some diurnal anthropoid species (e.g., orangutans, chimpanzees). These females, being relatively large-bodied, have little to fear from predators, and by feeding alone or with only one or two youngsters, they maximize their access to food, free from competition with others. In the case of the orangutan, this may be particularly important, as the female is effectively removing herself from competition with males who may be twice her size.

The various solutions that primate species have developed to deal with the problems of survival differ in complicated ways. Closely related species living in proximity to one another and exploiting many of the same resources can have very different types of social structure. It is only through continued research that primatologists will be able to sort out the intricate relationships between society and the natural environment.

Virtual Lab 6 provides an in-depth investigation of the behaviors of savanna baboons.

Five Monkey Species in the Kibale Forest, Uganda

One of the most detailed and controlled studies of primate socioecology was undertaken in the Kibale Forest (Fig. 6–3) of western Uganda (Struhsaker and Leyland, 1979). The five species thus far studied in detail are all varieties of Old World monkeys and include black-and-white colobus (*Colobus guereza*), red colobus (*Colobus badius*), mangabey (*Cercocebus albigena*), blue monkey (*Cercopithecus mitus*), and the redtail monkey (*Cercopithecus ascanius*). In addition to these five, there are also in the Kibale Forest two other monkey species as well as pottos, two species of galago, and chimpanzees (for a discussion of the latter, see Ghiglieri, 1984). Altogether there are 11 different nonhuman primate species at Kibale, and they display the

FIGURE 6–3

Kibale Forest habitat, Uganda.

■ Sympatric

Living in the same area; pertaining to two or more species whose habitats partly or largely overlap.

greatest number of individuals and highest primate biomass for any site yet described (Waser, 1987). In the study under discussion (Struhsaker and Leyland, 1979), comparisons are facilitated because all species were sampled using similar methodologies. This avoids the pitfall of making comparisons between highly variable research strategies, a problem usually unavoidable in making cross-species comparisons. Moreover, the research at Kibale is important because this region is probably the least disturbed habitat where primates have been studied long-term.

Although these species are **sympatric**, they differ with regard to anatomy, behavior, and dietary preference. Body weights vary considerably (3 to 4 kg for redtails and up to 7 to 10 kg for the mangabey and colobus species). Diet also differs, with the two colobus species primarily eating leaves (i.e., they are folivorous) and the other three species showing more concentration on fruits supplemented by insects.

Several aspects of social organization also vary among the five species. For example, the red colobus and mangabey have several adult males in the group, while only one fully adult male is typically present in the other species. Furthermore, all five species occasionally have solitary males moving independently of the bisexual groups, but bachelor groups do not typically form. Even among the mostly multimale bisexual species, there is a marked difference. In mangabeys, females constitute the permanent core of the group, with males transferring out. In red colobus, it is the females who transfer (with the males remaining the long-term residents) (Struhsaker and Leyland, 1987). Indeed, there is so much variability that Struhsaker and Leyland could find little correlation between social organization and feeding ecology.

More detailed analysis of feeding patterns showed even further differences. For instance, while both colobus species eat mostly leaves, they nevertheless exploit different resources. Black-and-white colobus eat mature leaf blades, some high in protein. Red colobus, on the other hand, eat a wider variety of leaves, but usually not mature ones, as well as fruits and shoots. Perhaps correlated with these dietary differences are the observations that black-and-white colobus spend less time feeding but more time resting; in contrast, red colobus range further and live in higher density (i.e., higher biomass). In addition, some species show dramatic variability from month to month. Among redtail monkeys, the proportion of fruit in the monthly diet varies from as low as 13 percent to as much as 81 percent (Richard, 1985).

Ecological patterns and social ramifications are unquestionably complicated. In the same forest at Kibale, the closely related colobus species show marked differences in social organization. (Black-and-white colobus are found in one-male groups, red colobus in multimale-multifemale groups; see Box 6–1.) Yet in another area (the Tana River Forest of Kenya), red colobus live in one-male groups (like black-and-white colobus at Kibale), and *both* males and females transfer

BOX 6–1

Types of Nonhuman Primate Social Groups*

1. *One male.* A single adult male, several adult females, and their offspring. This is the most common primate mating structure, in which only one male actively breeds (Jolly, 1985). Usually formed by a male joining a kin group of females. Females usually form the permanent nucleus of the group. Examples: guenons, gorillas, some pottos, some spider monkeys, patas.
2. *Multimale-multifemale.* Several adult males, several adult females, and their young. Several of the males reproduce. The presence of several males in the group may lead to tension and to a dominance hierarchy. Examples: some lemurs, macaques, mangabeys, savanna baboons, vervets, squirrel monkeys, some spider monkeys, chimpanzees.
3. *Monogamous pair.* A mated pair and its young. Usually arboreal, minimal sexual dimorphism, frequently territorial. Adults usually do not tolerate other adults of the same sex. Not found among great apes, and least common of the breeding structures among nonhuman primates. Examples: gibbons, indris, titis, sakis, owl monkeys, pottos.
4. *Polyandry.* One female and two males. Seen only in some New World monkeys (marmosets and tamarins).
5. *Solitary.* Individual forages for food alone. Seen in some nocturnal prosimians (aye-ayes, lorises, galagos). In some species, adult females may forage in pairs or may be accompanied by offspring. Also seen in orangutans.

Sources
Jolly, 1985; Napier and Napier, 1985.

---

*These are called breeding groups by Jolly and permanent groupings by Napier and Napier. There are also other groupings, such as foraging groups, hunting groups, all female or male groups, and so on. Like humans, nonhuman primates do not always maintain one kind of group; single male groups may sometimes form multimale groups and vice versa. Hamadryas baboons, for example, are described as living in one-male groups but "form herds of 100 or more at night when they move towards the safety of the steep cliffs where they sleep" (Napier and Napier, 1985, p. 61). Also, variability is seen in other forms, for example, red colobus monkeys.

(unlike either colobus species at Kibale)(Richard, 1985). The distinct impression one gathers from attempts to find correlations is that many primate species are exceedingly flexible regarding group composition, a fact that makes generalizing an extremely tentative undertaking at best.

Still, the highly controlled nature of the Kibale study makes some comparisons and provisional generalizations possible:

1. The omnivores (mangabeys, redtails, blues) move about more than the folivores (the two colobus species).
2. Among the omnivores there is an inverse relationship between body size and group size (i.e., the smaller the body size, the larger the group tends to be); also among the omnivores, there is a direct relationship between body size and **home range.**
3. Omnivores are spatially more dispersed than folivores.
4. Female sexual swelling (see p. 162) is obvious only in those species (red colobus and mangabeys) that live in multimale groups.
5. Feeding, spacing, group residency, dispersal, and reproductive strategies may be very different for males and females of the same species. These considerations have become a central focus of ecological and evolutionary research (see p. 148).

▮ **Home range**
The area exploited by an animal or social group; usually given for one year—or for the entire lifetime—of an animal.

Dohlinow, 1978). Sussman and colleagues (1995), as well as others, have questioned the actual prevalence of the practice, arguing that it is not particularly common. These authors have also postulated that if indeed male fitness is increased through the practice, such increases are negligible. Others (Struhsaker and Leyland, 1987; Hrdy, 1995) maintain that the incidence and patterning of infanticide by males are not only significant, but consistent with the assumptions established by sociobiological theory.

Evolutionary interpretations have also been applied to other types of reproductive strategies seen in primates. As you will see in our discussion of the limitations of evolutionary ecology below, there are controversies surrounding the issue, and they are not easy to resolve.

Evolutionary Ecology: Current Constraints

Evolutionary interpretations have had a dramatic impact on the direction of behavioral studies of nonhuman animals, including primates. But, even though most primatologists use theoretical models derived from evolutionary ecology today, the approach has not gone completely uncriticized. For example, Richard and Schulman (1982, pp. 243–244) listed the following limitations.

1. The lack of long-term data on the demography and social behavior of large groups of individually known animals
2. The lack of long-term, precise data on the distribution of resources in time and space
3. The nearly complete absence of information on genetic relatedness through the male line
4. The difficulty in assigning reproductive and other costs and benefits to particular behaviors
5. Our almost total ignorance of the genetics of primate social behavior

Some critics (e.g., Gould and Lewontin, 1978) have long questioned the ways in which the influences of natural selection on behavior have been interpreted. Is natural selection indeed a self-perfecting process? Of course, no one can say for certain, since we see only a small slice of possible evolutionary strategies among living animals; but evidence does suggest that natural selection often works simply "to get by." In this way, a host of marginal traits and behaviors could endure for substantial periods of time. The lemurs of Madagascar are a case in point. Just a few hundred years ago, the island was inhabited by a much greater array of lemur species, but human intervention caused rapid extinction of many forms. Consequently, the survivors (like the indri) have probably moved into a variety of habitats from which competitors had once excluded them. Without such competition, they now make do, but probably could not be described as particularly well adapted:

> The lemurs alive today inhabit forests from which many species, some of them probably competitors, have vanished. It is not difficult to imagine that the surviving lemurs have expanded their life-style to include foods and perhaps whole habitats from which they were once excluded by competitors. It does not matter that they do not make very good use of these new resources, so long as they do not have to compete with more efficient animals. In short, there is no reason to suppose that the distribution, feeding habits, and social organization of lemurs

today are the results of a long, slow evolutionary process, each species finely tuned to make the best of its environment. More likely, what we see are animals getting by and making ecological experiments after two thousand years of rapid evolutionary change. (Richard, 1985, pp. 356–358)

Of course, this is not an evolutionary situation that has had much time to reach a balance. But when we look at any modern primate population, can we be sure that it is not changing (perhaps rapidly)? Is it showing particularly functional adaptations, and if so, to which circumstances? Is the population in balance? Has it ever been in balance? Beyond these theoretical difficulties, evolutionary ecology must address the type of information needed to test hypotheses, and one obstacle to this goal is the lack of long-term data.

Indeed, among wild primates, the longest-term studies concern Old World monkeys (baboons at Amboseli or Gilgil in Kenya) or chimpanzees in Tanzania (Gombe and Mahale), but still encompass barely two complete generations. Data from captive or heavily provisioned populations (e.g., Japanese macaques) are more complete, but are difficult to interpret, given the potentially large disruption of behavior these animals have experienced.

In spite of these obstacles, the approaches of evolutionary ecology offer the best opportunity to understand how animal behavior has been shaped by natural selection. Thus, primatologists worldwide are now employing this perspective to interpret primate (including human) behavior.

Primate Social Groups

As you have seen, many different patterns of social groupings exist among the primates. Most typically, primate social groups include members of all ages and of both sexes, a composition that does not vary significantly during the annual cycle. This situation differs from that of most mammals, among whom adult males and females associate only during the breeding season and the young of either sex do not usually remain with the adults after reaching puberty.

Since many mammalian species do not live in permanent social groups, one might ask why most primates do. In addition to helping avoid predation, group living permits more effective defense of resources from other animals, especially members of the same species. Groups of related females may tolerate the presence of one or more males because of the role males frequently play in defending against predators or protecting food resources from other animals. And males tolerate females because of the reproductive opportunities they offer.

But there are disadvantages to group living. For one thing, permanent association with other animals increases the likelihood of intragroup competition for resources, and consequently, there are more opportunities for violence. Therefore, for the predation hypothesis to be correct, the risks of predation must outweigh the costs of intragroup competition and aggression.

We have already mentioned that the makeup of social groups is influenced by several factors, such as diet, body size, activity patterns (diurnal/nocturnal), availability of resources, and mating patterns. In addition to these, one other important consideration is dispersal. As is true of most mammals (and indeed, most vertebrates), members of one sex leave the group in which they were born (their natal group) about the time they reach puberty. There is considerable variability within and between species regarding which sex leaves, but male dispersal is the most common pattern in primates (e.g., ring-tailed lemurs, vervets, and macaques, to name a few). Female dispersal is seen in some colobus species, hamadryas baboons, chimpanzees, and mountain gorillas.

Dispersal may have more than one outcome. Typically, when females leave, they join another group. Males may do likewise, but in some species they may remain solitary for a time, or they may temporarily join an all-male "bachelor" group until they are able to establish a group of their own. But one common theme that emerges is that those individuals who disperse usually find mates outside their natal group. This commonality has led primatologists to conclude that the most valid explanations for dispersal are probably related to two major factors: reduced competition for mates (particularly between males) and, perhaps even more important, decreased likelihood of close inbreeding.

Members of the **philopatric** sex enjoy certain advantages. Individuals (of either sex) who remain in their natal group are able to establish long-term bonds with relatives and other animals, with whom they cooperate to protect resources or enhance their position within the social structure. This is well illustrated by chimpanzee males who permanently reside in their natal groups (see further discussion in Chapter 7).

Because some individuals remain together over a long period of time, members of a primate group get to know each other well. They learn—as they must—how to respond to a variety of actions that may be threatening, friendly, or neutral. In such social groups, individuals must be able to evaluate a situation before acting. Evolutionarily speaking, this would have placed selective pressure on social intelligence, which in turn would select for brains that could assess such situations and store the information. One of the results of such selection would be the evolution of proportionately larger and more complex brains, especially among the higher primates (i.e., anthropoids).

■ **Philopatric**
Remaining in one's natal group or home range as an adult. In most species, members of one sex disperse from their natal group as young adults, and members of the philopatric sex remain. In the majority of nonhuman primate species, the philopatric sex is female.

The concept of an ethogram, or a catalog of behaviors, is discussed in Virtual Lab 6, section II. Various behaviors of savanna baboons are presented in section III.

Primate Social Behavior

Because primates solve their major adaptive problems in a social context, we might expect them to participate in a number of activities to reinforce the integrity of the group. The better known of these activities are described in the sections that follow.

Dominance

Most primate societies are organized into **dominance hierarchies.** Dominance hierarchies impose a certain degree of order within groups by establishing parameters of individual behavior. Although aggression is frequently a means of increasing one's status, dominance usually serves to reduce the amount of actual physical violence. Not only are lower-ranking animals unlikely to attack or even threaten a higher-ranking one, but dominant animals are also frequently able to exert control simply by making a threatening gesture.

Individual rank or status may be measured by access to resources, including food items and mating partners. Dominant individuals are given priority by others, and they usually do not give way in confrontations.

Many (but not all) primatologists postulate that the primary benefit of dominance is the increased reproductive success of the individual. This observation would be true if it could be demonstrated that dominant males compete more successfully for mates than do subordinate males. However, there is also good evi-

■ **Dominance hierarchies**
Systems of social organization wherein individuals within a group are ranked relative to one another. Higher-ranking individuals have greater access to preferred food items and mating partners than lower-ranking individuals. Dominance hierarchies are sometimes referred to as "pecking orders."

dence that lower-ranking males of some species successfully mate; they just do so surreptitiously. Likewise, increased reproductive success can be postulated for high-ranking females, who have greater access to food than subordinate females. High-ranking females are provided with more energy for offspring production and care (Fedigan, 1983), and presumably their reproductive success is greater.

An individual's rank is not permanent and changes throughout life. It is influenced by many factors, including sex, age, level of aggression, amount of time spent in the group, intelligence, perhaps motivation, and sometimes the mother's social position (particularly true of macaques).

In species organized into groups containing a number of females associated with one or several adult males, the males are generally dominant to females. Within such groups, males and females have separate hierarchies, although very high ranking females can dominate the lowest-ranking males (particularly young males). There are exceptions to this pattern of male dominance. Among many lemur species, females are the dominant sex. Moreover, among species that form monogamous pairs (e.g., indris, gibbons), males and females are codominant.

All primates *learn* their position in the hierarchy. From birth, an infant is carried by its mother, and it observes how she responds to every member of the group. Just as important, it sees how others react to her. Dominance and subordination are indicated by gestures and behaviors, some of which are universal throughout the primate order (including humans), and this gestural repertoire is part of every youngster's learning experience.

Young primates also acquire social rank through play with age peers. As they spend more time with play groups, their social interactions widen. Competition and rough-and-tumble play allow them to learn the strengths and weaknesses of peers, and they carry this knowledge with them throughout their lives. Thus, through early contact with the mother and subsequent exposure to peers, young primates learn to negotiate their way through the complex web of social interactions that make up their daily lives.

Communication

Communication is universal among animals and includes scents and unintentional, **autonomic** responses and behaviors that convey meaning. Such attributes as body posture convey information about an animal's emotional state. For example, a crouched position indicates a certain degree of insecurity or fear, while a purposeful striding gait implies confidence. Moreover, autonomic responses to threatening or novel stimuli, such as raised body hair (most species) or enhanced body odor (gorillas), indicate excitement.

Many intentional behaviors also serve as communication. In primates, these include a wide variety of gestures, facial expressions, and vocalizations, some of which we humans share. Among many primates, a mild threat is indicated by an intense stare, and indeed, we humans find prolonged eye contact with strangers very uncomfortable. For this reason, people should avoid eye contact with captive primates. Other threat gestures are a quick yawn to expose canine teeth (baboons, macaques) (Fig. 6–5); bobbing back and forth in a crouched position (patas monkeys); and branch shaking (many monkey species). High-ranking baboons *mount* the hindquarters of subordinates to express dominance (Fig. 6–6). Mounting may also serve to defuse potentially tense situations by indicating something like, "It's okay, I accept your apology, I know you didn't intend to offend me."

Virtual Lab 6, section IV, includes an exercise that utilizes video clips of a savanna baboon mother and infant.

Communication
Any act that conveys information, in the form of a message, to another individual. Frequently, the result of communication is a change in the behavior of the recipient. Communication may not be deliberate but may be the result of involuntary processes or a secondary consequence of an intentional action.

Autonomic
Pertaining to physiological responses not under voluntary control. An example in chimpanzees would be the erection of body hair during excitement. An example in humans is blushing. Both convey information regarding emotional states, but neither is a deliberate behavior, and communication is not intended.

FIGURE 6–5

Adolescent male savanna baboon threatens photographer with a characteristic "yawn" that shows the canine teeth. Note also that the eyes are closed briefly to expose light, cream-colored eyelids. This has been termed the "eyelid flash."

FIGURE 6–6

One young male savanna baboon mounts another as an expression of dominance.

■ **Displays**

Sequences of repetitious behaviors that serve to communicate emotional states. Nonhuman primate displays are most frequently associated with reproductive or agonistic behavior.

FIGURE 6–7

Chimpanzee facial expressions. (Adapted with permission of the publishers from *The Chimpanzees of Gombe* by Jane Goodall, Cambridge, Mass.: Harvard University Press, © 1986 by the President and Fellows of Harvard College.)

There is also a variety of behaviors to indicate submission, reassurance, or amicable intentions. Submission is indicated by the crouched position (most primates) or presenting the hindquarters (baboons). Reassurance takes the form of touching, patting, and, in chimpanzees, hugging and holding hands. Grooming also serves in a number of situations to indicate submission or reassurance.

A wide variety of facial expressions indicating emotional states is seen in chimpanzees and bonobos (Fig. 6–7). These include the well-known play face (also seen in several other species), associated with play behavior, and the fear grin (seen in *all* primates) to indicate fear and submission.

Primates also use a wide array of vocalizations for communication. Some, such as the bark of a baboon that has just spotted a leopard, are unintentional startled reactions. Others, such as the chimpanzee food grunt, are heard only in specific contexts. Nevertheless, both serve the same function: They inform others, although not necessarily deliberately, of the possible presence of predators or food.

Primates (and other animals) also communicate through **displays**, which are more complicated, frequently elaborate combinations of behaviors. For example,

Relaxed

Relaxed with dropped lip

Horizontal pout face
(distress)

Fear grin
(fear/excitement)

Full play face

the exaggerated courtship dances of many male birds, often enhanced by colorful plumage, are displays. Common gorilla displays are chest slapping and the tearing of vegetation to indicate threat. Likewise, an angry chimpanzee, with hair bristling, may charge an opponent, while screaming, waving its arms, and tearing vegetation.

By describing a few communicative behaviors shared by many primates (including humans), we do not intend to convey that these gestures are dictated solely by genetic factors. Indeed, if primates are not reared within a relatively normal social context, such behaviors may not be performed appropriately, because the contextual manifestations of communicatory actions are *learned*. But the underlying *predisposition* to learn and use them and the motor patterns involved in their execution are genetically influenced, and these factors do have adaptive significance. Therefore, theories about how such expressive devices evolved focus on motor patterns and the original context in which they occurred.

Over time, certain behaviors and motor patterns that originated in specific contexts have assumed increasing importance as communicatory signals. For example, crouching initially aided in avoiding physical attack. In addition, this behavior conveyed that the individual was fearful, submissive, and nonaggressive. Thus, crouching became valuable not only for its primary function, but for its role in communication as well, and natural selection increasingly favored it for this secondary role. In such a manner, over time, the expressions of specific behaviors may thus become elaborated or exaggerated because of their value in enhancing communication. Moreover, many complex displays incorporate various combinations of **ritualized behaviors.**

Mounting, as seen in baboons, is a good example of a ritualized behavior. Higher-ranking individuals mount the hindquarters of more subordinate animals in the manner of copulation, not to mate, but to express dominance. (It should be noted that when mounting serves a communicatory function, mounters and mountees may be members of the same sex.) In most anthropoid species characterized by one-male or multimale groups, males (the mounters in the mating context) are socially dominant to females. Thus, in the context of communication, the mounter assumes the male reproductive role. Likewise, presentation of the hindquarters in solicitation of mounting indicates submission or subordination by the mountee. As communication, these behavior patterns are entirely removed from their original (reproductive) context, and they function instead to reinforce and clarify the respective social roles of individuals in specific interactions.

All nonhuman animals employ various vocalizations, body postures, and, to some degree, facial expressions that transmit information. However, the array of communicative devices is much richer among nonhuman primates, even though they do not use language in the manner of humans. Communication is important, for it truly is what makes social living possible. Through submissive gestures, aggression is reduced and physical violence is less likely. Likewise, friendly intentions and relationships are reinforced through physical contact and grooming. Indeed, it is in the familiar methods of nonverbal communication that we humans can see ourselves in other primate species most clearly.

Aggressive and Affiliative Interactions

Within primate societies, there is an interplay between **affiliative** behaviors that promote group cohesion and aggressive behaviors that can lead to group disruption. Conflict within a group frequently develops out of competition for resources, including mating partners and food items. Instead of actual attacks or

Ritualized behaviors
Behaviors removed from their original context and sometimes exaggerated to convey information.

Affiliative
Pertaining to amicable associations between individuals. Affiliative behaviors, such as grooming, reinforce social bonds and promote group cohesion.

Many affiliative behaviors can be seen in the video clips included in Virtual Lab 6, section IV.

fighting, most intragroup aggression occurs in the form of various signals and displays, frequently within the context of a dominance hierarchy. Likewise, the majority of such situations are resolved through various submissive and appeasement behaviors.

But, conflict is not always resolved peacefully, and it can have serious consequences. For example, high ranking female macaques frequently intimidate, harass, and even attack lower ranking females, particularly to restrict their access to food. High ranking females consistently chase subordinates away from food and have even been observed to take food from their mouths; these behaviors can result in weight loss and poorer nutrition in low ranking females. Even more important, these females exhibit lower reproductive success because they are less able to successfully rear offspring to maturity, in part because of their inability to obtain desired food items (Dittus, 1979).

Competition between males for mates frequently results in injury and, occasionally, in death. In species that have a distinct breeding season (e.g., squirrel monkeys) conflict between males is most common during that time. Male squirrel monkeys form coalitions in order to compete with other males and, when outright fighting occurs, injuries can be severe. In species not restricted to a mating season, competition between males can be an ongoing process. As you have seen, one-male social groups are common in primates, and a male who gains control over a group of females must constantly protect his own interests against the interests of other males attempting to overthrow him. While a majority of conflicts do not result in death, it does occur. In one very well-known example, Dian Fossey once found the skull of an adult male mountain gorilla in which was embedded a canine tooth of another male gorilla!

Even though conflict can be destructive, a certain amount of aggression is useful in maintaining order within groups and protecting either individual or group resources. Fortunately, to minimize actual violence and to defuse potentially dangerous situations, there is an array of affiliative or friendly behaviors that serve to reinforce bonds between individuals, and enhance group stability. Affiliative or friendly behaviors reduce levels of aggression by defusing potentially dangerous situations, reinforcing bonds between individuals, and promoting group cohesion.

Common affiliative behaviors include reconciliation, consolation, and simple amicable interactions between friends and relatives. Most such behaviors involve various forms of physical contact, such as touching, hand holding, hugging, and, among chimpanzees, kissing. In fact, physical contact is one of the most important factors in primate development and is crucial in promoting peaceful relationships in many primate social groups.

Grooming is one of the most important affiliative behaviors in many primate species. Although grooming occurs in other animal species, social grooming is mostly a primate activity, and it plays an important role in day-to-day life (Fig. 6–8). Because grooming involves using the fingers to pick through the fur of another individual (or one's own) to remove insects, dirt and other materials, it serves hygienic functions. But it is also an immensely pleasurable activity that individuals of some species (especially chimpanzees) engage in for considerable periods of time.

Grooming occurs in a variety of contexts. Mothers groom infants. Males groom sexually receptive females. Subordinate animals groom dominant ones, sometimes to gain favor. Friends groom friends. In general, grooming is comforting. It restores peaceful relationships between animals who have quarreled and provides reassurance during tense situations. In short, grooming reinforces social

Grooming

Picking through fur to remove dirt, parasites, and other materials that may be present. Social grooming is common among primates and reinforces social relationships.

(a)

(b)

(c)

(d)

FIGURE 6–8

*Grooming primates. (a) Patas monkeys;
female grooming male. (b) Longtail
macaques. (c) Savanna baboons.
(d) Chimpanzees.*

bonds and consequently helps to maintain and strengthen the structure of the group. For this reason, it has been called "the social cement of primates from lemur to chimpanzee" (Jolly, 1985, p. 207).

Conflict resolution through reconciliation is another important aspect of primate social behavior. Following a conflict, chimpanzee opponents frequently move, within minutes, to reconcile (de Waal, 1982). Reconciliation takes many forms, including hugging, kissing, and grooming. Even uninvolved individuals may take part, either grooming one or both participants or forming their own grooming parties. In addition, bonobos are unique in their use of sex to promote group cohesion, restore peace after conflicts, and relieve tension within the group (de Waal, 1987, 1989).

Because relationships are crucial to nonhuman primates, the bonds between individuals can last a lifetime. These relationships serve a variety of functions. Individuals of many species form alliances in which one supports another against a third. Alliances, or coalitions, as they are also called, can be used to enhance the status of members. For example, at Gombe, the male chimpanzee Figan achieved alpha status because of support from his brother (Goodall, 1986, p. 424). In fact, chimpanzees so heavily rely on coalitions and are so skillful politically that an entire book, appropriately titled *Chimpanzee Politics* (de Waal, 1982), is devoted to the topic.

Reproduction and Reproductive Strategies

A behavioral interaction between a female (who has recently mated) and a male can be seen in a video clip at the end of Virtual Lab 6, section II.

In most primate species, sexual behavior is tied to the female's reproductive cycle, with females sexually receptive to males only when they are in estrus. Estrus is characterized by behavioral changes that indicate a female is receptive. In Old World monkeys and apes that live in multimale groups, estrus is also accompanied by swelling and changes in color of the skin around the genital area. These changes serve as visual cues of a female's readiness to mate (Fig. 6–9).

Permanent bonding between males and females is not common among nonhuman primates. However, male and female savanna baboons sometimes form mating *consortships*. These temporary relationships last while the female is in estrus, and the two spend most of the time together, mating frequently. Moreover, lower-ranking baboon males often form "friendships" (Smuts, 1985) with females and occasionally may mate with them, although they may be driven away by high-ranking males when the female is most receptive.

Mating consortships are sometimes seen in chimpanzees and are particularly common among bonobos. In fact, a male and female bonobo may spend several weeks primarily in each other's company. During this time, they mate often, even when the female is not in estrus. These relationships of longer duration are not typical of chimpanzee (*Pan troglodytes*) males and females.

FIGURE 6–9

Estrous swelling of genital tissues in a female chimpanzee.

Such a male-female bond may result in increased reproductive success for both sexes. For the male, there is the increased likelihood that he will be the father of any infant the female conceives. At the same time, the female potentially gains protection from predators or others of her group and perhaps assistance in caring for offspring she may already have.

Reproductive Strategies

Reproductive strategies, and especially how they differ between the sexes, have been a primary focus of primate research. The goal of such strategies is to produce and successfully rear to adulthood as many offspring as possible.

Primates are among the most **K-selected** of mammal species. By this we mean that individuals produce only a few young, in whom they invest a tremendous amount of parental care. Contrast this pattern with **r-selected** species, where individuals produce large numbers of offspring but invest little or no energy in parental care. Good examples of r-selected species include insects, most fish, and, among mammals, mice and rabbits.

When we consider the degree of care required by young, growing primate offspring, it is clear that enormous investment by at least one parent is necessary, and it is usually the mother who carries most of the burden both before and after birth. Primates are totally helpless at birth. They develop slowly and are thus exposed to expanded learning opportunities within a *social* environment. This trend has been elaborated most dramatically in great apes and humans, and especially in the latter. Thus, what we see in ourselves and our close primate kin (and presumably in our more recent ancestors as well) is a strategy wherein a few "high-quality," slowly maturing offspring are produced through extraordinary investment by at least one parent, usually the mother.

Finding food and mates, avoiding predators, and caring for and protecting dependent young represent difficult challenges for nonhuman primates. Moreover, in most species, males and females employ different strategies to meet these challenges.

Female primates spend almost all their adult lives either pregnant, lactating, and/or caring for offspring, and the resulting metabolic demands are enormous. A pregnant or lactating female, although perhaps only half the size of her male counterpart, may require about the same number of calories per day. Even if these demands are met, her physical resources may be drained. For example, analysis of chimpanzee skeletons from Gombe National Park, in Tanzania, shows significant loss of bone and bone mineral in older females (Sumner et al., 1989).

Given these physiological costs, a female's best strategy is to maximize the amount of resources available to her and her offspring. Indeed, females of many primate species (gibbons, marmosets, and macaques, to name a few) are viciously competitive with other females and aggressively protect resources and territories. In other species, as we have seen, females distance themselves from others to avoid competition.

Males, however, face a separate set of challenges. Having little investment in the rearing of offspring (except in the case of monogamous pairs), it is to the male's advantage to secure as many mates and produce as many offspring as possible. By so doing, he is effectively increasing his genetic contribution to the next generation relative to other males.

One outcome of different mating strategies is **sexual selection**, a phenomenon first described by Charles Darwin. Sexual selection is a type of natural

---

Reproductive strategies
The complex of behavioral patterns that contributes to individual reproductive success. The behaviors need not be deliberate, and they often vary considerably between males and females.

K-selected
Pertaining to an adaptive strategy whereby individuals produce relatively few offspring, in whom they invest increased parental care. Although only a few infants are born, chances of survival are increased for each individual because of parental investments in time and energy. Examples of nonprimate K-selected species are birds and canids (e.g., wolves, coyotes, and dogs).

r-selected
Pertaining to an adaptive strategy that emphasizes relatively large numbers of offspring and reduced parental care (compared to K-selected species). (*K-selection* and *r-selection* are relative terms; e.g., mice are r-selected compared to primates but K-selected compared to many fish species.)

Sexual selection
A type of natural selection that operates on only one sex within a species. It is the result of competition for mates and it can lead to sexual dimorphism with regard to one or more traits.

selection that operates on only one sex, usually males, whereby the selective agent is male competition for mates and, in some species, mate choice in females. The long-term effect of sexual selection is to increase the frequency of those traits that lead to greater success in acquiring mates.

In the animal kingdom there are numerous male attributes that result from sexual selection. In some bird species, for example, males are much more brightly colored than females. For various reasons, female birds find those males with more vividly colored plumage more attractive as mates; thus, selection has increased the frequency of alleles that influence brighter coloration in males. However, not all bird species exhibit color dimorphism. Moreover, in some species, such as phalaropes, females compete for males and it is the males who sit on developing eggs. In phalaropes, sexual selection acts on females, who are more brightly colored than males. This example also illustrates the fact that given the necessity for predator avoidance, it is beneficial for those responsible for hatching the eggs to be as inconspicuous as possible.

Sexual selection in primates is most important in species characterized by multimale social groups, but it is a factor in any species where mating is polygynous and male competition for females is prominent. In these species, sexual selection produces dimorphism with regard to a number of traits, most noticeably body size. The males of many primate species are considerably larger than females (indeed, male gorillas and orangutans can be twice as large), and males also have larger canine teeth. Males of multimale societies also have relatively larger testes than males of other types of groups, presumably because of the potential need to produce greater numbers of sperm, which may ultimately compete with the sperm of other males when females mate with more than one individual.

Conversely, in species where mating is monogamous (e.g., gibbons) or where male competition is reduced, sexual dimorphism in canine and body size is either reduced or nonexistent, and relative testis size is smaller. For these reasons, the presence or absence of sexually dimorphic traits in a species is a reasonably good indicator of mating structure.

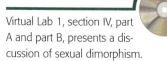

Virtual Lab 1, section IV, part A and part B, presents a discussion of sexual dimorphism.

Mothers and Infants

The basic social unit among all primates is the female and her infants (Fig. 6–10). Except in those species in which monogamy or **polyandry** occurs, males do not participate greatly in the rearing of offspring. Observations both in the field and in captivity suggest that the mother-offspring core provides the social group with its stability.

The mother-infant bond, one of the most basic themes running throughout primate social relations, begins at birth. Although the exact nature of the bonding process is not fully known, there appear to be predisposing innate factors that strongly attract the female to her infant, so long as she herself has had sufficiently normal experience with her own mother. This does not mean that primate mothers possess innate knowledge of how to care for an infant. Indeed, they do not. Monkeys and apes raised in captivity without contact with their own mothers not only do not know how to care for a newborn infant, but may also be afraid of it and attack and kill it. Even if they do not directly attack the infant, they may kill it indirectly through mishandling or improper nursing.

The crucial role of bonding between primate mothers and infants was clearly demonstrated by the Harlows (1959), who raised infant monkeys with surrogate

■ Polyandry
A mating system wherein a female continuously associates with more than one male (usually two or three) with whom she mates. Among non-human primates, this pattern is seen only in marmosets and tamarins.

(a)   (b)   (c)

(d)

(e)

mothers fashioned from wire or a combination of wire and cloth. Other monkeys were raised with no mothers at all. In one experiment, infants retained an attachment to their cloth-covered surrogate mother (Fig. 6–11). But those raised with no mother were incapable of forming lasting affectional ties. These deprived monkeys sat passively in their cages and stared vacantly into space. None of the motherless males ever successfully copulated, and those females who were (somewhat artificially) impregnated either paid little attention to offspring or reacted aggressively toward them (Harlow and Harlow, 1961). The point is that monkeys reared in isolation were denied opportunities to *learn* the rules of social behavior. Moreover, and just as essential, they were denied the all-important physical contact so necessary for normal primate psychological and emotional development.

FIGURE 6–10

Primate mothers with young. (a) Mongoose lemur. (b) Chimpanzee. (c) Patas monkey. (d) Orangutan. (e) Sykes monkey.

FIGURE 6–11

Infant macaque clinging to cloth mother.

▌ Alloparenting

A common behavior in many primate species whereby individuals other than the parent(s) hold, carry, and in general interact with infants.

FIGURE 6–12

Male savanna baboon carrying an infant. This is an example of alloparenting.

The importance of a normal relationship with the mother is demonstrated by field studies as well. From birth, infant primates are able to cling to their mother's fur, and they are in more or less constant physical contact with her for several months. During this critical period, the infant develops a closeness with the mother that does not always end with weaning. This closeness is often maintained throughout life (especially among some Old World monkeys). It is reflected in grooming behavior that continues between mother and offspring even after the young reach adulthood and have infants of their own.

In later studies, Suomi and colleagues emphasized that social isolation initiated early in life could have devastating effects on subsequent development and behavior for many species of primates. The primate deprivation syndrome that results from early isolation is characterized by displays of abnormal self-directed behavior, such as hugging oneself or rocking back and forth, and by gross deficits in all aspects of social behavior (Suomi et al., 1983, p. 190).

Although infants are mainly cared for by the mother, in some species adult males are also known to take more than a casual interest. This phenomenon has frequently been noted among male hamadryas and savanna baboons (Fig. 6–12). Male gibbons and siamangs are directly involved in the care of offspring, and among marmosets and tamarins, the males provide most of the direct infant care, only transferring them back to their mother for nursing.

What may be an extension of the mother-infant relationship has been called **alloparenting**, or "aunt" behavior. This type of behavior occurs in many animal species but is most richly expressed in primates, and some researchers believe that it is found among all social primates. Usually, alloparents crowd around an infant and attempt to groom, hold, or touch it. Some species, like the common langur, are well known for their aunts, and as many as eight females may hold an infant during its first day of life. Occasionally, rough treatment by inexperienced or aggressive animals can result in injury or

death to the infant. For this reason, mothers may attempt to shield infants from overly attentive individuals.

Several functions are suggested for alloparenting. If the mother dies, the infant stands a chance of being adopted by an alloparent or other individual of the group. Moreover, the practice may bind together the adults of the group. Also, it may simply be convenient for the mother to leave her infant occasionally with another female. Finally, the practice of alloparenting may assist in the training of young females for motherhood.

Summary

We have discussed many aspects of nonhuman primate behavior, such as social organization and dominance hierarchies, communication, aggression, affiliation, reproduction, reproductive strategies, and mother-infant relationships. We have also presented views of sexual selection and its role in influencing sexual dimorphism. These behaviors have been treated, to considerable extent, from an ecological perspective; specifically, we have attempted to show what features of the environment are most likely to be important in shaping primate social behavior.

Group size and composition are influenced by such environmental components as resource availability and predators. Moreover, many behaviors are seen as the result of natural selection; that is, they promote increased likelihood of survival and reproduction. Consequently, individuals should behave in ways that will maximize their own reproductive success relative to others. Although this does not imply that in mammals, and especially primates, there are genes for specific behaviors, it does suggest that genes may have mediating effects on behavior and that behavioral attributes have evolved in response to demands imposed by numerous ecological factors.

In the next chapter, we will explore how nonhuman primate behaviors, and the evolutionary factors that have shaped them, can provide information about early hominid behavior. These factors can also illuminate various aspects of behavior in modern humans.

Be sure to complete the self-quiz at the end of Virtual Lab 6.

Questions for Review

1. What factors should be considered if one approaches the study of nonhuman primate behavior from an ecological perspective?
2. What are some of the environmental factors believed to influence group size and social organization? Give two examples.
3. How could multimale, multifemale groupings be advantageous to species living in areas where predation pressure is high?
4. How may solitary foraging be advantageous to primates? Discuss two examples.
5. Define sociobiology. What is the main premise of this theory?
6. How may genetic factors influence behavior?
7. Discuss a primate behavior that has traditionally been used as an example of evolutionary ecology.
8. What are reproductive strategies, and what is their basic benefit?

2. If you wanted to become involved with primate research, where would you begin? Where would you find more information on primates or be able to observe their behavior? Across the country there are Regional Primate Research Centers. Use one of the Internet search engines to find some of these. Which one is closest to you? Whom would you contact at the center?

3. Choose one of the monkey species that live in Kibale Forest, Uganda, and see if you can find out more about them on the Internet. Write a short paper including everything you were able to find out about their ecology and behavior.

Models for Human Evolution

Introduction

Intelligence
Mental capacity; the ability to learn, reason, or comprehend and interpret information, facts, relationships, meanings, etc.; the capacity to solve problems, whether through the application of previously acquired knowledge or through insight.

As you learned in Chapter 5, one characteristic that distinguishes primates, as a group, from most other mammals is increased neurological complexity. Such physiological development is directly reflected in behavioral complexity or, to put it simply, **intelligence**. But while primatologists have documented hundreds of examples of primate intelligence, the question of why primates are so clever remains unanswered. One hypothesis is that the predilection to live in social groups was one of several factors that provided selective pressures favoring intelligence, especially *social* intelligence, as an adaptive strategy for primates.

Primates exhibit a propensity for forming long-term social bonds that frequently include complex alliances and friendships. This predisposition for complex social life provided a foundation for the evolution of the earliest hominids. One of the hallmarks of later hominid evolution is increased relative brain size, but the foundations of neurological complexity were laid long before bipedal hominids began making stone tools. Those foundations are still evident today in behavioral patterns shared by human and nonhuman primates.

Within the social sciences, human behavior has traditionally been considered separately from that of all other organisms, even other primates. This perspective has consistently avoided biological explanations for human behavior, emphasizing that most (if not all) of human behavior is *learned*.

Certainly, human behavior *is* predominantly learned. But the *ability to learn* and behave in complex ways is ultimately rooted in biological (genetic) factors, and natural selection has favored increased learning capacities and behavioral modification in the human lineage.

In the last two decades, there has been a growing consensus, particularly among primatologists, that certain human predispositions reflect patterns also seen in other primates (Cartmill, 1990; King, 1994; de Waal, 1996). Moreover, because we do share an evolutionary history with other primates, a useful approach in developing a better understanding of the evolution of human behavior is to identify in other species those factors that also produced specific patterns in humans. This approach places human behavior, although unarguably unique, within a biological and evolutionary context.

A biological perspective does not assume that all human abilities and behavioral patterns are genetically determined or unalterable. Rather, such an approach aids in explaining *how* certain patterns may have come about and what their adaptive significance might be. Within this framework, the plasticity of human behavior is clearly recognized and emphasized.

As Hinde (1987, p. 413) warns, "Attempting to draw parallels in behavior between human and nonhuman species is a dangerous pastime." Hinde proceeds to caution that owing to the number and diversity of primate species and human cultures, it is not difficult to find comparable behaviors in nonhuman and human primates. Once shared behavioral patterns have been identified, it is easy to support almost any hypothesis one develops, regardless of its validity. However, as Hinde further emphasizes, if one recognizes the risks and limitations of drawing comparisons between species, investigations of shared behavioral *patterns* and principles can be a fruitful endeavor.

All the considerations discussed in this chapter regarding the evolution of behavior in *all* primates (including humans) are ultimately grounded physiologically in the central nervous system. Moreover, the physiological organization of primate neurology is, in turn, directly correlated with growth development, body size, and metabolism, all components of what primatologists have termed **life history**.

Behavior and Human Origins

What does it mean to be human? There are several physical characteristics, such as adaptations for bipedal locomotion and an enlarged brain, that characterize humans and, to varying degrees, our hominid ancestors. But from a structural point of view, humans are not really that unique when compared with other primates, especially the great apes.

Clearly, it is behavioral attributes that most dramatically set humans apart, and long ago, culture became our strategy for coping with life's challenges. No other primate even comes close to the human ability to modify the environment. Communication through symbolic language is yet another uniquely human trait (see pp. 176–180 for a discussion of language capabilities in nonhuman primates). In addition, several other features differentiate humans from the majority of other primates, as summarized in the following list. Keep in mind that any one of these traits may be found in one or more other primate species, but only humans can claim them all:

1. Humans are bipedal. (Some apes occasionally walk bipedally, but they do not do it habitually.)
2. Humans live in permanent bisexual social groups with males often bonded to females.
3. Humans have large brains relative to body weight, and they are capable of complex learning. (All primates learn, as do all mammals, but none has the capacity for learning to the degree shown by humans.)
4. Partly as a consequence of neurological reorganization, humans can think symbolically, and they use language, a communication system that is symbolic in nature.
5. Also related to neurological reorganization, *culture* has become the fundamental hominid adaptive strategy.
6. Humans obtain food through some male-female division of labor. Moreover, food is actively transported back to a base camp (home) for purposes of sharing.
7. There is a relaxation of the estrous cycle and concealed ovulation in humans, so that females are sexually receptive throughout the year.

These traits are characteristic of all modern humans. Moreover, much of this complex is a reasonable theoretical framework within which we can investigate the early stages of hominid emergence. In fact, behavioral reconstructions are often central to theories that explain how hominids came to be hominids in the first place.

According to most experts, modern African apes and humans last shared a common ancestor somewhere between 8 and 5 million years ago (m.y.a.). Researchers believe that since that time, ape behavior has indeed changed, but these changes have not been as dramatic as those in hominids, who developed culture as a major adaptive strategy. Therefore, if we are interested in what hominid behavior might have been like before culture became a significant factor,

■ Life history
Basic components of an animal's development and physiology, viewed from an evolutionary perspective. Such key components include body size, proportional brain size, metabolism, and reproduction.

The evolution of many human traits is discussed in Virtual Labs 9–12.

and if we wish to know what behaviors may have led hominids to become dependent on culture, we may find clues in the behavior of our closest relatives.

Aspects of Life History and Body Size

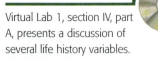

Virtual Lab 1, section IV, part A, presents a discussion of several life history variables.

In the last decade, primatologists have become increasingly interested in broad generalizations regarding primate lifestyles, maturation, and reproduction, topics that are all subsumed under the category of life history. A crucial factor that crosscuts all these aspects of life history is body size. By body size we mean some overall measure of body mass, sometimes given as a linear measure, such as stature, or (more critically) some estimate of weight. In modeling significant features of human evolution, a broad comparative perspective using data from other primates can be useful. We can obtain rough estimates of the body size of ancient hominids from preserved skeletal evidence, especially through extrapolation from joint size. In those rare instances where partial (or even mostly complete) skeletons are preserved, details concerning limb proportions, relative brain size, and so forth, can also be tentatively determined. As we will see in succeeding chapters, there are two quite famous partial skeletons (both from East Africa) now available for such reconstruction. (A third such discovery, in South Africa, was announced in December 1998, but this fossil has not yet been analyzed.)

Among living primates, body size is extraordinarily diverse, ranging from the tiny mouse lemur (66 g, or 2.4 ounces) to the massive gorilla (117 kg, or 258 pounds). And, of course, there is an array of species in between. Several critical features of primate life history are correlated with variation in adult body size. For example, small-bodied species tend to specialize in insectivorous diets, while only larger-bodied species are leaf eaters (i.e., folivorous). It should be noted that almost *all* species eat some fruit, but how this component is supplemented varies considerably and is correlated with body size. Supplementing a diet made up largely of fruits is necessary, for while they are high in calories, fruits lack protein. Primates thus acquire protein from other sources—insects, young buds, leaves, and shoots. In addition, some highly specialized species exploit exudates, that is, tree gums.

Small animals have very high energy needs (per unit of body mass), and for them, insects are an extremely efficient source of calories and protein. However, an animal can capture only so many insects per day, thus placing an upper limit on body size for species that rely heavily on insects to supplement their diet.

On the other hand, to process leaves (especially mature leaves containing cellulose), an animal needs a specialized gut with elongated intestines and/or a multichambered stomach. These physiological adaptations are necessary to digest large amounts of low-energy food, giving microorganisms (bacteria) the opportunity to break down cellulose and neutralize plant toxins. Primates that emphasize leaves in their diets (e.g., colobus monkeys and langurs) have larger overall body size than those that are primarily insectivorous (e.g., tarsiers and lorises).

Tied closely to these dietary factors, body size is also correlated with metabolic rate. The larger an animal is, the more efficient its thermal control will be (see Bergmann's rule, Chapter 15), and consequently, its metabolic rate will be lower than that of a smaller animal. "Thus large animals expend less energy and consequently need less food than small animals. Put more simply, two 5-kg (11-pound) monkeys require more food than a single 10-kg (22-pound) monkey" (Fleagle, 1999, p. 284). The content of the diet also frequently correlates with metabolism (usually measured as basal metabolic rate). On average, folivores have a lower metabolism than other primates—an especially relevant factor when comparing animals of roughly equal body size.

Locomotion and habitat preference, too, are partly correlated with overall body size. Most arboreal primates are small and practice some leaping. Larger arboreal primates tend to exhibit more suspensory behavior. And the largest primates of all tend to be at least partly terrestrial. Monkeys that weigh over 10 kg (22 pounds) are almost always *primarily* terrestrial in their habitat preference. These relationships, however, are not quite this simple. Adaptive solutions such as locomotor behavior are always compromises among competing requirements. While large size may facilitate a more efficient metabolism, it hinders arboreal locomotion and might therefore preclude access to some of the most nutritious food items, located at the ends of small terminal branches. On the ground, larger size might, in some cases, discourage predators, but it will also make the animal more conspicuous.

Body Size and Brain Size

Body size is closely correlated with brain size. Clearly, an animal the size of a chimpanzee 45 kg (100 pounds) has a larger brain than a squirrel monkey (adult weight, almost 1 kg or 2 pounds). However, in making such a superficial comparison of *absolute* brain size, one is ignoring the more important consideration of *proportional brain size.*

It has been known for some time that in mammals in general, not only is brain size tied directly to body size, but the relationship is not completely linear. In other words, in cross-species comparisons, as body weight increases, brain size does not necessarily increase at the same rate.

The predictable relationship between body and brain size has been called the index of **encephalization** (Jerison, 1973). The degree of encephalization can be a very powerful analytical tool, as it provides a gauge of the expected brain size for any given body size. Most primates fall close to the predicted curve, but there is one notable exception: *Homo sapiens.* Modern humans have a brain size well beyond that expected for a primate of similar body weight. It is this degree of encephalization that must be explained as a unique and central component of recent human evolution. Using these same analytical perspectives as applied to the fossil materials in the next several chapters, you will see that earlier members of genus *Homo* as well as more primitive hominids (*Australopithecus*) were not nearly as encephalized as modern *H. sapiens.*

Timing of growth also provides an interesting contrast. In nonhuman primates, the most rapid period of brain development occurs either before or immediately after birth. In humans, rapid growth occurs prior to and after birth—so that already large-brained neonates continue to show considerable brain expansion for at least the first year after birth. The metabolic costs of such rapid and sustained neurological growth are enormous, requiring more than 50 percent of the infant's metabolic output (Aiello, 1992).

Carefully controlled comparisons are essential in making cross-species generalizations regarding animals of differing sizes (a point to keep in mind when we discuss early hominids, most of which varied notably from *Homo sapiens* in body size). Such controls relate to considerations of what is called *scaling,* or (more technically) **allometry.** These allometric comparisons have now become increasingly important in understanding contemporary primate life history variables and adaptations. Moreover, similar approaches, as directly borrowed from these primate models, are now also routinely applied to interpretation of the primate/hominid fossil record.

▌ Encephalization

The proportional size of the brain relative to some other measure, usually some estimate of overall body size. More precisely, the term refers to increases in brain size beyond that which would be expected given the body size of a particular species.

▌ Allometry

Also called "scaling," the differential proportion among various anatomical structures. For example, the relative size of the brain changes during the development of an individual. Moreover, scaling effects must also be considered when comparing species.

At the Yerkes Regional Primate Research Center in Atlanta, Georgia, another chimp, Lana, worked with a specially designed computer keyboard with chips attached to keys. After six months, Lana recognized symbols for 30 words and was able to ask for food and answer questions through the machine (Rumbaugh, 1977). Also at Yerkes, two male chimpanzees, Sherman and Austin, have learned to communicate using a series of lexigrams, or geometric symbols, imprinted on a computer keyboard (Savage-Rumbaugh, 1986).

Dr. Francine Patterson, who taught ASL to Koko, a female lowland gorilla, reports that Koko uses more than 500 signs. Furthermore, Michael, an adult male gorilla also involved in the study, has a considerable sign vocabulary, and the two gorillas communicate with each other via signs.

In the late 1970s, a two-year-old male orangutan named Chantek (also at Yerkes) began to use signs after one month of training. Eventually, he acquired approximately 140 signs, which were sometimes used to refer to objects and persons not present. Chantek also invented signs and recombined them in novel ways, and he appeared to understand that his signs were *representations* of items, actions, and people (Miles, 1990).

Questions have been raised about this type of experimental work. Do the apes really understand the signs they learn? Are they merely imitating their trainers? Do they learn that a symbol is a name for an object or simply that executing a symbol will produce that object? Other unanswered questions concern the apes' use of grammar, especially when they combine more than just a few "words" to communicate.

Partly in an effort to address some of these questions and criticisms, psychologist Sue Savage-Rumbaugh taught the two chimpanzees Sherman and Austin to use symbols to categorize *classes* of objects, such as "food" or "tool." This was done in recognition of the fact that in previous studies, apes had been taught symbols for *specific* items. Savage-Rumbaugh reasoned that simply to use a symbol as a label is not the same thing as understanding the *representational value* of the symbol.

Sherman and Austin were taught to recognize familiar food items, for which they routinely used symbols, as belonging to a broader category referred to by yet another symbol, "food." They were then introduced to unfamiliar food items, for which they had no symbols, in order to see if they would place them in the food category. The fact that they both had perfect or nearly perfect scores further substantiated that indeed they could categorize unfamiliar objects. More importantly, it was clear that they were capable of assigning to unknown objects symbols that denoted membership in a broad grouping. This ability was a strong indication that the chimpanzees understood that the symbols were being used referentially.

However, subsequent work with Lana, who had different language experiences, did not prove as successful. Although Lana was able to sort actual objects into categories, she was unable to assign generic symbols to novel items (Savage-Rumbaugh and Lewin, 1994). Thus, it became apparent that the manner in which chimpanzees are introduced to language influences their ability to understand the representational value of symbols.

Throughout the relatively brief history of ape language studies, one often repeated assertion was that young chimpanzees must be *taught* to use symbols. This pattern was contrasted with the ability of human children to learn language spontaneously, through exposure, without being deliberately taught. Therefore, it was significant when Savage-Rumbaugh and her colleagues reported that Kanzi, an infant male bonobo, was *spontaneously* acquiring and using symbols at the age of

$2^1/2$ years (Savage-Rumbaugh et al., 1986) (Fig. 7–2). Kanzi's younger half-sister also began to use symbols spontaneously at 11 months of age. Both animals had been exposed to the use of lexigrams when they accompanied their mother to training sessions, but neither had received instruction and in fact were not involved in these sessions.

While the abilities shown by Kanzi and his sister reveal a remarkable degree of cognitive complexity, it nevertheless remains evident that apes do not acquire and use language in the same way humans do. Moreover, it appears that not all signing apes understand the referential relationship between symbol and object, person, or action. Nonetheless, there is abundant evidence that humans are not the only species capable of some degree of symbolic thought and complex communication.

FIGURE 7–2

The bonobo Kanzi, as a youngster, using lexigrams to communicate with human observers. (Photograph by Elizabeth Pugh)

From an evolutionary perspective, the ape language experiments may suggest clues to the origins of human language. It is quite likely that the last common ancestor that hominids shared with the African great apes possessed communication capabilities similar to those we now see in these species. If so, we need to elucidate the factors that enhanced the adaptive significance of these characteristics in our own lineage. It is equally important to explore why these pressures did not operate to the same degree in gorillas, chimpanzees, and bonobos.

For reasons we do not yet fully understand, communication became increasingly important during the course of human evolution, and natural selection favored anatomical and neurological changes that enhanced our ancestors' ability to use spoken language. However, this trend would not have been possible if early hominids had not already been predisposed to language development.

In nonhuman primates, vocalizations are not completely controlled by the **motor cortex.** However, some of the regions of the brain involved in human speech production *are* located in the motor cortex, and they direct movement of the mouth, larynx, and tongue, but *only as those movements pertain to language.* Damage to these neural tracts does not cause paralysis, as damage to other areas will do, but it will disturb speech, demonstrating that these structures are adapted to movements related specifically to speech production. However, human speech involves much more than simply the motor control of specific muscle groups.

In most humans, language function is located primarily in the left hemisphere of the brain, especially the left temporal lobe (see Fig. 7–3). In particular, two regions—*Wernicke's area* and *Broca's area*—are directly involved in the perception and production (respectively) of spoken language. But the perception and production of speech involves much more than these two areas, and use of written language requires still other neurological structures.

■ **Motor cortex**

That portion of the cortex pertaining to outgoing signals involved in muscle use. (The *cortex* of the brain, the outer layer, is composed of nerve cells or neurons.)

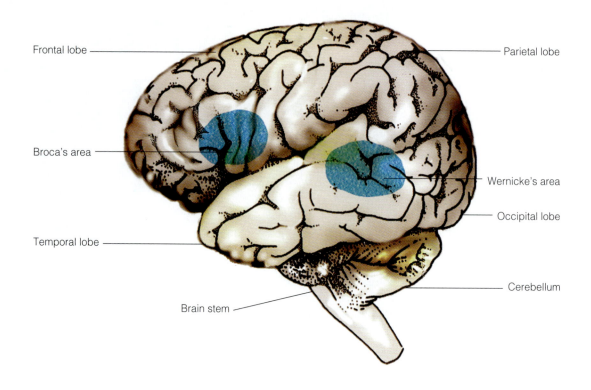

Frontal lobe

Broca's area

Temporal lobe

Brain stem

Parietal lobe

Wernicke's area

Occipital lobe

Cerebellum

FIGURE 7–3

Left lateral view of the human brain, showing major regions and areas involved in speech.

Association areas, composed of thousands of neural connections, integrate information sent from various parts of the cerebral cortex. Information relating to visual, olfactory, tactile, and auditory stimuli is first combined and then relayed to Broca's area, where it is translated for speech production. This remarkable human ability depends on interconnections between receiving areas for all sensory stimuli. While the brains of other species have such association areas, they do not have the ability to transform this information for the purpose of using language.

In discussions of human evolution, much emphasis is placed on increased brain size, both in relative and absolute terms. While increased brain size is certainly important, it was the *reorganization* of neurological structures that permitted the development of language. Although the study of comparative brain structure is still in its infancy, much current evidence suggests that *new* structures and novel connections have not been the basis for neurological differences among species. Rather, systematic reorganization, elaboration, and/or reduction of existing structures, as well as shifts in the proportions of existing connections, have been far more important (Deacon, 1992).

Some researchers argue that language capabilities appeared late in human evolution (i.e., with the wide dispersal of modern *Homo sapiens* some 100,000 to 30,000 years ago). Others postulate a much earlier origin, possibly with the appearance of the genus *Homo* some 2 m.y.a. Whichever scenario is true, language came about as complex and efficient forms of communication gained selective value in our lineage.

Primate Cultural Behavior

One important trait that makes primates, and especially chimpanzees and bonobos, attractive as models for behavior in early hominids may be called *cultural behavior*. Although many cultural anthropologists and others prefer to use the term *culture* to refer specifically to human activities, most biological anthropologists feel that it is appropriate to use the term in discussions of nonhuman primates as well.

Undeniably, there are many aspects of culture that are uniquely human, and one must be cautious when interpreting nonhuman animal behavior. But again, since humans are products of the same evolutionary forces that have produced other species, they can be expected to exhibit some of the same *behavioral patterns* seen in other species, particularly primates. However, because of increased brain size and learning capacities, humans express many characteristics to a greater degree. We would argue that the *aptitude for culture,* as a means of adapting to the natural environment, is one such characteristic.

Among other things, cultural behavior is *learned,* and it is passed from generation to generation—not biologically, but through learning. Whereas humans deliberately teach their young, free-ranging nonhuman primates (with the exception of a few reports) do not appear to do so. But at the same time, like young nonhuman primates, human children also acquire tremendous knowledge not from instruction, but through observation. Nonhuman primate infants, through observing their mothers and others, learn about food items, appropriate behaviors, and how to use and modify objects to achieve certain ends. In turn, their own offspring will observe their activities. What emerges is a *cultural tradition* that may eventually come to typify an entire group or even a species.

Two famous examples of cultural behavior were seen in a study group of Japanese macaques on Koshima Island. In 1952, Japanese researchers began provisioning the 22-member troop with sweet potatoes. The following year, a young female named Imo began washing her potatoes in a freshwater stream prior to eating them. Within three years, several monkeys had adopted the practice, but they had switched from using the stream to taking their potatoes to the ocean nearby. Perhaps they liked the salt seasoning!

In 1956, the Koshima primatologists began scattering wheat grains onto the sandy beach, and again, Imo introduced a novel behavior. Instead of picking out wheat grains one at a time (as the researchers had expected), Imo picked up handfuls of grain and sand and dropped them together into the water. The sand sank, the wheat kernels floated, and Imo simply scooped them off the water and ate them. Just as with potato washing, others adopted Imo's technique until the new behavior eventually became common throughout the troop.

The researchers proposed that dietary habits and food preferences are learned and that potato washing and wheat floating were examples of nonhuman culture. Because these practices arose as innovative solutions to problems, and they gradually spread through the troop until they became traditions, they were seen as containing elements of human culture.

Among chimpanzees we see more elaborate examples of cultural behavior in the form of *tool use*. This point is very important, for traditionally, tool use (along with language) was said to set humans apart from other animals.

Chimpanzees insert twigs and grass blades into termite mounds in a practice called "termite fishing" (Fig. 7–4). When termites seize the twig, the chimpanzee

Tool use by chimpanzees is discussed in Virtual Lab 11, section I.

(a)   (b)

FIGURE 7–4

(a) Female chimpanzee using a tool to "fish"
for termites at Gombe National Park,
Tanzania. (b) A chimpanzee at the
Sacramento Zoo also uses a tool in the
same manner as free-ranging animals.

withdraws it and eats the attached insects. Chimpanzees modify some of their
stems and twigs by stripping the leaves—in effect, manufacturing a tool from the
natural material. To some extent, chimpanzees even alter objects to a "regular and
set pattern" and have been observed preparing objects for later use at an out-of-
sight location (Goodall, 1986, p. 535). For example, a chimpanzee will very carefully select a piece of vine, bark, twig, or palm frond and modify it by removing
leaves or other extraneous material, then break off portions until it is the proper
length. Chimpanzees have also been seen making these tools even before the termite mound is in sight.

All this preparation has several implications. First, the chimpanzees are
engaged in an activity that prepares them for a future (not immediate) task at a
somewhat distant location, and this action implies planning and forethought.
Second, attention to the shape and size of the raw material indicates that chimpanzee toolmakers have a preconceived idea of what the finished product needs
to be in order to be useful. To produce a tool, even a simple tool, based on a concept is an extremely complex behavior. Scientists previously believed that such
behavior was the exclusive domain of humans, but now we must question this
very basic assumption.

Chimpanzees also crumple and chew handfuls of leaves, which they dip into
the hollow of a tree where water has accumulated. Then they suck the water from
their newly made "leaf sponges," water that otherwise would have been inacces-
sible to them. Leaves are also used to wipe substances from fur; twigs are sometimes used as toothpicks; stones may be used as weapons; and various objects,
such as branches and stones, may be dragged or rolled to enhance displays. Lastly,
sticks or leaves are used as aids in processing mammalian prey, but with one

exception these practices appear to be incidental. The one exception, observed in chimpanzees in the Tai forest (Ivory Coast), is the frequent use of sticks to extract marrow from long bones (Boesch and Boesch, 1989).

Chimpanzees in numerous West African study groups use hammerstones with platform stones to crack nuts and hard-shelled fruits (Boesch et al, 1994). However, it is important to note that neither the hammerstone nor the platform stone was deliberately manufactured.* Wild capuchin monkeys use leaves to extract water from cavities in trees (Phillips, 1998) and also smash objects against stones (Izawa and Mizuno, 1977), and their use of stones in captivity (both as hammers and anvils) has been reported (Visalberghi, 1990). (Stones serve as anvils when fruit or other objects are bashed against the rock surface.) In nature, chimpanzees are the only nonhuman animal to use stones both as hammers and anvils to obtain food. They are the only nonhuman primate that consistently and habitually makes and uses tools (McGrew, 1992).

Chimpanzees exhibit regional variation regarding both the types and methods of tool use. Use of stone hammers and platforms is confined to West African groups. And at central and eastern African sites, termites are obtained by means of stems and sticks, while at some West African locations, it appears that no tools are used in this context (McGrew, 1992).

Regional dietary preferences are also noted for chimpanzees (Nishida et al., 1983; McGrew, 1992). For example, oil palms are exploited for their fruits and nuts at many locations, including Gombe, but even though they are present in the Mahale Mountains, they are not utilized by the chimpanzees there. Such regional patterns in tool use and food preferences that are not related to environmental variation are reminiscent of the cultural variations characteristic of humans.

McGrew (1992) presents eight criteria for cultural behaviors in nonhuman species (Table 7–1). Of these, the first six were established by the pioneering cultural anthropologist Alfred Kroeber (1928); the last two were added by McGrew and Tutin (1978). McGrew (1992) demonstrates that Japanese macaques meet the first six criteria. However, all the macaque examples have developed, in

TABLE 7–1   Criteria for Cultural Acts in Other Species

Innovation	New pattern is invented or modified.
Dissemination	Pattern is acquired (through imitation) by another from an innovator.
Standardization	Form of pattern is consistent and stylized.
Durability	Pattern is performed without presence of demonstrator.
Diffusion	Pattern spreads from one group to another.
Tradition	Pattern persists from innovator's generation to the next.
Nonsubsistence	Pattern transcends subsistence.
Naturalness	Pattern is shown in absence of direct human influence.

Source: Adapted from Kroeber, 1928, and McGrew and Tutin, 1978. In McGrew, 1992.

---

*Observers of nonhuman primates rarely distinguish natural objects used as tools from modified objects deliberately manufactured for specific purposes. The term *tool* is usually employed in both cases.

■ Biological continuum
Refers to the fact that organisms are related through common ancestry and that behaviors and traits seen in one species are also seen in others to varying degrees. (When expressions of a phenomenon continuously grade into one another so that there are no discrete categories, they are said to exist on a continuum. Color is such a phenomenon.)

in many ways unquestionably unique, are nevertheless part of a **biological continuum.**

Where do humans fit, then, in this biological continuum? Are we at the top? The answer depends on the criteria used. Certainly, we are the most intelligent species, if we define intelligence in terms of problem-solving abilities and abstract thought. However, if we look more closely, we recognize that the differences between ourselves and our primate relatives, especially chimpanzees and bonobos, are primarily quantitative and not qualitative.

Although human brains are absolutely and relatively larger, neurological processes are functionally the same. The necessity of close bonding with at least one parent and the need for physical contact are essentially the same. Developmental stages and dependence on learning are strikingly similar. Indeed, even in the capacity for cruelty and aggression combined with compassion, tenderness, and altruism exhibited by chimpanzees, we see a close parallel to the dichotomy between "evil" and "good" so long recognized in ourselves. The main difference between how chimpanzees and humans express these qualities (and therefore the dichotomy) is one of degree. Humans are much more adept at cruelty and compassion, and humans can reflect on their behavior in ways that chimpanzees cannot. While chimpanzees may not understand the suffering they inflict on others, humans do. Likewise, while an adult chimpanzee may sit next to and protect a dying relative or friend, it does not appear to feel intense grief and a sense of loss to the extent a human normally does.

To arrive at any understanding of what it is to be human, it is vastly important to recognize that many of our behaviors are but elaborate extensions of those of our hominid ancestors and close primate relatives. The fact that so many of us prefer to bask in the warmth of the "sun belt" with literally millions of others reflects our heritage as social animals adapted to life in the tropics. And the "sweet tooth" seen in so many humans is a direct result of our earlier primate ancestors' predilection for high-energy sugar contained in desirably sweet, ripe fruit. Thus, it is important to recognize our primate heritage as we explore how humans came to be and how we continue to adapt.

Summary

Various aspects of nonhuman primate behavior and adaptation have been discussed as they pertain to modern humans and to human evolution. Such capacities as efficient communication (including language), affiliation, intergroup aggression, and cultural behavior are explained within an evolutionary framework. Although this does not imply that in mammals, and especially primates, there are genes for specific behaviors, it does suggest that genes may have mediating effects on behavior. Moreover, these capabilities and the similarity of their expression in many primate species argue for their adaptive significance in complex social settings.

Language and tool use, like most human capacities, can be seen as elaborations of patterns observed in many nonhuman primates. Humans reflect their evolutionary heritage as primates and stand as one component of a biological continuum. It is this evolutionary relationship, then, that accounts for many of the behaviors we have in common with prosimians, monkeys, and apes.

Questions for Review

1. How can aspects of human behavior be explained in terms of biological evolution without necessarily postulating that complex behaviors are under *strict* genetic control?
2. How is body size in primates related to diet and metabolism?
3. What is meant by encephalization? Give an example of how this concept would be useful in comparing different primate species.
4. How does human language differ from most nonhuman communication? What is the evidence to suggest that some nonhuman primates exhibit certain language abilities seen in humans?
5. Briefly discuss neurological changes that occurred in human evolution that relate to language function.
6. Discuss an example of between-group aggression. What is thought to have motivated the violence between two groups of chimpanzees at Gombe?
7. Discuss two examples of nonhuman primate cultural behavior. Why is our discovery of these behaviors important to studies of early human evolution?
8. Discuss the language acquisition studies using chimpanzees, bonobos, and gorillas. What are the implications of this research?
9. What do we mean when we state that humans are a part of a biological continuum? How does the view expressed in this statement differ from traditional views expressed by most people?
10. Why are anthropologists interested in cooperative hunting in chimpanzees?

Primates in Biomedical Research: Ethics and Concerns

The use of nonhuman animals for experimentation is an established practice, long recognized for its benefits to human beings as well as to nonhuman animals. Currently, an estimated 17 to 22 million animals are used annually in the United States for the testing of new vaccines and other methods of treating or preventing disease, as well as for the development of innovative surgical procedures. Nonhuman animals are also used in psychological experimentation and in the testing of consumer products.

Because of biological and behavioral similarities shared with humans, nonhuman primates are among those species most desired for biomedical research. According to figures from the United States Department of Agriculture (USDA), 42,620 primates were used in laboratory studies in 1991. On average, about 50,000 are used annually, with approximately 3,000 being involved in more than one study. The most commonly used primates are baboons, vervets, various macaque species, squirrel monkeys, marmosets, and tamarins. Because they are more costly than other species (such as mice, rats, rabbits, cats, and dogs), primates are usually reserved for medical and behavioral studies and not for the testing of consumer goods such as cosmetics or household cleaners. (It should be noted that many cosmetic companies assert that they no longer perform tests on animals.)

Although work with primates has certainly benefited humankind, these benefits are expensive, not only monetarily but in terms of suffering and animal lives lost. The development of the polio vaccine in the 1950s serves as one example of the costs involved. Prior to the 1950s, polio had killed and crippled millions of people worldwide. Now the disease is almost unheard of, at least in developed nations. But included in the price tag for the polio vaccine were the lives of 1.5 *million* rhesus macaques, mostly imported from India.

Unquestionably, the elimination of polio and other diseases is a boon to humanity, and such achievements are part of the obligation of medical research to promote the health and well-being of humans. But at the same time, serious questions have been raised about medical advances made at the expense of millions of nonhuman animals, many of whom are primates. Indeed, one well-known primatologist, speaking at a conference some years ago, questioned whether we can morally justify depleting populations of threatened species solely for the benefit of a single, highly overpopulated one.

This question will seem extreme, if not absurd, to many readers, especially in view of the fact that the majority of people would argue that *whatever* is necessary to promote human health and longevity is justified.

Leaving the broader ethical issues aside for a moment, one area of controversy regarding laboratory primates is housing. Traditionally, lab animals have been kept in small metal cages, usually one or two per cage. Cages are usually bare, except for food and water, and they are frequently stacked one on top of another, so that their inhabitants find themselves in the unnatural situation of having animals above and below them, as well as on each side.

The primary reason for small cage size is simple. Small cages are less expensive than large ones and they require less space (space is also costly). Moreover, sterile, unenriched cages (i.e., lacking objects for manipulation or play) are easier and therefore cheaper to clean. But for such curious, intelligent animals as primates, these easy-to-maintain facilities result in a deprivation that leads to depression, neurosis, and psychosis. (The application of these terms to a nonhuman context is criticized as being anthropomorphic by many who believe that nonhuman animals, including primates, cannot be said to have psychological needs.)

Chimpanzees, reserved primarily for AIDS and hepatitis B research, probably suffer more than any other species from inadequate facilities. In 1990, Jane Goodall published a description of conditions she encountered in one lab she visited in Maryland. In this facility, she saw two- and three-year-old chimpanzees housed, two together, in cages measuring 22 inches square and 24 inches high. Obviously, movement for these youngsters was virtually impossible, and they had been housed in this manner for over three months. At this same lab and others, adult chimps, infected with HIV or hepatitis, were confined alone for several years in small isolation chambers, where they rocked back and forth, seeing little and hearing nothing of their surroundings.

Fortunately, conditions are improving. There has been increased public awareness of existing conditions; and there is, among some members of the biomedical community, a growing sensitivity toward the special requirements of primates.

In 1991, amendments to the Animal Welfare Act were enacted to require all labs to provide minimum standards for the humane care of all "warm-blooded" animals. (For some reason, birds and rodents were not included in this category.) These minimum standards provide specific requirements for cage size based on weight of the animal. For example, primates weighing less than 2.2 pounds must have 1.6 square feet of floor space per animal, and the cage must be at least 20 inches high. Those weighing more than 55 pounds are allotted at least 25.1 square feet of floor space per animal and at least 84 inches (7 feet) of vertical space.

Clearly, the enclosures described above are not sufficiently large for normal locomotor activities, and this could certainly contribute to psychological stress. One method of reducing such stress is to provide cages with objects and climbing structures (even part of a dead branch is a considerable improvement and costs nothing). Several facilities are now implementing such procedures. Also, many laboratory staffs are now trained to provide enrichment for the animals in their care. Moreover, the Maryland lab that Dr. Goodall

observed no longer maintains chimpanzees in isolation chambers. Rather, they are now housed with other animals in areas measuring 80 cubic feet and are provided with enrichment devices.

Aside from the treatment of captive primates, there continues to be concern over the depletion of wild populations in order to provide research animals. Actually, the number of wild-caught animals used in research today is small compared to the numbers lost to habitat destruction and hunting for food. However, in the past, particularly in the 1950s and 1960s, the numbers of animals captured for research were staggering. In 1968, for example, 113,714 primates were received in the United States alone!

Fortunately, the number of animals imported into the United States has declined dramatically since the Convention on Trade in Endangered Species (CITES) was ratified in 1973 (see p. 137). In 1984, for example, the United States imported 13,148 primates (Mittermeier and Cheney, 1987). On average, the United States annually imports some 20,000 (some from breeding colonies in the country of origin). Although it would be best if no free-ranging primates were involved, at least these figures represent a substantial improvement since the 1960s.

It is important to note that biomedical research accounts for only a small part of the demand for primates captured in the wild. The exotic pet trade provides a much greater share of the market, both locally and internationally. But

even more important is the hunting or live capture of primates for human consumption. This is especially true in parts of West Africa and Asia. Moreover, in several Asian countries there is a growing demand for animal (including primate) products (body parts such as bones or brain tissue) for medicinal purposes.

In response to concerns for diminishing wild populations and regulations to protect them, a number of breeding colonies have been established in the United States and other countries to help meet demands for laboratory animals. Additionally, in 1986, the National Institutes of Health established the National Chimpanzee Breeding Program to provide chimpanzees primarily for AIDS and hepatitis B research.

Furthermore, in 1989, the United States Fish and Wildlife Service upgraded the status of wild chimpanzees from "threatened" to "endangered." The endangered status was not applied to animals born in captivity; the upgrade was intended to provide additional protection for free-ranging populations. Unfortunately, even with all the policies now in place, there is no guarantee that some wild-born chimpanzees will not find their way into research labs.

The animal rights movement has been described by many in the scientific community as "anti-science," or "anti-intellectual." Certainly, there are extremists in the animal rights movement for whom these labels are appropriate. But to categorize in this manner all who have concern for

experts to conclude that this evidence "shows that birds are not only *descended* from dinosaurs, they *are* dinosaurs (and reptiles)—just as humans are mammals, even though people are as different from other mammals as birds are from other reptiles" (Padian and Chiappe, 1998, p. 43) (Fig. 8–4b).

There are some doubters who remain concerned that the presence of feathers in dinosaurs (145–125 m.y.a.) might simply be a homoplasy (i.e., these creatures developed the trait independently from its appearance in birds). Certainly, the possibility of homoplasy must always be considered, as it can add considerably to the complexity of what seems like a straightforward evolutionary interpretation. Indeed, strict cladistic analysis assumes that homoplasy is not a common occurrence; if it were, perhaps no evolutionary interpretation could be very straightforward! In the case of the proposed relationship between some (theropod) dinosaurs and birds, the presence of feathers looks like an excellent example of a shared derived characteristic, which therefore *does* link the forms. Moreover, cladistic analysis emphasizes that several characteristics should be examined, since homoplasy might muddle an interpretation based on just one or two shared traits. In the bird-dinosaur case, several other characteristics further suggest their evolutionary relationship.

As we noted above, dinosaur paleontology continues to be a hotbed, fueled by dramatic new discoveries, reinterpretations, and ongoing disputes. Another spectacular new analysis (using ultraviolet light) of a 100 m.y.a. Italian theropod has revealed the presence of internal organs, including the intestines, liver, trachea, and some muscles (Ruben et al., 1999). Initial analysis has suggested this theropod dinosaur had a breathing mechanism quite different from birds, but, in some ways, similar to that of living crocodiles. Some researchers have thus argued that this new evidence casts some doubt on the theropod-dinosaur link. For the moment, however, the overall cladistic analysis of several other traits (following Padian and Chiappe, 1998) argues for a fairly close theropod-bird evolutionary relationship. (Note: to falsify this hypothesis a great deal of homoplasy in theropods on the one hand and birds on the other would have had to take place).

One last point needs to be mentioned. Traditional phylogenetic systematics illustrates the hypothesized evolutionary relationships using a *phylogeny*, more properly called a **phylogenetic tree**. Strict cladistic analysis, however, shows relationships in a **cladogram** (Fig. 8–5). If you examine these charts, you will see some obvious differences. A phylogenetic tree incorporates the dimension of

◼ Phylogenetic tree

A chart showing evolutionary relationships as determined by phylogenetic systematics. It contains a time component and implies ancestor-descendant relationships.

◼ Cladogram

A chart showing evolutionary relationships as determined by cladistic analysis. It is based solely on interpretation of shared derived characters. No time component is indicated, and ancestor-descendant relationships are *not* inferred.

FIGURE 8–5

Cladogram showing relationships of birds, dinosaurs, and other terrestrial vertebrates. Note that no time scale is utilized, and both living and fossil forms are shown along the same dimension (i.e., there is no indication of ancestor-descendant relationships).

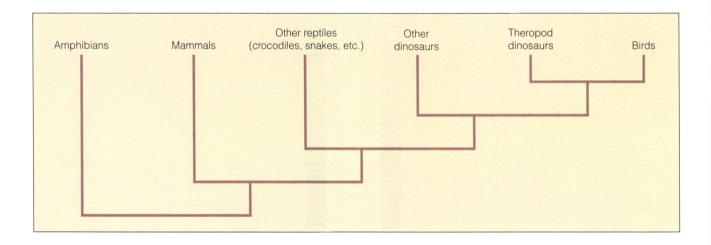

time, shown approximately in Figure 8–4. (Numerous other examples can be found in this and subsequent chapters.) A cladogram does not indicate time; all forms (fossil and modern) are indicated along one dimension. Phylogenetic trees usually attempt to make some hypotheses regarding ancestor-descendant relationships (e.g., theropods are ancestral to modern birds). Cladistic analysis (through cladograms) makes no attempt whatsoever to discern ancestor-descendant relationships. In fact, strict cladists are quite skeptical that the evidence really permits such specific evolutionary hypotheses to be scientifically confirmed (since there are many more extinct species than living ones).

In practice, most physical anthropologists (and other evolutionary biologists) utilize cladistic analysis to identify and assess the utility of traits and to make testable hypotheses regarding the relationships of groups of organisms. Moreover, they frequently extend this basic cladistic methodology to further hypothesize likely ancestor-descendant relationships shown relative to a time scale (i.e., in a phylogenetic tree). In this way, aspects of both traditional phylogenetic systematics and cladistic analyses are combined to produce a more complete picture of evolutionary history.

Vertebrate Evolutionary History: A Brief Summary

In addition to the staggering array of living and extinct life forms, biologists must also contend with the vast amount of time that life has been evolving on earth. Again, scientists have devised simplified schemes—but in this case to organize *time,* not organic diversity.

Geologists have formulated the **geological time scale** (Fig. 8–6), in which very large time spans are organized into eras and periods. Periods, in turn, can be broken down into epochs (as we will do later in our discussion of primate evolution). For the time span encompassing vertebrate evolution, there are three eras: the Paleozoic, the Mesozoic, and the Cenozoic. The first vertebrates are present in the fossil record dating to early in the Paleozoic 500 m.y.a. and probably go back considerably further. It is the vertebrate capacity to form bone that accounts for their more complete fossil record *after* 500 m.y.a.

During the Paleozoic, several varieties of fishes (including the ancestors of modern sharks and bony fishes), amphibians, and reptiles appeared. In addition, at the end of the Paleozoic, close to 250 m.y.a., several varieties of mammal-like reptiles were also diversifying. It is widely thought that some of these forms gave rise to the mammals.

The evolutionary history of vertebrates and other organisms during the Paleozoic and Mesozoic was profoundly influenced by geographical events. We know that the positions of the earth's continents have dramatically shifted during the last several hundred million years. This process, called **continental drift**, is explained by the geological theory of *plate tectonics,* which views the earth's crust as a series of gigantic moving and colliding plates. Such massive geological movements can induce volcanic activity (as, for example, all around the Pacific rim), mountain building (e.g., the Himalayas), and earthquakes. Living on the edge of the Pacific and North American plates, residents of the Pacific coast of the United States are acutely aware of some of these consequences, as illustrated by the explosive volcanic eruption of Mt. St. Helens or the frequent earthquakes in Alaska and California.

Virtual Lab 7, section I, part B, provides discussions and many examples of geological time. Be sure to view the information about geological dating techniques in part C.

■ **Geological time scale**
The organization of earth history into eras, periods, and epochs; commonly used by geologists and paleoanthropologists.

■ **Continental drift**
The movement of continents on sliding plates of the earth's surface. As a result, the position of large landmasses has shifted dramatically during earth's history.

An animation of plate tectonics is provided in Virtual Lab 7, section II, part A.

ERA	PERIOD	(Began m.y.a.)	EPOCH	(Began m.y.a.)
CENOZOIC	Quaternary	1.8	Holocene Pleistocene	0.01 1.8
CENOZOIC	Tertiary	65	Pliocene Miocene Oligocene Eocene Paleocene	5 23 34 55 65
MESOZOIC	Cretaceous	136		
MESOZOIC	Jurassic	190		
MESOZOIC	Triassic	225		
PALEOZOIC	Permian	280		
PALEOZOIC	Carboniferous	345		
PALEOZOIC	Devonian	395		
PALEOZOIC	Silurian	430		
PALEOZOIC	Ordovician	500		
PALEOZOIC	Cambrian	570		
PRE-CAMBRIAN				

FIGURE 8–6

Geological time scale.

▮ Ecological niches

The positions of species within their physical and biological environments, together making up the *ecosystem*. A species' ecological niche is defined by such components as diet, terrain, vegetation, type of predators, relationships with other species, and activity patterns, and each niche is unique to a given species.

Geologists, in reconstructing the earth's physical history, have established the prior (significantly altered) positioning of major continental landmasses. During the late Paleozoic, the continents came together to form a single colossal landmass called *Pangea* (Fig 8–7). In actuality, the continents had been drifting on plates, coming together and separating, long before the end of the Paleozoic (c. 225 m.y.a.), and to be more precise, the large landmass at this time should be called Pangea II. During the early Mesozoic, the southern continents (South America, Africa, Antarctica, Australia, and India) began to split off from Pangea, forming a large southern continent called *Gondwanaland*. Similarly, the northern continents (North America, Greenland, Europe, and Asia) were consolidated into a northern landmass called *Laurasia*. During the Mesozoic, Gondwanaland and Laurasia continued to drift apart and to break up into smaller segments. By the end of the Mesozoic (c. 65 m.y.a.), the continents were beginning to assume their current positions (Fig. 8–7b).

The evolutionary ramifications of this long-term continental drift were profound. Groups of land animals became effectively isolated from each other by large water boundaries, and the distribution of reptiles and mammals was significantly influenced by continental movements. Although not producing such dramatic continental realignments, the process continued through the Mesozoic and into the Cenozoic. The more specific effects of continental drift on early primate evolution are discussed later in this chapter.

During most of the Mesozoic, reptiles were the dominant land vertebrates, and they exhibited a broad expansion into a variety of **ecological niches**, which included aerial and marine habitats. No doubt, the most famous of these highly successful Mesozoic reptiles were the dinosaurs, which themselves evolved into a wide array of sizes and lifestyles. Dinosaur paleontology, never a boring field, has advanced several startling notions in recent years: that many dinosaurs were warm-blooded; that some varieties were quite social and probably also engaged in considerable parental care; that many forms became extinct as the result of major climactic changes to the earth's atmosphere from collisions with comets or asteroids; and finally, as previously discussed, that not all

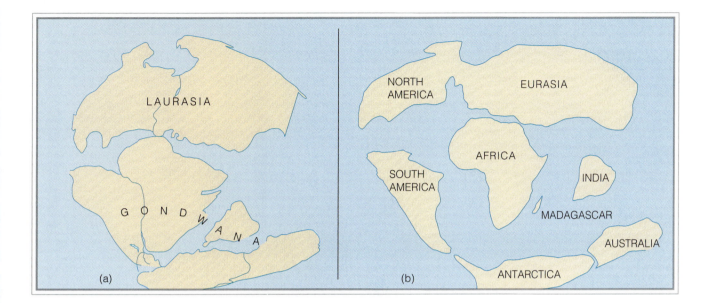

(a)

NORTH AMERICA

EURASIA

SOUTH AMERICA

AFRICA

INDIA

MADAGASCAR

AUSTRALIA

ANTARCTICA

LAURASIA

G O N D W A N A

(b)

dinosaurs became entirely extinct, with many descendants still living today (i.e., all modern birds). (See Figure 8–8 for a summary of major events in early vertebrate evolutionary history.)

The earliest mammals are known from fossil traces fairly early in the Mesozoic, but the first *placental* mammals cannot be positively identified until quite late in the Mesozoic, approximately 70 m.y.a. This highly successful mammalian adaptive radiation is thus almost entirely within the most recent era of geological history, the Cenozoic.

The Cenozoic is divided into two periods, the Tertiary (about 63 million years duration) and the Quaternary, from about 1.8 m.y.a. up to and including the present. Because this division is rather imprecise, paleontologists more frequently refer to the next level of subdivision within the Cenozoic, the **epochs**. There are seven epochs within the Cenozoic: the Paleocene, Eocene, Oligocene, Miocene, Pliocene, Pleistocene, and Holocene, the last often referred to as the Recent (see Fig 8–6).

FIGURE 8–7a, b

Continental drift. Changes in positions of the continental plates from late Paleozoic to late Eocene. (a) The position of the continents during the Mesozoic (c. 125 m.y.a.) Pangea is breaking up into a northern landmass (Laurasia) and a southern landmass (Gondwanaland). (b) The position of the continents at the beginning of the Cenozoic (c. 65 m.y.a.).

▌ Epochs

Categories of the geological time scale; subdivisions of periods. In the Cenozoic, epochs include Paleocene, Eocene, Oligocene, Miocene, Pliocene (from the Tertiary), and the Pleistocene and Holocene (from the Quaternary).

Mammalian Evolution

Following the extinction of dinosaurs and many other Mesozoic forms (at the beginning of the Cenozoic), there was a wide array of ecological niches open for the rapid expansion and diversification of mammals. The Cenozoic was an opportunistic time for mammals, and it is known as the Age of Mammals. Mesozoic mammals were small animals, about the size of mice, which they resembled superficially (Fig 8–9). The wide diversification of mammals in the Cenozoic saw the rise of the major lineages of all modern mammals. Indeed, mammals, along with birds, replaced reptiles as the dominant terrestrial vertebrates.

How do we account for the rapid success of the mammals? Several characteristics relating to learning and general flexibility of behavior are of prime importance.

PALEOZOIC							MESOZOIC		
Cambrian	Ordovician	Silurian	Devonian	Carbon-iferous	Permian		Triassic	Jurassic	Cretaceous
Trilobites abundant; also brachiopods, jellyfish, worms, and other invertebrates	First fishes; trilobites still abundant; graptolites and corals become plentiful; possible land plants	Jawed fishes appear; first air-breathing animals; definite land plants	Age of fish; first amphibians; first forests	First reptiles; radiation of amphibians; modern insects diversify	Reptile radiation; mammal-like reptiles	Major extinction event	Reptiles further radiate; first dinosaurs; egg-laying mammals	Great age of dinosaurs; flying and swimming dinosaurs; first toothed birds	Placental and marsupial mammals appear; first modern birds
570 m.y.a	500 m.y.a	430 m.y.a	395 m.y.a	345 m.y.a	280 m.y.a	225 m.y.a	190 m.y.a	136 m.y.a	65 m.y.a

(Major extinction event also noted at far right, after Cretaceous)

FIGURE 8–8

Time line of major events in early vertebrate evolution.

■ **Viviparous**

Giving birth to live young.

FIGURE 8–9

Mesozoic mammal. A speculative reconstruction of what a Mesozoic mammal might have looked like.

To process more information, mammals were selected for larger brains than those typically found in reptiles. In particular, the cerebrum became generally enlarged, especially the outer covering, the neocortex, which controls higher brain functions (Fig. 8–10). In some mammals, the cerebrum expanded so much that it came to comprise the majority of brain volume; moreover, the number of surface convolutions increased, creating more surface area and thus providing space for even more nerve cells (neurons). As we have already seen (in Chapter 7), this is a trend even further emphasized among the primates.

For such a large and complex organ as the mammalian brain to develop, a longer, more intense period of growth is required. Slower development can occur internally (*in utero*) as well as after birth. While internal fertilization, and especially internal development, are not unique to mammals, the latter is a major innovation among terrestrial vertebrates. Other forms (birds, most fish, and reptiles) incubate their young externally by laying eggs (i.e., they are oviparous), while mammals, with very few exceptions, give birth to live young and are thus said to be **viviparous**. Even among mammals, however, there is considerable variation among the major groups in how mature the young are at birth. As you will see, it is in mammals like ourselves, the *placental* forms, where development *in utero* goes the furthest.

Another distinctive feature of mammals is seen in the denti-

FISH BRAIN

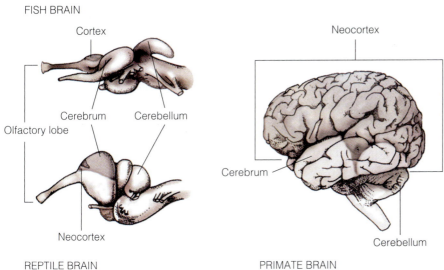

REPTILE BRAIN   PRIMATE BRAIN

FIGURE 8–10

Lateral view of the brain. The illustration shows the increase in the cerebral cortex of the brain. The cerebral cortex integrates sensory information and selects responses.

tion. While living reptiles consistently have similarly shaped teeth (called a *homodont* dentition), mammals have differently shaped teeth (Fig. 8–11). This varied pattern, termed a **heterodont** dentition, is reflected in the primitive mammalian array of dental elements, which includes 3 incisors, 1 canine, 4 premolars, and 3 molars for each quarter of the mouth. Since the upper and lower jaws are usually the same and are symmetrical for both sides, this "dental formula" is conventionally illustrated by dental quarter (see p. 113 for a more complete discussion of dental patterns as they apply to primates). Thus, with 11 teeth per quarter segment, the primitive mammalian dental complement includes a total of 44 teeth. Such a heterodont arrangement allows mammals to process a wide variety of foods. Incisors can be used for cutting, canines for grasping and piercing, and premolars and molars for crushing and grinding.

A final point regarding teeth relates to their disproportionate representation in the fossil record. As the hardest, most durable portion of a vertebrate skeleton, teeth have the greatest likelihood of becoming fossilized (i.e., mineralized). As a result, the vast majority of the available fossil data for most vertebrates, including primates, consists of teeth.

Another major adaptive complex that distinguishes contemporary mammals from reptiles is the maintenance of a constant internal body temperature. Also colloquially (and incorrectly) called warm-bloodedness, this central physiological adaptation is also seen in contemporary birds (and was also perhaps characteristic of many dinosaurs as well). In fact, many contemporary reptiles are able to approximate a constant internal body temperature through behavioral means (especially by regulating activity and exposing the body to the sun). In this sense, reptiles (along with birds and mammals) could be said to be *homeothermic*. Thus, the most important distinction in contrasting mammals (and birds) with reptiles is how the energy to maintain body temperature is produced and channeled. In reptiles, this energy is obtained directly from exposure (externally) to the sun; reptiles are thus said to be *ectothermic*. In mammals and birds, however, the energy is generated *internally* through metabolic activity (by processing food or by muscle action); mammals and birds are hence referred to as **endothermic.**

REPTILIAN (alligator): homodont

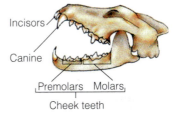

MAMMALIAN: heterodont

Incisors

Canine

Premolars   Molars
Cheek teeth

FIGURE 8–11

Reptilian and mammalian teeth.

Heterodont

Having different kinds of teeth; characteristic of mammals, whose teeth consist of incisors, canines, premolars, and molars.

Endothermic (*endo,* meaning "within" or "internal")

Able to maintain internal body temperature through the production of energy by means of metabolic processes within cells; characteristic feature of mammals, birds, and perhaps some dinosaurs.

Virtual Lab 7, section II, part B, provides a presentation of placental mammalian relationships.

Major Mammalian Groups

As briefly mentioned in Chapter 5, there are three major subgroups of living mammals: the egg-laying mammals, or monotremes (Fig. 8–12), the pouched mammals, or marsupials (Fig. 8–13), and the placental mammals. The monotremes are extremely primitive and are considered more distinct from marsupials or placentals than these latter are from each other.

The most notable distinction differentiating the marsupials from the placentals is the type of fetal development. In marsupials, the young are born extremely immature and must complete development in an external pouch. It has been suggested (Carroll, 1988) that such a reproductive strategy is more energetically costly than retaining the young for a longer period *in utero*. In fact, the latter is exactly what placental mammals have done through a more advanced placental connection (from which the group gets its popular name). But perhaps even more basic than fetal nourishment is the means to allow the mother to *tolerate* her young internally over an extended period. Marsupial young are born so quickly after conception that there is little chance for the mother's system to recognize and have an immune rejection of the fetal "foreign" tissue. But in placental mammals, such an immune response would occur were it not for the development of a specialized tissue that isolates the fetus from the mother's immune detection, thus preventing tissue rejection. Quite possibly, this innovation is the central factor in the origin and initial rapid success of placental mammals (Carroll, 1988).

In any case, with a longer gestation period, the central nervous system could develop more completely in the fetus. Moreover, after birth, the "bond of milk" between mother and young also would allow more time for complex neural structures to form. It should also be emphasized that from a *biosocial* perspective, this

FIGURE 8–12

The spiny anteater (a monotreme).

FIGURE 8–13

A wallaby with an infant in the pouch (marsupials).

dependency period not only allows for adequate physiological development, but also provides for a wider range of learning stimuli. That is, the young mammalian brain receives a vast amount of information channeled to it through observation of the mother's behavior and through play with age-mates. It is not sufficient to have evolved a brain capable of learning. Collateral evolution of mammalian social systems has ensured that young mammal brains are provided with ample learning opportunities and are thus put to good use.

Early Primate Evolution

The roots of the primate order go back to the beginnings of the placental mammal radiation circa 65 m.y.a. Thus, the earliest primates were diverging from quite early primitive placental mammals. We have seen (in Chapter 5) that strictly defining living primates using clear-cut derived features is not an easy task. The further back we go in the fossil record, the more primitive and, in many cases, the more generalized the fossil primates become. Such a situation makes classifying them all the more difficult.

As a case in point, the earliest identifiable primates were long thought to be a Paleocene group known as the plesiadapiforms (see the geological time scale in Fig. 8–6). You must remember, however, that much of our understanding, especially of early primates, is based on quite fragmentary evidence, mostly jaws and teeth. In just the last few years, much more complete remains of plesiadapiforms from Wyoming have been discovered, including a nearly complete skull and elements of the hand and wrist.

As a result of this more complete information, the plesiadapiforms have been removed from the primate order altogether. From distinctive features (shared derived characteristics) of the skull and hands, these Paleocene mammals are now thought to be closely related to the colugo (Fig. 8–14). The colugo is sometimes called a "flying lemur," a misnomer, really, as it is not a lemur, nor does it fly (it glides). This group of unusual mammals is probably closely linked to the roots of primates, but apparently was already diverged by Paleocene times.

Given these new and major reinterpretations, we are left with extremely scarce traces of the beginnings of primates. Scholars have suggested that some other recently discovered bits and pieces from North Africa *may* be those of a very small primitive primate. Until more evidence is found, and remembering the lesson of the plesiadapiforms, we will just have to wait and see.

A large array of fossil primates from the Eocene (55–34 m.y.a.) that display distinctive primate features have been identified. Indeed, primatologist Elwyn Simons (1972, p. 124) has called them "the first primates of modern aspect." These animals have been found primarily in sites in North America and Europe (which were then still connected). It is important to recall that the landmasses that connect continents, as well as the water boundaries that separate them, have obvious impact on the geographical distribution of such terrestrially bound animals as primates.

Some interesting late Eocene forms have also been found in Asia, which was joined to Europe by the end of the Eocene epoch. Looking at the whole array of Eocene primates, it is certain that they were (1) primates, (2) widely distributed, and (3) mostly extinct by the end of the Eocene. What is less certain is how any of them might be related to the living primates. Some of these forms are probably ancestors of the *prosimians*—the lemurs and lorises. Others are probably related to

Detailed presentations of fossil primates from the Paleocene, Eocene, and Oligocene are given in Virtual Lab 7, section III, parts A, B, and C. Animations of possible dispersal routes to the New World are given under "South American Oligocene Primates" in part C.

FIGURE 8–14
Colugo.

FIGURE 8–15

Location of the Fayum, an Oligocene primate site in Egypt.

Virtual Lab 7, section III, part B, "Eosimiids," provides a video of the excavations of Eocene anthropoid fossil primates from the Yuanqu Basin in China.

■ **Genus**

A group of closely related species.

Detailed discussions of fossil primates from the Fayum are found in Virtual Lab 7, section III, parts B and C. A virtual exercise on dating the Fayum primates is given in Virtual Lab 7, section I, part C under "Paleomagnetic Dating."

See screen 3 under "African Oligocene Primates" in Virtual Lab 7, section III, part C, to view a 3-D animation of the cranium of *Aegyptopithecus*.

the tarsier. New evidence of *anthropoid* origins has also recently been discovered in several sites from North Africa, the Persian Gulf, and China. These newly discovered fossils of late Eocene anthropoids have now shown that anthropoid origins were well established by 35 m.y.a.

The Oligocene (34–22.5 m.y.a.) has yielded numerous additional fossil remains of several different species of early anthropoids. Most of these forms are *Old World anthropoids,* all discovered at a single locality in Egypt, the Fayum (Fig. 8–15). In addition, from North and South America, there are a few known bits that relate only to the ancestry of New World monkeys. By the early Oligocene, continental drift had separated the New World (i.e., the Americas) from the Old World (Africa and Eurasia). Some of the earliest Fayum forms, nevertheless, *may* potentially be close to the ancestry of both Old and New World anthropoids. It has been suggested that late in the Eocene or very early in the Oligocene, the first anthropoids (primitive "monkeys") arose in Africa and later reached South America by "rafting" over the water separation on drifting chunks of vegetation. What we call "monkey," then, may have a common Old World origin, but the ancestry of New and Old World varieties remains separate after about 35 m.y.a. Our closest evolutionary affinities after this time are with other Old World anthropoids, that is, with Old World monkeys and apes.

The possible roots of anthropoid evolution are illustrated by different forms from the Fayum; one is the **genus** *Apidium.* By *genus* (*pl.,* genera) we mean a group of species that are closely related. In Chapter 2, we discussed Linnaeus' binomial system for designating different organisms (e.g., *Equus callabus* for the horse, *Pan troglodytes* for the chimp, and *Homo sapiens* for humans). The first term (always capitalized—*Equus, Pan, Homo*) is the genus. In paleontological contexts, when remains are fragmentary and usually separated by long time spans, often the best that can be achieved is to make genus-level distinctions (see p. 220 for further discussion).

Apidium, well known at the Fayum, is represented by several dozen jaws or partial dentitions and more than 100 specimens from the limb and trunk skeleton. Because of its primitive dental arrangement, some paleontologists have suggested that *Apidium* may lie near or even before the evolutionary divergence of Old and New World anthropoids. As so much fossil material of teeth and limb bones of *Apidium* has been found, some informed speculation regarding diet and locomotor behavior is possible. It is thought that this small, squirrel-sized primate ate mostly fruits and some seeds and was most likely an arboreal quadruped, adept at leaping and springing (Table 8–1).

The other genus of importance from the Fayum is *Aegyptopithecus.* This genus, also well known, is represented by several well-preserved crania and abundant jaws and teeth. The largest of the Fayum anthropoids, *Aegyptopithecus* is roughly the size of a modern howler monkey (13 to 20 pounds) (Fleagle, 1983)

TABLE 8–1	Inferred General Paleobiological Aspects of Oligocene Primates			
	Weight Range	Substratum	Locomotion	Diet
Apidium	750–1,600 g (2–3 lb)	Arboreal	Quadruped	Fruit, seeds
Aegyptopithecus	6,700 g (15 lb)	Arboreal	Quadruped	Fruit, some leaves?

After Fleagle, 1999.

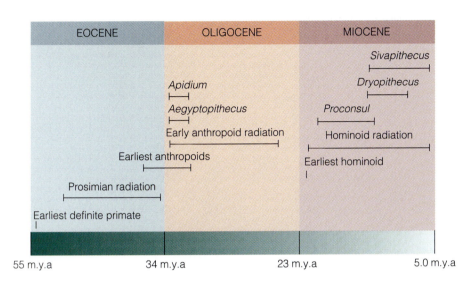

FIGURE 8–16
Major events in early primate evolution.

A phylogeny of primate evolution along with pronunciations of the names is provided under "Primate Relationships" in the glossary of Virtual Lab 7.

and is thought to have been a short-limbed, slow-moving arboreal quadruped (see Table 8–1). *Aegyptopithecus* is important because, better than any other known form, it bridges the gap between the Eocene fossils and the succeeding Miocene hominoids.

Nevertheless, *Aegyptopithecus* is a very primitive Old World anthropoid, with a small brain and long snout and not showing any derived features of either Old World monkeys or hominoids. Thus, it may be close to the ancestry of *both* major groups of living Old World anthropoids.

Found in geological beds dating to 35–33 m.y.a., *Aegyptopithecus* further suggests that the crucial evolutionary divergence of hominoids from other Old World anthropoids occurred *after* this time (Fig. 8–16).

Miocene Fossil Hominoids

During the approximately 18 million years of the Miocene (23–5 m.y.a.), a great deal of evolutionary activity took place. In Africa, Asia, and Europe, a diverse and highly successful group of hominoids emerged (Fig. 8–17). Indeed, there were many more forms of hominoids from the Miocene than are found today (now represented by the highly restricted groups of apes and one species of humans). In fact, the Miocene could be called "the golden age of hominoids." Many thousands of fossils have been found from dozens of sites scattered in East Africa, southwest Africa, southwest Asia, into western and southern Europe, and extending into southern Asia and China.

A problem arises in any attempt to simplify this complex evolutionary situation. For example, for many years paleontologists tended to think of these fossil forms as either "apelike" or "humanlike" and used modern examples as models. But as we have just noted, there are very few hominoids remaining. We should not rashly generalize from the living forms to the much more diverse fossil forms; otherwise, we obscure the evolutionary uniqueness of these animals. In addition, we should not expect all fossil forms to be directly or even particularly closely related to living varieties. Indeed, we should expect the opposite; that is, most lines vanish without descendants.

The Miocene fossil primates from the Old World are presented in Virtual Lab 7, section III, part D.

FIGURE 8–17

Miocene hominoid distribution, from fossils thus far discovered.

FIGURE 8–18

Proconsul africanus *skull (from early Miocene deposits on Rusinga Island, Kenya).*

Virtual Lab 7, section III, part D, provides 3-D animations of many of the important fossil primates from the Miocene.

Over the last three decades, the Miocene hominoid assemblage has been interpreted and reinterpreted. As more fossils are found, the evolutionary picture grows more complicated. The vast array of fossil forms has not yet been completely studied, so conclusions remain tenuous. Given this uncertainty, it is probably best, for the present, to group Miocene hominoids geographically:

1. *African forms (23–14 m.y.a.)*   Known especially from western Kenya, these include quite generalized, in many ways primitive, hominoids. The best-known genus is *Proconsul* (Fig. 8–18). In addition to the well-known East African early Miocene hominoids, a recent discovery (in 1992) in Namibia has further extended by over 1,800 miles the known range of African Miocene hominoids (Conroy et al., 1992).
2. *European forms (13–11 m.y.a.)*   Known from widely scattered localities in France, Spain, Italy, Greece, Austria, and Hungary, most of these forms are quite derived. However, this is a varied and not well understood lot. The best known of the forms are placed in the genus *Dryopithecus;* the Hungarian and Greek fossils are usually assigned to other genera.
3. *Asian forms (16–7 m.y.a.)*   The largest and most varied group from the Miocene fossil hominoid assemblage, geographically dispersed from Turkey through India/Pakistan and east to the highly prolific site Lufeng, in southern China, most of these forms are *highly* derived. The best-known genus is *Sivapithecus* (known from Turkey and Pakistan). The Lufeng material (now totaling more than 1,000 specimens) is usually placed in a separate genus from *Sivapithecus* (and is referred to as *Lufengpithecus*).

Four general points are certain concerning Miocene hominoid fossils: They are widespread geographically; they are numerous; they span a considerable portion of the Miocene, with *known* remains dated between 23 and 6 m.y.a.; and at present, they are poorly understood. However, we can reasonably draw the following conclusions:

1. These are hominoids—more closely related to the ape-human lineage than to Old World monkeys.

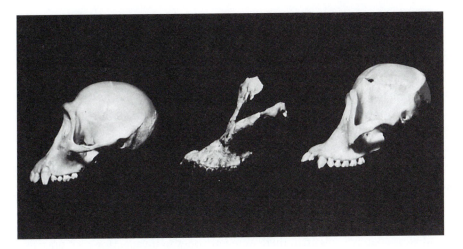

FIGURE 8–19

Comparison of Sivapithecus *cranium (center) with that of modern chimpanzee (left) and orangutan (right). The* Sivapithecus *fossil is specimen GSP 15000 from the Potwar Plateau, Pakistan, c. 8 m.y.a.*

2. Moreover, they are mostly **large-bodied hominoids**, that is, more akin to the lineages of orangutans, gorillas, chimpanzees, and humans than to smaller-bodied apes (i.e., gibbons).
3. Most of the Miocene forms thus far discovered are so derived as to be improbable ancestors of *any* living form.
4. One lineage that appears well established relates to *Sivapithecus* from Turkey and Pakistan. This form shows some highly derived facial features similar to the modern orangutan, suggesting a fairly close evolutionary link (Fig. 8–19).
5. There are no definite **hominids** yet discerned from any Miocene-dated locale. All the confirmed members of our family come from Pliocene beds and later. (The detailed story of hominid evolution will encompass much of the remainder of this text.)

Large-bodied hominoids

Those hominoids including the great apes (orangutans, chimpanzees, gorillas) and hominids, as well as all ancestral forms back to the time of divergence from small-bodied hominoids (i.e., the gibbon lineage).

Hominids

Colloquial term for members of the family Hominidae which includes all bipedal hominoids back to the divergence from African great apes.

Processes of Macroevolution

As noted earlier, evolution operates at both microevolutionary and macroevolutionary levels. We discussed evolution primarily from a microevolutionary perspective in Chapter 4; in this chapter our focus is on macroevolution. Below we discuss some macroevolutionary mechanisms that operate more on the whole species than on individuals or populations and which also take much longer than microevolutionary processes to have a noticeable impact.

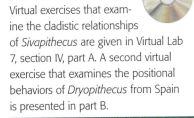

Virtual exercises that examine the cladistic relationships of *Sivapithecus* are given in Virtual Lab 7, section IV, part A. A second virtual exercise that examines the positional behaviors of *Dryopithecus* from Spain is presented in part B.

Adaptive Radiation

The potential capacity of a group of organisms to multiply is practically unlimited; its ability to increase its numbers, however, is regulated largely by the available resources of food, shelter, and space. As the size of a population increases, its food supply, shelter, and space decrease, and the environment will ultimately prove inadequate. Depleted resources engender pressures that will very likely induce some members of the population to seek an environment in which competition is considerably reduced and the opportunity for survival and reproductive success increased. This evolutionary tendency to exploit unoccupied habitats may eventually produce an abundance of diverse species.

■ **Adaptive radiation**
The relatively rapid expansion and diversification of life forms into new ecological niches.

An instructive example of the evolutionary process known as **adaptive radiation** may be seen in the divergence of the stem reptiles into the profusion of different forms of the late Paleozoic and especially those of the Mesozoic. It is a process that has taken place many times in evolutionary history when a life form has rapidly taken advantage, so to speak, of the many newly available ecological niches.

The principle of evolution illustrated by adaptive radiation is fairly simple, but important. It may be stated thus: *A species, or group of species, will diverge into as many variations as two factors allow: (1) its adaptive potential and (2) the adaptive opportunities of the available zones.*

In the case of reptiles, there was little divergence in the very early stages of evolution, when the ancestral form was little more than one among a variety of amphibian water-dwellers. In reptiles, a more efficient egg than that of amphibians (i.e., one that could incubate out of water) had developed, but although it had great adaptive potential, there were few zones to invade. However, once reptiles became fully terrestrial, there was a sudden opening of available zones—ecological niches—accessible to them.

This new kind of egg provided the primary adaptive trait that freed reptiles from their attachment to water. The adaptive zones for reptiles were not limitless; nevertheless, continents were now open to them with no serious competition from any other animal. The reptiles moved into the many different ecological niches on land (and to some extent in the air and sea), and as they adapted to these areas, they diversified into a large number of species. This spectacular radiation burst forth with such evolutionary rapidity that it may well be termed an adaptive explosion.

The rapid expansion of placental mammals at the beginning of the Cenozoic and the diversification of lemurs in Madagascar are other good examples of adaptive radiation. This latter (primate) example is particulary instructive. As we noted in Chapter 5, the contemporary array of 22 lemur species shows considerable diversity, both in size and in lifestyle (diet, degree of arboreality, etc.). Indeed, if we also include several other species that have become extinct in the last 1,000 years (following intensive human occupation of the island), the degree of lemur biodiversity was even greater—even including a ground-living form the size of a gorilla! The diversification of so many different kinds of lemur in Madagascar is explained by their adaptive radiation from a common ancestor, beginning up to 50 m.y.a. Without competition from other types of mammals, the lemurs fairly rapidly diversified and expanded into a number of varied niches in their isolated island home.

Generalized and Specialized Characteristics

Another aspect of evolution closely related to adaptive radiation involves the transition from generalized characteristics to specialized characteristics. These two terms refer to the adaptive potential of a particular trait: a trait that is adapted for many functions is said to be generalized, whereas a trait that is limited to a narrow set of ecological functions is said to be specialized.

For example, a generalized mammalian limb has five fairly flexible digits adapted for many possible functions (grasping, weight support, digging). In this respect, our hands are still quite generalized. On the other hand (or foot), there have been many structural modifications in our feet suited for the ecologically specialized function of stable weight support in an upright posture.

The terms *generalized* and *specialized* are also sometimes used when speaking of the adaptive potential of whole organisms. For example, the aye-aye of Madagascar is a highly specialized animal structurally adapted in its dentition for an ecologically narrow rodent/ woodpecker-like niche—digging holes with prominent incisors and removing insect larvae with an elongated finger.

The notion of adaptive potential is a relative judgment and can estimate only crudely the likelihood of one form evolving into one or more other forms. Adaptive radiation is a related concept, for only a generalized ancestor can provide the flexible evolutionary basis for such rapid diversification. Only a generalized species with potential for adaptation into varied ecological niches can lead to all the later diversification and specialization of forms into particular ecological niches.

An issue that we have already raised also bears on this discussion: the relationship of ancestral and derived characters. While not always the case, ancestral characters *usually* tend to be more generalized than specialized. And specialized characteristics are almost always also derived ones.

Modes of Evolutionary Change

The single most important evolutionary factor underlying macroevolutionary change is **speciation**, the process whereby new species first arise. As you will recall, we have defined a species as a group of *reproductively isolated* organisms, a characterization that follows the biological species concept (Mayr, 1970). According to this same view, the way new species are first produced involves some form of isolation. Picture a single species (baboons, for example) composed of several populations distributed over a wide geographical area. Gene exchange between populations (gene flow) will be limited if a geographical barrier such as an ocean or mountain range effectively separates these populations. This extremely important form of isolating mechanism is termed *geographical isolation*.

If one baboon population (A) is separated from another baboon population (B) by a mountain range, individual baboons of population A will not be able to mate with individuals from B (Fig. 8–20). As time passes (several generations), genetic differences will accumulate in both populations. If population size is small, we can predict that genetic drift will cause allele frequencies to change in both populations. Moreover, since drift is *random* in nature, we would not expect the effects to be the same. Consequently, the two populations will begin to diverge.

As long as gene exchange is limited, the populations can only become more genetically different with time. Moreover, further difference would be expected if

■ Speciation

The process by which new species are produced from earlier ones; the most important mechanism of macroevolutionary change.

FIGURE 8–20

A speciation model.

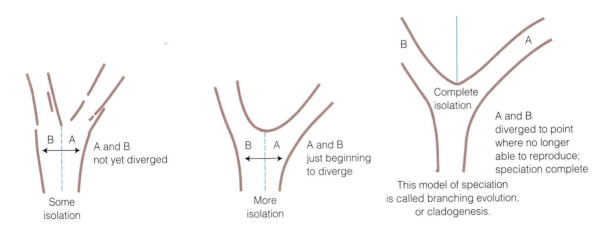

the baboon groups are occupying slightly different habitats. These additional genetic differences would be incorporated through the process of natural selection. Certain individuals in population A may be most reproductively fit in their own environment, but would show less reproductive success in the environment occupied by population B. Thus, allele frequencies will shift further, and the results, again, will be divergent in the two groups.

With the cumulative effects of genetic drift and natural selection acting over many generations, the result will be two populations that—even if they were to come back into geographical contact—could no longer interbreed. More than just geographical isolation might now apply. There may, for instance, be behavioral differences interfering with courtship—what we call *behavioral isolation*. Using our *biological* definition of species, we now would recognize two distinct species, where initially only one existed.

Until recently, the general consensus among evolutionary biologists was that microevolutionary mechanisms could be translated directly into the larger-scale macroevolutionary changes, especially speciation (also called *transspecific evolution*). A smooth gradation of change was assumed to run directly from microevolution into macroevolution. A representative view was expressed by a leading synthesist, Ernst Mayr: "The proponents of the synthetic theory maintain that all evolution is due to accumulation of small genetic changes, guided by natural selection, and that transspecific evolution is nothing but an extrapolation and magnification of events that take place within populations and species" (Mayr, 1970, p. 351).

In the last two decades, this view has been seriously challenged. Many theorists now believe that macroevolution cannot be explained solely in terms of accumulated microevolutionary changes. Consequently, these researchers are convinced that macroevolution is only partly understandable through microevolutionary models.

Gradualism vs. Punctuationalism   The traditional view of evolution has emphasized that change accumulates gradually in evolving lineages—the idea of phyletic gradualism. Accordingly, the complete fossil record of an evolving group (if it could be recovered) would display a series of forms with finely graded transitional differences between each ancestor and its descendant. The fact that such transitional forms are only rarely found is attributed to the incompleteness of the fossil record, or, as Darwin called it, "a history of the world, imperfectly kept, and written in changing dialect."

For more than a century, this perspective dominated evolutionary biology, but in the last 20 years, some biologists have called this notion into serious question. The evolutionary mechanisms operating on species over the long run are often not continuously gradual. In some cases, species persist for thousands of generations basically unchanged. Then, rather suddenly, at least in evolutionary terms, a "spurt" of speciation occurs. This uneven, nongradual process of long stasis and quick spurts has been termed **punctuated equilibrium** (Gould and Eldredge, 1977).

What the advocates of punctuated equilibrium are disputing are the tempo (rate) and mode (manner) of evolutionary change as commonly understood since Darwin's time. Rather than a slow, steady tempo, this alternate view postulates long periods of no change punctuated only occasionally by sudden bursts. From this observation, it was concluded that the mode of evolution, too, must be different from that suggested by classical Darwinists. Rather than gradual accumulation of small changes in a single lineage, advocates of punctuated equilibrium believe that an additional evolutionary mechanism is required to push the

⬛ Punctuated equilibrium
The concept that evolutionary change proceeds through long periods of stasis punctuated by rapid periods of change.

process along. They thus postulate *speciation* as the major influence in bringing about rapid evolutionary change.

How well does the paleontological record agree with the predictions of punctuated equilibrium? Indeed, considerable fossil data show long periods of stasis punctuated by occasional quite rapid changes (on the order of 10,000 to 50,000 years). The best supporting evidence for punctuated equilibrium has come from the fossilized remains of marine invertebrates. Intermediate forms are rare, not so much because the fossil record is poor, but because the speciation events and longevity of these transitional species were so short that we should not expect to find them very often.

How well, then, does the primate fossil record fit the punctuated equilibrium model? In studies of Eocene primates, rates of evolutionary change were shown to be quite gradual (Gingerich, 1985; Brown and Rose, 1987; Rose, 1991). In another study, here of Paleocene plesiadapiforms, evolutionary changes were also quite gradual. Although no longer considered primates, these forms show a gradual tempo of change in another, closely related group of mammals. The predictions consistent with punctuated equilibrium have thus far not been substantiated in those evolving lineages of primates for which we have adequate data to test the theory.

It would, however, be a fallacy to assume that evolutionary change in primates or in any other group must therefore be of a completely gradual tempo. Such is clearly not the case. In all lineages, the pace assuredly speeds up and slows down as a result of factors that influence the size and relative isolation of populations. In addition, environmental changes that influence the pace and direction of natural selection must also be considered. Nevertheless, in general accordance with the modern synthesis, microevolution and macroevolution need not be "decoupled," as some evolutionary biologists have recently suggested.

The Meaning of Genus and Species

Our discussion of fossil primates has introduced a variety of taxonomic names. We should pause at this point and ask why we use so many names like *Aegyptopithecus*, *Apidium*, and *Sivapithecus*. What do such names mean in evolutionary terms?

Our goal when applying genus, species, or other taxonomic labels to groups of organisms is to make meaningful biological statements about the variation that is present. When looking at populations of living or long-extinct animals, we are assuredly going to see variation. The situation is true of *any* sexually reproducing organism because of the factors of recombination (see Chapter 3). As a result of recombination, each individual organism is a unique combination of genetic material, and the uniqueness is usually reflected to some extent in the phenotype.

In addition to such *individual variation,* we see other kinds of systematic variation in all biological populations. *Age changes* certainly alter overall body size as well as shape in many mammals. One pertinent example for fossil hominoid studies is the great change in number, size, and shape of teeth from deciduous (milk) teeth (only 20 present) to the permanent dentition (32 present). It would be an obvious error to differentiate fossil forms solely on the basis of such age-dependent criteria. If one individual were represented just by milk teeth and another (seemingly very different) individual were represented just by adult teeth, they easily could be different-aged individuals from the *same* population.

Questions for Review

1. What are the two primary goals of organic classification?
2. What are the six major groups of vertebrates?
3. What are the two main approaches to the classification of organisms? Compare them.
4. What are the major eras of geological time over which vertebrates have evolved?
5. What primary features distinguish mammals—especially placental mammals—from other vertebrates?
6. What is meant by a homology? Contrast with analogy, using examples.
7. Why do evolutionary biologists concentrate on derived features rather than primitive ones? Give an example of each.
8. What are the seven epochs of the Cenozoic?
9. Why is it difficult to identify clearly very early primates from other primitive placental mammals?
10. How diversified and geographically widespread were hominoids in the Miocene?
11.. Humans are Old World anthropoids. What other groups are also Old World anthropoids?
12. Contrast the gradualist view of evolutionary change with a punctuationalist view. Give an example from primate evolution that supports one view or the other.
13. How are species defined? Discuss how the definition applies to both living and fossil groups.

Suggested Further Reading

Carroll, Robert L. 1988. *Vertebrate Paleontology and Evolution*. New York: Freeman.
Conroy, G. C. 1990. *Primate Evolution*. New York: Norton.
Fleagle, John. 1999. *Primate Adaptation and Evolution* 2nd ed. New York: Academic Press.
Jones, Steve, Robert Martin, and David Pilbeam (eds.). 1992. *The Cambridge Encyclopedia of Human Evolution*. New York: Cambridge University Press.

Additional Resources

Multimedia Tools

- **Virtual Laboratories for Physical Anthropology CD-ROM**
  The following concepts in this chapter are covered on the physical anthropology CD-ROM:
  taxonomy, classification (Virtual Lab 7.II)
  cladistic terminology (Virtual Lab 7.glossary)
  phenetics, cladistics (Virtual Lab7.II.A)
  vertebrates, cladistic analysis (Virtual Lab 7.II.A)

geologic time scale, era, period, epoch (Virtual Lab 7.I.B, C)

plate tectonics, animation (Virtual Lab 7.II.A)

cladistics, placental mammals (Virtual Lab 7.II.B)

fossil primates, Paleocene, Eocene, Oligocene (Virtual Lab 7.III.A, B, C)

Eocene, *Eosimias,* excavation, China (Virtual Lab 7.III.B)

Fayum, paleomagnetic dating, *Aegyptopithecus* (Virtual Lab 7.III.B, C; I.C)

Aegyptopithecus, 3-D animation (Virtual Lab 7.III.C)

primate phylogeny, pronunciations (Virtual Lab 7.glossary)

Miocene, hominoids, monkeys (Virtual Lab 7.III.D)

Miocene hominoids, 3-D animation (Virtual Lab 7.III.D)

cladistic analysis, positional behaviors (Virtual Lab 7.IV.A, B)

Wadsworth Anthropology Resource Center
http://anthropology.wadsworth.com
Visit Anthropology Online to obtain current updates in the field, surfing tips, career information and more. In addition, enrich your study
efforts with text-specific study aids arranged by chapter.

InfoTrac College Edition
http://www.infotrac-college.com/wadsworth

1. One of the most difficult problems facing evolutionary biologists is
   exactly how to define a species. Species are usually defined in terms
   of reproduction, but when looking at the span of time involved,
   other species concepts may be necessary. Read "Phylogenetics, molecular variation, and species concepts" by Jerrold I. Davis in *Bioscience,*
   available on InfoTrac College Edition. How does this article suggest
   that we define species?

2. Some of the best evidence for evolution is in the form of teeth,
   since they preserve so well. Read "Great Teeth" on InfoTrac College
   Edition. What changes have occurred in the evolution of mammalian teeth? What is unique about mammalian teeth as opposed
   to those of other animals? Can you find anything else about dental
   evolution on InfoTrac?

3. On InfoTrac College Edition, search for the keywords *evolution* and
   mammals. Choose one of the articles found by this search and read
   through it. What does this research reveal about evolution?

4. Now do the same search for the keywords *evolution* and *primates*.
   Choose a recent article about primate evolution. What does it reveal
   about primate evolution that is different from what is presented in
   the text?

5. Go to InfoTrac College Edition and read "Cladistic Analysis and
   Anthropoid Origins" by Bloch, et al., from *Science*. Draw an evolutionary tree based on the conclusions presented in this article. How
   do these conclusions differ from the traditional classifications of
   primates?

Internet Exercises
1. Visit the UC Museum of Paleontology (**http://www.ucmp.berkeley.
   edu/**). This site provides extensive online exhibits on geology, phylogeny, and mammalian evolution. Spend some time exploring the
   site. Then see what you can find to fill out the information in the
   text on mammalian evolution. When did mammals arise? When did

Introduction

In the last four chapters, we have seen how humans are classed as primates, both structurally and behaviorally, and how our evolutionary history coincides with that of other mammals and, specifically, with other primates. However, we are a unique kind of primate, and our ancestors have been adapted to a particular lifestyle for several million years. Some primitive hominoid may have begun this process more than 8 m.y.a., but there is much more definite hominid fossil evidence from Africa shortly after 5 m.y.a. The hominid nature of these remains is revealed by more than the morphological structure of teeth and bones; we know that these animals are hominids also because of the way they behaved—emphasizing once again the *biocultural* nature of human evolution. In this chapter, we will discuss the methods scientists use to explore the secrets of early hominid behavior and ecology, and we will demonstrate these methods through the example of the best-known early hominid site in the world: Olduvai Gorge in East Africa.

Definition of Hominid

If any of the Miocene hominoid fossils represent the earliest stages of hominid diversification, our definition of them as hominid must primarily be a *dental* one, for teeth and jaws are most of what we have of these Miocene forms. In fact, as we have seen in the previous chapter, *none* of the Miocene hominoid fossils discovered thus far is clearly hominid. Dentition is not the only way to describe the special attributes of our particular evolutionary radiation, and it certainly is not the most distinctive characteristic of its later stages. Modern humans and our hominid ancestors are distinguished from our closest living relatives (the great apes) by more obvious features than proportionate tooth and jaw size. For example, various scientists have pointed to such hominid characteristics as large brain size, bipedal locomotion, and toolmaking behavior as being significant (at some stage) in defining what makes a hominid a hominid (as opposed to a pongid or anything else).

It must be emphasized that not all these characteristics developed simultaneously. Quite the opposite, in fact, has been apparent in hominid evolution over the last 5 million years. This pattern, in which different physiological systems (and behavioral correlates) evolve at different rates, is called **mosaic evolution**. As we first pointed out in Chapter 1 and will discuss in more detail in Chapter 10, the most defining characteristic for all of hominid evolution is *bipedal locomotion*. Certainly for the earliest stages of the hominid lineage, skeletal evidence of bipedal locomotion is the only truly reliable indicator of hominid status. However, in later stages of hominid evolution, other features, especially those relating to neurology and behavior, do become highly significant (Fig. 9–1).

These behavioral aspects of hominid emergence—particularly toolmaking capacity—is what we wish to emphasize in this chapter. The important structural attributes of the hominid brain, teeth, and especially locomotor apparatus will be discussed in the next chapter, where we investigate early hominid anatomical adaptations in greater detail.

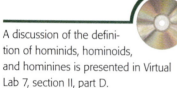

A discussion of the definition of hominids, hominoids, and hominines is presented in Virtual Lab 7, section II, part D.

■ Mosaic evolution
Rates of evolution in one functional system vary from those in other systems. For example, in hominid evolution, the dental system, locomotor system, and neurological system (especially the brain) all evolved at markedly different rates.

	Locomotion	Brain	Dentition	Toolmaking Behavior
(Modern *Homo sapiens*)	Bipedal: shortened pelvis; body size larger; legs longer; fingers and toes not as long	Greatly increased brain size—highly encephalized	Small incisors; canines further reduced; molar tooth enamel caps thick	Stone tools found after 2.5 m.y.a.; increasing trend of cultural dependency apparent in later hominids
(Early hominid)	Bipedal: shortened pelvis; some differences from later hominids, showing smaller body size and long arms relative to legs; long fingers and toes; probably capable of considerable climbing	Larger than Miocene forms, but still only moderately encephalized	Moderately large front teeth (incisors); canines somewhat reduced; molar tooth enamel caps very thick	In earliest stages unknown; no stone tool use prior to 2.5 m.y.a.; probably somewhat more oriented toward tool manufacture and use than chimpanzees
(Miocene, generalized hominoid)	Quadrupedal: long pelvis; some forms capable of considerable arm swinging, suspensory locomotion	Small compared to hominids, but large compared to other primates; a fair degree of encephalization	Large front teeth (including canines); molar teeth variable depending on species; some have thin enamel caps, others thick enamel caps	Unknown—no stone tools; probably had capabilities similar to chimpanzees

Time markers (right side): 0.5 m.y.a. — 1 m.y.a. — 2 m.y.a. — 3 m.y.a. — 4 m.y.a. — 20 m.y.a.

FIGURE 9–1

Mosaic evolution of hominid characteristics: a postulated time line.

Biocultural Evolution: The Human Capacity for Culture

When compared with other animals, the most distinctive behavioral feature of humans is our extraordinary elaboration of and dependence on culture. Certainly, other primates, and many other animals for that matter, modify their environments. As we saw in Chapter 7, chimpanzees especially are known for such behaviors as using termite sticks and sponges and even transporting rocks to crush nuts. Given such observations, it becomes tenuous to draw sharp lines between hominid toolmaking behavior and that exhibited by other animals.

Virtual Lab 11 is devoted to the archaeological record.

Another point to remember is that human culture, at least as it is defined in contemporary contexts, involves much more than toolmaking capacity. For humans, culture integrates an entire adaptive strategy involving cognitive, political, social, and economic components. The *material culture,* the tools and other items humans use, is but a small portion of this cultural complex.

Nevertheless, when examining the archaeological record of earlier hominids, what is available for study is almost exclusively certain remains of material culture, especially residues of stone tool manufacture. Thus, it is extremely difficult to learn anything about the earliest stages of hominid cultural development prior to the regular manufacture of stone tools. As you will see, this most crucial cultural development has been traced to approximately 2.5 m.y.a. Yet, hominids undoubtedly were using other kinds of tools (such as sticks) and displaying a whole array of other cultural behaviors long before this time. However, without any "hard" evidence preserved in the archaeological record, the development of these nonmaterial cultural components remains elusive.

The fundamental basis for human cultural elaboration relates directly to cognitive abilities. Again, we are not dealing with an absolute distinction, but a relative one. As you have learned, some other primates possess some of the symboling capabilities exhibited by humans. Nevertheless, modern humans display these abilities in a complexity several orders of magnitude beyond that of any other animal. Moreover, only humans are so completely dependent on symbolic communication and its cultural by-products that contemporary *Homo sapiens* could not survive without them.

When did the unique combination of cognitive, social, and material cultural adaptations become prominent in human evolution? We must be careful to recognize the manifold nature of culture and not expect it always to contain the same elements across species (as when compared to nonhuman primates) or through time (when trying to reconstruct ancient hominid behavior). Richard Potts (1993) has critiqued this overly simplistic perspective and suggests a more dynamic approach, one that incorporates many subcomponents (including aspects of behavior, cognition, and social interaction).

We know that the earliest hominids almost certainly did *not* regularly manufacture stone tools (at least, none that has been found!). The earliest members of the hominid lineage, perhaps dating back to approximately 7–5 m.y.a., could be referred to as **protohominids.** These protohominids may have carried objects such as naturally sharp stones or stone flakes, parts of carcasses, and pieces of wood. At minimum, we would expect them to have displayed these behaviors to at least the same degree as living chimpanzees.

Moreover, as you will see in the next chapter, by at least 4 m.y.a., hominids had developed one crucial advantage: They were bipedal and could therefore much more easily carry all manner of objects from place to place. Ultimately, the efficient exploitation of resources widely distributed in time and space would most likely have led to using "central" spots where key components, especially stone objects, were cached (Potts, 1991).

What is certain is that over a period of several million years, during the formative stages of hominid emergence, numerous components interacted, but not all developed simultaneously. As cognitive abilities developed, more efficient means of communication and learning resulted. Largely as a result of such neural reorganization, more elaborate tools and social relationships also emerged. These, in turn, selected for greater intelligence, which in turn selected for further neural elaboration. Quite clearly, then, these mutual dynamics are at the very heart of what we call hominid *biocultural* evolution.

■ Protohominids
The earliest members of the hominid lineage, as yet basically unrepresented in the fossil record; thus, their structure and behavior are reconstructed hypothetically.

The Strategy of Paleoanthropology

To understand human evolution adequately, we obviously need a broad base of information. The task of recovering and interpreting all the clues left by early hominids is the work of paleoanthropologists. Paleoanthropology is defined as the study of ancient humans. As such, it is a diverse *multidisciplinary* pursuit seeking to reconstruct every possible bit of information concerning the dating, structure, behavior, and ecology of our hominid ancestors. In just the last few years, the study of early humans has marshaled the specialized skills of many different kinds of scientists. Included in this growing and exciting adventure are geologists, archaeologists, physical anthropologists, and **paleoecologists** (Table 9–1).

Geologists, usually working with anthropologists, do the initial surveys to locate potential early hominid sites. Many sophisticated techniques can aid in this search, including aerial and satellite photography. Paleontologists are usually involved in this early survey work, for they can help find fossil beds containing faunal remains. Where conditions are favorable for the preservation of bone from such species as pigs and elephants, conditions may also be favorable for the preservation of hominid remains. In addition, paleontologists can (through comparison with known faunal sequences) give fairly quick estimates of the approximate age of fossil sites without having to wait for the more expensive and time-consuming analyses. In this way, fossil beds of appropriate geological ages (i.e., where hominid finds are most likely) can be isolated.

Once potential early hominid localities have been identified, much more extensive surveying begins. At this point, at least for some sites postdating 2.5 m.y.a., archaeologists take over in the search for hominid "traces." We do not necessarily have to find remains of early hominids themselves to know that they consistently occupied a particular area. Preserved material clues, or **artifacts**, also inform us directly and unambiguously about early hominid activities. Modifying rocks according to a consistent plan or simply carrying them around from one place to another (over fairly long distances) is characteristic of no other animal but a hominid. Therefore, when we see such behavioral evidence at a site, we know absolutely that hominids were present.

Because organic materials such as sticks and bones do not usually preserve in the archaeological record, we have no solid evidence of the earliest stages of hominid cultural modifications. On the other hand, our ancestors at some point showed a veritable fascination with stones, for these provided not only easily

A detailed discussion of how the fossil record is generated is given in Virtual Lab 7, section I, part D.

Paleoecologists
(*paleo*, meaning "old," and *ecology*, meaning "environmental setting") Scientists who study ancient environments.

Artifacts
Material traces of hominid behavior. Very old ones are usually made of stone or, occasionally, bone.

TABLE 9–1 Subdisciplines of Paleoanthropology

Physical Sciences	Biological Sciences	Social Sciences
Geology	Physical anthropology	Archaeology
Stratigraphy	Ecology	Ethnoarchaeology
Petrology	Paleontology (fossil	Cultural anthropology
(rocks, minerals)	animals)	Ethnography
Pedology (soils)	Palynology (fossil pollen)	Psychology
Geomorphology	Primatology	
Geophysics		
Chemistry		
Taphonomy		

accessible and transportable materials (to use as convenient projectiles to throw or to hold down objects, such as skins and windbreaks) but also the most durable and sharpest cutting edges available at that time. Luckily for us, stone is almost indestructible, and some early hominid sites are strewn with thousands of stone artifacts. The earliest artifact sites now documented are from the Gona and Bouri areas in northeastern Ethiopia, dating to 2.5 m.y.a. (Semaw et al., 1997; de Heinzelin et al., 1999). Other contenders for the "earliest" stone assemblage come from the adjacent Hadar and Middle Awash areas, immediately to the south in Ethiopia, dated 2.5–2.0 m.y.a.

If an area is clearly demonstrated to be a hominid site, much more concentrated research will then begin. We should point out that a more mundane but very significant aspect of paleoanthropology not shown in Table 9–1 is the financial one. Just the initial survey work in usually remote areas costs many thousands of dollars, and mounting a concentrated research project costs several hundred thousand dollars. Therefore, for such work to go on, massive financial support is required from government agencies and private donations. A significant amount of a paleoanthropologist's efforts and time is necessarily devoted to writing grant proposals or speaking on the lecture circuit to raise the required funds for this work.

Once the financial hurdle has been cleared, a coordinated research project can commence. Usually headed by an archaeologist or physical anthropologist, the field crew will continue to survey and map the target area in great detail. In addition, field crew members will begin to search carefully for bones and artifacts eroding out of the soil, take pollen and soil samples for ecological analysis, and carefully recover rock samples for use in various dating techniques. If, in this early stage of exploration, members of the field crew find a fossil hominid, they will feel very lucky indeed. The international press usually considers human fossils the most exciting kind of discovery, a situation that produces wide publicity, often ensuring future financial support. More likely, the crew will accumulate much information on geological setting, ecological data (particularly faunal remains), and, with some luck, archaeological traces (hominid artifacts).

After long and arduous research in the field, even more time-consuming and detailed analysis is required back in the laboratory. Archaeologists must clean, sort, label, and identify all artifacts, and paleontologists must do the same for all faunal remains. Knowing the kinds of animals represented, whether forest browsers, woodland species, or open-country forms, will greatly help in reconstructing the local *paleoecological* settings in which early hominids lived. In addition, analysis of pollen remains by a palynologist will further aid in a detailed environmental reconstruction. All these paleoecological analyses can assist in reconstructing the diet of early humans. Also, the **taphonomy** of the site must be worked out in order to understand its depositional history—that is, whether the site is of a *primary* or *secondary* **context**.

In the concluding stages of interpretation, the paleoanthropologist will draw together the following essentials:

1. *Dating*
     geological
     paleontological
     geophysical
2. *Paleoecology*
     paleontology
     palynology
     geomorphology
     taphonomy

▌ Taphonomy

(*taphos,* meaning "dead") The study of how bones and other materials came to be buried in the earth and preserved as fossils. A taphonomist studies the processes of sedimentation, the action of streams, preservation properties of bone, and carnivore disturbance factors.

▌ Context

The environmental setting where an archaeological trace is found. *Primary* context is the setting in which the archaeological trace was originally deposited. A *secondary* context is one to which it has been moved (e.g., by the action of a stream).

3. *Archaeological traces of behavior*
4. *Anatomical evidence from hominid remains*

From all this information, scientists will try to "flesh out" the kind of animal that may have been our direct ancestor, or at least a very close relative. In this final analysis, still further comparative scientific information may be needed. Primatologists may assist here by showing the detailed relationships between the anatomical structure and behavior of humans and that of contemporary non-human primates (see Chapters 6 through 8). Cultural anthropologists may contribute ethnographic information concerning the varied nature of human behavior, particularly ecological adaptations of those contemporary hunter-gatherer groups exploiting roughly similar environmental settings as those reconstructed for a hominid site.

The end result of years of research by dozens of scientists will (we hope) produce a more complete and accurate understanding of human evolution—how we came to be the way we are. Both biological and cultural aspects of our ancestors pertain to this investigation, each process developing in relation to the other.

Paleoanthropology in Action—Olduvai Gorge

Several paleoanthropological projects of the scope just discussed have recently been pursued in diverse places in the Old World (Fig. 9–2). The most important of these include David Pilbeam's work in the Miocene beds of the Potwar Plateau of western Pakistan (circa 13–7 m.y.a.); Don Johanson's projects at Hadar and other areas of Ethiopia (circa 3.7–1.6 m.y.a.), sponsored by the Institute of Human Origins; a recently intensified effort just south of Hadar in Ethiopia in an area called the Middle Awash (circa 5–4 m.y.a.), led by Berkeley paleoanthropologists Tim White and Desmond Clark; a now completed research project along the Omo River of southern Ethiopia (circa 4–1.5 m.y.a.), directed by F. Clark Howell; Richard and Meave Leakey's fantastically successful research near Lake Turkana (formerly Lake Rudolf) in northern Kenya (circa 4.2–1.5 m.y.a.); Mary Leakey's famous investigations at Olduvai Gorge in northern Tanzania (circa 1.85 m.y.a. to present); and finally the recent exploration by Phillip Tobias of hominid localities in southern Africa (the most important being Swartkrans, discussed in Chapter 10).

Of all these localities, the one that has yielded the finest quality and greatest abundance of paleoanthropological information concerning the behavior of early hominids has been Olduvai Gorge. First "discovered" in the early twentieth century by a German butterfly collector, Olduvai was soon scientifically surveyed and its wealth of paleontological evidence recognized. In 1931, Louis Leakey made his first trip to Olduvai Gorge and almost immediately realized its significance for studying early humans. From 1935, when she first worked there, until she retired in 1984, Mary Leakey directed the archaeological excavations at Olduvai.

Located in the Serengeti Plain of northern Tanzania, Olduvai is a steep-sided valley resembling a miniature version of the Grand Canyon. A deep ravine cut into an almost mile-high grassland plateau of East Africa, Olduvai extends more than 25 miles in total length. Climatically, the semiarid pattern of present-day Olduvai is believed to be similar to what it has been for the last 2 million years. The surrounding countryside is a grassland savanna broken occasionally by scrub bushes and acacia trees. It is noteworthy that this environment presently (as well as in the past)

FIGURE 9–2

Major paleoanthropological projects.

supports a vast number of mammals (such as zebra, wildebeest, and gazelle), representing an enormous supply of "meat on the hoof."

Geographically, Olduvai is located on the eastern branch of the Great Rift Valley of Africa. The geological processes associated with the formation of the Rift Valley make Olduvai (and other East African sites) extremely important to paleoanthropological investigation. Three results of geological rifting are most significant:

1. Faulting, or earth movement, exposes geological beds near the surface that are normally hidden by hundreds of feet of accumulated overburden.
2. Active volcanic processes cause rapid sedimentation, which often yields excellent preservation of bone and artifacts that normally would be scattered by carnivore activity and erosion forces.
3. Volcanic activity provides a wealth of radiometrically datable material.

As a result, Olduvai is the site of superb preservation of ancient hominids, portions of their environment, and their behavioral patterns in datable contexts, all of which are readily accessible.

The greatest contribution Olduvai has made to paleoanthropological research is the establishment of an extremely well documented and correlated *sequence* of geological, paleontological, archaeological, and hominid remains over the last 2 million years. At the very foundation of all paleoanthropological research is a well-established geological context. At Olduvai, the geological and paleogeographical situation is known in minute detail. Olduvai is today a geologist's delight, containing sediments in some places 350 feet thick, accumulated from lava flows (basalts), tuffs (windblown or waterborne fine deposits from nearby volcanoes), sandstones, claystones, and limestone conglomerates, all neatly stratified (Fig. 9–3). A hominid site can therefore be accurately dated relative to other sites in the Olduvai Gorge by cross-correlating known marker beds. At the most general geological level, the stratigraphic sequence at Olduvai is broken down into four major beds (Beds I–IV).

Paleontological evidence of fossilized animal bones also has come from Olduvai in great abundance. More than 150 species of extinct animals have been recognized, including fish, turtles, crocodiles, pigs, giraffes, horses, and many birds, rodents, and antelopes. Careful analysis of such remains has yielded voluminous information concerning the ecological conditions of early human habitats. In addition, the precise analysis of bones directly associated with artifacts can sometimes tell us about the diets and bone-processing techniques of early hominids. (There are some reservations, however; see Issue, pp. 253–254.)

The archaeological sequence is also well documented for the last 2 million years. Beginning at the ear-

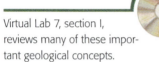

Virtual Lab 7, section I, reviews many of these important geological concepts.

FIGURE 9–3

View of the main gorge at Olduvai. Note the clear sequence of geological beds. The discontinuity to the right is a major fault line.

Mary Leakey (1913–1996)

Mary Leakey, one of the leading prehistorians of this century, spent most of the early part of her professional life living in the shadow of her famous husband, Louis Leakey. But to a considerable degree, Louis' fame is directly attributable to Mary. Justly known for his extensive fieldwork in Miocene sites along the shores of Lake Victoria in Kenya, Louis Leakey is quite often associated with important hominoid discoveries. However, it was Mary who, in 1948, found the best-preserved Proconsul skull ever discovered.

The names Louis Leakey and Olduvai Gorge are almost synonymous, but here, too, it was Mary who made the most significant single discovery—the "Zinj" skull in 1959. Mary had always been the supervisor of archaeological work at Olduvai while Louis was busily engaged in traveling, lecturing, or tending to the National Museums in Nairobi.

Mary Leakey did not come upon her archaeological career by chance. A direct descendant of John Frere (who, because of his discoveries in 1797, is called the father of Paleolithic archaeology), Mary always had a compelling interest in prehistory. Her talent in illustrating stone tools provided her entry into African prehistory and was the reason for her introduction to Louis in 1933. Throughout her career, she did all the tool illustrations for her publications, and she set an extremely high standard of excellence for all would-be illustrators of Paleolithic implements.

A committed, hard-driving woman of almost inexhaustible energy, Mary spent most of each year at Olduvai. Busily engaged seven days a week, she supervised ongoing excavations, as well as working on the monumental publications detailing the fieldwork already done.

Following her retirement from active fieldwork, Mary continued her research and writing at her home in Nairobi. As one of the great pioneers of modern archaeological research, her death in 1996 left a void for friends, colleagues, and admirers worldwide.

Photo courtesy of the L.S.B. Leakey Foundation

liest hominid site (circa 1.85 m.y.a.), there is already a well-developed stone tool kit, including chopping tools and some small flake tools (Leakey; 1971). Such a tool industry is called *Oldowan* (after Olduvai), and it continues into later beds with some small modifications, where it is called *Developed Oldowan*.

Finally, partial remains of several fossilized hominids have been found at Olduvai, ranging in time from the earliest occupation levels to fairly recent *Homo sapiens*. Of the more than 40 individuals represented, many are quite fragmentary, but a few are excellently preserved. While the center of hominid discoveries has now shifted to other areas of East Africa, it was the initial discovery by Mary Leakey of the *Zinjanthropus* skull at Olduvai in July 1959 that focused the world's attention on this remarkably rich area (Fig. 9–4). "Zinj" provides an excellent

A 3-D animation of this cranium is given in Virtual Lab 8, section I, part E.

FIGURE 9–4

Zinjanthropus skull, discovered by Mary Leakey at Olduvai Gorge in 1959. The skull and reconstructed jaw depicted here are casts at the National Museums of Kenya, Nairobi. As we will see in Chapter 10, this fossil is now included as part of the genus Australopithecus.

Virtual Lab 7, section I, part C, provides a discussion of geological dating methods including radioisotopic dating.

▊ **Chronometric dating**

(*chrono,* meaning "time," and *metric,* meaning "measure") A dating technique that gives an estimate in actual numbers of years.

▊ **Stratigraphy**

Study of the sequential layering of deposits.

You may wish to review the geological time scale in Virtual Lab 7, section I, part B.

example of how financial ramifications directly result from hominid fossil discoveries. Prior to 1959, the Leakeys had worked sporadically at Olduvai on a financial shoestring, making marvelous paleontological and archaeological discoveries. Yet, there was little support available for much needed large-scale excavations. However, following the discovery of "Zinj," the National Geographic Society funded the Leakeys' research, and within a year, more than twice as much dirt had been excavated than during the previous 30 years!

Dating Methods

One of the essentials of paleoanthropology is placing sites and fossils into a chronological framework. In other words, we want to know how old they are. How, then, do we date sites—or, more precisely, the geological strata in which sites are found? The question is both reasonable and important, so let us examine the dating techniques used by paleontologists, geologists, paleoanthropologists, and archaeologists.

Scientists use two kinds of dating for this purpose: relative and **chronometric** (also known as *absolute dating*). Relative dating methods tell us that something is older or younger than something else, but not by how much. If, for example, a cranium is found at a depth of 50 feet and another cranium at 70 feet at the same site, we usually assume that the specimen discovered at 70 feet is older. We may not know the date (in years) of either one, but we would know that one is older (or younger) than the other. Although this may not satisfy our curiosity about the actual number of years involved, it would give some idea of the evolutionary changes in cranial morphology (structure), especially if a number of crania at different levels are found and compared.

This method of relative dating is based on **stratigraphy** and was one of the first techniques to be used by scholars working with the vast period of geological time. Stratigraphy, in turn, is based on the law of superposition, which states that a lower stratum (layer) is older than a higher stratum. Given the fact that much of the earth's crust has been laid down by layer after layer of sedimentary rock, much like the layers of a cake, stratigraphy has been a valuable aid in reconstructing the history of the earth and the life upon it.

Stratigraphic dating does, however, have a number of problems. Earth disturbances, such as volcanic activity, river activity, and mountain building, may shift strata and the objects within them, and the chronology of the material may be difficult or even impossible to reconstruct. Furthermore, the time period of a particular stratum—that is, the length of time it took to accumulate—is not possible to determine with much accuracy.

Another method of relative dating is *fluorine analysis,* which applies only to bones (Oakley, 1963). Bones in the earth are exposed to the seepage of groundwater that usually contains fluorine. The longer a bone lies in the earth, the more fluorine it will incorporate during the fossilization process. Therefore, bones deposited at the same time in the same location should contain the same amount of fluorine. The use of this technique by Professor Oakley of the British Museum in the early 1950s exposed the Piltdown (England) hoax by demonstrating that a human skull was considerably older than the jaw (ostensibly also human) found with it (Weiner, 1955). A discrepancy in fluorine content led Oakley and others to a closer examination of the bones, and they found that the jaw was not that of a hominid at all but of a young adult orangutan!

Discovery of *Zinjanthropus,* July 17, 1959

That morning I woke with a headache and a slight fever. Reluctantly I agreed to spend the day in camp.

With one of us out of commission, it was even more vital for the other to continue the work, for our precious seven-week season was running out. So Mary departed for the diggings with Sally and Toots [two of their dalmatians] in the Land-Rover, and I settled back to a restless day off.

Some time later—perhaps I dozed off—I heard the Land-Rover coming up fast to camp. I had a momentary vision of Mary stung by one of our hundreds of resident scorpions or bitten by a snake that had slipped past the dogs.

The Land-Rover rattled to a stop, and I heard Mary's voice calling over and over: "I've got him! I've got him! I've got him!"

Still groggy from the headache, I couldn't make her out.

"Got what? Are you hurt?" I asked.

"Him, the man! Our man," Mary said. "The one we've been looking for (for 23 years). Come quick, I've found his teeth!"

Magically, the headache departed. I somehow fumbled into my work clothes while Mary waited.

As we bounced down the trail in the car, she described the dramatic moment of discovery. She had been searching the slope where I had found the first Oldowan tools in 1931, when suddenly her eye caught a piece of bone lodged in a rock slide. Instantly, she recognized it as part of a skull—almost certainly not that of an animal.

Her glance wandered higher, and there in the rock were two immense teeth, side by side. This time there was no question: They were undeniably human. Carefully, she marked the spot with a cairn of stones, rushed to the Land-Rover, and sped back to camp with the news.

The gorge trail ended half a mile from the site, and we left the car at a dead run. Mary led the way to the cairn, and we knelt to examine the treasure.

I saw at once that she was right. The teeth were premolars, and they had belonged to a human. I was sure they were larger than anything similar ever found, nearly twice the width of modern man's.

I turned to look at Mary, and we almost cried with sheer joy, each seized by that terrific emotion that comes rarely in life. After all our hoping and hardship and sacrifice, at last we had reached our goal—we had discovered the world's earliest known human.

Source

"Finding the World's Earliest Man," by L. S. B. Leakey, *National Geographic,* 118 (September 1960);431. Reprinted with permission of the publisher.

Unfortunately, fluorine is useful only with bones found at the same location. Because the amount of fluorine in groundwater is based on local conditions, it varies from place to place. Also, some groundwater may not contain any fluorine. For these reasons, comparing bones from different localities by fluorine analysis is impossible.

In both stratigraphy and fluorine analysis, the actual age of the rock stratum and the objects in it is impossible to calculate. To determine the age in years, scientists have developed a variety of chronometric techniques based on the phenomenon of radioactive decay. The theory is quite simple: Certain radioactive isotopes of elements are unstable, disintegrate, and form an isotopic variation of another element. Since the rate of disintegration follows a definite mathematical pattern, the radioactive material forms an accurate geological time clock. By measuring the amount of disintegration in a particular sample, scientists can calculate the number of years it took for that amount of decay to accumulate.

Chronometric techniques have been used for dating the immense age of the earth as well as artifacts less than 1,000 years old. Several techniques have been employed for a number of years and are now quite well known.

Uranium-238 (^{238}U) decays with a *half-life* of 4.5 billion years to form lead. That is, one-half of the original amount of ^{238}U is lost in 4.5 billion years and through various processes becomes lead. Therefore, if a sample of rock containing this element is analyzed and one-half of the uranium has been converted to lead, the age of that rock is 4.5 billion years. In another 4.5 billion years, half the remaining ^{238}U will have decayed. The isotope ^{238}U has proved a useful tool in dating the age of the formation of the earth.

Another chronometric technique involves potassium-40 (^{40}K), which has a half-life of 1.25 billion years and produces argon-40 (^{40}Ar). Known as the K/Ar or potassium-argon method, this procedure has been extensively used by paleoan-thropologists in dating materials in the 1- to 5-million-year range, especially in East Africa. In addition, a variant of this technique, the ^{40}Ar/^{39}Ar method, has recently been used to date a number of hominid localities. The ^{40}Ar/^{39}Ar method allows analysis of smaller samples (even single crystals), reduces experimental error, and is more precise than standard K/Ar dating. Consequently, it can be used to date a wide chronological range—indeed, the entire hominid record, even up to modern times. Recent applications have provided excellent dates for several early hominid sites in East Africa (discussed in Chapter 10) as well as somewhat later sites in Java (discussed in Chapter 11). In fact, the technique was recently used to date the famous Mt. Vesuvius eruption of A.D. 79 (which destroyed the city of Pompeii). Remarkably, the midrange date obtained by the ^{40}Ar/^{39}Ar tech-nique was A.D. 73, just six years from the known date (Deino et al., 1998)! Organic material, such as bone, cannot be measured by these techniques, but the rock matrix in which the bone is found can be. K/Ar was used to provide a minimum date for the deposit containing the *Zinjanthropus* cranium by dating a volcanic layer above the fossil.

Rocks that provide the best samples for K/Ar and ^{40}Ar/^{39}Ar are those heated to an extremely high temperature, such as that generated by volcanic activity. When the rock is in a molten state, argon, a gas, is driven off. As the rock cools and solid-ifies, potassium-40 continues to break down to argon, but now the gas is physi-cally trapped in the cooled rock. To obtain the date of the rock, it is reheated and the escaping gas measured.

A well-known radiometric method popular with archaeologists makes use of carbon-14 (^{14}C), with a half-life of 5,730 years. Carbon-14 has been used to date material from less than 1,000 years to as old as 75,000 years, although the proba-bility of error rises rapidly after 40,000 years. Since this technique applies to the latter stages of hominid evolution, its applications relate to material discussed in Chapters 12 and 13. In addition, other dating techniques (thermoluminescence and electron spin resonance) that are used for calibrating these latter time periods will be discussed in Chapter 12.

We should stress that none of these methods is precise, and each is beset with problems that must be carefully considered during laboratory measurement and the collection of material to be analyzed. Because the methods are imprecise, approximate dates are given as probability statements with a plus or minus factor. For example, a date given as 1.75 ± 0.2 million years should be read as having a 67 percent chance that the actual date lies somewhere between 1.55 and 1.95 mil-lion years (see Box 9–1).

There are, then, two ways in which the question of age may be answered. We can say that a particular fossil is *x* number of years old, a date determined usually either by K/Ar or ^{14}C chronometric dating techniques. Or we can say that fossil X lived before or after fossil Y, a relative dating technique.

BOX 9–1

Chronometric Dating Estimates

Chronometric dates are usually determined after several geological samples are tested. The dates that result from such testing are combined and expressed statistically. For example, say that five different samples are used to give the K/Ar date 1.75 ± 0.2 m.y. for a particular geological bed. The individual results from each of the five samples are totaled together to give an average date (here, 1.75 m.y.), and also the standard deviation is calculated (here, 0.20 m.y.; that is, 200,000 years). The dating estimate is then reported as the mean plus or minus (±) one standard deviation. For those of you who have taken statistics, you realize that (assuming a normal distribution) 67 percent of a distribution of dates is included within 1 standard deviation (±) of the mean. Thus, the chronometric results, as shown in the reported range, is simply a probability statement that 67 percent of the dates from all the samples tested fell within the range of dates from 1.55 to 1.95 m.y.a. You should carefully read chronometric dates and study the reported ranges. The smaller the range, probably the more samples that were analyzed. Smaller ranges mean more precise estimates; better laboratory controls will also increase precision.

Application of Dating Methods: Examples from Olduvai

Olduvai has been a rich proving ground for materials datable by numerous techniques, and as a result, it has some of the best-documented chronology for any hominid site in the Lower or Middle Pleistocene.

The potassium-argon (K/Ar) method is an extremely valuable tool for dating early hominid sites and has been widely used in areas containing suitable volcanic deposits (mainly in East Africa). At Olduvai, K/Ar has given several reliable dates of the underlying basalt and several tuffs in Bed I, including the one associated with the "Zinj" find (now dated at 1.79 ± 0.03 m.y.a.). When dating relatively recent samples (from the perspective of a half-life of 1.25 billion years for K/Ar, *all* paleoanthropological material is relatively recent), the amount of radiogenic argon (that argon produced by disintegration of a potassium isotope) is going to be exceedingly small. Experimental errors in measurement can therefore occur as well as the thorny problem of distinguishing the atmospheric argon normally clinging to the outside of the sample from the radiogenic argon. In addition, the initial sample may have been contaminated or argon leakage may have occurred while it lay buried.

Due to the potential sources of error, K/Ar dating must be cross-checked using other independent methods. Once again, the sediments at Olduvai provide some of the best examples of the use of many of these other dating techniques.

Fission-track dating is one of the most important techniques for cross-checking K/Ar determinations. The key to fission-track dating is that uranium-238 (^{238}U) decays regularly by spontaneous fission. By counting the proportion of uranium atoms that have fissioned (shown as microscopic tracks caused by explosive fission of ^{238}U nuclei), we can ascertain the age of a mineral or natural glass sample. One of the earliest applications of this technique was on volcanic pumice from Olduvai, giving a date of 2.30 (±0.28 m.y.a.)—in good accord with K/Ar dates. Fission-track dating has also been used to date baked earth and pottery from contexts as recently as 5,000 years ago from a site in Iran (Wagner, 1996).

Virtual Lab 7, section I, part C, provides a discussion of paleomagnetic dating and an interactive exercise.

■ **Paleomagnetism**
Dating method based on the shifting magnetic pole.

Another important means of cross-checking dates is called **paleomagnetism.** This technique is based on the constantly shifting nature of the earth's magnetic pole. Of course, the earth's magnetic pole is now oriented in a northerly direction, but this has not always been so. In fact, the orientation and intensity of the geomagnetic field have undergone numerous documented changes in the last few million years. From our present point of view, we call a northern orientation "normal" and a southern one "reversed." Major epochs (also called "*chrons*") of recent geomagnetic time are:

0.7 m.y.a.–present	Normal
2.6–0.7 m.y.a.	Reversed
3.4–2.6 m.y.a.	Normal
?–3.4 m.y.a.	Reversed

Paleomagnetic dating is accomplished by carefully taking samples of sediments that contain magnetically charged particles. Since these particles maintain the magnetic orientation they had when they were consolidated into rock (many thousands or millions of years ago), we have a kind of "fossil compass." Then the paleomagnetic *sequence* is compared against the K/Ar dates to check if they agree. Some complications may arise, for during an epoch, a relatively long period of time can occur when the geomagnetic orientation is the opposite of what is expected. For example, during the reversed epoch from 2.6 to 0.7 m.y.a. (the Matuyama epoch), there was an *event* lasting about 210,000 years when orientations were normal. (Because this phenomenon was first conclusively demonstrated at Olduvai, it is appropriately called the *Olduvai event.*) However, once these oscillations in the geomagnetic pole are worked out, the sequence of paleomagnetic orientations can provide a valuable cross-check for K/Ar and fission-track age determinations.

A final dating technique employed in the Lower Pleistocene beds at Olduvai and other African sites is based on the regular evolutionary changes in well-known groups of mammals. This technique, called *faunal correlation* or **biostratigraphy**, provides yet another means of cross-checking the other methods. Animals that have been widely used in biostratigraphic analysis in East and South Africa are fossil pigs (suids), elephants (proboscids), antelopes (bovids), rodents, and carnivores. From areas where dates are known (by K/Ar, for instance), approximate ages can be extrapolated to other lesser-known areas by noting which genera and species are present.

All these methods—potassium-argon, fission-track, paleomagnetism, and biostratigraphy—have been used in dating sites at Olduvai. So many different dating techniques are necessary because no single one is perfectly reliable by itself. Sampling error, contamination, and experimental error can all introduce ambiguities into our so-called "absolute" dates. However, the sources of error are different for each technique; therefore, cross-checking among several independent methods is the most reliable way of authenticating the chronology for early hominid sites.

■ **Biostratigraphy**
Dating method based on evolutionary changes within an evolving lineage.

An interactive exercise in faunal correlation is presented in Virtual Lab 7, section I, part C.

Excavations at Olduvai

Because the vertical cut of the Olduvai Gorge provides a ready cross section of 2 million years of earth history, sites can be excavated by digging "straight in" rather than first having to remove tons of overlying dirt (Fig. 9–5). In fact, sites are usually discovered by merely walking the exposures and observing what bones, stones, and so forth, are eroding out.

Several dozen hominid sites (at a minimum, they are bone and tool scatters) have been surveyed at Olduvai, and Mary Leakey extensively excavated close to 20 of these. An incredible amount of paleoanthropological information has come from these excavated areas, data that can be generally grouped into three broad categories of site types, depending on implied function:

1. *"Butchering" localities,* areas containing one or only a few individuals of a single species of large mammal associated with a scatter of archaeological traces. Two "butchering" sites, one containing an elephant and another containing a *Deinotherium* (a large extinct relative of the elephant), have been found at levels approximately 1.7 m.y.a. Both sites contain only a single animal, and it is impossible to ascertain whether the hominids actually killed these animals or exploited them (either for meat or, perhaps, to extract marrow) after they were already dead. A third butchering locality dated at approximately 1.2 m.y.a. shows much more consistent and efficient exploitation of large mammals by this time. Remains of 24 *Pelorovis* individuals (a giant extinct relative of the buffalo, with horn spans more than 10 feet across!) have been found here, and Louis Leakey suggested they were driven into a swamp by a band of hominids and then systematically slaughtered (Leakey, 1971). (*Note:* This is an interpretation that is no longer widely accepted.)

2. *Quarry localities,* areas where early hominids extracted their stone resources and initially fashioned their tools. At such sites, thousands of small stone fragments of only one type of rock are found, usually associated with no or very little bone refuse. At Olduvai, a 1.6- to 1.7-million-year-old area was apparently a chert (a rock resembling flint) factory site, where hominids came repeatedly to quarry this material.

3. *Multipurpose localities* (also called "campsites"), general-purpose areas where hominids possibly ate, slept, and put the finishing touches on their tools. The accumulation of living debris, including broken bones of many animals of several different species and many broken stones (some complete tools, some waste flakes), is a basic human pattern. As Glynn Isaac noted:

> The fact that discarded artifacts tend to be concentrated in restricted areas is itself highly suggestive. It seems likely that such patches of material reflect the organization of movement around a camp or home base, with recurrent dispersal and reuniting of the group at the chosen locality. Among living primates this pattern in its full expression is distinctive of man. The coincidence of bone and food refuse with the artifacts strongly implies that meat was carried back—presumably for sharing. (Isaac, 1976, pp. 27–28)

(See Issue, pp. 253–254 for a different interpretation.)

FIGURE 9–5

Excavations in progress at Olduvai. This site, more than 1 million years old, was located when a hominid ulna (arm bone) was found eroding out of the side of the gorge.

Virtual Lab 11, section III, part C, provides a discussion of the factors that influence the development of different archaeological localities.

Microliths
(*micro,* meaning "small," and *lith,* meaning "stone") Small stone tools usually produced from narrow blades punched from a core; found especially in Africa during the latter part of the Pleistocene.

Pressure flaking
A method of removing flakes from a core by pressing a pointed implement (e.g., bone or antler) against the stone.

FIGURE 9–9
Pressure flaking.

Microwear
Polishes, striations, and other diagnostic microscopic changes on the edges of stone tools.

Phytoliths
(*phyto,* meaning "hidden," and *lith,* meaning "stone") Microscopic silica structures formed in the cells of many plants, particularly grasses.

The manufacture of stone tools is depicted in Virtual Lab 11, section IV, with animation and video clips.

Virtual Lab 11, section IV, part C, discusses many of these aspects of bone alteration.

as the delicate **microliths** found in the uppermost beds at Olduvai (circa 17,000 y.a.), the superb Solutrean blades from Europe (circa 20,000 y.a.), and the expertly crafted Folsom projectile points from the New World (circa 10,000 y.a.) all require a mastery of stone matched by few knappers today.

Reproducing implements such as those mentioned above requires removal of extremely thin flakes, possible only through **pressure flaking**—for example, using a pointed piece of bone, antler, or hard wood and pressing firmly against the stone (Fig. 9–9).

Once the tools were manufactured, the ways our ancestors used them can be inferred through further experimentation. For example, archaeologists from the Smithsonian Institution successfully butchered an entire elephant (which had died in a zoo) using stone tools they had made for that purpose (Park, 1978). Others have cut down trees using stone axes they had made.

Ancient tools themselves may carry telltale signs of how they were used. In his graduate work at Oxford University, Lawrence Keeley, now at the University of Illinois, Chicago, performed a series of experiments in which he manufactured flint tools and then used them in diverse ways—whittling wood, cutting bone, cutting meat, and scraping skins (Keeley, 1980). Viewing those implements under a microscope at fairly high magnification revealed patterns of polishes, striations, and other kinds of **microwear** (Fig. 9–10). What is most intriguing is that these patterns vary, depending on how the implement was used and which material was worked. For example, Keeley was able to distinguish among implements used on bone, antler, meat, plant materials, or hides. In the latter case, he was even able to determine if the hides were fresh or dried! In addition, orientations of microwear markings are also indicative of the way in which the tool was used (e.g., for cutting or scraping). Evidence of microwear polish has been examined on even the extremely early hominid stone tools from Koobi Fora (East Lake Turkana), in Kenya (Keeley and Toth, 1981).

Recent advances in tool use studies include the application of scanning electron microscopy (SEM). Working at 10,000× magnification, researchers have found that the working edges of stone implements sometimes retain plant fibers and amino acids, as well as nonorganic residues, including **phytoliths.** Because phytoliths produced by different plant species are morphologically distinctive, there is good potential for identifying the botanical materials that came in contact with the tool during use (Rovner, 1983). Such work is most exciting, since for the first time, we may be able to make definite statements concerning the uses of ancient tools.

Analysis of Bone

Experimental archaeologists are also interested in the ways bone is altered by human and natural forces. Other scientists are vitally concerned with this process as well; in fact, it has engendered an entire new branch of paleoecology—taphonomy. In recent years, taphonomists have carried out comprehensive research on how natural factors influence bone deposition and preservation. In South Africa, C. K. Brain has collected data on contemporary African butchering practices, carnivore (dog) disturbances, and so forth, and has correlated these factors with the kinds and numbers of elements usually found in bone accumulations (Brain, 1981). In this way, he has been able to account for the accumulation of most (if not all) of the bones in South African cave sites. Likewise, in East African game parks, observations have been made on decaying animals to measure the effects of weathering, predator chewing, and trampling (Behrensmeyer et al., 1979).

Further insight into the many ways bone is altered by natural factors has come from experimental work in the laboratory (Boaz and Behrensmeyer, 1976). In an experiment conducted at the University of California, Berkeley, human bones were put into a running-water trough. Researchers observed how far different pieces were transported and how much damage was done. Application of such information is extremely useful in interpreting early hominid sites. For example, the distribution of hominid fossils at Olduvai suggests that less active water transport was prevalent there than in the Omo River Valley.

Detailed examination of bones may also provide evidence of butchering and bone breakage by hominids, including cut marks and percussion marks left by stone tools. Great care must be taken to distinguish scars left on bone by carnivore or rodent gnawing, weathering processes, hoof marks, or even normal growth. High magnification of a cut made by a stone tool may reveal a minutely striated and roughened groove scored into the bone's surface. Many such finds have been recognized at early hominid sites, including Olduvai Gorge (Bunn et al., 1980; Bunn, 1981; Potts and Shipman, 1981) (see Issue, pp. 253–254).

Reconstruction of Early Hominid Environments and Behavior

Now that we have reviewed the various methods used by paleoanthropologists to *collect* their varied data, we will turn to the intriguing ways this information is *interpreted*. We must caution that much of this interpretation is quite speculative and not as amenable to scientific verification as are more concrete sources of data (e.g., that relating to dating, geology, or hominid anatomy). (In Chapter 1, we discussed how hypotheses are developed and tested by scientists, noting the requirement that *scientific* explanations be falsifiable.)

However, paleoanthropologists are keenly interested in not just *how* early hominids evolved, but also *why* the process occurred in the manner that it did. Accordingly, the data available are frequently used as a basis for broad, speculative **scenarios** seeking to explain both early hominid adaptations to a changing environment as well as the new behaviors that these hominids adopted. Such scenarios are fascinating, and paleoanthropologists enjoy constructing them (and certainly many in the general public enjoy reading them). Without doubt, for scientists and laypersons alike, our curiosity inevitably leads to intriguing and sweeping generalizations. Nevertheless, in the following discussion, we will attempt, wherever possible, to focus on what is *known* from the paleoanthropological record itself and to separate that from the more speculative conclusions. You, too, should evaluate these explanations with a critical eye and attempt to discern the empirical basis for each type of reconstruction. It is important to go beyond accepting views merely because they are appealing (often because they are simple) or just because they seem *plausible*. We always need to ask ourselves what kinds of evidence support a particular contention, how generally the explanation fits the evidence (i.e., how consistent it is with different types of data from varied sources), and what types of *new* evidence might either help verify or potentially falsify the interpretation.

Environmental Explanations for Hominid Origins

As we saw in Chapter 8, there are no *definite* hominid remains yet discovered from any Miocene-dated context. From what we presently know, the earliest hominids

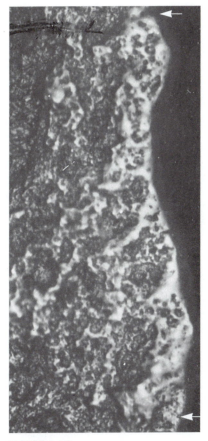

FIGURE 9–10

Microwear: the polish left on an experimental flint implement by scraping wood for 10 minutes. Bright, smooth areas are the microwear polish; dark, grainy areas are the unworn flint surface. Arrows indicate implement edge. (Magnification 200×)

■ Scenarios

General, speculative reconstructions derived from various scientific data. In paleoanthropology, scenarios are usually presented as imaginative reconstructions of early hominid behavior. Such interpretations are broader than typical scientific hypotheses and theories and are not as rigorously amenable to verification.

did not appear until early in the Pliocene (4–5 m.y.a.). What were the environmental conditions at this time and immediately prior to it? Can these general ecological patterns help explain the origins of the first hominids (as they diversified from other kinds of hominoids)?

Before continuing, we should provide one further caution. A common misconception that many students have is that a single large environmental change is related clearly to a major adaptive change in a type of organism (in other words, environmental change X produced adaptation Y in a particular life form). This oversimplification is a form of **environmental determinism**, and it grossly underestimates the true complexity of the evolutionary process. It is clear that the environment does influence evolutionary change, as seen in the process of natural selection. But organisms are highly complex systems, composed of thousands of genes, and any adaptive shift to changing environmental circumstances is likely to be a compromise, balancing several selective factors simultaneously (such as temperature requirements, amount and distribution of food and water, predators, and safe sleeping sites). Our discussion of the socioecological dynamics of nonhuman primate adaptations in Chapter 6 made this same point.

There is some evidence that at about the same time the earliest hominids were diverging, there *may* have been some major ecological changes occurring in Africa. Could these ecological and evolutionary changes be related to each other? As we will see, there is much debate regarding such a sweeping generalization. For most of the Miocene, Africa was generally tropical, with heavy rainfall persisting for most of the year; consequently, most of the continent was heavily forested. However, beginning later in the Miocene and intensifying up to the end of the epoch (about 5 m.y.a.), the climate became cooler, drier, and more seasonal.

We should mention as well that there were other regions of the world where paleoecological evidence reveals a distinct cooling trend at the end of the Miocene. However, our focus is on Africa, particularly East Africa, for it is from this region that we have the earliest evidence of hominid diversification. As already noted, one method used by paleoanthropologists to reconstruct environments is to analyze animal (faunal) remains and fossilized pollen. In addition, an innovative technique also studies the chemical pathways utilized by different plants. In particular, **stable carbon isotopes** are produced by plants in differing proportions, depending partly on temperature and aridity (plants adapted to warmer, wetter climates, such as most trees, shrubs, and tubers, versus plants requiring hotter, drier conditions, as typified by many types of grasses). Animals eat the plants, and the differing concentrations of the stable isotopes of carbon are incorporated into their bones and teeth, thus providing a "signature" of the general type of environment in which they lived.

It is from a combination of these analytical techniques that paleoecologists have gained a reasonably good handle on worldwide and continentwide environmental patterns of the past. For example, one model postulates that as climates grew cooler in East Africa 12–5 m.y.a., forests became less continuous. As a result, forest "fringe" habitats and transitional zones between forests and grasslands became more widespread. It is hypothesized that in such transitional environments, some of the late Miocene hominoids may have exploited more intensively the drier grassland portions of the fringe (these would be the earliest hominids); conversely, other hominoids concentrated more on the wetter portions of the fringe (these presumably were the ancestors of African great apes). In the incipient protohominids, further adaptive strategies would have followed, including bipedalism, increased tool use, dietary specialization (perhaps on hard items such as seeds and nuts), and changes in social organization.

▌ Environmental determinism
An interpretation that links simple environmental changes directly to a major evolutionary shift in an organism. Such explanations tend to be extreme oversimplifications of the evolutionary process.

▌ Stable carbon isotopes
Isotopes of carbon that are produced in plants in differing proportions, depending on environmental conditions. Through analyzing the proportions of the isotopes contained in fossil remains of animals (who ate the plants), it is possible to reconstruct aspects of ancient environments (particularly temperature and aridity).

Such assertions concerning interactions of habitat, locomotion, dietary changes, and social organization are not really testable (since we do not know which changes came first). Still, some of the more restricted contentions of this "climatic forcing" theory are amenable to testing; in fact, some of the more basic predictions of the model have not been verified. Most notably, further analyses using stable carbon isotopes from several East African localities suggest that during the late Miocene, environments across the area were consistently quite densely forested (i.e., grasslands never predominated, except perhaps at a local level).

You should be aware that there can be wide fluctuations at the local level pertaining to such factors as temperature, rainfall, vegetation, and the animals exploiting the vegetation. For example, local uplift can produce a rain shadow, dramatically altering rainfall and temperature in a region. River and related lake drainages also have major impacts in some areas, and these topographical features are often influenced by highly localized geological factors. To generalize about climates in Africa, good data from several regions are required.

It would thus appear, given current evidence and available analytical techniques, that our knowledge of the factors influencing the appearance of the *earliest* hominids is very limited. Considering the constraints, most hypotheses relating to potential factors are best kept restricted in scope and directly related to actual data. In this way, their utility can be more easily evaluated and they can be modified and built upon.

Changing Environments and Later Hominid Diversifications

From the Pliocene and early Pleistocene, we have much more data relating to hominids and the environments in which they lived. One innovative explanation has sought to link periods of hominid and other mammalian diversification (when new species appear) with regular shifts in the African environment. From her research in both South and East Africa, Elizabeth Vrba, of Yale University, noticed that the appearance of new species of antelope as well as hominids was correlated with three periods of increased aridity (at 2.5, 1.8, and 1.0 m.y.a.) (Vrba, 1988, 1995). Could the environment have played a significant role in stimulating mammalian (including hominid) evolution at several crucial stages? This view has come to be called the **evolutionary pulse theory** and has been supported from data in Africa and other regions.

However, more recent and highly detailed analyses of more than 400 paleontological sites located around Lake Turkana (in northern Kenya and southern Ethiopia) have cast doubt on some aspects of the evolutionary pulse theory. Anna Behrensmeyer and colleagues from the Smithsonian Institution collected data from more than 10,000 specimens from contexts dated to 4.4 m.y.a. to the present to see if any "spikes" in rates of extinction or appearance of new species were evident (Behrensmeyer et al., 1997). The key period pointed to by many proponents of the evolutionary pulse theory is around 2.5 m.y.a., since this is a time of considerable activity in the hominid lineage (including the first documented evidence of the genus *Homo*). Was there a general evolutionary pulse at 2.5 m.y.a. associated with climate change that impacted a wide variety of African mammals? The evidence for this time period from the Lake Turkana region does not support any such rapid evolutionary event. In fact, species turnover between 3 and 2 million years ago in this area was quite gradual, with no indication of a pulse. Some species associated with drier habitats persisted throughout this million-year time period.

■ Evolutionary pulse theory
A view that postulates a correlation of periods of hominid diversification during the Pliocene and early Pleistocene with major shifts in several African mammalian species. These changes in mammalian evolution, in turn, are thought to be related to periodic episodes of aridity.

Vrba's hypothesis suggested a series of rapid, continentwide environmental changes, which then stimulated accelerated evolutionary changes in various animals (including hominids) around 2.5 m.y.a. This view is intriguing and was initially bolstered by some paleontological data, especially those from South Africa. However, for the Turkana area, "the absence of a pulse from the best calibrated, fossil-rich deposits from this time period weakens the case for rapid climatic forcing of continent scale ecological change and faunal turnover" (Behrensmeyer et al., 1997, p. 1593). Nevertheless, this region is only one segment of Africa and may not indicate broad climatic trends occurring elsewhere on the continent. The evolutionary pulse theory is thus not yet clearly established, but the proposal has stimulated innovative further research. In this way, we can see scientific methodology working at its best. Better data analyzed with better controls *should* yield better explanations. Indeed, Vrba has suggested two other periods of evolutionary pulses, one of these occurring at 1.8 m.y.a. These periods of increased speciation and extinction are again thought to be associated with significant evolutionary changes among the hominids. Interestingly, the data from the Turkana region lends support to fairly rapid turnover in mammalian species at 1.8 m.y.a. Thus, there may have been a significant role played by broad climatic influences, at least during some stages of hominid evolution.

We should not, however, assume that for any period, environmental explanations can be simply applied. What we should conclude is that such broad environmental changes probably were just one factor among many influencing the evolution of early African hominids at different times and in different regions of the continent.

Why Did Hominids Become Bipedal?

As we have noted several times, the adaptation of hominids to bepedal locomotion was *the* most fundamental adaptive shift among the early members of our family. But what were the factors that initiated this crucial change? Ecological theories, similar to some of those just discussed, have long been thought to be central to the development of bipedalism. Clearly, however, environmental influences would have to occur *before* documented evidence of well-adapted bipedal behavior. In other words, the major shift would have been at the end of the Miocene or beginning of the Pliocene. Although the evidence indicates that no *sudden* wide ecological change took place at this time, locally forests probably did become patchier as rainfall became more seasonal. Given the changing environmental conditions, did hominids come to the ground to seize the opportunities offered in these more open habitats? Did bipedalism then quickly ensue, stimulated by this new way of life? At a very general level, the answer to these questions is yes. Obviously, hominids did at some point become bipedal, and this adaptation took place on the ground. Likewise, hominids are more adapted to mixed and open-country habitats than are our closest ape cousins. Successful terrestrial bipedalism probably made possible the further adaptation to more arid, open-country terrain. Still, this rendition simply tells us *where* hominids found their niche, not *why.*

As always, one must be cautious when speculating about causation in evolution. It is all too easy to draw superficial conclusions. For example, it is often surmised that the mere fact that ground niches were available (and perhaps lacked direct competitors) inevitably led the earliest hominids to terrestrial bipedalism. But consider this: There are plenty of mammalian species, including some nonhuman primates, that also live mostly on the ground in open country—and they are not bipedal. Clearly, beyond such simplistic environmental determinism, some more complex explanation for hominid bipedalism is required. There must have been something *more* than just an environmental opportunity to explain this adaptation to such a unique lifestyle.

Another issue sometimes overlooked in the discussion of early hominid bipedal adaptation is that these creatures did not suddenly become *completely* terrestrial. We know, for example, that all terrestrial species of nonhuman primates (e.g., savanna baboons, hamadryas baboons, patas monkeys; see Chapter 7) regularly seek out "safe sleeping sites" off the ground. These safe havens help protect against predation and are usually found in trees or on cliff faces. Likewise, early hominids almost certainly sought safety at night *in the trees,* even after they became well adapted to terrestrial bipedalism during daytime foraging. Moreover, the continued opportunities for feeding in the trees would most likely have remained significant to early hominids, well after they were also utilizing ground-based resources.

A variety of hypotheses to explain why hominids initially became bipedal have been suggested and are summarized in Table 9–2. The primary influences claimed to have stimulated the shift to bipedalism include the ability to carry objects (and offspring); hunting on the ground; gathering of seeds and nuts; feeding from bushes; better view of open country (to spot predators); long-distance walking; and provisioning by males of females with dependent offspring.

These are all creative scenarios, but once again are not very conducive to rigorous testing and verification. Nevertheless, two of the more ambitious scenarios

TABLE 9–2 Possible Factors Influencing the Initial Evolution of Bipedal Locomotion in Hominids

Factor	Speculated Influence	Comments
Carrying (objects, tools, weapons, infants)	Upright posture freed the arms to carry various objects (including offspring)	Charles Darwin emphasized this view, particularly relating to tools and weapons; however, evidence of stone tools is found much later in record than first evidence of bipedalism.
Hunting	As correlated with above theory, carrying weapons made hunting more efficient; in addition, long-distance walking may have been more energetically efficient (see below)	Systematic hunting is now thought not to have been practiced until after the origin of bipedal hominids (see Issue, Chapter 11)
Seed and nut gathering	Feeding on seeds and nuts occurred while standing upright	Model initially drawn from analogy with gelada baboons (see text)
Feeding from bushes	Upright posture provided access to seeds, berries, etc., in lower branches; analogous to adaptation seen in some specialized antelope	Climbing adaptation already existed as prior ancestral trait in earliest hominids (i.e., bush and tree feeding already was established prior to bipedal adaptation)
Visual surveillance	Standing up provided better view of surrounding countryside (view of potential predators as well as other group members)	Behavior seen occasionally in terrestrial primates (e.g., baboons); probably a contributing factor, but unlikely as "prime mover"
Long-distance walking	Covering long distances was more efficient for a biped than for a quadruped (during hunting or foraging); mechanical reconstructions show that bipedal walking is less energetically costly than quadrupedalism (this is not the case for bipedal *running*)	Same difficulties as with hunting explanation; long-distance foraging on ground also appears unlikely adaptation in *earliest* hominids
Male provisioning	Males carried back resources to dependent females and young	Monogamous bond suggested; however, most skeletal data appear to falsify this part of the hypothesis (see text)

chapter, we will survey the fossil hominid evidence in South and East Africa that informs us directly about human origins during the Plio-Pleistocene.

Questions for Review

1. Why are cultural remains so important in the interpretation of human evolution?
2. How are early hominid sites found, and what kind of specialist is involved in the excavation and analysis of paleoanthropological data?
3. What kinds of paleoanthropological information have been found at Olduvai Gorge? Why is this particular locality so rich in material?
4. What techniques have been used to date early hominid sites at Olduvai? Why is more than one technique necessary for accurate dating?
5. Why are context and association so important in the interpretation of archaeological remains?
6. What different activities can be inferred from the different kinds of sites at Olduvai? Discuss alternative views in the interpretation of these "sites."
7. How do archaeologists determine the functions of ancient stone tools?
8. What is a scenario? How does it differ from a scientific hypothesis? Give an example.
9. What environmental factors have been postulated as important in influencing the origins of the first hominids? How satisfactory are these explanations?
10. What are some of the factors thought to be important in influencing the early evolution of bipedal locomotion?

Suggested Further Reading

Binford, Lewis. 1981. *Bones: Ancient Men and Myths.* New York: Academic Press.
Leakey, Mary. 1984. *Disclosing the Past. An Autobiography.* Garden City, NJ: Doubleday.
Leakey, Richard. 1981. *The Making of Mankind.* New York: Dutton.
Rasmussen, D. T. (ed.). 1993. *The Origin and Evolution of Humans and Humaness.* Boston: Jones and Bartlett.
Willis, Delta. 1989. *The Hominid Gang: Behind the Scenes in the Search for Human Origins.* New York: Viking.

Additional Resources

Multimedia Tools

- **Virtual Laboratories for Physical Anthropology CD-ROM**
  The following concepts in this chapter are covered on the physical anthropology CD-ROM:
  hominids, hominoids, hominines (Virtual Lab 7.II.D)
  archaeology, culture (Virtual Lab 11)

fossil, fossilization, paleoecology, taphonomy (Virtual Lab 7.I.D)
stratigraphy, sedimentary rocks (Virtual Lab 7.I)
Zinjanthropus, Australopithecus boisei (Virtual Lab 8.I.E)
radioisotopic dating, K-Ar, Ar-Ar, Carbon-14 (Virtual Lab 7.I.C)
geological time scale (Virtual Lab 7.I.B)
paleomagnetic dating (Virtual Lab 7.I.C)
stratigraphic superposition, faunal correlation (Virtual Lab 7.I.C)
site use, quarry, butchering (Virtual Lab 11.III.C)
archaeological record, tool manufacture (Virtual Lab 11)
stone tools, 3-D animations (Virtual Lab 11.IV)
bone alteration, taphonomy (Virtual Lab 11.IV.C)
sexual dimorphism, early hominids (Virtual Lab 8.I)

- ## Wadsworth Anthropology Resource Center
  http://anthropology.wadsworth.com
  Visit Anthropology Online to obtain current updates in the field, surfing tips, career information and more. In addition, enrich your study efforts with text-specific study aids arranged by chapter.

- ## InfoTrac College Edition
  http://www.infotrac-college.com/wadsworth

  1. Search InfoTrac College Edition for *radioactive dating*. How many different methods are covered in the articles you found? Make a chart showing all the different methods of radiometric dating and the time scales they cover. Are there any major gaps in time that cannot be dated by radiometric methods?

  2. Archaeologists have sometimes identified living floors at prehistoric sites, suggesting that the artifacts found at a particular level were contemporaneous. Is this a logical conclusion to draw? Read "Testing the reality of a 'living floor' with archaeological data" by Harold Dibble, et al., *American Antiquity*. Are living floors really living floors? What evidence do the researchers present for their conclusions?

  3. Search InfoTrac College Edition for *tools, prehistoric*. What information can you learn about prehistoric toolmaking from the articles found in this search? Specifically, read "Hominid Hardware" by Shanti Meron. What can we learn about lithic technology from the finds described in this article? Finally, what other keywords can you think of that might help you find information about hominid tool-making and tool use?

  4. Search InfoTrac College Edition for *bipedalism*. What hypotheses are offered in these articles for the origins of bipedalism? Do you find any single hypothesis more convincing than the others? Why or why not?

- ## Internet Exercises

  1. Visit the Origins of Humankind Web site (**http://www.humanevolution.com/**) and choose one of the recent news stories in human evolution. Read through this story then visit one of the search engines to see if you can find anything else on the same topic. Finally, using the information from Origins of Humankind and any other site you find, write a summary of the news story and how this research has changed ideas about human evolution.

  2. You can also find news about paleoanthropology on either Anthropology in the News at Texas A&M (**http://www.tamu.edu/**

ISSUE

Are the Sites at Olduvai Really "Sites"? (continued)

consistently, what did they obtain from scavenging the kills of other animals? One obvious answer is, whatever meat was left behind. However, the position of the cut marks suggests that early hominids were often hacking at non-meat-bearing-portions of the skeletons. Perhaps they were simply after bone marrow, a substance not really being exploited by other predators (Binford, 1981).

Exciting new discoveries from the Bouri Peninsula of the Middle Awash of Ethiopia provide the best evidence yet for meat and marrow exploitation by early hominids. Dated to 2.5 m.y.a. (i.e., as old as the oldest known artifacts), antelope and horse fossils from Bouri show telltale incisions and breaks indicating bones were smashed to extract marrow and also cut, ostensibly to retrieve meat (de Heinzelin et al., 1999). The researchers who analyzed these materials have suggested that the greater dietary reliance on animal products may have been important in stimulating brain enlargement in the lineage leading to genus *Homo.*

Another new research twist relating to the reconstruction of early hominid diets has come from bio-chemical analysis of hominid teeth from South Africa (dating to about the same time range as hominids from Olduvai—or perhaps slightly

earlier). In an innovative application of stable carbon isotope analysis (see p. 244), Matt Sponheimer of Rutgers University and Julia Lee-Thorp of the University of Cape Town found that these early hominid teeth revealed telltale chemical signatures relating to diet (Sponheimer and Lee-Thorp, 1999). In particular, the proportions of stable carbon isotopes indicated these early hominids either ate grass products (such as seeds), or they ate meat/marrow from animals who, in turn, had eaten grass products (i.e., the hominids might well have derived a significant portion of their diet from meat or other animal products). This evidence comes from an exciting new perspective, for it provides a more *direct* indicator of early hominid diets. While it is not clear how much meat these early hominids consumed, these new data do suggest they were consistently exploiting more open regions of their environment.

Critical Thinking Questions

1. What types of evidence are available to interpret hominid behavior (specifically, meat acquisition) at Olduvai sites?
2. Which of the evidence in question 1 is prehistoric, and which relates to *modern* contexts?
3. What is *known* and what is *inferred* in regard to these behavioral interpretations?

4. Using Binford's model, how would you test the hypothesis that the distribution of broken animal bones at a 1.8 million year old site at Olduvai is primarily the result of hominid food-processing behavior?

Sources

Binford, Lewis R. 1981. *Bones: Ancient Men and Modern Myths.* New York: Academic Press.

_____. 1983. *In Pursuit of the Past.* New York: Thames & Hudson.

Bunn, Henry T. 1981. "Archaeological Evidence for Meat-Eating by Plio-Pleistocene Hominids from Koobi Fora and Olduvai Gorge." *Nature* 291:574–577.

de Heinzelin, Jean, J. Desmond Clark, Tim White, et al. 1999. "Environment and Behavior of 2.5-Million-Year-Old Bouri Hominids." *Science* 284:625–629.

Potts, Richard, and Pat Shipman. 1981. "Cutmarks Made by Stone Tools from Olduvai Gorge, Tanzania." *Nature* 291:577–580.

Shipman, Pat. 1983. "Early Hominid Lifestyle. Hunting and Gathering or Foraging and Scavenging?" Paper presented at 52nd Annual Meeting, American Association of Physical Anthropologists, Indianapolis.

Sponheimer, Matt and Julia A. Lee-Thorp. 1999. "Isotopic Evidence for the Diet of an Early Hominid, *Australopithecus africanus.*" *Science* 283:368–370.

10

Hominid Origins

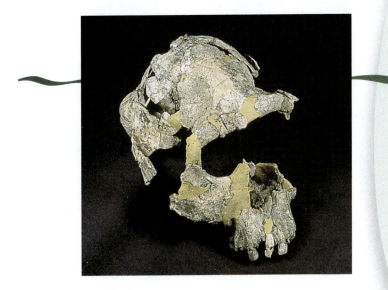

You may wish to review the geological time scale in Virtual Lab 7, section I, part B.

■ **Plio-Pleistocene**
Pertaining to the Pliocene and first half of the Pleistocene, a time range of 5–1 m.y.a. During this time period, the earliest fossil hominids have been found in Africa.

■ **Morphological**
Pertaining to the form and structure of organisms.

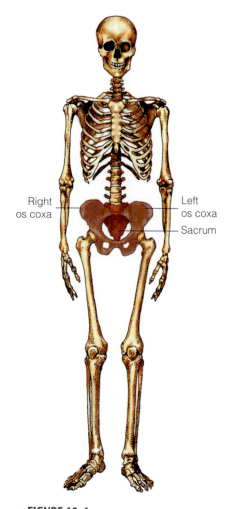

FIGURE 10–1

The human pelvis. Various elements shown on a modern skeleton.

Introduction

In Chapter 9, we discussed the techniques used by paleoanthropologists to collect and interpret basic background data relating to the evolution of early hominids. Such geological, ecological, and archaeological information helps us understand the environments and behaviors of the earliest members of the hominid family.

In this chapter, we turn to the physical evidence of the hominid fossils themselves. From the Pliocene epoch and the first half of the Pleistocene, a very large fossil collection of these early hominids has been found in Africa. Comprising the time span of 5–1 m.y.a., this period is usually referred to as the **Plio-Pleistocene**. These fossil hominids are a rich and varied lot, and their discovery has stimulated a great deal of interest among both the scientific community and the general public. Given these circumstances, it is perhaps no great surprise that the interpretation of these finds has also generated considerable controversy. Thus, in addition to reviewing the anatomical details revealed directly in the fossil material, we will also discuss and attempt to sort out the complex and frequently conflicting interpretations concerning the evolutionary patterns of Plio-Pleistocene hominids.

The Bipedal Adaptation

In our overview of behavioral reconstructions in early hominids, we highlighted several hypotheses that attempt to explain *why* bipedal locomotion first evolved in the hominids. Here we turn to the specific anatomical (i.e., **morphological**) evidence that shows us when, where, and how hominid bipedal locomotion evolved.

In our discussion of primate anatomical trends in Chapter 5, we noted that there is a general tendency in all primates for erect body posture and some bipedalism. However, of all living primates, efficient bipedalism as the primary form of locomotion is seen *only* in hominids. Functionally, the human mode of locomotion is most clearly shown in our striding gait, where weight is alternately placed on a single fully extended hind limb. This specialized form of locomotion has developed to a point where energy levels are used to near peak efficiency. Such is not the case in nonhuman primates, who move bipedally with hips and knees bent and maintain balance in a clumsy and inefficient manner.

Our mode of locomotion is indeed extraordinary, involving as it does an activity in which "the body, step by step, teeters on the edge of catastrophe" (Napier, 1967, p.56). The problem is to maintain balance on the "stance" leg while the "swing" leg is off the ground. In fact, during normal walking, both feet are simultaneously on the ground only about 25 percent of the time, and as speed of locomotion increases, this figure becomes even smaller.

To maintain a stable center of balance in this complex form of locomotion, many drastic structural/anatomical alterations in the basic primate quadrupedal pattern are required. The most dramatic changes are seen in the pelvis. The pelvis is composed of three elements: two *ossa coxae* (*sing.* os coxa) joined at the back to the sacrum (Fig. 10–1). In a quadruped, the ossa coxae are elongated bones positioned along each side of the lower portion of the spine and oriented more or less parallel to it. In hominids, the pelvis is comparatively much shorter and broader and extends around to the side (Fig. 10–2). This configuration helps to stabilize the line of weight transmission, in a bipedal posture, from the lower back to the hip joint (Fig. 10–3).

A number of consequences resulted from the remodeling of the pelvis during early hominid evolution. Broadening the two sides and extending them around

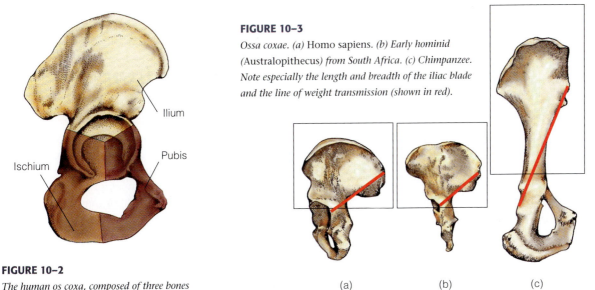

FIGURE 10–3

Ossa coxae. (a) Homo sapiens. *(b) Early hominid*
(Australopithecus) from South Africa. (c) Chimpanzee.
Note especially the length and breadth of the iliac blade
and the line of weight transmission (shown in red).

Ilium

Pubis

Ischium

(a)   (b)   (c)

FIGURE 10–2

The human os coxa, composed of three bones
(right side shown).

to the side and front of the body produced a basin-shaped structure that helps
support the abdominal organs (indeed, *pelvis* means "basin" in Latin). Moreover,
these alterations repositioned the attachments of several key muscles that act on
the hip and leg, changing their mechanical function. Probably the most important of these altered relationships is that involving the *gluteus maximus,* the
largest muscle in the body, which in humans forms the bulk of the buttocks. In
quadrupeds, the gluteus maximus is positioned to the side of the hip and functions to pull the thigh to the side, away from the body. But in humans, this muscle acts, along with the hamstrings, to extend the thigh, pulling it to the rear
during walking and running (Fig 10–4). Indeed, the gluteus maximus is a powerful extensor of the thigh and provides additional force, particularly during running and climbing.

Virtual Lab 9 presents a
detailed discussion of the
evolution of bipedalism.

The anatomy and function
of the pelvis is presented in
Virtual Lab 9, section I.

Be sure to view the animation of the gluteus medius in
Virtual Lab 9, section I, part A.

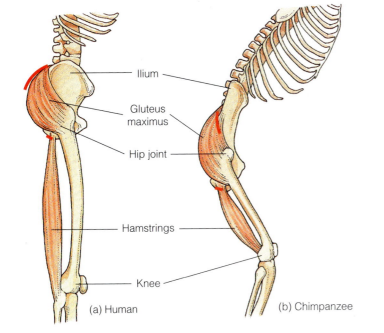

Ilium

Gluteus
maximus

Hip joint

Hamstrings

Knee

(a) Human   (b) Chimpanzee

FIGURE 10–4

Comparisons of important muscles that act to
extend the hip. Note that the attachment joint
(origin, shown in red) of the gluteus maximus
in humans (a) is farther in back of the hip
bone than in a chimpanzee standing bipedally
(b). Conversely, in chimpanzees, the ham-
strings are farther in back of the knee.

BOX 10-1

Major Features of Hominid Bipedalism

During hominid evolution, several major structural features throughout the body have been reorganized (from that seen in other primates) to facilitate efficient bipedal locomotion. These are illustrated here, beginning with the head and progressing to the foot: **1** The *foramen magnum* (shown in red) is repositioned farther underneath the head, so that the head is more or less balanced on the spine (and thus requires less robust neck muscles to hold the head upright). **2** The spine has two distinctive curves—a backward (thoracic) one and a forward (lumbar) one—that keep the trunk (and weight) centered above the pelvis. **3** The pelvis is shaped more in

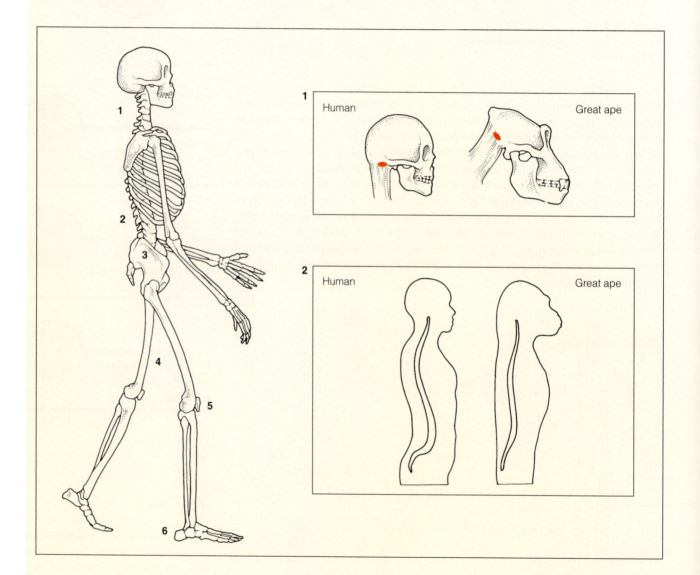

the form of a basin to support internal organs; moreover, the ossa coxae (specifically, iliac blades) are shorter and broader, thus stabilizing weight transmission. **4** Lower limbs are elongated, as shown by the proportional lengths of various body segments (e.g., in humans the thigh comprises 20 percent of body height, while in gorillas it comprises only 11 percent). **5** The femur is angled inward, keeping the legs more directly under the body; modified knee anatomy also permits full extension of this joint. **6** The big toe is enlarged and brought in line with the other toes; in addition, a distinctive longitudinal arch forms, helping absorb shock and adding propulsive spring.

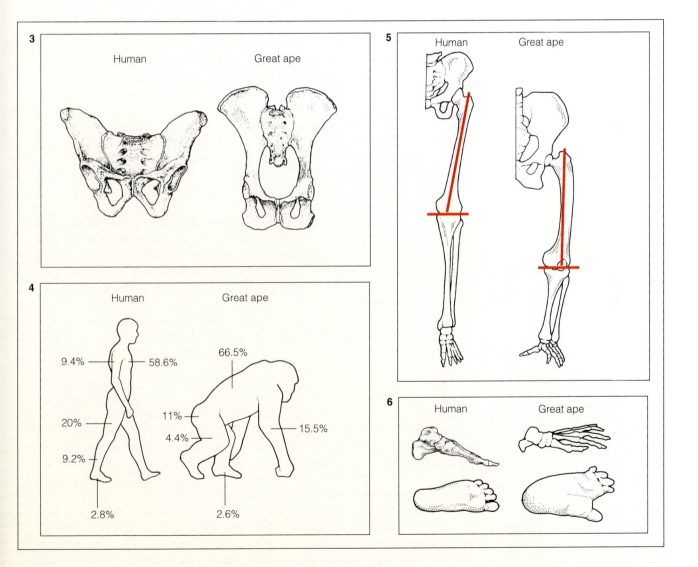

3
Human   Great ape

4
Human   Great ape
9.4%   58.6%
66.5%
20%   11%
4.4%   15.5%
9.2%
2.8%   2.6%

5
Human   Great ape

6
Human   Great ape

Foramen magnum
The opening at the base of the skull through which the spinal cord passes as it enters the body to descend through the vertebral column. In quadrupeds, it is located more to the rear of the skull, while in bipeds, it is located farther beneath the skull.

Virtual Lab 9, section II provides a discussion of the anatomy and function of the vertebral column.

The anatomy and function of the hominid femur is presented in Virtual Lab 9, section III.

Modifications also occurred in other parts of the skeleton as a result of the shift to bipedalism. The most significant of these are summarized in Box 10–1 and include (1) repositioning of the **foramen magnum**, the opening at the base of the skull through which the spinal cord emerges; (2) the addition of spinal curves that facilitate the transmission of the weight of the upper body to the hips in an upright posture; (3) shortening and broadening of the pelvis and the stabilization of weight transmission (discussed earlier); (4) lengthening of the hind limb, thus increasing stride length; (5) angling of the femur (thighbone) inward to bring the knees and feet closer together under the body; and (6) several structural changes in the foot, including the development of a longitudinal arch and realignment of the big toe in parallel with the other toes (i.e., it was no longer divergent).

As you can appreciate, the evolution of hominid bipedalism required complex anatomical reorganization. For natural selection to produce anatomical change of the magnitude seen in hominids, the benefits of bipedal locomotion must have been significant indeed. We mentioned in Chapter 9 several possible adaptive advantages that bipedal locomotion *may* have conferred upon early hominids. However, these all remain hypotheses (even more accurately, they could be called scenarios), and we lack adequate data with which to test the various proposed alternatives.

Still, given the anatomical alterations that efficient bipedalism necessitated, there must have been some major behavioral stimuli influencing its development. In the interpretation of evolutionary history, biologists are fond of saying that form follows function. In other words, during evolution, organisms do not undergo significant reorganization in structure *unless* these changes (over many generations) assist individuals in some functional capacity (and, in so doing, increase their reproductive success). Such changes did not necessarily occur all at once, but probably evolved over a fairly long period of time. Nevertheless, once behavioral influences initiated certain structural modifications, the process gained momentum and proceeded irreversibly.

We say that hominid bipedalism is *habitual* and *obligate*. By habitual, we mean that hominids, unlike any other primate, move bipedally as their standard and most efficient mode of locomotion. By obligate, we mean that hominids are committed to bipedalism and cannot locomote efficiently in any other manner. For example, the loss of grasping ability in the foot makes climbing much more difficult for humans (although by no means impossible). The central task, then, in trying to understand the earliest members of the hominid family is to identify anatomical features that indicate bipedalism and to interpret to what degree these organisms were committed to this form of locomotion (i.e., was it habitual and was it obligate?).

What structural patterns are observable in early hominids, and what do they imply regarding locomotor function? *All the major structural changes required for bipedalism are seen in early hominids from East and South Africa* (at least insofar as the evidence has thus far been reported). In particular, the pelvis, as clearly documented by several excellently preserved specimens, was dramatically remodeled to support weight in a bipedal stance (see Fig. 10–3b).

In addition, other structural changes shown in even the earliest definitive hominid postcranial remains further confirm the pattern seen in the pelvis. For example, the vertebral column (as known from specimens in East and South Africa) shows the same curves as in modern hominids. The lower limbs were also elongated and were apparently proportionately about as long as in modern humans (although the arms were longer). Further, the carrying angle of weight support from the hip to the knee was also very similar to that seen in *Homo sapiens*.

Fossil evidence of early hominid foot structure has come from two sites in South Africa, and especially important are some recently announced new fossils from Sterkfontein (Clarke and Tobias, 1995). These specimens, consisting of four articulating elements from the ankle and big toe, indicate that the heel and longitudinal arch were both well adapted for a bipedal gait. However, the paleoanthropologists (Ron Clarke and Phillip Tobias) who analyzed these remains also suggest that the large toe was *divergent,* unlike the hominid pattern shown in Box 10–1. If the large toe really did possess this anatomical position, it most likely would have aided the foot in grasping. In turn, this grasping ability (as in other primates) would have enabled early hominids to more effectively exploit arboreal habitats. Finally, since anatomical remodeling is always constrained by a set of complex functional compromises, a foot highly capable of grasping and climbing is *less* capable as a stable platform during bipedal locomotion. Some researchers therefore see early hominids as not necessarily obligate bipeds. Further investigation of the cave site in 1998 revealed a remarkable find, the remains of a nearly complete skeleton belonging to the same individual from which the foot came (see p. 278).

Further evidence for evolutionary changes in the foot skeleton comes from Olduvai Gorge in Tanzania, where a nearly complete hominid foot is preserved, and from Hadar in Ethiopia, where numerous foot elements have been recovered (Fig. 10–5). As in the remains from South Africa, the East African fossils suggest a well-adapted bipedal gait. The arches are developed, but some differences in the ankle also imply that considerable flexibility was possible (again, suggested for continued adaptation to climbing). As we will see, some researchers have recently concluded that many early forms of hominids probably spent considerable time in the trees. Moreover, they may not have been quite as efficient bipeds as has previously been suggested. Nevertheless, to this point, *all* the early hominids that have been identified from Africa are thought by most researchers to have been both habitual and obligate bipeds (notwithstanding the new evidence from South Africa, which will require further study).

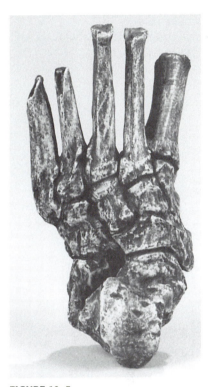

FIGURE 10–5

A nearly complete hominid foot (OH 8) from Olduvai Gorge, Tanzania.

Early Hominids in the Plio-Pleistocene

The beginnings of hominid differentiation almost certainly have their roots in the late Miocene (circa 10–5 m.y.a.). Sometime during the period between 8 and 5 m.y.a., hominids began to adapt more fully to their peculiar ground-living niche, and fossil evidence from this period would be most illuminating, particularly any remains indicating a bipedal adaptation. However, scant information is presently available concerning the course of hominid evolution during this significant 3-million-year gap. But beginning around 4.5 m.y.a., the fossil record picks up considerably. We now have a wealth of fossil hominid material from the Pliocene and the earliest stages of the Pleistocene (5–1 m.y.a.), and as noted, this whole span is usually referred to as the Plio-Pleistocene.

Virtual Lab 9, section IV, discusses the anatomy and function of the foot.

The East African Rift Valley

Stretching along a more than 1,200-mile trough extending through Ethiopia, Kenya, and Tanzania from the Red Sea in the north to the Serengeti Plain in the south is the eastern branch of the Great Rift Valley of Africa (Fig. 10–6). This massive geological feature has been associated with active mountain building, faulting, and vulcanism over the last several million years.

Because of these gigantic earth movements, earlier sediments (normally buried under hundreds of feet of earth and rock) were literally thrown to the

An interactive time line, map, and phylogeny (with pronunciations) are available throughout Virtual Lab 8.

FIGURE 10–6

The East African Rift Valley system and locations of major hominid sites.

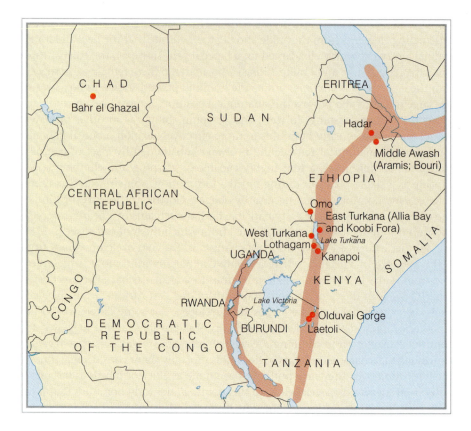

surface, where they became exposed to the trained eye of the paleoanthropologist. Such earth movements have exposed Miocene beds at sites in Kenya, along the shores of Lake Victoria, where abundant remains of early fossil hominoids have been found. In addition, Plio-Pleistocene sediments are also exposed all along the Rift Valley, and paleoanthropologists in recent years have made the most of this unique opportunity.

More than just exposing normally hidden deposits, rifting has stimulated volcanic activity, which in turn has provided a valuable means of chronometrically dating many sites in East Africa. Unlike the sites in South Africa (see pp. 283–285), those along the Rift Valley are *datable* and have thus yielded much crucial information concerning the precise chronology of early hominid evolution.

The Earliest East African Hominids

The site that focused attention on East Africa as a potential paleoanthropological gold mine was Olduvai Gorge in northern Tanzania. As discussed in great detail in Chapter 9, this site has offered unique opportunities because of the remarkable preservation of geological, paleontological, and archaeological records. Following Mary Leakey's discovery of "Zinj" in 1959 (and the subsequent dating of its site at 1.75 m.y.a. by the K/Ar method), numerous other areas in East Africa have been surveyed and several intensively explored. We will review the fossil discoveries from these sites as well as briefly discuss their chronological and geological context, beginning with the earliest.

Earliest Traces

The oldest specimen discovered to date, which several authorities identify as a *probable* hominid, comes from Lothagam in northern Kenya (see Fig. 10–6). This fossil is very fragmentary and consists of a portion of a lower jaw (mandible). In addition, in the time range 5–4 m.y.a., there are further scattered finds from two other sites in northern Kenya and from a third locality in northeastern Ethiopia. However, none of this fossil material is very definitive, since, as of yet, only a single (fragmentary) specimen has been recovered from each site (see Table 10–1 for a summary of discoveries).

Still, in the last five years, new and much more abundant discoveries have been made at three other localities, two in northern Kenya (Kanapoi and Allia Bay) and the other in Ethiopia (Aramis) (see Fig. 10–6). Finds from these three sites have added dramatically to our knowledge of the earliest stages of hominid emergence.

Ardipithecus from Aramis (Ethiopia)

One of the most exciting areas for future research in East Africa is the Afar Triangle of northeastern Ethiopia, where the Red Sea, Rift Valley, and Gulf of Aden all intersect. From this area have come many of the most important recent discoveries bearing on human origins. Several areas have yielded fossil remains in recent decades, and many potentially very rich sites are currently being explored. One of these sites just recently discovered, located in the region called the Middle Awash (along the banks of the Awash River), is called **Aramis**. Initial radiometric dating of the sediments places the hominid remains at 4.4 m.y.a., making this the earliest *collection* of hominids yet discovered.

Fossil remains from Aramis were excavated between 1992 and 1995 and include up to 50 different individuals (Wolpoff, 1999). This crucial and quite large

Virtual Lab 8, section I, part A, discusses the fossil evidence for the earliest hominids.

Aramis

(air´-ah-miss)

TABLE 10–1	Discoveries of Earliest Hominid* Fossil Remains			
Site	Dates (m.y.a.)	Taxonomic Designation	Fossil Sample	
Lothagam (Kenya)	5.8–5.6	Uncertain (possibly, *Ardipithecus*)	1 specimen (partial mandible)	
Mabaget (Kenya) (Chemeron Beds)	5.1–5.0	Uncertain	1 specimen (partial subadult humerus)	
Tabarin (Kenya) (Chemeron Beds)	5.0	Uncertain	1 specimen (partial mandible)	
Aramis (Ethiopia)	4.4	*Ardipithecus ramidus*	More than 50 individuals	
Kanapoi (Kenya)	4.2–3.9	*Australopithecus anamensis*	9 specimens	
Allia Bay (East Turkana) (Kenya)	3.9	*Australopithecus anamensis*	13 specimens	
Belohdelie (Ethiopia)	3.9–3.8	*Australopithecus afarensis*	5 pieces of cranium	

Note: In some cases, hominid status is not yet well established.

FIGURE 10–7

New hominid discoveries from Aramis. Alemayehu Asfaw is holding his discovery of an upper arm bone (humerus). In the background, team members search for other fragments; parts of all three bones of the upper appendage of one Ardipithecus ramidus *individual were discovered.*

©1994 Tim D. White\Brill Atlanta

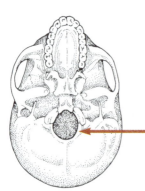

(a)

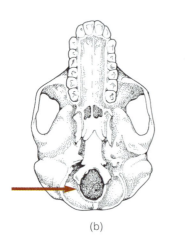

(b)

FIGURE 10–8

Position of the foramen magnum in (a) a human and (b) a chimpanzee. Note the more forward position in the human cranium.

collection includes several dental specimens as well as an upper arm bone (humerus) and some fragmentary cranial remains (Fig. 10–7). Most exciting of all, in 1995, 40 percent of a skeleton was discovered; however, the bones are all encased in limestone matrix, thus requiring a long and tedious process to remove the fossils intact from the cementlike material surrounding them. In fact, as of this writing, the Aramis remains (including the skeleton) have not yet been fully scientifically described. Nevertheless, details from initial reports are highly suggestive that these remains are, in fact, the *earliest* hominids yet to be found (except, perhaps, for some of the potential early "traces" mentioned earlier).

First of all, in an Aramis partial cranium, the *foramen magnum* is positioned farther forward in the base of the skull than is the case in quadrupeds (Fig. 10–8). Second, features of the humerus also differ from those seen in quadrupeds, indicating that the Aramis humerus did not function in locomotion to support weight (i.e., the upper limbs were free). From these two features, the provisional interpretation by Tim White, of the University of California, Berkeley, and his colleagues was that the Aramis individuals were *bipedal*. Moreover, initial interpretation of the partial skeleton (while not yet fully cleaned and reported) also suggests obligate bipedalism (Wolpoff, 1999).

Nevertheless, these were clearly quite primitive hominids, displaying an array of characteristics quite distinct from other members of our family. These primitive characteristics include flattening of the cranial base and relatively thin enamel caps on the molar teeth. From measurements of the humerus head, Wolpoff (1999) estimates a body weight of 42 kg (93 pounds); if this humerus comes from a male individual, this weight estimate is very similar to that hypothesized for other Plio-Pleistocene hominids (see Table 10–3, p. 281).

Thus, current conclusions (which will be either unambiguously confirmed or falsified as the skeleton is fully cleaned and studied) interpret the Aramis remains as the earliest hominids yet known (the mandible from Lothagam notwithstanding—and it is probably a member of the same species as the individuals from Aramis). These individuals from Aramis, although very primitive hominids, were apparently fully bipedal, although not necessarily in the same way that later hominids were.

Tim White and colleagues have recently argued (White et al., 1995) that the fossil hominids from Aramis are so primitive and so different from other early hominids that they should be assigned to a new genus (and, necessarily, a new species as well): *Ardipithecus ramidus*. Most especially, the thin enamel caps on the molars are in dramatic contrast to all other early hominids, who show quite thick enamel caps. These other early hominid forms (all somewhat later than *Ardipithecus*) are placed in the genus **Australopithecus**. Moreover, White and his associates have further suggested that as the earliest and most primitive hominid yet discovered, *Ardipithecus* may form the "sister-group" and thus possibly the root species for all later hominids. Another intriguing feature is that unlike the savanna habitat found at Olduvai and other East African hominid sites, the habitat at Aramis 4.4 m.y.a. was woodland. Perhaps we are seeing at Aramis the divergence of hominids very soon after they diverged from the African great apes!

▌ *Australopithecus*
An early hominid genus, known from the Plio-Pleistocene of Africa, characterized by bipedal locomotion, a relatively small brain, and large back teeth.

Australopithecus from East Africa

Several sites in Ethiopia, Kenya, and Tanzania have yielded remains of somewhat later hominids than the *Ardipithecus* remains from Aramis. Dating from 4.2 m.y.a. to approximately 1.4 m.y.a., most of these later East African fossils are included in the genus *Australopithecus*.* Note, however, that in the later half of this time span, some other specimens are placed in the genus *Homo*.

The earliest members of *Australopithecus* found to date come from two sites near Lake Turkana in northern Kenya (Allia Bay and Kanapoi). Like Aramis, these localities have only recently been fully explored, with the majority of discoveries coming during 1994 and 1995 (Leakey et al., 1995). Not as many specimens have been found at these two sites as at Aramis (see Table 10–1), but from what has been discovered, Meave Leakey and her colleagues have detected some interesting patterns. First, as with the Aramis specimens, limb bones indicate that these individuals were bipedal. Moreover, the molar teeth have thick enamel, like other members of *Australopithecus*.

However, there are also some primitive characteristics in these still quite early hominid specimens (dated 4.2–3.9 m.y.a.). For example, Leakey and colleagues point to such primitive features as a large canine, a **sectorial** lower first premolar (Fig. 10–9), and a small opening for the ear canal. Since these particular *Australopithecus* individuals have initially been interpreted as more primitive than all the later members of the genus, Meave Leakey and associates have provisionally assigned them to a separate species (*Australopithecus anamensis*). Further study and (with some luck) additional more complete remains will help decide whether such a distinction is warranted.

Slightly later and much more complete remains of *Australopithecus* have come from the sites of Hadar (in Ethiopia) and Laetoli (in Tanzania) (see Fig. 10–6). Much of this material has been known for some time (since the mid-1970s), and the fossils have been very well studied; indeed, in certain instances, they are quite famous. For example, the Lucy skeleton was discovered at Hadar in 1974, and the Laetoli footprints were first found in 1978. You will recall that we

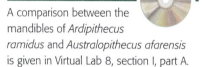
A comparison between the mandibles of *Ardipithecus ramidus* and *Australopithecus afarensis* is given in Virtual Lab 8, section I, part A.

▌ **Sectorial**
Adapted for cutting or shearing; among primates, refers to the compressed (side-to-side) first lower premolar, which functions as a shearing surface with the upper canine.

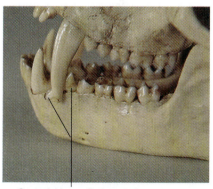
Sectorial lower first premolar

FIGURE 10–9

Left lateral view of the teeth of a male patas monkey. Note how the large upper canine shears against the elongated surface of the sectorial lower first premolar.

*Moreover, some paleoanthropologists place portions of the *Australopithecus* sample into another genus designated *Paranthropus* (see p. 289).

FIGURE 10–10

Hominid footprint from Laetoli, Tanzania. Note the deep impression of the heel and the large toe (arrow) in line (adducted) with the other toes.

Be sure to view the 3-D animations of the tibia of *Australopithecus anamensis* in Virtual Lab 8, section I, part A.

began this text with a brief discussion of the extraordinary footprint trail at Laetoli (see Fig. 1–1, p. 2). Literally thousands of footprints have been found at this remarkable site, representing more than 20 different kinds of animals (Pliocene elephants, horses, pigs, giraffes, antelope, hyenas, and an abundance of hares). Several hominid footprints have also been found, including a trail more than 75 feet long, made by at least two—and perhaps three—individuals (Leakey and Hay, 1979) (Fig 10–10).

Such discoveries of well-preserved hominid footprints are extremely important in furthering our understanding of human evolution. For the first time, we can make *definite* statements regarding the locomotor pattern and stature of early hominids. Initial analysis of these Pliocene footprints suggests a stature of about 4 feet 9 inches for the larger individual and 4 feet 1 inch for the smaller individual.

Studies of these impression patterns clearly show that the mode of locomotion of these hominids was bipedal (Day and Wickens, 1980). As we have discussed, the development of bipedal locomotion is the most important defining characteristic of early hominid evolution. Some researchers, however, have concluded that these early hominids were not bipedal in quite the same way that modern humans are. From detailed comparisons with modern humans, estimates of stride length, cadence, and speed of walking have been ascertained, indicating that the Laetoli hominids moved in a slow-moving ("strolling") fashion with a rather short stride (Chateris et al., 1981).

Two extraordinary discoveries at Hadar are most noteworthy. First, there is the Lucy skeleton (Fig. 10–11), found by Don Johanson eroding out of a hillside. This fossil is scientifically designated as Afar Locality (AL) 288-1, but is usually just called Lucy (after the Beatles' song "Lucy in the Sky with Diamonds"). Representing almost 40 percent of a skeleton, this is one of the three most complete individuals from anywhere in the world for the entire period before about 100,000 years ago.*

---

*The others are a specimen from Sterkfontein in South Africa (see p. 278) and a *H. erectus* skeleton from west of Lake Turkana, Kenya (see p. 314). Also note that the crushed and embedded skeleton from Aramis may be nearly as complete as Lucy.

The second find, a phenomenal discovery, came to light in 1975 at another Hadar locality. Don Johanson and his amazed crew found dozens of hominid bones scattered along a hillside. These bones represented at least 13 individuals, including 4 infants. Possibly members of one social unit, it has been argued that the members of this group died at about the same time, thus representing a "catastrophic" assemblage (White and Johanson, 1989). However, the precise deposition of the site has not been completely explained, so this assertion must be viewed as quite tentative. (In geological time, an "instant" could represent many decades or centuries.) Considerable cultural material has been found in the Hadar area—mostly washed into stream channels, but some stone tools have been reported in context at a site dated at 2.5 m.y.a., potentially making the findings among the oldest cultural evidence yet discovered.

Because the Laetoli area was covered periodically by ashfalls from nearby volcanic eruptions, accurate K/Ar dating is possible and has provided dates of 3.7–3.5 m.y.a. Dating from the Hadar region has not proved as straightforward; however, more complete dating calibration, using a variety of techniques (see Chapter 9), has determined a range of 3.9–3.0 m.y.a. for the hominid discoveries from this area (see Table 10–1).

Australopithecus afarensis from Laetoli and Hadar

Several hundred specimens, representing a minimum of 60 individuals (and perhaps as many as 100) have been removed from Laetoli and Hadar. At present, these materials represent the largest *well-studied* collection of early hominids known. This situation may well change with further discoveries and as analyses are completed for the Aramis, Kanapoi, and Allia Bay localities. Moreover, it has been suggested that fragmentary specimens from other locales in East Africa are remains of the same species as that found at Laetoli and Hadar. Most scholars refer to this species as *Australopithecus afarensis*.

Without question, *A. afarensis* is more primitive than any of the other **australopithecine** fossils from South or East Africa (discussed subsequently), although the recently described materials from Aramis (*Ardipithecus*) and Kanapoi and Allia Bay (*Australopithecus anamensis*) are even more primitive yet. By "primitive," we mean that *A. afarensis* is less evolved in any particular direction than are later occurring hominid species. That is, *A. afarensis* shares more primitive features with other early hominoids (such as *Dryopithecus* and *Sivapithecus*) and with living pongids than do later hominids, who display more derived characteristics.

For example, the teeth of *A. afarensis* are quite primitive. The canines are often large, pointed teeth. Moreover, the lower first premolar is semisectorial (i.e., it provides a shearing surface for the upper canine) and the tooth rows are parallel, even converging somewhat toward the back of the mouth (Fig. 10–12).

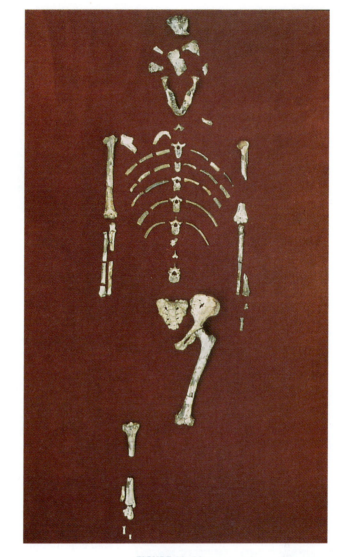

FIGURE 10–11

"Lucy," a partial hominid skeleton, discovered at Hadar in 1974. This individual is assigned to Australopithecus afarensis.

Virtual Lab 8, section I, part B, provides a discussion of *Australopithecus afarensis.*

■ **Australopithecine**

(os-tra-loh-pith´-e-seen) The colloquial name for members of the genus *Australopithecus*. The term was first used as a subfamily designation, but it is now most commonly used informally.

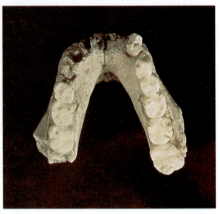

(a)   (b)

The cranial portions that are preserved, including a recently discovered specimen (shown in Fig. 10–13), also display several primitive hominoid characteristics, including a compound crest in the back as well as several primitive features
of the cranial base. Cranial capacity estimates for *A. afarensis* show a mixed pattern when compared to later hominids. A provisional estimate for the one partially complete cranium—apparently a large individual—gives a figure of 500 cm³,
but another, even more fragmentary cranium is apparently quite a bit smaller and
has been estimated at about 375 cm³ (Holloway, 1983). Thus, for some individuals (males?), *A. afarensis* is well within the range of other australopithecine species
(see Box 10–2), but others (females?) may have a significantly smaller cranial
capacity. However, a detailed depiction of cranial size for *A. afarensis* is not possible at this time; this part of the skeleton is unfortunately too poorly represented.
One thing is clear: *A. afarensis* had a small brain, probably averaging for the whole
species not much over 420 cm³.

On the other hand, a large assortment of postcranial pieces has been found at
Hadar. Initial impressions suggest that relative to lower limbs, the upper limbs are
longer than in modern humans (also a primitive hominoid condition). (This statement does not mean that the arms of *A. afarensis* were longer than the legs.) In
addition, the wrist, hand, and foot bones show several differences from modern
humans (Susman et al., 1985). Stature can now be confidently estimated:
A. afarensis was a short hominid. From her partial skeleton, Lucy is figured to be
only 3½ to 4 feet tall. However, Lucy—as demonstrated by her pelvis—was probably a female, and at Hadar and Laetoli, there is evidence of larger individuals as
well. The most economical hypothesis explaining this variation is that *A. afarensis*
was quite sexually dimorphic: The larger individuals are male and the smaller
ones, such as Lucy, are female. Estimates of male stature can be approximated
from the larger footprints at Laetoli, inferring a height of about 5 feet. If we accept
this interpretation, *A. afarensis* was a very sexually dimorphic form. In fact, for
overall body size, this species may have been as dimorphic as *any* living primate
(i.e., as much as gorillas, orangutans, or baboons).

In a majority of dental and cranial features, *A. afarensis* is clearly more primitive than later hominids. In fact, from the neck up, *A. afarensis* is so primitive that
without any evidence from the limbs, one would be hard-pressed to call it a
hominid at all (although the back teeth are large and heavily enameled, unlike
pongids, and the position of the foramen magnum indicates an upright posture).

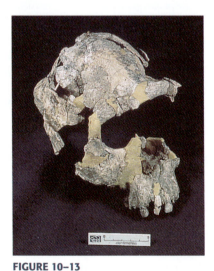

FIGURE 10–13

Australopithecus afarensis *cranium discovered at Hadar in 1992. This is the most complete* A. afarensis *cranium yet found.*

BOX 10–2

Cranial Capacity

ranial capacity, usually reported in cubic centimeters, is a measure of brain size or volume. The brain itself, of course, does not fossilize. However, the space once occupied by brain tissue (the inside of the cranial vault) does sometimes preserve, at least in those cases where fairly complete crania are recovered.

For purposes of comparison it is easy to obtain cranial capacity estimates for contemporary species (including humans) from analyses of skeletonized specimens in museum collections. From studies of this nature, estimated cranial capacities for modern hominoids have been determined as follows (Tobias, 1971, 1983):

	Range (cm³)	Average (cm³)
Human	1150–1750*	1325
Chimpanzee	285–500	395
Gorilla	340–752	506
Orangutan	276–540	411
Bonobo	—	350

*The range of cranial capacity for modern humans is very large—in fact, even greater than that shown (which approximates cranial capacity for the *majority* of contemporary *H. sapiens*).

These data for living hominoids can then be compared with those obtained from early hominids:

	Averages(s) (cm³)
Ardipithecus	Not presently known
Australopithecus anamensis	Not presently known
Australopithecus afarensis	420
Later australopithecines	410–530
Early members of genus *Homo*	631

As the tabulations indicate, cranial capacity estimates for australopithecines fall within the range of most modern great apes, and gorillas actually average slightly more than *A. afarensis.* It must be remembered, however, that gorillas are very large animals, whereas australopithecines probably weighed on the order of 100 pounds (see Table 10–3). Since brain size is partially correlated with body size, comparing such different-sized animals cannot be justified (see Chapter 7, p. 175, for a discussion of such *scaling* considerations). Compared to living chimpanzees (most of which are slightly larger than early hominids) and bonobos (which are somewhat smaller), australopithecines had *proportionately* about 10 percent bigger brains, and we would therefore say that these early hominids were more *encephalized* (see p. 175).

What, then, makes *A. afarensis* a hominid? The answer is revealed by its manner of locomotion. From the abundant limb bones recovered from Hadar and those beautiful footprints from Laetoli, we know unequivocally that *A. afarensis* walked bipedally when on the ground. Whether Lucy and her contemporaries still spent considerable time in the trees, and just how efficiently they walked, have become topics of some controversy. Most researchers, however, agree that *A. afarensis* was an efficient habitual biped while on the ground. These hominids were also clearly obligate bipeds, which would have hampered their climbing abilities but would not necessarily have precluded arboreal behavior altogether. As one physical anthropologist has surmised: "One could imagine these diminutive early hominids making maximum use of *both* terrestrial and arboreal resources in spite of their commitment to exclusive bipedalism when on the ground. The contention of a mixed arboreal and terrestrial behavioral repertoire would make adaptive sense of the Hadar australopithecine forelimb, hand, and foot morphology without contradicting the evidence of the pelvis" (Wolpoff, 1983b. p. 451).

The evolution of brain size in hominids is discussed in Virtual Lab 10, section IV, part B, and Virtual Lab 12, section I, part C.

The laboratory exercise in Virtual Lab 9, section V, focuses on the unique locomotor anatomy of *A. afarensis.*

Later East African Australopithecine Finds

An assortment of fossil hominids, including many specimens of later members of the genus *Australopithecus,* has been recovered from geological contexts with dates after 3 m.y.a. at several localities in East Africa. Up to 10 different such sites are now known (in the time range of 3–1 m.y.a.), but here we will concentrate on the three most significant ones: East Lake Turkana, West Lake Turkana (both in northern Kenya), and Olduvai Gorge (in northern Tanzania) (Table 10–2).

A significant new hominid discovery from another site in East Africa was announced in 1999 (Asfaw et al., 1999). Behane Asfaw, Tim White, and colleagues have discovered several fossils, dated to 2.5 m.y.a., of what they suggest may be yet another species of *Australopithecus* (termed *A. garhi; garhi,* meaning "surprise" in the Afar language). These important new finds come from the Bouri site in the Middle Awash region of Ethiopia, just south of Aramis. The hominid fossils, including an incomplete cranium and much of the limb skeleton (from another individual), are in several ways quite different from any other Plio-Pleistocene hominid. For example, the cranium combines a projecting face, fairly large front teeth, and very large back teeth. The limb proportions are also unusual, with long forelimbs (as in *A. afarensis*) but also with quite long hindlimbs (as in *Homo*). Finally, the hominids at Bouri were found close to animal bones displaying clear signs of butchering (see p. 254; see also cover photo).

Located very near the considerably older Allia Bay site on the east shore of Lake Turkana is Koobi Fora (Fig. 10–14). This latter locality, with sediments dating to 1.8–1.3 m.y.a., has provided specimens representing at least 100 individuals, and this fine sample includes several complete crania, many jaws, and an assortment of postcranial bones. Next to Olduvai, Koobi Fora has yielded the most information concerning the behavior of early hominids. More than 20 archaeological sites have been discovered, and excavation or testing has been done at 10 localities.

Across the lake, on the west side of Lake Turkana, are other deposits that recently have yielded new and very exciting discoveries. In addition, Olduvai

These hominid fossil localities can be found in the glossary of Virtual Lab 8.

TABLE 10–2   Summary of Later East African Hominid Discoveries

Site Name	Location	Age (m.y.a.)	Hominids
Olduvai	N. Tanzania	1.85–1.0	48 specimens; australopithecines; early *Homo*
Turkana	N. Kenya (eastern side of Lake Turkana)	1.9–1.3	More than 150 specimens; many australopithecines; several early *Homo*
	West side of Lake Turkana	2.5–1.6	1 cranium (australopithecine); 1 nearly complete skeleton (*Homo erectus*)
Middle Awash (Bouri)	N.E. Ethiopia	2.5	5 hominids; 1 cranium; parts of limb skeleton; (*A. garhi*)
Hadar	N.E. Ethiopia	3.9–3.0	Minimum of 40 individuals (maximum of 65); early australopithecines (*A. afarensis*)
Laetoli	N. Tanzania	3.7–3.5	24 hominids; early australopithecines (*A. afarensis*)

FIGURE 10-14

Excavations in progress at Koobi Fora, in East Lake Turkana, northern Kenya.

Gorge (discussed in detail in Chapter 9) has also yielded a considerable collection of early hominid fossils (see Table 10–2).

Australopithecines from Olduvai and Lake Turkana

Most fossil hominids from Olduvai, West Lake Turkana, and especially Koobi Fora are later in time than the *A. afarensis* remains from Laetoli and Hadar (by at least 500,000 years). It is thus not surprising that they are more derived, in some cases dramatically so. Also, these later hominids are considerably more diverse. Most researchers accept the interpretation that all the hominids from Laetoli and Hadar are members of a single taxon, *A. afarensis*. However, it is clear that the remains from the Turkana area and Olduvai collectively represent multiple taxa—two different genera and perhaps up to five or six different species. Current discussion on how best to sort this complex material is among the most vehement in paleoanthropology. Here we summarize the broad patterns of physical morphology. At the end of this chapter, we will take up the various schemes that attempt to interpret the fossil remains in a broader evolutionary context.

Following 2.5 m.y.a., later (and more derived) representatives of *Australopithecus* are found in East Africa. This is a most distinctive group that has popularly been known for some time as "robust" australopithecines. By "robust" it had generally been meant that these forms—when compared to other australopithecines—were larger in body size. However, recent, more controlled studies (Jungers, 1988; McHenry, 1988, 1992) have shown that all the species of *Australopithecus* overlapped considerably in body size. As you will see shortly, "robust" australopithecines have also been found in South Africa.

As a result of these new weight estimates, many researchers have either dropped the use of the term *robust* (along with its opposite, *gracile*) or presented it in quotation marks to emphasize its conditional application. We believe that the term *robust* can be used in this latter sense, as it still emphasizes important differences in the scaling of craniodental traits. In other words, even if they are not larger overall, robust forms are clearly robust in the skull and dentition.

FIGURE 10–15

The "black skull," WT 17000, discovered at West Lake Turkana in 1985. This specimen is provisionally assigned to Australopithecus aethiopicus. *It is called the "black skull" owing to the dark color from the fossilization (mineralization) process.*

■ **Sagittal crest**
Raised ridge along the midline of the cranium where the temporal muscle (which closes jaw) is attached.

Virtual Lab 8, section I, part C, provides a 3-D animation of WT 17000; section E provides 3-D animations of several specimens of *Australopithecus boisei.*

Virtual Lab 10 concerns the evolution of the genus *Homo* and provides many 3-D animations of important specimens.

■ ***Homo habilis***
    (hab´-ih-liss)
A species of early *Homo,* well known from East Africa, but perhaps also found in other regions.

Dating to approximately 2.5 m.y.a., the earliest representative of this robust group comes from northern Kenya on the west side of Lake Turkana. A complete cranium (WT 17000—"the black skull") was unearthed there in 1985 and has proved to be a most important discovery (Fig. 10–15). This skull, with a cranial capacity of only 410 cm³, has the smallest definitely ascertained brain volume of any hominid yet found and has other primitive traits reminiscent of *A. afarensis.* For example, there is a compound crest in the back of the skull, the upper face projects considerably, the upper dental row converges in back, and the cranial base is extensively pneumatized—that is, it possesses air pockets (Kimbel et al., 1988).

What makes the black skull so fascinating, however, is that mixed with this array of distinctively primitive traits are a host of derived ones linking it to other members of the robust group (including a broad face, a very large palate, and a large area for the back teeth). This mosaic of features seems to place skull WT 17000 between earlier *A. afarensis* on the one hand and the later robust species on the other. Because of its unique position in hominid evolution, WT 17000 (and the population it represents) has been placed in a new species, *Australopithecus aethiopicus.*

Around 2 m.y.a., different varieties of even more derived members of the robust lineage were on the scene in East Africa. As well documented by finds at Olduvai and Koobi Fora, robust australopithecines have relatively small cranial capacities (ranging from 510 to 530 cm³) and very large, broad faces with massive back teeth and lower jaws. The larger (probably male) individuals also show a raised ridge, called a **sagittal crest,** along the midline of the cranium. The first find of a recognized Pio-Pleistocene hominid in East Africa, in fact, was of a nearly complete robust australopithecine cranium, discovered in 1959 by Mary Leakey at Olduvai Gorge (see p. 234). As a result of Louis Leakey's original naming of the fossil (as *Zinjanthropus*), this find is still popularly referred to as "Zinj." However, it and other members of the same species in East Africa are now usually classified as *Australopithecus boisei.*

Early *Homo*

In addition to the robust australopithecine remains in East Africa, there is another contemporaneous Plio-Pleistocene hominid that is quite distinctive. In fact, as best documented by fossil discoveries from Olduvai and Koobi Fora, these materials have been assigned to the genus *Homo*—and thus are different from all species assigned to *Australopithecus.*

The earliest appearance of genus *Homo* in East Africa may be as ancient as that of the robust australopithecines. (As we have discussed, the black skull from West Turkana has been dated to approximately 2.5 m.y.a.) Recent reinterpretations of a temporal fragment from the Lake Baringo region of central Kenya have suggested that early *Homo* may also be close to this same antiquity (estimated age of 2.4 m.y.a) (Hill et al., 1992). More diagnostic remains of a lower jaw of early *Homo* have also recently been reported from Hadar, in Ethiopia, and are dated to 2.3 m.y.a. (Kimbel et al., 1996). Given that the robust australopithecine lineage was probably diverging at this time, it is not surprising to find the earliest representatives of the genus *Homo* also beginning to diversify.

The presence of a Plio-Pleistocene hominid with a significantly larger brain than seen in *Australopithecus* was first suggested by Louis Leakey in the early 1960s on the basis of fragmentary remains found at Olduvai Gorge. Leakey and his colleagues gave a new species designation to these fossil remains, naming them ***Homo habilis.***

The *Homo habilis* material at Olduvai ranges in time from 1.85 m.y.a. for the earliest to about 1.6 m.y.a. for the latest. Due to the fragmentary nature of the fossil remains, interpretations have been difficult and much disputed. The most immediately obvious feature distinguishing the *H. habilis* material from the australopithecines is cranial size. For all the measurable *H. habilis* skulls, the estimated average cranial capacity is 631 cm³ compared to 520 cm³ for all measurable robust australopithecines and 442 cm³ for the less robust species (McHenry, 1988) (see Box 10–2). *Homo habilis,* therefore, shows an increase in cranial size of about 20 percent over the larger of the australopithecines and an even greater increase over some of the smaller-brained forms (from South Africa, discussed shortly). In their initial description of *H. habilis,* Leakey and his associates also pointed to differences from australopithecines in cranial shape and in tooth proportions (larger front teeth relative to back teeth and narrower premolars).

The naming of this fossil material as *Homo habilis* ("handy man") was meaningful from two perspectives. First of all, Leakey inferred that members of this group were the early Olduvai toolmakers. If true, how do we account for a robust australopithecine like "Zinj" lying in the middle of the largest excavated area known at Olduvai? What was he doing there? Leakey suggested that he was the remains of a *habilis* meal! Excepting those instances where cut marks are left behind (see pp. 253–254), we must point out again that there is no clear way archaeologically to establish the validity of such a claim. However, the debate over this assertion serves to demonstrate that cultural factors as well as physical morphology must be considered in the interpretation of hominids as biocultural organisms. Secondly, and most significantly, by calling this group *Homo,* Leakey was arguing for at least *two separate branches* of hominid evolution in the Plio-Pleistocene. Clearly, only one could be on the main branch eventually leading to *Homo sapiens.* By labeling this new group *Homo* rather than *Australopithecus,* Leakey was guessing that he had found our ancestors.

Because the initial evidence was so fragmentary, most paleoanthropologists were reluctant to accept *H. habilis* as a valid taxon distinct from *all* australopithecines. Later discoveries, especially from Lake Turkana, of better-preserved fossil material have shed further light on early *Homo* in the Plio-Pleistocene (Fig. 10–16). The most important of this additional material is a nearly complete cranium (ER 1470) discovered at Koobi Fora (Fig. 10–17). With a cranial capacity of 775 cm³, this

FIGURE 10–16

The Kenyan team at East Lake Turkana. Kamoya Kimeu (driving) is the most successful fossil hunter in East Africa. He has been responsible for dozens of important discoveries.

FIGURE 10–17

A nearly complete early Homo *cranium from East Lake Turkana (ER 1470), one of the most important single fossil hominid discoveries from East Africa.*

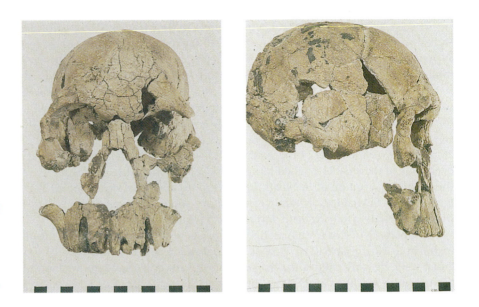

A 3-D animation of ER 1470 and discussions of early *Homo* are provided in Virtual Lab 10, section I, part A.

Virtual Lab 10, section IV, part A, provides a laboratory exercise that investigates the humero-femoral index of early *Homo,* including specimen OH 62.

individual is well outside the known range for australopithecines and actually overlaps the lower boundary for *Homo erectus.* In addition, the shape of the skull vault and face are in many respects unlike those of australopithecines. However, the face is still quite robust (Walker, 1976), and the fragments of tooth crowns that are preserved indicate that the back teeth in this individual were quite large. Dating of the Koobi Fora early *Homo* material places it contemporaneous with the Olduvai remains, that is, about 1.8–1.6 m.y.a.

Other Plio-Pleistocene sites also have revealed possible early members of the genus *Homo* (Fig. 10–18). From the Omo in southern Ethiopia, scattered remains of a few teeth and small cranial fragments are similar in pattern to other comparable early *Homo* material. In addition, a recently discovered very partial skeleton from Olduvai Gorge (OH 62) is extremely small-statured (probably less than 4 feet tall) and has several primitive aspects in its limb proportions (Johanson et al., 1987).

On the basis of evidence from Olduvai and particularly from Koobi Fora, we can reasonably postulate that one or more species of early *Homo* were present in East Africa probably by 2.4 m.y.a., developing in parallel with at least one line of australopithecines. These two hominid lines lived contemporaneously for a minimum of 1 million years, after which the australopithecine lineage apparently disappeared forever. At the same time, probably the early *Homo* line was evolving into a later form, *Homo erectus,* which in turn developed into *H. sapiens.*

Central Africa

In 1995, another new early hominid discovery was announced from a rather surprising location—Chad, in central Africa (Brunet et al., 1995) (see Fig. 10–6). From an area called the Bahr el Ghazal (Arabic for "River of the Gazelles"), a partial hominid mandible was discovered in association with faunal remains tentatively dated to 3.5–3.0 m.y.a. (Further confirmation will have to await radiometric dating, assuming that appropriate materials become available.) The preliminary analysis suggests that this fossil is an australopithecine with closest affinities to *A. afarensis.* What makes this find remarkable is its geographical location, more than 1,500 miles west of the previously established range of early hominids!

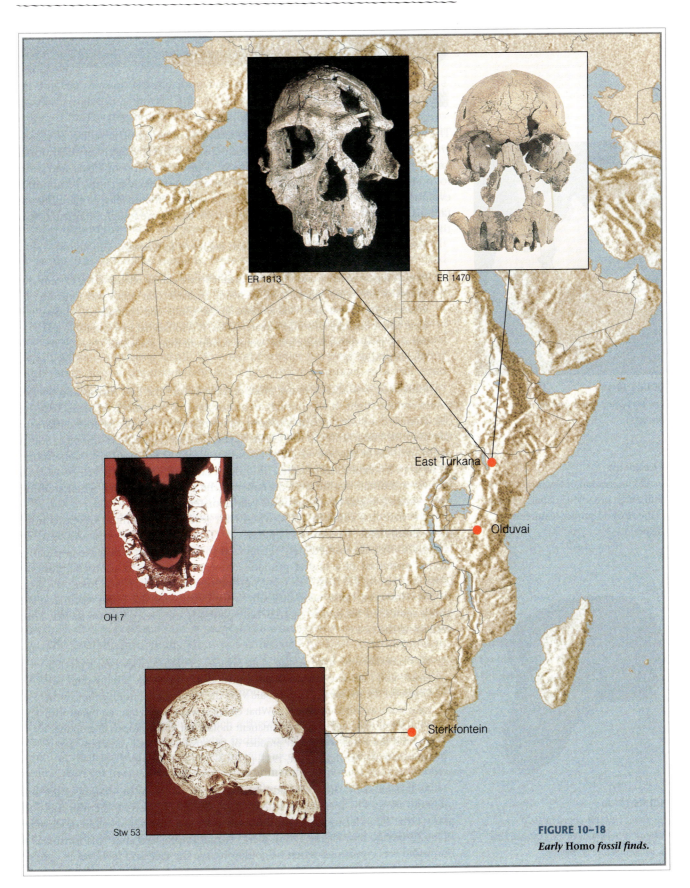

ER 1813

ER 1470

East Turkana

Olduvai

OH 7

Sterkfontein

Stw 53

FIGURE 10–18
Early Homo *fossil finds.*

FIGURE 10–21
Robert Broom.

■ **Sterkfontein**
(sterk´-fon-tane)

■ **Kromdraai**
(kromm´-dry)

■ **Swartkrans**
(swart´-kranz)

■ **Makapansgat**
(mak-ah-pans´-gat)

The South African hominids
are discussed in Virtual Lab 8,
section I, parts D and F. These sections
include several 3-D animations.

Further Discoveries of South African Hominids

Soon after publication of his controversial theories, Dart found a strong ally in Robert Broom (Fig. 10–21). A Scottish physician and part-time paleontologist, Broom's credentials as a fossil hunter had been established earlier with his highly successful paleontological work on early mammal-like reptiles in South Africa.

Although interested, Broom was unable to participate actively in the search for additional australopithecines until 1936. From two of Dart's students, Broom learned of another commercial limeworks site, called **Sterkfontein**, not far from Johannesburg. Here, as at Taung, the quarrying involved blasting out large sections with dynamite, leaving piles of debris that often contained fossilized remains. Accordingly, Broom asked the quarry manager to keep his eyes open for fossils, and when Broom returned to the site in August 1936, the manager asked, "Is this what you are looking for?" Indeed it was, for Broom held in his hand the endocast of an adult australopithecine—exactly what he had set out to find! Looking further over the scattered debris, Broom was able to find most of the rest of the skull of the same individual.

Such remarkable success, just a few months after beginning his search, was not the end of Broom's luck, for his magical touch was to continue unabated for several more years. In 1938, he learned of another australopithecine site at **Kromdraai**, about 1 mile from Sterkfontein, and following World War II (1948), he found yet another, **Swartkrans**, in the same vicinity. A final australopithecine site, **Makapansgat**, was excavated in 1947 by Raymond Dart, who returned to the fossil-discovering stage after an absence of over 20 years.

Numerous extremely important discoveries came from these additional sites, discoveries that would eventually swing the tide of intellectual thought to the views that Dart expressed back in 1925. Particularly important was a nearly complete cranium and pelvis, both found at Sterkfontein in 1947. As the number of discoveries accumulated, it became increasingly difficult to simply write the australopithecines off as aberrant apes.

By 1949, at least 30 hominid individuals were represented from five South African sites, and leading scientists were coming to accept the australopithecines as hominids. With this acceptance also came the necessary recognition that hominid brains had their greatest expansion *after* earlier changes in teeth and locomotor systems. In other words, once again we see that the rate of evolution in one functional system of the body varies from that of other systems, thus displaying the *mosaic* nature of human evolution.

Since the 1950s, exploration of the South African hominid sites has continued, and numerous important discoveries were made in the 1970s and 1980s. The most spectacular new find was made in 1998 at Sterkfontein, where the remains of a virtually complete australopithecine skeleton were found by Ron Clarke and his associates from the University of Witwatersrand. Most of the remains are still embedded in the surrounding limestone matrix and will require several months for removal, cleaning, and reconstruction.

As we will discuss in more detail shortly, dating of all the South African Plio-Pleistocene sites has proved most difficult; estimates for the Sterkfontein australopithecine skeleton are between 3.6 and 2.5 m.y.a. Even before the remains have been fully excavated, this is still recognized as an unusual and highly significant find. Because such complete individuals are so rare in the hominid fossil record, this discovery has tremendous potential to shed more light on the precise nature of early hominid locomotion. For example, will the rest of the skeleton confirm what foot bones of the same individual have implied regarding arboreal climbing in this bipedal hominid? (See p. 261.) Moreover, relative proportions of brain size compared to body size, better estimates of overall body size, relative proportions of the limbs, and much more can be more accurately assessed from such a completely preserved skeleton.

Hominids from South Africa

The Plio-Pleistocene hominid discoveries from South Africa are most significant. First, they were the initial hominid discoveries in Africa and helped point the way to later finds in East Africa. Second, morphology of the South African hominids shows broad similarities to the forms in East Africa, but with several distinctive features, which argues for separation at least at the species level. Finally, there is a large assemblage of hominid fossils from South Africa, and exciting discoveries are still being made (Fig. 10–22).

Today, the evidence from South Africa continues to accumulate. In the last few years alone, more than 150 *new* specimens have come to light at Sterkfontein, including another well-preserved cranium found in 1989 (Conroy et al., 1998). In addition, several important new discoveries have been made at Swartkrans. A truly remarkable collection of early hominids, the remains from South Africa exceed 1,500 (counting all teeth as separate items), and the number of individuals is now more than 200.

From an evolutionary point of view, the most meaningful remains are those of the pelvis, which now include portions of nine ossa coxae (see p. 257). Remains of the pelvis are so important because, better than any other area of the body, this structure displays the unique requirements of a bipedal animal (as in modern humans *and* in our hominid forebears).

"Robust" Australopithecines   In addition to the discoveries of *A. aethiopicus* and *A. boisei* in East Africa, there are also numerous finds of robust australopithecines in South Africa from sites at Kromdraai and most especially at Swartkrans. Like their East African cousins, the South African robust forms also have small cranial capacities (the only measurable specimen equals 530 cm³), large broad faces, and very large premolars and molars (although not as massive as in East Africa). Owing to the differences in dental proportions, as well as important differences in facial architecture (Rak, 1983), most researchers now agree that there is a species-level difference between the later East African robust variety (*A. boisei*) and the South African group (*A. robustus*).

Despite these differences, all members of the robust lineage appear to be specialized for a diet made up of hard food items, such as seeds and nuts. For many years, paleoanthropologists (e.g., Robinson, 1972) had speculated that robust australopithecines concentrated their diet on heavier vegetable foods than those seen in the diet of other early hominids. More recent research that included examining microscopic polishes and scratches on the teeth (Kay and Grine, 1988) has confirmed this view.

"Gracile" Australopithecines   Another variety of australopithecine (also small-brained, but not as large-toothed as the robust varieties) is known from Africa. However, while the robust lineage is represented in both East and South Africa, this other (gracile) australopithecine form is known only from the southern part of the continent. First named *A. africanus* by Dart for the single individual at

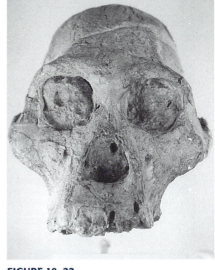

FIGURE 10–22

A gracile australopithecine cranium from Sterkfontein (Sts 5). Discovered in 1947, this specimen is the best-preserved gracile skull yet found in South Africa.

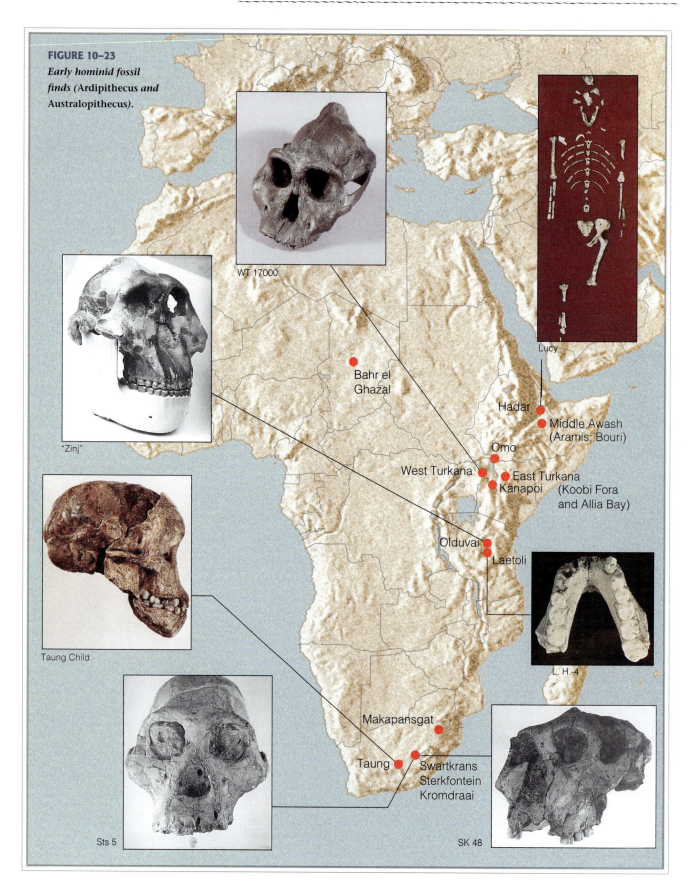

FIGURE 10–23
Early hominid fossil finds (Ardipithecus and Australopithecus).

WT 17000

Lucy

"Zinj"

Bahr el Ghazal

Hadar

Middle Awash (Aramis; Bouri)

Omo

West Turkana

East Turkana (Koobi Fora and Allia Bay)

Kanapoi

Olduvai

Laetoli

Taung Child

L. H.-4

Makapansgat

Taung

Swartkrans
Sterkfontein
Kromdraai

Sts 5

SK 48

| TABLE 10–3 | Estimated Body Weights and Stature in Plio-Pleistocene Hominids | | | |

| | Body Weight | | Stature | |
	Male	Female	Male	Female
A. afarensis	45 kg (99 lb)	29 kg (64 lb)	151 cm (59 in.)	105 cm (41 in.)
A. africanus	41 kg (90 lb)	30 kg (65 lb)	138 cm (54 in.)	115 cm (45 in.)
A. robustus	40 kg (88 lb)	32 kg (70 lb)	132 cm (52 in.)	110 cm (43 in.)
A. boisei	49 kg (108 lb)	34 kg (75 lb)	137 cm (54 in.)	124 cm (49 in.)
H. habilis	52 kg (114 lb)	32 kg (70 lb)	157 cm (62 in.)	125 cm (49 in.)

Source: After McHenry, 1992.

A discussion of body mass and the methods for estimating it for fossil specimens is given in Virtual Lab 10, section III, part B.

Taung, this australopithecine is also found at Makapansgat and especially at Sterkfontein (Fig. 10–23).

Traditionally, it had been thought that there was a significant variation in body size between the gracile and robust forms. But as mentioned earlier and shown in Table 10–3, there is not much difference in body size among the australopithecines. In fact, most of the differences between the robust and gracile forms are found in the face and dentition.

The facial structure of the gracile australopithecines is more lightly built and somewhat dish-shaped compared to the more vertical configuration seen in robust specimens. As we noted earlier, in robust individuals, a raised ridge along the midline of the skull is occasionally observed. Indeed, at Sterkfontein, among the larger individuals (males?), a hint of such a sagittal crest is also seen. This structure provides additional attachment area for the large temporal muscle, which is the primary muscle operating the massive jaw below. Such a structure is also seen in some modern apes, especially male gorillas and orangutans; however, in most australopithecines, the temporal muscle acts most efficiently on the back of the mouth and is therefore not functionally equivalent to the pattern seen in great apes—where the emphasis is more on the front teeth (see Fig 10–24).

The most distinctive difference observed between gracile and robust australopithecines is in the dentition. Compared to modern humans, they both have relatively large teeth, which are, however, definitely hominid in pattern. In fact, more emphasis is on the typical back-tooth grinding complex among these early forms than is seen in modern humans; therefore, if anything, australopithecines are "hyperhominid" in their dentition. Robust forms emphasize this trend to an extreme degree, showing deep jaws and much-enlarged back teeth, particularly the molars, leaving little room in the front of the mouth for the anterior teeth (incisors and canines). Conversely, the gracile australopithecines have proportionately larger front teeth compared to the size of their back teeth. The contrast is seen most clearly in the relative size of the canine compared to the first premolar: In robust individuals, the first premolar is clearly a much larger tooth than the small canine (about twice as large), whereas in gracile specimens, it only averages abut 20 percent larger than the fairly good-sized canine (Howells, 1973).

These differences in the relative proportions of the teeth and jaws best define a gracile, as compared to a robust, australopithecine. In fact, most of the

(a) Hominid (robust australopithecine)

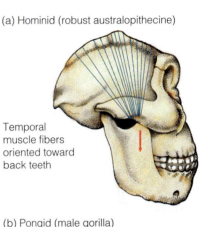

Temporal muscle fibers oriented toward back teeth

(b) Pongid (male gorilla)

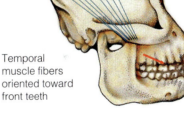

Temporal muscle fibers oriented toward front teeth

FIGURE 10–24

Sagittal crests and temporal muscle orientations. Hominid compared to pongid. (Line of greatest muscle force is shown in red.)

Virtual Lab 8 provides many comparisons of the craniodental features of the gracile and robust australopithecines. The laboratory exercise in section II investigates the features and diet of *Australopithecus boisei.*

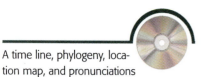

A time line, phylogeny, location map, and pronunciations for the Plio-Pleistocene hominids are given in the glossary of Virtual Lab 8.

FIGURE 10–25

Time line of major Plio-Pleistocene hominid sites. Note that most dates are approximations. Question marks indicate those estimates that are most tentative.

differences in skull shape we have discussed can be directly attributed to contrasting jaw function in the two forms. Both the sagittal crest and broad vertical face of the robust form are related to the muscles and biomechanical requirements of the heavy back tooth chewing adaptation seen in this animal.

Early *Homo* in South Africa   As in East Africa, early members of the genus *Homo* have also been found in South Africa, apparently living contemporaneously with australopithecines. At both Sterkfontein and Swartkrans, fragmentary remains have been recognized as most likely belonging to *Homo*. In fact, Ron Clarke (1985) has shown that the key fossil of early *Homo* from Sterkfontein (Stw 53) is nearly identical to the OH 24 *Homo habilis* cranium from Olduvai.

However, a problem with both OH 24 and Stw 53 is that while most experts agree that they belong to the genus *Homo*, there is considerable disagreement as to whether they should be included in the species *habilis*. The relationships of the Plio-Pleistocene fossil hominids to one another and the difficulties of such genus and species interpretation will be discussed in the following sections. A time line for all the Plio-Pleistocene sites discussed in the text is shown in Figure 10–25.

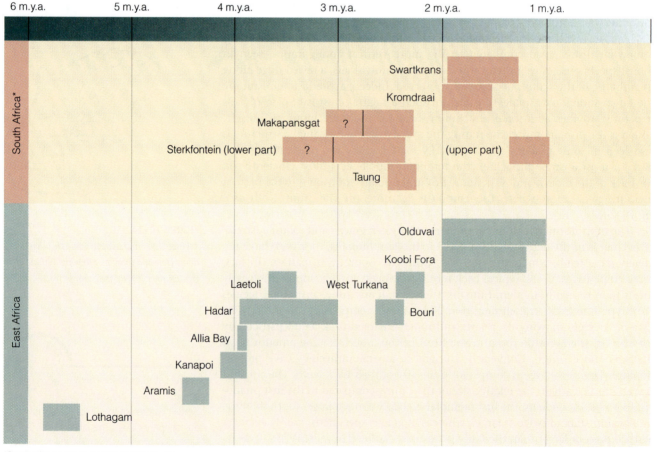

*South African dates are very approximate.

Geology and Dating Problems in South Africa

While the geological and archaeological context in East Africa is often straightforward, the five South African early hominid sites are much more complex geologically. All were discovered by commercial quarrying activity, which greatly disrupted the geological picture and, in the case of Taung, completely destroyed the site.

The hominid remains are found with thousands of other fossilized bones embedded in limestone cliffs, caves, fissures, and sinkholes. The limestone was formed by millions of generations of shells of marine organisms during the Precambrian—more than 2 billion years ago—when South Africa was submerged under a shallow sea. Once deposited, the limestones were cut through by percolating groundwater from below and rainwater from above, forming a maze of caves and fissures often connected to the surface by narrow shafts. Through these vertical shafts and horizontal cave openings, bones either fell or were carried in, where they conglomerated with sand, pebbles, and soil into a cementlike matrix call *breccia*.

As the cave fissures filled in, they were constantly subjected to further erosion forces from above and below, so that caves would be partially filled, then closed to the surface for a considerable time, then reopened again to commence accumulation thousands of years later. All this activity yields an incredibly complex geological situation that can be worked out only after the most detailed kind of paleoecological analysis.

Since bones accumulated in these caves and fissures largely by accidental processes, it seems likely that none of the South African australopithecine sites are *primary* hominid localities. In other words, unlike East Africa, these are not areas where hominids organized activities, scavenged food, and so on.

Just how did all the fossilized bone accumulate, and, most particularly, what were the ancient hominids doing there? In the case of Swartkrans, Sterkfontein, and Kromdraai, the bones probably accumulated through the combined activities of carnivorous leopards, saber-toothed cats, and hyenas. Moreover, the unexpectedly high proportion of primate (baboon and hominid) remains suggests that these localities were the location (or very near the location) of primate sleeping sites, thus providing ready primate prey for various predators (Brain, 1981).

Raymond Dart argued enthusiastically for an alternative explanation, suggesting that the hominids camping at Makapansgat regularly used bone, tooth, and horn remains as tools, which he called the **osteodontokeratic** culture complex. Analogies with the food habits of modern African foragers indicate that the bone accumulation at Makapansgat may be accounted for simply by hominid and carnivore eating practices. More recent paleoecological work at Makapansgat has thrown Dart's assertions into even greater doubt. Apparently, remains accumulated here primarily in a similar fashion to Sterkfontein and Swartkrans—through a narrow shaft entrance (Fig. 10–26). Therefore, large animals could have entered but not departed the deep subterranean cavern. Makapansgat, like Sterkfontein and Swartkrans, probably also represents the accumulated debris of carnivore activity (perhaps hyenas) outside the cave entrance. So little is left of the final site, Taung, that accurate paleoecological reconstructions are not feasible.

Owing to the complex geological picture, as well as lack of appropriate material such as volcanic deposits for chronometric techniques, dating the

■ Osteodontokeratic
(*osteo*, meaning "bone," *donto*, meaning "tooth," and *keratic*, meaning "horn")

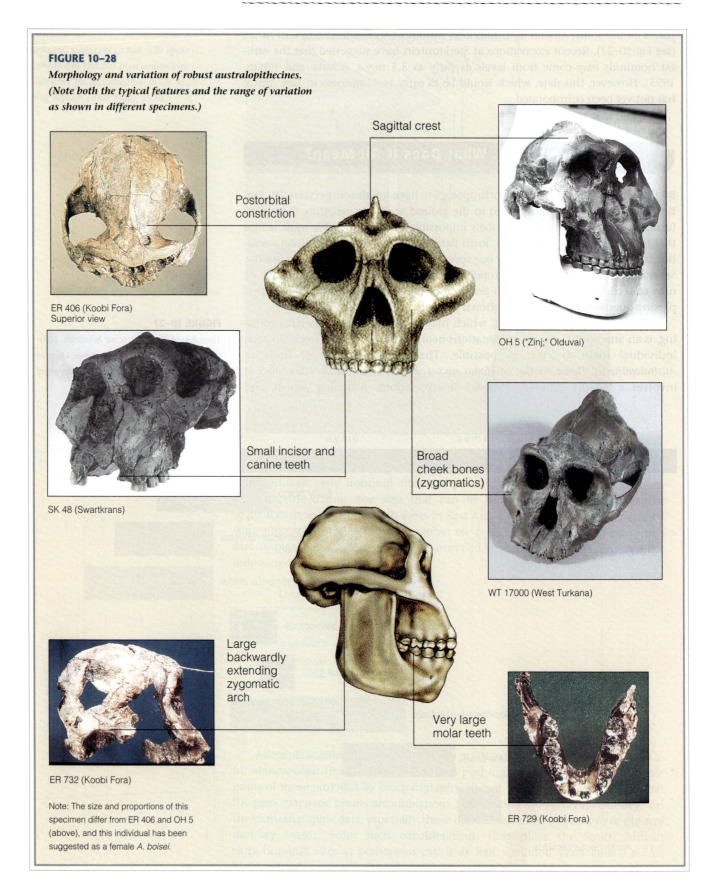

FIGURE 10–28

Morphology and variation of robust australopithecines. (Note both the typical features and the range of variation as shown in different specimens.)

Sagittal crest

Postorbital constriction

ER 406 (Koobi Fora)
Superior view

OH 5 ("Zinj;" Olduvai)

SK 48 (Swartkrans)

Small incisor and canine teeth

Broad cheek bones (zygomatics)

WT 17000 (West Turkana)

Large backwardly extending zygomatic arch

Very large molar teeth

ER 732 (Koobi Fora)

Note: The size and proportions of this specimen differ from ER 406 and OH 5 (above), and this individual has been suggested as a female *A. boisei*.

ER 729 (Koobi Fora)

specific names to fossil finds is more than just a convenience; when we attach a particular label, such as *A. boisei*, to a particular fossil, we should be fully aware of the biological implications of such an interpretation.

Even more basic to our understanding of human evolution, the use of taxonomic nomenclature involves interpretations of fossil relationships. For example, the two fossils "Zinj" and ER 406 (see Fig. 10–28) are both usually called *A. boisei*. What we are saying here is that they are both members of one interbreeding species. These two fossils can now be compared with others, like Sts 5 from Sterkfontein (see Fig. 10–22), which is usually called *A. africanus*. What we are implying now is that "Zinj" and ER 406 are more closely related to each other than *either* is to Sts 5. Furthermore, that Sts 5 (*A. africanus*) populations were incapable of successfully interbreeding with *A. boisei* populations is a direct biological inference of this nomenclature.

We can carry the level of interpretation even further. For example, fossils such as ER 1470 (see Fig. 10–17) are called early *Homo* (*Homo habilis*). We are now making a genus-level distinction, and two basic biological implications are involved:

1. *A. africanus* (Sts 5) and *A. boisei* ("Zinj" and ER 406) are more closely related to each other than either is to ER 1470 (Fig. 10–29).
2. The distinction between the groups reflects a basic difference in adaptive level (see Chapter 8).

From the time that fossil sites are first located to the eventual interpretation of hominid evolutionary events, several steps are necessary. Ideally, they should follow a logical order, for if interpretations are made too hastily, they confuse important issues for many years. Here is a reasonable sequence:

1. Selecting and surveying sites
2. Excavating sites and recovering fossil hominids
3. Designating individual finds with specimen numbers for clear reference
4. Cleaning, preparing, studying, and describing fossils
5. Comparing with other fossil material—in chronological framework if possible
6. Comparing fossil variation with known ranges of variation in closely related groups of living primates and analyzing ancestral and derived characteristics
7. Assigning taxonomic names to fossil material

The task of interpretation is still not complete, for what we really want to know in the long run is what happened to the populations represented by the fossil remains. Indeed, in looking at the fossil hominid record, we are looking for our ancestors. In the process of eventually determining those populations that are our most likely antecedents, we may conclude that some hominids are on evolutionary side branches. If this conclusion is accurate, those hominids necessarily must have become extinct. It is both interesting and relevant to us as hominids to try to find out what influenced some earlier members of our family to continue evolving while others died out.

Continuing Uncertainties—Taxonomic Issues

As previously discussed, paleoanthropologists are crucially concerned with making biological interpretations of variation found in the hominid fossil

Comparisons of the craniodental features of the Plio-Pleistocene hominid shown in Fig. 10–28 are also presented in Virtual Lab 8.

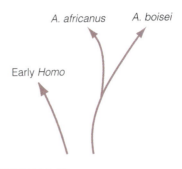

FIGURE 10–29

Phylogenetic interpretation. Early Homo *is generically distinct from australopithecines.*

record. Most especially, researchers endeavor to assign extinct forms to particular genera and species. We saw that for the diverse array of Miocene hominoids, the evolutionary picture is exceptionally complex. As new finds accumulate, there is continued uncertainty even as to family assignment, to say nothing of genus and species!

For the Plio-Pleistocene, the situation is considerably clearer. First, there is a larger fossil sample from a more restricted geographical area (South and East Africa) and from a more concentrated time period (spanning 3.4 million years, from 4.4 to 1.0 m.y.a.). Second, more complete specimens exist (e.g., "Lucy"), and we thus have good evidence for most parts of the body. Accordingly, there is considerable consensus on several basic aspects of evolutionary development during the Plio-Pleistocene. Researchers agree unanimously that these forms are hominids (members of the family Hominidae). And as support for this point, all these forms are seen as habitual, well-adapted bipeds, committed at least in part to a terrestrial niche. Moreover, researchers generally agree as to genus-level assignments for most of the forms (although *Ardipithecus* has been so recently named as to not yet be fully evaluated and accepted, and there is also some disagreement regarding how to group the robust australopithecines).

As for species-level designations, little consensus can be found. Indeed, as new fossils have been discovered (e.g., the "black skull"), the picture seems to muddy further. Once again, we are faced with a complex evolutionary process. In attempts to deal with it, we impose varying degrees of simplicity. In so doing, we hope to understand evolutionary developments more clearly—not just for introductory students, but also for professional paleoanthropologists and textbook authors! Nevertheless, evolution is not a simple process, and disputes and disagreements are bound to arise, especially in making such fine-tuned interpretations as species-level designations.

Consider the following ongoing topics of interest and occasional disagreement among paleoanthropologists dealing with Plio-Pleistocene hominids. You should realize, however, that such continued debate is at the heart of scientific endeavor; indeed, it provides a major stimulus for further research. Here, we raise questions regarding five areas of taxonomic interpretation. In general, there is still reasonably strong agreement on these points and we follow, where possible, the current consensus as reflected in recent publications (Grine, 1988a; Klein, 1989; Conroy, 1997; Fleagle, 1999).

1. ***Is* Ardipithecus *a hominid? If so, is* Ardipithecus *really generically distinct from* Australopithecus?**
   Only tentative clues from the cranium and upper limb have thus far suggested that the 4.4-million-year-old fossils from Aramis were bipedal. Descriptions of the more complete skeleton (including a pelvis) have not yet been published. However, from what is known and what has been initially reported, it appears that these forms were bipedal and thus should be classified as hominids. Much more detailed analysis will need to be completed before it can be concluded how habitual and obligate the bipedal adaptation was. Also uncertain is the genus status of these new finds. Again, from what is known, especially of the dentition (showing thin enamel on the back teeth), the Aramis finds do look quite different from *any* known *Australopithecus* species.

2. ***How many species are there at Hadar and Laetoli (i.e., is* Australopithecus afarensis *one species)?***
   Some paleoanthropologists argue that what has been described as a single species (especially regarding the large Hadar sample) actually represents at

least two separate species (taxa). However, it is clear that all australopithecines were highly variable, and thus the pattern seen at Hadar might well represent a single, highly dimorphic species. Most scholars accept this interpretation, and it is best, for the moment, to follow this more conservative view. As a matter of good paleontological practice, it is desirable not to overly "split" fossil samples until compelling evidence is presented.

3. *Is Australopithecus anamensis (from Allia Bay and Kanapoi) a separate species from Australopithecus afarensis?*
   The fossil discoveries of *A. anamensis* have thus far been quite fragmentary. When we compare them with the much better known *A. afarensis* materials, the anatomical differences in the Allia Bay and Kanapoi specimens are by no means striking. Thus, until more complete remains are discovered, it is best to be cautious and regard the new species designation (*Australopithecus anamensis*) as a tentative hypothesis and one requiring further confirmation.

4. *How many genera of australopithecines are there?*
   Many years ago, a plethora of genera was suggested by Robert Broom and others. However, in the 1960s and 1970s, most researchers agreed to "lump" all these forms into *Australopithecus*. With the discovery of early members of the genus *Homo* in the 1960s (and its general recognition in the 1970s), most researchers also recognized the presence of our genus in the Plio-Pleistocene as well (Fig. 10–30).

   In the last decade, there has been an increasing tendency to resplit some of the australopithecines. Recognizing that the robust group (*aethiopicus, boisei,* and *robustus*) forms a distinct evolutionary lineage (clade), many researchers (Grine, 1988a; Wood et al., 1994) have argued that the generic term *Paranthropus* should be used to set these robust forms apart from *Australopithecus* (now used in the strict sense).

   We agree that there are adequate grounds to make a genus-level distinction, given the evolutionary distinctiveness of the robust clade as well as its apparent adaptive uniqueness (see Fig 10–28). However, for *closely related taxa*, such as we are dealing with here, making this type of interpretation is largely arbitrary. (See discussion, pp. 219–221.) The single genus *Australopithecus* has been used for four decades in the wider sense (to include all robust forms), and because it simplifies terminology, we follow the current consensus and continue the traditional usage—*Australopithecus* for all small-brained Plio-Pleistocene hominids with large, thickly enameled teeth (particularly molars) and including all five recognized species: *A. afarensis, A. aethiopicus, A. africanus, A. robustus,* and *A. boisei.*

5. *How many species of early Homo existed?*
   Here is another species-level type of interpretation that is unlikely to be resolved soon. Yet, as it strikes closer to home (our own genus) than the issue for robust australopithecines, the current debate is generating more heat.

See Virtual Labs 8 and 10 for 3-D animations of these various Plio-Pleistocene hominid species.

FIGURE 10–30

Plio-Pleistocene hominids.

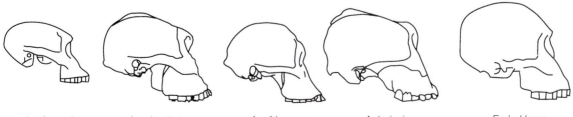

A. afarensis   A. robustus   A. africanus   A. boisei   Early *Homo*

Whether we find resolution or not, the *form* of the conflicting views is instructive. The main issue is again interpreting whether variation is *inter-* or *intraspecific*. For those anthropologists who include all the early *Homo* remains from Africa within *one* species (e.g., Tobias, 1991), the considerable variation is thought largely to be due to sexual dimorphism. However, many other researchers (a growing consensus, in fact) see too much variation among the specimens to be explained as part of just one species (even a highly variable one). These paleoanthropologists (Lieberman et al., 1988; Wood, 1992a) thus argue that there was *more than one species* of early *Homo.**
We agree that more than one species is probably represented, but for simplicity suggest referring to all the specimens as "early *Homo.*"

Putting It All Together

■ **Phylogeny**

A schematic representation showing ancestor-descendant relationships, usually in a chronological framework.

The interpretation of our paleontological past in terms of which fossils are related to other fossils and how they are all related to modern humans is usually shown diagrammatically in the form of a **phylogeny**. Such a diagram is a family tree of fossil evolution. (Note that strict practioners of cladistics prefer to use cladograms; see pp. 200–205.) This kind of interpretation is the eventual goal of evolutionary studies, but it is the final goal, only after adequate data are available to understand what is going on.

Another, more basic way to handle these data is to divide the fossil material into subsets. This avoids (for the moment) what are still problematic phylogenetic relationships. Accordingly, for the Plio-Pleistocene hominid material from Africa, we can divide the data into four broad groupings:

Set I. Basal hominids (4.4 m.y.a.)   The earliest (and most primitive) collection of remains that have been classified as hominids are those from Aramis. These fossils have, for the moment, been assigned to *Ardipithecus ramidus* and are hence provisionally interpreted as being generically distinct from all the other Plio-Pleistocene forms (listed in sets II–IV). Analysis thus far indicates that these forms were bipedal, but with a primitive dentition. Brain size of *A. ramidus* is not yet known, but was almost certainly quite small.

Set II. Early, primitive *Australopithecus* (4.2–3.0 m.y.a.)   This grouping comprises one well-known species, *A. afarensis*, especially well documented at Laetoli and Hadar. Slightly earlier, closely related forms (perhaps representing a distinct second species) come from Allia Bay (East Turkana) and Kanapoi and are provisionally called "*Australopithecus anamensis.*" Best known from analysis of the *A. afarensis* material, these hominids are characterized by a small brain, large teeth (front and back), and a bipedal gait (probably still allowing for considerable climbing).

Set III. Later, more derived *Australopithecus* (2.5–1.4 m.y.a.; possibly as early as 3.5 m.y.a.)   This group is composed of numerous species (most experts recognize at least three; some subdivide this material into five or more species). Remains have come from several sites in both South and East Africa. All of these forms have very large back teeth and do not show appreciable brain enlargement (i.e., encephalization) compared to *A. afarensis*.

Set IV. Early *Homo* (2.4–1.8 m.y.a.)   The best known specimens are from East Africa (East Turkana and Olduvai), but early remains of *Homo* have also been

*The species names *Homo habilis* and *Homo rudolfensis* are the ones most commonly used for designating two different species of early *Homo*.

found in South Africa (Sterkfontein and possibly Swartkrans). This group is composed of possibly just one, but probably more than one, species. Early *Homo* is characterized (compared to *Australopithecus*) by greater encephalization, altered cranial shape, and smaller (especially molars) and narrower (especially premolars) teeth.

Although hominid fossil evidence has accumulated in great abundance, the fact that so much of the material has been discovered so recently makes any firm judgments concerning the route of human evolution premature. However, paleo-anthropologists are certainly not deterred from making their "best guesses," and diverse hypotheses have abounded in recent years. The vast majority of more than 300 fossils from East Africa is still in the descriptive and early analytical stages. At this time, the construction of phylogenies of human evolution is analogous to building a house with only a partial blueprint. We are not even sure how many rooms there are! Until the existing fossil evidence has been adequately studied, to say nothing about possible new finds, speculative hypotheses must be viewed with a critical eye.

In Figure 10–31, we present several phylogenies representing different and opposing views of hominid evolution. We suggest that you not attempt to

FIGURE 10–31

Phylogenies of hominid evolution.

PHYLOGENY A
A. afarensis common ancestor theory
(after Johanson and White, 1979)

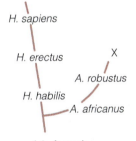

Note: Afarensis postulated as common ancestor to all Plio-Pleistocene hominids.

PHYLOGENY B
Multiple lineage early divergence
(after Senut and Tardieu, 1985)

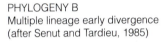
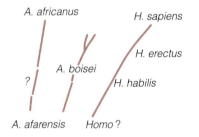

Note: Major split occurs before *A. afarensis.* Possible multiple lineages in Plio-Pleistocene.

PHYLOGENY C
A. africanus common ancestor theory
(after Skelton et al., 1986)

Note: Major split occurs after *A. africanus.* Therefore, *A. africanus* is seen as still in our lineage as well as that of more derived australopithecines.

PHYLOGENY D
Early robust lineage
(after Delson, 1986, 1987; Grine, 1993)

PHYLOGENY E
Ardipithecus as probable root species for later hominids (and also incorporating other recent modifications) (after Skelton and McHenry, 1992; Wolpoff, 1999)

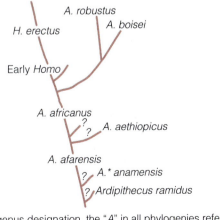

* For genus designation, the "*A*" in all phylogenies refers to *Australopithecus.*

memorize them, for they *all* could be out of date by the time you read this book. It will prove more profitable to look at each one and assess the biological implications involved. Also, note which groups are on the "main line" of human evolution (the one including *Homo sapiens*) and which are placed on extinct side branches.

Interpreting the Interpretations

All the schemes in Figure 10–31 postdate 1979, when *A. afarensis* was first suggested as the most likely common ancestor of all later hominids (Johanson and White, 1979). Since the early 1980s, most paleoanthropologists have accepted this view. One exception is shown in phylogeny B (after Senut and Tardieu, 1985), but this position—based on the premise that *A. afarensis* is actually more than one species—has not been generally supported.

We have not included evolutionary schemes prior to 1979, as they do not account for the crucial discoveries at Hadar and Laetoli of *Australopithecus afarensis*. These now-outdated models frequently postulated *A. africanus* as the common ancestor of later *Australopithecus* (robust varieties) and early *Homo*. In modified form, this view is still continued in some respects (see phylogeny C).

Indeed, probably the most intractable problems for interpretation of early hominid evolution involve what to do with *A. aethiopicus* and *A. africanus*. Carefully look at the different evolutionary reconstructions to see how various researchers deal with these complicated issues. Finally, the newest finds from Aramis (*Ardipithecus*) and from Allia Bay and Kanapoi (*Australopithecus anamensis*) will need to be incorporated into these schemes. Phylogeny E is an initial attempt to do so, but only points up how frequently hominid evolutionary interpretations need to be reevaluated and substantially revised.

Summary

After so much detail relating to hominid evolution in the Plio-Pleistocene, you may feel frustrated by what must seem to be endlessly changing and conflicting interpretations. However, after 75 years of discoveries of early hominids in Africa, there are several general points on which most researchers agree:

1. *A. afarensis* is the earliest hominid, at present with substantial definite supporting evidence. We can anticipate, however, that *Ardipithecus* will soon supplant *A. afarensis* for this status of earliest definite (and widely accepted) hominid.
2. *A. afarensis*, as defined, probably represents only one species.
3. *A. afarensis* is probably ancestral to all later hominids (or is very closely related to the species that is).
4. *A. aethiopicus* is ancestral solely to the "robust" group (clade), linking it with earlier *afarensis* as well as with one (or both) later robust species.
5. All australopithecines were extinct by 1 m.y.a. (or shortly before).
6. All australopithecine species (presumably early *Homo* as well) were highly variable, showing extreme sexual dimorphism.

7. Since there is so much intraspecific variation, on average there was not much difference in body size among australopithecine species.

8. *A. africanus* was probably not the last common ancestor of the robust lineage *and* genus *Homo*. That is, phylogeny C is probably not entirely correct. Indeed, the robust "lineage" may actually be more than one group, or clade. As phylogeny E suggests, *A. aethiopicus* may have diverged earlier, prior to *A. africanus*.

9. All forms (*Australopithecus* and early *Homo*) were small-brained (as compared to later species of the genus *Homo*); nevertheless, all early hominids are more encephalized than apes of comparable body size.

10. Most forms (including some members of early *Homo*) had large back teeth.

11. There was substantial parallelism (homoplasy) in physical traits among early hominid lineages.

12. Given the current state of knowledge, there are several equally supportable phylogenies. In fact, in a recent publication, three leading researchers (Bill Kimbel, Tim White, and Don Johanson, 1988) make this point; moreover, they note that of four possible phylogenetic reconstructions they present (various modifications of phylogenies D and E), they have not reached agreement among themselves as to which is the most likely.

As this list makes clear, we have come a long way in reaching an understanding of Plio-Pleistocene hominid evolution. Nevertheless, a truly complete understanding is not at hand. Such is the stuff of science!

Questions for Review

1. In East Africa, all the early hominid sites are found along the Rift Valley. Why is this significant?

2. (a) Why is postcranial evidence (particularly the lower limb) so crucial in showing the australopithecines as definite hominids? (b) What particular aspects of the australopithecine pelvis and lower limb are hominid-like?

3. In what ways are the remains of *Ardipithecus ramidus* and *Australopithecus anamensis* primitive? How do we know that these forms are hominids?

4. Why are some Plio-Pleistocene hominids from East Africa called "early *Homo*" (or *H. habilis*)? What does this imply for the evolutionary relationships of the australopithecines?

5. What kinds of dating techniques have been used in South Africa?

6. Why is the dating control better in East Africa than in South Africa?

7. Discuss the first thing you would do if you found an early hominid fossil and were responsible for its formal description and publication. What would you include in your publication?

8. Discuss two current disputes regarding taxonomic issues concerning early hominids. Try to give support for alternative positions.

9. Why would one use the taxonomic term *Paranthropus* in contrast to *Australopithecus*?

10. What is a phylogeny? Construct one for early hominids (4.4–1 m.y.a.). Make sure you can describe what conclusions your scheme makes. Also, try to defend it.

11. Discuss at least two alternative ways that *A. africanus* is currently incorporated into phylogenetic schemes.

12. What are the most recently discovered of the Plio-Pleistocene hominid materials, and how are they, for the moment, incorporated into a phylogenetic scheme? How secure do you think this interpretation is?

Suggested Further Reading

Conroy, Glenn C. 1997. *Reconstructing Human Origins. A Modern Synthesis*. New York: Norton.

Corruccini, Robert S., and Russel L. Ciochon (eds.). 1994. *Integrative Paths to the Past: Paleoanthropology Advances in Honor of F. Clark Howell*. Englewood Cliffs, NJ: Prentice Hall.

Delson, Eric (ed.). 1985. *Ancestors: The Hard Evidence*. New York: Liss.

Grine, Fred (ed.). 1988. *Evolutionary History of the Robust Australopithecines*. New York: de Gruyter.

Rak, Yoel. 1983. *The Australopithecine Face*. New York: Academic Press.

Wolpoff, Milford H. 1999. *Paleoanthropology*. 2nd ed. Boston: McGraw-Hill.

Additional Resources

Multimedia Tools

■ **Virtual Laboratories for Physical Anthropology CD-ROM**
The following concepts in this chapter are covered on the physical anthropology CD-ROM:
geological time scale (Virtual Lab 7.I.B)
bipedalism, hominids (Virtual Lab 9)
pelvis, ilium, hip (Virtual Lab 9.I)
gluteus medius, animation (Virtual Lab 9.I.A)
vertebral column, sacrum, lumbar curvature (Virtual Lab 9.II)
femur, knee, bicondylar angle (Virtual Lab 9.III)
foot, calcaneus, phalanges (Virtual Lab 9.IV)
time line, map, phylogeny (Virtual Lab 8)
Aramis, Tabarin, Lothagam (Virtual Lab 8.I.A)
Ardipithecus ramidus, Australopithecus afarensis (Virtual Lab 8.I.A)
Australopithecus anamensis, 3-D animations (Virtual Lab 8.I.A)
Australopithecus afarensis, Hadar, Laetoli (Virtual Lab 8.I.B)
brain size, encephalization (Virtual Labs 10.IV.B, 12.I.C)
anatomy, *A. afarensis*, locomotion (Virtual Lab 9.V)
hominid fossil localities (Virtual Lab 8.glossary)
3-D animation, *Australopithecus boisei, Australopithecus aethiopicus* (Virtual Lab 8.I.C, E)
3-D animation, *Homo* (Virtual Lab 10)
3-D animation, early *Homo, ER 1470* (Virtual Lab 10.I.A)
humerofemoral index, early *Homo* (Virtual Lab 10.IV.A)
3-D animation, *Australopithecus africanus, Australopithecus robustus* (Virtual Lab 8.I.D, F)
body mass (Virtual Lab 10.III.B)

3-D animation, *gracile, robust, Australopithecus boisei* (Virtual Lab 8.II)
time line, phylogeny, location map, pronunciations (Virtual Lab 8.
   glossary)
craniodental features, Plio-Pleistocene hominids (Virtual Lab 8)
3-D animations, Plio-Pleistocene hominids (Virtual Labs 8; 10)

- **Wadsworth Anthropology Resource Center**
  http://anthropology.wadsworth.com
  Visit Anthropology Online to obtain current updates in the field, surfing tips, career information and more. In addition, enrich your study
  efforts with text-specific study aids arranged by chapter.

- **InfoTrac College Edition**
  http://www.infotrac-college.com/wadsworth
  1. Search InfoTrac College Edition for news on *Australopithecus*. Choose
     one story, read it, and write a page about the contribution of this
     piece of research to what we know about early hominid evolution.
  2. Review the Plio-Pleistocene hominid sites mentioned in the text.
     Can you find research about any of these sites on InfoTrac College
     Edition. (Hint: use PowerTrac.) What was found at these sites? To
     what taxon or taxa are these finds attributed?
  3. The genus *Homo* appears to have originated in Africa, but fairly quickly
     dispersed from this continent to colonize other parts of the Old World.
     Exactly when this happened, however, is much debated. One opinion
     on this issue can be found in "The African emergence and early Asian
     dispersals of the genus *Homo*" by Roy Larick and Russell L. Ciochon,
     American Scientist. Read this article. What does it say about not only
     when, but also why and how hominids left Africa?

- **Internet Exercises**
  1. Search the Internet for information regarding one of the very earliest
     hominid sites, Aramis, Kanapoi, or Allia Bay. What information have
     you learned that supplements the material in the textbook? Also,
     search the news sites including ScienceDaily (**http://www.
     sciencedaily.com**). What new information has come out regarding
     these sites or any other early hominid sites since this text was
     written?
  2. Take the Lucy Test! (**http://www.cen.uiuc.edu/~priestle/aa/
     index.html**). In order to help you learn about the differences
     between pongids, hominids, and humans, this site has been created
     to allow *you* to compare the three. Work through this comparison
     exercise. How did you do? Did you think the australopithecine was
     more like humans or like pongids? Having done this exercise, con-
     sider how paleoanthropologists interpret such data.
  3. Visit National Geographic Outpost (**http://www.
     nationalgeographic.com/outpost/**). Research by Lee Berger in
     Botswana is profiled on this National Geographic site. Start with the
     field journal. What would it be like to do field work in paleoanthro-
     pology? Then go to the Interpretation Station. What did Berger and
     his crew find?
  4. Visit the TalkOrigins archive's FAQ on fossil hominids (**http://www.
     talkorigins.org/faqs/fossil-hominids.html**). Read the section on

A discussion of *Homo erectus* is given in the Species Gallery in Virtual Lab 10, section I, part B. Be sure to click on the Extra Information text icon for each specimen.

Introduction

In Chapter 10, we traced the earliest evidence of hominid evolution by reviewing the abundant fossil material from Africa that documents the origins of *Australopithecus* and *Homo* during the Pliocene and early Pleistocene. In this chapter, we take up what might be called the next stage of hominid evolution, the appearance and dispersal of *Homo erectus* (Fig. 11–2).

Homo erectus was a widely distributed species that also had a long temporal record, spanning over 1 million years. Our discussion focuses on the defining physical characteristics of *Homo erectus* compared with what came immediately before (early *Homo*) and what came immediately after (*Homo sapiens*). As we have emphasized, hominid evolution has long been characterized by a biocultural interaction. Thus, it is only through explaining the behavioral capacities of *Homo erectus* (in concert with morphological change) that we can understand the success of this hominid species. For this reason, we also highlight some of the abundant archaeological evidence and related biocultural reconstructions that have so long occupied and fascinated paleoanthropologists.

Homo erectus: Terminology and Geographical Distribution

The discoveries of fossils now referred to as *H. erectus* go back to the nineteenth century. Later in this chapter, we will discuss in some detail the historical background of these earliest discoveries in Java and the somewhat later discoveries in China. From this work, as well as presumably related finds in Europe and North Africa, a variety of taxonomic names were suggested. The most significant of these earlier terms were *Pithecanthropus* (for the Javanese remains) and *Sinanthropus* (for the fossils from northern China). In fact, you may still see these terms in older sources or occasionally used colloquially and thus placed in quotation marks (e.g., "*Pithecanthropus*").

It is important to realize that taxonomic *splitting* (which this terminology reflects) was quite common in the early years of paleoanthropology. Only after World War II and with the incorporation of the modern synthesis (see p. 90) into paleontology did more systematic biological thinking come to the fore. Following this trend, in the early 1950s all the material previously referred to as "Pithecanthropus," "Sinanthropus," and so forth, was included in a single species of genus *Homo—H. erectus*. This reclassification proved to be a most significant development on two counts:

1. It reflected the incorporation of modern evolutionary thinking into hominid paleontology.
2. The simplification in terminology, based as it was on sound biological principles, refocused research away from endless arguments regarding classification to broader populational, behavioral, and ecological considerations.

Discoveries in the last few decades have established *well-dated* finds of *H. erectus* in East Africa from geological contexts radiometrically dated as old as 1.8 m.y.a. In addition, new dates first published in 1994 by geologists from the Berkeley Geochronology Laboratory (Swisher et al., 1994) have suggested that two localities in Java are as old as those in East Africa (with dates of 1.8 and 1.6

m.y.a.). These early dates have come as somewhat of a surprise to many paleo-anthropologists, but as you will see, there is now growing evidence for an early dispersal of hominids outside of Africa—that is, one *well before* 1 m.y.a.

Current interpretations thus view the first hominid dispersal out of Africa as occurring between 1.5 and 2 m.y.a. A likely route would have taken these hominids through southwestern Asia, and there are some intriguing hints from the Ubeidiya site in Israel that this route was indeed exploited quite early on. The most conclusive evidence from Ubeidiya is archaeological, including a number of stone tools dated (by paleomagnetism and faunal correlation) to 1.4–1.3 m.y.a. In addition, there are some fragmentary hominid remains, including cranial pieces and two teeth. Unfortunately, the association of these hominid remains with the tools at a date prior to 1 m.y.a. is uncertain. Consequently, there is not yet *definitive* fossil evidence of *H. erectus* (or a close relative) from Southwest Asia. Nevertheless, the Ubeidiya archaeological discoveries are highly suggestive and fit with the overall emerging pattern of an early hominid dispersal from Africa.

More than likely, these first continental migrants were members of *H. erectus* or a group very closely related to *H. erectus* (although an earlier dispersal of a more primitive member of genus *Homo* cannot be ruled out). What the current evidence most economically suggests is that *Homo erectus* migrated out of East Africa, eventually to occupy South and North Africa, southern and northeastern Asia, and perhaps Europe as well. A recent, not yet fully described hominid mandible from the Dmanisi site in the Republic of Georgia has been provisionally dated to 1.8–1.6 m.y.a. (Fig. 11–1). In other words, if this as yet unconfirmed date should prove accurate, this fossil would be as early as any *H. erectus* discovery in Java and about as old as East African remains as well! Another new find pushing back the antiquity of hominids in Europe has come from the 500,000-year-old Boxgrove site in southern England, where a hominid tibia (shinbone) was unearthed in 1994. And still another recent find (1994), from the Ceprano site in central Italy, may be the best evidence yet of *H. erectus* in Europe (Ascenzi et al., 1996). Provisional dating of a partial cranium from this important site suggests a date greater than 700,000 years ago. The primary researchers, as well as Rightmire (1998), conclude that cranial morphology places this specimen quite close to *H. erectus*.

Finally, some other fossil remains from Spain, also discovered in 1994 and announced in 1995, may well be the oldest hominids yet found in western Europe (see Fig. 11–2 for locations of these hominid sites). From the Gran Dolina site in the highly productive Atapuerca region of northern Spain, where numerous, somewhat more recent hominid fossils have also been discovered (discussed in Chapter 12), several fragments of at least four individuals have been found (Carbonell et al., 1995). The dating, based on paleomagnetic determinations (see p. 238), places the Gran Dolina hominids at approximately 780,000 y.a.* (Parés and Pérez-González, 1995). If this dating is further corroborated, these early Spanish finds would be *at least* 250,000 years older than any other hominid yet discovered in western Europe. Because all the 36 pieces thus far identified are quite fragmentary, the taxonomic assignment of these fossils still remains problematic. Initial analysis, however, suggests that they probably are *not H. erectus,* except perhaps for the Ceprano cranium. Whether any of these early European hominids belong within the species *Homo erectus* thus still remains to be determined.

The dispersal of *Homo erectus* from Africa was influenced by climate, topography, water boundaries, and access to food and other resources. Paleoenvironmental reconstructions are thus of crucial importance in understanding the

Virtual Lab 10 includes an interactive map showing the distribution of *Homo erectus.* This can be accessed on every specimen screen.

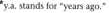

FIGURE 11–1
Dmanisi mandible.

---

*y.a. stands for "years ago."

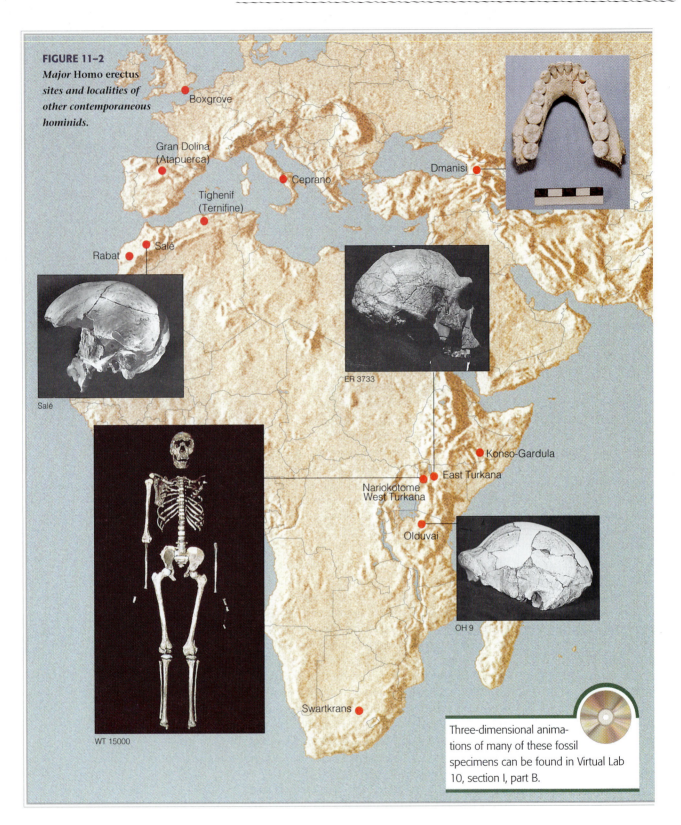

FIGURE 11–2

Major Homo erectus sites and localities of other contemporaneous hominids.

Boxgrove

Gran Dolina (Atapuerca)

Ceprano

Dmanisi

Tighenif (Ternifine)

Rabat

Salé

Salé

ER 3733

Konso-Gardula

East Turkana

Nariokotome West Turkana

Olduvai

WT 15000

OH 9

Swartkrans

Three-dimensional animations of many of these fossil specimens can be found in Virtual Lab 10, section I, part B.

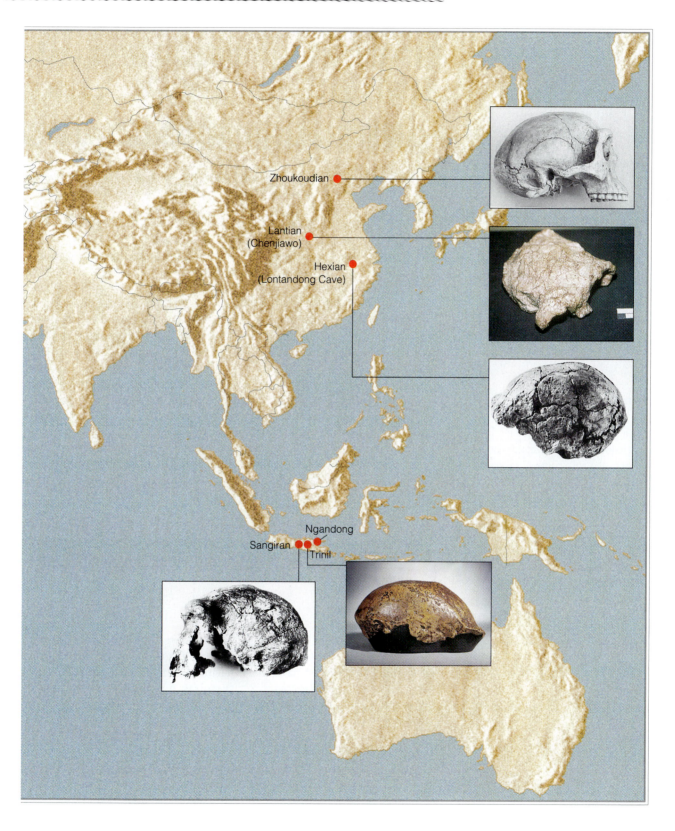

expansion of *H. erectus* to so many parts of the Old World. The long temporal span of *H. erectus* begins very early in the **Pleistocene** and extends to fairly late in that geological epoch. To comprehend the world of *Homo erectus,* we must understand how environments shifted during the Pleistocene.

The Pleistocene (1.8 m.y.a.–10,000 y.a.)

During much of the Pleistocene (also known as the Age of Glaciers or Ice Age), large areas of the Northern Hemisphere were covered with enormous masses of ice, which advanced and retreated as the temperature fell and rose. An early classification of glacial (and interglacial) Europe divided the Pleistocene into four major glacial periods. However, climatic conditions varied in different areas of Europe, and distinctive glacial periods are also now known for the North Sea, England, and eastern Europe, not to mention Asia and North America. New dating techniques have revealed a much more complex account of glacial advance and retreat, and the many oscillations of cold and warm temperatures during the Pleistocene affected both plants and animals: "The Pleistocene record shows that there were about 15 major cold periods and 50 minor advances during its [more than] 1.5-m.y. duration, or one major cold period every 100,000 years" (Tattersal et al., 1988, p. 230).

The Pleistocene, which lasted more than 1.75 million years, was a significant period in hominid evolutionary history and encompassed the appearance and disappearance of *Homo erectus.* By the end of the Pleistocene, modern humans had already appeared, dependence on culture had dramatically increased, and domestication of plants and animals—one of the great cultural revolutions of human history—was either about to commence or had already begun. Given this background on the time span in which *H. erectus* evolved and lived, let us examine more closely this predecessor of *H. sapiens.*

The Morphology of *Homo erectus*

Brain Size

Homo erectus differs in several respects from both early *Homo* and *Homo sapiens.* The most obvious feature is cranial size (which, of course, is closely related to brain size). Early *Homo* had cranial capacities ranging from as small as 500 cm³ to as large as 800 cm³. *H. erectus,* on the other hand, shows considerable brain enlargement, with a cranial capacity of 750 to 1,250 cm³ (with a mean of approximately 900 cm³). However, in making such comparisons, we must bear in mind two key questions: What is the comparative sample, and what were the overall body sizes of the species being compared?

In relation to the first question, you should recall that many scholars are now convinced that there was more than one species of early *Homo* in East Africa around 2 m.y.a. If so, only one of these could have been ancestral to *H. erectus.* (Indeed, it is possible that neither species gave rise to *H. erectus* and that perhaps we have yet to find direct evidence of the ancestral species.) Taking a more optimistic view that at least one of these fossil groups is a likely ancestor of later hominids, the question still remains—which one? If we choose the smaller-

■ Pleistocene
The epoch of the Cenozoic from 1.8 m.y.a. until 10,000 y.a. Frequently referred to as the Ice Age, this epoch is associated with continental glaciations in northern latitudes.

A time line icon that gives the ages for early *Homo* is available on every screen in Virtual Lab 10. You may wish to review the geological time scale in Virtual Lab 7, section I, part B.

Virtual Lab 10, section IV, part B, provides an interactive laboratory exercise on the evolution of relative brain size.

bodied sample of early *Homo* as our presumed ancestral group, then *H. erectus* shows as much as a 40 percent increase in cranial capacity. However, if the comparative sample is the larger-bodied group of early *Homo* (as exemplified by skull 1470, from East Turkana), then *H. erectus* shows a 25 percent increase in cranial capacity.

As we previously discussed in Chapter 7, brain size is closely tied to overall body size (a relationship termed *encephalization*). We have made a point of the increase in *H. erectus* brain size; however, it must be realized that *H. erectus* was also considerably larger overall than earlier members of the genus *Homo*. In fact, when *H. erectus* is compared with the larger-bodied early *Homo* sample, *relative* brain size is about the same (Walker, 1991). Furthermore, when considering the relative brain size of *H. erectus* in comparison with *H. sapiens,* it is seen that *H. erectus* was considerably less encephalized than later members of the genus *Homo*.

Body Size

As we have just mentioned, another feature displayed by *H. erectus,* compared to earlier hominids, is a dramatic increase in body size. For several decades, little was known of the postcranial skeleton of *H. erectus*. However, with the discovery of a nearly complete skeleton in 1984 from **Nariokotome** (on the west side of Lake Turkana in Kenya) and its recent detailed analysis (Walker and Leakey, 1993), the data base is now much improved. From this specimen (and from less complete individuals at other sites), some *Homo erectus* adults are estimated to have weighed well over 100 pounds, with a mean adult stature of about 5 feet 6 inches (McHenry, 1992; Ruff and Walker, 1993). Another point to keep in mind is that *Homo erectus* was quite sexually dimorphic—at least as indicated by the East African specimens. Thus, for male adult body size, weight and stature in some individuals may have been considerably greater than the average figures just mentioned. In fact, it is estimated that if the Nariokotome boy had survived, he would have attained an adult stature of over 6 feet (Walker, 1993).

Associated with the large stature (and explaining the significant increase in body weight) is also a dramatic increase in robusticity. In fact, this characteristic of very heavy body build was to dominate hominid evolution not just during *H. erectus* times, but through the long transitional era of archaic *Homo sapiens* as well. Only with the appearance of anatomically modern *H. sapiens* do we see a more gracile skeletal structure, which is still characteristic of most modern populations.

Cranial Shape

The cranium of *Homo erectus* displays a highly distinctive shape, partly as a result of increased brain size, but probably more correlated with significant body size (robusticity). The ramifications of this heavily built cranium are reflected in thick cranial bone (most notably in Asian specimens) and large browridges (supraorbital tori) in the front of the skull and a projecting **nuchal torus** at the rear (Fig. 11–3).

The vault is long and low, receding back from the large browridges with little forehead development. Moreover, the cranium is wider at the base compared with earlier *or* later species of genus *Homo*. The maximum breadth is below the ear opening, giving a pentagonal contour to the cranium (when viewed from behind). In contrast, both early *Homo* crania and *H. sapiens* crania have more vertical sides, and the maximum width is *above* the ear openings.

Virtual Lab 10, section III, part B, provides an interactive exercise that teaches you how to estimate body mass from a fossil hominid femur.

Nariokotome
(nar´-ee-oh-ko´-tow-may)

An interactive exercise on skeletal robusticity is presented in Virtual Lab 10, section III, part A.

Virtual Lab 10, section II, part A, discusses the distinctive cranial shape of *Homo erectus*. Many of these anatomical terms are also given in the glossary of Virtual Lab 10.

Nuchal torus
(nuke´-ul, pertaining to the neck) A projection of bone in the back of the cranium where neck muscles attach, used to hold up the head. The nuchal torus is a distinctive feature of *H. erectus*.

points briefly covered in his original paper. He also brought along the actual fossil material, which gave scientists an opportunity to examine the evidence. As a result, many opponents became more sympathetic to his views.

However, to this day, questions about the finds remain: Does the femur really belong with the skullcap? Did the field crew dig through several layers, thus mixing the remains? Moreover, some anthropologists think that the Trinil femur is relatively recent and representative of modern *H. sapiens,* not *H. erectus.*

Despite the still-unanswered questions, there is general acceptance that Dubois was correct in identifying the skull as representing a previously undescribed species; that his estimates of cranial capacity were reasonably accurate; that *"Pithecanthropus erectus,"* or *H. erectus* as we call it today, is the ancestor of *H. sapiens;* and that bipedalism preceded enlargement of the brain.

By 1930, the controversy had faded, especially in the light of important new discoveries near Peking (Beijing), China, in the late 1920s (discussed shortly). Similarities between the Beijing skulls and Dubois' *"Pithecanthropus"* were obvious, and scientists pointed out that the Java form was not an "apeman," as Dubois contended, but rather was closely related to modern *Homo sapiens.*

One might expect that Dubois would welcome the finds from China and the support they provided for the human status of *"Pithecanthropus,"* but Dubois would have none of it. He refused to recognize any connection between Beijing and Java and described the Beijing fossils as "a degenerate Neanderthaler" (von Koenigswald, 1956, p. 55). He also refused to accept the classification of *"Pithecanthropus"* in the same species with later finds from Java.

Homo erectus from Java

Six sites in eastern Java have yielded all the *H. erectus* fossil remains found to date on that island. The dating of these fossils has been hampered by the complex nature of Javanese geology. It has been generally accepted that most of the fossils belong in the Middle Pleistocene and are less than 800,000 years old. However, as we noted earlier, new dating estimates have suggested one find (from Modjokerto) to be close to 1.8 m.y.a. and another fossil from the main site of Sangiran to be approximately 1.6 m.y.a.

At Sangiran, where the remains of at least five individuals have been excavated, the cranial capacities of the fossils range from 813 cm³ to 1,059 cm³. Another site called Ngandong has also been fruitful, yielding the remains of 12 crania (Fig. 11–6). The dating here is also confusing, but the Upper Pleistocene has been suggested, which may explain the larger cranial measurements of the Ngandong individuals as well as features that are more modern than those found on other Javanese crania. Newly published dates for the Ngandong site are very recent, remarkably so, in fact. Using two specialized dating techniques (discussed in Chapter 13; see p. 366), Swisher and colleagues from the Berkeley Geochronology Laboratory have determined from animal bones found at the site (and presumably associated with the hominids) a date ranging from about 50,000 years ago to as recently as 25,000 years ago (Swisher et al., 1996). If these dates are further confirmed, it would show a *very* late survival of *Homo erectus* in Java, long after they had disappeared elsewhere. They would thus be contemporary with *Homo sapiens*—which, by this time, had expanded widely in the Old World (see Chapter 12).

We cannot say much about the *H. erectus* way of life in Java. Very few artifacts have been found, and those have come mainly from river terraces, not from pri-

FIGURE 11–6

Rear view of a Ngandong skull. Note that the cranial walls slope downward and outward (or upward and inward), with the widest breadth low on the cranium, giving it a pentagonal form.

See Virtual Lab 10, section I, part B, for a 3-D animation and discussion of this specimen.

mary sites: "On Java there is still not a single site where artifacts can be associated with *H. erectus*" (Bartstra, 1982, p. 319).

Peking (Beijing)

The story of Peking *H. erectus* is another saga filled with excitement, hard work, luck, and misfortune. Europeans had known for a long time that "dragon bones," used by the Chinese as medicine and aphrodisiacs, were actually ancient mammal bones. In 1917, the Geological Survey of China decided to find the sites where these dragon bones were collected by local inhabitants and sold to apothecary shops. In 1921 a Swedish geologist, J. Gunnar Andersson, was told of a potentially fruitful fossil site in an abandoned quarry near the village of **Zhoukoudian.** A villager showed Andersson's team a fissure in the limestone wall, and within a few minutes they found the jaw of a pig: "That evening we went home with rosy dreams of great discoveries" (Andersson, 1934, pp. 97–98).

A young Chinese geologist, Pei Wenshong, took over the excavation in 1929 and began digging out the sediment in one branch of the lower cave, where he found one of the most remarkable fossil skulls to be recovered up to that time. One of the Chinese workers tells the story:

> We had got down about 30 meters deep. . . . It was there the skull-cap was sighted, half of it embedded in loose earth, the other in hard clay. The sun had almost set . . . . The team debated whether to take it out right away or to wait until the next day when they could see better. The agonizing suspense of a whole day was felt to be too much to bear, so they decided to go on. (Jia, 1975, pp. 12–13)

Pei brought the skull to anatomist Davidson Black (Fig 11–7). Because the fossil was embedded in hard limestone, it took Black four months of hard, steady work to free it from its tough matrix. The result was worth the labor. The skull, that of a juvenile, was thick, low, and relatively small, but in Black's mind there was no doubt it belonged to an early hominid. The response to this discovery, quite unlike that which greeted Dubois almost 40 years earlier, was immediate and enthusiastically favorable.

Franz Weidenreich (Fig 11–8), a distinguished anatomist well known for his work on European fossil hominids, succeeded Black. After Japan invaded China in 1933, Weidenreich decided to move the fossils from Beijing to prevent them from falling into the hands of the Japanese. Weidenreich left China in 1941, taking excellent prepared casts, photographs, and drawings of the Peking material with him. After he left, the bones were packed, and arrangements were made for the U.S. Marine Corps in Beijing to take them to the United States. The bones never reached the United States, and they have never been found. To this day, no one knows what happened to them, and their location remains a mystery.

Zhoukoudian *Homo erectus*

In their recent book (1990), Jia and Huang list the total fossil remains of *H. erectus* unearthed at the Zhoukoudian Cave as of 1982 (Fig. 11–9):

    14 skullcaps (only 6 relatively complete) (Fig. 11–10)
    6 facial bones (including maxillae, palates, and zygomatic bone fragments)

■ **Zhoukoudian**
(zhoh´-koh-dee´-en)

FIGURE 11–7
Davidson Black, responsible for the first study of the Zhoukoudian fossils.

FIGURE 11–8
Franz Weidenreich.

15 mandibles (mostly one side, only one
   nearly complete, many fragments)
122 isolated teeth
38 teeth rooted in jaws
3 humeri (upper arm bones, only 1 well
   preserved, the rest in fragments)
1 clavicle (both ends absent)
1 lunate (wrist bone)
7 femurs (only 1 well preserved)
1 tibia (shinbone, fragmentary)
(and over 100,000 artifacts)

These remains belong to upward of 40 male and female adults and children and constitute a considerable amount of evidence, the largest number of *H. erectus* specimens found at any one site. With the meticulous work by Weidenreich, the Zhoukoudian fossils have led to a good overall picture of the eastern *H. erectus* of China.

Peking *H. erectus*, like that from Java, possesses typical *H. erectus* features, including the supraorbital torus in front and the nuchal torus behind; also, the skull is keeled by a sagittal ridge, the face protrudes, the incisors are shoveled, and the molars contain large pulp cavities. Again, like the Javanese forms, the skull shows the greatest breadth near the bottom. (These similarities were recognized long ago by Black and Weidenreich.)

Cultural Remains   More than 100,000 artifacts have been recovered from this vast site that was occupied intermittently for almost 250,000 years. According to the Chinese (Wu and Lin, 1983, p.86), Zhoukoudian "is one of the sites with the longest history of habitation by man or his ancestors." The occupation of the site has been divided into three cultural stages:

*Earliest Stage (460,000–420,000 y.a.)** The tools are large, close to a pound in weight, and made of soft stone, such as sandstone.

Middle Stage (370,000–350,000 y.a.) Tools become smaller and lighter (under a pound), and these smaller tools comprise approximately two-thirds of the sample.

Final Stage (300,000–230,000 y.a.) Tools are still small, and the tool materials are of better quality. The coarse quartz of the earlier periods is replaced by a finer quartz, sandstone tools have almost disappeared, and flint tools increase in frequency by as much as 30 percent.

The early tools are crude and shapeless but become more refined over time. Common tools at the site are choppers and chopping tools, but retouched flakes were fashioned into scrapers, points, burins, and awls (Fig 11–11).

Stone was not the only material used by *H. erectus* at Zhoukoudian; these hominids also utilized bone and probably horn. Found in the cave were antler fragments, which had been hacked into pieces. Antler bases might have served as

FIGURE 11–9
Zhoukoudian Cave. The grid on the wall was drawn for purposes of excavation. The entrance to the cave can be seen near the grid.

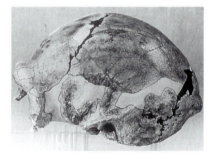

FIGURE 11–10
H. erectus *(specimen from Zhoukoudian). From this view, the supraorbital torus, low vault of the skull, and nuchal torus can clearly be seen.*

A 3-D animation and discussion of this specimen from Zhoukoudian is given in Virtual Lab 10, section I, part B.

*These dates should be considered tentative until more precise chronometric techniques are available.

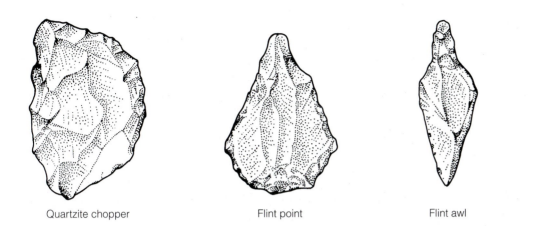

Quartzite chopper   Flint point   Flint awl   Graver or burin

hammers and the sharp tines as digging sticks. Also found in abundance were many deer skulls lacking facial bones as well as antlers, thus leaving only the braincases intact. Jia suggests that because the skulls show evidence of repeated whittling and over 100 specimens were discovered, all similarly shaped, "it is reasonable to infer they served as 'drinking bowls.'" He goes on to conjecture that the braincases of the Beijing *H. erectus* fossils "retain similar characteristics and probably served the same purpose."

The way of life at Zhoukoudian has traditionally been described as that of hunter-gatherers who killed deer and horses as well as other animals and gathered fruits, berries, and ostrich eggs. Fragments of charred ostrich eggshells, the abundant deposits of hackberry seeds unearthed in the cave, and the flourishing plant growth surrounding the cave all suggest that meat was supplemented by the gathering of herbs, wild fruits, tubers, and eggs. Layers of ash in the cave, over 18 feet deep at one point, suggest fire and hearths, but whether Beijing hominids could actually make fire is unknown. Wu and Lin (1983, p. 94) state that "Peking Man was a cave dweller, a fire user, a deer hunter, a seed gatherer and a maker of specialized tools," but several questions about Zhoukoudian *H. erectus* remain unanswered.

Did *H. erectus* at Zhoukoudian use language? If by language we mean articulate speech, it is unlikely. Nevertheless, some scholars believe that speech originated early in hominid evolution; others argue that speech did not originate until up to 200,000 years later in the Upper Paleolithic, with the origin of anatomically modern humans (see Chapter 13). We agree with Dean Falk when she writes, "Unfortunately, what it is going to take to *settle* the debate about when language originated in hominids is a time machine. Until one becomes available, we can only speculate about this fascinating and important question" (1989, p. 141).

Did these hominids wear clothes? Almost surely clothing of some type, probably in the form of animal skins, was worn. Winters in Beijing are harsh today and appear to have been bitter during the Middle Pleistocene as well. Moreover, awls were found at Zhoukoudian, and one of the probable bone tools may be a needle.

What was the life span of *H. erectus* at Zhoukoudian? Apparently, not very long, and infant and childhood mortality was probably very high. Studies of the fossil remains reveal that almost 40 percent of the bones belong to individuals under the age of 14, and only 2.6 percent are estimated to be in the 50- to 60- year age-group (Jia, 1975).

This picture of Zhoukoudian life has been challenged by archaeologist Lewis Binford and colleagues (Binford and Ho, 1985; Binford and Stone, 1986a, 1986b).

FIGURE 11–11

Chinese tools from Middle Pleistocene sites.
(Adapted from Wu and Olsen, 1985.)

Binford and his colleagues reject the description of Beijing *H. erectus* as hunters and argue that the evidence clearly points to them as scavengers. As we saw in Chapter 9, the controversy of early hominids as hunters or scavengers has engaged the attention of paleoanthropologists, and the matter is not yet settled. Binford and his colleagues also do not accept that the Beijing hominids were clearly associated with fire, except in the later phases of occupation (about 250,000 y.a.).

Other Chinese Sites

More work has been done at Zhoukoudian than at any other Chinese site. Nevertheless, there are other hominid sites worth noting. Three of the more important sites, besides Zhoukoudian, are Chenjiawo and Gongwangling (both in Lantian County and sometimes referred to as Lantian) and Lontandong Cave in Hexian County (often referred to as the Hexian find) (see Table 11–1).

At Chenjiawo, an almost complete mandible containing several teeth was found in 1963. It is quite similar to those from Zhoukoudian but has been provisionally dated at about 650,000 y.a. If the dating is correct, this specimen would be older than the Beijing material. The following year, a partial cranium was discovered at Gongwangling, not far from Chenjiawo. Provisionally dated to as much as 1.15 m.y.a. (Etler and Tianyuan, 1994), the Gongwangling specimen may be the oldest Chinese *Homo erectus* fossil yet known.

TABLE 11–1   *H. Erectus* Fossils from China

Designation	Site	Age* (Years Ago)	Material	Cranial Capacity (cm³)	Year Found	Remarks
Hexian	Longtandong Cave, Anhui	250,000	Calvarium, skull fragments, mandible fragments, isolated teeth	1,025	1980–81	First skull found in southern or southwest China
Zhoukoudian (Peking)	Zhoukoudian Cave, Beijing	500,000–200,000	5 adult crania, skull fragments, facial bones, isolated teeth, postcranial pieces (40+ individuals)	850–1,225; avg: 1,010	1927–ongoing	Most famous fossils in China and some of the most famous in the world
Yunxian	Longgudong Cave, Hubei	?500,000	Isolated teeth		1976–82	
Yunxian	Quyuanhekou	350,000	2 mostly complete (but crushed) crania	Undetermined	1989	The most complete crania from China, but still requiring much restoration
Lantian	Chenjiawo, Lantian	650,000	Mandible		1963	Old female
Lantian	Gongwangling, Lantian	800,000–1,150,000	Calvarium, facial bones	780	1964	Female over 30; oldest *H. erectus* found so far in China

Sources: *Atlas of Primitive Man in China* (1980); Lisowski, 1984; Pope, 1984; Wu and Dong, 1985; Etler and Tianyuan, 1994.
*These are best estimates; authorities differ.

Perhaps the most significant find was made in 1980 at Lontandong Cave, where remains of several individuals were recovered. One of the specimens is a well-preserved cranium (with a cranial capacity of about 1,025 cm³) lacking much of its base. Dated roughly at 250,000 y.a., it is not surprising that this Hexian cranium displays several advanced features. The cranial constriction, for example, is not as pronounced as in earlier forms, and certain temporal and occipital characteristics are "best compared with the later forms of *H. erectus* at Zhoukoudian" (Wu and Dong, 1985, p. 87).

In June 1993, Li Tianyuan and Dennis Etler reported that two relatively complete skulls were discovered in 1989 at a hominid site in Yunxian County. The date given for the site is 350,000 y.a., which, if correct, would make these the most complete crania of this great antiquity in China (Fig 11–12).

The Yunxian crania are both large and robust, considerably exceeding in size those from Zhoukoudian. In general, the Yunxian individuals fit within *Homo erectus*, but in the facial region especially they also show some interesting advanced features. A few of these features suggest to some scholars "a mid-facial morphology similar to that of modern Asians" (Etler and Tianyuan, 1994, p. 668).

Unfortunately, both skulls are still covered with a hard calcareous matrix, and critics argue that until the skulls are cleaned and the crushed parts properly put together, it is too early to make accurate assessments. In any case, these Yunxian crania will ultimately provide considerable data to help clarify hominid evolution in China and perhaps elsewhere in the Old World as well.

A number of archaeological sites have been excavated in China, and early stone tools have been found in numerous locations in widely separated areas. At present, there is little reason to believe that *H. erectus* culture in these provinces differed much from that described at Zhoukoudian.

The Asian crania from both Java and China are mainly Middle Pleistocene fossils and share many similar features, which may be explained by *H. erectus* migration from Java to China about 800,000 years ago. African *H. erectus* forms are generally older than most Asian forms and are not as similar to them as Asian forms (i.e., from Java and China) are to each other.

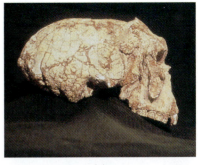

(a)

(b)

FIGURE 11–12

(a) EV 9002 (Yunxian, China). The skull is in better shape than its companion, and its lateral view clearly displays features characteristic of H. erectus: *flattened vault, receding forehead (frontal bone), angulated occiput, and supraorbital torus. (b) EV 9001 (Yunxian). Unfortunately, the skull was crushed, but it preserves some lateral facial structures absent in EV 9002.*

East Africa

Olduvai   Back in 1960, Louis Leakey unearthed a fossil skull at Olduvai (OH 9) that he identified as *H. erectus*. Skull OH 9 from Upper Bed II is dated at 1.4 m.y.a. and preserves a massive cranium but is faceless except for a bit of nose below the supraorbital torus. Estimated at 1,067 cm³, the cranial capacity of OH 9 is the largest of all the African *Homo erectus* specimens. The browridge is huge, the largest known for any hominid in both thickness and projection, but the vault walls are thin. This latter characteristic of fairly thin cranial vault bones is seen in most east African *H. erectus* specimens, and in this respect, they differ from Asian *H. erectus* (in which cranial vaults are thick).

East Turkana   Some 400 miles north of Olduvai Gorge, on the northern boundary of Kenya, is Lake Turkana. Explored by Richard Leakey and colleagues since 1969, the eastern shore of the lake has been a virtual gold mine for australopithecine, early *Homo*, and *H. erectus* fossil remains.

The most significant *H. erectus* discovery from East Turkana is ER 3733, an almost complete skull lacking a mandible (Fig. 11–13). Discovered in 1974, the specimen has been given a firm date of close to 1.8 m.y.a. The cranial capacity is estimated at 848 cm³, at the lower end of the range for *H. erectus*, but this is not

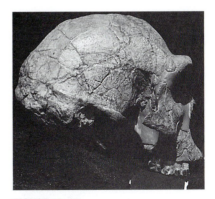

FIGURE 11–13

ER 3733, the most complete East Turkana H. erectus *cranium.*

■ **Acheulian**

(ash´-oo-lay-en)

Pertaining to a stone tool industry of the Lower and Middle Pleistocene characterized by a large proportion of bifacial tools (flaked on both sides). Acheulian tool kits are very common in Africa, Southwest Asia, and western Europe, but are nearly absent elsewhere. (Also spelled "Acheulean.")

Specimens from East Africa and their 3-D animations are presented in Virtual Lab 10, section I, part B.

A 3-D animation of the skull of the Nariokotome specimen is given in Virtual Lab 10, section I, part B. An interactive virtual exercise that concerns the limb proportions of *Homo erectus* in relationship to those of other hominid species is given in section IV, part A.

Be sure to consider this alternative phylogeny (with pronunciations of the species' names) that is presented in the glossary of Virtual Lab 10 under Phylogeny of *Homo.*

surprising considering its early date. The cranium generally resembles Asian *H. erectus* in many features (but with some important differences, discussed shortly).

Not many tools have been found at *H. erectus* sites in East Turkana. Oldowan types of flakes, cobbles, and core tools have been found, and the introduction of **Acheulian** tools about 1.4 m.y.a. replaced the Oldowan tradition.

West Turkana* In August 1984, Kamoya Kimeu (see p. 273), a member of Richard Leakey's team, lived up to his reputation as an outstanding fossil hunter and discovered a small piece of skull near the base camp on the west side of Lake Turkana. Leakey and his colleague, Alan Walker of Pennsylvania State University, excavated the site known as Nariokotome in 1984 and again in 1985 (see Box 11–1).

The dig was a resounding success. The workers unearthed the most complete *H. erectus* skeleton yet found (Fig. 11–14). Known properly as WT 15000, the all but complete skeleton includes facial bones and most of the postcranial bones, a rare finding indeed for *H. erectus,* since these particular elements are scarce at other *H. erectus* sites.

Another remarkable feature of the find is its age. Its dating is based on the chronometric dates of the geological formation in which the site is located and is set at about 1.6 million years. The skeleton is that of a boy about 12 years of age and 5 feet 3 inches tall. Had he grown to maturity, his height, it is estimated, would have been more than 6 feet, taller than *H. erectus* was heretofore thought to have been. The postcranial bones appear to be quite similar, though not identical, to those of modern humans. The cranial capacity of WT 15000 is estimated at 880 cm³; brain growth was nearly complete, and it is estimated that the boy's adult cranial capacity would have been approximately 909 cm³ (Begun and Walker, 1993).

Ethiopia In southern Ethiopia, the 1991 Paleoanthropological Inventory of Ethiopia team of international scientists discovered a site, Konso-Gardula (KGA), containing a remarkable abundance of Acheulian tools, a hominid upper third molar, and an almost complete mandible with several cheek teeth. Both specimens are attributed to *H. erectus* "because they lack specialized characteristics of robust *Australopithecus*" (Asfaw et al., 1992).

The mandible is robust and is dated to about 1.3 m.y.a. The Acheulian stone tools, mainly bifaces and picks, are made of quartz, quartzite, and volcanic rock.

🌿 Summary of East African *H. erectus*

The *Homo erectus* remains from East Africa show several differences from the fossil samples from Java and China. The African specimens (as exemplified by ER 3733, presumably a female, and WT 15000, presumably a male) are not as strongly buttressed in the cranium (by supraorbital or nuchal tori) and do not have such thick cranial bones as seen in Asian representatives of *H. erectus*. These differences, as well as others observed in the postcranial skeleton, have so impressed some researchers that they in fact argue for a *separate* species status for the African *H. erectus* remains (as distinct from the Asian samples). Bernard Wood, the leading proponent of this view, has suggested that the name *Homo ergaster* be used for the African remains; *H. erectus* would then be reserved solely for the Asian material

---

*WT is the symbol for West Turkana, that is, the west side of Lake Turkana. The east side is designated by ER—East Rudolf. Rudolf was the former name of the lake. (See p. 270.)

BOX 11-1

The Nariokotome Skeleton—
A Boy for All Seasons

The discovery of the spectacularly well-preserved skeleton from Nariokotome on the west side of Lake Turkana has allowed considerable new insight into key anatomical features of *Homo erectus*. Since its recovery in 1984 and 1985, detailed studies have been undertaken, and recent publication of the results (Walker, 1993; Walker and Leakey, 1993) allows some initial conclusions to be drawn. Moreover, the extraordinary quality of the remains has also allowed anthropologists to speculate on some major behavioral traits of *H. erectus* in Africa (and, more generally, of the entire species).

The remains comprise an almost complete skeleton, lacking only most of the small bones of the hands and feet and the unfused ends of long bones. This degree of preservation is remarkable, and this individual is the most complete skeleton of *any* fossil hominid yet found from before about 100,000 y.a. (after which deliberate burial facilitated much improved preservation). This superior preservation may well have been aided by rapid sedimentation in what is thought to have been an ancient shallow swamp. Once the individual died, his skeleton would have been quickly covered up, but some disturbance and breakage nevertheless did occur—from chewing by catfish, but most especially from trampling by large animals wading in the swamp 1.6 m.y.a.

As we have discussed, the individual was not fully grown when he died. His age (11 to 13 years—Walker, 1993) is determined by the stage of dental eruption (his permanent canines are not yet erupted) and by union of the ends of long bones. Moreover, as we have noted, this young *Homo erectus* male was quite tall (5 feet 3 inches), and using modern growth curve approximations, his adult stature would have been over 6 feet had he lived to full maturity.

More than simply tall, the body proportions of this boy's skeleton are intriguing. Reconstructions suggest that he had a linear build with long appendages, thus conforming to predictions of *Allen's rule* for inhabitants of hot climates (see Chapter 15). Further extrapolating from this observation, Alan Walker also suggests that *H. erectus* must have had a high sweating capacity to dissipate heat (in the modern human fashion). (See pp. 423–424 for a discussion of heat adaptation in humans.)

The boy's limb proportions suggest a quite warm mean annual temperature (90 °F/30 °C) in East Africa 1.6 m.y.a. Paleoecological reconstructions confirm this estimate of tropical conditions (much like the climate today in northern Kenya).

Another fascinating anatomical clue is seen in the beautifully preserved vertebrae. The opening through which the spinal cord passes (the neural canal; see Appendix A) is quite small in the thoracic elements. The possible behavioral corollaries of this reduced canal (as compared to modern *H. sapiens*) are also intriguing. Ann MacLarnan (1993) has proposed that the reduced canal argues for reduced size of the spinal cord, which in turn may suggest less control of the muscles between the ribs (the intercostals). One major function of these muscles is the precise control of breathing during human speech. From these data and inferences, Alan Walker has concluded that the Nariokotome youth (and *H. erectus* in general) was not fully capable of human articulate speech. (As an argument regarding language potential, this conclusion will no doubt spark considerable debate.)

A final interesting feature can be seen in the pelvis of this adolescent skeleton. It is very narrow and is thus correlated with a narrow bony birth canal. Walker (1993) again draws a behavioral inference from this anatomical feature. He estimates that a newborn with a cranial capacity no greater than a mere 200 cm³ could have passed through this pelvis. As we showed elsewhere, the adult cranial capacity estimate for this individual was slightly greater than 900 cm³—thus arguing for significant postnatal growth of the brain (exceeding 75 percent of its eventual size, again mirroring the modern human pattern). Walker speculates that this slow neural expansion (compared to other primates) leads to delayed development of motor skills and thus a prolonged period of infant/child dependency (what Walker terms "secondary altriciality"). Of course, as with other speculative behavioral scenarios, critics will no doubt find holes in this reconstruction. One point you should immediately note is that this specimen is the immature pelvis of a male. Thus, the crucial dimensions of an adult female *H. erectus* pelvis remain unknown. Nevertheless, they could not have departed too dramatically from the dimensions seen at Nariokotome—unless one accepts an extreme degree of sexual dimorphism in this species.

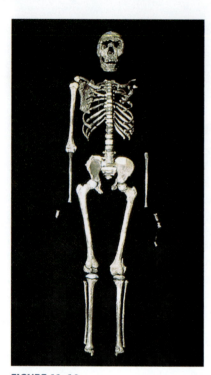

FIGURE 11–14

WT 15000 from Nariokotome, Kenya: the most complete H. erectus *specimen yet found.*

(Wood, 1991). In addition, the very early dates now postulated for the dispersal of *H. erectus* into Asia (Java) would argue for a more than 1-million-year separate history for Asian and African populations.

Nevertheless, this species division has not been generally accepted, and the current consensus (reflected in this text) is to continue to refer to all these hominids as *Homo erectus* (Kramer, 1993; Conroy, 1997; Rightmire, 1998). As with the Plio-Pleistocene samples, we accordingly will have to accommodate a considerable degree of intraspecific variation within this species. Wood has concluded, regarding variation within such a broadly defined *H. erectus* species, "It is a species which manifestly embraces an unusually wide degree of variation in both the cranium and postcranial skeleton" (Wood, 1992a, p. 329).

South Africa

A mandible was found among fossil remains collected at Swartkrans in South Africa in the 1940s and 1950s. This specimen, SK 15, was originally assigned to *"Telanthropus capensis,"* but is now placed within the genus *Homo* (there is, however, disagreement about its species designation). Rightmire (1990) suggests that it may be linked with *Homo erectus,* but others are not certain. If it is *H. erectus,* it would demonstrate that *H. erectus* inhabited South Africa as well as the other regions documented by other more complete fossil finds.

North Africa

With evidence from China and Java, it appears clear that *H. erectus* populations, with superior tools and weapons and presumably greater intelligence than their predecessors, had expanded their habitat beyond that of early hominids. The earliest evidence for *H. erectus,* 1.8–1.6 m.y.a., comes from East Africa and Java and about 1 million years later in China. Early dispersal of *H. erectus* to Europe (prior to 1 m.y.a.) may also have occurred. It is not surprising, therefore, that *H. erectus* migrations would have taken them to northwest Africa as well.

North African remains, consisting almost entirely of mandibles (or mandible fragments) and a partial parietal bone, have been found at Ternifine (now Tighenif), Algeria, and in Morocco, at Sidi Abderrahman and Thomas Quarries. The three Ternifine mandibles and the parietal fragment are quite robust and have been dated to about 700,000 y.a. The Moroccan material is not as robust as Ternifine and may be a bit younger, at 500,000 years. In addition, an interesting cranium was found in a quarry north of Salé, in Morocco. The walls of the skull vault are thick, and several other features resemble those of *H. erectus.* Some features suggest that Salé is *H. sapiens,* but a date of 400,000 y.a. and an estimated cranial capacity of about 900 cm^3 throw doubt on that interpretation.

Europe

The situation in Europe during the Pleistocene appears especially complex. With accumulating evidence suggesting dispersal of the first hominids to Europe in the Lower Pleistocene (i.e., prior to 700,000 y.a.), there is a growing realization that some of the earliest European hominids should perhaps be included within the species *H. erectus* (particularly the remains from Dmanisi and Ceprano, since the morphology of these specimens suggests at least a provisional assignment to

H. erectus; see p. 299). The slightly later remains from Atapuerca, in Spain (Gran Dolina site), are not as clearly similar to *Homo erectus,* and Spanish researchers have suggested placing them in a completely different species of hominid ("*Homo antecessor*"). Clearly, such an interpretation will require considerable more evaluation (and verification) before it could become widely accepted. We should note that all of this early Pleistocene European fossil material is both fragmentary and quite recently discovered. Thus, all current interpretations are, for the moment, both tentative and controversial.

After about 400,000 y.a., the European fossil hominid record becomes increasingly abundant. Nevertheless, interpretations relating to the proper taxonomic assessment of many of these remains have been debated, in some cases for decades. In recent years, several of these somewhat later (i.e., Middle Pleistocene) specimens have been placed within a grouping of early *Homo sapiens* referred to as "archaic *Homo sapiens*." Needless to say, Needless to say, not everyone agrees. These enigmatic archaic *H. sapiens* are discussed in Chapter 13. A time line for the *H. erectus* discoveries discussed in this chapter as well as other finds of more uncertain status is shown in Figure 11–15.

Technological and Population Trends in the Middle Pleistocene

Technological Trends

Many researchers have noted the remarkable stasis of the physical and cultural characteristics of *Homo erectus* populations, which seemed to change so little in the more than 1.5 million years of their existence. There is, however, dispute on this point. Some scholars (Rightmire, 1981) see almost no detectable changes in cranial dimensions over more than 1 million years of *H. erectus* evolution. Other paleoanthropologists (e.g., Wolpoff, 1984), who use different methodologies to date and subdivide their samples, draw a different conclusion, seeing some significant long-term morphological trends. Accepting a moderate position, we can postulate that there were some changes: The brain of later *H. erectus* was somewhat larger, the nose more protrusive, and the body not as robust as in earlier forms. Moreover, there were modifications in stone tool technology.

Expansion of the brain presumably enabled *H. erectus* to develop a more sophisticated tool kit than seen among earlier hominids. The important change in this kit was a core worked on both sides, called a *biface* (known widely as a hand axe or cleaver; Fig 11–16). The biface had a flatter core than the roundish earlier Oldowan pebble tool. And, probably even more important, this *core* tool was obviously a target design, that is, the main goal of the toolmaker. This greater focus and increased control enabled the stoneknapper to produce sharper, straighter edges, resulting in a more efficient implement. This Acheulian stone tool became standardized as the basic *H. erectus* all-purpose tool (with only minor modification) for more than a million years. It served to cut, scrape, pound, dig, and more—a most useful tool that has been found in Africa, parts of Asia, and later in western Europe.

Like populations elsewhere, *H. erectus* in China manufactured choppers and chopping tools as their core tools, and like other *H. erectus* toolmakers, fashioned scrapers and other small tools (Fig. 11–17), but they did not regularly manufacture bifaces. Interestingly, while the Acheulian is known from Africa as early as 1.4 m.y.a.

Virtual Lab 11 treats many of the issues of the early archaeological record and includes 3-D animations of stone tools.

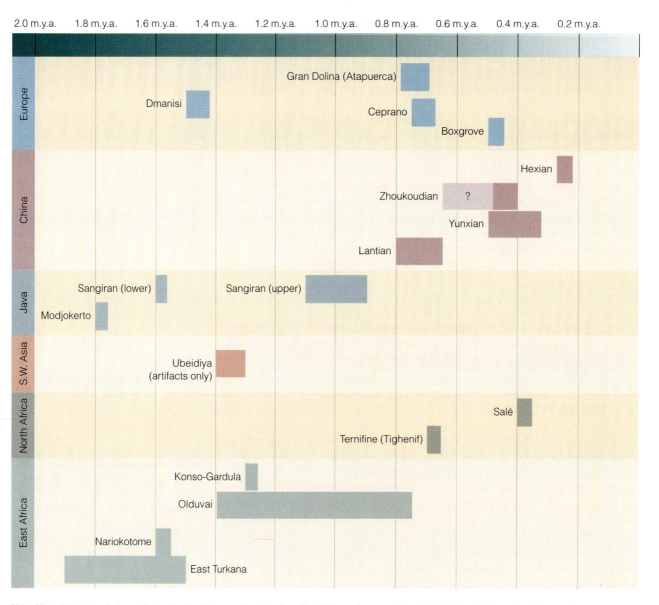

Note: Most dates are only imprecise estimates. However, the dates from East African sites are radiometrically determined and are thus much more secure. In addition, the early dates from Java are also radiometric and are gaining wide acceptance, although some researchers (e.g., Wolpoff, 1999) suggest that they are not secure and may be later than shown.

FIGURE 11–15

Time line for Homo erectus discoveries and other contemporary hominids. Note that most dates are approximations.

and persisted there and in western Europe and southwestern Asia for over 1 million years, this industry has *never* been found in eastern Europe or East Asia. Why there was such a long period of cultural distinctiveness has never been completely explained. It has been thought that other kinds of raw materials for tools were employed (bamboo, perhaps, in China). Another possibility suggested by the redating of the early Java sites is that *H. erectus* left Africa *prior* to the development of the Acheulian, and after reaching Asia, some groups continued to remain culturally isolated in certain regions.

In early days, toolmakers employed a stone hammer (simply an ovoid-shaped stone about the size of an egg or a bit larger) to remove flakes from the core, thus leaving deep scars. Later, they used other materials, such as wood and bone. They learned to use these new materials as soft hammers, which gave them more control over flaking, thus leaving shallow scars, sharper edges, and a more symmetrical form. Toward the end of the Acheulian industry, toolmakers blocked out a core with stone hammers and then switched to wood or bone for refining the edges. This technique produced more elegant-appearing and pear-shaped implements (see pp. 241–242).

Evidence of butchering is widespread at *H. erectus* sites, and in the past, such evidence has been cited in arguments for consistent hunting. For example, at the Olorgesailie site in Kenya (Fig. 11–18), dated at approximately 800,000 y.a., thousands of Acheulian hand axes have been recovered in association with remains of large animals, including giant baboons (now extinct). However, the assumption of consistent hunting has been challenged, especially by archaeologists who argue that the evidence does not prove the hunting hypothesis. Instead, they suggest that *H. erectus* was primarily a scavenger, a hypothesis that also has not yet been proved conclusively. We thus discuss *H. erectus* as a potential hunter *and* scavenger. It is crucial to remember, too, that *gathering* of wild plant foods was also practiced by *H. erectus* groups (as evidenced by the seeds at Zhoukoudian). Indeed, probably a majority of the calories they consumed came from such gathering activities.

Moreover, as we have seen, the mere *presence* of animal bones at archaeological sites does not prove that hominids were killing animals or even necessarily exploiting meat. Thus, in making interpretations of early hominid sites, we must consider a variety of alternatives. As Stanford University archaeologist Richard Klein has concluded regarding Middle Pleistocene sites, the interpretations are far from clear: "In sum, the available data do not allow us to isolate the relative roles of humans, carnivores, and factors such as starvation, accidents, and stream action in creating bone assemblages. . . . Certainly, as presently understood, the sites do not tell us how successful or effective *Homo erectus* was at obtaining meat" (1989, p. 221).

Population Trends

One of the fascinating qualities of *H. erectus* was a penchant for travel. From the relatively close confines of East Africa, *H. erectus* dispersed widely in the Old World. By the time *H. sapiens* appeared a million or more years later, *H. erectus* had migrated to South and North Africa. And even earlier, some groups had moved from Africa to Asia and perhaps to Europe as well.

The life of hunter-scavengers (and still, no doubt, *primarily* gatherers) was nomadic, and the woodland and savanna that covered the southern tier of Asia would have been an excellent environment for *H. erectus* (as it was similar to the econiche of their African ancestors). As the population grew, small groups budded off and moved on to find their own resource areas. This process, repeated again and again, led *H. erectus* east, crossing to Java, arriving there, it seems, as early as the most ancient known sites in East Africa itself.

Once in Java, it had been assumed that *H. erectus* would have found it impossible to venture farther south or east, since during the Pleistocene, deep water channels presumably separated Java completely from more southerly islands and Australia. However, recent reinterpretation (and firmer radiometric dates) of stone tools found on the island of Flores, 375 miles east of Java, has prompted some paleoanthropologists to reconsider this assumption (Gibbons, 1998). With a suggested date of 750,000 y.a. for these tools, it raises a most unexpected possibility: Could

FIGURE 11–16

Acheulian biface ("hand axe"), a basic tool of the Acheulian tradition.

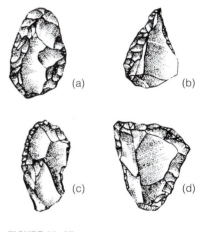

FIGURE 11–17

Small tools of the Acheulian industry. (a) Side scraper. (b) Point. (c) End scraper. (d) Burin.

Reconstructions of the dietary behaviors of early *Homo* and their relationship to the archaeological record are discussed in Virtual Lab 11.

(a)

(b)

FIGURE 11–18

(a) A Middle Pleistocene butchering site at Olorgesailie, Kenya, excavated by Louis and Mary Leakey, who had the catwalk built for observers. (b) A close-up of the Acheulian tools, mainly hand axes, found at the site.

ancient *H. erectus* at this *very* early period construct ocean-going vessels (rafts?) that could navigate over deep, fast-moving waters?

While initial dating of the Flores stone materials appears reasonably good (using fission-track dating; see p. 237), the conclusion that the finds *prove* such seemingly advanced capabilities for *H. erectus* is not yet generally accepted. A number of troublesome issues remain to be resolved, first of which is whether the lithic materials from Flores are *deliberate* tools or are simply naturally fractured rock. This latter possibility would argue against *H. erectus* (or any other hominid) having expanded south or east beyond Java at such an early date. Of course, the most unambiguous evidence would be fossil discoveries of *H. erectus* itself.

When we look back at the evolution of *H. erectus,* we realize how significant this early human's achievements were. It was *H. erectus* who increased in body size with more efficient bipedalism; who embraced culture wholeheartedly as a strategy of adaptation; whose brain was reshaped and increased in size to within *H. sapiens* range; who became a more efficient scavenger and likely hunter with greater dependence on meat; who apparently established more permanent bases; who perhaps could build vessels to cross open water; and who probably used fire and may have also controlled it. In short, it was *H. erectus,* committed to a cultural way of life, who transformed hominid evolution to human evolution; or as Foley states, "The appearance and expansion of *H. erectus* represented a major change in adaptive strategy that influenced the subsequent process and pattern of human evolution" (1991, p. 425).

Summary

Homo erectus remains are found in geological contexts dating from about 1.8 million to about 200,000 years ago (and perhaps much later), a period of more than

1.5 million years. The first finds were made by Dubois in Java, and later discoveries came from China and Africa. Differences from early *Homo* are notable in *H. erectus'* larger brain, taller stature, robust build, and changes in facial structure and cranial buttressing.

The long period of *H. erectus'* existence was marked by a remarkably uniform technology over space and time. Nevertheless, compared to earlier hominids, *H. erectus* introduced more sophisticated tools and probably ate novel and/or differently processed foods, using these new tools and probably fire as well. They were also able to move into different environments and successfully adapt to new conditions.

Originating in East Africa, *H. erectus* migrated in several directions: south and northwest in Africa and east to Java and China. The evidence from China, especially Zhoukoudian, supports a *H. erectus* way of life that included gathering, scavenging, hunting, and controlled use of fire (but note that there is not complete agreement about this archaeological reconstruction).

It is generally assumed that some *H. erectus* populations evolved to *H. sapiens*, since many fossils, such as Ngandong (and others discussed in Chapter 12), display both *H. erectus* and *H. sapiens* features. There remain questions about *H. erectus* behavior (e.g., did they hunt?) and about evolution to *H. sapiens* (was it gradual or rapid, and which *H. erectus* populations contributed genes to *H. sapiens*?). The search for answers continues.

Questions for Review

1. Describe the Pleistocene in terms of (a) relationship to glacial sequences and (b) the dating of fossil hominids.
2. Describe *Homo erectus*. How is *H. erectus* anatomically different from early *Homo*? From *H. sapiens*?
3. In what areas of the world have *Homo erectus* fossils been found?
4. In comparing *H. erectus* with earlier hominids, why is it important to specify which comparative sample is being used?
5. What was the intellectual climate in Europe in the latter half of the nineteenth century, especially concerning human evolution?
6. Why do you think there was so much opposition to Dubois' interpretation of the hominid fossils he found in Java?
7. Why do you think Zhoukoudian *H. erectus* was enthusiastically accepted, whereas the Javanese fossils were not?
8. What questions are still being asked about Dubois' finds? Explain.
9. Describe the way of life of *H. erectus* at Zhoukoudian as suggested in the text. What disagreements have been voiced about this conjecture?
10. *H. erectus* has been called the first human. Why?
11. What is the *H. erectus* evidence from Africa, and what questions of human evolution does the evidence raise?
12. Can you suggest any reason why the earliest remains of *H. erectus* have come from East Africa?
13. *H. erectus* migrated to various points in Africa and vast distances to eastern Asia and elsewhere. What does this tell you about the species?
14. What kinds of stone tools have been found at *H. erectus* sites?

Man, the Hunter;
Woman, the Gatherer?

Anthropologists have long been concerned with the behavioral evolution of our species. Accompanying changes in anatomy (limb structure, dentition, brain size and shape) were changes in mating patterns, social structure, cultural innovations, and, eventually, language. In fact, changes in these behavioral complexes are what mostly *explain* the concomitant adaptations in human biological structure.

We are, then, vitally interested in the behavioral adaptations of our early hominid ancestors. In seeking to reconstruct the behavioral patterns of these early hominids, anthropologists use inferences drawn from modern primates, social carnivores, and hunting-gathering peoples. In addition, they derive information directly from the paleoanthropological record (see Chapter 9).

Despite numerous attempts at such behavioral reconstructions, the conclusions must remain largely speculative. In point of fact, behavior does not fossilize. Accordingly, researchers must rely considerably on their imaginations in creating scenarios of early hominid behavioral evolution (see p. 243). In such an atmosphere, biases often emerge; these biased renditions, in turn, stimulate heated debates and alternative scenarios—often as narrow as those being attacked.

Among the most controversial topics in anthropology, and one that has displayed some of the most glaring biases, is the debate concerning origins of hominid gender-role differences. Did early hominid males

have characteristically different behavioral adaptations from their female counterparts? Did one sex dominate the frontier of early hominid cultural innovation? And if one sex did lead the way, which one?

A now well-known rendition of early hominid behavioral development was popularized in the 1960s and 1970s. According to this "man, the hunter" theory, the hunting of large animals by males was the central stimulus of hominid behavioral evolution. Such widely read works as *The Naked Ape* (1967), by Desmond Morris, and *The Hunting Hypothesis* (1976) and other books by Robert Ardrey maintain that early apish-looking forms *became* hominids as a result of a hunting way of life. As Ardrey states, "Man is man, and not a chimpanzee, because for millions upon millions of evolving years we killed for a living" (1976, p. 10).

In this reconstruction, the hunting of large, dangerous mammals by cooperating groups of males fostered the development of intelligence, language, tools, and bipedalism. In this scenario, increased intelligence accompanied by the development of weapons is also blamed for the roots of human aggressiveness, murder, and warfare.

This "man, the hunter" scenario further suggests that while the males are leading the vanguard in hominid evolution, females remain mostly sedentary, tied to the home base by the burden of dependent young. Females may have contributed some wild plant foods to the group's subsistence, but this is not seen as a particularly challenging (and certainly

not a very noble) endeavor. In this situation of marked division of labor, sexual relationships quickly changed. Males, constantly away from the home base (and thus away from the females, too), could not keep a watchful eye over their mates. In order to better ensure fidelity, monogamy came into being. In this way, a male would be assured that the young in which he invested were his own. This important factor of male-female bonding as a product of differential foraging patterns has more recently been restated by Owen Lovejoy (1981) (see p. 248).

From the female's point of view, it would be beneficial to maintain a close bond with a provisioning male. Consequently, she would want to appear "attractive," and thus, through time, the female breasts and buttocks would become more conspicuous. Besides rearing their young and being attractive sex objects, females were useful to males in another way. Groups of male hunters living in the same area might occasionally come into potentially dangerous competition for the same resources. As a means of solidifying political ties between groups, the males would thus routinely exchange females (by giving or "selling" their daughters to neighboring bands).

Thus, in a single stroke, this complex of features accounts for human intelligence, sexual practices, and political organization.

As might be expected, such a male-centered scenario did not go unchallenged. Ignoring females or relegating them to a definitely inferior role in human behavioral evolution drew sharp criticism from several quarters. As Sally Slocum notes:

So, while the males were out hunting, developing all their skills, learning to cooperate, inventing language, inventing art, creating tools and weapons, the poor dependent females were sitting back at the home base having one child after another and waiting for the males to bring home the bacon. While this reconstruction is certainly ingenious, it gives one the decided impression that only half the species— the male half—did any evolving. In addition to containing a number of logical gaps, the argument becomes somewhat doubtful in the light of modern knowledge of genetics and primate behavior. (Slocum, 1975, p. 42)

In fact, such a rigid rendering of our ancestors' behavior does not stand up to critical examination. Hunting is never defined rigorously. Does it include only large, terrestrial mammals? What of smaller mammals, sea mammals, fish, and birds? In numerous documented human societies, females actively participate in exploiting these latter resources.

Moreover, nonhuman primates do not conform to predictions derived from the "man, the hunter" model. For example, among chimpanzees, females do most of the tool-making, not the males. Finally in most nonhuman primates (most mammals, for that matter), it is the females—not the males—who choose with whom to mate.

Granting that the hunting hypothesis does not work, what alternatives have been proposed? As a reaction to male-centered views,

Elaine Morgan (1972) advanced the "aquatic hypothesis." In this rendition, females are seen as the pioneers of hominid evolution. But rather than having the dramatic changes of hominid evolution occur on the savanna, Morgan has them take place on the seashore. As females lead the way to bipedal locomotion, cultural innovation, and intellectual development, the poor males are seen as splashing pitifully behind.

Unfortunately, this scenario has less to back it up than the hunting hypothesis. Not a shred (even a watery one) of evidence has ever been discovered in the contexts predicted by the aquatic theory. Little is accomplished by such unsubstantiated overzealous speculation. Chauvinism—whether male or female—does not elucidate our origins and only obscures the evolutionary processes that operated on the *whole* species.

Another interesting aspect of these different behavioral "theories" has been pointed out by cultural anthropologist Misia Landau. She notes that these theories are like mythical stories with a hero emerging (from the forest) and ultimately conquering the challenges of existence (by boldly going bipedally onto the savanna). It could also be noted that in most of these myths, traditionally the hero is a male who acts to defend, provide for, and inseminate the females (who, otherwise, are not given much consideration).

What can we conclude from all these arguments? While the pattern is not as rigid as the hunting hypothesis advocates would have us believe, in the vast majority of

human societies, hunting of large, terrestrial mammals is almost always a male activity. In fact, a comprehensive cross-cultural survey shows that of 179 societies, males do the hunting exclusively in 166, both sexes participate in 13, and in *no* group is hunting done exclusively by females (Murdock, 1965).

In addition, there is some incipient division of labor in foraging patterns among chimpanzees. Females tend to concentrate more on termiting, while hunting is done mostly by males. Early hominids, expanding upon such a subsistence base, eventually adapted a greater sexual division of labor than is found in any other primate. Two points, however, must be kept in mind. First, both the gathering of wild plant foods and the hunting of animals would have been indispensable components of the diet. Consequently, *both* males and females always played a significant role. Secondly, the strategies must always have been somewhat flexible. With a shifting, usually unpredictable resource base, nothing else would have worked. As a result, males probably always did a considerable amount of gathering, and in most foraging societies they still do. Moreover, females—while not usually engaged in the stalking and killing of large prey—nonetheless contribute significantly to meat acquisition. Once large animals have been killed, there still remain the arduous tasks of butchering and transport back to the home base. In many societies, women and men participate equally in these activities.

A balanced view of human behavioral evolution must avoid simplistic

Man, the Hunter;
Woman, the Gatherer? (continued)

and overly rigid scenarios. As stated by Adrienne Zihlman, a researcher concerned with reconstructing early hominid behavior:

Both sexes must have been able to care for young, protect themselves from predators, make and use tools, and freely move about the environment in order to exploit available resources widely distributed through space and time. It is this range of behaviors—the overall behavioral flexibility of both sexes—that may have been the primary ingredient of early hominids' success in the savanna environment. (Zihlman, 1981, p. 97)

Following the notion developed by Landau that much of the literature on the evolution of human behavior resembles storytelling, anthropologist Linda Fedigan concluded her own comprehensive review of the topic (1986):

People will not stop wanting to hear origin stories and scientists will not cease to write scholarly tales. But we can become aware of the symbolic content of our stories, for much as our theories are not independent of our beliefs, so our behavior is not independent of our theories of human society. In these origin tales, we try to coax the material evidence into telling us about the past,

but the narrative we weave about the past also tells us about the present.

Critical Thinking Questions

1. What do we mean when we say, "Behavior does not fossilize"?
2. Exactly, what is it that *does* fossilize?
3. What is meant by male (or female) chauvinism? Do you detect elements of chauvinism in any of the views discussed here?
4. Select a feature of early hominid adaptation (e.g., bipedal locomotion or sexual dimorphism, where males are considerably larger than females) and construct your own behavioral explanation of how it might have evolved. (Do so in two different ways. First, restrict yourself to only firm evidence. Then be as speculative as possible, giving full vent to your imagination. Lastly, compare your two reconstructions and evaluate the *scientific* merit of each.)

Sources

Ardrey, Robert. 1976. *The Hunting Hypothesis.* New York: Atheneum.

Dahlberg, Frances (ed.). 1981. *Woman the Gatherer.* New Haven: Yale University Press.

Fedigan, Linda. 1986. "The Changing Role of Woman in Models of Human Evolution." *Annual Review of Anthropology* 15: 25–66.

Landau, Misia. 1986. "Human Evolution as Narrative." *American Scientist* 72: 262–268.

Lovejoy, C. Owen. 1981. "The Origin of Man." *Science* 211: 341–350.

Morgan, Elaine. 1972. *The Descent of Woman.* New York: Stein and Day.

Morris, Desmond. 1967. *The Naked Ape.* New York: McGraw-Hill.

Murdock, G. P. 1965. *Culture and Society.* Pittsburgh: University of Pittsburgh Press.

Slocum, Sally. 1975. "Woman the Gatherer: Male Bias in Anthropology," *Toward an Anthropology of Women,* R. R. Reiter, ed. New York: Monthly Review Press, pp. 36–50.

Zihlman, Adrienne L. 1981. "Women as Shapers of the Human Adaptation," *Woman the Gatherer,* op. cit., pp. 75–120.

The evidence for and consequences of sexual dimorphism in early *Homo* are discussed in Virtual Lab 10, section III, part C.

Neandertals and Other Archaic *Homo sapiens*

Introduction

In Chapter 11, we saw that *H. erectus* was present in Africa approximately 1.8 m.y.a. and also in Java at about this same time. Except for new finds at Dmanisi in the Republic of Georgia, and Ceprano in Italy, we also noted that *H. erectus* fossils thus far are very scarce in Europe, although several routes could easily have provided access. A major difficulty in accurately assessing finds is that a number of fossils from Europe—as well as Africa, China, and Java—display *both H. erectus* and *H. sapiens* features.

These particular forms, possibly representing some of the earliest members of our species, fall into the latter half of the Middle Pleistocene, from about 400,000 to 130,000 years ago, and are often referred to as **archaic *H. sapiens*.** The designation *H. sapiens* is used because the appearance of some derived sapiens traits suggests that these hominids are transitional forms. In most cases, these early archaic *H. sapiens* also retain some *H. erectus* features mixed with those derived features that distinguish them as *H. sapiens*. However, as they do not possess the full suite of derived characteristics diagnostic of **anatomically modern *H. sapiens*,** we classify them as archaic forms of our species. In general, we see in several different areas of the Old World through time a morphological trend from groups with more obvious *H. erectus* features to later populations displaying more diagnostic *H. sapiens* features.

When we speak of evolutionary trends and transitions from one species to another—for example, from *H. erectus* to *H. sapiens*—we do not wish to imply that such changes were in any way inevitable. In fact, most *H. erectus* populations never evolved into anything else. *Some* populations of *H. erectus* did apparently undergo slow evolutionary changes, and thus, some populations of what we call archaic *H. sapiens* emerge as transitional forms. In turn, *some* of these archaic *H. sapiens* populations suggest evolutionary change in the direction of anatomically modern *H. sapiens*.

In this chapter, we attempt, where the data permit, to focus on those populations that provide clues regarding patterns of hominid evolutionary change. We would like to ascertain *where* such transformations took place, *when* they occurred, and *what* the adaptive stimuli were (both cultural and biological) that urged the process along.

There are still significant gaps in the fossil data, and we certainly do not have a complete record of all the transitional stages; nor are we ever likely to possess anything approaching such a complete record. What we will do in this chapter is to paint the evolution of later hominids in fairly broad strokes to show the general trends.

Early Archaic *H. sapiens*

Many early archaic forms show morphological changes compared with *H. erectus*. These derived changes are reflected in brain expansion; increased parietal breadth (the basal portion of the skull is no longer the widest area, and therefore, the shape of the skull as seen from the rear is no longer pentagonal); some decrease in the size of the molars; and general decrease in cranial and postcranial robusticity.

A difficulty of major significance concerns exactly how to classify all this Middle Pleistocene hominid material. Here we take a conservative taxonomic approach and classify *all* of the specimens (as archaic forms) within the species

■ Archaic *H. sapiens*
Earlier forms of *Homo sapiens* (including Neandertals) from the Old World that differ from *H. erectus* but lack the full set of characteristics diagnostic of modern *H. sapiens*.

■ Anatomically modern *H. sapiens*
All modern humans and some fossil forms, perhaps dating as early as 200,000 y.a.; defined by a set of derived characteristics, including cranial architecture and lack of skeletal robusticity; usually classified at the subspecies level as *Homo sapiens sapiens*.

A discussion of archaic *Homo sapiens* is given in the species gallery in Virtual Lab 10, section I, part C. Be sure to click on the Extra Information text icon for each specimen.

Virtual Lab 10 includes a traditional phylogeny button that is accessible on each screen of the species gallery in section I, part C. Be sure to consider an alternative phylogeny (with pronunciations of the species' names) that is presented in the glossary of Virtual Lab 10 under Phylogeny of *Homo*.

Homo sapiens. However, a growing number of paleoanthropologists (e.g., Stringer, 1995; Larick and Ciochon, 1996; Rightmire, 1998) disagree with this interpretation and prefer to classify most, if not all, of the individuals into other species of the genus *Homo*. In this view, some of the earlier archaic forms could be ancestral to modern humans, but the later ones most likely would not be. As in other debates of this nature discussed in previous chapters, the essential issue concerns interpretation of intra- as compared to interspecific variation. We will return to this crucial topic at the end of this chapter.

A further complication in understanding archaic *H. sapiens* is that there is considerable variation both within and between samples of these hominids. Moreover, they are geographically very widely dispersed. In fact, archaic *H. sapiens* fossils have been found on the three continents of Africa, Asia, and Europe. In Europe, the well-known Neandertals are included in this category. (Neandertals are not found anywhere *except* Europe and western Asia.)

Africa

In Africa, archaic *H. sapiens* fossils have been found at several sites (Figs. 12–1 and 12–2). One of the best known is Broken Hill (Kabwe). At this site in Zambia, a complete cranium, together with other cranial and postcranial elements belonging to several individuals, was discovered.

In this and other African early archaic specimens, a mixture of older and more recent traits can be seen. The skull's massive supraorbital torus (one of the largest of any hominid), low vault, and prominent occipital torus recall those of *H. erectus.* On the other hand, the occipital region is less angulated, the cranial vault bones are thinner, and the cranial base is essentially modern. Dating estimates of Broken Hill and most of the other early archaic *H. sapiens* from Africa have ranged throughout the Middle and Upper Pleistocene, but recent estimates have given dates for most of the localities in the range of 150,000–125,000 y.a.

A total of eight other archaic *H. sapiens* crania from South and East Africa also show a combination of *H. erectus* and *H. sapiens* characteristics, and they are all mentioned in the literature as being similar to Broken Hill. The most important of these African finds come from the sites of Florisbad and Elandsfontein in South Africa, Laetoli in Tanzania, and Bodo in Ethiopia (see Fig. 12–2). The general similarities in all these African archaic *H. sapiens* may signify a fairly close genetic relationship of hominids from East and South Africa. It is also possible—although it seems most unlikely—that several populations were evolving in a somewhat similar way from *H. erectus* to a more *H. sapiens*-looking morphology.

We should point out that the evolutionary path of these hominids did not take a Neandertal turn. It seems that there were no Neandertals in Africa—nor were there any in the Far East (see Table 12–1).

Asia

China   Like their counterparts in Europe and Africa, Chinese archaic *H. sapiens** also display both earlier and later characteristics. Chinese paleoanthropologists suggest that archaic *H. sapiens* traits, such as a sagittal ridge (see p. 304) and flattened nasal bones, are shared with *H. erectus*, especially those specimens from

FIGURE 12–1

Broken Hill (Kabwe). Note the very heavy supraorbital torus.

Three-dimensional animations of many of these fossil specimens can be found in Virtual Lab 10, section I, part C.

---

*Chinese anthropologists prefer the term "early *Homo sapiens*" instead of "archaic *H. sapiens.*"

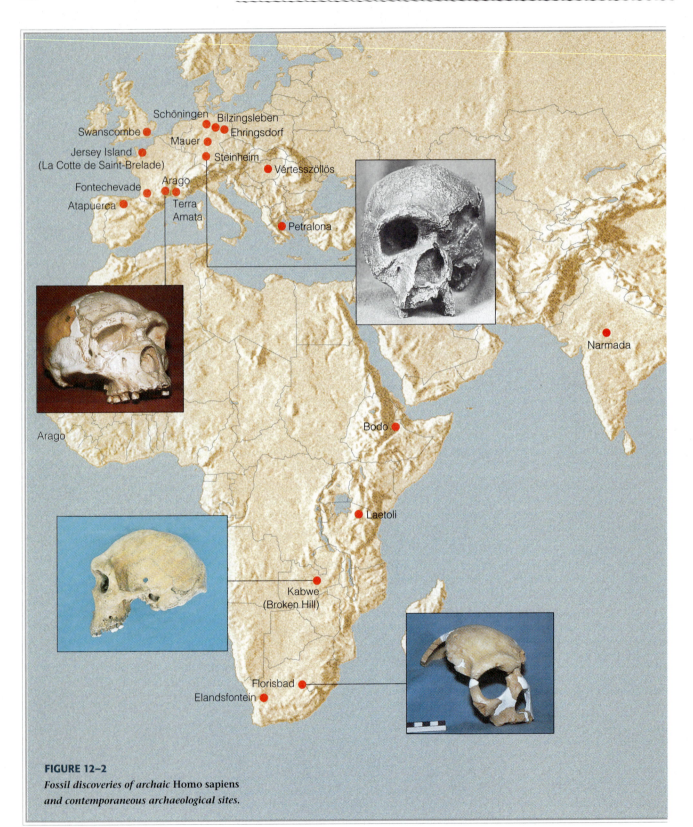

FIGURE 12–2

Fossil discoveries of archaic Homo sapiens *and contemporaneous archaeological sites.*

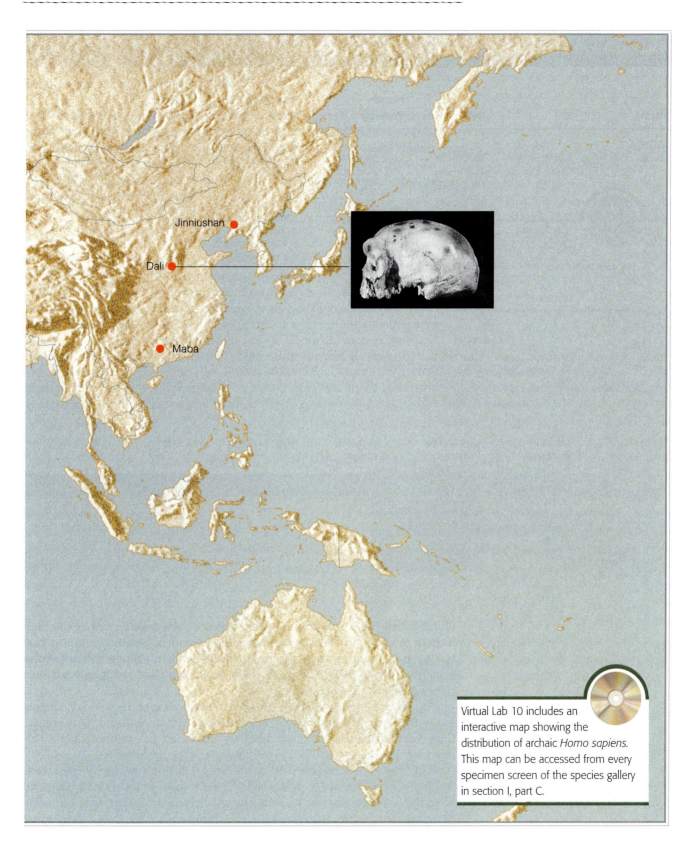

Jinniushan

Dali

Maba

Virtual Lab 10 includes an interactive map showing the distribution of archaic *Homo sapiens.* This map can be accessed from every specimen screen of the species gallery in section I, part C.

The earliest archaic *H. sapiens* representatives from Europe show some resemblance to *H. erectus* in the robusticity of the mandible, thick cranial bones, pronounced occipital torus, heavy supraorbital torus, receding frontal bone, greatest parietal breadth near the base of the skull, and large teeth. (They, of course, also have one or more *H. sapiens* characteristics.) Examples of these early archaic forms from Europe include fossils from Steinheim, Swanscombe, and Vértesszöllös (see Fig. 12–2). Later European archaic representatives also possess some *H. erectus* characteristics, but they also have one or more of the following traits: larger cranial capacity, more rounded occipital area, parietal expansion, and reduced tooth size (see Table 12–2).

The later group, essentially from the later half of the Middle Pleistocene, overlaps to some extent with the earlier group. From an evolutionary point of view, this later group may have evolved from the earlier one, and since many of these individuals display traits unique to Neandertals, they may in turn have given rise to the Neandertals. Examples of this somewhat later European transitional group include specimens from Fontechevade (France) and Ehringsdorf (Germany), as well as recent discoveries from Atapuerca, in northern Spain, in the same region as the newly discovered more ancient remains discussed in Chapter 11. This last site (called Sima de los Huesos), dated to approximately 300,000 y.a., has yielded the largest sample yet of archaic *Homo sapiens* from anywhere in the world and includes the remains of at least 32 individuals (among which are several excellently preserved crania) (Arsuaga et al., 1993, 1997; Kunzig, 1997). Excavations continue at this remarkable site, where bones have somehow accumulated within a deep chamber inside a cave. There are also large numbers of carnivore remains (bear, fox), but these fossils are generally in separate locations from where the hominids were found. From initial descriptions completed, the hominid morphology has been interpreted as showing several indications of an early Neandertal-like pattern (arching browridges, projecting midface, and other features) (Rightmire, 1998).

A Review of Middle Pleistocene Evolution (circa 400,000–125,000 y.a.)

Like the *erectus/sapiens* mix in Africa and China, the fossils from Europe also exhibit a mosaic of traits from both species (Fig. 12–4). However, it is important to note that the fossils from each continent differ; that is, the mosaic Chinese forms are not the same as those from Africa or Europe. Some European fossils, assumed to be earlier, are more robust and possess more similarities to *H. erectus* than to modern *H. sapiens*. The later Middle Pleistocene European fossils appear to be more Neandertal-like, but the uncertainty of dates prevents a clear scenario of the Middle Pleistocene evolutionary sequence.

The physical differences from *H. erectus* are not extraordinary. Bones remain thick, the supraorbital torus is prominent, and vault height shows little increase. There is, however, a definite increase in brain size and a change in the shape of the skull from pentagonal to globular as seen from the rear. There is also a trend, especially with the later Middle Pleistocene forms, toward less occipital angulation. It is interesting to note that in Europe, the changes move toward a Neandertal *H. sapiens* pattern, but in Africa and Asia, toward modern *H. sapiens*.

Be sure to study the cranial and postcranial morphology of archaic *Homo sapiens* in Virtual Lab 10, sections II and III.

TABLE 12–2   Archaic *Homo sapiens* in Europe*

Name	Site	Date*	Human Remains	Associated Finds	Cranial Capacity (cm³)	Comments
Arago (Tautavel)	Cave site near Tautavel, Verdouble Valley, Pyrenees, southeastern France	400,000–300,000 y.a.; date uncertain	Face; parietal perhaps from same person; many cranial fragments; up to 23 individuals represented	Upper Acheulian artifacts, animal bones	1,150	Thick supra-orbital torus, pronounced alveolar prognathism; parietal resembles Swanscombe
Bilzingsleben	Quarry at Bilzingsleben, near Erfurt, Germany	425,000–200,000 y.a., probably 280,000 y.a.	Skull fragments and teeth	Flake industry, plant and animal remains	Insufficient material	Resembles *H. erectus* in some features
Atapuerca	Sima de los Huesos, northern Spain	320,000–190,000 y.a. probably 300,000 y.a.	Minimum of 32 individuals; including some nearly complete crania	Many carnivore remains, but at different levels from human remains	Highly variable; small indiv., 1,125; larger indiv., 1,390 (probably reflects sexual dimorphism)	Several resemblances to Neandertals; oldest evidence of deliberate disposal of dead; largest sample of archaic *H. sapiens* at any site
Petralona	Cave near Petralona, Khalkidhiki, northeastern Greece	300,000–200,000 y.a.; date uncertain	Nearly complete skull	None	1,190–1,220	Mosaic; some bones resemble Neandertal, Broken Hill, and *H. erectus*
Steinheim	Gravel pit at Steinheim, Germany	Mindel-Riss Interglacial—300,000–250,000 y.a.; date uncertain	Nearly complete skull, lacking mandible	No artifacts, some animal bones	1,100	Pronounced supraorbital torus, frontal low, occipital rounded
Swanscombe	Swanscombe, Kent, England	Mindel-Riss Interglacial—300,000–250,000 y.a.; date uncertain	Occipital and parietals	Middle Acheulian artifacts, animal bones	1,325 (estimate)	Bones thick like *H. erectus*; occipital resembles Neandertal
Ehringsdorf	Fossil quarry; travertine deposits, eastern Germany	245,000–190,000 y.a.	Minimum of 9 individuals, including partial cranium	Mousterian artifacts	1,450	Resembles Neandertals in some respects
Vértesszöllös	Near village of Vértesszöllös, 30 miles west of Budapest, Hungary	210,000–160,000 y.a.; date uncertain	Adult occipital bone, fragments of infant teeth	Flake and pebble tools, animal bones	1,115–1,434 (estimate)	Occipital thick (*H. erectus* trait), but size and angulation suggest *H. sapiens*

*Also see Figure 12–3.

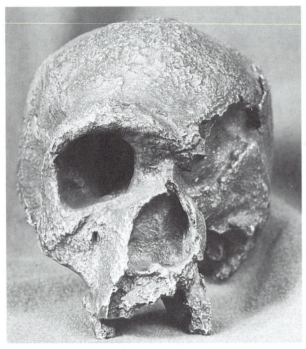

(a)

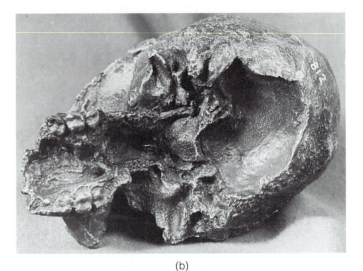

(b)

FIGURE 12–4

Cast of an archaic Homo sapiens *skull from Germany (Steinheim). (a) Frontal view showing damaged skull. (b) Basal view showing how the foramen magnum was enlarged, apparently for removal of the brain, perhaps for dietary or ritualistic purposes.*

Middle Pleistocene Culture

The Acheulian technology of *H. erectus* persevered in the Middle Pleistocene with relatively little change until near the end of the period, when it became slightly more sophisticated. The hand axe, almost entirely absent in China in the Lower Pleistocene, remained rare in the Middle Pleistocene, and choppers and flake tools continued to be the basic tools. Bone, a very useful tool material, apparently went practically unused by archaic *H. sapiens*. Stone flake tools similar to those of the earlier era persisted, perhaps in greater variety. Archaic *H. sapiens* in Africa and Europe invented a method—the Levallois technique (Fig. 12–5)—for controlling flake size and shape. Requiring several coordinated steps, this was no mean feat and suggests to many scholars increased cognitive abilities in late archaic *H. sapiens* compared to earlier archaic forms.

Interpretation of the distribution of artifacts during the later Middle Pleistocene has generated considerable discussion among archaeologists. We have noted (in Chapter 11) that there is a general geographical distribution characteristic of the Lower Pleistocene, with bifaces (mostly hand axes) found quite often in sites in Africa, but only very rarely at sites in most of Asia, and not at all among the rich assemblage at Zhoukoudian (see p. 308). Moreover, where hand axes proliferate, the stone tool industry is referred to as Acheulian, while at localities without hand axes, various other terms are used (e.g., "chopper/chopping tool"—a misnomer, since most of the tools are actually flakes).

Acheulian assemblages have been found at many African sites as well as numerous European ones (e.g., Swanscombe in England and Arago in France). Nevertheless, the broad geographical distribution of what we call Acheulian should not blind us to the considerable intraregional diversity in stone tool industries. For example, while a variety of European sites do show a typical Acheulian complex, rich in bifacial hand axes and cleavers, other contemporaneous ones—for example, Bilzingsleben in Germany and Vértesszöllös in Hungary—do not. At these latter two sites, a variety of small retouched flake tools and flaked pebbles of various sizes were found, but no hand axes.

It thus appears that different stone tool industries coexisted in some areas for long periods. Various explanations (Villa, 1983) have been offered to account for this apparent diversity: (1) The tool industries were produced by different peoples (i.e., different cultures, perhaps hominids that also differed biologically); (2) the tool industries represent different types of activities carried out at separate locales; (3) the presence (or absence) of specific tool types—bifaces—represents the availability (or unavailability) of appropriate local stone resources.

Archaic *H. sapiens* continued to live both in caves and in open-air sites, but may have increased their use of caves. Did archaic *H. sapiens* control fire? Klein (1989, p. 255) suggests they did. He writes that there was a "concentration of burnt bones in depressions 50–60 cm across at Vértesszöllös" and that "fossil hearths have also been identified at Bilzingsleben and in several French caves that were probably occupied by early *H. sapiens*." Chinese archaeologists insist that many Middle Pleistocene sites in China contain evidence of human-controlled fire. However, not everyone is convinced.

That archaic *H. sapiens* built temporary structures is revealed by concentrations of bones, stones, and artifacts at several sites. Here, they manufactured artifacts and exploited the area for food. The stones may have been used to support the sides of a shelter.

In the Lazaret Cave in the city of Nice, in southern France, a shelter about 36 feet by 11 feet was built against the cave wall, and skins probably were hung over a framework of poles as walls for the shelter. The base was supported by rocks and large bones, and inside the shelter were two hearths. The hearth charcoal suggests that the hominid occupants used slow-burning oak and boxwood, which produced easy-to-rekindle embers. Very little stone waste was found inside the shelter, suggesting that they manufactured tools outside, perhaps because there was more light.

Archaeological evidence clearly alludes to the utilization of many different food sources, such as fruits, vegetables, seeds, nuts, and bird eggs, each in its own season. Marine life was also exploited. From Lazaret and Orgnac (southern France) comes evidence of freshwater fishing for trout, perch, and carp. The most detailed reconstruction of Middle Pleistocene life in Europe, however, comes from evidence at Terra Amata, on the southern coast of France (de Lumley and de Lumley, 1973; Villa, 1983). From this site has come fascinating evidence relating to short-term, seasonal visits by archaic *H. sapiens* who built flimsy shelters (Fig. 12–6), gathered plants, exploited marine resources, and possibly hunted medium-sized and large mammals.

The hunting capabilities of these early members of *H. sapiens,* as for earlier hominids, remain open to dispute. What seems clear is that the evidence does not yet unambiguously establish widely practiced advanced abilities. In earlier professional discussions (as well as in earlier editions of our texts), archaeological evidence from Terra Amata (in France) and Torralba and Ambrona (in Spain) was used to argue for significantly advanced hunting skills for archaic *H. sapiens* in Europe. However, reconstruction of these sites by Richard Klein and others has now cast doubt on those prior conclusions. Once again, we see that application of scientific rigor (which is simply good critical thinking) makes us question assumptions. And in so doing, we frequently must conclude that other less dramatic (and less romantic) explanations fit the evidence as well as or better than those based on initial imaginative scenarios.

A possible exception to the current, much more conservative view of the hunting skills of archaic *H. sapiens* comes from an archaeological site excavated

Nodule

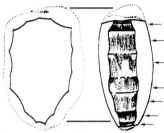

The nodule is chipped on the perimeter.

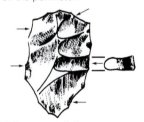

Flakes are radially removed from top surface.

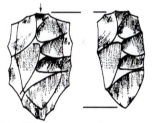

A final blow at one end removes a large flake.

FIGURE 12–5

The Levallois technique.

Virtual Lab 11 includes 3-D animations of many stone tools and their manufacture.

FIGURE 12–6

Cutaway of Terra Amata hut (reconstruction). Note the hearth (arrow), the stone scatters where people sat making tools, the poles that supported the roof, and the stones at the base of the hut supporting the sides. (Adapted from de Lumley, 1969.)

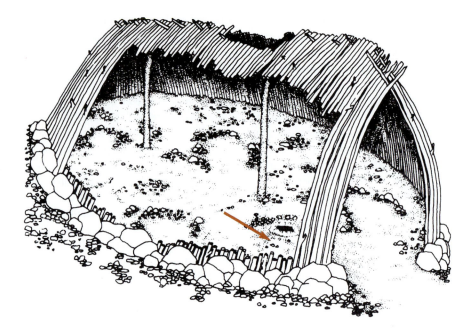

on the Channel Island of Jersey off the west coast of France (see Fig. 12–2). In a cave site called La Cotte de Saint-Brelade, many skeletal remains of large mammals (mammoth and woolly rhinoceros) were found in association with stone flakes. Unlike the remains from the sites mentioned earlier, the animals sampled at La Cotte de Saint-Brelade represent primarily subadults and adults in prime age (*not* what one would expect in naturally occurring accumulations). Moreover, the preserved elements also exhibit the kind of damage that further suggests hominid activities. Directly killing such large animals may not have been within the capabilities of the hominids (archaic *H. sapiens*?) who occupied this site. Thus, K. Scott, who led the excavations, has suggested that these early hominids may have driven their prey off a nearby cliff, bringing certain prized parts back to the cave for further butchering (Scott, 1980).

Another recent and exceptional find is also challenging assumptions regarding hunting capabilities of archaic *H. sapiens* in Europe. From the site of Schöningen in Germany, three remarkably well preserved wooden spears were discovered in 1995 (Thieme, 1997). As we have noted before, fragile organic remains (such as wood) can rarely be preserved more than a few hundred years; yet these beautifully crafted implements are provisionally dated to 380,000–400,000 y.a.! Beyond this surprisingly ancient date, the spears are intriguing on a variety of other counts. Firstly, they are all large (about 6 feet long), very finely made, selected from hard spruce wood, and expertly balanced. Each spear would have required considerable planning, time, and skill to manufacture. Further, the weapons were most likely used as throwing spears, presumably to hunt large animals. Of interest in this context, bones of numerous horses were also recovered at Schöningen. Archaeologist Hartmut Thieme has thus concluded that "the spears strongly suggest that systematic hunting, involving foresight, planning and the use of appropriate technology, was part of the behavioural repertoire of pre-modern hominids" (1997:807). Therefore, as with the remains from La Cotte de Saint-Brelade, these extraordinary spears from Schöningen make a strong case for advanced hunting skills, practiced by at least some archaic *Homo sapiens* populations.

As documented by the fossil hominid remains as well as artifactual evidence from archaeological sites, the long period of transitional hominids in Europe was to continue well into the Upper Pleistocene (after 125,000 y.a.). However, the evolution of archaic *H. sapiens* was to take a unique turn with the appearance and expansion of the Neandertals.

Neandertals: Late Archaic *H. sapiens* (130,000–35,000 y.a.)

Since their discovery more than a century ago, the Neandertals have haunted the best-laid theories of paleoanthropologists. They fit into the general scheme of human evolution, and yet they are misfits. Classified as *H. sapiens,* they are like us and yet different. It is not an easy task to put them in their place.*

While Neandertal fossil remains have been found at dates approaching 130,000 y.a., in the following discussion of Neandertals, we refer to those populations that lived especially during the last glaciation, which began about 75,000 y.a. and ended about 10,000 y.a. (Fig. 12–7). We should also note that the evolutionary roots of Neandertals apparently reach quite far back in western Europe, as evidenced by the 300,000 y.a. remains from Sima de los Huesos, Atapuerca, in northern Spain. The majority of fossils have been found in Europe, where they have been most studied, and our description of Neandertals is based primarily on those specimens from western Europe, who are usually called *classic* Neandertals. Not all Neandertals—including others from eastern Europe and western Asia and those from the interglacial that preceded the last glacial—entirely conform to our description of the classic morphology. They tend to be less robust, perhaps because the climate in which they lived was not as cold as western Europe during the last glaciation.

One striking feature of Neandertals is brain size, which in these hominids actually was larger than that of *H. sapiens* today. The average for contemporary *H. sapiens* centers around 1,400 cm³, while for Neandertals it was 1,520 cm³. The larger size may be associated with the metabolic efficiency of a larger brain in cold weather. The Inuit (Eskimo) brain also averages larger than that of other modern human populations (about the size of the Neandertal brain). It should also be pointed out that the larger brain size in both archaic and contemporary *Homo sapiens* in populations adapted to *cold* climates is partially correlated with larger body size, which has also evolved among these groups (see Chapter 15).

The classic Neandertal cranium is large, long, low, and bulging at the sides. Viewed from the side, the posterior portion of the occipital bone is somewhat bun-shaped, but the marked occipital angle typical of many *H. erectus* crania is absent. The forehead rises more vertically than that of *H. erectus,* and the browridges arch over the orbits instead of forming a straight bar (Fig. 12–8).

Compared with anatomically modern humans, the Neandertal face stands out. It projects almost as if it were pulled forward. This feature can be seen when the distance of the nose and teeth from the eye orbits is compared with that of modern *H. sapiens.* Postcranially, Neandertals were very robust, barrel-chested, and powerfully muscled. This robust skeletal structure, in fact, dominates

Neandertals are discussed in Virtual Lab 10, section I, part C.

The intriguing relationship between brain size and body mass is investigated in Virtual Lab 10, section IV, part B.

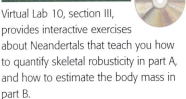

Virtual Lab 10, section III, provides interactive exercises about Neandertals that teach you how to quantify skeletal robusticity in part A, and how to estimate the body mass in part B.

Homo sapiens neanderthalensis is the subspecific designation for Neandertals, although not all paleoanthropologists agree with this terminology. (The subspecies for anatomically modern *H. sapiens* is designated as *Homo sapiens sapiens.*) *Thal,* meaning "valley," is the old spelling and is kept in the species designation (the "h" was always silent and not pronounced). The modern spelling is *tal* and is now used this way in Germany; we shall adhere to contemporary usage in the text with the spelling *Neandertal.*

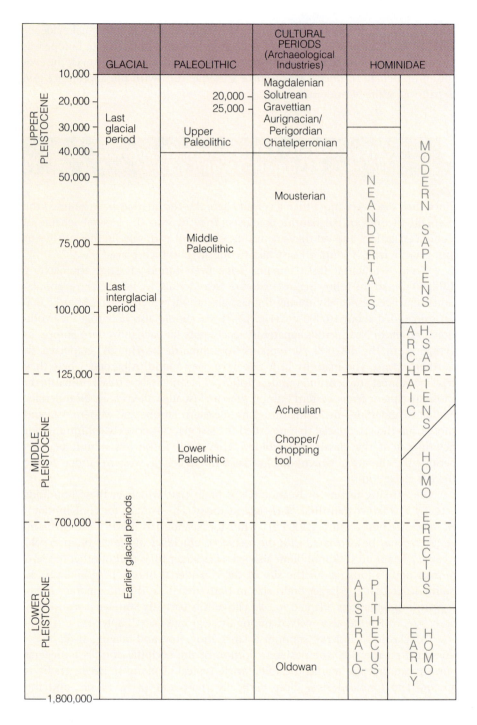

hominid evolution from *H. erectus* through archaic *H. sapiens*. Nevertheless, the Neandertals appear particularly robust, with shorter limbs than seen in most modern *H. sapiens* populations. Both the facial anatomy and robust postcranial structure of Neandertals have been interpreted by Erik Trinkaus (of Washington University in St. Louis) to reflect adaptation to rigorous living in a cold climate.

For about 100,000 years, Neandertals lived in Europe and western Asia (Fig. 12–9), and their coming and going has raised more questions and controversies than perhaps any other hominid group. Neandertal forebears date back to the

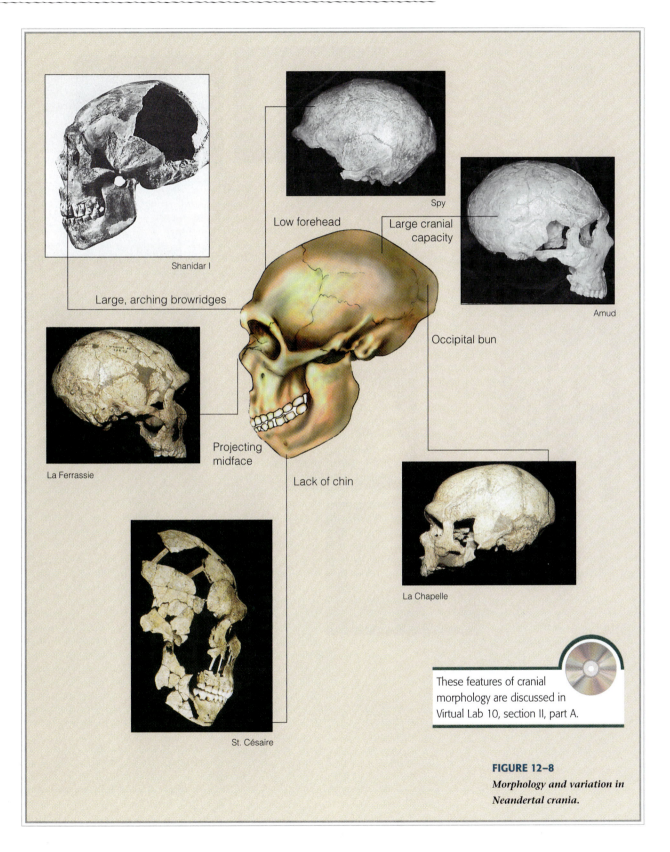

Shanidar I

Large, arching browridges

Low forehead

Spy

Large cranial capacity

Amud

Occipital bun

La Ferrassie

Projecting midface

Lack of chin

La Chapelle

St. Césaire

These features of cranial morphology are discussed in Virtual Lab 10, section II, part A.

FIGURE 12–8

Morphology and variation in Neandertal crania.

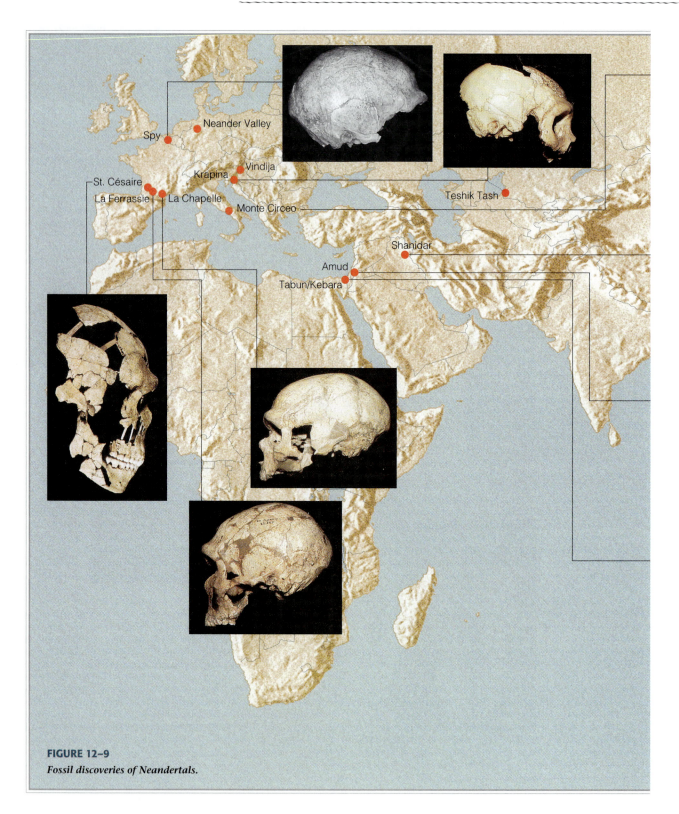

FIGURE 12–9
Fossil discoveries of Neandertals.

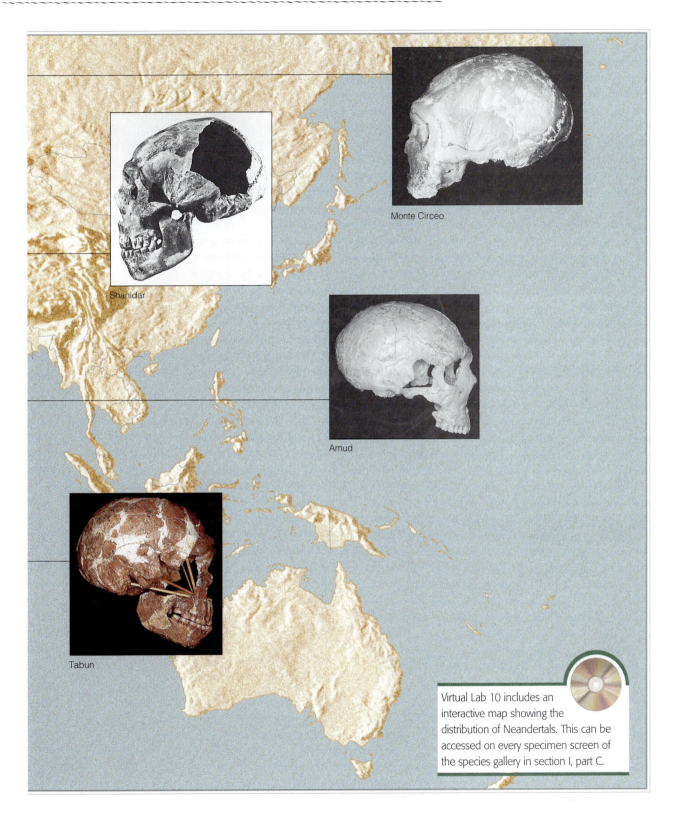

Monte Circeo

Shanidar

Amud

Tabun

Virtual Lab 10 includes an interactive map showing the distribution of Neandertals. This can be accessed on every specimen screen of the species gallery in section I, part C.

■ **Flexed**
The position of the body in a bent orientation, with the arms and legs drawn up to the chest.

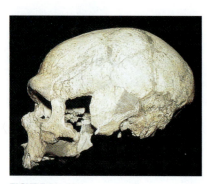

FIGURE 12–10
La Chapelle-aux-Saints. Note the occipital bun, projecting face, and low vault.

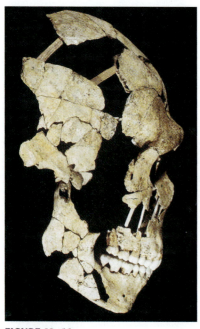

FIGURE 12–11
St. Césaire, among the "last" Neandertals.

■ **Upper Paleolithic**
A cultural period associated with early modern humans and distinguished by technological innovation in various stone tool industries. Best known from western Europe, similar industries are also known from central and eastern Europe and Africa.

later archaic *H. sapiens*. But these were transitional forms, and it is not until the last interglacial that Neandertals were fully recognizable.

Neandertal takes its name from the Neander Valley, near Düsseldorf, Germany. In 1856, workmen quarrying limestone caves in the valley came across some fossilized bones. The owner of the quarry believed them to be bear and gave them to a natural science teacher, who realized that they were not the remains of a cave bear, but rather the remains of an ancient human. Exactly what the bones represented became a *cause célèbre* for many years, and the fate of "Neandertal Man," as the bones were named, hung in the balance until later finds provided more evidence.

What swung the balance in favor of accepting the Neander Valley specimen as a genuine hominid fossil were other nineteenth-century finds similar to it. What is more important, the additional fossil remains brought home the realization that a form of human different from nineteenth-century Europeans had in fact once existed.

France and Spain

One of the most important Neandertal discoveries was made in 1908 at La Chapelle-aux-Saints in southwestern France. A nearly complete skeleton was found buried in a shallow grave in a **flexed** position, with several fragments of nonhuman long bones placed over the head, and over them, a bison leg. Around the body were flint tools and broken animal bones.

The skeleton was turned over for study to a well-known French paleontologist, Marcellin Boule, who published his analysis in three copious volumes. Boule depicted the La Chapelle Neandertal as a brutish, bent-kneed, not fully erect biped. As a result of this exaggerated interpretation, some scholars, and certainly the general public, concluded that all Neandertals were highly primitive creatures.

Why did Boule draw these conclusions from the La Chapelle skeleton? Apparently, he misconstrued Neandertal posture owing to the presence of spinal osteoarthritis in this older male. In addition, and probably more important, Boule and his contemporaries found it difficult to accept fully as a human ancestor an individual who appeared to depart, however slightly, from the modern pattern: "With the over-emphasis of the nonmodern features of the La Chapelle-aux-Saints skeleton, it became a much less likely candidate for the forefather of the succeeding Upper Paleolithic forms" (Brace and Montagu, 1977, p. 219).

The skull of this male, who was possibly at least 40 years of age when he died, is very large, with a cranial capacity of 1,620 cm³. As is typical for western European "classic" forms, the vault is low and long, the supraorbital ridges are immense, with the typical Neandertal arched shape, the forehead is low and retreating, and the face is long and projecting. The back of the skull is protuberant and bun-shaped (Figs. 12–8 and 12–10).

La Chapelle, however, is not a typical Neandertal, but an unusually robust male that "evidently represents an extreme in the Neandertal range of variation" (Brace et al., 1979, p. 117). Unfortunately, this skeleton, which Boule claimed did not even walk completely erect, was widely accepted as "Mr. Neandertal." But not all Neandertal materials express the suite of "classic Neandertal" traits to the degree seen in La Chapelle.

Some of the most recent of the western European Neandertals come from St. Césaire in southwestern France and are dated at about 35,000 y.a. (Figs. 12–11 and 12–12). The bones were recovered from a bed including discarded chipped blades, hand axes, and other stone tools of an **Upper Paleolithic** tool industry associated

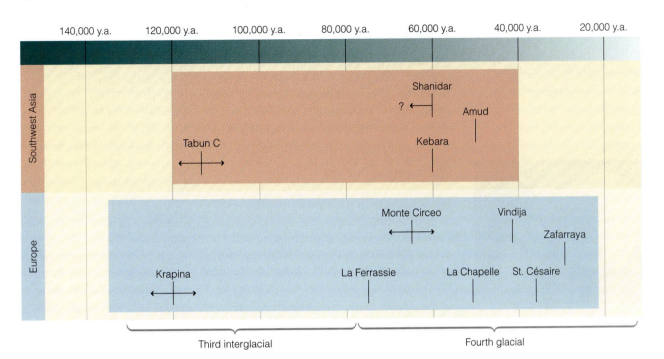

FIGURE 12–12

Time line for Neandertal (Homo sapiens neanderthalensis) fossil discoveries.

See Virtual Lab 10, section I, part C, for a 3-D animation and discussion of the La Chapelle-aux-Saints specimen.

with Neandertals. Another site, Zafarraya Cave in southern Spain, may provide yet a more recent time range for Neandertal occupation in Europe. During the 1980s and 1990s, a few pieces of hominid individuals were found at Zafarraya that have been interpreted as Neandertal in morphology. What is most interesting, however, is the *date* (as determined by radiocarbon dating) suggested for the site. French archaeologist Jean-Jacques Hublin, who has excavated the site, asserts that the date is close to 29,000 y.a.—a full 6,000 years later than St. Césaire. If this date is confirmed, the Zafarraya hominids would gain the distinction of being the most recent Neandertals thus far discovered.

The St. Césaire and Zafarraya sites are fascinating for several reasons. Anatomically modern humans were living in western Europe by about 35,000 y.a. or a bit earlier. Therefore, it is possible that Neandertals and modern *H. sapiens* were living in close proximity for several thousand years. How did these two groups interact? Evidence from a number of French sites (Harrold, 1989) indicates that Neandertals borrowed technological methods and tools (such as blades) from the anatomically modern populations and thereby modified their own tools, creating a new industry, the **Chatelperronian.** However, such an example of cultural diffusion does not specify *how* the diffusion took place. Did the Neandertals become assimilated into modern populations? Did the two groups interbreed? It would also be interesting to know more precisely how long the coexistence of Neandertals and modern *H. sapiens* lasted.* No one knows the answers to these questions, but it has been suggested that an average annual difference of 2 percent mortality between the two populations (i.e., modern *H. sapiens* lived longer than Neandertals) would have resulted in the extinction of the Neandertals in approximately 1,000 years (Zubrow, 1989).

■ **Chatelperronian**

Pertaining to an Upper Paleolithic tool industry found in France and Spain, containing blade tools and associated with Neandertals.

---

*For a fictionalized account of the meeting between Neandertals and anatomically modern humans, see Bjorn Kurten's *Dance of the Tiger. A Novel of the Ice Age*. Another novel on the subject is Jean M. Auel's *Clan of the Cave Bear*. Several movies have also been made on this theme.

It should be noted that not all paleoanthropologists agree with the notion of the coexistence of Neandertals and Upper Paleolithic modern humans. For example, in a recent paper, David Frayer of the University of Kansas states: "There is still *no human fossil evidence* which supports the coexistence of Neanderthal and Upper Paleolithic forms in Europe" (emphasis added) (1992, p. 9). That is, despite the indications of cultural diffusion noted here, no European site has yet produced directly associated remains of *both* types of humans.

Central Europe

There are quite a few other European classic Neandertals, including significant finds in central Europe. At Krapina, Croatia, an abundance of bones (1,000 fragments, representing up to 70 individuals) and 1,000 stone tools or flakes have been recovered (Trinkaus and Shipman, 1992). Krapina is an old site, perhaps the earliest showing the full "classic" Neandertal morphology, dating back to the third interglacial (estimated at 130,000–110,000 y.a.). Moreover, despite the relatively early date, the characteristic Neandertal features of the Krapina specimens (although less robust) are similar to the western European finds (Fig. 12–13). Krapina is also important as an intentional burial site, one of the oldest on record.

Another interesting site in central Europe is Vindija, about 30 miles from Krapina. The site is an excellent source of faunal, cultural, and hominid materials stratified in *sequence* throughout much of the Upper Pleistocene. Neandertal fossils, consisting of some 35 specimens, are tentatively dated at about 42,000 y.a. Even though some of their features approach the morphology of early modern south-central European *H. sapiens,* the overall pattern is definitely Neandertal. However, these modified Neandertal features, such as smaller browridges and slight chin development, may also be seen as an evolutionary trend toward modern *H. sapiens.*

Fred Smith, of Northern Illinois University, takes the view that variation in Vindija cranial features points to a trend continuing on to the later anatomically modern specimens found in the upper levels of the cave. Does Vindija support the proposition that the origin of *H. sapiens* could have occurred here in central Europe? Smith does not insist on this interpretation and suggests that anatomically modern *Homo sapiens* could have come from elsewhere. But he does believe that there is at least some morphological and genetic continuity between the samples found in the lower and upper levels of the cave.

Western Asia

Israel   In addition to European Neandertals, there are numerous important discoveries from southwest Asia. Several specimens from Israel display some modern features and are less robust than the classic Neandertals of Europe, but again the overall pattern is Neandertal. The best known of these discoveries is from Tabun (Mugharet-et-Tabun, "Cave of the Oven") at Mt. Carmel, a short drive south from Haifa (Fig. 12–14). Tabun, excavated in the early 1930s, yielded a female skeleton, recently dated by thermoluminescence (TL) at about 120,000–110,000 y.a. If this dating proves accurate, it places the Tabun find as clearly contemporary with early modern *H. sapiens* found in nearby caves. (TL dating is discussed on p. 366.)

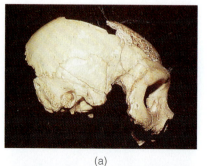

(a)

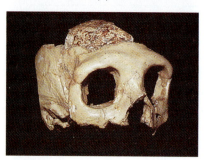

(b)

FIGURE 12–13

Krapina C. (a) Lateral view showing characteristic Neandertal traits. (b) Three-quarters view.

FIGURE 12–14
Excavation of the Tabun Cave, Mt. Carmel, Israel.

A more recent Neandertal burial, a male discovered in 1983, comes from Kebara, a neighboring cave of Tabun at Mt. Carmel. Although the skeleton is incomplete—the cranium and much of the lower limbs are missing—the pelvis, dated to 60,000 y.a., is the most complete Neandertal pelvis so far recovered. Also recovered at Kebara is a hyoid bone, the first from a Neandertal, and this find is especially important from the point of view of reconstructing language capabilities.*

Iraq   A most remarkable site is Shanidar, in the Zagros Mountains of northeastern Iraq, where partial skeletons of nine individuals—males and females, seven adults and two infants—were found, four of them deliberately buried. One of the more interesting individuals is Shanidar 1, a male who lived to be approximately 30 to 45 years old, a considerable age for a prehistoric human (Fig. 12–15). His stature is estimated at 5 feet 7 inches, with a cranial capacity of 1,600 cm³. This individual shows several fascinating features:

FIGURE 12–15
Shanidar 1. Does he represent an example of Neandertal compassion for the disabled?

> There had been a crushing blow to the left side of the head, fracturing the eye socket, displacing the left eye, and probably causing blindness on that side. He also sustained a massive blow to the right side of the body that so badly damaged the right arm that it became withered and useless; the bones of the shoulder blade, collar bone, and upper arm are much smaller and thinner than those on the left. The right lower arm and hand are missing, probably not because of poor preservation . . . but because they either atrophied and dropped off or because they were amputated. (Trinkaus and Shipman, 1992, p. 340)

*The Kebara hyoid is identical to that of modern humans, suggesting that Neandertals did not differ from *H. sapiens sapiens* in this key element.

In addition to these injuries, there was damage to the lower right leg (including a healed fracture of a foot bone). The right knee and left leg show signs of pathological involvement, and these changes to the limbs and foot may have left this man with a limping gait.

How such a person could perform normal obligations and customs is difficult to imagine. However, both Ralph Solecki, who supervised the work at Shanidar Cave, and Erik Trinkaus, who has carefully studied the Shanidar remains, believe that to survive, he must have been helped by others: "A one-armed, partially blind, crippled man could have made no pretense of hunting or gathering his own food. That he survived for years after his trauma was a testament to Neandertal compassion and humanity" (Trinkaus and Shipman, 1992, p. 341).*

Central Asia

Uzbekistan   About 1,600 miles east of Shanidar in Uzbekistan, in a cave at Teshik-Tash, is the easternmost Neandertal discovery. The skeleton is that of a nine-year-old boy who appears to have been deliberately buried. It was reported that he was surrounded by five pairs of wild goat horns, suggesting a burial ritual or perhaps a religious cult, but owing to inadequate published documentation of the excavation, this interpretation has been seriously questioned. The Teshik-Tash individual, like some specimens from Croatia and southwest Asia, also shows a mixture of Neandertal traits (heavy browridges and occipital bun) and modern traits (high vault and definite signs of a chin).

As noted, the Teshik-Tash site represents the easternmost location presently established for Neandertals. Thus, based on current evidence, it is clear that the geographical distribution of the Neandertals extended from France eastward to central Asia, a distance of about 4,000 miles.

Culture of Neandertals

Neandertals, who lived in the cultural period known as the Middle Paleolithic, are usually associated with the **Mousterian** industry (although the Mousterian industry is not always associated with Neandertals). In the early part of the last glacial period, Mousterian culture extended across Europe and North Africa into the former Soviet Union, Israel, Iran, and as far east as Uzbekistan and perhaps even China. Moreover, in Africa, the contemporaneous Middle Stone Age industry is broadly similar to the Mousterian.

Technology

Neandertals improved on previous prepared-core techniques (i.e., the Levallois) by inventing a new variation. They trimmed a flint nodule around the edges to form a disk-shaped core. Each time they struck the edge, they produced a flake, continuing this way until the core became too small and was discarded. Thus, the Neandertals were able to obtain more flakes per core than their predecessors. They then trimmed (retouched) the flakes into various forms, such as scrapers, points, and knives (Fig.12–16).

■ **Mousterian**
Pertaining to the stone tool industry associated with Neandertals and some modern *H. sapiens* groups; also called Middle Paleolithic. This industry is characterized by a larger proportion of flake tools than is found in Acheulian tool kits.

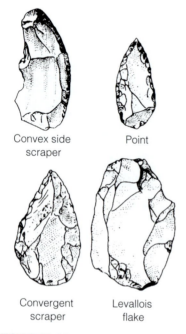

Convex side scraper   Point

Convergent scraper   Levallois flake

FIGURE 12–16
Mousterian tools. (After Bordes.)

---

*K. A. Dettwyler (1991) asserts that Shanidar 1 could have survived without assistance and that there is no solid evidence that compassion explains this individual's survival.

Neandertal craftspeople elaborated and diversified traditional methods, and there is some indication of development in the specialization of tools used in skin and meat preparation, hunting, woodworking, and hafting. There is, however, still nearly a complete absence of bone tools, in strong contrast to the succeeding cultural period, the Upper Paleolithic. Nevertheless, Neandertals advanced their technology, which tended to be similar in basic tool types over considerable geographical distances, far beyond that of *H. erectus*. It is quite possible that their modifications in technology helped provide a basis for the remarkable changes of the Upper Paleolithic (discussed in the next chapter).

Settlements

People of the Mousterian culture lived in a variety of open sites, caves, and rock shelters. Living in the open on the cold tundra suggests the building of structures, and there is some evidence of such structures (although the last glaciation must have destroyed many open sites). At the site of Moldova, in the Ukraine (now an independent state and neighbor of Russia), archaeologists found traces of an oval ring of mammoth bones enclosing an area of about 26 by 16 feet and which may have been used to weigh down the skin walls of a temporary hut or tent. Inside the ring are traces of a number of hearths, hundreds of tools, thousands of waste flakes, and many bone fragments, quite possibly derived from animals brought back for consumption.

Evidence of life in caves is abundant. Windbreaks of poles and skin were probably erected at the cave mouth for protection against severe weather. Fire was in general use by this time and was no doubt used for cooking, warmth, light, and keeping predators at bay.

How large were Neandertal settlements, and were they permanent or temporary? These questions are not yet answered, but Binford (1981) suggests that the settlements were used repeatedly for short-term occupation.

Subsistence

Neandertals were successful hunters, as the abundant remains of animal bones at their sites demonstrate. But while it is clear that Neandertals could hunt large mammals, they may not have been as efficient at this task as were Upper Paleolithic hunters. Inferring from his detailed work in the Middle East, Harvard anthropologist Ofer Bar-Yosef (1994) has concluded that only after the beginning of the Upper Paleolithic was the spear-thrower, or atlatl (see p. 375), invented. Moreover, shortly thereafter, the bow and arrow may have greatly facilitated efficiency (and safety) in hunting large mammals. Lacking such long-distance weaponry, and thus mostly limited to close-proximity spears, Neandertals may have been more prone to serious injury—a hypothesis recently given some intriguing support by paleoanthropologists Thomas Berger and Erik Trinkaus. Berger and Trinkaus (1995) analyzed the pattern of trauma (particularly fractures) in Neandertals and compared it with that seen in contemporary human samples. Interestingly, the pattern in Neandertals—especially the relatively high proportion of head and neck injuries—matched most closely to that seen in contemporary rodeo performers. Berger and Trinkaus thus conclude, "The similarity to the rodeo distribution suggests frequent close encounters with large ungulates unkindly disposed to the humans involved" (Berger and Trinkaus, 1995, p. 841).

Reconstructions of the dietary behaviors of later *Homo* and their relationship to the archaeological record are discussed in Virtual Lab 11.

Meat was, of course, not the only component of Neandertal diet. Evidence (from Shanidar, for example) indicates that Neandertals gathered as well, consuming berries, nuts, and other plants.

It is assumed that in the bitter cold of the last glacial period, Neandertals wore clothing, and they probably had developed methods of curing skins. But since there is no evidence of sewing equipment, the clothing was probably of simple design, perhaps something like a poncho.

We know much more of European Middle Paleolithic culture than of any prior period, as it has been studied longer by more scholars. In recent years, however, Africa has been a target not only of physical anthropologists (as we have seen copiously documented in earlier chapters), but also of archaeologists, who have added considerably to our knowledge of African Pleistocene hominid history. In many instances, the technology and assumed cultural adaptations were similar in Africa to those in Europe and southwest Asia. We will see in the next chapter that the African technological achievements also kept pace with (or even preceded) those in western Europe.

Symbolic Behavior

There are a variety of hypotheses concerning the speech capacities of Neandertals. Many of these views are highly contradictory, with some scholars arguing that Neandertals were incapable of human speech. Nevertheless, the current consensus is that Neandertals were capable of articulate speech, even perhaps fully competent in the range of sounds produced by modern humans. However, this conclusion is not to argue that because Neandertals *could* speak, they necessarily had the same language capacities as modern *Homo sapiens*. A major contemporary focus among paleoanthropologists is the apparently sudden expansion of modern *H. sapiens* (discussed in Chapter 13) and various explanations for the success of this group. Moreover, at the same time we are explaining how and why *H. sapiens sapiens* expanded its geographical range, we are left with the further problem of explaining what happened to the Neandertals. In making these types of interpretations, a growing number of paleoanthropologists suggest that *behavioral* differences are the key.

Upper Paleolithic *H. sapiens* is hypothesized to have possessed some significant behavioral advantages that Neandertals (and other archaic *H. sapiens*) lacked. Was it some kind of new and expanded ability to symbolize, communicate, organize social activities, elaborate technology, obtain a wider range of food resources, or care for the sick or injured, or was it some other factor? Were there, compared with *H. sapiens sapiens,* neurological differences that limited the Neandertals and thus contributed to their demise?

The direct anatomical evidence derived from Neandertal fossils is not especially helpful in specifically answering these questions. Ralph Holloway (1985) has maintained that Neandertal brains (at least as far as the fossil evidence suggests) do not differ significantly from that of modern *H. sapiens*. Moreover, Neandertal vocal tracts and other morphological features, compared with our own, do not appear seriously to have limited them. Furthermore, a recent study of the size of a small opening in the base of the skull (the hypoglossal canal; see Figure A–4 in Appendix A) has shed new insight on Neandertal speech capabilities. Richard Kay, Matt Cartmill, and Michelle Balow of Duke University measured the size of this canal in a variety of fossil hominids as well as in modern humans and great apes (Kay et al., 1998). The size of the hypoglossal canal may be particularly significant to speech production, since the main nerve supply for the tongue passes through this opening. The Duke researchers found that Neandertals (and other archaic *H. sapiens*) had hypoglossal canals as large as those seen in modern humans, arguing that Neandertal speech capabilities would not have been hampered in this respect. Interestingly, however, in earlier hominids (*Australopithecus* and early *Homo*), the hypoglossal canal was much smaller—in fact, similar in size to that seen in chimpanzees. Another recent study (DeGusta et al., 1999), however, has cast considerable doubt on all these assertions (see p. 386).

Most of the reservations about advanced cognitive abilities in Neandertals have come from archaeological data. Interpretation of Neandertal sites, when compared with succeeding Upper Paleolithic sites (especially as documented in western Europe), have led to several intriguing contrasts, as shown in Table 12–3.

On the basis of this type of behavioral and anatomical evidence, Neandertals in recent years have increasingly been viewed as an evolutionary dead end.

TABLE 12–3   Cultural Contrasts* Between Neandertals and Upper Paleolithic *Homo sapiens sapiens*

Neandertals	Upper Paleolithic *H. sapiens sapiens*
TOOL TECHNOLOGY Numerous flake tools; few, however, apparently for highly specialized functions; use of bone, antler, or ivory very rare; relatively few tools with more than one or two parts	Many more varieties of stone tools; many apparently for specialized functions; frequent use of bone, antler, and ivory; many more tools comprised of two or more component parts
HUNTING EFFICIENCY AND WEAPONS No long-distance hunting weapons; close-proximity weapons used (thus, more likelihood of injury)	Use of spear-thrower and bow and arrow; wider range of social contacts, perhaps permitting larger, more organized hunting parties (including game drives)
STONE MATERIAL TRANSPORT Stone materials transported only short distances—just "a few kilometers" (Klein, 1989)	Stone tool raw materials transported over much longer distances, implying wider social networks and perhaps trade
ART Artwork uncommon; usually small; probably mostly of a personal nature; some items perhaps misinterpreted as "art"; others may be intrusive from overlying Upper Paleolithic contexts; cave art absent	Artwork much more common, including transportable objects as well as elaborate cave art; well executed, using a variety of materials and techniques; stylistic sophistication
BURIAL Deliberate burial at several sites; graves unelaborated; graves frequently lack artifacts	Burials much more complex, frequently including both tools and remains of animals

*The contrasts are more apparent in some areas (particularly western Europe) than others (eastern Europe, Near East). Elsewhere (Africa, eastern Asia), where there were no Neandertals, the cultural situation is quite different (see p. 381). Moreover, even in western Europe, the cultural transformations were not necessarily abrupt, but may have developed more gradually from Mousterian to Upper Paleolithic times. For example, Straus (1995) argues that many of the Upper Paleolithic features were not consistently manifested until after 20,000 y.a.

Whether their disappearance and ultimate replacement by anatomically modern Upper Paleolithic peoples (with their presumably "superior" culture) was solely the result of cultural differences or was also influenced by biological variation cannot at present be determined.

An intriguing possibility for future research has recently been initiated. After several years of experimentation, German researchers and their American colleagues were successfully able to extract, amplify, and sequence DNA from a Neandertal fossil (Krings et al., 1997). The investigators removed a small piece of bone from the humerus of the original Neander Valley fossil and compared the mitochondrial DNA (mtDNA) sequences with those from samples of contemporary humans as well as chimpanzees. The initial results indicate that the Neandertal DNA is considerably *more* different from the contemporary human samples than these latter are from each other (on average, about three times as much). Furthermore, tentative estimates of the time of divergence of the Neandertal lineage from that of modern humans are put at 690,000–550,000 years ago. From these findings, the researchers support the emerging view that Neandertals did *not* contribute genetically to contemporary human populations (and may, in fact, have been a separate species from *Homo sapiens*). These results and interpretations are, however, tentative. Further DNA samples from other Neandertals as well as from early *Homo sapiens sapiens* fossils would be highly informative. At present, it is difficult to judge how "anomalous" any ancient human is, given the extremely small degree of genetic diversity seen among *all* contemporary humans (see Chapter 14).

The implications of the ancient mtDNA that was recovered from a Neandertal are discussed in Virtual Lab 10, section I, part C.

Burials

It has been known for some time that Neandertals deliberately buried their dead. Indeed, the spectacular discoveries at La Chapelle, Shanidar, and elsewhere were the direct results of ancient burial, thus facilitating much more complete preservation. Such deliberate burial treatment extends back at least 90,000 years at Tabun. Moreover, some form of consistent "disposal" of the dead (but not necessarily below-ground burial) is evidenced at Atapuerca, Spain, where at least 32 individuals comprising more than 700 fossilized elements were found in a cave at the end of a deep vertical shaft. From the nature of the site and the accumulation of hominid remains, Spanish researchers are convinced that the site demonstrates some form of human activity involving deliberate disposal of the dead (Arsuaga et al., 1997).

The provisional 300,000-year-old age for Atapuerca suggests that Neandertals (more precisely, their immediate precursors) were, by the Middle Pleistocene, handling their dead in special ways, a behavior thought previously to have emerged only much later (in the Upper Pleistocene). And, apparently as far as current data indicate, this practice is seen in western European contexts well before it appears in Africa or in eastern Asia. For example, in the archaic *H. sapiens* sites at Laetoli, Kabwe, and Florisbad (discussed earlier), deliberate disposal of the dead is not documented. Nor is it seen in African early modern sites (e.g., Klasies River Mouth, dated at 120,000–100,000 y.a.; see p. 366).

Nevertheless, in later contexts (after 35,000 y.a.) in Europe, where anatomically modern *H. sapiens* (*H. sapiens sapiens*) remains are found in clear burial contexts, their treatment is considerably more complex than is seen in Neandertal burials. In these later (Upper Paleolithic) sites, grave goods, including bone and stone tools as well as animal bones, are found more consistently and in greater concentrations. Because many Neandertal sites were excavated in the nineteenth or early twentieth century, before the development of more rigorous archaeological methods, there are questions regarding numerous purported burials. Nevertheless, the evidence seems quite clear that deliberate burial was practiced at La Chapelle, La Ferrassie (eight graves), Tabun, Amud, Kebara, Shanidar, and Teshik-Tash (as well as at several other localities, especially in France). Moreover, in many instances, the *position* of the body was deliberately modified and placed in the grave in a flexed posture (see p. 342). Such a flexed position has been found in 16 of the 20 best-documented Neandertal burial contexts (Klein, 1989).

Finally, the placement of supposed grave goods in burials, including stone tools, animal bones (such as cave bear), and even arrangements of flowers, together with stone slabs on top of the burials, have all been postulated as further evidence of Neandertal symbolic behavior. However, in many instances, again due to poor excavation documentation, these assertions are questionable. Placement of stone tools, for example, is occasionally seen, but apparently was not done consistently. In those 33 Neandertal burials for which adequate data exist, only 14 show definite association of stone tools and/or animal bones with the deceased (Klein, 1989). It is not until the next cultural period, the Upper Paleolithic, that we see a major behavioral shift, as demonstrated in more elaborate burials and development of art.

Evolutionary Trends in the Genus *Homo*

To understand the evolution of the various forms of *Homo sapiens* discussed in this chapter, it is useful to briefly review general trends of evolution in the genus *Homo* over the last 2 million years. In doing so, we see that at least three major *transitions* have taken place. Paleoanthropologists are keenly interested in interpreting the nature of these transitions, as they inform us directly regarding human origins. In addition, such investigations contribute to a broader understanding of the mechanics of the evolutionary process—at both the micro- and macroevolutionary levels.

The first transition of note was from early *Homo* to *Homo erectus*. This transition was apparently geographically restricted to Africa and appears to have been quite rapid (lasting 200,000 years at most, perhaps considerably less). It is important to recall that such a transition by no means implies that all early *Homo* groups actually evolved into *H. erectus*. In fact, many paleoanthropologists (part of a growing consensus) suggest that there were more than one species of early *Homo*. Clearly, only one could be ancestral to *H. erectus*. Even more to the point, only *some* populations of this one species would have been part of the genetic transformation (speciation) that produced *Homo erectus*.

The second transition is more complex and is the main topic of this chapter. It is the gradual change in populations of *H. erectus* grading into early *H. sapiens* forms—what we have termed archaic *H. sapiens*. This transition was not geographically restricted, as there is evidence of archaic *H. sapiens* widespread in the Old World (in East and South Africa, in China, India, and Java, and in Europe). Moreover, the transition appears not to have been rapid, but rather quite slow and uneven in pace from area to area. The complexity of this evolutionary transition creates ambiguities for our interpretations and resulting classifications.

For example, in Chapter 11, we included the Ngandong (Solo) material from Java within *Homo erectus*. However, there are several derived features in many of these specimens that suggest, alternatively, that they could be assigned to *Homo sapiens*. The dating (just recently indicating a date of only 29,000 y.a.) would argue that if this is a *H. erectus* group, it is a *very* late remnant, probably isolated *H. erectus* population surviving in southern Asia long after archaic *H. sapiens* populations were expanding elsewhere. Whatever the interpretation of Ngandong—either as a late *H. erectus* or as a quite primitive (i.e., not particularly derived) archaic *H. sapiens*—the conclusion is actually quite arbitrary (after all, the evolutionary process is continuous). We, by the nature of our classifications, have to draw the line *somewhere*.

Another important ramification of such considerations relates to understanding the nature of the *erectus/sapiens* transition itself. In Java, the transition (with late-persisting *H. erectus* genetic components) appears to have been slower than, for example, in southern Africa or in Europe. Nowhere, however, does this transition appear to have been as rapid as that which originally produced *H. erectus*. Why should this be so? To answer this question, we must refer back to basic evolutionary mechanisms (discussed in Chapters 3 and 4). First, the environments certainly differed from one region of the Old World to another during the time period 350,000–100,000 y.a. And recall that by the beginning of this time period, *H. erectus* populations had been long established in eastern and southern Asia, in North and East Africa, and in Europe. Clearly, we would not expect the same environmental conditions in northeast China as we would in Indonesia. Accordingly, natural selection could well have played a *differential* role, influencing the frequencies of alternative alleles in different populations in a pattern similar (but more intensive) to that seen in environmental adaptations of contemporary populations (see Chapter 15).

Second, many of these populations (in Java, southernmost Africa, and glacial Europe) could have been isolated and thus probably quite small. Genetic drift, therefore, also would have played a role in influencing the pace of evolutionary change. Third, advance or retreat of barriers, such as water boundaries or glacial ice sheets, would dramatically have affected migration routes.

Thus, it should hardly come as a surprise that some populations of *H. erectus* evolved at different rates and in slightly different directions from others. Some limited migration almost certainly occurred among the various populations. With sufficient gene flow, the spread of those few genetic modifications that distinguish the earliest *H. sapiens* eventually did become incorporated into widely separated populations. This, however, was a long, slow, inherently uneven process.

What, then, of the third transition within the genus *Homo*? This is the transition from archaic *H. sapiens* to anatomically modern *H. sapiens*—and it was considerably *faster* than the transition we have just discussed. How quickly anatomically modern forms evolved and exactly *where* this happened is a subject of much contemporary debate—and is the main topic of the next chapter.

Taxonomic Issues

As we discussed in Chapter 11, (and briefly at the beginning of this chapter), there is considerable debate regarding how to classify much of the *Homo* fossil material prior to 35,000 years ago. Our view, followed throughout the discussions in Chapters 10 through 12, proposes a minimum number of species and thus interprets the evolutionary processes influencing the genus *Homo* in a fairly straightforward manner.

However, this interpretation might well be *too* simplistic, and certainly, many paleoanthropologists now suggest much more diversity and complexity in the evolution of our genus. Accordingly, several new species of *Homo* have been proposed. In this text, we have classified the *Homo* fossil materials into three recognized species: *H. habilis*, *H. erectus*, and *H. sapiens*. We further noted that *H. habilis* might well be only one of two species of what we collectively called "early *Homo*." Moreover, in this chapter we made a clear distinction between archaic forms of *H. sapiens* and anatomically modern forms (*H. sapiens sapiens*). A diagrammatic phylogeny representing this interpretation is shown in Figure 12–17a.

Remember, however, that this is a conservative interpretation, implying a minimum amount of species diversity. This scheme is just about as simple as most paleoanthropologists are willing to consider seriously. Yet, there is another view, proposed by Milford Wolpoff of the University of Michigan, which is even more simple (Fig. 12–17b). Wolpoff argues that subsequent to early *Homo*, only one species (*H. sapiens*) should be recognized. In other words, Professor Wolpoff sinks *H. erectus* into *H. sapiens*. Given the significant anatomical (and probably behavioral) differences between *H. erectus* and *H. sapiens*, Wolpoff's suggestion has not received much support from other paleoanthropologists (see particularly the discussion in Rightmire, 1998).

At the other end of the spectrum are views expressed by a number of researchers who subdivide the *Homo* material into a variety of species. In fact, at every major stage of the evolution of *Homo* over the last 2 million years, some professional opinion has argued seriously for more than one species. First, as noted in Chapter 10 (p. 290), early *Homo* is now frequently subdivided into two different species (usually named *H. habilis* and *H. rudolfensis*). Second, as briefly discussed in Chapter 11, what is usually called *H. erectus* is also partitioned into two species (*H. erectus* and *H. ergaster*, the latter referring solely to African specimens). And third (and most relevant to the present discussion), various forms of archaic *H. sapiens* have been assigned by other paleoanthropologists to two or three additional species of *Homo* (some researchers think even more species might be represented).

The major issues relating to these interpretations (and consequent classifications) of what we have termed "archaic *Homo sapiens*" are as follows:

Be sure to consider an alternative phylogeny of archaic *Homo sapiens* (with pronunciations of the species' names) that is presented in the glossary of Virtual Lab 10 under Phylogeny of *Homo*.

FIGURE 12–17

(a) Phylogeny showing evolution of genus Homo, *as discussed in the text. Only very modest species diversity is implied. (Contrast with Figure 12–18.) (b) Highly simplified view of evolution of genus* Homo *with minimal species diversity. (After Wolpoff, 1999.)*

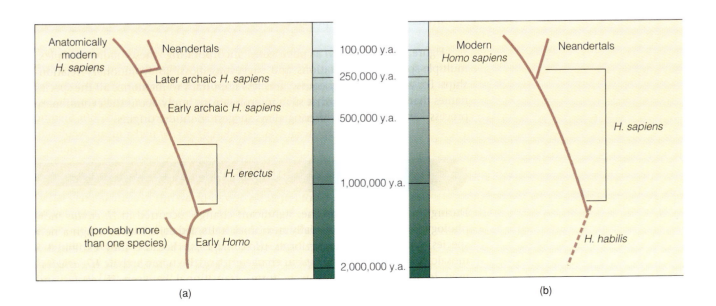

(a)   (b)

11. What two major transitions within the genus *Homo* have been discussed in this chapter and in Chapter 11? Compare these transitions for geographical distribution as well as for aspects of evolutionary pace.

12. Discuss why some paleoanthropologists subdivide the archaic *H. sapiens* material into more than one species. What does this interpretation imply biologically?

Suggested Further Reading

Mellars, Paul. 1995. *The Neanderthal Legacy. An Archaeological Perspective from Western Europe.* Princeton, NJ: Princeton University Press.

Shreeve, James. 1995. *The Neandertal Enigma.* New York: Morrow.

Stiner, Mary C. 1995. *Honor Among Thieves. A Zooarchaeological Study of Neandertal Ecology.* Princeton, NJ: Princeton University Press.

Stringer, Christopher, and Clive Gamble. 1993. *In Search of the Neanderthals.* New York: Thames and Hudson.

Trinkaus, Erik, and Pat Shipman. 1993. *The Neandertals: Changing the Image of Mankind.* New York: Knopf.

Additional Resources

Multimedia Tools

Virtual Laboratories for Physical Anthropology CD-ROM
The following concepts in this chapter are covered on the physical anthropology CD-ROM:
archaic *Homo sapiens* (Virtual Lab 10.I.C)
pronunciations, phylogeny (Virtual Lab 10.I.C; glossary)
archaic *Homo sapiens,* 3-D animations (Virtual Lab 10.I.C)
geographical distribution (Virtual Lab 10.I.C)
time line (Virtual Lab 10.I.C)
cranial shape, tooth size, skeletal robusticity, body mass, sexual dimorphism (Virtual Labs 10.II, III)
archaeology, stone tools (Virtual Lab 11)
Neandertals, 3-D animations (Virtual Lab 10.I.C)
brain size, body mass (Virtual Lab 10.IV.B)
skeletal robusticity, body mass (Virtual Lab 10.III.A, B)
cranial morphology (Virtual Lab 10.II.A)
geographical distribution (Virtual Lab 10.I.C)
La Chapelle-aux-Saints, Neandertal, 3-D animation (Virtual Lab 10.I.C)
archaeology, stone tools, dietary reconstruction (Virtual Lab 11)
mtDNA, Neandertal (Virtual Lab 10.I.C)
pronunciations, phylogeny (Virtual Lab 10;glossary)

■ **Wadsworth Anthropology Resource Center**
http://anthropology.wadsworth.com
Visit Anthropology Online to obtain current updates in the field, surfing tips, career information and more. In addition, enrich your study efforts with text-specific study aids arranged by chapter.

■   **InfoTrac College Edition**
    http://www.infotrac-college.com/wadsworth

1. Use PowerTrac to find articles which have in their text a discussion of Atapuerca, the archaic human site in Spain. This search should pull up a number of relevant articles. Read several of these. What can we learn about archaic humans from the remains at this site? What were these humans like? Should we call them Neandertals? Write a short paper describing the finds at Atapuerca and their importance in the study of human evolution.

2. Choose any other archaic human in the site and use PowerTrac to find research on this site. What was found at the site? Was there evidence of cultural behavior as well as skeletal remains. Write a short paper on the site you have researched, summarizing its contribution to our understanding of paleoanthropology.

3. Using InfoTrac College Edition search for the subject *Neanderthal* (InfoTrac spells Neanderthal with the *h*, the older spelling—using the newer will pull up fewer references). Have there been any recent discoveries of Neandertals or recent research on this group? What does this research conclude about the place of Neandertals in human evolution?

4. Read "Genetic Evidence on Modern Human Origins" by Alan R. Rogers and Lynn B. Jorder, *Human Biology,* InfoTrac College Edition. Which of the major theories of modern human origins do these authors believe the genetic evidence supports or refutes? Why?

■   **Internet Exercises**

1. Archaic forms of *Homo sapiens* are the subject of much debate, especially those in Europe, which may have given rise to either Neandertals or more modern humans. One site that has provided many fossils of this type is Arago, or Tautavel, in France. Visit the site for this cave at **http://www.culture.fr/culture/arcnat/ tautavel/en/index.htm** and read about the fossils found there and the circumstances surrounding the discovery of the site. Compare these fossils with pictures of Neandertals. Look at the section where Arago's face is reconstructed to see what it might have looked like in life. Write a paragraph or so describing how this individual looks similar to or different from anyone whom you might see on the street.

2. Visit the Skeletal Explorer's Photo Gallery (**http://www.sew. csuohio.edu/public/sew/gallery/paleontology/index.htm**). Choose a photo of an archaic *Homo sapiens* (challenge enough there!) and click on it to see a close-up of the fossil. Write a one-page description of the morphology of the fossil. What aspects of its morphology make us consider this fossil to be an archaic rather

than a modern form of *Homo sapiens?* Now click on a fossil of a modern *Homo sapiens.* Does this skull look similar to that of a modern person's?

3. Visit Neandertals: A Cyber Perspective (**http://thunder.indstate. edu/~ramanank/index.html**). Read through this site. Afterwards, write a short paper on the cultural capacities of Neandertals. What do we know about Neandertal cultural behavior? How similar was Neandertal behavior to that of modern humans? How was it different?

Homo sapiens sapiens

A discussion of modern *Homo sapiens* is given in the species gallery in Virtual Lab 12, section I, part B. Be sure to click on the Extra Information text icon for each specimen. You may wish to review the information on archaic *Homo sapiens* in section I, part A.

Introduction

In this chapter, we discuss anatomically modern humans, taxonomically known as *Homo sapiens sapiens*. As we discussed in Chapter 12, in some areas evolutionary developments produced early archaic *H. sapiens* populations exhibiting a mosaic of *H. erectus* and *H. sapiens* traits. In some regions, the trend emphasizing *H. sapiens* characteristics continued, and possibly as early as 200,000 y.a., transitional forms (between early archaic and anatomically modern forms) appeared in Africa. Given the nature of the evidence and ongoing ambiguities in dating, it is not possible to say exactly when anatomically modern *H. sapiens* first appeared. However, the transition and certainly the wide dispersal of *H. sapiens sapiens* in the Old World appear to have been relatively rapid evolutionary events. Thus, we can ask several basic questions:

1. *When* (approximately) did *H. sapiens sapiens* first appear?
2. *Where* did the transition take place? Did it occur in just one region or in several?
3. *What* was the pace of evolutionary change? How quickly did the transition occur?
4. *How* did the dispersal of *H. sapiens sapiens* to other areas of the Old World (outside that of origin) take place?

These questions concerning the origins and early dispersal of *Homo sapiens sapiens* continue to fuel much controversy among paleoanthropologists. And it is no wonder, for members of early *Homo sapiens sapiens* are our *direct* kin and are thus closely related to all contemporary humans. They are much like us skeletally, genetically, and (most likely) behaviorally as well. In fact, it is the various hypotheses relating to the behavioral capacities of our most immediate predecessors that have most fired the imagination of scientists and laypeople alike. In every major respect, these are the first hominids that we can confidently refer to as "fully human."

In this chapter, we will also discuss archaeological evidence from the *Upper Paleolithic* (see p. 342). This evidence will allow us to better understand technological and social developments during the period when modern humans arose and quickly came to dominate the planet.

The evolutionary story of *Homo sapiens sapiens* is really a biological autobiography of us all. It is a story that still has many unanswered questions; but several theories have been proposed that seek to organize the diverse information that is presently available.

The Origin and Dispersal of *Homo sapiens sapiens* (Anatomically Modern Human Beings)

There are two major theories that attempt to organize and explain modern human origins: the complete replacement model and the regional continuity model. These two views are quite distinct and in some ways diametrically opposed to each other. Moreover, the popular press has further contributed to a wide and incorrect perception of irreconcilable argument on these points by "opposing" scientists. Indeed, there is a third theory, which we call the partial replacement model, that is a compromise hypothesis incorporating some aspects of the two major theories. Because so much of our contemporary view of modern human origins is driven by the debates linked to these differing theories, let us begin by briefly reviewing each. We will then turn to the fossil evidence itself to see what it can contribute to resolving the questions we have posed.

The Complete Replacement Model (Recent African Evolution)

The complete replacement model, developed by British paleoanthropologists Christopher Stringer and Peter Andrews (1988), is based on the origin of modern humans in Africa and later replacement of populations in Europe and Asia (Fig. 13–1). In brief, this theory proposes that anatomically modern populations arose in Africa within the last 200,000 years, then migrated from Africa, completely *replacing* populations in Europe and Asia. This model does not take into account any transition from archaic *H. sapiens* to modern *H. sapiens* anywhere in the world except Africa. A critical deduction of the Stringer and Andrews theory is that it considers the appearance of anatomically modern humans as a biological speciation event. Thus, in this view there could be no admixture of migrating African modern *H. sapiens* with local populations because the African modern humans were a *biologically* different species. In a taxonomic context, all of the "archaic *H. sapiens*" populations outside Africa would, in this view, be classified as belonging to different species of *Homo* (e.g., the Neandertals would be classified as *H. neanderthalensis;* see p. 354 for further discussion). While this speciation explanation fits nicely with, and in fact helps explain, *complete* replacement, Stringer has more recently stated that he is not dogmatic regarding this issue. Thus, he suggests that there may have been potential for interbreeding, but he argues that very little apparently took place.

A crucial source of supporting evidence for the African origin hypothesis (and complete replacement elsewhere) has come from genetic data obtained from living peoples. Underlying this approach is the assumption that genetic patterning seen in contemporary populations will provide clues to relationships and origins of ancient *Homo sapiens*. However, as with numerous prior attempts to evaluate such patterning from data on human polymorphisms (e.g., ABO, HLA—see Chapter 14), the obstacles are enormous.

A recent innovation uses genetic sequencing data derived directly from DNA. The most promising application has come not from the DNA within the nucleus, but from DNA found in the cytoplasm, that is, mitochondrial DNA (mtDNA; see Chapter 3). You may recall that mitochondria are organelles found in the cell, but outside the nucleus. They contain a set of DNA, dissimilar from nuclear DNA, inherited only through the mother. Thus, mtDNA does not undergo the genetic recombination that occurs in nuclear DNA during meiosis.

Using mtDNA gathered from a number of different populations, scientists at the University of California, Berkeley, constructed "trees" (something like a family tree) that, they claimed, demonstrated that the entire population of the world today descended from a single African lineage. However, the methodology of these molecular biologists has been faulted. Using the same mtDNA material, other scientists constructed many trees that differed from those of the Berkeley group, and some of them are *without African roots* (i.e., the same data can be used statistically to show that *H. sapiens* arose in Asia, *not* in Africa).

This question of the applicability of the mtDNA evidence continues to generate considerable disagreement. Paleoanthropologist Robert Corruccini of Southern Illinois University has been unimpressed with the entire approach,

Virtual Lab 12 provides an animation of the Complete Replacement Model in section II, part C.

An interactive laboratory exercise that investigates the use of mtDNA in phylogenetic reconstruction is included in Virtual Lab 12 under section II, part B.

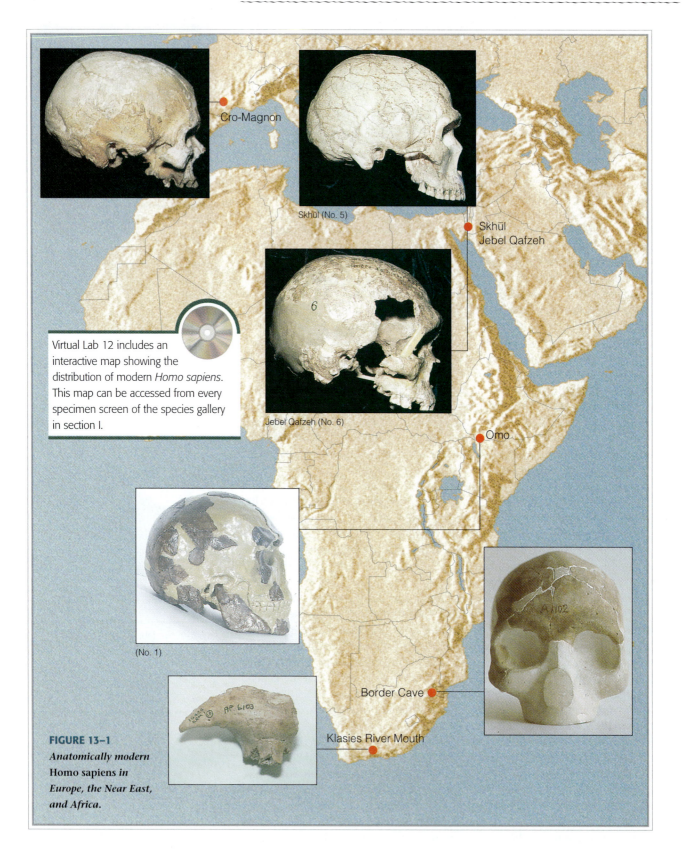

Cro-Magnon

Skhūl (No. 5)

Skhūl
Jebel Qafzeh

6

Virtual Lab 12 includes an
interactive map showing the
distribution of modern *Homo sapiens*.
This map can be accessed from every
specimen screen of the species gallery
in section I.

Jebel Qafzeh (No. 6)

Omo

(No. 1)

Border Cave

FIGURE 13–1

*Anatomically modern
Homo sapiens in
Europe, the Near East,
and Africa.*

Klasies River Mouth

stating that "critical shortcomings of molecular population genetic assumptions and of analysis . . . render any mtDNA conclusions virtually useless to ruminations about human evolution" (Corruccini, 1994, p. 698). Likewise, Glenn Conroy (1997) has critiqued many of the oversimplifications inherent in the genetic data and consequent interpretations. However, molecular anthropologist Mark Stoneking of Pennsylvania State University (and one of the founders of this approach) remains much more confident in the general reliability of the mtDNA results, especially as they show a much greater diversity among contemporary African groups as compared to other world populations. Stoneking thus concludes: "Because non-African populations that predate the mtDNA ancestor apparently did not contribute mtDNAs to contemporary human populations, it follows that the spread of modern populations was accomplished with little or no admixture with resident non-African populations. If it were otherwise, there should be evidence of much more divergent mtDNA types in contemporary human populations" (Stoneking, 1993, pp. 66–67).

Recently, some further genetic data have helped bolster some of the main tenets of the complete replacement model. A team of Yale, Harvard, and University of Chicago researchers (Dorit et al., 1995) has investigated variation in the Y chromosome, finding *much* less variation in humans than in other primates. And another group of Yale researchers (Tishkoff et al., 1996), looking at DNA sequences on chromosome 12, again found much more variation among contemporary Africans than is seen in all the remainder of the world combined. Finally, the recent report of the distinctive nature of Neandertal mtDNA (see p. 350) also argues that substantial replacement took place. Nevertheless, some geneticists find the results unconvincing (e.g., Ayala, 1995; Templeton, 1996), and many paleoanthropologists (agreeing with the views expressed by Corruccini and Conroy) are extremely skeptical of the main conclusions derived from the genetic data (see Box 13–1 for further discussion).

The Partial Replacement Model

The partial replacement model also begins with African early archaic *H. sapiens*. Later, also in Africa, anatomically modern *H. sapiens* populations first evolved. This theory, proposed by Gunter Bräuer of the University of Hamburg, postulates the earliest dates for African modern *Homo sapiens* at over 100,000 y.a. Bräuer sees the initial dispersal of *H. sapiens sapiens* out of South Africa as significantly influenced by shifting environmental conditions and thus as a gradual process. Moving into Eurasia, modern humans hybridized, probably to a limited degree, with resident archaic groups, and eventually replaced them. The disappearance of archaic humans was therefore due to both hybridization and replacement and was a gradual and complex process. This model includes components of regional continuity, hybridization, and replacement, with the emphasis on replacement.

The Regional Continuity Model (Multiregional Evolution)

The regional continuity model is most closely associated with paleoanthropologist Milford Wolpoff of the University of Michigan and his associates (Thorne and Wolpoff, 1992; Wolpoff et al., 1994). These researchers suggest that local populations (not all, of course) in Europe, Asia, and Africa continued their indigenous evolutionary development from archaic *H. sapiens* to anatomically modern

Virtual Lab 12 provides an animation of the Regional Continuity Model (Multiregionalism) in section II, part D.

The Garden of Eden Hypothesis

Gathering samples of mtDNA from placentas of women whose ancestors lived in Africa, Asia, Europe, Australia, and New Guinea, biologists Allan Wilson, Rebecca Cann, and Mark Stoneking, from the University of California, Berkeley, postulated a distinctive genetic pattern for each area. They then compared the diversity of the various patterns (Cann et al., 1987).

They found the greatest variation among Africans and therefore postulated Africa to have been the home of the oldest human populations (the assumption is that the longer the time, the greater the accumulation of genetic variation). They also found that the African variants contained only African mtDNA, whereas those from other areas all included at least one African component. Therefore, the biologists concluded, there must have been a migration initially from Africa, ultimately to all other inhabited areas of the world. By counting the number of genetic mutations and applying the *rate* of mutation, Rebecca Cann and her associates calculated a date for the origin of anatomically modern humans: between 285,000 and 143,000 years ago—in other words, an average estimate of about 200,000 years ago. Indeed, a further contention of the mtDNA researchers is that the pattern of variation argues that all modern humans shared in common a single African female lineage that lived sometime during this time range. Thus was born the popularized concept of "mitochondrial Eve."

Not all scientists, by any means, agree with this scenario. The estimated rate of mutations may be incorrect, and therefore, the proposed date of migration out of Africa would also be in error. Secondly, differing population size in Africa, compared to elsewhere, would complicate interpretations (Relethford and Harpending, 1994). Also, secondary migration, outside Africa, could disrupt the direct inheritance of the African maternal line. Even more troubling are the inherent biases in the statistical technique used to identify the primary population relationships ("trees"). Recent reanalyses of the data suggest that the situation is not nearly as clear-cut as originally believed.

Scrutiny of the mitochondrial DNA–based model of modern human origins came when the approach was attempted by other laboratories using similar techniques and statistical treatments. In February 1992, three different papers were published by different teams of researchers, all of which severely challenged the main tenets of the hypotheses as proposed by Wilson, Cann, and Stoneking. The most serious error was a failure to recognize how many *equally valid* results could be deduced statistically from the *same set* of original data. In science, as we have remarked before, beyond the data themselves, the methodological treatments (especially statistical models) greatly influence both the nature and *confidence limits* of the results.

The central conclusion that Africa alone was the *sole* source of modern humans could still be correct. Yet, now it had to be admitted that dozens (indeed, thousands) of other equally probable renditions could be derived from the supposedly unambiguous mitochondrial data. Thus, barely a few months after the original researchers had proposed their most systematic statement of their hypotheses, the entire perspective (especially its statistical implications) was shaken to its very foundations—and, in many people's eyes, falsified altogether.

An interesting twist regarding this entire reassessment is that the team from Pennsylvania State University that challenged the initial results was joined in its critique by Mark Stoneking, one of the original formulators of the now-questioned hypothesis. A viable scientific perspective, so well illustrated here, is that new approaches (or refined applications) often necessitate reevaluation of prior hypotheses. It takes both objectivity and courage to admit miscalculations. By so doing, an even more permanent and

Be sure to review the interactive laboratory exercise that investigates the use of mtDNA in Virtual Lab 12 under section II, Part B.

humans. A question immediately arises: How is it possible for different local populations around the globe to evolve with such similar morphology? In other words, how could anatomically modern humans arise separately in different continents and end up physically (and genetically) so similar? The multiregional model explains this phenomenon by (1) denying that the earliest modern *H. sapiens* populations originated *exclusively* in Africa and challenging the notion of complete replacement and (2) asserting that some gene flow (migration) between positive legacy helps contain the inherent personal biases that sometimes have so divided the study of human origins.

On the basis of these new studies, many have proclaimed that mitochondrial Eve is dead—and perhaps the complete replacement hypothesis with her. As could be expected, the proponents of the African origin view are not yet ready to bury Eve or significantly alter their confidence in the complete replacement hypothesis.

As the debate continues, new lines of evidence and new techniques are being pursued: more ways to sequence both mitochondrial and nuclear DNA; more complete evidence of human polymorphisms; genetic sequence data for the Y chromosome; and, it is hoped, more reliable statistical techniques to interpret these complex data. The new data for the Y chromosome are particularly interesting. Since the Y chromosome is inherited *paternally* (and thus also is *not* recombined), its pattern of genetic diversity makes for an excellent complement to the maternally inherited mtDNA. Biologist Robert Dorit of Yale University, along with his team of researchers, sequenced a portion of the Y chromosome. Surprisingly, they found absolutely *no* variation in this region, but did see much more Y chromosome variation in great apes (chimpanzees, gorillas, orangutans). Dorit suggests that this lack of variation indicates a recent origin for *Homo sapiens*. He notes at the same time, however, that "the lack of variation in the Y chromosome regions we examined also makes it impossible for us to reconstruct the geographic location of the last common ancestor" (Henahan, 1995).

Further evidence along these lines has come from another group of Yale biologists led by Sarah Tishkoff (Tishkoff et al., 1996). Tishkoff and her colleagues have been investigating genetic patterns within nuclear DNA (their research target is a region on chromosome 12). Assembling a very large sample of data (1,600 individuals from 42 populations), Tishkoff and her team found by far the most variation among contemporary Africans. (Of 24 possible variants, 21 of these were found in Africa; Europe and the Middle East displayed only 3; Asia, the Pacific Islands, and the New World together displayed a mere 2.) Tishkoff draws the same conclusion as that proposed by both the mtDNA and the Y chromosome researchers—that all modern humans are the result of a single recent evolutionary event. (Tishkoff, in fact, places the date at 100,000–70,000 y.a., even more recent than that suggested by the mtDNA evidence.) Moreover, the results from the chromosome 12 DNA polymorphisms, like those relating to mtDNA, suggest that Africa was the geographical source for all modern humans.

What can we then conclude? Results are still tentative, but various studies are now corroborating one another. First, we can conclude that *Homo sapiens* is not a very genetically variable species; indeed, genetically, we are quite a homogeneous lot (a point we will emphasize further in Chapters 14 and 15). By some estimates, comparisons with other primates suggest that human mtDNA is only about 1/40 to 1/50 as variable as the mtDNA of chimpanzees (Cann et al., 1994)! Does human genetic homogeneity imply a *recent* origin for all *H. sapiens sapiens*? Perhaps. At the least, these increasingly consistent genetic data argue that it is unlikely that the present genetic patterning in *H. sapiens* can be traced back to the early dispersal of *H. erectus* out of Africa (circa 1.8 m.y.a.). It would appear that there must have been one or more later dispersals as well. But how much later? The broadest time limits so far indicated by various genetic techniques would suggest a time frame in the range of 850,000–100,000 y.a. (with the greatest probabilities between 450,000 and 100,000 y.a.). If you were inclined to make a wager on the probabilities of the time of the last major dispersal of hominids, somewhere in this latter range looks like a good bet.

archaic populations was extremely likely, and consequently, modern humans cannot be considered a species separate from archaic forms.

Through gene flow and local selection, according to the multiregional hypothesis, local populations would *not* have evolved totally independently from one another, and such mixing would have "prevented speciation between the regional lineages and thus maintained human beings as a *single,* although obviously **polytypic** (see p. 413), species throughout the Pleistocene" (Smith et al., 1989).

■ **Polytypic**

Referring to species composed of populations that differ with regard to the expression of one or more traits.

Three-dimensional animations and discussions of many of these fossil specimens can be found in Virtual Lab 12, section I, part B.

■ **Provenience**
In archaeology, the specific location of a discovery, including its geological context (also spelled "provenance").

Be sure to study the cranial and postcranial morphology in Virtual Lab 12, section I, part C, in order to understand the dramatic changes in body mass, skeletal robusticity, and brain size that accompany the origin of modern *Homo sapiens*. This section includes several interactive exercises.

A variety of dating techniques is discussed in Virtual Lab 12, section II, part A. The text button provides a review of radioisotopic techniques.

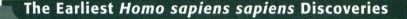

The Earliest *Homo sapiens sapiens* Discoveries

Current evidence strongly indicates that the earliest modern *H. sapiens* fossils come from Africa, but not everyone agrees on the dates or designations or precisely which specimens are the modern and which are the archaic forms. With this cautionary note, we continue our discussion, but there undoubtedly will be corrections as more evidence is gathered.

Africa

In Africa, several early fossil finds have been interpreted as fully anatomically modern forms (see Fig. 13–1). These specimens come from the Klasies River Mouth on the south coast (which could be the earliest find), Border Cave slightly to the north, and Omo Kibish 1 in southern Ethiopia. With the use of relatively new techniques, all three sites have been dated to about 120,000–80,000 y.a. **Provenience** at Border Cave is uncertain, and the fossils may be younger than at the other two sites (see Table 13–1 and Fig. 13–5). Some paleoanthropologists consider these fossils to be the earliest known anatomically modern humans. Problems with dating, provenience, and differing interpretations of the evidence have led other paleoanthropologists to question whether the *earliest* modern forms (Fig. 13–2) really did evolve in Africa. Other modern *H. sapiens* individuals, possibly older than these Africans, have been found in the Near East.

TABLE 13–1	Additional Techniques for Dating Middle and Upper Pleistocene Sites	
Technique	**Physical Basis**	**Examples of Use**
Uranium series dating	Radioactive decay of short-lived uranium isotopes	To date limestone formations (e.g., stalagmites) and ancient ostrich eggshells; to estimate age of Jinniushan site in China and Ngandong site in Java, both corroborated by ESR dates
Thermoluminescence (TL) dating	Accumulation of trapped electrons within certain crystals released during heating	To date ancient flint tools (either deliberately or accidentally heated); to provide key dates for the Qafzeh site
Electron spin resonance (ESR) dating	Measurement (counting) of accumulated trapped electrons	To date dental enamel; to corroborate dating of Qafzeh, Skhūl, and Tabun sites in Israel, Ngandong site in Java, and Klasies River Mouth and Border Cave sites in South Africa

Source: Cook et al., 1984; Aiken et al., 1993.

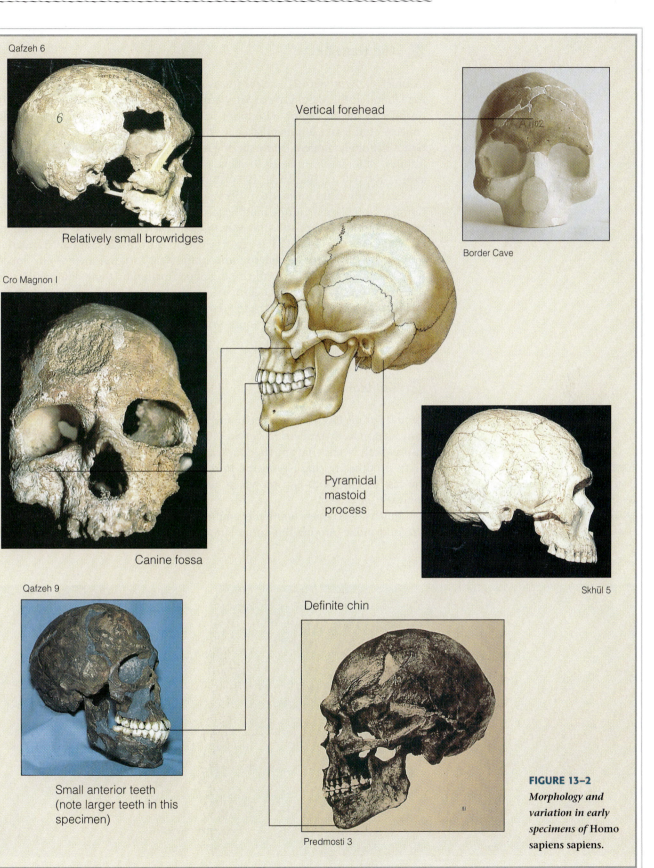

Qafzeh 6

Relatively small browridges

Cro Magnon I

Canine fossa

Qafzeh 9

Small anterior teeth
(note larger teeth in this
specimen)

Vertical forehead

Border Cave

Pyramidal
mastoid
process

Skhūl 5

Definite chin

Predmosti 3

FIGURE 13–2

*Morphology and
variation in early
specimens of* Homo
sapiens sapiens.

The Near East

In Israel, early modern *H. sapiens* fossils (the remains of at least 10 individuals) were found in the Skhūl Cave at Mt. Carmel (Figs. 13–3 and 13–4a), very near the Neandertal site of Tabun. Also from Israel, the Qafzeh Cave has yielded the remains of at least 20 individuals (Fig. 13–4b). Although their overall configuration is definitely modern, some specimens show certain archaic (i.e., Neandertal) features. Skhūl has been dated to about 115,000 y.a., and Qafzeh has been placed around 100,000 y.a. (Bar-Yosef, 1993, 1994) (Fig. 13–5).

Such early dates for modern specimens pose some problems for those advocating local replacement (the multiregional model). How early do archaic *H. sapiens* populations (Neandertals) appear in the Near East? A recent chronometric calibration for the Tabun Cave suggests a date as early as 120,000 y.a. Neandertals thus may *slightly* precede modern forms in the Near East, but there would appear to be considerable overlap in the timing of occupation by these different *H. sapiens* forms. And recall, the modern site at Mt. Carmel (Skhūl) is very near the Neandertal site (Tabun). Clearly, the dynamics of *Homo sapiens* evolution in the Near East are highly complex, and no simple model may explain later hominid evolution adequately.

Central Europe

Central Europe has been a source of many fossil finds, including numerous fairly early anatomically modern *H. sapiens*. At several sites, it appears that some fossils display both Neandertal and modern features, which supports the regional continuity hypothesis (from Neandertal to modern). Such continuity apparently was the case at Vindija in Croatia, where typical Neandertals were found in earlier contexts (see p. 344).

Smith (1984) offers another example of local continuity from Mladeč, in the Czech Republic. Among the earlier European modern *H. sapiens* fossils, dated to

FIGURE 13–3

(a) Mt. Carmel, studded with caves, was home to H. sapiens sapiens *at Skhūl (and to Neandertals at Tabun and Kebara). (b) Skhūl Cave.*

(a)

(b)

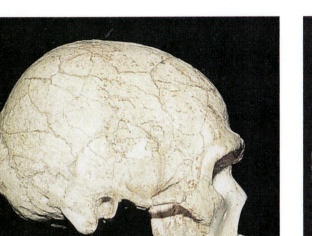

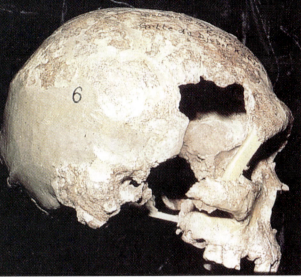

(a)   (b)

about 33,000 y.a., the Mladeč crania display a great deal of variation, probably in part due to sexual dimorphism. Although each of the crania (except for one of the females) displays a prominent supraorbital torus, it is reduced from the typical Neandertal pattern. Even though there is some suggestion of continuity from Neandertals to modern humans, Smith is certain that, given certain anatomical features, the Mladeč remains are best classified as *H. sapiens sapiens*. Reduced mid-facial projection, a higher forehead, and postcranial elements "are clearly modern *H. sapiens* in morphology and not specifically Neandertal-like in a single feature" (Smith, 1984, p. 174).

Western Europe

This area of the world and its fossils have received the greatest paleoanthropological attention for several reasons, one of which is probably serendipity. Over the last century and a half, many of the scholars interested in this kind of research happened to live in western Europe, and the southern region of France happened to be a fossil treasure trove. Also, early on, discovering and learning about human ancestors caught the curiosity and pride of the local population.

Because of this scholarly interest beginning back in the nineteenth century, a great deal of data accumulated, with little reliable comparative information available from elsewhere in the world. Consequently, theories of human evolution were based almost exclusively on the western European material. It has only been in recent years, with growing evidence from other areas of the world and with the application of new dating techniques, that recent human evolutionary dynamics have been seriously considered on a worldwide basis.

There are many anatomically modern human fossils from western Europe going back 40,000 years or more, but by far the best-known sample of western European *H. sapiens* is from the **Cro-Magnon** site. A total of eight individuals were discovered in 1868 in a rock shelter in the village of Les Eyzies, in the Dordogne region of southern France (Gambier, 1989).

FIGURE 13–4

(a) Skhūl 5. (b) Qafzeh 6. These specimens from Israel are thought to be representatives of early modern Homo sapiens. *The vault height, forehead, and lack of prognathism are modern traits.*

See Virtual Lab 12, section I, part B, for a 3-D animation and discussion of the Skhūl 5 specimen.

■ **Cro-Magnon**

(crow mah´yon)

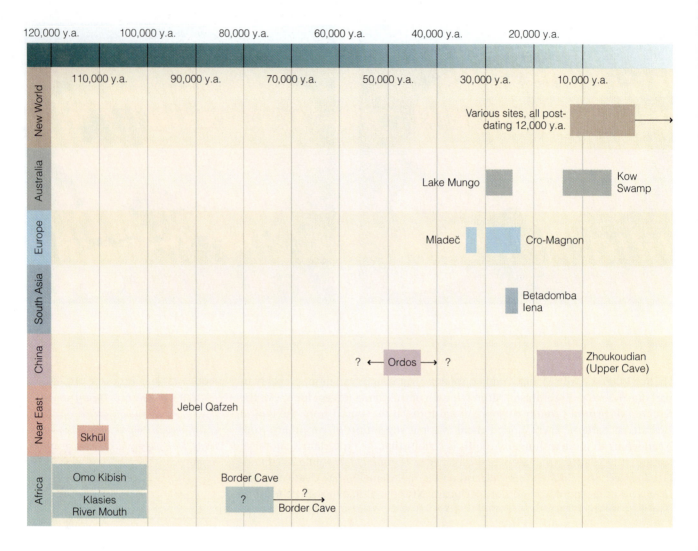

FIGURE 13–5

Time line of Homo sapiens sapiens *discoveries. Note that most dates are approximations. Question marks indicate those estimates that are most tentative.*

A time line that gives the ages for modern and archaic *Homo sapiens* is available from the species gallery in Virtual Lab 12, section I. Be sure to view the detailed screen.

■ **Aurignacian**

Pertaining to an Upper Paleolithic stone tool industry in Europe beginning at about 40,000 y.a.

Associated with an **Aurignacian** tool assemblage, an Upper Paleolithic industry, the Cro-Magnon materials, dated at 30,000 y.a., represent the earliest of France's anatomically modern humans. The so-called "Old Man" (Cro-Magnon I) became the archetype for what was once termed the Cro-Magnon, or Upper Paleolithic, "race" of Europe (Fig.13–6). Actually, of course, there is no such race, and Cro-Magnon I is not typical of Upper Paleolithic western Europeans, and not even all that similar to the other two male skulls that were found at the site.

Considered together, the male crania reflect a mixture of modern and archaic traits. Cro-Magnon I is the most gracile of the three—the supraorbital tori of the other two males, for example, are more robust. The most modern-looking is the female cranium, the appearance of which may be a function of sexual dimorphism.

The question of whether continuous local evolution produced anatomically modern groups directly from Neandertals in some regions of Eurasia is far from settled. From central Europe, variation seen in the Mladeč and Vindija fossils indicate a combination of both Neandertal and modern characteristics and may suggest gene flow between the two different *H. sapiens* groups. However, tracing such relatively minor genetic changes—considering the ever-present problems of dating, lack of fossils, and fragmented fossil finds—may well prove impossible.

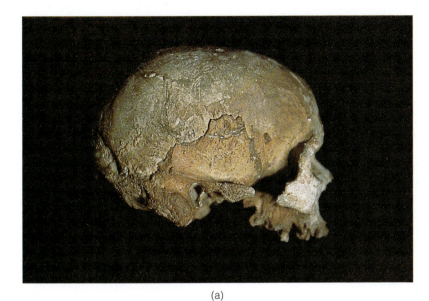

(a)

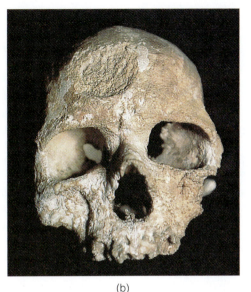

(b)

Asia

There are six early anatomically modern human localities in China, the most significant of which are Upper Cave at Zhoukoudian and Ordos. The fossils from these sites are all fully modern, and most are considered to be of quite late Upper Pleistocene age. Upper Cave at Zhoukoudian has been dated to between 18,000 and 10,000 y.a. The Ordos find was discovered at Dagouwan, Inner Mongolia, and may be the oldest anatomically modern material from China, perhaps dating to 50,000 y.a. or more (Etler, personal communication) (Fig. 13–5).

In addition, the Jinniushan skeleton discussed in Chapter 12 (see p. 330) has been suggested by some researchers (Tiemel et al., 1994) as hinting at modern features in China as early as 200,000 y.a. If this date (as early as that proposed for direct antecedents of modern *H. sapiens* in Africa) should prove accurate, it would cast doubt on the complete replacement model. Indeed, quite opposed to the complete replacement model and more in support of regional continuity, Chinese paleoanthropologists see a continuous evolution from Chinese *H. erectus* to archaic *H. sapiens* to anatomically modern humans. This view is supported by Wolpoff, who mentions that materials from Upper Cave at Zhoukoudian "have a number of features that are characteristically regional" and that these features are definitely not African (1989, p. 83).*

In addition to the well-known finds from China, anatomically modern remains have also been discovered in southern Asia. At Batadomba Iena, in southern Sri Lanka, modern *Homo sapiens* finds have been dated to 25,500 y.a. (Kennedy and Deraniyagala, 1989).

Australia

During glacial times, the Indonesian islands were joined to the Asian mainland, but Australia was not. It is likely that by 50,000 y.a., Sahul—the area including

FIGURE 13–6

Cro-Magnon 1 (France). In this specimen, modern traits are quite clear. (a) Lateral view. (b) Frontal view. (Courtesy of David Frayer.)

See Virtual Lab 12, section I, part B, for a 3-D animation and discussion of the Cro-Magnon I specimen.

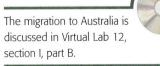

The migration to Australia is discussed in Virtual Lab 12, section I, part B.

---

*Wolpoff's statement supports his regional continuity hypothesis. His reference to Africa is a criticism of the complete replacement hypothesis.

New Guinea and Australia—was inhabited by modern humans. Bamboo rafts may have been the means of crossing the sea between islands, which would not have been a simple exercise. Just where the future Australians came from is unknown, but Borneo, Java, and New Guinea have all been suggested.

Archaeological sites in Australia have been dated to at least 55,000 y.a. (Roberts et al., 1990), but the oldest human fossils themselves have been dated to about 30,000 y.a. These oldest Australians are from Lake Mungo, where the remains of two burials (one individual was first cremated) date to 25,000 y.a. and at least 30,000 y.a., respectively (Fig. 13–7). The crania are rather gracile with, for example, only moderate development of the supraorbital torus.

Unlike these more gracile early Australian forms are the Kow Swamp people, who are thought to have lived between about 14,000 and 9,000 years ago (Fig. 13–8). The presence of certain archaic traits, such as receding foreheads, heavy supraorbital tori, and thick bones, are difficult to explain, since these features contrast with the postcranial anatomy, which matches that of recent native Australians.

The New World

There have been considerable, and often heated, arguments regarding the *earliest* entry of humans into the New World. It must be remembered that the ancestors of Native Americans reached the New World through multiple migrations over the Bering Land Bridge over many millennia. Regarding the first migration, all claims of great antiquity (prior to 30,000 y.a.) have now been refuted. Nevertheless, there are still varied claims that archaeological materials (i.e., evidence of artifacts) put the date of the initial migration at prior to 15,000 y.a. Such claims have come from evidence excavated at widely scattered locales (e.g., from the Yukon, Pennsylvania, and Peru). Because of concerns about accurate dating or the nature of the artifacts (were they actually made by humans?), these reports, too, have been subjected to rigorous scrutiny. As a result, these claims are not considered well established at this time.

The most indisputable proof would, of course, be actual hominid finds in clear, datable contexts. As with the earliest confirmed archaeological discoveries, direct evidence indicating the greatest antiquity for hominids anywhere in the New World goes back only about 12,000 years. From the broader perspective of human evolution, we must emphasize that all the hominid material found thus far is obviously fully modern *Homo sapiens*. This fact should come as no surprise, given the relatively late entry of *Homo sapiens* into the Americas, perhaps as much as 40,000 years after hominids had reached Australia.

Technology and Art in the Upper Paleolithic

The archaeological record of modern *Homo sapiens* is discussed in Virtual Lab 11.

Europe

The cultural period known as the Upper Paleolithic began in western Europe approximately 40,000 years ago (Fig. 13–9). Upper Paleolithic cultures are usually divided into five different industries based on stone tool technologies: (1) Chatelperronian, (2) Aurignacian, (3) Gravettian, (4) Solutrean, and (5) Magdalenian. Major environmental shifts were also apparent during this

Virtual Lab 12, section I, part B, presents animations of the hypothetical routes of the migration to the New World as well as a discussion of the major sites in the Americas.

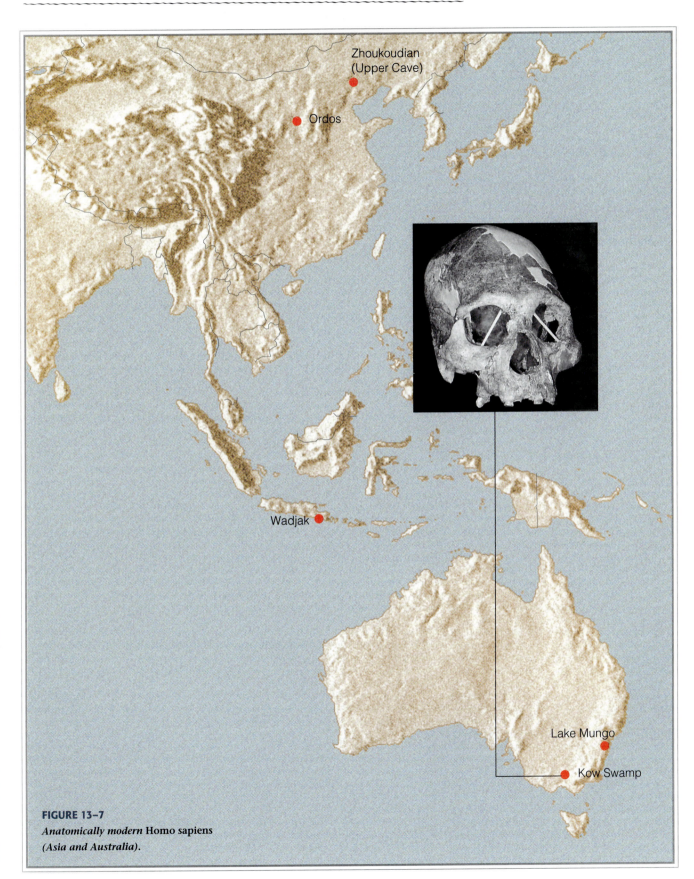

FIGURE 13–7

Anatomically modern Homo sapiens
(Asia and Australia).

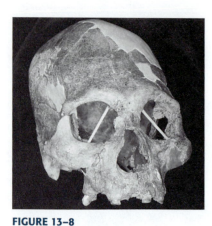

FIGURE 13–8

Kow Swamp (Australia). Note the considerable robusticity in this relatively late Australian Homo sapiens sapiens *cranium.*

period. During the last glacial period, at about 30,000 y.a., a warming trend lasting several thousand years partially melted the glacial ice. The result was that much of Eurasia was covered by tundra and steppe, a vast area of treeless country dotted with lakes and marshes. In many areas in the north, permafrost prevented the growth of trees but permitted the growth, in the short summers, of flowering plants, mosses, and other kinds of vegetation. This vegetation served as an enormous pasture for herbivorous animals, large and small, and carnivorous animals fed off the herbivores. It was a hunter's paradise, with millions of animals dispersed across expanses of tundra and grassland, from Spain through Europe and into the Russian steppes.

Large herds of reindeer roamed the tundra and steppes along with mammoths, bison, horses, and a host of smaller animals that served as a bountiful source of food. In addition, humans exploited fish and fowl systematically for the first time, especially along the southern tier of Europe. It was a time of relative affluence, and ultimately Upper Paleolithic people spread out over Europe, living in caves and open-air camps and building large shelters. Large dwellings with storage pits have been excavated in the former Soviet Union, with archaeological evidence of social status distinctions (Soffer, 1985). During this period, either western Europe or perhaps portions of Africa achieved the highest population density in human history up to that time.

In Eurasia, cultural innovations allowed humans for the first time to occupy easternmost Europe and northern Asia. In these areas, even during glacial warming stages, winters would have been long and harsh. Human groups were able to tolerate these environments probably because of better constructed structures as well as warmer, better fitting *sewn* clothing. The evidence for wide use of such tailored clothing comes from many sites and includes pointed stone tools such as awls and (by at least 19,000 y.a.) bone needles as well. Especially noteworthy is the clear evidence of the residues of clothing (including what has been interpreted as a cap, a shirt, a jacket, trousers, and moccasins) in graves at the 22,000-year-old Sungir site, located not far from Moscow (Klein, 1989).

Humans and other animals in the mid-latitudes of Eurasia had to cope with shifts in climatic conditions, some of which were quite rapid. For example, at 20,000 y.a. another climatic "pulse" caused the weather to become noticeably colder in Europe and Asia as the continental glaciations reached their maximum extent for this entire glacial period (called the Würm in Eurasia). Meanwhile, the southern continents, too, experienced widespread climatic effects. Notably, in Africa around 20,000 y.a. it became significantly wetter, thus permitting reoccupation of areas in the north and south that had previously been abandoned.

As a variety of organisms attempted to adapt to these changing conditions, *Homo sapiens* had a major advantage: the elaboration of an increasingly sophisticated technology (and probably other components of culture as well). Indeed, probably one of the greatest challenges facing numerous late Pleistocene mammals was the ever more dangerously equipped humans—a trend that has continued to modern times.

The Upper Paleolithic was an age of technological innovation and can be compared to the past few hundred years in our recent history of amazing technological change after centuries of relative inertia. Anatomically modern humans of the Upper Paleolithic not only invented new and specialized tools (Fig. 13–10), but, as we have seen, also greatly increased the use of, and probably experimented with, new materials, such as bone, ivory, and antler.

Solutrean tools are good examples of Upper Paleolithic skill and perhaps aesthetic appreciation as well (Fig. 13–10b). In this lithic

FIGURE 13–9

Cultural periods of the European Upper Paleolithic and their approximate beginning dates.

GLACIAL	UPPER PALEOLITHIC (beginnings)	CULTURAL PERIODS
W Ü R M	17,000 –	Magdalenian
	21,000 –	Solutrean
	27,000 –	Gravettian
	33,000 –	Aurignacian Chatelperronian
	Middle Paleolithic	Mousterian

(stone) tradition, stoneknapping developed to the finest degree ever known. Using a pressure-flaking technique (see p. 242), the artist/technicians made beautiful parallel-sided lance heads, expertly flaked on both surfaces, with such delicate points that they can be considered works of art that quite possibly never served, or were intended to serve, a utilitarian purpose.

The last stage of the Upper Paleolithic, known as the **Magdalenian**, saw even more advances in technology. The spear-thrower (Fig. 13–11), a wooden or bone hooked rod (called an *atlatl*), acted to extend the hunter's arm, thus enhancing the force and distance of a spear throw. For catching salmon and other fish, the barbed harpoon is a clever example of the craftsperson's skill. There is also evidence that the bow and arrow may have been used for the first time during this period. The introduction of the punch technique (Fig. 13–12) provided an abundance of standardized blank stone flakes that could be fashioned into **burins** (see Fig. 13–10a) for working wood, bone, and antler; borers for drilling holes in skins, bones, and shells; and blades for knives with serrated or notched edges for scraping wooden shafts into a variety of tools.

The elaboration of many more specialized tools by Upper Paleolithic peoples probably made more resources available to them and may also have had an impact on the biology of these populations. C. Loring Brace of the University of Michigan has suggested that with more efficient tools used for food processing, anatomically modern *H. sapiens* would not have required the large front teeth (incisors) seen in earlier populations. With relaxed selection pressures (no longer favoring large anterior teeth), incorporation of random mutations would through time lead to reduction of dental size and accompanying facial features. In particular, the lower face became less prognathic (as compared to archaic specimens) and thus produced the concavity of the cheekbones called a *canine fossa* (see Fig. 13–2). Moreover, as the dental-bearing portion of the lower jaw regressed, the buttressing below would have become modified into a *chin,* that distinctive feature seen in anatomically modern *H. sapiens.*

In addition to their reputation as hunters, western Europeans of the Upper Paleolithic are even better known for their symbolic representation, what has commonly been called "art." Certainly, in the famous caves of France and Spain (discussed below), we easily relate to an aesthetic property of the images—one that *may* have been intended by the people who created them. But here we cannot be certain. Our own cultural perspectives create labels (and categories) such as "art," which in itself *assumes* aesthetic intent. While such a cultural orientation is obviously a recognizable part of Western culture, many other contemporary peoples would not relate to this concept within their own cultural context. Furthermore, prehistoric peoples during the Upper Paleolithic did not necessarily create their symbols as true artistic representations. Rather, these representations may have served a variety of quite utilitarian and/or social functions—as do contemporary highway signs or logos on a company's letterhead. Would we call these symbols art?

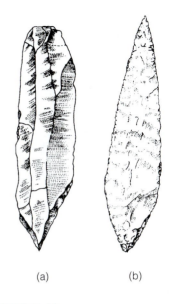

(a)   (b)

FIGURE 13–10

(a) Burin. A very common Upper Paleolithic tool. (b) Solutrean blade. This is the best-known work of the Solutrean tradition. Solutrean stonework is considered the most highly developed of any Upper Paleolithic industry.

■ **Magdalenian**
Pertaining to the final phase (stone tool industry) of the Upper Paleolithic in Europe.

■ **Burins**
Small, chisel-like tools (with a pointed end) thought to have been used to engrave bone, antler, ivory, or wood.

FIGURE 13–11

Spear-thrower (atlatl). Note the carving.

(a) A large core is selected and the top portion is removed by use of a hammerstone.

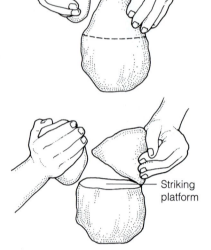

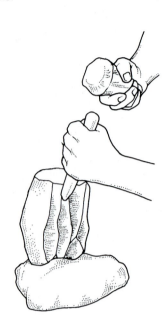

(e) The result is the production of highly consistent sharp blades, which can be used, as is, as knives; or they can be further modified (retouched) to make a variety of other tools (such as burins, scrapers, and awls).

— Striking platform

(b) The objective is to create a flat surface called a striking platform.

(c) Next, the core is struck by use of a hammer and punch (made of bone or antler) to remove the long narrow flakes (called blades).

(d) Or the blades can be removed by pressure flaking.

FIGURE 13–12

The punch blade technique.

Virtual Lab 11, section IV, part B, provides a 3-D animation of blade production.

Given these uncertainties, archaeologist Margaret Conkey of the University of California, Berkeley, refers to Upper Paleolithic cave paintings, sculptures, engravings, and so forth, as "visual and material imagery" (Conkey, 1987, p. 423). We will continue to use the term *art* to describe many of these prehistoric representations, but you should recognize that we do so mainly as a cultural convention—and perhaps a limiting one.

Moreover, the time depth for these prehistoric forms of symbolic imagery is quite long, encompassing the entire Upper Paleolithic (from at least 35,000 to 10,000 y.a.). Over this time span there is considerable variability in style, medium, content, and no doubt meaning as well. In addition, there is an extremely wide geographical distribution of symbolic images, best known from many parts of Europe, but now also well documented from Siberia, North Africa, South Africa, and Australia. Given the 25,000-year time depth of what we call "Paleolithic art" and its nearly worldwide distribution, there is indeed marked variability in expression.

In addition to cave art, there are numerous examples of small sculptures excavated from sites in western, central, and eastern Europe. Beyond these quite well known figurines, there are numerous other examples of what is frequently termed "portable art," including elaborate engravings on tools and tool handles (Fig. 13–13). Such symbolism can be found in many parts of Europe and was already well established early in the Aurignacian (by 35,000 y.a.). Innovations in symbolic representations also benefited from, and probably further stimulated, technological advances. New methods of mixing pigments and applying them were important in rendering painted or drawn images. Bone and ivory carving and engraving were made easier with the use of special stone tools (see Fig. 13–10). At two sites in the Czech Republic, Dolni Vestonice and Predmosti (both dated at 27,000 y.a.), small animal figures were fashioned from fired clay—the first documented use of ceramic technology anywhere (and preceding later pottery invention by more than 15,000 years!).

Female figurines, popularly know as Venuses, were sculpted not only in western Europe, but in central and eastern Europe and Siberia as well. Some of these figures were realistically carved, and the faces appear to be modeled after actual women (Fig. 13–14). Other figurines may seem grotesque, with sexual characteristics exaggerated, perhaps for fertility or other ritual purposes (Fig. 13–15).

It is, however, during the final phases of the Upper Paleolithic, particularly during the Magdalenian, that European prehistoric art reached its climax. Cave art is now known from more than 150 separate sites, the vast majority from southwestern France and northern Spain. Apparently, in other areas the rendering of such images did not take place in deep caves. Peoples in central Europe, China, Africa, and elsewhere certainly may have painted or carved representations on rockfaces in the open, but these images long since would have eroded. Thus, it is fortuitous that the people of at least one of the many sophisticated cultures of the Upper Paleolithic chose to journey below ground to create their artwork, preserving it not just for their immediate descendants, but for us as well.

In Lascaux Cave of southern France, immense wild bulls dominate what is called the Great Hall of Bulls, and horses, deer, and other animals adorn the walls in black, red, and yellow, drawn with remarkable skill. In addition to the famous cave of Lascaux, there is equally exemplary art from Altamira Cave in Spain.

FIGURE 13–13

Magdalenian bone artifact. Note the realistic animal engraving on this object, the precise function of which is unknown.

(a)　　　　(b)

FIGURE 13–14

Venus of Brassempouy. Upper Paleolithic artists were capable of portraying human realism (shown here) as well as symbolism (depicted in Fig 13–15). (a) Frontal view. (b) Lateral view.

FIGURE 13–15

Venus of Willendorf, Austria.

Indeed, discovered in 1879, Altamira was the first example of advanced cave art recorded in Europe. Filling the walls and ceiling of the cave are superb portrayals of bison in red and black, the "artist" taking advantage of bulges to give a sense of relief to the paintings. The cave is a treasure of beautiful art whose meaning has never been satisfactorily explained. It could have been religious or magical, a form of visual communication, or art for the sake of beauty.

Yet another spectacular example of cave art from western Europe was discovered in late 1994. On December 24, a team of three French cave explorers chanced upon a fabulous discovery in the valley of the Ardèche at Combe d'Arc (Fig. 13–16). Inside the cave, called the Grotte Chauvet after one of its discoverers, preserved unseen for perhaps 20,000 years, are many hundreds of images, including stylized dots, stenciled human handprints, and most dramatically, hundreds of animal representations. Included are depictions of such typical Paleolithic subjects as bison, horse, ibex, auroch, deer, and mammoth. But quite surprisingly, there are also numerous images of animals rarely portrayed elsewhere—such as rhino, lion, and bear. Three animals seen at Grotte Chauvet—a panther, a hyena, and an owl—have never before been documented at cave sites (Fig. 13–17). The artwork, at least after provisional study, seems to consistently repeat several stylistic conventions, causing French researchers to suggest that the images all may have been produced by the same artist. Provisional dating has placed the paintings during the Aurignacian (perhaps more than 30,000 y.a.), and thus Grotte Chauvet may be considerably earlier than the Magdalenian sites of Lascaux and Altamira. The cave was found as Paleolithic peoples had left it, and the initial discoverers, as well as archaeologists, have been careful not to disturb the remains. Among the archaeological traces already noted are dozens of footprints on the cave floor, produced by bears as well as by humans. We do not know yet how far the cave extends or what crucial artifactual remains lie along the floor.

A familiar motif seen at Grotte Chauvet and elsewhere is the representation of human hands, usually in the form of outlines. Apparently, the technique used was to liquefy the pigment and blow it onto a hand held flat against the cave wall. At one site in France, at least 159 such hand outlines were found (Leroi-Gourhan, 1986). Another stylistic innovation was the partial sculpting of a rock face—in what is called bas-relief (a technique used much later, for example, by the ancient Greeks at the Parthenon). Attaining depths up to 6 inches, some of the Paleolithic sculptures were quite dramatic and were attempted on a fairly grand scale. In one rock shelter in southwest France, several animals (including mountain goats, bison, reindeer, and horses) and one human figure were depicted in bas-relief. Interestingly, these representations were carved in an area also used as a living site—quite distinct from the special-purpose contexts in the deep cave locations. These bas-reliefs were executed throughout the Magdalenian, always in areas immediately adjacent to those of human habitation.

Strikingly, subject matter seems to differ by location and type of art motif. In portable art, common themes are horses and reindeer as well as stylized human figures; rarely are bison represented. However, in cave contexts, bison and horses are frequently seen, but almost never do we see reindeer (although in Europe, reindeer were probably the most common meat source). Cave artists were thought heretofore to have depicted carnivores only rarely, but the new finds at Grotte Chauvet give us a further perspective on the richness *and* diversity of Paleolithic art.

Ever since ancient art was discovered, attempts have been made to interpret the sculptures, paintings, and other graphic material found in caves or on rocks and tools at open-air archaeological sites. One of the early explanations of Upper Paleolithic art emphasized the relationship of paintings to hunting. Hunting ritu-

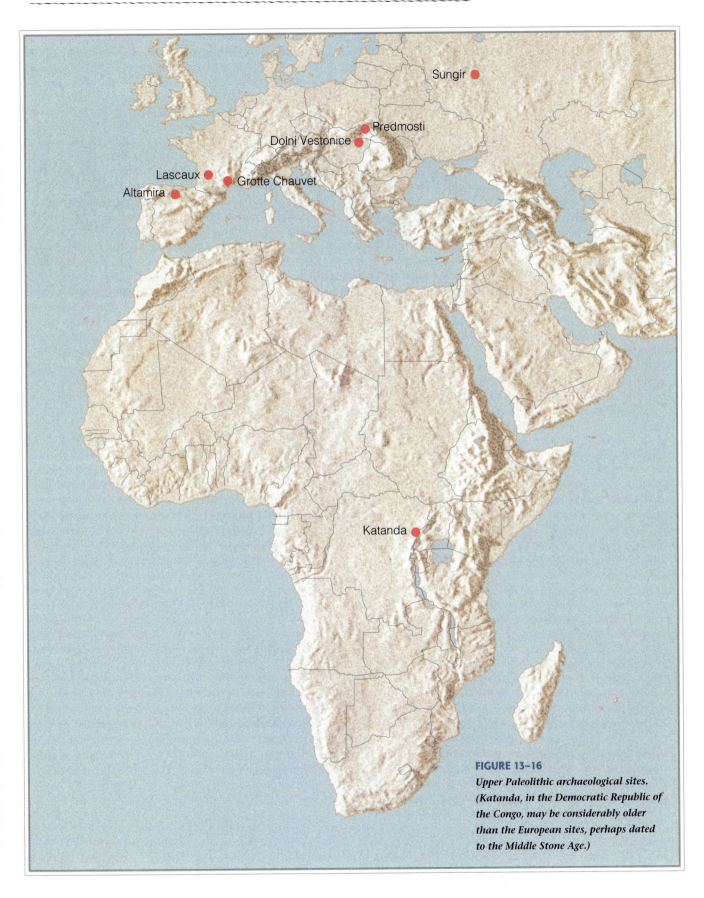

FIGURE 13–16

Upper Paleolithic archaeological sites. (Katanda, in the Democratic Republic of the Congo, may be considerably older than the European sites, perhaps dated to the Middle Stone Age.)

(a)

(b)

FIGURE 13–17

Cave art. (a) Bear. Grotte Chauvet, France.
(b) Aurochs and rhinoceros, Grotte Chauvet.

als were viewed as a kind of imitative magic that would increase prey animal populations or help hunters successfully find and kill their quarry. As new hypotheses were published, their applicability and deficiencies were discussed. When many of these new hypotheses faded, others were expounded, and the cycle of new hypotheses followed by critiques continued.

Among these hypotheses, the association of religious ritual and magic is still considered viable because of the importance of hunting in the Upper Paleolithic. Nevertheless, other ideas about these graphics have been widely discussed, including the viewing of Upper Paleolithic art from a male/female perspective and the consideration of a prevalent dots-and-lines motif as a notational system associated with language, writing, or a calendar (Marshack, 1972). Other perspectives and ongoing questions include why certain areas of caves were used for painting, but not other, similar areas; why certain animals were painted, but not others; why males were painted singly or in groups, but women only in groups; why males were painted near animals, but women never were; and why groups of animals were painted in the most acoustically resonant areas. (Were rituals perhaps performed in areas of the cave with the best acoustic properties?) It should be noted that given the time depth, different contexts, and variable styles of symbolic representations, no *single* explanation regarding their meaning is likely to prove adequate. As one expert has concluded, "It is clear that there can no longer be a single 'meaning' to account for the thousands of images, media, contexts, and uses of what we lump under the term 'paleolithic art'" (Conkey, 1987, p. 414).

A recent explanation for the florescence of cave art in certain areas has been suggested by archaeologists Clive Gamble (1991) and Lawrence Straus (1993), who point to the severe climatic conditions during the maximum (coldest interval) of the last glacial, around 20,000–18,000 y.a. It was during this period in southwestern France and northern Spain that most of the cave art was created. Straus notes that wherever there are clusters of living sites, there are cave art sanctuaries and residential sites with abundant mobile art objects. The caves could have been meeting places for local bands of people and locations for group activities. Bands could share hunting techniques and knowledge, and paintings and engravings served as "encoded information" that could be passed on across generations. Such information, Straus argues, would have been crucial for dealing with the severe conditions of the last glacial period.

Africa

Early accomplishments in rock art, perhaps as early as in Europe, are seen in southern Africa (Namibia), where a site containing such art is dated between 28,000 and 19,000 y.a. In addition, evidence of portable personal adornment is seen as early as 38,000 y.a. in the form of beads fashioned from ostrich eggshells.

In terms of stone tool technology, microliths (thumbnail-sized stone flakes hafted to make knives, saws, etc.) and blades characterize Late Stone Age* African industries. There was also considerable use of bone and antler in central Africa, perhaps some of it quite early. Recent excavations in the Katanda area of the eastern portion of the Democratic Republic of the Congo have shown remarkable development of bone craftsmanship. In fact, preliminary reports by Alison Brooks of George Washington University, and John Yellen of the National Science Foundation, have demonstrated that these technological achievements rival those of the more renowned European Upper Paleolithic (Yellen et al., 1995).

The most important artifacts discovered at Katanda are a dozen intricately made bone tools excavated from three sites along the Semiliki River (not far from Lake Rutanzige—formerly, Lake Edward) (Fig. 13–16). These tools, made from the ribs or long bone splinters of large mammals, apparently were first ground to flatten and sharpen them, and then some were apparently precisely pressure-flaked (see p. 242) to produce a row of barbs. In form these tools are similar to what have been called "harpoons" from the later Upper Paleolithic of Europe (Magdalenian, circa 15,000 y.a.). Their function in Africa, as well, is thought to have been for spearing fish, which archaeological remains indicate were quite large (catfish weighing up to 150 pounds!). In addition, a few carved bone rings with no barbs were also discovered, but their intended function (if indeed they were meant to have a utilitarian function at all) remains elusive.

The dating of the Katanda sites is crucial for drawing useful comparisons with the European Upper Paleolithic. However, the bone used for the tools retained no measurable nitrogen and thus proved unsuitable for radiocarbon dating (perhaps it was too old and beyond the range of this technique). As a result, the other techniques now used for this time range—thermoluminescence, electron spin resonance, and uranium series dating (see p. 366)—were all applied. Among these techniques, the results proved consistent, indicating dates between 180,000 and 75,000 y.a.†

You may wish to review these dating techniques in Virtual Lab 12, section II, part A.

However, there remain some difficulties in establishing the clear association of the bone implements with the materials that have supplied the chronometric age estimates. Indeed, Richard Klein, a coauthor of one of the initial reports (Brooks et al., 1995), does not accept the suggested great antiquity for these finds and believes they may be much younger. Nevertheless, if the early age estimates should hold up, we once again will look *first* to Africa as the crucial source area for human origins—not just for biological aspects, but for cultural aspects as well.

Summary of Upper Paleolithic Culture

As we look back at the Upper Paleolithic, we can see it as the culmination of 2 million years of cultural development. Change proceeded incredibly slowly for most of the Pleistocene, but as cultural traditions and materials accumulated, and the

*The Late Stone Age in Africa is equivalent to the Upper Paleolithic in Eurasia.

†If these dates prove accurate, Katanda would actually be earlier than Late Stone Age (and thus be referrable to the Middle Stone Age).

brain (and, we assume, intelligence) expanded and reorganized, the rate of change quickened.

Cultural evolution continued with the appearance of early archaic *H. sapiens* and moved a bit faster with later archaic *H. sapiens*. Neandertals in Eurasia and their contemporaries elsewhere added deliberate burials, technological innovations, and much more.

Building on existing cultures, late Pleistocene populations attained sophisticated cultural and material heights in a seemingly short (by previous standards) burst of exciting activity. In Europe and central Africa particularly, there seem to have been dramatic cultural innovations that saw big game hunting, potent new weapons (including harpoons, spear-throwers, and possibly the bow and arrow), body ornaments, needles, "tailored" clothing, and burials with elaborate grave goods (the latter might indicate some sort of status hierarchy).

This dynamic age was doomed, or so it appears, by the climatic changes of about 10,000 y.a. As the temperature slowly rose and the glaciers retreated, animal and plant species were seriously impacted, and humans were thus affected as well. As traditional prey animals were depleted or disappeared altogether, other means of obtaining food were sought.

Grinding hard seeds or roots became important, and as familiarity with plant propagation increased, domestication of plants and animals developed. Dependence on domestication became critical, and with it came permanent settlements, new technology, and more complex social organization.

The long road from hominid origins, from those remarkable footprints engraved into the African savanna, has now led by millions of chance evolutionary turnings to ourselves, anatomically modern human beings. But this road is not yet finished. We are the inheritors, both biologically and culturally, of our hominid forebears. Now, for the first time in human evolution, perhaps we have some choice in the direction our species may take. The continuing story of human evolution and the ways we study contemporary population diversity will be the topics of the remainder of this text.

Summary

The interactive lab exercise in Virtual Lab 12, section III, takes you on an expedition to discover early modern human fossils in China and evaluate the finds.

The date and location of the origin of anatomically modern human beings have been the subjects of a fierce debate for the past decade, and the end is not in sight. One hypothesis (complete replacement) claims that anatomically modern forms first evolved in Africa more than 100,000 y.a. and then, migrating out of Africa, completely replaced archaic *H. sapiens* in the rest of the world. Another school (regional continuity) takes a diametrically different view and maintains that in various geographical regions of the world, local groups of archaic *H. sapiens* evolved directly to anatomically modern humans. A third hypothesis (partial replacement) takes a somewhat middle position, suggesting an African origin but also accepting some later hybridization outside of Africa.

The Upper Paleolithic was an age of extraordinary innovation and achievement in technology and art. Many new and complex tools were introduced, and their production indicates fine skill in working wood, bone, and antler. It was a period that might be compared, for its time, to the past few hundred years of our own technological advances.

Cave art in France and Spain displays the masterful ability of Upper Paleolithic painters, and beautiful sculptures have been found at many European sites. Sophisticated symbolic representations have also been found in Africa and elsewhere. Upper Paleolithic *Homo sapiens* displayed amazing development in a relatively short period of time. The culture produced during this period led the way to still newer and more complex cultural techniques and methods.

Questions for Review

1. What characteristics define anatomically modern *H. sapiens?*
2. How do the characteristics of modern *H. sapiens* compare with those of archaic *H. sapiens?*
3. What are the three major theories that seek to explain the origin and dispersal of *Homo sapiens sapiens?* Compare and critically discuss these three views.
4. How have data from mitochondrial DNA been used to support an African origin of *H. sapiens sapiens?* What other genetic data have recently been analyzed, and how do they accord with the mtDNA results?
5. Discuss (and compare) the early evidence of anatomically modern humans from two different regions.
6. It is said that the Upper Paleolithic was a time of technological innovation. Support this statement with specific evidence, and compare the Upper Paleolithic with cultural data from earlier in the Pleistocene.
7. From which regions has cave art, dating to the Upper Pleistocene, been discovered? Particularly for the cave art of Europe, what explanations of its meaning have been proposed?

Suggested Further Reading

Aitken, M. J., C. B. Stringer, and P. A. Mellars (eds.). 1993. *The Origin of Modern Humans and the Impact of Chronometric Dating.* Princeton, NJ: Princeton University Press.

Klein, Richard. 1989. *The Human Career: Human Biological and Cultural Origins.* Chicago: University of Chicago Press.

Nitecki, Matthew H., and Doris V. Nitecki (eds.). 1994. *Origins of Anatomically Modern Humans.* New York: Plenum.

Smith, Fred, and Frank Spencer (eds.). 1984. *The Origin of Modern Humans.* New York: Liss.

Wolpoff, Milford. 1999. *Paleoanthropology.* 2nd ed. New York: McGraw-Hill.

Additional Resources

Multimedia Tools

- **Virtual Laboratories for Physical Anthropology CD-ROM**
  The following concepts in this chapter are covered on the physical anthropology CD-ROM:
  modern *Homo sapiens* (Virtual Lab 12.I.A, B)
  Complete Replacement Model (Virtual Lab 12.II.C)
  mtDNA, phylogeny (Virtual Lab 12.II.B)
  geographical distribution (Virtual Lab 12.I)
  Regional Continuity Model (Virtual Lab 12.II.D)

mtDNA, phylogeny (Virtual Lab 12.II.B)

modern *Homo sapiens,* 3-D animations (Virtual Lab 12.I.B)

cranial shape, body mass, skeletal robusticity, body mass, brain size
   (Virtual Lab 12.I.C)

ESR, thermoluminescence, fission-track, dating (Virtual Labs 12.II.A)

Skhūl 5, 3-D animation (Virtual Lab 12.I.B)

time line (Virtual Labs 12.I.A, B)

Cro-Magnon I, 3-D animation (Virtual Lab 12.I.B)

Australia, migration (Virtual Lab 12.I.B)

New World, migration (Virtual Lab 12.I.B)

archaeology, stone tools, dietary reconstruction (Virtual Lab 11)

archaeology, blade production (Virtual Lab 11.IV.B)

virtual expedition, modern humans (Virtual Lab 12.III)

InfoTrac College Edition
http://www.infotrac-college.com/wadsworth

1. Read "Genetic Evidence on Modern Human Origins" by Alan R.
   Rogers and Lynn B Jorder, *Human Biology,* from InfoTrac College
   Edition. Which of the major theories of modern human origins do
   these authors argue the genetic evidence supports or refutes? Why?

2. Choose one of the Upper Paleolithic industries mentioned in the text
   and in Figure 13.9. Search InfoTrac College Edition for recent
   research on an archaeological site of this industry. Write a short
   paper summarizing the research on this site and the stone tool industry found there.

3. One of the more interesting questions about Paleolithic art is how
   the pigments were made for the cave paintings. An article by Angela
   Minzoni-Deroche, et al., "The working of pigment during the
   Aurignacian period," available on InfoTrac College Edition sheds
   some light on this issue. Read this article, and then report on how
   Paleolithic peoples made their paints.

4. InfoTrac College Edition has a category, Language and Languages,
   Origin. Go to this category and read several of the articles found.
   How do these articles contribute to the information in the text
   regarding language origins?

Internet Exercises

1. Visit Peter Brown's Paleoanthropology Pages at the University of New
   England, in Australia (**http://metz.une.edu.au/~pbrown3/palaeo.
   html**). What can you learn about the origin of the Australian populations from this site? When was Australia first populated? By whom?
   Can you construct a time line of the important finds in Australia?

2. Some of the most recently discovered cave paintings are those at
   Grotte Chauvet in France. These paintings were completed between
   30,000 and 32,000 years ago. Visit the site on the Web at **http://
   www.culture.fr/culture/arcnat/chauvet/en/gvpda-d.htm**. Examine
   the photographs of the cave paintings and read the text. What is portrayed in the pictures? What do you think might have motivated the
   people to make the images? What do you think they were trying to
   communicate?

3. Read "The Great DNA Hunt" at the *Archaeology Magazine* Web site
   (**http://www.he.net/~archaeol/9609/abstracts/dna.html**). How
   does this article shed light on genetic evidence relating to modern
   human origins?

The Evolution of Language

One of the most distinctive behavioral attributes of all modern humans is our advanced ability to use highly sophisticated symbolic language. Indeed, it would be impossible to imagine human social relationships or human culture without language.

When did language evolve? First, we should define what we mean by *full* human language. As we discussed in Chapter 7 (see pp. 176–180), nonhuman primates have shown some elements of language. For example, some chimpanzees, gorillas, and bonobos display abilities to manipulate symbols and a rudimentary understanding of grammar. Nevertheless, the full complement of skills displayed by humans includes the extensive use of arbitrary symbols, sophisticated grammar, and a complex *open* system of communication (see p. 176).

Most scholars are comfortable attributing such equivalent skills to early members of *H. sapiens sapiens*, as early as 200,000–100,000 years ago. In fact, several researchers hypothesize that the elaborate technology and artistic achievements, as well as the rapid dispersal of anatomically modern humans, were directly a result of behavioral advantages—particularly full language capabilities. This rapid expansion of presumably culturally sophisticated modern *H. sapiens* (and consequent disappearance of other hominids) has sometimes been termed "the human revolution."

Of course, this hypothesis does not deny that earlier hominids had some form of complex communication; almost everyone agrees that even the earliest hominids did (at least as complex as that seen in living apes). What is not generally agreed upon is just when the full complement of human language capacity *first* emerged. Indeed, the controversy relating to this process has and will continue to ferment, since there is no clear answer to the question. The available evidence is not sufficient to establish clearly the language capabilities of any fossil hominid. We have discussed in Chapter 7 that there are neurological foundations for language and that these features relate more to brain reorganization than to simple increase in brain size. Moreover, as far as *spoken* language is concerned, during hominid evolution there were also physiological alterations of the vocal tract (in particular, a lower position of the larynx as compared to other primates).

Yet, we have no complete record of fossil hominid brains or their vocal tracts. We do have *endocasts* (see p. 276), which preserve a few external features of the brain. For example, there are several preserved endocasts of australopithecines from South Africa. However, the information is incomplete and thus subject to varying interpretations. (For example, did these hominids possess language? If not, what form of communication did they display?) Evidence from the vocal tract is even more elusive.

In such an atmosphere of fragmentary data, a variety of conflicting hypotheses have been proposed. Some paleoanthropologists argue that early australopithecines (3 m.y.a.) had language. Others think that such capabilities were first displayed by early *Homo* (perhaps 2 m.y.a.). Still others suggest that language did not emerge fully until the time of *Homo erectus* (2–1 m.y.a.), or perhaps it was archaic forms of *H. sapiens* (such as the Neandertals) who first displayed such skills. And finally, a number of researchers assert that language first developed *only* with the appearance of *H. sapiens sapiens*.

Because the question of language evolution is so fundamental to understanding human evolution (indeed, what it *means* to be human), a variety of creative techniques have been applied to assess the (limited) evidence that is available. We have already mentioned the analysis of endocasts (see p. 348 for further discussion of limitations of analysis). Other researchers have suggested that the size of the vertebral canal in the thoracic region of the spine might be related to precise muscle control of breathing and thus an indicator of certain language skills. This conclusion was drawn from features of the *H. erectus* skeleton from Nariokotombe (see p. 313). Lastly, and perhaps most informative of all, other paleoanthropologists have recently presented provisional data on the size of the hypoglossal canal at the base of the cranium (the size of the canal is thought to reflect the degree of neurological control of the tongue). As we noted earlier (see p. 349), investigators have so far suggested that australopithecines and early *Homo* (with small canals) did not have full articulate language, but that archaic *H. sapiens* (Neandertals) and early *H. sapiens sapiens* probably did (these latter showing canals as large as those of contemporary people).

Subsequent to the initial suggestion that size of the hypoglossal canal might reflect speech capabili-

The Evolution of Language (continued)

ties (Kay et al., 1998), the hypothesis has been further tested using a much wider sample of nonhuman primates, fossil hominids, and modern humans (DeGusta et al., 1999). These new data do *not* confirm the hypothesis, and, in fact, seriously question it. For example, many nonhuman primates have hypoglossal canals as large as humans; similarly, some early hominids (members of *Australopithecus*) also have canals as large as contemporary humans. Perhaps even more revealing, the size of the canal, as shown in dissections of human cadavers, does not appear correlated with the size of the (hypoglossal) nerve running through it. Further studies might help resolve some of these issues, but, for the moment, the initial hypothesis concerning the utility of hypoglossal canal size for estimating speech abilities has been seriously weakened.

A final line of inquiry has also focused on language (i.e., speech) by reconstructing in various fossil hominids the presumed position of the larynx within the vocal tract. As first proposed by Lieberman and Crelin (Lieberman and Crelin, 1971; Lieberman, 1992) and more recently by Laitman (Laitman et al., 1993), it is argued that Neandertals and other members of archaic *H. sapiens* could not articulate full speech, since the larynx would have been positioned higher in the throat than is seen in *H. sapiens sapiens*. This inference is based on indirect reconstruction of the vocal tract from the contours of the cranial base. Again, the evidence is far from unambiguous, and interpretations are often varied (and contentious; see, for example, Falk, 1975; Frayer, 1993). Given these

uncertainties, most paleoanthropologists have been reluctant to conclude exactly what *speech* capabilities Neandertals had. The most *direct* evidence was discovered in 1983 and includes an adult Neandertal *hyoid bone* (from Kebara cave in Israel; see p. 345). This important structure, which supports the larynx, is identical in this Neandertal to that seen in modern humans. Given this information, it would be most imprudent to argue that Neandertals could not articulate full human speech. Nevertheless, simply because Neandertals *could* speak in a fully articulate manner does not necessarily argue that they communicated with the entire array of contemporary human symbolic language. We have noted in Chapter 12 several probable behavioral contrasts of Neandertals with Upper Paleolithic *H. sapiens sapiens*. Was language ability among these contrasts and perhaps the most important difference? Does more advanced language capabilities help explain the rapid success of modern humans in displacing other hominids? Does language, then, mostly account for the human revolution? Surely, these are fascinating and important questions. Perhaps someday we will be able to answer them in a comprehensive, scientifically rigorous manner.

Critical Thinking Questions

1. What is meant by human language? How does it differ from communication seen in great apes?
2. What direct evidence (fossil and archaeological) is used to suggest that early hominids had

language capabilities? How sufficient is this evidence?
3. What kind of evidence would convince you that an earlier hominid (Neandertals, for example) did or did not possess language?

Sources

Falk, Dean. 1975. "Comparative Anatomy of the Larynx in Man and the Chimpanzee: Implications for Language in Neandertal." *American Journal of Physical Anthropology* 43:123–132.

Frayer, D. W. 1993. "On Neanderthal Crania and Speech: Response to Lieberman." Current Anthropology 34:721.

Kay, R. F., M. Cartmill, and M. Balow. 1998. "The Hypoglossal Canal and the Origins of Human Vocal Behavior" (abstract). *American Journal of Physical Anthropology, Supplement* 26:137.

Laitman, J. T., J. S. Reidenberg, D. R. Friedland, et al. 1993. "Neandertal Upper Respiratory Specializations and Their Effect upon Respiration and Speech" (abstract). *American Journal of Physical Anthropology* 16:129.

Lieberman, Phillip. 1992. "On Neanderthal Speech and Neanderthal Extinction." *Current Anthropology* 33:409–410.

Lieberman, P., and E. S. Crelin. 1971. "On the Speech of Neanderthal Man." *Linguistic Inquiries* 2:203–222.

MacLarnon, Ann. 1993. "The Vertebral Canal of KNM-WT 15000 and the Evolution of the Spinal Cord and Other Canal Contents." In: A. Walker and R. E. Leakey (eds.), "The Nariokotombe *Homo erectus* Skeleton." Cambridge: Harvard University Press, pp. 359–390.

Microevolution in Modern Human Populations

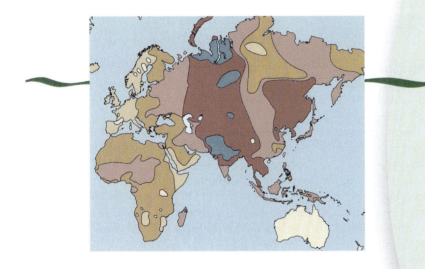

Introduction

In the last chapter, we completed our overview of hominid evolution. The dispersal of *Homo sapiens sapiens* was the last major event in our lineage relating to what we have termed *macroevolution*. However, the evolution of our species did not conclude at this point, but has in fact continued over the last several thousand years. This ongoing process of evolutionary change is part of what is referred to as *microevolution*.

How is microevolution evaluated and measured in contemporary species? In earlier chapters, we discussed the mechanisms of inheritance and the manner in which heritable characteristics influence evolutionary change. In this chapter, we will demonstrate how these genetic principles lie at the very foundation of the evolutionary process. Moreover, we will show how these factors interact to produce evolutionary change in contemporary human populations. As with all other organisms, the variation exhibited by *Homo sapiens* can be understood within this contemporary evolutionary framework. Evolutionary change not only characterizes the human past, but also continues as a major factor shaping human beings today. In this explicit evolutionary context, physical anthropologists are able to assess larger patterns of human population diversity.

Human Populations

As we defined it in Chapter 4, a *population* is a group of interbreeding individuals. More precisely, a population is the group within which one is most likely to find a mate. As such, a population is marked by a degree of genetic relatedness and shares a common **gene pool.**

In theory, this is a straightforward concept. In every generation, the genes (alleles) are mixed by recombination and rejoined through mating. What emerges in the next generation is a direct product of the genes going into the pool, which in turn is a product of who is mating with whom.

In practice, however, defining and describing human populations is difficult. The largest population of *Homo sapiens* that could be described is the entire species. All members of a species are *potentially* capable of interbreeding, but are incapable of fertile interbreeding with members of other species. Our species is thus a *genetically closed system*. The problem arises not in describing who potentially can interbreed, but in isolating exactly the pattern of those individuals who are doing so.

Factors that determine mate choice are geographical, ecological, and social. If individuals are isolated on a remote island in the middle of the Pacific, there is not much chance of their finding a mate outside the immediate vicinity. Such **breeding isolates** are fairly easily defined and are a favorite target of microevolutionary studies. Geography plays a dominant role in producing these isolates by rather strictly determining the range of available mates. But even within these limits, cultural rules can easily play a deciding role by prescribing who is most appropriate among those who are potentially available.

Human population segments within the species are defined as groups with relative degrees of **endogamy** (marrying/mating within the group). These are, however, not totally closed systems. Gene flow often occurs between groups, and individuals may choose mates from distant localities. With the modern advent of

■ Gene pool

The total complement of genes shared by reproductive members of a population.

The central importance of the concept of a population is discussed in Virtual Lab 2, section I, part A.

■ Breeding isolates

Populations that are clearly isolated geographically and/or socially from other breeding groups.

■ Endogamy

Mating with individuals from the same group.

rapid transportation, greatly accelerated rates of **exogamy** (marrying/mating outside the group) have emerged.

Most humans today are not so clearly defined as members of particular populations as they would be if they belonged to a breeding isolate. Inhabitants of large cities may appear to be members of a single population, but within the city borders, social, ethnic, and religious boundaries crosscut in a complex fashion to form smaller population segments. In addition to being members of these highly open local population groupings, we are simultaneously members of overlapping gradations of larger populations—the immediate geographical region (a metropolitan area or perhaps an entire state), a section of the country, the whole nation, and, ultimately, the whole species.

Population Genetics

Once specific human populations have been identified, the next step is to ascertain what evolutionary forces, if any, are operating on this group. To determine whether evolution is taking place at a given locus, we measure allele frequencies for specific traits and compare these observed frequencies with a set predicted by a mathematical model: the **Hardy-Weinberg theory of genetic equilibrium**. This model provides us with a baseline set of evolutionary expectations under *known* conditions.

The Hardy-Weinberg theory of genetic equilibrium postulates a set of conditions in a population where *no* evolution occurs. In other words, none of the forces of evolution are acting, and all genes have an equal chance of recombining in each generation (i.e., there is random mating of individuals). More precisely, the hypothetical conditions that such a population would be *assumed* to meet are as follows:

1. The population is infinitely large. This condition eliminates the possibility of random genetic drift or changes in allele frequencies due to chance.
2. There is no mutation. Thus, no new alleles are being added by molecular changes in gametes.
3. There is no gene flow. There is no exchange of genes with other populations that can alter allele frequencies.
4. Natural selection is not operating. Specific alleles confer no advantage over others that might influence reproductive success.
5. Mating is random. There are no factors that influence who mates with whom. Thus, any female is assumed to have an equal chance of mating with any male.

If all these conditions are satisfied, allele frequencies will not change from one generation to the next (i.e., no evolution will take place), and a permanent equilibrium will be maintained as long as these conditions prevail. An evolutionary "barometer" is thus provided that may be used as a standard against which actual circumstances are compared. Similar to the way a typical barometer is standardized under known temperature and altitude conditions, the Hardy-Weinberg equilibrium is standardized under known evolutionary conditions.

Note that the idealized conditions that define the Hardy-Weinberg equilibrium are just that: an idealized, *hypothetical* state. In the real world, no actual population would fully meet any of these conditions. But do not be confused by this

■ Exogamy
Mating pattern whereby individuals obtain mates from groups other than their own.

■ Hardy-Weinberg theory of genetic equilibrium
The mathematical relationship expressing—under ideal conditions—the predicted distribution of alleles in populations; the central theorem of population genetics.

Virtual Lab 2, section III, part A, provides a virtual exercise on the Hardy-Weinberg equation.

distinction. By explicitly defining the genetic distribution that would be *expected* if *no* evolutionary change were occurring (i.e., in equilibrium), we can compare the *observed* genetic distribution obtained from actual human populations. The evolutionary barometer is thus evaluated through comparison of these observed allele and genotype frequencies with those expected in the predefined equilibrium situation.

If the observed frequencies differ from those of the expected model, then we can say that evolution is taking place at the locus in question. The alternative, of course, is that the observed and expected frequencies do not differ sufficiently to state unambiguously that evolution is occurring at a locus in a population. Indeed, frequently this is the result that is obtained, and in such cases, population geneticists are unable to delineate evolutionary changes at the particular locus under study. Put another way, geneticists are unable to reject what statisticians call the *null hypothesis* (where "null" means nothing, a statistical condition of randomness).

The simplest situation applicable to a microevolutionary study is a genetic trait that follows a simple Mendelian pattern and has only two alleles (*A, a*). As you recall from earlier discussions, there are then only three possible genotypes: *AA, Aa, aa*. Proportions of these genotypes (*AA:Aa:aa*) are a function of the *allele frequencies* themselves (percentage of *A* and percentage of *a*). To provide uniformity for all genetic loci, a standard notation is employed to refer to these frequencies:

Frequency of dominant allele *(A)* = *p*
Frequency of recessive allele *(a)* = *q*

Since in this case there are only two alleles, their combined total frequency must represent all possibilities. In other words, the sum of their separate frequencies must be 1:

p + q = 1 (100% of alleles at the locus in question)
(Frequency   (Frequency
of *A* alleles)   of *a* alleles)

To ascertain the expected proportions of genotypes, we compute the chances of the alleles combining with one another into all possible combinations. Remember, they all have an equal chance of combining, and no new alleles are being added.

These probabilities are a direct function of the frequency of the two alleles. The chances of all possible combinations occurring randomly can be simply shown as

$$\begin{array}{r} p + q \\ \times \quad p + q \\ \hline pq + q^2 \\ p^2 + pq \\ \hline p^2 + 2pq + q^2 \end{array}$$

Mathematically, this is known as a binomial expansion and can also be shown as

$$(p + q)(p + q) = p^2 + 2pq + q^2$$

What we have just calculated is simply:

Allele Combination	Genotype Produced	Expected Proportion in Population
Chances of *A* combining with *A*	*AA*	$p \times p = p^2$
Chances of *A* combining with *a*;	*Aa*	$p \times q$
a combining with *A*	*aA*	$p \times q$ $= 2pq$
Chances of *a* combining with *a*	*aa*	$q \times q = q^2$

Thus, p^2 is the frequency of the *AA* genotype, $2pq$ is the frequency of the *Aa* genotype, and q^2 is the frequency of the *aa* genotype, where p is the frequency of the dominant allele and q is the frequency of the recessive allele in a population.

Calculating Allele Frequencies: An Example

How geneticists use the Hardy-Weinberg formula is best demonstrated through an example. Let us assume that a population contains 200 individuals, and we will use the MN blood group locus as the gene to be measured. This gene produces a blood group antigen—similar to ABO—located on red blood cells. Because the *M* and *N* alleles are codominant, we can ascertain everyone's phenotype by taking blood samples and observing reactions with specially prepared antisera. From the phenotypes, we can then directly calculate the *observed* allele frequencies. So let us proceed.

All 200 individuals are tested, and the results are shown in Box 14–1. Although the match between observed and expected frequencies is not perfect, it is close enough statistically to satisfy equilibrium conditions. Since our population is not a large one, sampling may easily account for the small observed deviations. Our population is therefore probably in equilibrium (i.e., at this locus, it is not evolving). At the minimum, what we can say scientifically is that we cannot reject the null hypothesis.

A detailed discussion of blood groups is given in Virtual Lab 2, section III, part B. You may wish to review these data in section II, part E.

Evolution in Action: Modern Human Populations

Once a population has been defined, a population geneticist will ascertain whether allele frequencies are stable (i.e., in genetic equilibrium) or whether they are changing. As we have seen, the Hardy-Weinberg formula provides the tool to establish whether allele frequencies are indeed changing. What factors initiate changes in allele frequencies? There are a number of factors, including those that:

1. Produce new variation (i.e., *mutation*)
2. Redistribute variation through *gene flow* or *genetic drift*
3. Select "advantageous" allele combinations that promote reproductive success—that is, *natural selection*

Note that factors 1 and 2 constitute the first stage of the evolutionary process, as first emphasized by the modern synthesis, while factor 3 is the second stage, natural selection (see p. 90). There is yet another factor, as implied by the condition of genetic equilibrium that under idealized conditions all matings are

BOX 14–1

Calculating Allele Frequencies in a Hypothetical Population

Observed Data:

Genotype	Number of individuals*	Percent	Number of Alleles M	N
MM	80	40	160	0
MN	80	40	80	80
NN	40	20	0	80
Totals	200	100	240 +	160 = 400
		Proportion:	.6 +	.4 = 1

Observed Allele Frequencies:

$$M = .6(p)$$
$$N = .4(q)$$
$(p + q$ should equal 1, and they do)

Expected Frequencies: What are the predicted genotypic proportions if genetic equilibrium (no evolution) applies to our population? We simply apply the Hardy-Weinberg formula: $p^2 + 2pq + q^2$.

p^2	=	(.6)(.6)	= .36
$2pq$	=	2(.6)(.4) = 2(.24)	= .48
q^2	=	(.4)(.4)	= .16
Total			1.00

There are only three possible genotypes (*MM:MN:NN*), so the total of the relative proportions should equal 1; as you can see, they do.

Comparing Frequencies: How do the expected frequencies compare with the observed frequencies in our population?

	Expected Frequency	Expected Number of Individuals	Observed Frequency	Actual Number of Individuals with Each Genotype
MM	.36	72	.40	80
MN	.48	96	.40	80
NN	.16	32	.20	40

*Each individual has two alleles; thus a person who is *MM* contributes two *M* alleles to the total gene pool. A person who is *MN* contributes one *M* and one *N*. One hundred individuals, then, have 200 alleles for the *MN* locus.

Nonrandom mating
Patterns of mating in a population in which individuals choose mates preferentially.

random. Thus, the evolutionary alteration (i.e., deviation from equilibrium) is called **nonrandom mating.**

Nonrandom Mating

Although sexual recombination does not itself alter *allele frequencies,* any consistent bias in mating patterns can alter the *genotypic proportions.* By affecting the frequencies of genotypes, nonrandom mating causes deviations from Hardy-

Weinberg expectations of the proportions p^2, $2pq$, and q^2. It therefore sets the stage for the action of other evolutionary factors, particularly natural selection.

One variety of nonrandom mating, called **positive assortative mating**, occurs when individuals of like phenotype mate more often than expected by random mating predictions. Because individuals with like phenotypes are also similar to some degree in genotype, positive assortative mating increases the amount of homozygosity in the population and reduces heterozygosity (p^2 and q^2 greater than expected; $2pq$ less than expected).

The most consistent mating biases documented in the United States deal with stature and IQ. Of course, both these traits are influenced by environment as well as heredity (see p. 88), and observed correlations also reflect socioeconomic status (generating like environments). Eye color in a Swedish population and hair color in a Lapp group have shown significant degrees of correlation among married couples. Moreover, several studies in the United States and Britain have shown significant correlations for several other phenotypic traits (see Table 14–1).

The opposite of positive assortative mating is **negative assortative mating**, or mating with an individual who is phenotypically dissimilar. Theoretically, if this occurs more than expected by random mating predictions, it should increase the amount of heterozygosity in the population while reducing homozygosity. Curt Stern (1973) suggested that redheaded persons marry each other less often than would be expected, but this has not been substantiated; nor has any other instance of negative assortative mating been conclusively demonstrated in human populations.

A third type of nonrandom mating in humans that can disrupt expected genotypic proportions occurs when relatives mate more often than expected. Called **inbreeding** or consanguinity, such mating will increase the amount of homozygosity, since relatives who share close ancestors will more than likely also share more alleles than would two nonrelated individuals. In reality, inbreeding is just an extreme form of positive assortative mating.

All living societies have some sort of incest taboo banning matings between very close relatives such as between parent and child or brother and sister. Therefore, such matings usually occur less frequently than predicted under random mating conditions (which postulates that these matings, like all others, have a certain probability of occurring).

■ Positive assortative mating
A type of nonrandom mating in which individuals of like phenotype mate more often than predicted under random mating conditions.

■ Negative assortative mating
A type of nonrandom mating in which individuals of unlike phenotype mate more often than predicted under random mating conditions.

■ Inbreeding
A type of nonrandom mating in which relatives mate more often than predicted under random mating conditions.

TABLE 14–1	Positive Correlations Between Husbands and Wives in the United States and Britain	
IQ		.47
Ear lobe length*		.40
Waist circumference		.38
Stature		.28
Hip circumference		.22
Weight		.21
Neck circumference		.20

*This is not to say that prospective mates go around measuring or even paying particular attention to each other's ear lobes. Correlation for this trait may be residual of assortative mating for overall size or for certain head dimensions. It also may mean absolutely nothing. If one measures enough traits, statistically some will appear associated strictly on the basis of chance.

Source: Lerner and Libby, 1976, p. 369.

Whether incest is strictly prohibited by social proscriptions or whether biological factors also interact to condition against such behavior has long been a topic of heated debate among anthropologists. For numerous social, economic, and ecological reasons, exogamy is an advantageous strategy for hunting and gathering bands. Moreover, selective pressures may also play a part, since highly inbred offspring have a greater chance of expressing a genetic disorder and thereby lowering their reproductive fitness. In addition, inbreeding reduces variability among offspring, potentially reducing reproductive success (Murray, 1980). In this regard, an interesting note is that incest avoidance is widespread among vertebrates (Parker, 1976). Moreover, detailed studies of free-ranging chimpanzees indicate that they avoid incestuous matings within their family group (Goodall, 1968); in fact, adults of at least one sex in most primate species consistently establish themselves and then mate within groups other than the one in which they were reared (see p. 155). Apparently, both biological factors (in common with other primates) and uniquely human cultural factors have interacted during hominid evolution to produce this universal behavior pattern among contemporary societies.

Conversely, in certain societies inbreeding among fairly close relations such as cousins is actively encouraged or is unavoidable owing to the small number of potential mates available. A famous case of the latter situation occurred on Pitcairn Island among descendants of the mutineers of the *Bounty* and their Tahitian wives. Only a small founding population (23 or 24) initially settled this tiny island, and this group was still further reduced by intragroup violence. As a result, young men and women of the ensuing generations usually chose spouses with whom they shared several common ancestors. On Pitcairn there was no choice but to partake in considerable inbreeding.

On the other hand, there are some areas where inbreeding, although avoidable, is still actively encouraged. In some parts of Japan, among certain social classes, first-cousin marriages make up almost 10 percent of all marriages, and in the Andhra Pradesh area of India, among certain castes, uncle-niece unions also make up about 10 percent of marriages.

It must be kept in mind, however, that such considerable inbreeding is the exception rather than the rule among human populations. In fact, most groups seem to work very hard at maintaining exogamy, actively promoting exchange of marriage partners between groups. For example, many polar Inuit (Eskimo) groups live in small geographically separate isolates. Despite this, through socially established rules, very little inbreeding occurs. As a general rule, then, most human populations do not inbreed if they can help it.

Inbreeding has important medical consequences in addition to its influence on genetic equilibrium. When relatives mate, their offspring have an increased probability of inheriting two copies of potentially harmful recessive alleles from a relative that they share in common, such as a grandparent. Many potentially deleterious genes normally "masked" in heterozygous carriers may be expressed in offspring of consanguineous matings and thereby "exposed" to the action of natural selection. Among offspring of first-cousin matings in the United States, the risk of congenital disorders is 2.3 times greater than it is for the overall population. Matings between especially close relatives—incest—often lead to multiple genetic defects.

Human Polymorphisms

The ABO and MN blood groups, as well as the traits discussed earlier in Chapter 4, are *Mendelian* traits. That is, the phenotype of each of these traits can unambiguously be linked to the action of a single locus. These simple genetic mechanisms are much more straightforward than the polygenic traits usually associated with studies of human **racial** variation (discussed in Chapter 15). In fact, the difficulty in tracing the genetic influence on such characteristics as skin color or face shape has led some human biologists to avoid investigations of such polygenic traits. Although physical anthropologists, by tradition, have been keenly interested in explaining such variation, we have seen a trend toward greater concentration on those traits with a clearly demonstrated genetic mechanism (i.e., Mendelian characteristics).

Of greatest use in contemporary studies of human variation are those traits that can be used to document genetic differences among various populations. Such genetic traits are called **polymorphisms.** A genetic trait is a polymorphism "when two or more alleles at a given genetic locus occur with appreciable frequencies in a population" (Bodmer and Cavalli-Sforza, 1976, p. 308). How much is "appreciable" is a fairly arbitrary judgment, but it is usually placed at 1 percent. In other words, if a population is sampled for a particular trait, and frequencies for more than one allele are higher than 1 percent, the trait (more precisely, the locus that governs the trait) is polymorphic. The limit of 1 percent is an attempt by population geneticists to control for mutation effects, which normally add new alleles at rates far below our 1 percent level. To explain this pattern of variation, beyond mutation, some *additional* evolutionary factor(s), such as gene flow, drift, natural selection, must also have been at work.

Clearly, then, the understanding of human genetic polymorphisms demands evolutionary explanations. As students of human evolution, physical anthropologists use these polymorphisms as their principal tool to understand the dynamics of evolution in modern populations. Moreover, by utilizing these polymorphisms and comparing allele frequencies in different populations, we can begin to reconstruct the evolutionary events that link human populations with one another. Several polymorphisms are now well known in humans, including those determined from analysis of blood.

ABO

With the first use of transfusions as a medical practice around the turn of the century, serious problems were immediately recognized. Some patients had severe reactions, such as agglutination (clumping) of their blood cells, kidney failure, and even death. In the year 1900, Karl Landsteiner showed that the underlying cause of these incompatibilities was a genetic trait. As you know, this trait, called the ABO blood system, is expressed phenotypically in individuals as antigens located on the surface of their red blood cells (see p. 80). The blood group (i.e., what antigens a person has) is directly determined by his or her genotype for the ABO locus. The complications sometimes resulting from transfusions are due to *antigen-antibody* reactions. In a highly specific fashion, the body can recognize foreign antigens (proteins) and combat their invasion by producing specific antibodies that deactivate the foreign substances. Such an *immune response* is normally beneficial, for it is the basis of fighting infections caused by bacteria or viruses.

Usually, antibodies must be produced when foreign antigens are introduced. However, in the case of ABO, naturally occurring antibodies are already present in the blood serum at birth. Actually, no antibodies are probably "natural," although they may be (as in ABO) stimulated early in fetal life.

The ABO system is most interesting from an anthropological perspective because the frequencies of the three alleles (*A, B, O*) vary tremendously among human populations. As the distribution maps indicate (Fig. 14–1), *A* or *B* rarely

■ **Racial**

In biology, pertaining to populations of a species that differ from other populations of the same species with regard to some aspects of outwardly expressed phenotype. Such phenotypic variation within a species is usually associated with differences in geographical location.

■ **Polymorphism**

A genetic trait governed by a locus with more than one allele in appreciable frequency. That is, the locus has two or more alleles, each with a frequency of at least 1 percent.

Virtual Lab 2, section II, part E, provides a detailed review of Mendelian genetics.

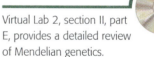

An interactive exercise about ABO blood groups is provided in Virtual Lab 2, section III, part B.

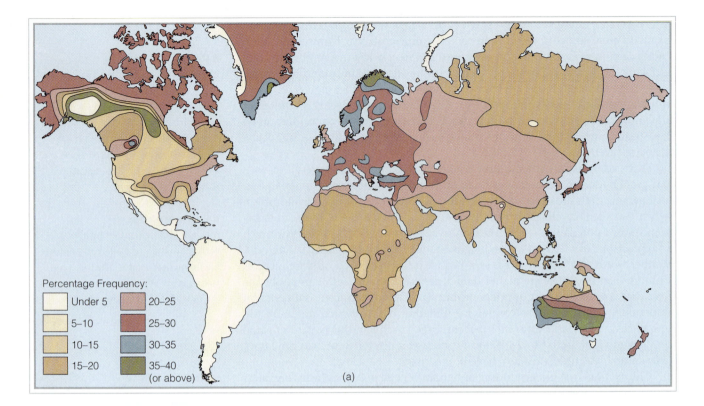

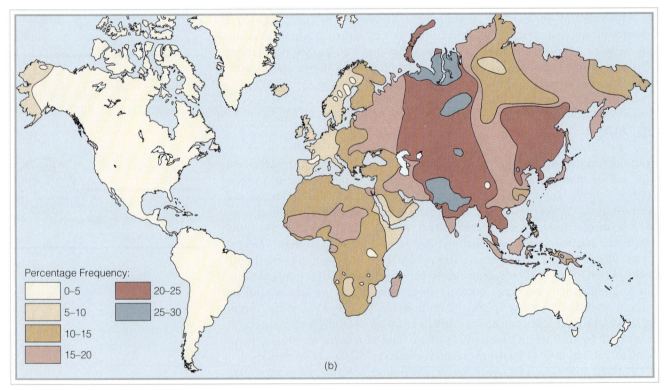

FIGURE 14–1

ABO blood group system. (a) Distribution of the A allele in the indigenous populations of the world.
(b) Distribution of the B allele in the indigenous populations of the world. (After Mourant et al., 1976.)

approaches a frequency of 50 percent; frequencies for these two alleles are usually considerably below this figure. Most human groups, however, are polymorphic for all three alleles. Occasionally, as in native South American Indians, frequencies of *O* reach 100 percent, and this allele is said to be "fixed" in this population. Indeed, in most native New World populations, *O* is at least 80 percent and is usually considerably higher. Unusually high frequencies of *O* are also found in northern Australia, and some islands off the coast show frequencies of 90 percent and higher. Since these frequencies are considerably greater than for presumably closely related mainland populations, founder effect is probably the evolutionary agent responsible.

In general, the lowest values for *O* found in the world are in eastern Europe and central Asia. As you might expect, frequencies for *A* and *B* can be relatively higher only where *O* tends to be lower. Generally, *B* is the rarest of the three alleles, and except among the Inuit, it appears to have been completely absent in the pre-Columbian New World. Moreover, the allele has apparently been introduced into Australia only in recent times.

The *B* allele reaches its highest peak in Eurasia, where its distribution is the inverse of *O*. Values up to 20 percent and occasionally slightly higher are found in a broad area in central Asia, western Siberia, and central Mongolia. The highest reported frequencies for *B* are found in the Himalaya area, reaching a peak of 25 to 30 percent. Generally, the frequency of *B* declines gradually in populations the farther westward they are in Eurasia. This pattern of gradual shift in allele frequency over space is called a **cline** (see p. 416 for further discussion).

The *A* allele has two interesting peaks, one among Blackfoot Indians and surrounding groups in North America and the other distributed over almost the entire Australian continent. With frequencies greater than 50 percent, the Blackfoot display the highest frequencies of *A* anywhere in the world. Certainly, they are divergent from other North American groups, who all have very high frequencies of *O* (and therefore low frequencies of *A*). How did *A* increase so much among this one tribe and its close neighbors compared to surrounding populations? Possibly drift (founder effect) is the answer, possibly some unknown selective factor. No one knows.

In Australia, except for the northern part, frequencies of *A* are generally high—particularly in central Australia, where they are 40 percent or higher. One tribe has especially high frequencies of *A* (53 percent), significantly higher than any surrounding group. Once again, is founder effect responsible? Over the rest of Australia, frequencies of *A* are fairly even in distribution and gradually decrease as populations become further removed from the center of the continent.

We must point out that distributions of alleles for a single genetic trait like ABO do not conclusively demonstrate genetic relationships between populations. For example, the North American Blackfoot and central Australian Mandjiljara have similar frequencies of *A,* but are obviously not closely related. On the other hand, in South Africa, the San have lower *B* frequencies than some of their close neighbors, with whom they share fairly close genetic ties. To understand *patterns* of population relationships, it is absolutely necessary to consider allele frequency distributions for several traits simultaneously (see p. 416).

Why do frequencies of the ABO alleles vary so much in different populations? In some cases, as with the islands off northern Australia and perhaps with the Blackfoot, drift may be the key factor. However, the even distribution of alleles (as *B* in Eurasia, *A* in Australia) indicates that selection may also be playing an important role, for the regularity in the frequency distributions is thought to mirror gradual changes in environments.

▌Cline

Gradual change in frequency of genotypes and phenotypes over geographical space.

Virtual Lab 2, section III, part A, provides a discussion of the critical factors underlying population genetics including genetic drift.

If, in fact, selection is operating, what are the specific factors involved? Unfortunately, unlike sickle-cell traits, there is not as yet any proven association between ABO frequencies and *any* selective agent (such as a particular disease). There are, however, some clues. For example, *A* individuals have significantly more stomach cancer and pernicious anemia, while *O* individuals have more gastric and duodenal ulcers (Vogel, 1970). Such chronic diseases as these are not that common; indeed, they probably do not affect reproductive success very much, since they occur so late in life.

On the other hand, infectious diseases (as already shown for malaria) are potentially selective factors of enormous significance. Some interesting associations between ABO frequencies and incidence of smallpox, tuberculosis, syphilis, bubonic plague, cholera, and leprosy have been suggested. Moreover, it has also been suggested that *O* individuals are more attractive to mosquitoes and are thus bitten more often than *A*, *B*, or *AB* individuals (Wood et al., 1972). Here, too, could be an important contributing factor for infectious diseases, since many—including malaria, yellow fever, and typhus—are transmitted by insects (Brues, 1990). As yet, none of these associations is well substantiated. Consequently, the evolutionary factors influencing the distribution of ABO alleles are still largely a mystery.

Rh

Another group of antigens found on red blood cells is the *Rh system,* named after the rhesus monkeys that initially provided the blood cells with which to make antiserum. Developed in 1940 by Wiener and Landsteiner (a full 40 years after the latter's discovery of ABO), this antiserum was then tested in a large sample of white Americans, in which 85 percent reacted positively.

The individuals showing such a positive agglutination reaction are usually called Rh-positive (Rh$^+$), and those whose blood does not agglutinate with the antiserum are called Rh-negative (Rh$^-$). These standardized designations refer to an apparently simple two-allele system, with *DD* and *Dd* resulting in Rh$^+$ and the recessive *dd* resulting in Rh$^-$.

Clinically, the Rh factor—like ABO—can lead to serious complications. However, the greatest problem is not so much the incompatibilities following transfusions as those between a mother and her developing fetus (see Box 14–2). For most significant medical applications, Rh$^+$ and Rh$^-$ phenotypes are accounted for by the three genotypes already noted (*DD, Dd, dd*). However, the actual genetics of the Rh system are a good deal more complex than explained by just two alleles at one locus. The famous English population geneticist Sir R. A. Fisher suggested that the Rh system is actually three closely linked loci with at least two alleles each.

The distribution of the various allele combinations within the Rh system (which may be pictured as large genes) varies considerably among human populations. Generally, Rh$^-$ (*d*) is quite high in European groups, averaging around 40 percent. African populations also have a fair amount of polymorphism at the *D* locus, with frequencies of Rh$^-$ centering around 25 percent. Native Americans and Australians, on the other hand, are almost 100 percent Rh$^+$.

Other Red Blood Cell Antigen Systems

MN   The pattern of inheritance of the MN blood group that we have referred to previously is very straightforward and is thus a favorite tool in population genetics research. There are three genotypes—*MM, MN, NN*—all clearly ascertainable at the phenotypic level using antisera obtained from rabbits. Clinically, no observable complications arise as a result of transfusions or mother-fetus incompatibilities; the MN system is anthropologically important because of its variable distribution among human populations.

Almost all human populations are polymorphic (i.e., having both *M* and *N* in "appreciable" frequencies), but the relative frequency of the two alleles varies tremendously. In some areas of Australia, *M* is as low as 2 percent, contrasted with many areas of the New World, where frequencies exceed 90 percent and even reach 100 percent in some areas. The allele *M* is also found in quite high frequency in Arabia, Siberia, and portions of Southeast Asia.

In addition to ABO, Rh, and MN, there are several other polymorphic red blood cell antigen systems. While not clinically significant like ABO or Rh, many of these are important for anthropological studies of population variation. Table 14–2 lists the major antigen systems of human red blood cells.

Polymorphisms in White Blood Cells

An important polymorphic trait called the HLA (human lymphocyte antigen) system has been discovered on some white blood cells (lymphocytes). Of great medical importance, HLA loci affect histocompatibility, or recognition and rejection of foreign tissues—the reason skin grafts and organ transplants are usually rejected. Genetically, the HLA system is exceedingly complex, and researchers are still discovering further subtleties within it. There are at least seven closely linked loci on chromosome 6 making up the HLA system. Taken together, there are already well over 100 antigens known within the system, with a potential of at least 30 million different genotypes (Williams, 1985; Bodmer, 1995). By far, this is the most polymorphic of any known human genetic system.

The component loci of the HLA system function together as a kind of "supergene." In addition to the components of the HLA loci themselves, many other factors affecting immune response are known to exist in the same region of chromosome 6. Altogether, the whole system is called the *major histocompatibility complex* (MHC).

The geographical distribution of the various MHC alleles is not yet well known. Some interesting patterns, however, are apparent. For example, Lapps, Sardinians, and Basques show deviations from frequencies of HLA alleles in other European populations, paralleling evidence for ABO, Rh, and MN. In addition, many areas in New Guinea and Australia are quite divergent, possibly suggesting the effects of drift. It is imperative, however, that care be taken in postulating genetic relatedness from restricted polymorphic information. Otherwise, such obviously ridiculous links as some proposed from HLA data (e.g., Tibetans and Australians; Inuit with some New Guineans) would obscure the evolutionary process in human populations (Livingstone, 1980). Since HLA is involved in the superfine detection and deactivation of foreign antigens, selection relative to infectious diseases (particularly those caused by viruses) may also play a significant role in the distribution of HLA alleles.

Evidence is still tentative, but some HLA antigens are apparently associated with susceptibility to certain diseases. Most severe forms of diabetes, a disease of the spine called ankylosing spondylitis, as well as multiple sclerosis and some varieties of hay fever, all probably result from individuals developing an autoimmune response to their own HLA antigens.

TABLE 14–2 Other Blood Group Systems Used in Human Microevolutionary Studies

Major Systems	Number of Known Antigens
P	3
Lutheran	2
Kell-Cellano	5
Lewis	2
Duffy	2
Kidd	2
Diego	1
Auberger	1
Xg (sex-linked)	1
Dombrock	1
Stolzfus	1

Source: Lerner and Libby, 1976, p. 354.

BOX 14–2

Mother-Fetus Incompatibilities

A mother-fetus incompatibility occurs when the system of the mother is immunized by cells from a fetus and forms antibodies that then raise problems for that fetus or future ones.

For the Rh trait, complications occur only when the mother is Rh⁻ (*dd*) and the father Rh⁺ (*DD* or *Dd*). Actually, the other loci can also cause incompatibilities, but 95 percent of the problems are due to the D locus.

European populations are the most polymorphic for Rh, and around 13 percent of all matings are at risk. Not all those at risk, however, run into problems. Only about 6 percent of those potentially in danger have any complications. With new preventive treatment, this figure can be expected to decline even further.

The problem of incompatibility arises only if the mother is Rh⁻ and her fetus is Rh⁺. Usually, there are no serious effects in the first pregnancy, for the mother's system has not been immunized. Transfer along the placental boundary does not generally include blood cells, except in the case of rupture. Ruptures, however, do occur normally at birth, so that fetal blood enters the mother's system, stimulating the production of antibodies. Such antibodies do not occur naturally, as in the ABO system, but are produced "on the spot" quite quickly. About 70 percent of all Rh⁻ people have the capability of producing significant amounts of these antibodies, and it requires only one drop of blood to stimulate the process!

When the next pregnancy occurs, transfer of the antibodies from the mother's system takes place across the placental boundary into the fetus. Here is the real problem: The anti-Rh⁺ antibodies react with the fetal blood, causing cell destruction. Consequently, the fetus will be born with a severe malady called *hemolytic disease of the newborn,* which produces severe anemia with accompanying "oxygen starvation." Because of the lack of oxygen, such newborns are sometimes called "blue babies." In recent decades, doctors, prepared in advance for such complications, administered massive transfusions and often saved the infant. However, previous to modern medical treatment, this disease was probably nearly always fatal. Such incompatibilities were thus fairly common in polymorphic populations and should have exerted a powerful selection pressure.

More recently, physicians have sought to prevent incompatibilities by administering serum containing anti-Rh⁺ antibodies to women at risk after their first birth. These antibodies quickly destroy any fetal red blood cells as they enter the mother's circulation, thereby preventing her from forming her own antibodies. Since the serum given the mother is a passive form of immunization (to her), it will shortly leave her bloodstream. Thus, she does not produce any long-acting antibodies, and the quite low risk of first pregnancies should not be increased in future pregnancies.

It should also be mentioned that mother-fetus incompatibilities result from ABO as well. However, these are considerably rarer than Rh complications, with less than 0.1 percent of newborns affected. It is possible, though, that some ABO incompatibilities go undetected owing to early fetal death.

A very interesting relationship appears to exist between Rh and ABO incompatibilities. Surprisingly, if the fetus is *both* ABO and Rh incompatible with the mother, the effects are less than if the incompatibility were for only one trait. ABO incompatibility seems to buffer the potentially very serious effects of Rh immunization. How this occurs is still unknown, but possibly the naturally occurring anti-A and/or anti-B antibodies coat and inactivate incoming cells, thus preventing them from stimulating the Rh immune response in the mother's system.

Miscellaneous Polymorphisms

An interesting genetically controlled variation in human populations was discovered by accident in 1931. When the artificially synthesized chemical phenylthiocarbamide (PTC) was dropped in a laboratory, some researchers were able to smell it, while others could not. It was later established that there is a dichotomy among humans regarding those who can versus those who cannot taste PTC. Although tasters vary considerably in sensitivity, most report a very bitter,

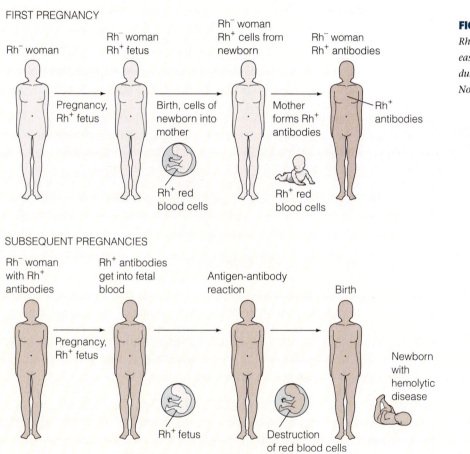

FIRST PREGNANCY

Rh⁻ woman

Rh⁻ woman
Rh⁺ fetus

Rh⁻ woman
Rh⁺ cells from
newborn

Rh⁻ woman
Rh⁺ antibodies

Pregnancy,
Rh⁺ fetus

Birth, cells of
newborn into
mother

Mother
forms Rh⁺
antibodies

Rh⁺
antibodies

Rh⁺ red
blood cells

Rh⁺ red
blood cells

SUBSEQUENT PREGNANCIES

Rh⁻ woman
with Rh⁺
antibodies

Rh⁺ antibodies
get into fetal
blood

Antigen-antibody
reaction

Birth

Pregnancy,
Rh⁺ fetus

Newborn
with
hemolytic
disease

Rh⁺ fetus

Destruction
of red blood cells

FIGURE 1

Rh incompatibility and hemolytic disease of the newborn: the series of events during first and later pregnancies. (After Novitski, 1977.)

unpleasant sensation. The pattern of inheritance follows a Mendelian model, with the inability to taste behaving as a simple recessive. In most populations, a majority of individuals are tasters, but the frequency of nontasters varies dramatically—from as low as 5 percent in Africa to as high as 40 percent in India.

The evolutionary function of this polymorphism is not known, although the fact that it is also seen in some other primates argues that it has a long history. Obviously, evolution has not acted to produce discrimination for an artificial substance recently concocted by humans. The observed variation *may* reflect selection for taste discrimination of other, more significant substances. Indeed, taste discrimination, which may allow the avoidance of many toxic plants (which frequently are bitter), may well be an important evolutionary consideration.

Another puzzling human polymorphism is the variability seen in earwax, or cerumen. Earwax is found in human groups in two basic varieties: (1) yellow and sticky with a good deal of lipids (fats and fatlike substances) and (2) gray and dry with fewer lipids. Cerumen variation appears also to be inherited as a simple Mendelian trait with two alleles (sticky is dominant; dry is recessive). Interestingly, frequencies of the two varieties of earwax vary considerably among human populations. In European populations, about 90 percent of individuals typically have the sticky variety, while in northern China, only about 4 percent are of this type.

How do we explain these differences? Even between very large groups there are consistent differences in cerumen type, arguing that drift is an unlikely causal mechanism. However, it is difficult to imagine what kind of selective pressure would act directly on earwax. Perhaps, like that previously suggested for PTC discrimination, earwax variation is an incidental expression of a gene controlling something more adaptively significant. Suggestions along these lines have pointed to the relation of cerumen to other body secretions, especially those affecting odor. Certainly, other mammals, including nonhuman primates, pay considerable attention to smell stimuli. Although the sense of smell is not as well developed in humans as in other mammals, humans still process and utilize olfactory (smell) stimuli. Thus, it is not impossible that during the course of human evolution, genes affecting bodily secretions (including earwax) came under selective influence.

Polymorphisms at the DNA Level

Geneticists and physical anthropologists over the last 50 years have used somewhat indirect techniques to study human polymorphisms, observing some *phenotypic* products. For example, the ABO antigens are phenotypic products (quite immediate ones) of the DNA locus coding for them. In the last decade, with the revolution in DNA technology, much more *direct* means have become available by which to study human genetic variation.

The use of mtDNA in studies of modern human origins is presented in a virtual exercise in Virtual Lab 12, section II, part B.

mtDNA   In addition to the DNA found in the nucleus (nuclear DNA), human (and other eukaryotic) cells contain another kind of DNA. This DNA, found in the cytoplasm, is contained within the organelles called mitochondria—and is thus called *mitochondrial DNA (mtDNA)*. While nuclear DNA is extraordinarily long, containing an estimated 3 billion nucleotides, mtDNA is much shorter, containing only 16,500 nucleotides. Using special enzymes (restriction enzymes, derived from bacteria) that cut the DNA in specific locations, researchers have been able to sequence much of the mtDNA genome. Thus, it has become possible to compare variation among individuals and among populations. Ongoing work is establishing that some mtDNA regions are more variable than others but that for the *total* mtDNA genome, variation within *Homo sapiens* is apparently much less pronounced than in other species (e.g., chimpanzees). The possible evolutionary reasons for this surprising finding might relate to a quite recent origin of all modern *Homo sapiens* from a restricted ancestral population base (thus producing genetic drift/founder effect). The evolutionary ramifications of such a process on the dispersal of modern humans was discussed in Chapter 13 (see p. 364).

Nuclear DNA   As with mtDNA analysis, the use of restriction enzymes has permitted much greater precision in direct study of the DNA contained within human chromosomes, that is, nuclear DNA. This work has been greatly facilitated as part of the continuing intense research of the *Human Genome Project.* Untangling the entire human genetic complement is obviously an enormous undertaking, but to date, considerable insight has been gained regarding human variation *directly at the DNA level.* By cutting the DNA of different individuals and comparing the results, researchers have observed great variation in the length of the DNA fragments at numerous DNA sites. Accordingly, these genetic differences (caused by variable DNA sequences) are referred to as **restriction fragment length polymorphisms (RFLPs).** In addition to providing direct evidence of human genetic variation, the RFLPs are also of vital importance in mapping other loci (e.g., that for cystic fibrosis) to specific regions of specific chromosomes.

■ Restriction fragment length polymorphisms (RFLPs)
Variation among individuals in the length of DNA fragments produced by enzymes that break the DNA at specific sites.

Human Biocultural Evolution

We have defined culture as the human strategy of adaptation. Human beings live in cultural environments that are continually modified by human activity; thus, evolutionary processes are understandable only within this *cultural* context. You will recall that natural selection pressures operate within specific environmental settings. For humans and many of our hominid ancestors, this means an environment dominated by culture. For example, the sickle-cell allele has not always been an important genetic factor in human populations. In fact, human cultural modification of environments apparently provided the initial stimulus. Before the development of agriculture, humans rarely, if ever, lived close to mosquito breeding areas. With the development and spread to Africa of **slash-and-burn agriculture,** perhaps in just the last 2,000 years, penetration and clearing of tropical rain forests occurred. As a result of deforestation, open, stagnant pools provided prime mosquito breeding areas in close proximity to human settlements.

The relationship between malaria and sickle-cell anemia is provided in a virtual exercise in Virtual Lab 2, section III, part B.

Malaria, for the first time, struck human populations with its full impact, and as a selective force it was powerful indeed. No doubt, humans attempted to adjust culturally to these circumstances, and numerous biological adaptations also probably came into play. The sickle-cell trait is one of these biological adaptations. However, there is a definite cost involved with such an adaptation. Carriers have increased resistance to malaria and presumably higher reproductive success, but some of their offspring may be lost through the genetic disease sickle-cell anemia. So there is a counterbalancing of selective forces with an advantage for carriers *only* in malarial environments. The genetic patterns of recessive traits such as sickle-cell anemia are discussed in Chapter 4 (see p. 83).

Following World War II, extensive DDT spraying by the World Health Organization began systematically to wipe out mosquito breeding areas in the tropics. As would be expected, malaria decreased sharply, and also as would be expected, the frequency of the sickle-cell allele also seemed on the decline. The intertwined story of human cultural practices, mosquitoes, malarial parasites, and the sickle-cell allele is still not finished. Forty years of DDT spraying killed many mosquitoes, but, at the same time, natural selection has been acting on these insect populations. Because of the tremendous amount of genetic diversity among insects, as well as their short generation span, several DDT-resistant strains have arisen and spread in the last few years (Fig. 14–2). Accordingly, malaria is

■ Slash-and-burn agriculture
A traditional land-clearing practice whereby trees and vegetation are cut and burned. In many areas, fields are abandoned after a few years and clearing occurs elsewhere.

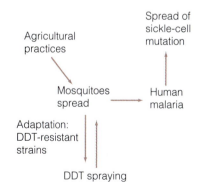

FIGURE 14–2
Evolutionary interactions affecting the frequency of the sickle-cell allele.

again on the rise, with several hundred thousand new cases reported in India, Africa, and Central America.

A genetic trait (such as sickle-cell trait) that provides a reproductive advantage to the heterozygote in certain environments is a clear example of natural selection in action among human populations. The precise evolutionary mechanism in the sickle-cell example is termed a **balanced polymorphism.** A polymorphism, as we have defined it, is a trait with more than one allele in appreciable frequency. So when an allele like that for sickle-cell is found in a population in frequencies approaching 10 percent, the trait is clearly polymorphic. The sickle-cell allele has a higher frequency than can be accounted for by mutation *alone* and thus demands a fuller evolutionary explanation. In this case, the additional mechanism is natural selection.

This brings us back to the other part of the term *balanced polymorphism*. By "balanced," we are referring to the interaction of selective pressures operating in a malarial environment. Some individuals (mainly homozygous normals) will be removed by the infectious disease malaria and some (homozygous recessives) will die of the inherited disease sickle-cell anemia. Those with the highest reproductive success are the heterozygous carriers. But what alleles do they carry? Clearly, they are passing *both* the "normal" allele as well as the sickle-cell allele to offspring, thus maintaining both alleles at fairly high frequencies (*above* the minimum level for polymorphism). Since one allele in this population will not significantly increase in frequency over the other allele, this situation will reach a balance and persist, at least as long as malaria continues to be a selective factor.

Two other traits that may also be influenced by the selective agent of malaria are G-6-PD deficiency and the thalassemias (results of several different mutations that act to block hemoglobin production). However, in both these cases, evidence of natural selection is not as strong as with the sickle-cell allele. The primary evidence suggesting a link with malaria is the geographical concordance of increased frequency of these traits with areas (especially around the Mediterranean) that historically have had a high incidence of malarial infection (see Box 14–3).

Another example of human biocultural evolution concerns the ability to digest milk. In all human populations, infants and young children can digest milk, an obvious necessity for any young mammal. A major ingredient of milk is the sugar *lactose,* which is broken down by humans and other mammals by the enzyme *lactase.* (The action of digestive enzymes and their role in human nutrition will be discussed in more detail in Chapter 16). In most mammals, including humans, the gene coding for lactase production "switches off" by adolescence. If too much milk is then ingested, it ferments in the large intestine, leading to diarrhea and severe gastrointestinal upset. Among many African and Asian populations—a majority of humankind today—most adults are intolerant of milk (Table 14–3).

Recent evidence has suggested a simple dominant mode of inheritance for **lactose intolerance.** The environment also plays a role in expression of the trait—that is, whether a person will be lactose-intolerant—since intestinal bacteria can somewhat buffer the adverse effects. Because these bacteria will increase with previous exposure, some tolerance can be acquired, even in individuals who genetically have become lactase-deficient.

Why do we see variation in lactose tolerance among human populations? Throughout most of hominid evolution, no milk was available after weaning. Perhaps, in such circumstances, continued action of an unnecessary enzyme might inhibit digestion of other foods. Therefore, there *may* be a selective advantage for the gene coding for lactase production to switch off. The question can then be asked: Why can some adults (the majority in some populations) tolerate

■ **Balanced polymorphism**
The maintenance of two or more alleles in a population due to the selective advantage of the heterozygote.

TABLE 14–3 Frequencies of Lactose Intolerance

Population Group	Percent
U.S. whites	2–19
Finnish	18
Swiss	12
Swedish	4
U.S. blacks	70–77
Ibos	99
Bantu	90
Fulani	22
Thais	99
Asian Americans	95–100
Native Australians	85

Source: Lerner and Libby, 1976, p. 327.

■ **Lactose intolerance**
The inability to digest fresh milk products; caused by the discontinued production of *lactase,* the enzyme that breaks down lactose, or milk sugar.

BOX 14–3

Other Genetic Traits Possibly Associated with Malaria

In many parts of the world, malaria has been an extremely important selective factor over the last several thousand years. Sickle-cell is probably only one of several inherited traits that have spread because they provide resistance. It must be noted, however, that none of these other traits have been documented as well as sickle-cell, nor has there been conclusive experimental evidence comparable to the work of A. C. Allison (see p. 97). Concordance between higher incidence of these genetic traits with geographical areas exhibiting high malarial infection provides *indirect* evidence of possible association in the following:

1. Hemoglobin C—produced by an allele at the same locus as that for Hb^A and Hb^S; distributed in Africa mainly in the west but with a few pockets of high incidence in the south. Hb^C is found in many populations where Hb^S is also present. Possibly this allele provides resistance to another strain of malaria and *both* alleles occur in populations exposed to multiple varieties of malaria (Weiss and Mann, 1981).

2. Thalassemia—a general term for several inherited disorders. Rather than a defect in the hemoglobin molecule itself, thalassemias involve a block in hemoglobin production (absence of, or deficient production of, the alpha or beta globin molecules). There are probably a variety of genetic mechanisms (mutations) that can lead to thalassemia, including point mutations, deletions, and disruption of gene regulation. For example, one variety of thalassemia (β^+) is caused by inadequate production of mRNA; consequently, protein synthesis of the beta hemoglobin chain is disrupted. The most harmful expression of this disease syndrome is seen in homozygotes, producing severe anemia. In heterozygotes, there are little, if any, harmful effects. Geographical evidence suggests a possible connection between thalassemia and malaria, with the highest frequencies of the disease found among populations around the Mediterranean. The severe form of beta-thalassemia affects as many as 1 percent of newborns in some parts of southern Europe. Tentative experimental evidence suggests that in heterozygotes, thalassemia—like sickle-cell—provides an inadequate environment for malarial infestation and proliferation (Friedman and Trager, 1981).

3. G-6-PD—glucose-6-phosphate dehydrogenase—an enzyme in red blood cells; individuals with a genetically caused deficiency do not produce this enzyme. The gene for this trait is on the X chromosome (i.e., X-linked), and some populations are up to 60 percent deficient (Bodmer and Cavalli-Sforza, 1976). First discovered by adverse reactions with severe anemia when individuals were given certain antimalarial drugs, anemia can also result from exposure to some foods (fava beans, for example). Distribution is again correlated with malarial areas, but apparently the alleles that cause the deficiency in southern Europe are different from those in sub-Saharan Africa. At the biochemical level, G-6-PD deficiency may act like thalassemia, producing a cellular environment not conducive to malarial infection. When exposed to certain drugs or foods (particularly fava beans), individuals with G-6-PD deficiency may have a severe anemic reaction. It is possible, however, that heterozygous carriers may actually increase malarial resistance by eating such foods—potentially an extremely important biocultural interaction (Friedman and Trager, 1981).

milk? The distribution of lactose-tolerant populations is very interesting, revealing the probable influence of cultural factors on this trait.

European groups, who are generally lactose-tolerant, are partially descended from groups of the Middle East. Often economically dependent on pastoralism, these groups raised cows and/or goats and no doubt drank considerable quantities of milk. In such a cultural environment, strong selection pressures would act to shift allele frequencies in the direction of more lactose tolerance. Modern European descendants of these populations apparently retain this ancient ability.

Even more informative is the distribution of lactose tolerance in Africa. For example, groups such as the Fulani and Tutsi, who have been pastoralists probably for thousands of years, have much higher rates of lactose tolerance than nonpastoralists.

As we have seen, the geographical distribution of lactose tolerance is related to a history of cultural dependence on milk products. There are, however, some populations that rely on dairying but are not characterized by high rates of lactose tolerance. It has been suggested that such populations traditionally have consumed their milk produce as cheese and other derivatives in which the lactose has been broken down by bacterial action (Durham, 1981).

The interaction of human cultural environments and changes in lactose tolerance among human populations is another example of biocultural evolution. In the last few thousand years, cultural factors have initiated specific evolutionary changes in human groups. Such cultural factors have probably influenced the course of human evolution for at least 3 million years, and today they are of paramount importance.

Summary

In this chapter, we have discussed human variation from an evolutionary perspective. We have focused on the contemporary trend to describe simple genetic polymorphisms that can be measured for allele frequencies as well as emphasizing genetic data obtained directly from analysis of mitochondrial and nuclear DNA.

Moreover, we have reviewed the theoretical basis of the *population genetics* approach, the subdiscipline of physical anthropology that seeks to *measure* genetic diversity among humans. Data on polymorphic traits can be used to understand aspects of human microevolution. For humans, of course, culture also plays a crucial evolutionary role, and the sickle-cell trait and lactose intolerance are thus discussed from an explicit biocultural perspective.

Questions for Review

1. How is a population defined? Discuss why, in human groups, defining particular populations can be very difficult.
2. What is meant by genetic equilibrium?
3. What is meant by nonrandom mating? Give two examples, and discuss how relevant such factors are in human evolution.
4. How has the sickle-cell allele come to be common in some parts of the world? Why is it thought to be a good example of natural selection?
5. What biocultural interactions have occurred that help explain the distribution of lactose intolerance?
6. Discuss how genetic drift may have influenced the geographical distribution of the *A, B,* and *O* alleles.

Suggested Further Reading

Bodmer, W. F., and L. L. Cavalli-Sforza. 1976. *Genetics, Evolution and Man.* San Francisco: Freeman.

Cummings, Michael R. 2000. *Human Heredity: Principles and Issues.* 5th ed. Pacific Grove: Brooks/Cole.

Durham, W. 1991. *Coevolution: Genes, Culture and Human Diversity.* Stanford: Stanford University Press.

Lewontin, R. 1974. *The Genetic Basis of Evolutionary Change.* New York: Columbia University Press.

Additional Resources

 ### Multimedia Tools

- **Virtual Laboratories for Physical Anthropology CD-ROM**
  The following concepts in this chapter are covered on the physical anthropology CD-ROM:
  population (Virtual Lab 2.I.A)
  Hardy-Weinberg (Virtual Lab 2.III.A)
  blood groups (Virtual Labs 2.II.E, III.B)
  Mendelian genetics (Virtual Lab 2.II.E)
  ABO blood groups (Virtual Lab 2.III.B)
  genetic drift (Virtual Lab 2.III.A)
  mtDNA, modern human origins (Virtual Lab 12.II.B)
  malaria, sickle-cell anemia (Virtual Lab 2.III.B)

- **Wadsworth Anthropology Resource Center**
  http://anthropology.wadsworth.com
  Visit Anthropology Online to obtain current updates in the field, surfing tips, career information and more. In addition, enrich your study efforts with text-specific study aids arranged by chapter.

- **InfoTrac College Edition**
  http://www.infotrac-college.com/wadsworth
  1. On InfoTrac College Edition, search for *human population genetics.* What does this search find? Choose one article and report on the gene(s) studied and the distribution of that gene in the population investigated. Is an explanation offered for the distribution seen?
  2. Just as you searched the Internet at large for information regarding the sickle-cell trait, research this trait on InfoTrac College Edition. Go especially to the subdivision of the sickle-cell subject, *genetic aspects.* Were you able to learn yet more about the trait?
  3. Read "Phylogenetic analysis of the evolution of lactose digestion in adults" by Holden and Mace, *Human Biology,* Oct. 1997, v69 n5 p605(24), available on InfoTrac College Edition. According to this article, which populations have high frequencies of lactose tolerance and which are generally lactose intolerant. What is the evolutionary explanation offered for this distribution?

Internet Exercises

1. Natural selection and genetic drift can both change the frequencies of different alleles in a population over a short period of time. This site, designed at the University of Tennessee at Martin, **http://fmc.utm.edu/~rirwin/NatSelModIntro.htm**, allows you to experiment with evolutionary mechanisms. Try this exercise with each of the different animals offered. Does evolution proceed differently with the different animals?

2. Is there evidence of evolution in humans? Of course, there is. The best and most clear example known is that of the sickle-cell trait and sickle-cell anemia. This topic is covered in some detail in the text, but all the information you might want about it is available on the Internet. Search for sickle-cell disease using one or more of the search engines. Who tends to develop sickle-cell anemia? Why? What causes it? Can sickle-cell anemia be prevented? Can it be predicted? Try to answer all these questions in a one-page essay on the disease and the trait.

3. Visit Online Mendelian Inheritance in Man (OMIM—**http://www3. ncbi.nlm.nih.gov/Omim/**) and search for any trait that you think might be inherited by simple Mendelian Inheritance. What did you learn about the inheritance of this trait? For what sorts of further questions/research might OMIM be useful?

Human Variation and Adaptation

Introduction

In Chapter 14, we began our discussion of biological variation in modern human populations, which in turn was based on the genetic principles discussed in Chapters 3 and 4. More specifically, Chapter 14 concerned certain Mendelian characteristics, how they vary among humans, and the underlying genetic factors that influence them, especially at the level of the population.

In this chapter, we continue our discussion of human diversity, beginning with a section on past and current views of human phenotypic variation that primarily deals with the concept of race. The traits that were traditionally used to classify humans into racial groups are polygenic. Hence, our discussion focuses on certain polygenic characteristics and emphasizes their adaptive value. We also discuss adaptation to numerous environmental factors, such as temperature, altitude, and infectious disease. Infectious disease has exerted enormous selective pressures on our species and continues to do so today. Thus, we offer a few examples of how infectious disease has altered allele frequencies in some populations. We also consider some of the many cultural and environmental factors that are currently changing the distribution and prevalence of infectious disease. Lastly, there is a discussion of HIV/AIDS that emphasizes evolutionary factors, including recently reported discoveries of genetically determined resistance to HIV.

Historical Views of Human Variation

The first step toward understanding natural phenomena is the ordering of variation into categories that can then be named, discussed, and perhaps studied. Historically, when different groups of people came into contact with one another, they offered explanations for the phenotypic variations they saw, and because skin color was so noticeable, it was one of the more frequently explained traits, and most systems of racial classification came to be based on it.

As early as 1350 B.C., the ancient Egyptians had classified humans on the basis of skin color: red for Egyptian, yellow for people to the east, white for those to the north, and black for Africans from the south (Gossett, 1963, p. 4). In the sixteenth century, after the discovery of the New World, Europe embarked on a period of intense exploration and colonization in both the New and Old Worlds. Resulting from this contact was an increased awareness of human diversity.

As you learned in Chapter 2, the discovery of the New World was of major importance in altering the views of Europeans, who had perceived the world as static and nonchanging. One of the most influential discoveries of the early European explorers was that the Americas were inhabited by people, some of whom were dark-skinned (compared to most Europeans). Furthermore, these people were not Christian, and they were not considered "civilized" by Europeans. At first, Native Americans were thought to be Asian, and since Columbus believed that he had discovered a new route to India, he called them "Indians." (This term was later applied to indigenous, dark-skinned populations of Australia as well.)

By the late eighteenth century, Europeans and European Americans were asking questions that challenged traditional Christian beliefs. They wanted to know if other groups belonged to the same species as themselves; that is, were Native Americans and other indigenous peoples indeed human? Were they descendants of Adam and Eve, or had there been later creations of non-Europeans? If the latter were true, then Native Americans had to represent a different species, or else the Genesis account of creation could not be taken literally.

Two schools of thought, known as **monogenism** and **polygenism**, devised responses. In the monogenist view, all humans were descended from a single, original pair (Adam and Eve). Insisting on the **plasticity** of human structure, monogenists contended that local environmental conditions, such as climate and terrain, could modify the original form, resulting in observable phenotypic differences between populations. Monogenist views were initially attractive to many, for they did not conflict with the Genesis version of creation.

The polygenist view, on the other hand, argued that all populations did not descend from a single, original pair, but from a number of pairs. Also, polygenists saw such a wide gap in the physical, mental, and moral attributes between themselves and other peoples that they were sure that outsiders belonged to different species. Furthermore, polygenists did not accept the monogenist notion of plasticity of physical traits, and they rejected the proposition that climate and environment were modifying influences.

Throughout the eighteenth and nineteenth centuries, European and American scientists concentrated primarily on describing and classifying biological diversity as observed in humans as well as in nonhuman species. The first scientific attempt to categorize the newly discovered variation among humans was Linnaeus' taxonomic classification, which placed humans into four separate groupings (Linnaeus, 1758) (Table 15–1). Linnaeus assigned behavioral and intellectual qualities to each group, with the least complimentary descriptions going to African blacks. This ranking was typical of the period and reflected the almost universal European view that Europeans were superior to all other peoples. (To be fair, we should note that the Europeans were not—and are not—the only people guilty of *ethnocentrism*. Most, if not all, human societies participate in the belief that their own culture is superior to others.)

Johann Friedrich Blumenbach (1752–1840), a German anatomist, classified humans into five categories or races (See Table 15–1). Although Blumenbach's categories came to be described simply as white, yellow, red, black, and brown, he also used criteria other than skin color. Moreover, Blumenbach emphasized that divisions based on skin color were arbitrary and that many traits, including skin color, were not discrete phenomena. Blumenbach pointed out that to attempt to classify all humans using such a system would be to omit completely all those who did not neatly fall into a specific category. Furthermore, he and other scientists recognized that traits such as skin color showed overlapping expression between groups. At the time, it was thought that racial taxonomies should be based on characteristics unique to particular groups and uniformly expressed within them. Some scientists, taking the polygenist view, attempted to identify certain physical traits that were thought to be stable or that did not appear to be influenced by external environmental factors. Therefore, these so-called *nonadaptive* traits should exhibit only minimal within-group variation and could thus be used to typify entire populations. Shape of the skull was incorrectly believed to be one such characteristic, and the fallacy of this assumption was not demonstrated until the early twentieth century (Boas, 1912).

In 1842, Anders Retzius, a Swedish anatomist, developed the *cephalic index* as a method of describing the shape of the head. The cephalic index, derived by dividing maximum head breadth by maximum length and multiplying by 100, gives the ratio of head breadth to length. (It is important to note that the cephalic index does not measure head size.) Compared to the statistical methods in use today, the cephalic index seems simplistic and typological, but in the nineteenth century, it was viewed as a sophisticated scientific tool. Furthermore, because

■ Monogenism

The theory that all human populations are descended from one pair (Adam and Eve), but they differ from one another because they have occupied different habitats. This concept was an attempt to explain phenotypic variation between groups, but did not imply evolutionary change.

■ Polygenism

A theory, opposed to monogenism, that stated that human races were not all descended from Adam and Eve. Instead, there had been several original human pairs, each giving rise to a different group. Thus, human races were considered to be separate species.

■ Plasticity

The capacity to change; in a physiological context, the ability of systems or organisms to make alterations in order to respond to differing conditions.

TABLE 15–1   Racial Classification Schemes

Linnaeus, 1735	Stanley M. Garn, 1965

Linnaeus, 1735

Homo europaeus
Homo afer (Africans)
Homo asiaticus
Homo americanus (Native Americans)

Blumenbach, 1781

Caucasoid	Ethiopian
Mongoloid	American
Malay	

E. A. Hooton, 1926

PRIMARY RACE

White	Mongoloid
Mediterranean	Classic Mongoloid
Ainu	Arctic Mongoloid
Keltic	Malay-Mongoloid
Nordic	Indonesian
Alpine	
East Baltic	

Negroid
  African Negro
  Nilotic Negro
  Negrito

Stanley M. Garn, 1965

GEOGRAPHICAL RACES: "a collection of race populations, separated from other such collections by major geographical barriers."

Amerindian	Melanesian-Papuan	Indian
Polynesian	Australian	European
Micronesian	Asiatic	African

LOCAL RACE: "a breeding population adapted to local selection pressures and maintained by either natural or social barriers to gene interchange."

These are examples of local races; there are many, many more:

Northwest European	East African	North Chinese
Northeast European	Bantu	Extreme Mongoloid
Alpine	Tibetan	Hindu
Mediterranean		

MICRORACES: Not well defined but apparently refers to neighborhoods within a city or a city itself, since "marriage or mating is a mathematical function of distance. With millions of potential mates, the male ordinarily chooses one near at hand."

■ **Dolichocephalic**
Having a long, narrow head in which the width measures less than 75 percent of the length.

■ **Brachycephalic**
Having a broad head in which the width measures more than 80 percent of the length.

■ **Biological determinism**
The concept that phenomena, including various aspects of behavior (e.g., intelligence, values, morals) are governed by biological (genetic) factors; the inaccurate association of various behavioral attributes with certain biological traits, such as skin color.

people could be neatly categorized by a single number, it provided an extremely efficient method for describing and ordering phenotypic variation. Individuals with an index of less than 75 had long, narrow heads and were termed **dolichocephalic**. **Brachycephalic** individuals, with broad heads, had an index of over 80; and those whose indices were between 75 and 80 were *mesocephalic*.

Northern Europeans tended to be dolichocephalic, while southern Europeans were brachycephalic. Not surprisingly, these results led to heated and nationalistic debate over whether one group was superior to the other. Furthermore, when it was shown that northern Europeans shared their tendency to long, narrow heads with several African populations, the cephalic index ceased to be considered such a reliable indicator of race.

By the mid-nineteenth century, monogenists were beginning to reject their somewhat egalitarian concept of race in favor of a more hierarchical view. Populations were ranked essentially on a scale based on skin color (along with size and shape of the head), with Africans at the bottom. Moreover, Europeans themselves were ranked so that northern, light-skinned populations were considered superior to their southern, more olive-skinned neighbors.

The fact that non-Europeans were not Christian and were seen as "uncivilized" implied an inferiority of character and intellect. This view was based in a concept now termed **biological determinism**, which in part holds that there is an association between physical characteristics and such attributes as intelligence, morals, values, abilities, and even social and economic differences between groups. In other words, cultural variations are *inherited* in the same manner as biological variations. It follows, then, that there are inherent behavioral and cognitive differences between groups and that some groups are *by nature* superior to others. Following this logic, it is a simple matter to justify the persecution and even enslavement of other peoples simply because their appearance differs from what is familiar.

After 1850, biological determinism was a constant theme underlying common thinking as well as scientific research in Europe and the United States. Deterministic (and what we today would call racist) views were held to some extent by most people, including such notable figures as Thomas Jefferson, Georges Cuvier, Benjamin Franklin, Charles Lyell, Abraham Lincoln, Charles Darwin, and Oliver Wendell Holmes. Commenting on this usually deemphasized characteristic of notable historical figures, Stephen J. Gould (1981, p. 32) emphasizes that "all American culture heroes embraced racial attitudes that would embarrass public-school mythmakers."

Francis Galton (1822–1911), a cousin of Charles Darwin, shared the increasingly common fear among Europeans that "civilized society" was being weakened by the failure of natural selection to eliminate unfit and inferior individuals (Greene, 1981, p. 107). Galton wrote and lectured on the necessity of "race improvement" and suggested governmental regulation of marriage and family size, an approach he called **eugenics.**

Although eugenics had its share of critics, its popularity flourished in the years following World War I and especially throughout the 1930s. The movement was increasingly popular in Europe and the United States, but nowhere was it more popular than in Germany, where the viewpoint took a disastrous turn. The idea of a "pure race" (see Issue, pp. 435–436) was increasingly extolled as a means of reestablishing a strong and prosperous state. Eugenics was seen as a scientific rationale for purging Germany of its "unfit," and many of Germany's scientists continued to support the policies of racial purity and eugenics during the Nazi period (Proctor, 1988, p. 143), when they served as justification for condemning millions of people to death.

But at the same time, many scientists were turning away from racial typologies and classification in favor of a more evolutionary approach. No doubt for some, this shift in direction was motivated by their growing concerns over the goals of the eugenics movement. Probably more important, however, was the synthesis of Mendelian genetics and Darwin's theories of natural selection during the 1930s. This breakthrough influenced all the biological sciences, and many physical anthropologists began to apply evolutionary principles to the study of human variation.

■ Eugenics
The philosophy of "race improvement" through the forced sterilization of members of some groups and increased reproduction among others; an overly simplified, often racist, view that is now discredited.

The Concept of Race

All contemporary humans are members of the same **polytypic** species, *Homo sapiens.* A polytypic species is one composed of local populations that differ with regard to the expression of one or more traits. Moreover, *within* local populations there is a great deal of phenotypic (and genotypic) variation between individuals. Most species are polytypic, and consequently, there is no species "type" to which all members *exactly* conform.

In discussions of human variation, people have traditionally clumped together various attributes such as skin color, shape of the face, shape of the nose, hair color, hair form (curly, straight), and eye color. People possessing particular combinations of these and other traits have been placed together into categories associated with specific geographical localities. Such categories are called *races.*

■ Polytypic
Referring to species composed of populations that differ with regard to the expression of one or more traits.

We all think we know what we mean by the word *race,* but in truth, the term has had a wide assortment of meanings since it gained common usage in English in the 1500s. It has been used synonymously with *species,* as in "the human race," or to refer to a more limited grouping of individuals all descended from a single individual (e.g., "the race of Abraham").

Since the 1600s, race has also referred to various culturally defined groups, and this meaning still enjoys popular usage. For example, one hears "the English race" or "the Japanese race," where the reference is actually to nationality. Another often-heard phrase is "the Jewish race," when the speaker is really talking about a particular ethnic and religious identity.

Thus, while *race* is usually used as a biological term, or at least one with biological connotations, it is also one with enormous social significance. Moreover, there is still a widespread perception that there is an association between certain physical traits (skin color, in particular) and numerous cultural attributes (such as language, occupational preferences, or even morality). Therefore, in many cultural contexts, a person's social identity is strongly influenced by the manner in which he or she expresses those physical traits traditionally used to define "racial groups." Characteristics such as skin color are highly visible, and they facilitate an immediate and superficial designation of individuals into socially defined categories. However, so-called racial traits are not the only phenotypic expressions that contribute to social identity. Sex and age are also critically important. But aside from these two variables, an individual's biological and/or ethnic background is still inevitably a factor that influences how he or she is initially perceived and judged by others.

The use of expressions of national origin (e.g., African, Asian) or the terms *ethnic* or *ethnicity* as substitutes for racial labels and *race* has become more common in recent years, both within and outside anthropology. Within anthropology, the term *ethnicity* was proposed in the early 1950s as a means of avoiding the more emotionally charged term *race.* Strictly speaking, ethnicity refers to cultural factors, and for this reason, some have objected to its use in discussions that also include biological characteristics. However, the fact that the words *ethnicity* and *race* are used interchangeably reflects the social importance of phenotypic expression and demonstrates once again how phenotype is associated with culturally defined variables.

In its most common biological usage, race refers to geographically patterned phenotypic variation within a species. By the seventeenth century, naturalists had begun to describe races in plants and nonhuman animals, because they recognized that when populations of a species occupied different regions, they sometimes differed from one another in the expression of one or more traits. But even today, there are no established criteria by which races of plants and animals are to be assessed. To a biologist studying nonhuman forms, the degree of genetic difference necessary for racial distinctions is a subjective issue, determined in part by the investigator. However, if we are to apply the term to humans, we must elucidate the degree of genetic difference that exists between individuals *within* populations, as well as *between* populations.

Prior to World War II, most studies of human variation focused on phenotypic variation between large, geographically defined populations, and these studies were largely descriptive. Since that time, the emphasis has shifted to the examination of differences in allele frequencies within and between populations, as well as the adaptive significance of phenotypic and genotypic variation. This shift in focus occurred partly as a result of the modern synthesis in biology (see p. 90), which was based on the recognition of the fundamental importance of the *interaction* of natural selection and other factors, such as gene flow, mutation, and drift, to the process of evolution.

Application of evolutionary principles to the study of modern human variation replaced the nineteenth-century view of race *based solely on observed phenotype*. Additionally, the genetic emphasis dispelled previously held misconceptions that races were fixed biological entities that did not change over time and that were composed of individuals who all conformed to a particular *type*.

Clearly, there are phenotypic differences between humans, and these differences roughly correspond to particular geographical locations. It is unlikely that anyone would mistake a person of Asian descent for one of northern European ancestry. But certain questions must be asked: Is there any adaptive significance attached to observed phenotypic variation? Is genetic drift a factor? What is the degree of underlying genetic variation that influences it? And how important is that genetic variation? These questions place considerations of human variation within a contemporary evolutionary framework.

Although, in part, physical anthropology has its roots in attempts to explain human diversity, anthropologists have never been in complete agreement on the topic of race. Even attempts to reach a consensus in defining the term have frequently failed. Among physical anthropologists there is still sometimes heated debate over whether it is justifiable to apply racial concepts to humans at all.

Today, some anthropologists recognize population patterning corresponding to at least three major racial groups, each composed of several subgroupings. However, no contemporary scholar subscribes to pre-Darwinian and pre-modern synthesis concepts of races (human and nonhuman) as fixed biological entities, the members of which all conform to specific types. Among those who accept the validity of the race concept, there are various viewpoints. Many who continue to use broad racial categories do not view them as particularly important, especially from a genetic perspective, because the amount of genetic variation accounted for by differences *between* groups is vastly exceeded by the variation that exists *within* groups (see p. 417). But given these considerations, there are those who see variation in outwardly expressed phenotype, because of its potential adaptive value, as worthy of investigation and explanation within the framework of evolutionary principles (Brues, 1991).

Forensic anthropologists in particular find the phenotypic criteria associated with race to have practical applications because they are frequently called on by law enforcement agencies to assist in the identification of human skeletal remains. Inasmuch as unidentified human remains are often those of crime victims, and their analysis may lead to courtroom testimony, identification must be as accurate as possible. The most important variables in such identification are the individual's sex, age, stature, and "racial" or "ethnic" background. Using metric and nonmetric criteria, forensic anthropologists employ a number of techniques for establishing broad population affinity, and they are generally able to do so with about 80 percent accuracy.

On the other side of the issue, there are numerous physical anthropologists who argue that race is a meaningless concept when applied to humans. Race is seen as an outdated creation of the human mind that attempts to simplify biological complexity by organizing it into categories. Thus, human races are a product of the human tendency to superimpose order on complex natural phenomena. While classification may have been an acceptable approach some 150 years ago, it is viewed as no longer valid given the current state of genetic and evolutionary science.

Objections to racial taxonomies have also been raised because classification schemes are *typological* in nature, meaning that categories are discrete and based on stereotypes or ideals that comprise a specific set of traits. Thus, in general, typologies are inherently misleading, because there are always many individuals in any grouping who do not conform to all aspects of a particular type.

In any so-called racial group, there will be individuals who fall into the normal range of variation for another group with regard to one or several characteristics. For example, two people of different ancestry might vary with regard to skin color, but they could share any number of other traits, such as height, shape of head, hair color, eye color, or ABO blood type. In fact, they could easily share more similarities with each other than they do with many members of their own populations.

Moreover, as we have stressed, because the characteristics that have traditionally been used to define races are polygenic, they exhibit a continuous range of expression. It thus becomes difficult, if not impossible, to draw discrete boundaries between populations with regard to many traits. This limitation becomes clear if you ask yourself, "At what point is hair color no longer dark brown but medium brown, or no longer light brown but blond?"

The scientific controversy over race is not likely to disappear. It has received considerable attention outside academia in popular magazines such as *Newsweek* and *Discover*. But in spite of all the scientific discussion that has ensued, among the general public, variations on the theme of race will undoubtedly continue to be the most common view of human biological and cultural variation. Given this fact, it falls to anthropologists and biologists to continue to explore the issue so that, to the best of our abilities, accurate information regarding human variation is available for anyone who seeks informed explanations of complex phenomena.

Contemporary Interpretations of Human Population Diversity

By the 1960s, the study of *clinal distributions* of individual polymorphic traits had become a popular alternative to the racial approach. As discussed in Chapter 14, a cline is a gradual change in the frequency of a single trait, or allele, in populations dispersed over geographical space. In humans, the various expressions of many polymorphic traits exhibit a more or less continuous distribution from one geographical region to another. The distribution of the *A* and *B* alleles in the Old World, discussed in Chapter 14, provides a good example of a clinal distribution (see Fig. 14–1, p. 396). Clinal distributions are generally thought to reflect microevolutionary influences of natural selection and/or gene flow. Thus, interpretations are explicitly framed in evolutionary terms.

Utilizing single traits can be informative regarding potential influences of natural selection or gene flow, but this approach has limitations when we try to sort out population relationships. As noted in our discussion of the HLA polymorphisms, single traits *by themselves* often can yield confusing interpretations regarding likely population relationships. What is needed, then, is a method to analyze a larger, more consistent body of data—that is, to look at several traits simultaneously. Such a *multivariate* approach makes ready use of digital computers.

An excellent example of the contemporary multivariate approach to human diversity was undertaken by Harvard population geneticist R. D. Lewontin (1972). Lewontin calculated population differences in allele frequency for 17 polymorphic traits. In his analysis, Lewontin immediately faced a dilemma: Which groups (populations) should he contrast, and how should they be weighted? That is, should larger population segments, such as Arabs, carry the same weight in the analysis as small populations, such as the one from the island Tristan da Cunha? After considerable deliberation, Lewontin decided to break down his sample into seven geographical areas, and he included several equally weighted population samples within each (Table 15–2). He then calculated how much of the total genetic variability within our species could be accounted for by these population subdivisions.

The results are surprising. Only 6.3 percent of the total genetic variation is explained by differences among major populations (Lewontin's seven geographical units). In other words, close to 94 percent of human genetic diversity occurs *within* these very large groups. The larger population subdivisions within the geographical clusters (e.g., within Caucasians: Arabs, Basques, Welsh) account for another 8.3 percent. Thus, geographical and local "races" together account for just 15 percent of all human genetic variation, leaving the remaining 85 percent unaccounted for.

The vast majority of genetic differences among human beings is explicable in terms of differences from one village to another, one family to another, and, to a very significant degree, one person to another—even within the same family. Of course, when you recall the high degree of genetic polymorphism combined with the vast number of combinations resulting from recombination during meiosis (discussed in Chapter 3), all this individual variation should not be surprising.

Our superficial visual perceptions tell us that race does exist. But the visible phenotypic traits most frequently used to make racial distinctions (skin color, hair form, nose shape, etc.) may very well produce a highly biased sample, not giving an accurate picture of the actual pattern of *genetic variation*. Simple polymorphic traits provide a more objective basis for accurate biological comparisons of human groups, and they indicate that the traditional concept of race is very limited. Indeed, Lewontin concludes his analysis with a ringing condemnation of traditional studies: "Human racial classification is of no social value and is positively destructive of social and human relations. Since such racial classification is now seen to be of virtually no genetic or taxonomic significance either, no justification can be offered for its continuance" (Lewontin, 1972, p. 397).

However, not all population geneticists are this critical. After all, Lewontin did find that about 6 percent of human variation is accounted for by the large geographical population segments traditionally called major "races." Whereas this is certainly a minority of all human genetic variation, it is not necessarily biologically insignificant.

If one feels compelled to continue to classify humankind into large geographical segments, population genetics offers some aid in isolating consistent patterns of genetic variation. Following and expanding on the approach used by Lewontin,

TABLE 15–2	Population Groupings Used by Lewontin in Population Genetics Study (1972)
Geographical Group	**Examples of Populations Included**
Caucasians	Arabs, Armenians, Tristan da Cunhans
Black Africans	Bantu, San, U.S. blacks
Asians	Ainu, Chinese, Turks
South Asians	Andamanese, Tamils
Amerinds	Aleuts, Navaho, Yanomama
Oceanians	Easter Islanders, Micronesians
Australians	All treated as a single group

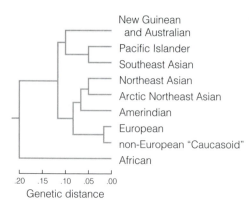

New Guinean
  and Australian
Pacific Islander
Southeast Asian
Northeast Asian
Arctic Northeast Asian
Amerindian
European
non-European "Caucasoid"
African

.20   .15   .10   .05   .00
Genetic distance

FIGURE 15–1

Genetic tree (dendrogram) showing population relationships. This dendrogram was constructed by population geneticists (Cavalli-Sforza et al., 1988) using 44 polymorphic traits.

population geneticist L. L. Cavalli-Sforza, of Stanford University, and colleagues evaluated 44 different polymorphic traits ascertained in 42 different human sample populations. From the results, these researchers constructed a "tree" (technically called a dendrogram) depicting the relationships of these samples as part of larger populations (Cavalli-Sforza et al., 1988) (Fig. 15–1). Analysis of mitochondrial DNA has produced similar results, especially showing greater genetic diversity among African populations than among other groups (Stoneking, 1993). Because mtDNA is passed solely through the maternal line (and thus does not undergo recombination), it provides certain advantages in reconstructing population relationships. Nevertheless, as a single genetic component, it acts like one large locus; thus, mtDNA results must be supplemented by other genetic data.

Comparative data from nuclear DNA studies (RFLPs or restriction fragment length polymorphisms; see Chapter 14) in conjunction with the studies discussed here are thus potentially illuminating. Initial analysis comparing 80 RFLPs in eight different groups (Mountain et al., 1993) again produced patterns quite similar to those established for the traditional polymorphisms and for mtDNA. However, another recent large-scale study (Jia and Chakraborty, 1993) of DNA markers among 59 different groups (and including about 12,000 individuals) found the vast majority of variation (up to 98.5 percent) occurring *within* populations at the *individual* level. These latest data dramatize even further the results obtained by Lewontin, leading one geneticist to conclude, "These results indicate that individual variation in DNA profiles overwhelm any interpopulational differences, no matter how the populations are ethnically or racially classified" (Cummings, 1994, p. 500). And while not quite as overwhelming, *all* the genetically based studies cited here support Lewontin's initial results, strongly indicating that the great majority of human variation does occur within human populations—not between them.

Racism

The most detrimental outcome of biological determinism is racism. Racism is based on the false belief that such factors as intellect and various cultural attributes are inherited along with physical characteristics. Such beliefs also rest on the assumption that one's own group is superior to other groups.

Because we have already alluded to certain aspects of racism, such as the eugenics movement, notions of racial purity, and persecution of people based on racial or ethnic misconceptions, we will not belabor the point here. However, it is important to point out that racism is hardly a thing of the past, nor is it restricted to European and American whites. Racism is a cultural phenomenon, and it is found worldwide.

Ultimately, racism is one of the more dangerous aspects of human behavior because it frequently leads to violence, warfare, terrorism, and genocide. We have seen recent manifestations of racism in many cities in the United States. The rioting that occurred in Los Angeles in 1992 after the acquittal of white police officers accused of beating Rodney King, a black suspect, was a clear example of the tensions among the diverse populations of large urban centers. In the past few years, there has been an increase in racial slurs and hate speech on radio talk shows and, perhaps especially, on the Internet. Sadly, the twentieth century has provided numerous examples of ethnic/racial conflict, but it is important to mention that while in some cases, there may have been some phenotypic differences between these groups, virtually all these conflicts were due to *ethnic* differences between the participants. The unspeakable genocide of the Holocaust during World War II, in Cambodia in the 1970s, and in Rwanda in 1994, as well as the tragedies of Bosnia, Croatia, and Kosovo all bespeak the tragic outcomes of intolerance of groups we call "others," however we define the term.

What we observe when we see biological variations between populations (and individuals) are the traces of our evolutionary past. Different expressions of traits such as skin color, eye color, and shape of the face are the results of biological adaptations that human ancestors made to local environmental conditions in a process that began perhaps several hundred thousand years ago. Instead of using these differences as a basis for prejudice and persecution, we should recognize them for what they are: a preserved record of how evolutionary forces shaped our species to meet the varied environmental challenges it faced while expanding its geographical range over most of the planet.

We end this brief discussion of racism with an excerpt from an article, "The Study of Race," by Sherwood Washburn, a well-known physical anthropologist at the University of California, Berkeley. Although written some years ago, the statement is as fresh and applicable today as it was when it was written:

> Races are products of the past. They are relics of times and conditions which have long ceased to exist.
>
> Racism is equally a relic supported by no phase of modern science. We may not know how to interpret the form of the Mongoloid face, or why Rh is of high incidence in Africa, but we do know the benefits of education and of economic progress. We . . . know that the roots of happiness lie in the biology of the whole species and that the potential of the species can only be realized in a culture, in a social system. It is knowledge and the social system which give life or take it away, and in so doing change the gene frequencies and continue the million-year-old interaction of culture and biology. Human biology finds its realization in a culturally determined way of life, and the infinite variety of genetic combinations can only express themselves efficiently in a free and open society. (Washburn, 1963, p. 531)

Intelligence

As we have shown, belief in the relationship between phenotype and specific behavioral attributes is popular even today, but evidence is lacking that personality or any other behavioral trait differs genetically *between* human groups. Most scientists would agree with this last statement, but one question that has produced controversy both inside scientific circles and among laypeople is whether populations vary with regard to **intelligence**.

Both genetic and environmental factors contribute to intelligence, although it is not yet possible to measure accurately the percentage each contributes. What can be said is that IQ scores and intelligence are not the same thing; IQ scores can change during a person's lifetime, and average IQ scores of different populations overlap. Such differences in IQ scores as do exist between groups are difficult to interpret, given the problems inherent in the design of the IQ tests. Moreover, complex cognitive abilities, however measured, are influenced by multiple loci and are thus strikingly polygenic.

Innate factors set limits and define potentials for behavior and cognitive ability in any species. In humans, the limits are broad and the potentials are not fully known. Individual abilities result from complex interactions between

■ Intelligence
Mental capacity; ability to learn, reason, or comprehend and interpret information, facts, relationships, meanings, etc.; the capacity to solve problems, whether through the application of previously acquired knowledge or through insight.

genetic and environmental factors. One product of this interaction is learning, and the ability to learn has genetic or biological components. Undeniably, there are differences between individuals regarding these biological components. However, elucidating what proportion of the variation in test scores is due to biological factors probably is not possible. Moreover, innate differences in abilities reflect individual variation *within* populations, not inherent differences *between* groups. Comparing populations on the basis of IQ test results is a misuse of testing procedures, and there is no convincing evidence *whatsoever* that populations vary with regard to cognitive abilities, regardless of the assertions in some publications.

The Adaptive Significance of Human Variation

Today, physical anthropologists view human variation as the result of such evolutionary factors as genetic drift, founder effect, gene flow, and adaptation (through natural selection) to environmental conditions, both past and present. Although cultural adaptations have certainly played a vital role in the evolution of *Homo sapiens,* in this discussion we are primarily concerned with biological factors.

All organisms must maintain the normal functions of internal organs, tissues, and cells in order to survive, and this task must be accomplished within the context of an ever-changing environment. Even during the course of a single, seemingly uneventful day, there are numerous fluctuations in temperature, wind, solar radiation, humidity, and so on. Physical activity also places **stress** on physiological mechanisms. The body must accommodate all these changes by compensating in some manner to maintain internal constancy, or **homeostasis**, and all life forms have evolved physiological mechanisms that, within limits, achieve this goal.

Physiological response to environmental change is, to some degree, influenced by genetic factors. We have already defined adaptation as a functional response to environmental conditions in populations and individuals. In a narrower sense, adaptation refers to *long-term* evolutionary (i.e., genetic) changes that characterize all individuals within a population or species.

Examples of long-term adaptations in *Homo sapiens* include some physiological responses to heat (sweating) and deeply pigmented skin in tropical regions. Such characteristics are the results of evolutionary change in species or populations and they do not vary as the result of short-term environmental change. For example, the ability to sweat is not lost in people who spend their lives in predominantly cool areas. Likewise, individuals born with deeply pigmented skin will not become pale, even if never exposed to intense sunlight.

Short-term physiological response to environmental change, which is also genetically influenced, is called **acclimatization**. Tanning, which occurs in all people, is a form of acclimatization. Another example is the very rapid increase in hemoglobin production that occurs when lowland natives travel to higher elevations. This increase provides the body with more oxygen in an environment where oxygen is less available. In both these examples, the physiological change is temporary. Tans fade once exposure to sunlight is reduced; and hemoglobin production drops to original levels on return to lower altitudes.

In the following discussion, we present some examples of how humans respond to environmental challenges. Some of these examples illustrate adaptations that characterize the entire species. Others illustrate adaptations seen in only some populations. And still others illustrate the process of acclimatization.

▌ Stress
In a physiological context, any factor that acts to disrupt homeostasis; more precisely, the body's response to any factor that threatens its ability to maintain homeostasis.

▌ Homeostasis
A condition of balance, or stability, within a biological system, maintained by the interaction of physiological mechanisms that compensate for changes (both external and internal).

▌ Acclimatization
Physiological response to changes in the environment that occurs during an individual's lifetime. Such responses may be short-term. The capacity for acclimatization may typify an entire population or species. This capacity is under genetic influence and thus is subject to evolutionary factors such as natural selection.

Solar Radiation, Vitamin D, and Skin Color

Skin color is often cited as an example of adaptation and natural selection in human populations. In general, skin color in populations, especially prior to about 1500, follows a particular geographical distribution, especially in the Old World. Figure 15–2 illustrates that populations with the greatest amount of pigmentation are found in the tropics, while lighter skin color is associated with more northern latitudes, particularly the inhabitants of northwestern Europe.

Skin color is influenced by three substances: hemoglobin, carotene, and, most important, the pigment *melanin*. Melanin is a granular substance produced by specialized cells in the epidermis called *melanocytes*. All humans appear to have approximately the same number of melanocytes. It is the amount of melanin and the size of melanin granules that vary.

Melanin has the capacity to absorb potentially dangerous ultraviolet (UV) rays that are present (although not visible) in sunlight. Because of this ability, melanin provides protection from overexposure to ultraviolet radiation, which can cause genetic mutations in skin cells. These mutations may ultimately lead to skin cancer, which, if left untreated, can eventually spread to other organs and result in death.

As already mentioned, exposure to sunlight triggers a protective mechanism in the form of temporarily increased melanin production (acclimatization). (The visible manifestation of this increase is a tan.) This protective response occurs in all humans except albinos, who carry a genetic mutation that prevents their melanocytes from producing melanin (Fig. 15–3). Moreover, tanning is limited in many fair-complexioned people of northern European descent who do produce

The adaptive significance of skin color is presented as a virtual exercise in Virtual Lab 2, section IV.

FIGURE 15–2

Geographical distribution of skin color among the indigenous populations of the world. (After Biasutti, 1959.)

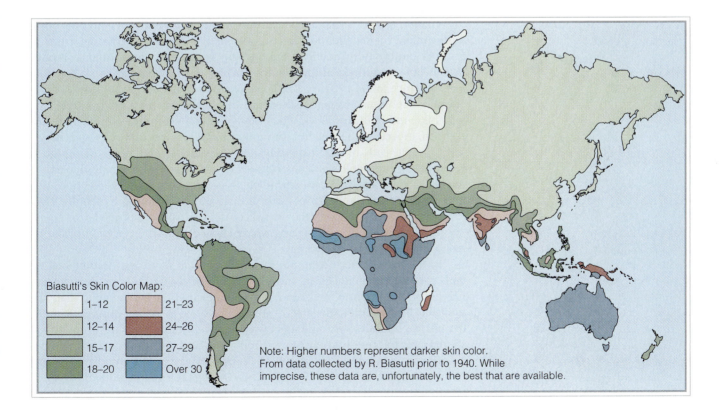

Biasutti's Skin Color Map:

1–12	21–23
12–14	24–26
15–17	27–29
18–20	Over 30

Note: Higher numbers represent darker skin color. From data collected by R. Biasutti prior to 1940. While imprecise, these data are, unfortunately, the best that are available.

FIGURE 15–3

An African albino.

small amounts of melanin, but have a reduced capacity for such temporary increases in melanin production.

Natural selection appears to have favored dark skin in areas nearest to the equator, where the sun's rays are most direct and thus where exposure to UV light is most intense. In considering the potentially harmful effects of ultraviolet radiation from an *evolutionary* perspective, three points must be kept in mind: (1) Early hominids lived mostly in the tropics, where solar radiation is more intense than in temperate areas like northwestern Europe; (2) unlike modern city dwellers, most earlier hominids spent the majority of time outdoors; and (3) early hominids did not wear clothing that would have provided some protection from the sun. Given these conditions, ultraviolet radiation could indeed have been a powerful agent selecting for optimum levels of melanin production in early human ancestors.

As hominids migrated out of Africa into Europe and Asia, selective pressures changed. In particular, those populations that eventually occupied northern Europe encountered cold temperatures and cloudy skies sometimes during the summer as well as in winter. Winter also meant fewer hours of daylight, and with the sun well to the south, solar radiation was indirect. Moreover, since physiological adaptations were not sufficient to meet the demands of living in colder climates, these populations had undoubtedly adopted certain cultural practices, such as using fire and wearing animal skins and other types of clothing. As a consequence of reduced exposure to sunlight, the advantages provided by deeply pigmented skin in the tropics were no longer important, and selection for melanin production may have been relaxed (Brace and Montagu, 1977).

However, relaxed selection for dark skin is probably not adequate to explain the very depigmented skin seen especially in some northern Europeans. More than likely, another factor, the need for adequate amounts of vitamin D, was also critical. The theory concerning the possible role of vitamin D, known as the *vitamin D hypothesis*, offers the following explanation.

Vitamin D plays a vital role in the mineralization and normal growth of bone during infancy and childhood and is available in a few foods, including fish oils, egg yolk, butter, cream, and liver. But the body's primary source of vitamin D is its own ability to synthesize it through the interaction of UV light and a cholesterol-like substance found in skin cells. Therefore, if normal bone growth is to occur, adequate exposure to sunlight is essential. Insufficient amounts of vitamin D during childhood result in *rickets,* which leads to bone deformities throughout the skeleton, especially the weight-bearing bones of the lower extremity and pelvis. Thus, people with rickets frequently have bowed legs and pelvic deformities. Pelvic deformities are of particular concern for women, for they can lead to a narrowing of the birth canal, which, in the absence of surgical intervention, frequently results in the death of both mother and fetus during childbirth. This example illustrates the potential for rickets as a significant selective factor favoring less pigmented skin in regions where climate and other factors operate to reduce exposure to UV radiation.

In the past, reduced exposure to sunlight would have been detrimental to darker-skinned individuals in more northern latitudes. In these individuals, higher concentrations of melanin filtered out much of the UV radiation that was available. If, in addition, the diets of groups that came to inhabit northern Europe did not provide adequate amounts of vitamin D, selective pressures would have shifted even further over time to favor less pigmented skin.

There is substantial evidence, both historically and in contemporary populations, to support the vitamin D hypothesis. During the latter decades of the nineteenth century, black inhabitants of northern U.S. cities suffered a higher incidence of rickets than whites. Northern blacks were also more commonly affected than blacks living in the South, where exposure to sunlight is greater. (The supplementation of milk with vitamin D was initiated to alleviate this problem.) Another example is seen in Britain, where darker-skinned East Indians and Pakistanis show a higher incidence of rickets than whites (Molnar, 1983).

Perhaps more social importance has been attached to variation in skin color than to any other single human biological trait. In point of fact, there is no reason this should be so. Aside from its probable adaptive significance relative to UV radiation, skin color is no more important physiologically than many other biological characteristics. But from an evolutionary perspective, skin color provides an outstanding example of how the forces of natural selection have produced geographically patterned variation as the consequence of two conflicting selective forces: the need for protection from overexposure to UV radiation, on the one hand, and the need for adequate UV exposure for vitamin D synthesis on the other.

The Thermal Environment

Mammals and birds have evolved complex mechanisms to maintain a constant internal body temperature. While reptiles must rely on exposure to external heat sources to raise body temperature and energy levels, mammals and birds possess physiological mechanisms that, within certain limits, increase or reduce the loss of body heat. The optimum body temperature for normal cellular functions is species-specific, and for humans it is approximately 98.6° F.

Homo sapiens is found in a wide variety of habitats, with thermal environments ranging from exceedingly hot (in excess of 120° F) to bitter cold (less than −60° F). In such extremes, particularly cold, human life would not be possible without cultural innovations. But even accounting for the artificial environments in which we live, such external conditions place the human body under enormous stress.

Response to Heat   All available evidence suggests that the earliest hominids evolved in the warm-to-hot savannas of East Africa. The fact that humans cope better with heat than they do with cold is testimony to the long-term adaptations to heat that evolved in our ancestors.

In humans, as well as certain other species, such as horses, sweat glands are distributed throughout the skin. This wide distribution of sweat glands makes possible the loss of heat at the body surface through evaporative cooling, a mechanism that has evolved to the greatest degree in humans.

The capacity to dissipate heat by sweating is seen in all human populations to an almost equal degree, with the average number of sweat glands per individual (approximately 1.6 million) being fairly constant. However, there is variation in that persons not generally exposed to hot conditions do experience a period of acclimatization that initially involves significantly increased perspiration rates (Frisancho, 1993). An additional factor that enhances the cooling effects of sweating is increased exposure of the skin through reduced amounts of body hair. We do not know when in our evolutionary history loss of body hair began, but it represents a species-wide adaptation.

Heat reduction through evaporation can be expensive, and indeed dangerous, in terms of water and sodium loss. Up to 3 liters of water can be lost by an average human engaged in heavy work in high heat. The importance of this fact can be appreciated if you consider that the loss of 1 liter of water is approximately equivalent to losing 1.5 percent of total body weight, and loss of 10 percent of body weight can be life threatening.

■ **Vasodilation**
Expansion of blood vessels, permitting increased blood flow to the skin. Vasodilation permits warming of the skin and also facilitates radiation of warmth as a means of cooling. Vasodilation is an involuntary response to warm temperatures, various drugs, and even emotional states (blushing).

Another mechanism for radiating body heat is **vasodilation**, whereby capillaries near the skin's surface widen to permit increased blood flow to the skin. The visible effect of vasodilation is flushing, or increased redness of the skin, particularly of the face, accompanied by warmth. But the physiological effect is to permit heat, carried by the blood from the interior of the body, to be emitted from the skin's surface to the surrounding air. (Some drugs, including alcohol, also produce vasodilation, which accounts for the increased redness and warmth of the face in some people.)

Body size and proportions are also important in regulating body temperature. In fact, there seems to be a general relationship between climate and body size and shape in birds and mammals. In general, within a species, body size (weight) increases as distance from the equator increases. In humans, this relationship holds up fairly well, but there are numerous exceptions.

Two rules that pertain to the relationship between body size, body proportions, and climate are *Bergmann's rule* and *Allen's rule.*

1. *Bergmann's rule (concerns the relationship of body mass or volume to surface area):* Among mammals, body size tends to be greater in populations that live in colder climates. This is because as mass increases, the relative amount of surface area decreases proportionately. Because heat is lost at the surface, it follows that increased mass allows for greater heat retention and reduced heat loss.

2. *Allen's rule (concerns shape of body, especially appendages):* In colder climates, shorter appendages, with increased mass-to-surface ratios, are adaptive because they are more effective at preventing heat loss. Conversely, longer appendages, with increased surface area relative to mass, are more adaptive in warmer climates because they promote heat loss.

According to these rules, the most suitable body shape in hot climates is linear with long arms and legs. In a cold climate, a more suitable body type is stocky with shorter limbs. Considerable data gathered from several human populations generally conform to these principles. In colder climates, body mass tends, on average, to be greater and characterized by a larger trunk relative to arms and legs (Roberts, 1973). People living in the Arctic tend to be short and stocky, while many sub-Saharan Africans, especially the East African pastoralists, are tall and linear (Fig. 15–4). But there is much human variability regarding body proportions, and not all populations conform so obviously to Bergmann's and Allen's rules.

Response to Cold   Human physiological responses to cold increase heat production and enhance heat retention. Of the two, heat retention is more efficient because less energy is required. This is an important point because energy is derived from dietary sources. Unless food resources are abundant, and in winter they frequently are not, any factor that conserves energy can have adaptive value.

Short-term responses to cold include increased metabolic rate and shivering, both of which generate body heat, at least for a short time. **Vasoconstriction**, another short-term response, restricts heat loss and conserves energy. In addition, humans possess a subcutaneous (beneath the skin) fat layer that serves as insulation throughout the body. Behavioral modifications include increased activity, increased food consumption, and assuming a curled-up position.

Increases in metabolic rate (the rate at which cells break up nutrients into their components) release energy in the form of heat. Shivering also generates muscle heat, as does voluntary exercise. But these methods of heat production are expensive because they require an increased intake of nutrients to provide needed

■ **Vasoconstriction**
Narrowing of blood vessels to reduce blood flow to the skin. Vasoconstriction is an involuntary response to cold and reduces heat loss at the skin's surface.

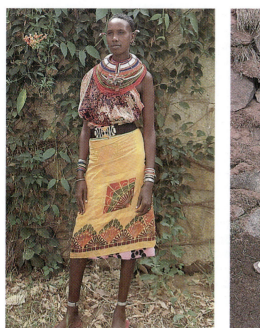

(a)

(b)

FIGURE 15–4
(a) This African woman has the linear proportions characteristic of many inhabitants of sub-Saharan Africa. (b) By comparison, the Inuit woman is short and stocky. These two individuals serve as good examples of Bergmann's and Allen's rules.

energy. (Perhaps this explains why we tend to have a heartier appetite during the winter and why we also tend to increase our intake of fats and carbohydrates, the very sources of energy our bodies require.)

In general, people exposed to chronic cold (meaning much or most of the year) maintain higher metabolic rates than those living in warmer climates. The Inuit (Eskimo) people living in the Arctic maintain metabolic rates between 13 and 45 percent higher than observed in non-Inuit control subjects (Frisancho, 1993). Moreover, the highest metabolic rates are seen in inland Inuit, who are exposed to even greater cold stress than coastal populations. Traditionally, the Inuit had the highest animal protein and fat diet of any population in the world. Such a diet, necessitated by the available resource base, served to maintain the high metabolic rates required by exposure to chronic cold.

Vasoconstriction restricts capillary blood flow to the surface of the skin, thus reducing heat loss at the body surface. Because retaining body heat is more economical than creating it, vasoconstriction is very efficient, provided temperatures do not drop below freezing. However, if temperatures do fall below freezing, continued vasoconstriction can allow the skin temperature to decrease to the point of frostbite or worse.

Long-term responses to cold vary among human groups. For example, in the past, desert-dwelling native Australian populations were subjected to wide temperature fluctuations from day to night. As they wore no clothing and did not build shelters, their only protection from nighttime temperatures that hovered only a few degrees above freezing was provided by sleeping fires. They experienced continuous vasoconstriction throughout the night that permitted a degree of skin cooling most people would find extremely uncomfortable. But there was no threat of frostbite, and continued vasoconstriction helped prevent excessive internal heat loss.

By contrast, the Inuit experience intermittent periods of vasoconstriction and vasodilation. This compromise provides periodic warmth to the skin that helps prevent frostbite in below-freezing temperatures. At the same time, because vasodilation is intermittent, energy loss is restricted, with more heat retained at the body's core.

The preceding examples illustrate but two of the many ways in which human populations vary with regard to adaptation to cold. Although all humans respond to cold stress in much the same manner, there is variation in how adaptation and acclimatization are manifested.

High Altitude

Today, perhaps as many as 25 million people live at altitudes above 10,000 feet. In Tibet, permanent settlements exist above 15,000 feet, and in the Andes, they can be found as high as 17,000 feet (Fig. 15–5).

At such altitudes, multiple factors produce stress on the human body. These include **hypoxia** (reduced available oxygen), more intense solar radiation, cold, low humidity, wind (which amplifies cold stress), a reduced nutritional base, and rough terrain. Of these, hypoxia exerts the greatest amount of stress on human physiological systems, especially the heart, lungs, and brain.

Hypoxia results from reduced barometric pressure. It is not that there is less oxygen in the atmosphere at high altitudes; rather, it is less concentrated. Therefore, to obtain the same amount of oxygen at 9,000 feet as at sea level, people must make certain physiological alterations aimed at increasing the body's ability to transport and utilize efficiently the oxygen that is available.

People who reside at higher elevations, especially recent immigrants, display a number of manifestations of their hypoxic environment. Reproduction, in particular, is affected through increased rates of infant mortality, miscarriage, and prematurity. In Colorado, for example, infant deaths are nearly twice as common above 8,200 feet (2,500 m) as at lower elevations. Low birth weight is also more common and is attributed to decreased fetal growth due to impaired maternal-fetal transport of oxygen (Moore and Regensteiner, 1983).

■ **Hypoxia**
Lack of oxygen. Hypoxia can refer to reduced amounts of available oxygen in the atmosphere (due to lowered barometric pressure) or to insufficient amounts of oxygen in the body.

FIGURE 15–5
(a) La Paz, Bolivia, at just over 12,000 feet above sea level, is home to 1 million people. (b) A household in northern Tibet, situated at an elevation of over 15,000 feet above sea level.

(a)

(b)

Compared to populations at lower elevations, lifelong residents of high altitude display slowed growth and maturation. Other differences include larger chest size, associated, in turn, with greater lung volume and larger hearts.

High-altitude natives and nonnatives exhibit certain differences in acclimatization and adaptation to hypoxia. Frisancho (1993) calls these different responses "adult acclimatization" and "developmental acclimatization." *Adult acclimatization* occurs upon exposure to high altitude in people born at low elevation. The responses may be short-term modifications, depending on duration of stay, but they begin within hours of the altitude change. These changes include an increase in respiration rate, heart rate, and production of red blood cells. (Red blood cells contain hemoglobin, the protein responsible for transporting oxygen to organs and tissues.)

Developmental acclimatization occurs in high-altitude natives during growth and development. (Note that this type of acclimatization is present only in people who grow up in high-altitude areas, not in those who moved there as adults.) In addition to greater lung capacity, people born at high altitudes are more efficient than migrants at diffusing oxygen from blood to body tissues. Hence, they do not rely as heavily on increased red cell formation as do newcomers. Developmental acclimatization serves as a good example of physiological plasticity by illustrating how, within the limits set by genetic factors, development can be influenced by environment.

There is evidence that some *populations* have also genetically adapted to high altitudes. Indigenous peoples of Tibet who have inhabited regions higher than 12,000 feet for around 25,000 years may have made genetic (i.e., evolutionary) accommodations to hypoxia. Altitude does not appear to affect reproduction in these people to the degree it does in other populations. Infants have birth weights as high as those of lowland Tibetan groups and higher than those of recent (20 to 30 years) Chinese immigrants. This fact may be the result of alterations in maternal blood flow to the uterus during pregnancy (Moore et al., 1994).

Another line of evidence concerns the utilization of glucose (blood sugar). Glucose is critical because it is the only source of energy used by the brain, and it is also utilized, although not exclusively, by the heart. Both highland Tibetans and the Quechua (inhabitants of high-altitude regions of the Peruvian Andes) burn glucose in a way that permits more efficient use of oxygen. This implies the presence of genetic mutations in the mitochondrial DNA that directs how cells use glucose. It also implies that natural selection has acted to increase the frequency of these advantageous mutations in these groups.

There is no certain evidence that Tibetans and Quechua have made evolutionary changes to accommodate high-altitude hypoxia. Moreover, the genetic mechanisms that underlie these populations' unique abilities have not been identified. The new data are intriguing, however, and strongly suggest that selection has operated to produce evolutionary change in these two groups. If further study supports these findings, we have an excellent example of evolution in action producing long-term adaptation at the population level.

Infectious Disease

Infection, as opposed to other disease categories, such as degenerative or genetic disease, is a category that includes those pathological conditions caused by microorganisms (viruses, bacteria, and fungi). Throughout the course of human evolution, infectious disease has exerted enormous selective pressures on populations and thus has influenced the frequency of certain alleles that affect the immune response. Indeed, it would be difficult to overemphasize the importance of infectious disease as an agent of natural selection in human populations. But as important as infectious disease has been, its role in this regard is not very well documented.

The effects of infectious disease on humans are mediated culturally as well as biologically. Innumerable cultural factors, such as architectural styles, subsistence techniques, exposure to domesticated animals, even religious practices, all affect how infectious disease develops and persists within and between populations.

Until about 10,000 to 12,000 years ago, all humans lived in small nomadic hunting and gathering groups. As these groups rarely remained in one location more than a few days at a time, they had minimal contact with refuse heaps that house disease **vectors.** But with the domestication of plants and animals, people became more sedentary and began living in small villages. Gradually, villages became towns, and towns, in turn, developed into densely crowded, unsanitary cities.

As long as humans lived in small bands, there was little opportunity for infectious disease to have much impact on large numbers of people. Even if an entire local group or band were wiped out, the effect on the overall population in a given area would have been negligible. Moreover, for a disease to become **endemic** in a population, sufficient numbers of people must be present. Therefore, small bands of hunter-gatherers were not faced with continuous exposure to endemic disease.

But with the advent of settled living and association with domesticated animals, opportunities for disease increased. As sedentary life permitted larger group size, it became possible for some diseases to become permanently established in some populations. Moreover, exposure to domestic animals, such as cattle, provided an opportune environment for the spread of such maladies as tuberculosis. The crowded, unsanitary conditions that characterized parts of all cities until the late nineteenth century, and that persist in much of the world today, further added to the disease burden borne by human inhabitants.

Malaria provides perhaps the best-documented example of how disease can act to change allele frequencies in human populations. In Chapter 4, you saw how malaria has operated in some African and Mediterranean populations to alter allele frequencies at the locus governing hemoglobin formation. In spite of extensive long-term eradication programs, malaria still poses a serious threat to human health. Indeed, the World Health Organization estimates the number of people currently infected with malaria to be between 300 and 500 million worldwide. This number is increasing, also, as drug-resistant strains of the disease-causing microorganism become more common (Olliaro et al., 1995).

Another example of the selective role of infectious disease is indirectly provided by AIDS (acquired immune deficiency syndrome). In the United States, the first cases of AIDS were reported in 1981. Since that time, perhaps as many as 1.5 million people have been infected by HIV (human immunodeficiency virus), the agent that causes AIDS. As of December 1998, nearly 412,000 had died.

But most of the burden of AIDS is borne by developing countries, where 95 percent of all HIV-infected people live. Worldwide, an estimated 33.4 million people are living with HIV infection, and an estimated 14 million have died.

A few words about viral infection are warranted here. Unlike bacteria, viruses are not living cells. Most viruses are composed of strands of DNA encased within a protein shell. Once a virus enters a host's body, it invades target cells and inserts its own DNA into the cell's cytoplasm. By thus gaining control of some cellular functions, the viral DNA directs the cell to produce virus particles. The new viruses eventually spill out to invade other cells, frequently killing the original host cell in

■ Vectors
Agents that serve to transmit disease from one carrier to another. Mosquitoes are vectors for malaria, just as fleas are vectors for bubonic plague.

■ Endemic
Continuously present in a population.

Virtual Lab 2, section III, part B, provides a discussion of the human adaptive response to malaria.

the process. In response to viral assault, the host's immune system mounts various defenses, which, if successful, keep the infection under control and the host symptom free. In fact, immune response is the basis for vaccination (more accurately called immunization). Because viruses do not respond to antibiotic treatment, immunization is the only effective method of fighting viral disease.

HIV was first identified and described in 1985, at which time it was assigned to a family of viruses called *retroviruses*. Retroviruses contain RNA instead of DNA, and they are unique in their ability to convert their RNA to DNA once they have entered a target cell. They are also unique in that the newly formed viral DNA becomes incorporated directly into the host cell's nuclear or chromosomal DNA. Since the 1970s, when retroviruses were first identified, a number of species-specific forms have been identified, including those that cause disease in cats, sheep, horses, cattle, monkeys, and humans. In general, retroviruses cause various forms of leukemia or, as in the case of HIV, they directly attack immune cells and cause immune deficiencies. The reason that HIV is so lethal is that it attacks the very cells capable of combating it.

HIV is transmitted from person to person through the exchange of bodily fluids, usually blood or semen. It is not spread through casual contact with an infected person. Within six months of infection, most persons test positive for anti-HIV antibodies, meaning that their immune system has recognized the presence of foreign antigens and has responded by producing antibodies. However, serious HIV-related symptoms may not appear for years. HIV is a "slow virus" in that it may persist in a host's body for years before the onset of severe illness. This asymptomatic state is called a "latency period," and the average latency period in the United States is over 11 years.

Like all viruses, HIV must invade certain types of cells and alter the functions of those cells to produce more virus particles in a process that eventually leads to cell destruction. (The manner in which HIV accomplishes this task is different from that of many other viruses.) HIV can attack various types of cells, but it especially targets so-called T4 helper cells, which are major components of the immune system. As HIV infection spreads and T4 cells are destroyed, the patient's immune system begins to fail. Consequently, he or she begins to exhibit symptoms caused by various **pathogens** that are commonly present but usually kept in check by a normal immune response. When an HIV-infected person's T cell count drops to a level that indicates immune suppression, and when symptoms of "opportunistic" infections appear, the patient is said to have AIDS.

By the early 1990s, scientists were aware of a number of patients who had been HIV positive for 10 to 15 years, but who continued to show few if any symptoms. Awareness of these patients led researchers to suspect that some individuals possess a natural immunity or resistance to HIV infection. This was shown to be true in late 1996 with the publication of two different studies (Dean et al., 1996; Samson et al., 1996) that demonstrated a mechanism for resistance to HIV.

These two reports describe a genetic mutation that concerns a major protein "receptor site" on the surface of certain immune cells, including T4 cells. (Receptor sites are protein molecules that enable HIV and other viruses to invade cells.) In this particular situation, the mutant allele results in a malfunctioning receptor site to which HIV is unable to bind, and current evidence now strongly suggests that individuals who are homozygous for this allele may be completely resistant to many types of HIV infection. In heterozygotes, infection may still occur, but the course of HIV disease is markedly slowed.

Interestingly, and for unknown reasons, the mutant allele occurs mainly in people of European descent, among whom its frequency is about 10 percent. Samson and colleagues (1996) reported that in the Japanese and West African samples they studied, the mutation was absent, but Dean and colleagues (1996)

■ Pathogens
Substances or microorganisms, such as bacteria, fungi, or viruses, that cause disease.

reported an allele frequency of about 2 percent among African Americans. These researchers speculate that the presence of the allele in African Americans may be entirely due to genetic admixture (gene flow) with American whites. Moreover, they suggest that this polymorphism exists in Europeans as a result of selective pressures favoring an allele that originally occurred as a rare mutation. But, it is critical to note, the original selective agent was *not* HIV. Instead, it was some other, as yet unidentified pathogen that requires the same receptor site as HIV.

O'Brien and Dean (1997) believe that a devastating epidemic of some type occurred well after humans migrated out of Africa and perhaps as recently as about 4,000 years ago. They assume that this event occurred in north-central Europe and in what is now Russia, because these are the regions where the mutant allele reaches its highest frequencies (around 13 percent) today. But the low population density of northern Europe at that time makes an epidemic unlikely. Perhaps the mutant allele increased in frequency because of some endemic infectious disease or even recurring episodes of infection over a long period of time. Regardless of how these events occurred, the receptor site mutation provides an excellent example of how a mutation that has been favored by selection because it provides protection against one disease can also increase resistance to another condition, in this case, AIDS.

The Continuing Impact of Infectious Disease

It is important to realize that humans and pathogens exert selective pressures on each other, creating a dynamic relationship between disease organisms and their human (and nonhuman) hosts. Just as disease exerts selective pressures on host populations to adapt, microorganisms also evolve and adapt to various pressures exerted on them by their hosts.

Evolutionarily speaking, it is to the advantage of any pathogen not to be so virulent as to kill its host too quickly. If the host dies shortly after becoming infected, the viral or bacterial agent may not have time to reproduce and infect other hosts. Thus, selection sometimes acts to produce resistance in host populations and/or to reduce the virulence of disease organisms, to the benefit of both. However, hosts exposed for the first time to a new disease frequently die in huge numbers. Such exposure was a major factor in the decimation of indigenous New World populations after contact with Europeans introduced smallpox into Native American groups. And, this has been the case with the current worldwide spread of HIV.

Of the known disease-causing organisms, HIV provides the best documented example of evolution and adaptation in a pathogen. It is also one of several examples of interspecies transfer of infection. For these reasons, we focus much of this discussion of evolutionary factors and infectious disease on HIV and AIDS.

HIV is the most mutable and genetically variable virus known. The type of HIV responsible for the AIDS epidemic is HIV-1, which in turn, is divided into three major subtypes comprising at least 10 different varieties that vary genetically from one population to another (Hu et al., 1996; Gao, 1999). Another, far less common type, is HIV-2, which is present only in populations of West Africa. HIV-2 also exhibits a wide range of genetic diversity and, while some strains cause AIDS, others are far less virulent.

Since the late 1980s researchers have been comparing the DNA sequences of HIV and a closely related retrovirus called *simian immunodeficiency virus* (SIV). SIV is found in chimpanzees and several African monkey species. Like HIV, SIV is genetically variable and each strain appears to be specific to a given species and even subspecies of primate. SIV produces no symptoms in the African monkeys and chimpanzees that are its traditional hosts, but when injected into Asian monkeys, it eventually causes immune suppression, AIDS-like symptoms, and death. These findings indicate that the various forms of SIV have shared a long evolutionary history (perhaps several hundred thousand years) with a number of African primate species, and that the latter are able to accommodate this virus which is deadly to their Asian relatives. Moreover, these results substantiate long held hypotheses that SIV and HIV evolved in Africa.

Comparisons of the DNA sequences of HIV-2 and the form of SIV found in one monkey species (the sooty mangabey) revealed that, genetically, these two viruses are almost identical. These findings led to the generally accepted conclusion that HIV-2 evolved from sooty mangabey SIV. Moreover, sooty mangabeys are hunted for food and also kept as pets in West-central Africa and the transmission of SIV to humans probably occurred through bites and the butchering of monkey carcasses.

But, although the origin of HIV-2 was established, there was continuing debate over which primate species had been the source of HIV-1. Recently, a group of medical researchers (Gao et al., 1999) compared DNA sequences of HIV-1 and the form of SIV found in chimpanzees indigenous to West central Africa. The results of this research have demonstrated that HIV-1 almost certainly evolved from the strain of chimpanzee SIV that infects the subspecies *Pan troglodytes troglodytes,* which is indigenous to central Africa.

Unfortunately for both species, chimpanzees are routinely hunted for food in parts of West Africa (see p. 136). Consequently, the most probable explanation for the transmission of SIV from chimpanzees to humans was, as with sooty mangabeys, the hunting and butchering of chimpanzees (Gao et al., 1999; Weiss and Wrangham, 1999). The DNA evidence further suggests that there were at least three separate human exposures to chimpanzee SIV and, at some point, the virus was altered to the form we call HIV. When chimpanzee SIV was transmitted to humans is unknown. The oldest evidence of human infection is a frozen, HIV-positive blood sample that was taken from a West African patient in 1959. There are also a few documented cases of AIDS infection by the late 1960s and early 1970s. Therefore, although human exposure to SIV/HIV probably occurred many times in the past, the virus did not become firmly established in humans until the latter half of the twentieth century.

From this SIV/HIV example you can appreciate how, through the adoption of various cultural practices, humans have radically altered patterns of infectious disease. Here, then, is another example of biocultural evolution in our species. The interaction of cultural and biological factors has influenced microevolutionary change in humans (as in the example of sickle-cell anemia) to accommodate altered relationships with disease organisms.

Until the twentieth century, infectious disease was the number one cause of death in all human populations. Even today, in many developing countries, as much as half the mortality is due to infectious disease, compared to about 10 percent in the United States. In the United States and other developed nations, with improved living conditions and sanitation and especially with the widespread use of antibiotics beginning in the late 1940s, infectious disease gave way to heart disease and cancer as the leading causes of death.

Optimistic predictions held that infectious disease would be a thing of the past in developed countries and, with the introduction of antibiotics and improved living standards, in developing nations as well. But by the mid-1980s, such predictions were increasingly seen to be wrong. Between 1980 and 1992, the number of deaths in the United States in which infectious disease was the underlying cause rose from 41 to 65 per 100,000, an increase of 58 percent (Pinner et al., 1996). During that same period, there was a 25 percent increase in infectious disease mortality among people aged 65 and older, from 271 to 338 per 100,000. And deaths due to respiratory tract infections rose from 25 to 30 deaths per 100,000.

Additionally, AIDS contributed substantially to the increase in mortality due to infectious disease in the United States between 1980 and 1992. By 1992, AIDS was the leading cause of death in men aged 25 to 44 years. As of 1998, mortality due to AIDS had decreased significantly, but even when subtracting the effect of AIDS in mortality rates, there was still a 22 percent increase in mortality rates due to infectious disease between 1980 and 1992 (Pinner et al., 1996).

A discussion of antibiotic resistance is provided in Virtual Lab 2, section III, part B.

Increase in the prevalence of infectious disease is perhaps partly due to the overuse of antibiotics. It is estimated that half of all antibiotics prescribed in the United States are used to treat viral conditions such as colds and flu. Because antibiotics are completely ineffective against viruses, such therapy not only is useless, it may also have dangerous long-term consequences. There is a growing concern in the biomedical community over the effects of antibiotic and pesticide use, practices that have flourished since the 1950s. Antibiotics have exerted selective pressures on bacterial species that have, over time, developed antibiotic-resistant strains (an excellent example of natural selection). Consequently, the past few years have seen the *reemergence* of many bacterial diseases, including influenza, pneumonia, tuberculosis, and cholera, in forms that are less responsive to treatment.

Tuberculosis is now listed as the world's leading killer of adults by the World Health Organization (Colwell, 1996). In fact, the number of tuberculosis cases has risen 28 percent since the mid-1980s worldwide, with an estimated 10 million infected in the United States alone. Although not all infected persons develop active disease, an estimated 30 million are believed to have died from TB in the 1990s worldwide. One very troubling aspect of the increase in tuberculosis infection is that newly developed strains of *Mycobacterium tuberculosis,* the bacterium that causes TB, are resistant to antibiotics and other treatments.

Cholera, a dangerous and often fatal gastrointestinal disease caused by *Vibrio cholerae,* a bacterium found in sewage-contaminated water, has periodically occurred in epidemic proportions throughout history, including outbreaks in the nineteenth century in New York, Philadelphia, and London. Currently, cholera claims about 100,000 lives annually in Asia alone, and an antibiotic-resistant strain, first identified in India in 1992, is spreading throughout Southeast Asia. Recent cholera outbreaks throughout much of South America, India, Bangladesh, China, and parts of Southeast Asia have been partly attributed to rising ocean temperatures, lack of sanitation, and overcrowding.

Various treatments for nonbacterial conditions have also become ineffective. One such example is the appearance of chloroquin-resistant malaria, which has rendered chloroquin (the traditional preventive medication) virtually useless in some parts of Africa. And many insect species have developed resistance to commonly used pesticides.

In addition to threats posed by resistant strains of pathogens, there are other factors that may contribute to the emergence (or reemergence) of infectious disease. Scientists are becoming increasingly concerned over the potential for global warming to expand the geographical range of numerous tropical disease vectors such as mosquitoes. And the destruction of natural environments not only contributes to global warming, it also has the potential of causing disease vectors formerly restricted to local areas to spread to new habitats.

One other factor associated with the rapid spread of disease and directly related to technological change is the mixing of people at an unprecedented rate. Indeed, an estimated 1 million people per day cross national borders by air (Lederberg, 1996)! In addition, new road construction and wider availability of

BOX 15–1

Overpopulation

I f we had to point to one challenge facing humanity, a problem to which virtually all others (water and air pollution, toxic waste, environmental destruction, global warming, and depletion of the ozone layer) are tied, it would be human population growth. Currently we are trapped in a destructive cycle of our own making. Population size has skyrocketed in our species as we have increased our ability to produce food surpluses. As population size increases, more land is converted to crops, pasture, and construction, providing for yet more humans. Additionally, through twentieth-century medical advances, we have reduced mortality at both ends of the life cycle. Thus, fewer people die in childhood, and, having survived to adulthood, the survivors live longer than ever before. Although these advances are unquestionably beneficial to individuals (who has not benefited from medical technology?), it is also clear that there are significant consequences detrimental to the species and to the planet.

Population size, if left unchecked, increases exponentially, that is, as a function of some percent, like compound interest in a bank account. Currently, human population increases worldwide at an annual rate of about 1.8 percent, but in many developing countries the rate is more than 3 percent.

Around 10,000 years ago, scientists estimate, only about 5 million people inhabited the earth (not even half as many as live in Los Angeles County or New York City today). By A.D. 1650, there were perhaps 500 million, and by 1800, 1 billion. In other words, between 10,000 years ago and A.D. 1650 (a period of 9,650 years), population size doubled seven and a half times. On average, then, from 1650 to 1800 it doubled again, which means that doubling time had been reduced to 150 years (Ehrlich and Ehrlich, 1990). And in the 37 years between 1950 and 1987, world population doubled from 2 billion to 4 billion.

Dates and associated population estimates up to the present are as follows: mid-1800s, 1 billion; 1930s, 2 billion; mid-1960s, 3 billion; mid-1980s, 4 billion; present, 6.0 billion (Fig. 1). To state this problem in terms we can appreciate, we add 90 to 95 million people to the world's population every year: an additional 1 billion people every 11 years and roughly a quarter of a million every day!

The most recent United Nations International Conference on Population and Development set as its goal the development of a plan to contain the world's population to about 7.3 billion by the year 2015 and to prevent future growth. Otherwise, by the year 2050, human numbers will approach 8 to 10 billion. The United Nations plan emphasizes women's education, health, and rights throughout the world, but it has met with stiff resistance from groups opposed to abortion and contraception. Certainly it is to be hoped that population growth can be curtailed. Otherwise, humans will continue to face new adaptive challenges posed by the increased crowding, changing disease patterns, and environmental degradation that accompany unprecedented numbers of people.

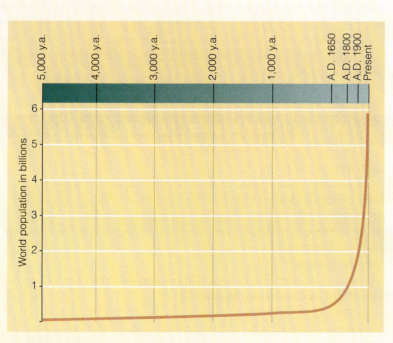

Figure 1 is a line graph depicting exponential growth of human population size worldwide. Note that for almost all of the last 5,000 years, the number of humans increased very slowly. It was not until 1650 that population size was even half a billion (500 million). The rapid increase to 1 billion by about 1850 is, in part, attributable to the Industrial Revolution.

motor-driven vehicles allow more people (armies, refugees, truck drivers, etc.) to travel farther and faster than ever before.

Fundamental to all these factors is human population size which, as it continues to soar, causes more environmental disturbance and, through additional human activity, adds further to global warming (see Box 15–1). Moreover, in developing countries, where as much as 50 percent of mortality is due to infectious disease, overcrowding and unsanitary conditions increasingly contribute to increased rates of communicable illness. One could scarcely conceive of a better set of circumstances for the appearance and spread of communicable disease, and it remains to be seen if scientific innovation and medical technology are able to meet the challenge.

It is still not clear what the long-term consequences of twentieth-century antibiotic therapy, pesticide-based eradication programs, environmental change, and human population growth will be on disease patterns. But there are many scientists who fear that we may not be able to develop new antibiotics and treatments fast enough to keep pace with the appearance of potentially deadly new bacteria and other pathogens. Thus, we have radically altered the course of evolution in some microbial species, just as they have altered our own evolutionary course in the past and clearly continue to do so in the present.

Summary

In this chapter, we have investigated some of the ways in which humans differ from one another, both within and between populations. We explored how this variation has been approached historically in terms of racial typologies and as a function of adaptation to a number of environmental factors, including solar radiation, heat, cold, and high altitude. We have also considered infectious disease, with particular emphasis on AIDS, and the dynamic relationship between pathogens and human hosts.

The topic of human variation is very complicated, and the biological and cultural factors that have contributed to that variation and that continue to influence it are manifold. But from an explicitly evolutionary perspective, it is through the investigation of changes in allele frequencies in response to environmental conditions that we will continue to elucidate the diverse adaptive potential that characterizes our species.

Questions for Review

1. What is a polytypic species?
2. What is a biological definition of race? Why is race socially important?
3. What is biological determinism?
4. What was the eugenics movement, and what were its goals?
5. How did eighteenth- and nineteenth-century European scientists deal with human phenotypic variation?
6. What is homeostasis?
7. Under what conditions might light skin color be adaptive? Under what conditions might dark skin color be adaptive?

8. What physiological adjustments do humans show in coping with cold stress?
9. What physiological adjustments do humans show in coping with heat stress?
10. What do body size and shape have to do with adaptation to climate?
11. What are Bergmann's and Allen's rules?
12. How has infectious disease influenced human evolution?
13. How has susceptibility to HIV been shown to vary between populations? What genetic and biological factors have led to this variation?
14. What is a cline, and how does a clinal approach to human phenotypic variation differ from a racial approach?
15. What components of high-altitude environments are most challenging to humans?
16. What are two effects of exposure to high altitude?
17. Discuss current culturally mediated factors that may contribute to the spread of infectious disease. Provide examples.

Suggested Further Reading

Bodmer, W. F., and L. L. Cavalli-Sforza. 1976. *Genetics, Evolution, and Man.* San Francisco: Freeman.

Discover. 1994. Special Issue: The Science of Race. 15 (November).

Frisancho, A. Roberto. 1993. *Human Adaptation and Accommodation.* Ann Arbor: University of Michigan Press.

Gould, Stephen Jay. 1981. *The Mismeasure of Man.* New York: Norton.

Jacoby, R., and N. Glauberman (eds). 1995. *The Bell Curve Debate.* New York: Times Books.

Journal of the American Medical Association, 1996. Entire issue, 275 (January 17). (Numerous articles pertaining to climate change and reemergence of infectious diseases.)

Leffell, David J., and Douglas E. Brash. 1996. "Sunlight and Skin Cancer." *Scientific American* 275(1): 52–59.

Nesse, Randolph M. and George C. Williams. 1998. "Evolution and the Origins of Disease." *Scientific American* 279(5): 86–93.

O'Brien, Stephen J. and Michael Dean. 1997. "In Search of AIDS-Resistance Genes." *Scientific American* 277(3): 44–51.

Ramenofsky, Ann F. 1992. "Death by Disease." *Archaeology* 45(2): 47–49.

Additional Resources

Multimedia Tools

- **Virtual Laboratories for Physical Anthropology CD-ROM**
  The following concepts in this chapter are covered on the physical anthropology CD-ROM:
  skin color, adaptation (Virtual Lab 2.IV)
  malaria, sickle-cell anemia (Virtual Lab 2.III.B)
  antibiotic resistance (Virtual Lab 2.III.B)

■ **Wadsworth Anthropology Resource Center**
http://anthropology.wadsworth.com
Visit Anthropology Online to obtain current updates in the field, surf-ing tips, career information and more. In addition, enrich your study efforts with text-specific study aids arranged by chapter.

■ **InfoTrac College Edition**
http://www.infotrac-college.com/wadsworth

1. Read "DNA Studies Challenge the Meaning of Race" by Eliot Marshall, *Science,* Oct 23, 1998 v282 i5389 p654(1) on InfoTrac College Edition. What does this article say about race? Now click on the LINK button to find more information on this topic. Given what you have learned, how would you define race? Is this a useful cate-gory of biological or social distinction?

2. InfoTrac College Edition provides many articles about eugenics and its effect on public policy. Search for *eugenics,* and read at least one article. Write a short (one-page) paper about how eugenics has affected politics and public policy. One good article to choose might be "Closets Full of Bones" by Peter Quinn, in *America,* or there are many other interesting articles relevant to this question.

3. Search InfoTrac College Edition for *human adaptation.* Choose one of these articles and, after reading it, write a brief report on the adapta-tion discussed, and how it may have evolved. If you do not find what you are looking for with this search, what other kinds of searches might you do to find articles about human adaptation? (hint: use PowerTrac)

■ **Internet Exercises**

1. Race is a sensitive topic in anthropology today. The Internet provides a good deal of information about race, racial distinctions, and the human variation that underlies the race concept. Just to get an idea of the scope of information on race, visit Yahoo! or another web search engine or index and search for the word *race.* How many dif-ferent pages did you find? What is the range of different topics in these sites? Now search for *human variation.* How are these sites dif-ferent from those you found when you searched for *race?*

2. Visit the American Anthropological Association Web site (**http://www.ameranthassn.org**) and read the AAA statement on "Race" and the statement on the "Misuse of 'Scientific Findings' to promote Bigotry and Racial and Ethnic Hatred and Discrimination." Following the statement on race is the question, "Should the AAA adopt a position paper on 'Race'?" Now that you have finished this chapter, write an answer to this question.

Racial Purity:
A False and Dangerous Ideology

During the late nineteenth and early twentieth centuries, a growing sense of nationalism was sweeping Europe and the United States. At the same time, an increased emphasis on racial purity had been coupled with the more dangerous aspects of what is termed "biological determinism" (see page 412). The concept of pure races is based, in part, on the notion that in the past, races were composed of individuals who conformed to idealized types and who were similar in appearance and intellect. Over time, some variation had been introduced into these pure races through interbreeding with other groups, and increasingly, this type of "contamination" was seen as a threat to be avoided.

In today's terminology, pure races would be said to be genetically homogenous, or to possess little genetic variation. Everyone would have the same alleles at most of their loci. Actually, we do see this situation in "pure breeds" of domesticated animals and plants, developed *deliberately* by humans through selective breeding. We also see many of the detrimental consequences of such genetic uniformity in various congenital abnormalities, such as hip dysplasia in some breeds of dogs.

With our current understanding of genetic principles, we are able to appreciate the potentially negative outcomes of matings between genetically similar individuals. For example, we know that inbreeding increases the likelihood of offspring who are homozygous for certain deleterious recessive alleles. We also know that decreased genetic variation in a species diminishes the

potential for natural selection to act, thus compromising that species' ability to adapt to certain environmental fluctuations. Furthermore, in genetically uniform populations, individual fertility can be seriously reduced, potentially with disastrous consequences for the entire species. Thus, even if pure human races did exist at one time (and they did not), theirs would not have been a desirable condition genetically, and they most certainly would have been at an evolutionary disadvantage.

During the latter half of the nineteenth century, many Americans and Europeans had come to believe that nations could be ranked according to technological achievement. It followed that the industrial societies of the United States and Europe were considered to be the most advanced and to have attained a "higher level of civilization" owing to the "biological superiority" of their northern European forebears. This concept arose in part from the writings of Herbert Spencer, a British philosopher who misapplied the principles of natural selection to societies in a doctrine termed "social Darwinism." Spencer believed that societies evolved, and through competition, "less endowed" cultures and the "unfit" people in them would be weeded out. Indeed, it was Spencer who coined the much abused (and almost always misused) phrase "survival of the fittest," and his philosophy became widely accepted on both sides of the Atlantic, where its principles accorded well with notions of racial purity.

In northern Europe, particularly Germany, and in the United States,

"racial superiority" was increasingly embodied in the so-called "Aryan race." *Aryan* is a term that is still widely used, albeit erroneously, with biological connotations. Actually, "Aryan" does not refer to a biological unit or Mendelian population, as the majority of people who use the term intend it. Rather, it is a linguistic term that refers to an ancient language group that was ancestral to the Indo-European family of languages. (Among the many and varied modern Indo-European languages are Hindi, Persian, Greek, Polish, German, and English.)

By the early twentieth century, the "Aryans" had been transformed into a mythical super race of people whose noble traits were embodied in an extremely idealized "nordic type." The true "Aryan" was held to be tall, blond, blue-eyed, strong, industrious, and "pure in spirit." "Nordics" were extolled as the developers of all ancient "high" civilizations and as the founders of modern industrialized nations. In Europe, there was growing emphasis on the superiority of northwestern Europeans as the modern representatives of "true Nordic stock," while southern and eastern Europeans were viewed as inferior.

In the United States, there prevailed the strongly held opinion that America was originally settled by Christian "Nordics." Prior to about 1890, the majority of newcomers to the United States had come from Germany, Scandinavia, and Britain (including Ireland). But by the 1890s, the pattern of immigration had changed. The arrival of increasing numbers of Italians, Turks,

Racial Purity: A False and Dangerous Ideology (continued)

Greeks, and Jews among the thousands of newcomers raised fears that society was being contaminated by immigration from southern and eastern Europe.

Moreover, in the United States, there were additional concerns about the large population of former slaves and their descendants. As African Americans left the South in increasing numbers to work in the factories of the North, many unskilled white workers felt economically threatened by new competition. It was no coincidence that the Ku Klux Klan, which had been inactive for a number of years, was revived in 1915 and by the 1920s was preaching vehement opposition to blacks, Jews, and Catholics in support of the supremacy of the white, Protestant, "Nordic race." These sentiments were widespread in the general population, although they did not always take the extreme form extolled by the Klan. One result of these views was the Immigration Restriction Act of 1924, which was aimed at curtailing the immigration of "non-Nordics," including Italians, Jews, and eastern Europeans, in order to preserve America's "Nordic" heritage.

To avoid the further "decline of the superior race," many states practiced policies of racial segregation until the mid-1950s. Particularly in the South, segregation laws resulted in an almost total separation of whites and blacks, except where blacks were employed as servants or laborers. Moreover, *antimiscegenation* laws prohibited marriage between whites and blacks in over half the states, and unions between whites and Asians were frequently illegal as well. In several states, marriage between whites and blacks was punishable either as a misdemeanor or a felony, and astonishingly, some of these laws were not repealed until the late 1950s or early 1960s. Likewise, in Germany by 1935, the newly instituted Nuremberg Laws forbade marriage or sexual intercourse between so-called "Aryan" Germans and Jews.

The fact that belief in racial purity and superiority led ultimately to the Nazi death camps in World War II is undisputed (except for continuing efforts by certain white supremacist and neo-Nazi organizations). It is one of the great tragedies of the twentieth century that some of history's most glaring examples of discrimination and viciousness were perpetrated by people who believed that their actions were based in scientific principles. In reality, such beliefs constitute nothing more than myth. There is absolutely no evidence to suggest that pure human races ever existed. Indeed, such an idea flies in the face of everything we know about natural selection, recombination, and gene flow. The degree of genetic uniformity throughout our species (compared to some other species), as evidenced by mounting data from mitochondrial and nuclear DNA analysis, argues strongly that there has always been gene flow between human populations and that genetically homogenous races are nothing more than fabrication.

The numerous abuses committed in the name of racial purity in the twentieth century were, in part, outgrowths of the rise of nationalism in Europe and the United States during the late nineteenth century. Unfortunately, however, prejudice based on a belief in racial purity and superiority is alive and well. The dogma preached by such white supremacist groups as White Aryan Resistance is no different from that espoused by the Nazi leadership in pre-World War II Germany. The dangers of such thinking have been manifested in incalculable human suffering. As we stand at the threshold of the twenty-first century, we can but wonder if the generations who will see it to its conclusion will have learned from the mistakes of their predecessors.

Critical Thinking Questions

1. Given what you know about evolutionary factors, discuss why the notion of "pure races" is inaccurate. Also discuss why you think the concept of racial purity has been (and remains) so prevalent.

2. What is the concept of an "Aryan race," and why is it incorrect? Is this concept dead today?

16

The Anthropological Perspective on the Human Life Course

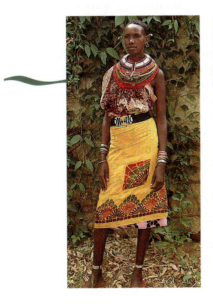

FIGURE 16–2

Skeletal age: epiphyseal union in the humerus. Some regions of the humerus exhibit some of the earliest fusion centers in the body, while others are among the latest to complete fusion (not until late adolescence).

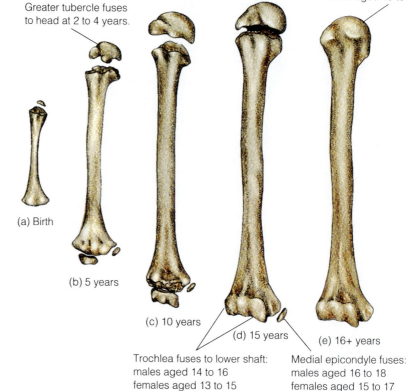

Greater tubercle fuses to head at 2 to 4 years.

Head fuses to shaft: males aged 16 to 18 females aged 15 to 17

(a) Birth

(b) 5 years

(c) 10 years

(d) 15 years

(e) 16+ years

Trochlea fuses to lower shaft: males aged 14 to 16 females aged 13 to 15

Medial epicondyle fuses: males aged 16 to 18 females aged 15 to 17

▮ Ossification

Process by which cartilage cells are replaced by bone cells.

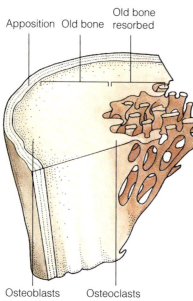

Apposition   Old bone   Old bone resorbed

Osteoblasts deposit new bone cells

Osteoclasts remove old bone cells

FIGURE 16–3

Bone cells are deposited on the outer portion of a bone by osteoblasts. In the interior of the shaft of the bone, osteoclasts remove bone, enlarging the marrow cavity.

✺ Bone Growth

Initially, the "skeleton" of the human fetus is made entirely of cartilage. This cartilage skeleton is sometimes referred to as a "model" of what the bony skeleton will look like. During growth, the cartilage cells are gradually broken down and replaced by bone cells in a process known as **ossification.** A newborn infant has more than 600 centers of bone growth in the body. During childhood, many segments of bone are connected to each other by cartilage, which decays more rapidly than bone deteriorates after death. As the child grows and the cartilage is replaced by bone, segments fuse to form adult bones, thus reducing the number of separate pieces. By the time growth is completed, there are approximately 206 bones.

Figure 16–2 shows the process of ossification of the humerus, or upper arm bone. The shaft is referred to as the *diaphysis,* and the ends are called the *epiphyses* (*sing.,* epiphysis). Growth in one end is completed when the epiphysis unites with the diaphysis. There are two types of cells responsible for bone growth. The *osteoclasts* remove or destroy bone or cartilage cells, while the *osteoblasts* deposit new bone cells. Growth of a bone occurs not only in length, as we have been discussing, but also in width. The shaft of the femur of an infant is much thinner than that of an adult, and the hollow interior is also much smaller. For the shaft to widen and for the interior to increase in size, osteoclasts must destroy bone in the inner part of the shaft while osteoblasts are continually depositing bone on the outer surface (Fig. 16–3). Such "appositional" growth continues throughout life, well after growth in length has been completed.

The epiphyses at the ends of long bones unite with their shafts in fairly pre-dictable patterns, enabling an anthropologist to estimate the age at death of young individuals from skeletal remains. For example, growth is completed in the elbow region in most people by approximately age 19 (a bit earlier in girls than in boys). What this means is that the epiphysis on the **distal** end of the humerus has united with the humeral shaft and the epiphyses at the **proximal** ends of the radius and ulna (lower arm bones) have united with their shafts (Fig. 16–4). By age 20 (again with some sex difference), the epiphyses have united in the hip and ankle regions. The epiphyses in the shoulder region do not unite until age 23, and the very last epiphyses to unite are in the medial clavicle, the projecting parts of the collarbone near the base of the throat.

Stature

Increased stature is a common indicator of health status in children because it is easy to assess under most circumstances. There are two ways in which increases in height are typically plotted on a graph. One way is to plot a *distance curve,* show-ing the height obtained in a given year. (Fig. 16–5a is a typical distance curve for height in an American girl.) Obvious growth spurts can be seen in early infancy and at puberty. Typically, well-nourished humans grow fairly rapidly during the first two trimesters (6 months) of fetal development, but growth slows during the third trimester. After birth, the rate of growth increases and remains fairly rapid for about four years, at which time it decreases again to a relatively slow, steady level that is maintained until puberty. At puberty, there is a very pronounced increase in growth. During this so-called **adolescent growth spurt,** Western teenagers typically grow 9 to 10 cm per year. Subsequent to the adolescent growth spurt, the rate of growth declines again and remains slower until adult stature is achieved by the late teens.

Another way to describe growth is to plot the amount of increase in height gained each year. This produces *a velocity curve* and depicts the growth spurts even more clearly (Fig. 16–5b). If we were to plot the height distance and velocity curves for a chimpanzee, a baboon, and a dog, we would see that the curves are different for each species. Some have argued that the human growth curve, with its characteristic spurt at adolescence, is unique to our species. Others argue that chimpanzees show small but significant spurts at puberty, making their curves similar to those of humans and suggesting that the adolescent growth spurt may be a characteristic that predates the separation of the chimpanzee and human evolutionary paths, approximately 5 to 7 million years ago. Nevertheless, no other mammal shows this characteristic to the same degree as do modern humans. In addition to total height, parts of the body (e.g., limbs, organs) also show similar growth curves, with rapid increases in the first trimester of gestation, during the first four years of life, and again at puberty.

Growth curves for boys and girls are significantly different, with the adoles-cent growth spurt occurring approximately two years earlier in girls than in boys (reflected in the fact that the ends of long bones unite earlier in girls than in boys). At birth, there is slight **sexual dimorphism** in many body measures (e.g., height, weight, head circumference, and body fat), but the major divergence in these characteristics does not occur until puberty. Table 16–1 shows the differ-ences between these measures for boys and girls at birth and at age 18. Boys are slightly larger than girls at birth and are even more so at age 18, except in the last two measures, triceps skinfold and subscapular skinfold. These two measurements give information on body fat content and are determined by a special skinfold

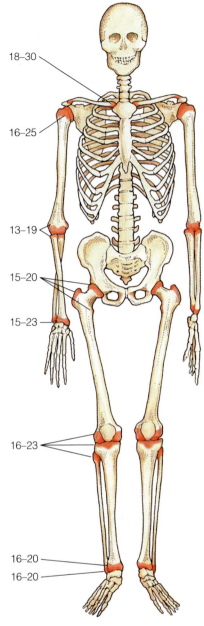

FIGURE 16–4

Ages of epiphyseal union. For example, the epiphyses unite in the elbow between ages 13 and 19.

▌ **Distal**

The end of a bone that is farthest from the point at which the bone attaches to the body. For example, the elbow is at the distal end of the humerus.

Proximal

The end of a bone that is closest to the point at which the bone attaches to the body. For example, the head of the humerus is on the proximal end.

Adolescent growth spurt

The period during adolescence in which well-nourished teens typically increase in stature at greater rates than at other points in the life cycle.

Sexual dimorphism

Differences in physical characteristics between males and females of the same species. For example, humans are slightly sexually dimorphic for body size, with males being taller, on average, than females of the same population.

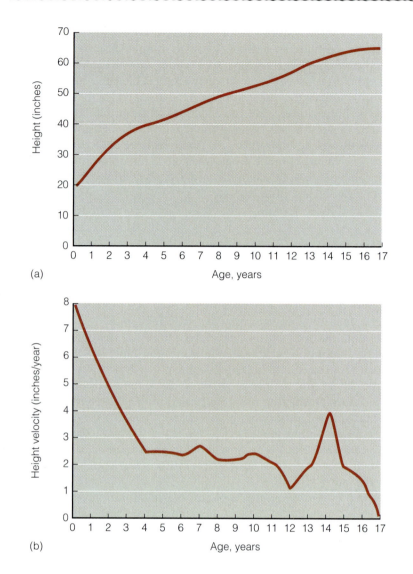

(a)

(b)

FIGURE 16–5

Distance and velocity curves of growth in height for a healthy American girl.

measuring caliper. The triceps skinfold measure is taken by gently pinching the skin and fat underneath the upper arm, and the subscapular measurement is taken by gently pinching the skin and fat below the shoulder blade. The measures in Table 16–1 reflect differences not only in the more obvious characteristics of height and weight, but also in body composition, with girls generally having more body fat than boys at all ages.

An individual's adult stature is influenced by genetics, health, and nutrition. In other words, children who experience good health and adequate nutrition during their growing years are much more likely to reach their genetic potential for height. On the other hand, children who are malnourished or experience prolonged periods of ill health may not reach that potential. In general, members of higher socioeconomic groups in a given population have taller average stature than members of lower socioeconomic groups, reflecting the impact of culture and economic status on the processes of growth and development (Bogin, 1998). This, then, is a good example of how growth is a result of biocultural processes.

TABLE 16–1	Some Measurements of Size at Birth and at Age 18 for Children Born in the United States			
	Boys		**Girls**	
	Birth	**18**	**Birth**	**18**
Recumbent length (cm)*	49.9	181.1	49.3	166.7
Weight (kg)*	3.4	69.9	3.3	55.6
Head circumference (cm)[†]	34.8	55.9	34.1	54.9
Triceps skinfold (mm)	3.8[††]	8.5[§]	4.1[††]	17.5[§]
Subscapular skinfold (mm)	3.5[††]	10.0[§]	3.8[††]	12.0[§]

* Hamill et al., 1977
[†] Nellhaus, 1968.
[††] Johnston and Beller, 1976.
[§] Johnson et al., 1981.

Source: From Bogin, 1988:22.

Brain Growth

The head is a relatively large part of the body at birth. The continued growth of the brain after birth occurs at a rate far greater than that of any other part of the body, with the exception of the eyeball. At birth, the human brain is about 25 percent of its adult size. By 6 months of age, the brain has doubled in size, reaching 50 percent of adult size. It reaches 75 percent of adult size at age $2^{1}/2$ years, 90 percent at age 5 years, and 95 percent by age 10 years. There is only a very small spurt at adolescence, making the brain an exception to the growth curves characteristic of most other parts of the body. As we will see later in this chapter, this pattern of brain growth, including the relatively small amount of growth before birth, is unusual among primates and other mammals. By contrast, the typical picture for most mammalian species is that at least 50 percent of adult brain size has been achieved prior to birth. For humans, however, the narrow pelvis necessary for walking bipedally provides limits on the size of the fetal head that can be delivered through it. That limitation, in addition to the value of having most brain growth occur in the more stimulating environment outside the womb, has resulted in human infants being born with far less of their total adult brain size than most other mammals. (As we saw in Chapter 11, this pattern of delayed maturation was probably already established in hominid evolution by 1.5 m.y.a.)

Nutritional Effects on Growth and Development

Nutrition has an impact on human growth at every stage of the life cycle. During pregnancy, for example, a woman's diet can have a profound effect on the development of her fetus and the eventual health of the child. Moreover, the effects are transgenerational, because a woman's own supply of eggs is developed while she herself is *in utero*. Thus, if a woman is malnourished during pregnancy, the eggs that develop in her female fetus may be damaged in a way that will impact the health of her future grandchildren.

Basic Nutrients for Growth and Development

Nutrients needed for growth, development, and body maintenance are organized into five major categories: proteins, carbohydrates, lipids (fats), vitamins, and minerals. As you learned in Chapter 3, *proteins,* composed of amino acids (see p. 49), are the major structural components of such structures as muscles, skin, hair, and most of the organs of the body. Antibodies and enzymes are proteins, as are most hormones. When you eat a meal, stomach and pancreatic enzymes break the protein down into the 20 amino acids described in Chapter 3. The amino acids are then absorbed into the bloodstream through the walls of the small intestine and are transported to other cells in the body, where they will be used in the synthesis of new proteins (the process by which this occurs is described in Chapter 3).

Carbohydrates are important sources of energy needed to run the body. Good sources of carbohydrates are potatoes, beans, and grains. Carbohydrate digestion begins in the mouth and continues in the small intestine, where simple sugars are absorbed into the bloodstream through the walls of the small intestine in a manner similar to that for amino acids. From there they are transported to the liver, where all are converted into glucose, the primary source of energy for the body. Indeed, glucose is the only source of energy utilized by the brain. The hormone insulin is responsible for regulating glucose levels in the blood and tissues. The condition in which insufficient amounts of insulin are produced or the cells are unable to respond to the insulin that is available is referred to as *diabetes*. We shall see later that diabetes, the eighth leading cause of death in the United States, is a disorder of relatively recent origin (Eaton, Shostak, and Konner, 1988). Glucose that is not needed for other functions is either converted into *glycogen,* a polysaccharide stored in the liver and muscles, or converted into fat. When levels of glucose fall too low, the glycogen can then be reconverted into glucose.

Lipids comprise the third major nutrient category and include fats and oils. Fats are broken down into fatty acids and are absorbed into the bloodstream through the walls of the small intestine. These fatty acids are then further broken down and stored until needed for energy.

Vitamins are another category of nutrients needed for growth and for a healthy, functioning body. Vitamins serve as components of enzymes that speed up chemical reactions. There are two categories of vitamins: those that are water-soluble (the B vitamins and vitamin C) and those that, like fats, are not soluble in water but are soluble in fat (vitamins A, D, E, and K). The fat-soluble vitamins can be stored, so a deficiency of any of them is slow to develop. Because water-soluble vitamins are excreted in urine, very little is stored; these vitamins must be consumed almost daily in order to maintain health.

Unlike other nutrients, minerals are not organic, but they, too, contribute to normal functioning and health. The minerals needed in the greatest quantity include calcium (this mineral alone makes up 2 percent of our body weight, mostly in the skeleton and teeth), phosphorus, potassium, sulfur, sodium, chlorine, and magnesium. Our requirements for iron are comparatively low, but this mineral plays a critical role in oxygen transport. Iron-deficiency anemia is one of the most common nutritional deficiency diseases worldwide, especially in women of reproductive age, whose iron needs are greater than those of men. Other essential minerals include iodine, zinc, manganese, copper, cobalt, fluoride, molybdenum, selenium, and chromium.

Evolution of Nutritional Requirements

Our nutritional requirements have coevolved with the types of food that were available to human ancestors throughout our evolutionary history. Because the earliest mammals and the first primates were probably insect-eaters, humans have inherited the ability to digest and process animal protein. Early primates also evolved the ability to process most vegetable material. Our more immediate ape-like ancestors were primarily fruit-eaters, so we are able to process fruits. Furthermore, human needs for specific vitamins and minerals reflect these ancestral nutritional adaptations. A good example is our requirement for vitamin C, also known as ascorbic acid. Vitamin C plays an important role in the metabolism of all foods and in the production of energy. It is a crucial organic compound for all animals—so crucial, in fact, that most animals are able to manufacture, or *synthesize,* it internally and need not depend on dietary sources. It is likely that most of the early primates were able to make their own vitamin C. As the monkeys evolved, however, they began to eat more leaves and fruits and less animal protein; thus, they were getting adequate amounts of vitamin C in their diets. At some point in early primate evolution (about 35 m.y.a.; see Chapter 8), it is hypothesized that some individuals "lost" the ability to synthesize vitamin C, perhaps through a genetic mutation. This loss would not have been disadvantageous as long as dietary sources of vitamin C were regularly available. In fact, it may have been selectively advantageous to conserve the energy required for the manufacture of vitamin C, so that natural selection favored those individuals in a species who were unable to synthesize it. Eventually, all descendants of these early higher primates (i.e., modern monkeys, apes, and humans) were unable to synthesize vitamin C and became dependent entirely on external (food) sources.

Through much of the course of human evolution, the inability to manufacture vitamin C was never a problem because of the abundance of the vitamin in the human diet. It has been estimated that the average daily intake of vitamin C for preagricultural people was 440 mg, compared to an approximate 90 mg in the current American diet (Eaton and Konner, 1985). When people get insufficient amounts of vitamin C, they often develop **scurvy**, a disease that was probably extremely rare or absent in preagricultural populations (agriculture arose approximately 10,000 to 12,000 years ago). Symptoms of scurvy include abnormal bleeding of gums, slowed healing of wounds, loss of energy, anemia, and abnormal formation of bones and teeth. Scurvy was probably not very common in the past except in extreme northern regions. Today, the condition occasionally appears in infants who are fed exclusively on powdered or canned milk that does not have supplemental vitamin C.

Humans also lack the ability to synthesize some of the amino acids that are necessary for growth and maintenance of the body. As noted in Chapter 3, there are 20 amino acids that make up the proteins of all living things. Plants synthesize all the amino acids, but animals must get some or all from the foods they consume. *Lactobacillus,* for example, is a bacterium that lives in milk; since it can get all 20 amino acids from the milk it consumes, it is not necessary that they be synthesized and, in fact, it is unable to synthesize any of them. Because adult humans cannot synthesize eight of the amino acids in sufficient quantities, we must get them from the foods we eat ; they are thus referred to as the eight **essential amino acids** (for infants, there are nine). Interestingly, the amounts of each of the amino acids we need parallel the amounts present in animal protein, suggesting that food from animal sources may have been an important component of ancestral hominid diets when our specific nutrient requirements were

█ Scurvy
Disease resulting from a dietary deficiency of vitamin C. It may result in anemia, poor bone growth, abnormal bleeding and bruising, and muscle pain.

█ Essential amino acids
The eight (nine for infants) amino acids that must be ingested by humans for normal growth and body maintenance; include tryptophan, leucine, lysine, methionine, phenylalanine, isoleucine, valine, and threonine (histidine for infants).

evolving. Biologically, most humans can best meet their amino acid requirements from animal sources, but meat consumption is expensive, in both ecological and economic terms. By combining vegetables such as legumes and grains, humans can obtain the eight essential amino acids in the correct proportions (Fig. 16–6). Thus, most contemporary populations meet their need for protein by eating enough variety of vegetable foods so that adequate proportions of amino acids are achieved. Examples of familiar cuisines that reflect these combinations include beans and corn in Mexico, beans and rice in Caribbean cultures, rice and lentils in India, and black-eyed peas and cornbread in the southern United States.

An example of biological and cultural interaction in meeting nutritional requirements is seen in the traditional methods for processing corn into tortillas or hominy. Wherever corn is a major part of the diet, it is usually associated with a high incidence of the disease **pellagra**, which results from a deficiency of the vitamin niacin (vitamin B$_3$). The exception to this pattern is the Americas, where corn was originally domesticated and where pellagra is not common. The reason for the lower prevalence of pellagra appears to be the practice of adding lime or ashes to the cornmeal when making tortillas or hominy. These additives increase the availability of niacin in the corn so that it can be absorbed by the body (Katz et al., 1974). Unfortunately, when corn was exported to the rest of the world, this particular technology was not exported with it.

Because humans can use cultural responses to adapt to environmental challenges, does that mean that culture has enabled us as a species to transcend the limitations placed on us by our biology? At this stage of human history, it seems that we are still constrained by our evolved nutritional requirements. These requirements reflect adaptation to a food base that included a great deal of variety. Not only did we evolve against a background of variety, we are now "stuck with" requirements for variety. As agriculture has evolved and population size

■ **Pellagra**

Disease resulting from a dietary deficiency of niacin (vitamin B$_3$). Symptoms include dermatitis, diarrhea, dementia, and death (the "four Ds").

FIGURE 16–6

Complementarity of beans and wheat. (Adapted from Scientific American, *1976.)*

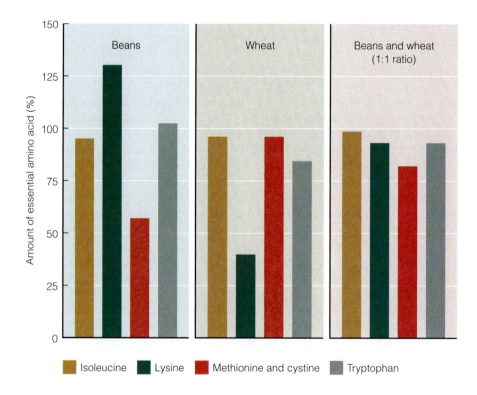

expanded, however, the human food base has become narrower, leading to the appearance of nutritional deficiency disease, which, like scurvy and pellagra, probably did not exist in the evolutionary past (i.e., prior to the development of agriculture).

Diets of Humans Before Agriculture

The preagricultural diet, while perhaps high in animal protein, was low in fats, particularly saturated fats (Table 16–2). The diet was also high in complex carbohydrates (including fiber), low in salt, and high in calcium. We do not need to be

TABLE 16–2 Selected Meats in Agricultural and Preagricultural Diets

	Meat (100 g portion)	Protein (g)	Fat (g)
Domestic meat	Prime lamb loin	14.7	32.0
	Ham	15.2	29.1
	Regular hamburger	17.9	21.2
	Choice sirloin steak	16.9	26.7
	Pork loin	16.4	28.0
Wild game	Goat	20.6	3.8
	Cape buffalo	—	2.8
	Warthog	—	4.2
	Horse	20.5	3.7
	Wild boar	16.8	8.3
	Beaver	30.0	5.1
	Muskrat	27.2	4.1
	Caribou	—	2.4
	Moose	—	1.5
	Kangaroo	—	1.2
	Turtle	26.8	3.9
	Opossum	33.6	4.5
	Wildebeest	—	5.4
	Thomson's gazelle	—	1.6
	Kob (waterbuck)	—	3.1
	Pheasant	24.3	5.2
	Rabbit	21.0	5.0
	Impala	—	2.6
	Topi	—	2.2
	Deer	21.0	4.0
	Bison	25.0	3.8

Note: Dashes indicate that data are not available.
Source: From Eaton, Shostak, and Konner, 1988.

reminded that the contemporary American diet has the opposite configuration of the one just described. It is high in saturated fats and salt and low in complex carbohydrates, fiber, and calcium (Table 16–3). There is very good evidence that many of today's diseases in industrialized countries are related to the lack of fit between our diet today and the one with which we evolved (Eaton, Shostak, and Konner, 1988).

Many of our biological and behavioral characteristics evolved because in the past they contributed to adaptation; but today these same characteristics may be maladaptive. An example is our ability to store fat. This capability was an advantage in the past, when food availability often alternated between abundance and scarcity. Those who could store fat during the times of abundance could draw on those stores during times of scarcity and remain healthy, resist disease, and, for women, maintain the ability to reproduce. Today, people with adequate economic resources spend much of their lives with a relative abundance of foods. Considering the number of disorders associated with obesity, the formerly positive ability to store extra fat has now turned into a liability. Our "feast or famine" biology is now incompatible with the constant feast many of us indulge in today.

It is clear that both deficiencies and excesses of nutrients can cause health problems and interfere with growth and development. Certainly, many people in all parts of the world, both industrialized and developing, suffer from inadequate supplies of food of any quality. We read daily of thousands dying from starvation due to drought, warfare, or political instability. We have noted that the agricultural revolution is partly responsible for some of the problems with food and health we see today. The blame must be placed not only on the narrowed food base that resulted from the emergence of agriculture, but also on the increase in human population that occurred when people began to settle in permanent villages and have more children. Today, the crush of billions of humans almost completely dependent on cereal grains means that millions face undernutrition, malnutrition, and even starvation.

Table 16–3   Preagricultural, Contemporary American, and Recently Recommended Dietary Composition

	Preagricultural Diet	Contemporary Diet	Recent Recommendations
Total dietary energy (%)			
Protein	33	12	12
Carbohydrate	46	46	58
Fat	21	42	30
Alcohol	~0	(7–10)	–
P:S ratio*	1.41	0.44	1
Cholesterol (mg)	520	300–500	300
Fiber (g)	100–150	19.7	30–60
Sodium (mg)	690	2,300–6,900	1,000–3,300
Calcium (mg)	1,500–2,000	740	800–1,500
Ascorbic acid (mg)	440	90	60

*Polyunsaturated: saturated fat ratio.

🌿 Undernutrition and Malnutrition

By **undernutrition**, we mean an inadequate quantity of food; in other words, not enough calories are consumed to support normal health. There is, of course, a great deal of variation in what constitutes an "adequate" diet (factors such as age, health, and activity levels all affect this determination), but it has been estimated that between 16 and 63 percent of the world's population are undernourished.

Malnutrition refers to an inadequate amount of some key element in the diet, such as proteins, minerals, or vitamins. In underdeveloped countries, protein malnutrition is the most common variety. The hallmark of severe protein malnutrition is *kwashiorkor,* a disease manifested by tissue swelling (especially in the abdominal area, giving its victims the typical "swollen belly" profile), anemia, loss or discoloration of hair, and apathy. A related syndrome, *marasmus,* is caused by the combined effects of protein *and* calorie deficiency.

More than causing discomfort, malnutrition greatly affects reproduction and infant survival. Malnourished mothers have difficult labor, more premature births, more children born with birth defects, higher prenatal mortality, and generally lower birth weights of newborns. Given all these potential physiological difficulties, it is surprising that overall **fertility** among malnourished mothers is not disrupted more than it is. Moderate chronic malnutrition (unless malnutrition becomes exceedingly severe, approaching starvation) has only a small effect on the number of live births (Bongaarts, 1980).

Children born to malnourished mothers are at a disadvantage even at birth. They are smaller and behind in most aspects of physical development. After birth, if malnutrition persists, such children fall further behind because of their mothers' generally poor **lactation**. Growth processes often slow down greatly when environmental insults are severe (malnutrition and/or disease). Later on, a period of accelerated growth (called the **catch-up period**) can make up some of the deficit. There are certain critical periods, however, in which growth in certain tissues is normally very rapid. If a severe interruption occurs during one of these periods, the individual may never catch up completely. For example, malnutrition during the last trimester of fetal life or during the first year of infancy can have marked effects on brain development. Autopsies of children who have died from complications of severe malnutrition have shown reduced brain size and weight, as well as fewer numbers of brain cells (Frisancho, 1978).

Deficiencies of specific nutrients are common in some parts of the world. **Beriberi,** caused by a deficiency of the vitamin thiamine (vitamin B_1), is the fourth leading cause of death in the Philippines. It is associated with the refined rice commonly eaten in the Philippines. Ironically, unrefined rice is an excellent source of thiamine, but the vitamin is removed during processing. This is an example of how cultural values may undermine biological adaptations. That is, refined white rice is seen as more pure and of higher social value than the more nutritious unrefined rice. Similarly, refined white bread was once more valued in the United States than the unrefined whole wheat bread.

Mineral deficiencies are also common today. Iron-deficiency anemia is a leading cause of pregnancy complications in many parts of the world, including the United States. Insufficient iodine causes **goiter** in adults and **cretinism** (a form of mental retardation) in infants whose mothers were deprived during pregnancy. Goiters form in the neck area when the thyroid gland enlarges as it tries to compensate for a lack of iodine in the diet. Goiters are most common in inland areas of the world, where soils are low in iodine; people living near the sea normally get sufficient iodine in their diets. In modern times, however, iodine is routinely

■ **Undernutrition**
A diet insufficient in quantity (calories) to support normal health.

■ **Malnutrition**
A diet insufficient in quality (i.e., lacking some essential component) to support normal health.

■ **Fertility**
Production of offspring; distinguished from *fecundity,* which is the ability to produce children. For example, a woman in her early 20s is probably fecund, but she is not actually fertile unless she has had children.

■ **Lactation**
The production of milk in mammals.

■ **Catch-up period**
A period of time during which a child who has experienced delayed growth because of malnutrition, undernutrition, or disease can increase in height to the point of his or her genetic potential.

■ **Beriberi**
Disease resulting from a dietary deficiency of thiamine (vitamin B_1). Symptoms include nerve damage and cardiovascular problems.

■ **Goiter**
Enlargement of the thyroid gland resulting from a dietary deficiency of iodine.

■ **Cretinism**
Mental and growth retardation in infants resulting from iodine deficiency in the mother during pregnancy.

added to salt, dramatically reducing the incidence of iodine deficiency worldwide. An interesting relationship between the ability to taste PTC (see p. 400) and certain foods that are known to interfere with iodine absorption (they are said to be *goitrogenic*) suggests that this polymorphism may be subject to natural selection. These foods include members of the cabbage family (e.g., broccoli, cauliflower, and Brussels sprouts) and peanuts. They contain chemicals similar to PTC, so that the tasters are more likely to avoid these foods than nontasters. In areas of iodine-deficient soils, it is adaptive to restrict consumption of goitrogenic foods. Thus, PTC tasting may be favorably selected over nontasting in those areas.

In summary, our nutritional adaptations were shaped in an environment that included times of scarcity alternating with times of abundance. The variety of foods consumed was so great that nutritional deficiency diseases were rare. Small amounts of animal foods were probably an important part of the diet in many parts of the world. In northern latitudes, subsequent to approximately 1 million years ago, meat was an important part of the diet, but because such meat was low in fats, the negative effects of high meat intake that we see today did not occur. Our diet today is often incompatible with the adaptations that evolved in the millions of years preceding the development of agriculture. The consequences of that incompatibility include both starvation and obesity.

Other Factors Influencing Growth and Development

Genetics

No matter how much you eat in your lifetime or how excellent your health, you will not be able to exceed your genetic potential for stature and a number of other physiological parameters. Genetic factors set the underlying limitations and potentialities for growth and development, but the life experience and environment of the organism determine how the body grows within those parameters. How do we assess the relative contributions of genes and the environment in their effects on growth? One of the most common sources of information comes from studies of monozygotic and dizygotic twins. Monozygotic ("identical") twins come from the union of a single sperm and ovum and share 100 percent of their genes. Dizygotic ("fraternal") twins come from separate ova and sperm and share only 50 percent of their genes, just as any other siblings from the same parents. If monozygotic twins with identical genes but different growth environments are exactly the same in stature at various ages (i.e., show perfect correlation or concordance for stature), then we can conclude that genes are the primary, if not the only, determinants of stature. Most studies of twins reveal that under normal circumstances, stature is "highly correlated" for monozygotic twins, leading to the conclusion that stature is under fairly strong genetic control (Table 16–4). Weight, on the other hand, seems to be more strongly influenced by diet, environment, and individual experiences than by genes.

There are a few specific genes that have a direct effect on growth (the gene controlling achondroplastic dwarfism, for example; see Table 4–3), but for the most part, the regulation of growth and development involves many genes; that is, growth and development are the result of polygenic inheritance (see Chapter 4). Some of these genes occur in clusters known as **homeobox genes** that have predictable influences on growth in large numbers of species and thus may have

■ **Homeobox genes**
A group of genes found in vertebrates that plays a major role in the embryonic development of such structures as the vertebral column, limbs, and gut.

TABLE 16–4   Correlation Coefficients for Height Between Monozygotic (MZ) and Dizygotic (DZ) Twin Pairs from Birth to Age 8.

Age	Total *n*	MZ	DZ Same sex	DZ Different Sex
Birth	629	0.62	0.79	0.67
3 months	764	0.78	0.72	0.65
6 months	819	0.80	0.67	0.62
12 months	827	0.86	0.66	0.58
24 months	687	0.89	0.54	0.61
3 years	699	0.93	0.56	0.60
5 years	606	0.94	0.51	.068
8 years	444	0.94	0.49	0.65

Source: From Wilson, 1979, after Bogin, 1988:163.

been highly conserved throughout evolution. For example, a set of homeobox genes known as *Hox* genes, found in vertebrates, has been identified as directing the growth of specific regions of the body such as the vertebral column, limbs, and gut. These *Hox* genes are in turn influenced by other regulatory genes that influence cell division and other complex interactions (Ulijaszek, 1998). It is best to think of the genes behind growth and development as part of a very complex hierarchy, where one set of genes affects another, and so on. At all of these stages, environmental factors such as nutrition and disease can have an influence on the resulting phenotype. Furthermore, mutations in some of these *Hox* genes are known to cause disease in humans, most commonly developmental disorders (Weiss, Stock, and Zhao, 1998).

Hormones

One of the primary ways in which genes have an effect on growth and development is through their effects on hormones. Hormones are substances produced in one cell that have an effect on another cell. Most hormones are produced by *endocrine* glands and then transported in the bloodstream; almost all have an effect on growth. The hypothalamus (located at the base of the forebrain) can be considered the relay station, control center, or central clearinghouse for most hormonal action. This control center receives messages from the brain and endocrine glands and sends out messages that stimulate hormonal action. Most of the hormonal messages transmitted from the hypothalamus result in the inhibition or release of other hormones.

One of the primary targets of the inhibiting and releasing hormones of the hypothalamus is the pituitary gland, located in a pocket of bone just behind the eyes. It has two parts, the anterior pituitary and the posterior pituitary. The anterior pituitary produces hormones that regulate reproduction (FSH and LH), milk production (prolactin), metabolism (ACTH), and growth (GH). The posterior pituitary produces hormones that control water balance (vasopressin) and uterine and breast involvement in labor and nursing (oxytocin).

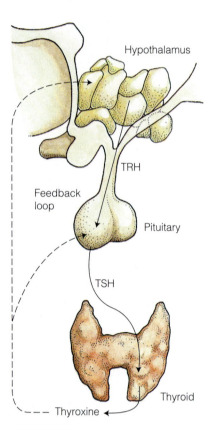

FIGURE 16–7

Example of a feedback loop. When thyroxine levels in the blood fall too low, the hypothalamus releases TRH (thyrotropin-releasing hormone), which goes to the anterior pituitary, triggering the release of TSH (thyroid-stimulating hormone). TSH causes thyroxine to be released from the thyroid gland. Release of TRH and TSH is then inhibited.

Many of the following variables are discussed within a comparative mammalian context in Virtual Lab 1, section IV, part A.

We can use the hormone thyroxine, produced by the thyroid glands in the neck, to illustrate the action of hormones and the communication system among the endocrine glands (Fig. 16–7) (Crapo, 1985). Thyroxine regulates metabolism and aids in body heat production. When thyroxine levels fall too low for normal metabolism, the brain senses this and sends a message to the hypothalamus. The hypothalamus reacts by releasing TRH, or thyrotropin-releasing hormone. TRH goes to the anterior pituitary, where it stimulates the release of TSH, or thyroid-stimulating hormone. TSH then goes to the thyroid gland, stimulating it to release thyroxine. When the brain senses that the levels of thyroxine are adequate, it sends signals that inhibit the further release of TRH and TSH. In many ways, this process is similar to what your household thermostat does: When it senses that the temperature has dropped too low for comfort, it sends a message to the furnace to begin producing more heat; when the temperature reaches or exceeds the preset level, the thermostat sends another message to turn the furnace off.

Two other hormones that are important in growth include growth hormone and insulin. Growth hormone, secreted by the anterior pituitary, promotes growth and has an effect on just about every cell in the body. Tumors and other disorders can result in excessive or insufficient amounts of growth hormone secretion which in turn can result in gigantism or dwarfism. As noted previously, insulin is produced by the pancreas and regulates the use of glucose in the body.

Environmental Factors

Environmental factors, such as altitude and climate, have effects on growth and development. Perhaps the primary influence of such external factors comes from their effects on nutrition, but there is evidence of independent effects as well. For example, as noted in Chapter 15, infant birth weight is lower at high altitude, even when such factors as nutrition, smoking, and socioeconomic status are taken into consideration. In the United States, the percentage of low-birth-weight (LBW) infants (those weighing less than 2,500 g, or 5.7 pounds) is about 6.5 percent at sea level, rising to 10.4 percent at 5,000 feet and almost 24 percent above 10,000 feet. In a Bolivian study, the mean birth weight was 3,415 g (7.8 pounds) at low elevations and 3,133 g (7.1 pounds) at high elevations (Haas et al., 1980). Most studies of children have found that those at high elevations are shorter and lighter than those at low elevations.

In general, populations in cold climates tend to be heavier and have longer trunks and shorter extremities than populations in tropical areas. This reflects Bergmann's and Allen's rules, discussed in Chapter 15. Exposure to sunlight also appears to have an effect on growth, most likely through its effects on vitamin D production. Children tend to grow more rapidly in times of high sunlight concentration (i.e., in the summer in temperate regions and in the dry season in monsoonal tropical regions). Vitamin D, necessary for skeletal growth, requires sunlight for its synthesis (see p. 422).

The Human Life Cycle

Not all animals have clearly demarcated phases in their lives; moreover, among mammals, humans have more such phases than do other species (Fig. 16–8). Protozoa, among the simplest of animals, have only one phase; many inverte-

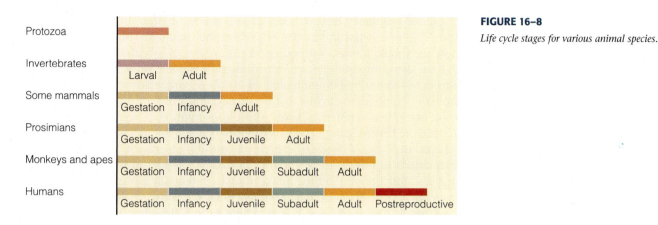

FIGURE 16–8

Life cycle stages for various animal species.

brates have two: larval and adult. Almost all mammals have at least three phases (gestation, infancy, and adulthood). Most primates have four phases: gestation, infancy, juvenile (usually called childhood in humans), and adult. Monkeys, apes, and humans add a phase between the juvenile phase and adulthood that is referred to as the subadult period (adolescence, or teenage, in humans). Finally, for humans there is the addition of a sixth phase in women, the postreproductive years following menopause. One could argue that during the course of primate evolution, more recently evolved forms have longer life spans and more divisions of the life span into phases, or stages.

Most of these life cycle stages are well marked by biological transitions. Gestation begins with conception and ends with birth; infancy is the period of nursing; childhood, or the juvenile phase, is the period from weaning to sexual maturity (puberty in humans); adolescence is the period from puberty to the end of growth; adulthood is marked by the birth of the first child and/or the completion of growth; and menopause is recognized as having occurred one full year after the last menstrual cycle. These biological markers are similar among higher primates, but for humans, there is an added complexity: They occur in cultural contexts that define and characterize them. Puberty, for example, has very different meanings in different cultures. A girl's first menstruation (menarche) is often marked with ritual and celebration, and a change in social status typically occurs with this biological transition. Likewise, menopause is often associated with a rise in status for women in non-Western societies, whereas it is commonly seen as a negative transition for women in many Western societies. As we shall see, collective and individual attitudes toward these life cycle transitions have an effect on growth and development.

Conception and Pregnancy

The biological aspects of conception and gestation can be discussed in a fairly straightforward way, drawing information from what is known about reproductive biology at the present time: A sperm fertilizes an egg; the resulting zygote travels through a uterine (fallopian) tube to become implanted in the uterine lining; and the embryo develops until it is mature enough to survive outside the womb, at which time birth occurs. But this is clearly not all there is to human pregnancy and birth. Female biology may be largely similar the world over, but cultural rules and practices are the primary determinants of who will get pregnant, as well as when, where, how, and by whom.

Once pregnancy has occurred, there is much variation in how the woman should behave, what she should eat, where she should and should not go, and how she should interact with other people. Almost every culture known, including our own, imposes dietary restrictions on pregnant women. Many of these appear to serve an important biological function, particularly that of keeping the woman from ingesting toxins that would be dangerous for the fetus. (Alcohol is a good example of a potential toxin whose consumption in pregnancy is discouraged in the United States.) Food aversions to coffee, alcohol, and other bitter substances that many women experience during pregnancy may be evolved adaptations to protect the embryo from toxins. The nausea of early pregnancy may also function to limit the intake of foods potentially harmful to the embryo at a critical stage of development (Profet, 1988; Williams and Nesse, 1991).

Thus, it appears that our biological heritage includes adaptations that improve pregnancy outcome, but we reinforce these with cultural restrictions that improve it even more (or in some cases make it worse). This is not to say that every food restriction or aversion of pregnancy is adaptive; but many are likely to prove advantageous if evaluated carefully. For example, many of the foods forbidden to women during pregnancy are proteins, such as eggs and chicken. Restriction of these items may at first seem maladaptive, since proteins are important for fetal growth and development. But they also cause stress on the mother's kidneys, which are already under great strain during pregnancy. Thus, physicians in the United States often advise against consumption of excess protein.

Gestation length in humans and in our closest relatives, chimpanzees and gorillas, is very similar, although for other life cycle stages, human spans are almost twice those of chimpanzees and gorillas. Ashley Montagu (1961), Stephen Jay Gould (1977), and others have suggested that the human gestation period may actually be about 15 to 18 months, but we are delivered "early" in order to be born at all—a necessity considering the large size of the fetal human head compared to the relatively narrow maternal pelvis. Extending the gestation period by another 6 to 9 months would bring it more in line with what would be expected from looking at other life cycle stages (Fig. 16–9).

Perhaps the most obvious difference between human and other primate infants at birth is the degree of brain development (Table 16–5). The human brain at birth is about one-fourth as large as it will be in adulthood, measuring approximately 350 cm³. By 1 year, it will have more than doubled in size, tripling by age 3. In contrast, nonhuman primate infants are born with brains averaging one-half the size of adults of their species.

FIGURE 16–9

Primate age spans.

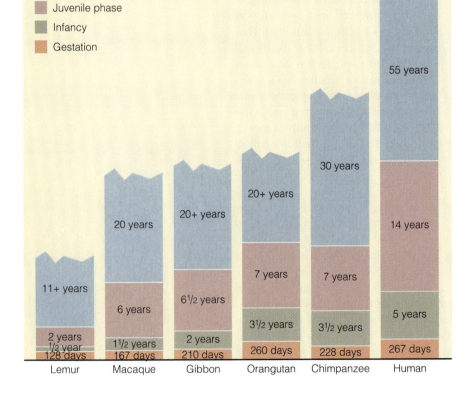

An undeveloped brain seems necessary for birth to occur through a narrow pelvis, but it may also be advantageous for other reasons. For a species as dependent on learning as we are for survival, it may be adaptive for most of our brain growth to take place in the presence of environmental stimuli rather than in the relatively unstimulating uterus. This may be particularly true for a species dependent on language. The language centers of the brain develop in the first three years of life, when the brain is undergoing its rapid expansion; these three years are considered a critical period for the development of language in the human child.

 Birth

Birth is an event that is celebrated with ritual in almost every culture studied. In fact, the relatively little fanfare associated with childbirth in the United States is unusual by world standards. Because risk of death for both mother and child is so great at birth, it is not surprising that it is surrounded with ritual significance. Perhaps because of the high risk of death, we tend to think that birth is far more difficult in humans than it is in other mammals. But since almost all primate infants have large heads relative to body size, birth is challenging to many primates (Fig. 16–10).

TABLE 16–5 Neonatal Brain Weight as a Percentage of Adult Brain Weight for Selected Mammalian Species	
Mammal	Neonatal Brain Weight (%)
Harbor porpoise	38
California seal	50
Horse	52
Llama	76
Cow	44
Galago	40
Howler	57
Spider monkey	58
Rhesus macaque	68
Hamadryas baboon	40
Common chimpanzee	36
Gorilla	56
Human	26

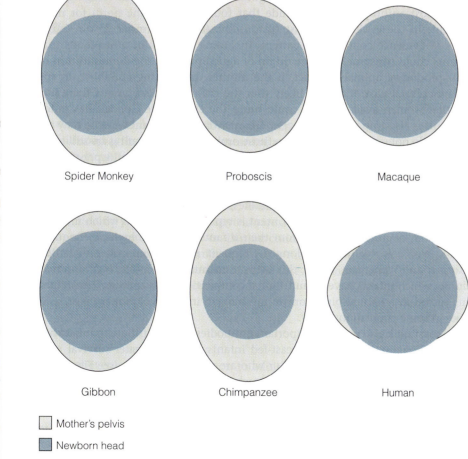

Spider Monkey   Proboscis   Macaque

Gibbon   Chimpanzee   Human

☐ Mother's pelvis
☐ Newborn head

FIGURE 16–10

The relation between the average diameter of the birth canal of adult females and average head length and breadth of newborns of the same species. (After Jolly, 1985.)

TABLE 16–6   Providing for Juveniles

	Percent of Those Who Survive	
	Weaning	Adolescence
Lion	28	15
Baboon	45	33
Macaque	42	13
Chimpanzee	48	38
Provisioned macaques	82	58
Human Populations		
!Kung*	80	58
Yanomamo †	73	50
Paleoindian ††	86	50

* A hunting and gathering population of southern Africa.
† Horticultural population of South America.
†† Preagricultural people of the Americas.

Source: Adapted from Lancaster and Lancaster, 1983.

and is usually the marker of this transition in cultures where the event is ritually celebrated.

A number of factors affect the onset of puberty in humans, including genetic patterns (children tend to become mature at about the same age as their parents), nutrition, disease, and stress. In humans and other primates, females reach sexual maturity before males do.

For girls, it appears that a certain amount of body fat is necessary for menarche and the maintenance of ovulation (Frisch, 1988). Both diet and activity levels affect the accumulation of body fat. This may explain the trend toward the lower age of menarche that has been noted in human populations in the last hundred years and the tendency for girls who are very active and thin to mature later than those who are heavier and less active. High activity and low body fat also characterize many ballet dancers and marathon runners, who often cease to menstruate during periods of intense training. Since pregnancy and nursing require an increase in caloric consumption, body fat may serve as a signal to the body that there is enough caloric reserve to support a pregnancy. When the levels of body fat fall too low, ovulation may cease temporarily to prevent initiation of a pregnancy that is likely to fail.

Adolescence is the time between puberty and the completion of physical growth or the social recognition of adulthood. This social recognition may result from marriage, bearing a child, or a particular accomplishment. In nonhuman primates, the equivalent stage is defined in males as the time from which they are capable of fertilization to the time when physical growth is complete. At this point, they have male-specific features and size and are recognized as adults by other members of the social group. Females begin to engage in sexual behavior, exhibiting signs of sexual receptivity before they are capable of bearing young. These early cycles are usually not ovulatory and define the period of adolescence for them. Adulthood comes with the first pregnancy.

Adolescence
The time in the human life cycle between puberty and the completion of growth, or adulthood.

Adulthood

Pregnancy and child care occupy much of a woman's adult life in most cultures, as they likely did in the evolutionary past. For most women, the years from menarche to menopause are marked monthly by menstruation, except when they are pregnant or nursing. A normal menstrual cycle has two phases: the follicular phase, in which the egg is preparing for ovulation, marked by high estrogen production; and the luteal phase, during which the uterus is preparing for implantation, marked by high progesterone production. If the egg is not fertilized, progesterone production drops off and menstruation, the shedding of the uterine lining, occurs. A woman who never becomes pregnant may have as many as 400 cycles between menarche and menopause. Because reliable contraceptives were unavailable in the preagricultural past, this high number of menstrual cycles is probably a relatively recent phenomenon. It has been suggested, in fact, that highly frequent menstrual cycling may be implicated in several cancers of female reproductive organs, especially of the breast, uterus, and ovaries (Eaton et al., 1994). During the course of human evolution, females may have had as few as 60 menstrual cycles in their entire lives, unless they were sterile or not sexually active.

In addition to caring for children, women in the majority of world cultures also participate in economic activities. Adulthood for men typically includes activities related to subsistence, religion, politics, and family. Women may be equally or less involved in these activities, depending on the culture.

During adulthood, the status of an individual may change as new skills are acquired or new achievements made. Where such records are kept, status may be defined by chronological age, as seen in the common pattern of retirement at age 65 or 70 in the United States.

For women, **menopause**, or the end of menstruation, is a sign of entry into a new phase of the life cycle. Estrogen and progesterone production begins to decline toward the end of the reproductive years until ovulation (and thus menstruation) ceases altogether. This occurs at approximately age 50 in all parts of the world. Throughout human evolution, the majority of females (and males) did not survive to age 50; thus, few women lived much past menopause. But today, this event occurs when women have as much as one-third of their active and healthy lives ahead of them. As already noted, such a long period of postreproductive time is not found in other primates. Female chimpanzees and monkeys experience decreased fertility in their later years, but most continue to have monthly cycles until their deaths. Occasional reports of menopause in apes and monkeys have been noted, but it is far from a routine and expected event.

Why do human females have such a long period during which they can no longer reproduce? One theory relates to parenting. Since it takes about 12 to 15 years before a child becomes independent, it has been argued that females are biologically "programmed" to live 12 to 15 years beyond the birth of their last child (Mayer, 1982). This suggests that the maximum human life span for preagricultural humans was about 65 years, a figure that corresponds to what is known for contemporary hunter-gatherers and for prehistoric populations. Another theory regarding menopause suggests that it was not itself favored by natural selection; rather it is an artifact of the extension of the human life span. Some have suggested that the maximum life span of the mammalian egg is 50 years (you will recall that all the ova are already present before birth; see p. 443). Thus, although the human life span has increased in the last several hundred years, the reproductive life span has not.

■ **Menopause**

The end of menstruation in human women, usually occurring at around age 50.

Senescence
The process of physiological decline in body function that occurs with aging.

Pleiotropic genes
Genes that have more than one effect; genes that have different effects at different times in the life cycle.

Aging

To some extent, aging is something we do throughout our entire lives. But we usually think of aging as **senescence**, the process of physiological decline in all systems of the body that occurs toward the end of the life course. Actually, throughout adulthood, there is a gradual decline in the cell's ability to synthesize proteins, in immune system function, in muscle mass (with a corresponding increase in fat mass) and strength, and in bone mineral density (Lamberts et al., 1997). This decline is associated with an increase in risk for the chronic degenerative diseases that are usually listed as the causes of death in industrialized nations.

Relative to most other animals, humans have a long life span (Table 16–7). The maximum life span potential, estimated to be about 120 years, has probably not changed in the last several thousand years, although life expectancy at birth (the average length of life) has increased significantly in the last 100 years, probably due to the decreased influence of infectious diseases, which typically take their toll on the young (Crews and Harper, 1998). Clearly, advances in medicine, public health, and technology have contributed to the increase in life expectancy among most human populations. Can we assume that further advances will lead to an increase in the life span? Will scientific advances eventually mean that humans can live 150, 200, even 300 years? Most scholars think not.

You remember from Chapter 2 that natural selection favors characteristics that increase reproductive success in individuals. Thus, most causes of death that have their effects after the reproductive years will not necessarily be subjected to forces of natural selection. One explanation for why we age and are affected by chronic degenerative diseases like atherosclerosis, cancers, and hypertension is that genes that enhance reproductive success in earlier years (and thus were favored by natural selection) may have detrimental effects in later years. These are referred to as **pleiotropic genes**, meaning that they have multiple effects at different times in the life span or under different conditions (Williams, 1957). For example, genes that enhance the function of the immune system in the early

TABLE 16–7   Maximal Life Spans for Selected Species

Organism	Approximate maximum life span (in years)
Bristlecone pine	5000
Tortoise	170
Rockfish	140
Human	120
Blue whale	80
Indian elephant	70
Gorilla	39
Domestic dog	34
Rabbit	13
Rat	5

Source: Stini, 1991.

years may also damage tissue so that cancer susceptibility increases in later life (Nesse and Williams, 1994).

Pleiotropy may help us understand evolutionary reasons for aging, but what are the causes of senescence in the individual? Much attention has been focused recently on free radicals, highly reactive molecules that can damage cells. Protection against these by-products of normal metabolism is provided by antioxidants such as vitamins A, C, and E and by a number of enzymes (Kirkwood, 1997). Ultimately, damage to DNA can occur, which in turn contributes to the senescence of cells, the immune system, and other functional systems of the body. Additionally, there is evidence that programmed cell death is also a part of the normal processes of development that can obviously contribute to senescence.

Far more important than genes in the aging process, however, are lifestyle factors, such as smoking, physical activity, diet, and medical care. Life expectancy at birth varies considerably from country to country and among socioeconomic classes within a country. Throughout the world, women have higher life expectancies than men. A Japanese girl born in 1997, for example, can expect to live to age 84, a boy to age 77. Girls and boys born those same years in the United States have life expectancies of 79 and 73, respectively. In contrast to these children in industrialized nations, girls and boys born in Mali have life expectancies of only 48 and 45, respectively.

Postreproductive years are somewhat well defined for women, but "old age" is a very ambiguous concept. In the United States, we tend to associate old age with physical ailments and decreased activity. Thus, a person who is vigorous and active at age 70 might not be regarded as "old," whereas another who is frail and debilitated at age 55 may be considered old.

One reason we are concerned with this definition is that old age is generally regarded negatively and is typically unwelcome in the United States, a culture noted for its emphasis on youth. This attitude is quite different from many other societies, where old age brings with it wealth, higher status, and new freedoms, particularly for women. This is because high status is often correlated with knowledge, experience, and wisdom, which are themselves associated with greater age in most societies. Such has been the case throughout most of history, but today, in technologically developed countries, knowledge is changing so rapidly that the old may no longer control the most relevant knowledge.

By and large, people today are living longer than they did in the past because, in part, they are not dying from infectious diseases. The top five killers in the United States, for example, are heart disease, cancer, stroke, accidents, and chronic obstructive lung disease. Together these account for 75 percent of deaths (Eaton, Shostak, and Konner, 1988). All these conditions are considered "diseases of civilization" in that most can be accounted for by conditions in the modern environment that were not present in the past. Examples include cigarette smoke, air and water pollution, alcohol, automobiles, high-fat diets, and environmental carcinogens. It should be noted, however, that the high incidence of these diseases is also a result of people living to older ages because of factors such as improved hygiene, regular medical care, and new medical technologies.

The final phase of the life cycle, if we can call it that, is death. Humans all over the world celebrate this transition, often with great fanfare and expense. Some people interpret evidence from Neandertal remains to mean that ritual treatment of the dead may go back as far as 100,000 years in human history (see Chapter 12). Death is a less ambiguous transition than any of the others previously described, although there is great variation in what is believed to happen to the individual after death. There is also variability in mortuary practices surrounding the disposal of the physical remains. Most common are cremation and burial.

Are We Still Evolving?

In many ways, it seems that culture has enabled us to transcend most of the limitations imposed on us by our biology. But that biology was shaped during millions of years of evolution in environments very different from those in which most of us live today. There is, to a great extent, a lack of fit between our biology and our twenty-first-century cultural environment. Our expectations that scientists can easily and quickly discover a "magic bullet" to enable us to resist any disease that arises have been painfully dashed with rising death tolls from AIDS in many parts of the world. Drug-resistant strains of diseases we once controlled, such as tuberculosis, pneumonia, shigella, salmonella, gonorrhea, and syphilis, are having significant impact on the health of people all over the world. These "new" diseases have themselves evolved in response to antibiotics, a human-induced agent of selection. Scientists believe that the crisis in antibiotic-resistant diseases will get even worse before it gets better (Neu, 1992). Thus, human innovations are now the major agents of selection operating on our species (and most others) today.

Socioeconomic and political concerns have powerful effects on our species today. Whether you die of starvation or succumb to disorders associated with overconsumption depends a great deal on where you live, what your socioeconomic status is, and how much power and control you have over your life, factors not likely to be related to biology. This also has an effect on whether or not you are killed in a war or spend most of your life in a safe, comfortable community. Whether or not you are exposed to one of the "new" pathogens such as HIV or tuberculosis has a lot to do with your lifestyle and other cultural factors, but whether or not you die from it or fail to reproduce because of it still has a lot to do with your biology. The 4.3 million children dying annually from respiratory infections are primarily those in the developing world, with limited access to adequate medical care, clearly a cultural factor. But in those same areas, lacking that same medical care, are millions of other children who are not getting the infections or are not dying from them. Presumably, among the factors affecting this difference is resistance afforded by genes. By considering this simple example, we can see that gene frequencies are still changing from one generation to the next in response to selective agents such as disease; thus our species is still evolving.

Whether we will become a different species or become extinct as a species (remember, that is the fate of almost everything that has ever lived on earth) is not something we can answer. Whether our brains will get larger, our hands will evolve solely to push buttons, or we will change genetically so that we no longer have to eat food is the stuff of science fiction, not anthropology. But as long as new pathogens appear, or new environments are introduced by technology, there is little doubt that the human species will continue to evolve or will become extinct, just as every other species on earth has done.

Culture has enabled us to transcend many limits imposed by our biology, and today people who never would have been able to do so in the past are surviving and having children. This, in itself, means we are evolving. How many of you would be reading this text if you had been born under conditions of 500 years ago?

Summary

This chapter has reviewed the fundamental concepts of growth and development in the human life course and how those processes occur within the contexts of both biology and culture. Diet has an important effect on growth, and human nutritional needs themselves result from biocultural evolution. The preagricultural human diet was reviewed, with the suggestion that many of our contemporary ills may result from incompatibilities between our evolved nutritional needs and the foods that are currently consumed. In particular, the preagricultural diet was probably high in complex carbohydrates and fiber and low in fat and sodium. Diets for many contemporary people are low in complex carbohydrates and fiber and high in fat and sodium. This type of diet has been implicated in many current health problems.

The human life cycle can be divided into six phases: gestation, infancy, juvenile, subadult, adult, and postreproductive. Each is fairly well defined by biological markers. Pregnancy lasts about nine months in humans, and infants are born with only about one-fourth of their adult brain size. This means that human infants are helpless at birth and therefore dependent on their parents for a long time. Birth is a bit more challenging for humans than for other mammals because of the very close correspondence between maternal pelvic size (narrow because of bipedalism) and fetal head size (large, even though the brain is relatively undeveloped). Infancy is the period of nursing, approximately four years for most humans and apes. The unusually long period of childhood in humans is important as the time in which social and technological skills are acquired. Sexual maturation is apparent at puberty, but full adult status is not achieved until growth has been completed and childbearing capabilities are reached. The last phase of the human life cycle, the postreproductive period, is marked in women by menopause, the cessation of menstruation and ovulation.

Questions for Review

1. What is meant by the analogy "Water is to fish as culture is to humans"?
2. Describe how a bone grows.
3. What is sexual dimorphism? List some examples in humans.
4. Briefly describe human brain growth.
5. What are essential amino acids? Develop a scenario for how our need for these amino acids might have evolved.
6. Give two examples of ways in which culture and biology interact in meeting human nutritional requirements.
7. What were the characteristics of the preagricultural human diet? What are the major differences today?
8. How does gestation length compare in humans and apes? Why is it shorter in humans than might be expected?
9. Why is nursing important for infant health? What is the proposed relationship between nursing and ovulation?
10. What is the proposed significance of providing food for children beyond the age of weaning?
11. What biological changes occur in males and females at puberty? What role does body fat appear to play in females?
12. What are some of the proposed explanations for menopause in human females?
13. What are some of the causes of senescence in humans?
14. Are we still evolving? What evidence is there that we are still subject to the forces of evolution?

Suggested Further Reading

Bogin, Barry. 1988. *Patterns of Human Growth.* Cambridge: Cambridge University Press.

Cohen, Mark Nathan. 1989. *Health and the Rise of Civilization.* New Haven: Yale University Press.

Crews, D. E., and R. M. Garutto (eds.). 1994. *Biological Anthropology and Aging: An Emerging Synthesis.* New York: Oxford University Press.

Diamond, Jared. 1992. *The Third Chimpanzee: The Evolution and Future of the Human Animal.* New York: Harper Collins.

Eaton, S. Boyd, Marjorie Shostak, and Melvin Konner. 1988. *The Paleolithic Prescription.* New York: Harper & Row.

Mascie-Taylor, C. G. N., and G. W. Lasker (eds.). 1991. *Applications of Biological Anthropology to Human Affairs.* Cambridge: Cambridge University Press.

Riddle, Robert D., and Clifford J. Tabin. 1999. "How Limbs Develop." *Scientific American* 280 (2): 74–79.

Shipman, Pat, Alan Walker, and David Bichell. 1985. *The Human Skeleton.* Cambridge, MA: Harvard University Press.

Sinclair, D. 1989. *Human Growth After Birth.* New York: Oxford University Press.

Stini, W. A., 1991. "Biology of Human Aging." *In Applications of Biological Anthropology to Human Affairs,* C. G. N. Mascie-Taylor and G. W. Lasker (eds.). Cambridge: Cambridge University Press.

Tanner, James M. 1990. *Foetus into Man: Physical Growth from Conception to Maturity.* 2d ed., Cambridge, MA: Harvard University Press.

Trevathan, Wenda R. 1987. *Human Birth: An Evolutionary Perspective.* Hawthorne, NY: Aldine de Gruyter.

Trevathan, W. R., E. O. Smith, and J. J. McKenna (eds.). 1999. *Evolutionary Medicine.* New York: Oxford University Press.

Ulijaszek, S. J., F. E. Johnston, and M. A. Preece (eds.). 1998. *The Cambridge Encyclopedia of Human Growth and Development.* Cambridge, England: Cambridge University Press.

Wallace, Douglas C. 1997. "Mitochondrial DNA in Aging and Disease." *Scientific American* 277(2): 40–47

Additional Resources

Multimedia Tools

- **Virtual Laboratories for Physical Anthropology CD-ROM**
  The following concepts in this chapter are covered on the physical anthropology CD-ROM:
  brain weight, longevity, gestation, age at first reproduction (Virtual Lab 1.IV.A)

- **Wadsworth Anthropology Resource Center**
  http://anthropology.wadsworth.com
  Visit Anthropology Online to obtain current updates in the field, surfing tips, career information, and more. In addition, enrich your study efforts with text-specific study aids arranged by chapter.

■ ⚙ **InfoTrac College Edition**
http://www.infotrac-college.com/wadsworth

1. One of the stages of growth is adolescence. To look at this stage in a little more detail, read "Growth and Normal Puberty" from *Pediatrics,* on InfoTrac College Edition. How does growth during adolescence usually proceed? Think about your own adolescence and puberty. How does your own development correspond to the averages?

2. Read "Why Women Change" by Jared Diamond, from *Discover,* on InfoTrac College Edition. How does Diamond propose that menopause evolved? Does this explanation concur with the theory proposed in the text?

3. How long can people live, and what determines maximum life span? Read "Evolution, mutations, and human longevity: European royal and noble families" by Gavrilova et al., in *Human Biology,* on InfoTrac College Edition. What evidence do these authors propose for the evolution of human longevity?

4. Choose one of the nutritional disorders listed in the text and see what more you can learn about this disorder using InfoTrac College Edition. Write a short report on the disorder: what causes it, and what can be done to prevent it.

■ 🌐 **Internet Exercises**

1. Visit the Paleolithic Diet Page (**http://www.panix.com/ ~paleodiet/**). This is a general resource for many Web sites relating to nonmodern diet and nutrition. Visit a couple of the links on this page. How would you characterize the Paleolithic diet? You might even try out one of the Paleolithic recipes.

2. Nutrition and general health both have a major impact on growth and development, yet the levels of nutrition vary significantly in different cultures and different areas of the world. The World Health Organization (**http://www. who.org**) studies health and nutrition around the world and has some comparative information available on their Web site. Browse around the site and see what you can find. Then visit the Global Health Pages (**http://www.who.int/whosis/ hfa/index.html**) and choose two countries (besides the United States) from the list of countries for which health and nutrition statistics are available. Compare these countries with the United States (use the data tables). What nutritional and health concerns exist in these countries that do not cause much concern in the United States?

3. Visit the American Museum of Natural History's Electronic Newspaper's Story on Aging (**http://www.amnh.org/enews/aging/ a43.html**). How does human longevity vary around the world? What are the causes of the differences? Follow the link to the evolution of aging. How long could different species of hominid live in the past? How long might we be able to live in the future?

Appendix A
Atlas of Primate
Skeletal Anatomy

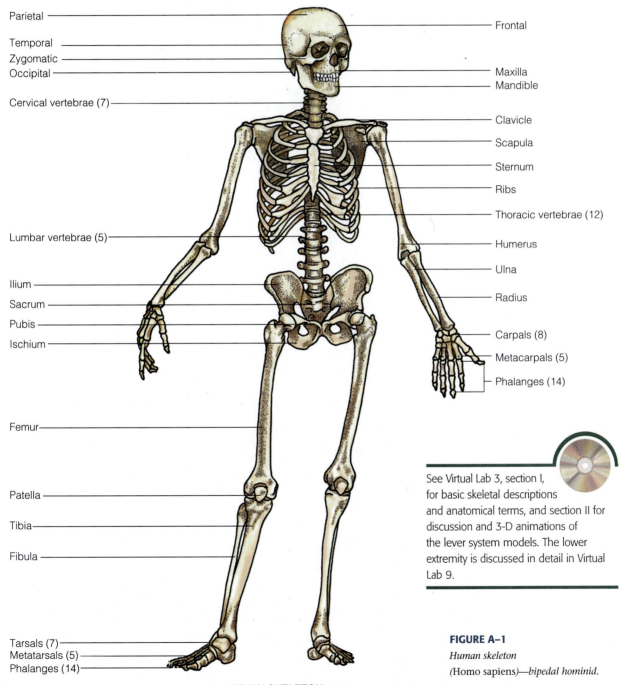

Parietal

Temporal

Zygomatic

Occipital

Cervical vertebrae (7)

Lumbar vertebrae (5)

Ilium

Sacrum

Pubis

Ischium

Femur

Patella

Tibia

Fibula

Tarsals (7)
Metatarsals (5)
Phalanges (14)

Frontal

Maxilla
Mandible

Clavicle

Scapula

Sternum

Ribs

Thoracic vertebrae (12)

Humerus

Ulna

Radius

Carpals (8)

Metacarpals (5)

Phalanges (14)

HUMAN SKELETON

See Virtual Lab 3, section I,
for basic skeletal descriptions
and anatomical terms, and section II for
discussion and 3-D animations of
the lever system models. The lower
extremity is discussed in detail in Virtual
Lab 9.

FIGURE A–1

*Human skeleton
(Homo sapiens)—bipedal hominid.*

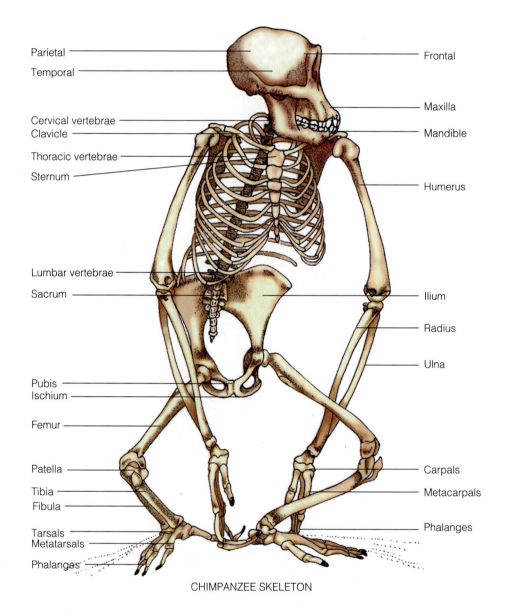

Parietal

Temporal

Cervical vertebrae

Clavicle

Thoracic vertebrae

Sternum

Lumbar vertebrae

Sacrum

Pubis

Ischium

Femur

Patella

Tibia

Fibula

Tarsals

Metatarsals

Phalanges

Frontal

Maxilla

Mandible

Humerus

Ilium

Radius

Ulna

Carpals

Metacarpals

Phalanges

CHIMPANZEE SKELETON

FIGURE A–2

Chimpanzee skeleton
(Pan troglodytes)—knuckle-walking pongid.

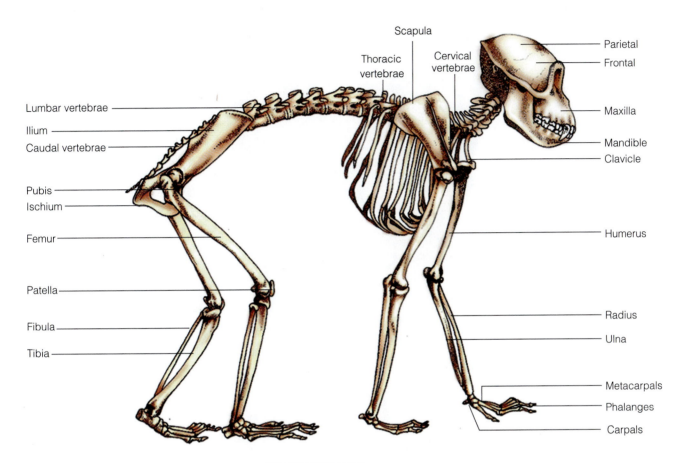

MONKEY SKELETON

FIGURE A–3

Monkey skeleton (rhesus macaque; Macaca mulatta)—a typical quadrupedal primate.

See Virtual Lab 3 for a detailed discussion and virtual exercise on the role of the forelimb in locomotion, and Virtual Lab 4 for a virtual exercise on relative limb lengths

FIGURE A–4

Human cranium.
(continued on next page)

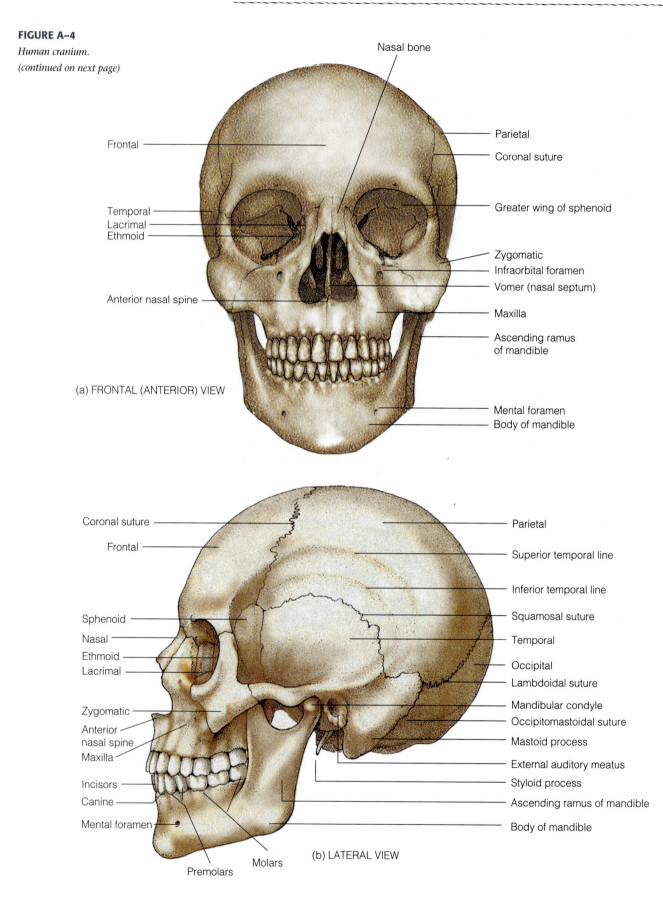

Nasal bone

Frontal

Parietal

Coronal suture

Temporal

Lacrimal

Ethmoid

Greater wing of sphenoid

Zygomatic

Infraorbital foramen

Vomer (nasal septum)

Anterior nasal spine

Maxilla

Ascending ramus
of mandible

(a) FRONTAL (ANTERIOR) VIEW

Mental foramen

Body of mandible

Coronal suture

Frontal

Parietal

Superior temporal line

Inferior temporal line

Sphenoid

Nasal

Ethmoid

Lacrimal

Squamosal suture

Temporal

Occipital

Lambdoidal suture

Zygomatic

Anterior
nasal spine

Maxilla

Mandibular condyle

Occipitomastoidal suture

Mastoid process

Incisors

Canine

External auditory meatus

Styloid process

Ascending ramus of mandible

Mental foramen

Body of mandible

Premolars

Molars

(b) LATERAL VIEW

FIGURE A–4

Human cranium. (continued)

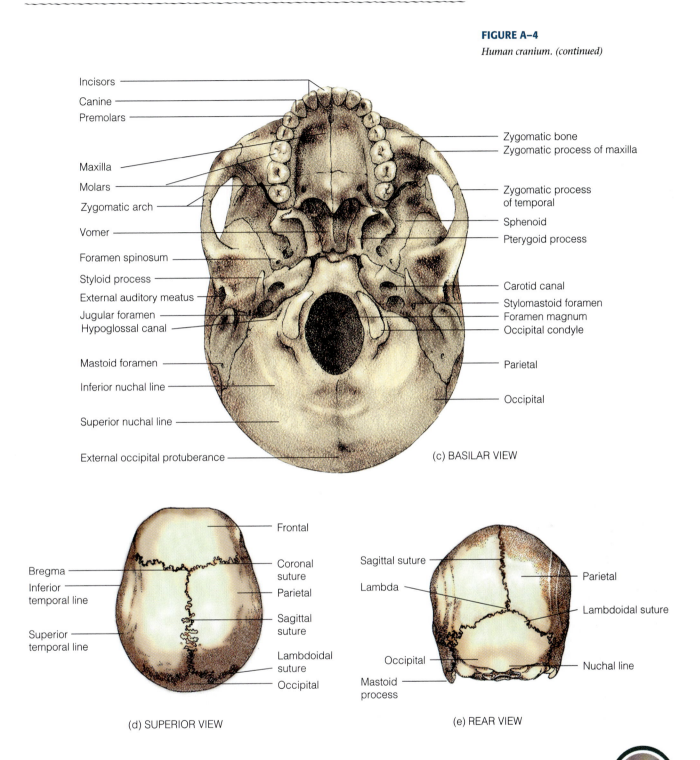

Incisors

Canine

Premolars

Maxilla

Molars

Zygomatic arch

Vomer

Foramen spinosum

Styloid process

External auditory meatus

Jugular foramen

Hypoglossal canal

Mastoid foramen

Inferior nuchal line

Superior nuchal line

External occipital protuberance

Zygomatic bone

Zygomatic process of maxilla

Zygomatic process of temporal

Sphenoid

Pterygoid process

Carotid canal

Stylomastoid foramen

Foramen magnum

Occipital condyle

Parietal

Occipital

(c) BASILAR VIEW

Bregma

Inferior temporal line

Superior temporal line

Frontal

Coronal suture

Parietal

Sagittal suture

Lambdoidal suture

Occipital

(d) SUPERIOR VIEW

Sagittal suture

Lambda

Occipital

Mastoid process

Parietal

Lambdoidal suture

Nuchal line

(e) REAR VIEW

Cranial, mandibular, and dental anatomy are covered in Virtual Lab 5, section II. You can test your knowledge with the virtual exercise in section III.

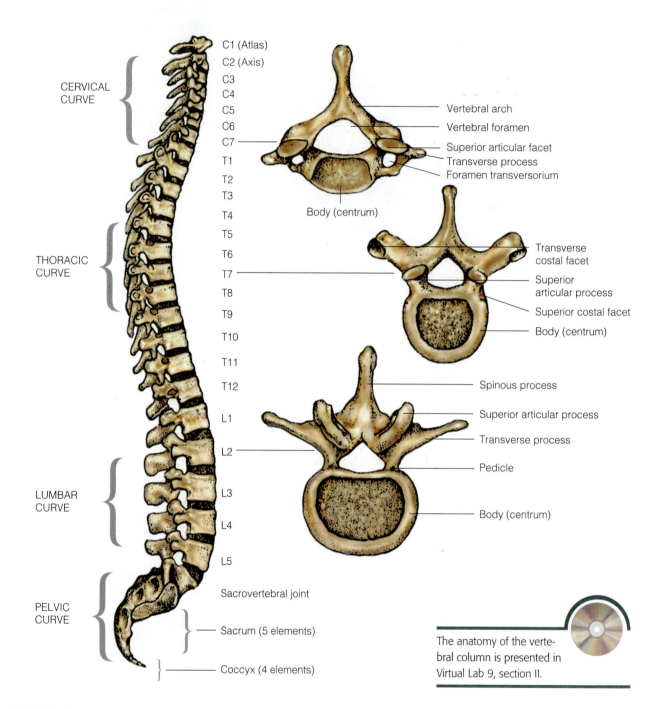

CERVICAL CURVE

THORACIC CURVE

LUMBAR CURVE

PELVIC CURVE

C1 (Atlas)
C2 (Axis)
C3
C4
C5
C6
C7
T1
T2
T3
T4
T5
T6
T7
T8
T9
T10
T11
T12
L1
L2
L3
L4
L5
Sacrovertebral joint
Sacrum (5 elements)
Coccyx (4 elements)

Vertebral arch
Vertebral foramen
Superior articular facet
Transverse process
Foramen transversorium
Body (centrum)

Transverse costal facet
Superior articular process
Superior costal facet
Body (centrum)

Spinous process
Superior articular process
Transverse process
Pedicle
Body (centrum)

The anatomy of the vertebral column is presented in Virtual Lab 9, section II.

FIGURE A–5

Human vertebral column (lateral view) and representative cervical, thoracic, and lumbar vertebrae (superior views).

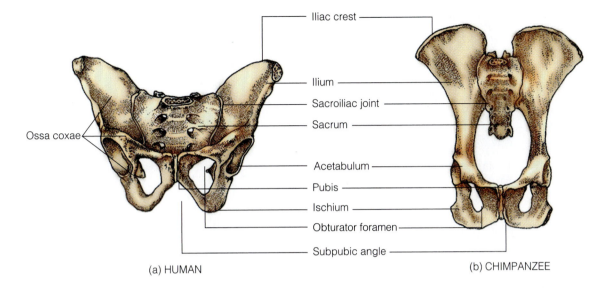

Iliac crest

Ilium

Sacroiliac joint

Sacrum

Acetabulum

Pubis

Ischium

Obturator foramen

Subpubic angle

Ossa coxae

(a) HUMAN

(b) CHIMPANZEE

FIGURE A–6

Pelvic girdles.

The anatomy of the pelvis is presented in Virtual Lab 9, section I.

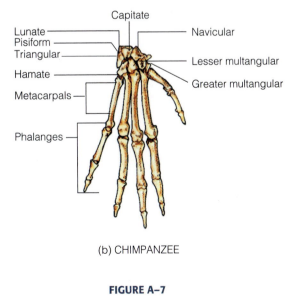

Pisiform

Triangular

Hamate

Capitate

5th metacarpal

Phalanges

Lunate

Navicular

Greater multangular

Lesser multangular

1st metacarpal

Capitate

Lunate
Pisiform
Triangular

Hamate

Metacarpals

Phalanges

Navicular

Lesser multangular

Greater multangular

(a) HUMAN

(b) CHIMPANZEE

FIGURE A–7

Hand anatomy.

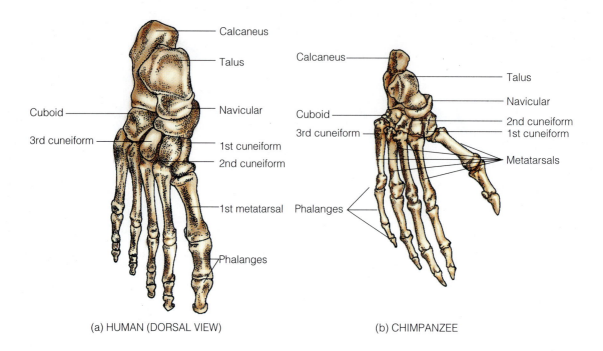

(a) HUMAN (DORSAL VIEW)

(b) CHIMPANZEE

The anatomy and function of the foot is presented in Virtual Lab 9, section IV.

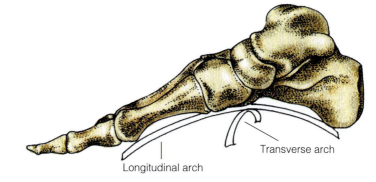

(c) HUMAN (MEDIAL VIEW)

FIGURE A–8

Foot (pedal) anatomy.

Multimedia Tools

■ **Virtual Laboratories for Physical Anthropology CD-ROM**
The following concepts in Appendix A are covered on the physical anthropology CD-ROM:
skeleton, anatomical terms, lever system models (Virtual Labs 3.I, II; 9)
forelimb, limb lengths (Virtual Labs 3, 4)
skull, cranium, mandible, dentition (Virtual Lab 5.II, III)
vertebral column (Virtual Lab 9.II)
pelvic anatomy (Virtual Lab 9.I)
foot anatomy (Virtual Lab 9.IV)

Appendix B

- Swanscombe
- Boxgrove
- St. Césaire
- La Chapelle
- Cro Magnon
- Atapuerca
- Salé
- Rabat
- Tighenif
- Spy
- Neander Valley
- Heidelberg (Mauer)
- Krapina
- Arago
- Petralona
- Amud
- Skhul/Tabun
- Dmanisi
- Shanidar
- Teshik Tash
- Jinniushan
- Zhoukoudian
- Lantian
- Dali
- Hexian
- Maba
- Bahr el Ghazal
- Hadar
- Aramis
- Bodo
- Konso-Gardula
- Omo
- Kanapoi
- East and West Turkana
- Olduvai/Laetoli
- Sangiran
- Trinil
- Ngandong
- Broken Hill
- Makapansgat
- Sterkfontein/Swartkrans/Kromdraai
- Taung
- Border Cave
- Florisbad
- Klasies River Mouth
- Lake Mungo
- Kow Swamp

1. SLOVENIA
2. CROATIA
3. BOSNIA AND HERZEGOVINA
4. ALBANIA
5. MACEDONIA

GEOGRAPHIC DISTRIBUTION OF LIVING NONHUMAN PRIMATES

WORLD POLITICAL MAP

180° 160°W 140°W 120°W 100°W 80°W 60°W 40°W 20°W

80°N

GREENLAND
(KALAALLIT NUNAAT)
(Den.)

ARCTIC CIRC

ALASKA
(U.S.)

60°N

ICELAND

UNITED
KINGDOM

IRELAND
(EIRE)

CANADA

40°N

*Atlantic
Ocean*

UNITED STATES

PORTUGAL SPAIN

AZORE IS.
(Port.)

MOROCCO

CANARY IS.
(Sp.)

TROPIC OF CANCER

MEXICO

BAHAMAS

CUBA
HAITI

DOMINICAN REP.

20°N

HAWAII
(U.S.)

CAPE VERDE IS.

MAURITANIA

BELIZE
HONDURAS
JAMAICA

PUERTO
RICO (U.S.)

ANTIGUA & BARBUDA
GUADELOUPE (Fr.)
DOMINICA
MARTINIQUE (Fr.)
BARBADOS
GRENADA
TRINIDAD & TOBAGO

SENEGAL

GAMBIA

BURKIN
FASO

GUATEMALA
EL SALVADOR
NICARAGUA

NETHERLANDS
ANTILLES (Neth.)

GUINEA BISSAU

GUINEA

IVORY
COAST

*Pacific
Ocean*

COSTA RICA

VENEZUELA

PANAMA

COLOMBIA

GUYANA

SURINAME
FRENCH GUIANA
(Fr.)

SIERRA LEONE

LIBERIA

EQUATOR

ECUADOR

EQUATORIA

GALAPAGOS IS.
(Ecuador)

0°

WESTERN
SAMOA

BRAZIL

AMERICAN
SAMOA (U.S.)

SOCIETY IS.
(Fr.)

FRENCH
POLYNESIA
(Fr.)

PERU

TONGA

TAHITI (Fr.)

BOLIVIA

20°S

TROPIC OF CAPRICORN

PARAGUAY

PITCAIRN IS.
(U.K.)

EASTER ISLAND
(Chile)

CHILE

*Atlantic
Ocean*

URUGUAY

| 0 | 500 | 1000 | 1500 miles |
| 0 | 1000 | | 2000 kms |

Equatorial Scale

ARGENTINA

40°S

FALKLAND IS.
(U.K.)

60°S

ANTARCTIC CIRCLE

80°S

180° 160°W 140°W 120°W 100°W 80°W 60°W 40°W 20°W

Arctic Ocean

80°N

NORWAY
SWEDEN
FINLAND
RUSSIA
60°N
ESTONIA
(Rus.)
LATVIA
LITHUANIA
DENMARK
BELARUS
NETH.
GERMANY
POLAND
BEL.
LUX.
CZECH REP.
SLOVAKIA
UKRAINE
KAZAKHSTAN
MONGOLIA
FRANCE
AUS.
HUNG.
MOLDOVA
SWITZERLAND
ROMANIA
UZBEKISTAN
40°N
ITALY
YUGO.
BULGARIA
KYRGYZSTAN
GEORGIA
Mediterranean Sea
GREECE
ARMENIA
AZERBAIJAN
TAJIKISTAN
TURKEY
TURKMENISTAN
CHINA
JAPAN
NORTH KOREA
Pacific Ocean
CYPRUS
SYRIA
LEBANON
ISRAEL
IRAQ
IRAN
AFGHANISTAN
SOUTH KOREA
TUNISIA
JORDAN
KUWAIT
PAKISTAN
ALGERIA
LIBYA
EGYPT
BAHRAIN
QATAR
U.A.E.
NEPAL
BHUTAN
TAIWAN
TROPIC OF CANCER
SAUDI ARABIA
OMAN
INDIA
BANGLADESH
MYANMAR (BURMA)
LAOS
HONG KONG (U.K.)
MACAU (Port.)
20°N
NORTHERN MARIANA ISLANDS (U.S.)
NIGER
CHAD
SUDAN
ERITREA
YEMEN
THAILAND
VIETNAM
PHILIPPINES
REPUBLIC OF THE MARSHALL ISLANDS
BENIN
NIGERIA
DJIBOUTI
CAMBODIA
TOGO
CENTRAL AFRICAN REP.
ETHIOPIA
SOMALIA
GUINEA
SRI LANKA
BRUNEI
GABON
UGANDA
MALAYSIA
FEDERATED STATES OF MICRONESIA
SAO TOME & PRINCIPE
CONGO
RWANDA
KENYA
MALDIVES
Borneo
EQUATOR
0°
DEMOCRATIC REPUBLIC OF THE CONGO
BURUNDI
Sumatra
SINGAPORE
CABINDA (Angola)
TANZANIA
INDONESIA
PAPUA NEW GUINEA
SOLOMON ISLANDS
SEYCHELLES
TUVALU
ANGOLA
COMOROS IS.
Indian Ocean
MALAWI
ZAMBIA
MOZAMBIQUE
VANUATU
FIJI
ZIMBABWE
MADAGASCAR
NEW CALEDONIA (Fr.)
20°S
NAMIBIA
BOTSWANA
MAURITIUS
TROPIC OF CAPRICORN
WALVIS BAY (Status to be determined)
AUSTRALIA
SWAZILAND
SOUTH AFRICA
LESOTHO

NEW ZEALAND
40°S

1. SLOVENIA
2. CROATIA
3. BOSNIA AND HERZEGOVINA
4. ALBANIA
5. MACEDONIA

60°S

ANTARCTIC CIRCLE

ANTARCTICA
80°S

20°E 40°E 60°E 80°E 100°E 120°E 140°E 160°E 180°

Glossary

Acclimatization   Physiological response to changes in the environment that occurs during an individual's lifetime. Such responses may be short-term. The capacity for acclimatization may typify an entire population or species. This capacity is under genetic influence and thus is subject to evolutionary factors such as natural selection.

Acheulian (ash´-oo-lay-en)   Pertaining to a stone tool industry of the Lower and Middle Pleistocene characterized by a large proportion of bifacial tools (flaked on both sides). Acheulian tool kits are very common in Africa, Southwest Asia, and western Europe, but are nearly absent elsewhere. (Also spelled "Acheulean.")

Adaptation   Functional response of organisms or populations to the environment. Adaptation results from evolutionary change (specifically, as a result of natural selection).

Adaptive niche   The entire way of life of an organism: where it lives, what it eats, how it gets food, etc.

Adaptive radiation   The relatively rapid expansion and diversification of life forms into new ecological niches.

Adolescence   The time in the human life cycle between puberty and the completion of growth, or adulthood.

Adolescent growth spurt   The period during adolescence in which well-nourished teens typically increase in stature at greater rates than at other points in the life cycle.

Affiliative   Pertaining to amicable associations between individuals. Affiliative behaviors, such as grooming, reinforce social bonds and promote group cohesion.

Allele frequency   In a population, the percentage of all the alleles at a locus accounted for by one specific allele.

Alleles   Alternate forms of a gene. Alleles occur at the same locus on homologous chromosomes and thus govern the same trait. However, because they are different, their action may result in different expressions of that trait. The term is often used synonymously with *gene*.

Allometry   Also called "scaling," the differential proportion among various anatomical structures. For example, the relative size of the brain changes during the development of an individual. Moreover, scaling effects must also be considered when comparing species.

Alloparenting   A common behavior in many primate species whereby individuals other than the parent(s) hold, carry, and in general interact with infants.

Altruism   Behaving in a manner that benefits another individual but at some potential risk or cost to oneself.

Amino acids   Small molecules that are the components of proteins.

Analogies   Similarities between organisms based strictly on common function with no assumed common evolutionary descent.

Anatomically modern *H. sapiens*   All modern humans and some fossil forms, perhaps dating as early as 200,000 y.a.; defined by a set of derived characteristics, including cranial architecture and lack of skeletal robusticity; usually classified at the subspecies level as *Homo sapiens sapiens*.

Ancestral (primitive)   Referring to characters inherited by a group of organisms from a remote ancestor and thus not diagnostic of groups (lineages) branching subsequent to the time the character first appears.

Anthropocentric   Viewing non-human phenomena in terms of human experience and capabilities. Emphasizing the importance of humans over everything else.

Anthropoids   Members of the sub-order of Primates, the *Anthropoidea*. Traditionally, the suborder includes monkeys, apes, and humans.

Anthropology   The field of inquiry that studies human culture and evolutionary aspects of human biology; includes cultural anthropology, archaeology, linguistics, and physical anthropology.

Anthropometry   Measurement of human body parts. When osteologists measure skeletal elements, the term *osteometry* is often used.

Antigens   Large molecules found on the surface of cells. Several different loci governing antigens on red and white blood cells are known. Foreign antigens provoke an immune response in individuals.

Arboreal   Tree-living; adapted to life in the trees.

Arboreal hypothesis   The traditional view that primate characteristics can be explained as a consequence of primate diversification into arboreal habitats.

Archaic *H. sapiens*   Earlier forms of *Homo sapiens* (including Neandertals) from the Old World that differ from *H. erectus* but lack the full set of characteristics diagnostic of modern *H. sapiens.*

Artifacts   Objects or materials made or modified for use by hominids. The earliest artifacts tend to be tools made of stone or, occasionally, bone.

Association   What an archaeological trace is found with.

Aurignacian   Pertaining to an Upper Paleolithic stone tool industry in Europe beginning at about 40,000 y.a.

Australopithecine   (os-tra-loh-pith´-e-seen) The colloquial name for members of the genus *Australopithecus.* The term was first used as a subfamily designation, but it is now most commonly used informally.

Australopithecus   An early hominid genus, known from the Plio-Pleistocene of Africa, characterized by bipedal locomotion, a relatively small brain, and large back teeth.

Autonomic   Pertaining to physiological responses not under voluntary control. An example in chimpanzees would be the erection of body hair during excitement. An example in humans is blushing. Both convey information regarding emotional states, but neither is a deliberate behavior, and communication is not intended.

Autosomes   All chromosomes except the sex chromosomes.

Balanced polymorphism   The maintenance of two or more alleles in a population due to the selective advantage of the heterozygote.

Beriberi   Disease resulting from a dietary deficiency of thiamine (vitamin B_1). Symptoms include nerve damage and cardiovascular problems.

Binocular vision   Vision characterized by overlapping visual fields provided by forward-facing eyes; essential to depth perception.

Binomial nomenclature   (*binomial,* meaning "two names") In taxonomy, the convention established by Carolus Linnaeus whereby genus and species names are used to refer to species. For example, *Homo sapiens* refers to human beings.

Biocultural evolution   The mutual, interactive evolution of human biology and culture; the concept that biology makes culture possible and that developing culture further influences the direction of biological evolution; a basic concept in understanding the unique components of human evolution.

Biological continuum   Refers to the fact that organisms are related through common ancestry and that behaviors and traits seen in one species are also seen in others to varying degrees. (When expressions of a phenomenon continuously grade into one another so that there are no discrete categories, they are said to exist on a continuum. Color is such a phenomenon.)

Biological determinism   The concept that phenomena, including various aspects of behavior (e.g., intelligence, values, morals) are governed by biological (genetic) factors; the inaccurate association of various behavioral attributes with certain biological traits, such as skin color.

Biostratigraphy   Dating method based on evolutionary changes within an evolving lineage.

Bipedally   On two feet. Walking habitually on two legs is the single most distinctive feature of the Hominidae.

Brachiation   A form of locomotion in which the body is suspended beneath the hands and support is alter-

nated from one forelimb to the other; arm swinging.

Brachycephalic   Having a broad head in which the width measures more than 80 percent of the length.

Breeding isolates   Populations that are clearly isolated geographically and/or socially from other breeding groups.

Burins   Small, chisel-like tools (with a pointed end) thought to have been used to engrave bone, antler, ivory, or wood.

Catastrophism   The view that the earth's geological landscape is the result of violent cataclysmic events. This view was promoted by Cuvier, especially in opposition to Lamarck.

Catch-up period   A period of time during which a child who has experienced delayed growth because of malnutrition, undernutrition, or disease can increase in height to the point of his or her genetic potential.

Centromere   The constricted portion of a chromosome. After replication, the two strands of a double-stranded chromosome are joined at the centromere.

Cercopithecines   (serk-oh-pith´-eh-seens) The subfamily of Old World monkeys that includes baboons, macaques, and guenons.

Chatelperronian   Pertaining to an Upper Paleolithic tool industry found in France and Spain, containing blade tools and associated with Neandertals.

Childhood   The phase of the life cycle between weaning and puberty.

Chordata (Chordates)   The phylum of the animal kingdom that includes vertebrates.

Chromatin   The loose, diffuse form of DNA seen during interphase. When condensed, chromatin forms into chromosomes.

Chromosomes   Discrete structures composed of DNA and protein found only in the nuclei of cells. Chromosomes are only visible under magnification during certain phases of cell division.

Chronometric dating (*chrono*, meaning "time," and *metric*, meaning "measure") A dating technique that gives an estimate in actual numbers of years.

Cladistics   An approach to classification that seeks to make rigorous evolutionary interpretations based solely on analysis of certain types of homologous (i.e., derived) characters.

Cladogram   A chart showing evolutionary relationships as determined by cladistic analysis. It is based solely on interpretation of shared derived characters. No time component is indicated, and ancestor-descendant relationships are *not* inferred.

Classification   In biology, the ordering of organisms into categories, such as phyla, orders, and families, to show evolutionary relationships.

Cline   Gradual change in frequency of genotypes and phenotypes over geographical space.

Clone   An organism that is genetically identical to another organism. The term may also be used to refer to genetically identical DNA segments and molecules.

Codominance   The expression of two alleles in heterozygotes. In this situation, neither allele is dominant or recessive, so that both influence the phenotype.

Codon   A triplet of messenger RNA bases that refers to a specific amino acid during protein synthesis.

Colobines   (kole´-uh-beans) The subfamily of Old World monkeys that includes the African colobus monkeys and Asian langurs.

Communication   Any act that conveys information, in the form of a message, to another individual. Frequently, the result of communication is a change in the behavior of the recipient. Communication may not be deliberate but may be the result of involuntary processes or a secondary consequence of an intentional action.

Complementary   Referring to the fact that DNA bases form base pairs in a precise manner. For example, adenine can bond only to thymine. Thus, these two bases are said to be *complementary* because one requires the other to form a complete DNA base pair.

Conspecifics   Members of the same species.

Context   The environmental setting where an archaeological trace is found. *Primary* context is the setting in which the archaeological trace was originally deposited. A *secondary* context is one to which it has been moved (e.g., by the action of a stream).

Continental drift   The movement of continents on sliding plates of the earth's surface. As a result, the position of large landmasses has shifted dramatically during earth's history.

Continuum   A set of relationships in which all components fall along a single integrated spectrum. All life reflects a single *biological* continuum.

Core   Stone reduced by flake removal, and not necessarily a "tool" itself.

Core area   The portion of a home range containing the highest concentration and most reliable supplies of food and water. The core area is frequently the area that will be defended.

Cretinism   Mental and growth retardation in infants resulting from iodine deficiency in the mother during pregnancy.

Culture   All aspects of human adaptation, including technology, traditions, language, and social roles. Culture is learned and transmitted from one generation to the next by nonbiological means.

Cusps   The elevated portions (bumps) on the chewing surfaces of premolar and molar teeth.

Cytoplasm   The portion of the cell contained within the cell membrane, excluding the nucleus. The cytoplasm consists of a semifluid material and contains numerous structures involved with cell function.

Data   (*sing.*, datum) Facts from which conclusions can be drawn; scientific information.

Deoxyribonucleic acid (DNA)   The double-stranded molecule that contains the genetic code. DNA is a main component of chromosomes.

Derived (modified)   Referring to characters that are modified from the ancestral condition and thus *are* diagnostic of particular evolutionary lineages.

Development   Differentiation of cells into different types of tissues and their maturation.

Diploid   Referring to the full complement of chromosomes in a somatic cell—two of each pair.

Direct percussion   Striking a core or flake with a hammerstone.

Displays   Sequences of repetitious behaviors that serve to communicate emotional states. Nonhuman primate displays are most frequently associated with reproductive or agonistic behavior.

Distal   The end of a bone that is farthest from the point at which the bone attaches to the body. For example, the elbow is at the distal end of the humerus.

Diurnal   Active during the day.

Dolichocephalic   Having a long, narrow head in which the width measures less than 75 percent of the length.

Dominance hierarchies   Systems of social organization wherein individuals within a group are ranked relative to one another. Higher-ranking individuals have greater access to preferred food items and mating partners than lower-ranking individuals. Dominance hierarchies are sometimes referred to as "pecking orders."

Dominant   Describing a trait governed by an allele that can be expressed in the presence of another, different allele (i.e., in heterozygotes). Dominant alleles prevent the expression of recessive alleles in heterozygotes. (This is the definition of *complete* dominance.)

Ecological   Pertaining to the relationship between organisms and all aspects of their environment.

Ecological niches   The positions of species within their physical and biological environments, together making up the *ecosystem*. A species' ecological niche is defined by such components as diet, terrain, vegetation, type of predators, relationships with other species, and activity patterns, and each niche is unique to a given species.

Empirical   Relying on experiment or observation; from the Latin *empiricus,* meaning "experienced."

Encephalization   The proportional size of the brain relative to some other measure, usually some estimate of overall body size. More precisely, the term refers to increases in brain size beyond that which would be expected given the body size of a particular species.

Endemic   Continuously present in a population.

Endocast   A solid impression of the inside of the skull, often preserving details relating to the size and surface features of the brain.

Endogamy   Mating with individuals from the same group.

Endothermic   (*endo,* meaning "within" or "internal") Able to maintain internal body temperature through the production of energy by means of metabolic processes within cells; characteristic feature of mammals, birds, and perhaps some dinosaurs.

Environmental determinism   An interpretation that links simple environmental changes directly to a major evolutionary shift in an organism. Such explanations tend to be extreme oversimplifications of the evolutionary process.

Enzymes   Specialized proteins that initiate and direct chemical reactions in the body.

Epochs   Categories of the geological time scale; subdivisions of periods. In the Cenozoic, epochs include Paleocene,

Eocene, Oligocene, Miocene, Pliocene (from the Tertiary), and the Pleistocene and Holocene (from the Quaternary).

Essential amino acids   The eight (nine for infants) amino acids that must be ingested by humans for normal growth and body maintenance; include tryptophan, leucine, lysine, methionine, phenylalanine, isoleucine, valine, and threonine (histidine for infants).

Estrus   (ess´-truss) Period of sexual receptivity in female mammals (except humans); correlated with ovulation. When used as an adjective, the word is spelled "estrous."

Ethnocentric   Viewing other cultures from the inherently biased perspective of one's own culture. Ethnocentrism often results in cultures being seen as inferior to one's own.

Ethnographies   Detailed descriptive studies of human societies. In cultural anthropology, an ethnography is traditionally the study of a non-Western society.

Eugenics   The philosophy of "race improvement" through forced sterilization of members of some groups and encouraged reproduction among others; an overly simplified, often racist, view that is now discredited.

Evolution   A change in the genetic structure of a population. The term is also frequently used to refer to the appearance of a new species. (Modern genetic definition: A change in the frequency of alleles from one generation to the next.)

Evolutionary pulse theory   A view that postulates a correlation of periods of hominid diversification during the Pliocene and early Pleistocene with major shifts in several African mammalian species. These changes in mammalian evolution, in turn, are thought to be related to periodic episodes of aridity.

Evolutionary systematics   A traditional approach to classification (and evolutionary interpretation) in which presumed ancestors and descendants

are traced in time by analysis of homologous characters.

Evolutionary trends   Overall characteristics of an evolving lineage, such as the primates. Such trends are useful in helping categorize the lineage as compared to other lineages (i.e., other placental mammals).

Exogamy   Mating pattern whereby individuals obtain mates from groups other than their own.

Fertility   Production of offspring; distinguished from *fecundity,* which is the ability to produce children. For example, a woman in her early 20s is probably fecund, but she is not actually fertile unless she has had children.

Fitness   Pertaining to natural selection, a measure of *relative* reproductive success of individuals. Fitness can be measured by an individual's genetic contribution to the next generation compared to that of other individuals.

Fixity of species   The notion that species, once created, can never change; an idea diametrically opposed to theories of biological evolution.

Flake   Thin-edged fragment removed from a core.

Flexed   The position of the body in a bent orientation, with the arms and legs drawn up to the chest.

Foramen magnum   The opening at the base of the skull through which the spinal cord passes as it enters the body to descend through the vertebral column. In quadrupeds, it is located more to the rear of the skull, while in bipeds, it is located farther beneath the skull.

Forensic anthropology   An applied anthropological approach dealing with legal matters. Physical anthropologists work with coroners and others in the analysis and identification of human remains.

Founder effect   Also called the *Sewall Wright effect,* a type of genetic drift in which allele frequencies are altered in small populations that are taken from, or are remnants of, larger populations.

Free-ranging   Pertaining to non-captive animals living in their natural habitat, largely free from constraints imposed by humans.

Frugivorous   (fru-give´-or-us) Having a diet composed primarily of fruit.

Gametes   Reproductive cells (eggs and sperm in animals) developed from precursor cells in ovaries and testes.

Gene   A sequence of DNA bases that specifies the order of amino acids in an entire protein or, in some cases, a portion of a protein. A gene may be made up of hundreds or thousands of DNA bases.

Gene flow   Exchange of genes between populations.

Gene pool   The total complement of genes shared by reproductive members of a population.

Genetic drift   Evolutionary changes—that is, changes in allele frequencies—produced by random factors. Genetic drift is a result of small population size.

Genetics   The study of gene structure and action and the patterns of inheritance of traits from parent to offspring. Genetic mechanisms are the underlying foundation for evolutionary change.

Genome   The entire genetic makeup of an individual or of a species. In humans, it is estimated that each individual possesses approximately 3 billion DNA nucleotides.

Genotype   The genetic makeup of an individual. Genotype can refer to an organism's entire genetic makeup or to the alleles at a particular locus.

Genus   A group of closely related species.

Geological time scale   The organization of earth history into eras, periods, and epochs; commonly used by geologists and paleoanthropologists.

Goiter   Enlargement of the thyroid gland resulting from a dietary deficiency of iodine.

Grooming   Picking through fur to remove dirt, parasites, and other materials that may be present. Social grooming is common among primates and reinforces social relationships.

Growth   Increase in mass or number of cells.

Haploid   Referring to a half set of chromosomes, one member of each pair. Haploid sets are found in gametes.

Hardy-Weinberg theory of genetic equilibrium   The mathematical relationship expressing—under ideal conditions—the predicted distribution of alleles in populations; the central theorem of population genetics.

Hemizygous   (*hemi*, meaning "half") Having only one member of a pair of alleles. Because males have only one X chromosome, all their X-linked alleles are hemizygous. All recessive alleles on a male's X chromosome are expressed in the phenotype.

Hemoglobin   A protein molecule that occurs in red blood cells and binds to oxygen molecules.

Heterodont   Having different kinds of teeth; characteristic of mammals, whose teeth consist of incisors, canines, premolars, and molars.

Heterozygous   Having different alleles at the same locus on members of a chromosome pair.

Home range   The area exploited by an animal or social group; usually given for one year—or for the entire lifetime—of an animal.

Homeobox genes   A group of genes found in vertebrates that plays a major role in the embryonic development of such structures as the vertebral column, limbs, and gut.

Homeostasis   A condition of balance, or stability, within a biological system, maintained by the interaction of physiological mechanisms that compensate for changes (both external and internal).

Hominidae   The taxonomic family to which humans belong; also includes other, now extinct, bipedal relatives.

Hominids   Colloquial term for members of the family Hominidae which includes all bipedal hominoids back to the divergence from African great apes.

Hominoidea   The formal designation for the superfamily of anthropoids that includes apes and humans.

Hominoids   Members of the superfamily Hominoidea. The group includes apes and humans.

Homo habilis   (hab´-ah-liss) A species of early *Homo,* well known from East Africa, but perhaps also found in other regions.

Homologies   Similarities between organisms based on descent from a common ancestor.

Homologous   Referring to members of chromosome pairs. Homologous chromosomes carry loci that govern the same traits. During meiosis, homologous chromosomes pair and exchange segments of DNA. They are alike with regard to size, position of centromere, and banding pattern.

Homoplasy   (*homo*, meaning "same," and *plasy*, meaning "growth") The separate evolutionary development of similar characteristics in different groups of organisms.

Homozygous   Having the same allele at the same locus on both members of a chromosome pair.

Hormones   Substances (usually proteins) that are produced by specialized cells and that travel to other parts of the body, where they influence chemical reactions and regulate various cellular functions.

Human Genome Project   An international effort aimed at sequencing and mapping the entire human genome.

Hybrids   Offspring of mixed ancestry; heterozygotes.

Hypothesis   (*pl.,* hypotheses) A provisional explanation of a phenomenon. Hypotheses require verification.

Hypoxia   Lack of oxygen. Hypoxia can refer to reduced amounts of available oxygen in the atmosphere (due to lowered barometric pressure) or to insufficient amounts of oxygen in the body.

Inbreeding   A type of nonrandom mating in which relatives mate more often than predicted under random mating conditions.

Infancy   The phase of the life cycle from birth until weaning, usually about four years in humans and great apes.

Intelligence   Mental capacity; ability to learn, reason, or comprehend and interpret information, facts, relationships, meanings, etc.; the capacity to solve problems, whether through the application of previously acquired knowledge or through insight.

Interphase   The portion of a cell's cycle during which metabolic processes and other cellular activities occur. Chromosomes are not visible as discrete structures at this time. DNA replication occurs during interphase.

Interspecific   Between species; refers to variation beyond that seen within the same species to include additional aspects seen between two different species.

Intraspecific   Within species; refers to variation seen within the same species.

Ischial callosities   Patches of tough, hard skin on the buttocks of Old World monkeys and chimpanzees.

K-selected   Pertaining to an adaptive strategy whereby individuals produce relatively few offspring, in whom they invest increased parental care. Although only a few infants are born, chances of survival are increased for each individual because of parental investments in time and energy. Examples of non-primate K-selected species are birds and canids (e.g., wolves, coyotes, and dogs).

Karyotype   The chromosomal complement of an individual or that which is typical for a species. Usually displayed in a photomicrograph, the chro-

mosomes are arranged in pairs and according to size and position of the centromere.

Knappers   Those who flake stone tools.

Lactation   The production of milk in mammals.

Lactose intolerance   The inability to digest fresh milk products; caused by the discontinued production of *lactase,* the enzyme that breaks down lactose, or milk sugar.

Large-bodied hominoids   Those hominoids including the great apes (orangutans, chimpanzees, gorillas) and hominids, as well as all ancestral forms back to the time of divergence from small-bodied hominoids (i.e., the gibbon lineage).

Life history   Basic components of an animal's development and physiology, viewed from an evolutionary perspective. Such key components include body size, proportional brain size, metabolism, and reproduction.

Linked   Describing genetic loci or genes located on the same chromosome.

Lithic   (*lith,* meaning "stone") Referring to stone tools.

Locus   (*pl.,* loci) (pronounced lo´-kus and lo-sigh´) The position on a chromosome where a given gene occurs. The term is sometimes used interchangeably with *gene,* but this usage is technically incorrect.

Macaques   (muh-kaks´) Group of Old World monkeys made up of several species, including rhesus monkeys.

Macroevolution   Changes produced only after many generations, such as the appearance of a new species.

Magdalenian   Pertaining to the final phase (stone tool industry) of the Upper Paleolithic in Europe.

Malnutrition   A diet insufficient in quality (i.e., lacking some essential component) to support normal health.

Mammalia   The technical term for the formal grouping (class) of mammals.

Material culture   The physical manifestations of human activities; includes tools, art, and structures. As the most durable aspects of culture, material remains make up the majority of archaeological evidence of past societies.

Meiosis   Cell division in specialized cells in ovaries and testes. Meiosis involves two divisions and results in four daughter cells, each containing only half the original number of chromosomes. These cells can develop into gametes.

Menarche   The first menstruation in girls, usually occurring in the early to mid-teens.

Mendelian traits   Characteristics that are influenced by alleles at only one genetic locus. Examples include many blood types, such as ABO. Many genetic disorders, including sickle-cell anemia and Tay-Sachs disease, are also Mendelian traits.

Menopause   The end of menstruation in human women, usually occurring at around age 50.

Messenger RNA (mRNA)   A form of RNA that is assembled on a sequence of DNA bases. It carries the DNA code to the ribosome during protein synthesis.

Metazoa   Multicellular animals; a major division of the animal kingdom.

Microevolution   Small changes occurring within species, such as a change in allele frequencies.

Microliths   (*micro,* meaning "small," and *lith,* meaning "stone") Small stone tools usually produced from narrow blades punched from a core; found especially in Africa during the latter part of the Pleistocene.

Microwear   Polishes, striations, and other diagnostic microscopic changes on the edges of stone tools.

Midline   An anatomical term referring to a hypothetical line that divides the body into right and left halves.

Mitochondria   (*sing.,* mitochondrion) Organelles found in the cytoplasm of cells that are responsible for producing energy for cellular functions.

Mitosis   Simple cell division; the process by which somatic cells divide to produce two identical daughter cells.

Molecules   Structures made up of two or more atoms. Molecules can combine with other molecules to form more complex structures.

Monogenism   The theory that all human populations are descended from one pair (Adam and Eve), but they differ from one another because they have occupied different habitats. This concept was an attempt to explain phenotypic variation between groups, but did not imply evolutionary change.

Morphological   Pertaining to the form and structure of organisms.

Morphology   The form (shape, size) of anatomical structures; can also refer to the entire organism.

Mosaic evolution   Rates of evolution in one functional system vary from those in other systems. For example, in hominid evolution, the dental system, locomotor system, and neurological system (especially the brain) all evolved at markedly different rates.

Motor cortex   That portion of the cortex pertaining to outgoing signals involved in muscle use. (The *cortex* of the brain, the outer layer, is composed of nerve cells or neurons.)

Mousterian   Pertaining to the stone tool industry associated with Neandertals and some modern *H. sapiens* groups; also called Middle Paleolithic. This industry is characterized by a larger proportion of flake tools than is found in Acheulian tool kits.

Mutation   A change in DNA. Technically, mutation refers to changes in DNA bases as well as changes in chromosome number and/or structure.

Natural selection   The mechanism of evolutionary change first articulated by Charles Darwin; refers to genetic change or changes in the frequencies of certain traits in populations due to differential reproductive success between individuals.

Negative assortative mating   A type of nonrandom mating in which individuals of unlike phenotype mate more often than predicted under random mating conditions.

Nocturnal   Active during the night.

Nondisjunction   The failure of homologous chromosomes or chromosome strands to separate during cell division.

Nonrandom mating   Patterns of mating in a population in which individuals choose mates preferentially.

Nuchal torus   (nuke´-ul, pertaining to the neck) A projection of bone in the back of the cranium where neck muscles attach, used to hold up the head. The nuchal torus is a distinctive feature of *H. erectus*.

Nucleotides   Basic units of the DNA molecule, composed of a sugar, a phosphate, and one of four DNA bases.

Nucleus   A structure (organelle) found in all eukaryotic cells. The nucleus contains chromosomes (nuclear DNA).

Ossification   Process by which cartilage cells are replaced by bone cells.

Osteodontokeratic   (*osteo,* meaning "bone," *donto,* meaning "tooth," and *keratic,* meaning "horn")

Osteology   The study of skeletal material. Human osteology focuses on the interpretation of the skeletal remains of past groups. The same techniques are used in paleoanthropology to study early hominids.

Paleoanthropology   The interdisciplinary approach to the study of earlier hominids—their chronology, physical structure, archaeological remains, habitats, etc.

Paleoecologists   (*paleo,* meaning "old," and *ecology,* meaning "environmental setting") Scientists who study ancient environments.

Paleomagnetism   Dating method based on the shifting magnetic pole.

Paleopathology   The branch of osteology that studies the traces of disease and injury in human skeletal (or, occasionally, mummified) remains.

Paleospecies   Species defined from fossil evidence, often covering a long time span.

Paradigm   A cognitive construct or framework within which we explain phenomena. Paradigms shape our world view. They can change as a result of technological and intellectual innovation.

Pathogens   Substances or microorganisms, such as bacteria, fungi, or viruses, that cause disease.

Pedigree chart   A diagram showing family relationships in order to trace the hereditary pattern of particular genetic (usually Mendelian) traits.

Pellagra   Disease resulting from a dietary deficiency of niacin (vitamin B_3). Symptoms include dermatitis, diarrhea, dementia, and death (the "four Ds").

Phenotypes   The observable or detectable physical characteristics of an organism; the detectable expressions of genotypes.

Phenotypic ratio   The proportion of one phenotype to other phenotypes in a group of organisms. For example, Mendel observed that there were approximately three tall plants for every short plant in the F_2 generation. This is expressed as a phenotypic ratio of 3:1.

Philopatric   Remaining in one's natal group or home range as an adult. In most species, members of one sex disperse from their natal group as young adults, and members of the philopatric sex remain. In the majority of non-human primate species, the philopatric sex is female.

Phylogenetic tree   A chart showing evolutionary relationships as determined by phylogenetic systematics. It contains a time component and implies ancestor-descendant relationships.

Phylogeny   A schematic representation showing ancestor-descendant relationships, usually in a chronological framework.

Phytoliths   (*phyto,* meaning "hidden," and *lith,* meaning "stone") Microscopic silica structures formed in the cells of many plants, particularly grasses.

Plasticity   The capacity to change; in a physiological context, the ability of systems or organisms to make alterations in order to respond to differing conditions.

Pleiotropic genes   Genes that have more than one effect; genes that have different effects at different times in the life cycle.

Pleiotropy   A situation whereby several seemingly unrelated phenotypic effects are influenced by the action of a single gene.

Pleistocene   The epoch of the Cenozoic from 1.8 m.y.a. until 10,000 y.a. Frequently referred to as the Ice Age, this epoch is associated with continental glaciations in northern latitudes.

Plio-Pleistocene   Pertaining to the Pliocene and first half of the Pleistocene, a time range of 5–1 m.y.a. During this time period, the earliest fossil hominids have been found in Africa.

Point mutation   A chemical change in a single base of a DNA sequence.

Polar body   A small nonviable cell that is a product of meiosis in females.

Polyandry   A mating system wherein a female continuously associates with more than one male (usually two or three) with whom she mates. Among nonhuman primates, this pattern is seen only in marmosets and tamarins.

Polygenic   Referring to traits that are influenced by genes at two or more loci. Examples of such traits are stature, skin color, and eye color. Many polygenic traits are also influenced by environmental factors.

Polygenism   A theory, opposed to monogenism, that stated that human races were not all descended from Adam and Eve. Instead, there had been several original human pairs, each giving rise to a different group. Thus, human races were considered to be separate species.

Polymerase chain reaction (PCR)   A method of producing thousands of copies of a DNA segment using the enzyme DNA polymerase.

Polymorphism   A genetic trait governed by a locus with more than one allele in appreciable frequency. That is, the locus has two or more alleles, each with a frequency of at least 1 percent.

Polypeptide chain   A sequence of amino acids that may act alone or in combination as a functional protein.

Polytypic   Referring to species composed of populations that differ with regard to the expression of one or more traits.

Population   Within a species, a community of individuals where mates are usually found.

Positive assortative mating   A type of nonrandom mating in which individuals of like phenotype mate more often than predicted under random mating conditions.

Prehensility   Grasping, as by the hands and feet of primates.

Pressure flaking   A method of removing flakes from a core by pressing a pointed implement (e.g., bone or antler) against the stone.

Primates   Members of the mammalian order Primates (pronounced "pry-may´-tees"), which includes prosimians, monkeys, apes, and humans. When the term is used colloquially, it is pronounced "pry´-mates."

Primatologists   Scientists who study the evolution, anatomy, and behavior of nonhuman primates. Those who study primate behavior in noncaptive animals are usually trained as anthropologists.

Primatology   The study of the biology and behavior of nonhuman primates (prosimians, monkeys, and apes).

Primitive   Referring to a trait or combination of traits present in an ancestral form (*see,* ancestral).

Principle of independent assortment   The distribution of one pair of alleles into gametes does not influence the distribution of another pair. The genes controlling different traits are inherited independently of one another.

Principle of segregation   Genes (alleles) occur in pairs (because chromosomes occur in pairs). During gamete production, the members of each gene pair separate, so that each gamete contains one member of each pair. During fertilization, the full number of chromosomes is restored, and members of gene or allele pairs are reunited.

Prosimians   Members of a suborder of Primates, the *Prosimii* (pronounced "pro-sim´-ee-eye"). Traditionally, the suborder includes lemurs, lorises, and tarsiers.

Protein synthesis   The assembly of chains of amino acids into functional protein molecules. The process is directed by DNA.

Proteins   Three-dimensional molecules that serve a wide variety of functions through their ability to bind to other molecules.

Protohominids   The earliest members of the hominid lineage, as yet basically unrepresented in the fossil record; thus, their structure and behavior are reconstructed hypothetically.

Provenience   In archaeology, the specific location of a discovery, including its geological context (also spelled "provenance").

Proximal   The end of a bone that is closest to the point at which the bone attaches to the body. For example, the head of the humerus is on the proximal end.

Punctuated equilibrium The concept that evolutionary change proceeds through long periods of stasis punctuated by rapid periods of change.

Quadrupedal Using all four limbs to support the body during locomotion; the basic mammalian (and primate) form of locomotion.

Quantitatively In a manner involving measurements of quantity and including such properties as size, number, and capacity. When data are quantified, they are expressed numerically and are capable of being tested statistically.

r-selected Pertaining to an adaptive strategy that emphasizes relatively large numbers of offspring and reduced parental care (compared to K-selected species). (*K-selection* and *r-selection* are relative terms; e.g., mice are r-selected compared to primates but K-selected compared to many fish species.)

Racial In biology, pertaining to populations of a species that differ from other populations of the same species with regard to some aspects of outwardly expressed phenotype. Such phenotypic variation within a species is usually associated with differences in geographical location.

Random assortment The chance distribution of chromosomes to daughter cells during meiosis; along with recombination, the source of variation resulting from meiosis.

Recessive Describing a trait that is not expressed in heterozygotes; also refers to the allele that governs the trait. For a recessive allele to be expressed, there must be two copies of the allele (i.e., the individual must be homozygous).

Recombination (crossing over) The exchange of genetic material between homologous chromosomes during meiosis.

Replicate To duplicate. The DNA molecule is able to make copies of itself.

Reproductive strategies The complex of behavioral patterns that contributes to individual reproductive success. The behaviors need not be deliberate, and they often vary considerably between males and females.

Reproductive success The number of offspring an individual produces and rears to reproductive age; an individual's genetic contribution to the next generation, as compared to the contributions of other individuals.

Restriction fragment length polymorphisms (RFLPs) Variation among individuals in the length of DNA fragments produced by enzymes that break the DNA at specific sites.

Rhinarium (rine-air´-ee-um) The moist, hairless pad at the end of the nose seen in most mammalian species. The rhinarium enhances an animal's sense of smell.

Ribonucleic acid (RNA) A single-stranded molecule, similar in structure to DNA. The three forms of RNA are essential to protein synthesis.

Ribosomes Structures found in the cytoplasm that are essential to the manufacture of proteins.

Ritualized behaviors Behaviors removed from their original context and sometimes exaggerated to convey information.

Sagittal crest Raised ridge along the midline of the cranium where the temporal muscle (which closes the jaw) is attached.

Scenarios General, speculative reconstructions derived from various scientific data. In paleoanthropology, scenarios are usually presented as imaginative reconstructions of early hominid behavior. Such interpretations are broader than typical scientific hypotheses and theories and are not as rigorously amenable to verification.

Science A body of knowledge gained through observation and experimentation; from the Latin *scientia*, meaning "knowledge."

Scientific method A research method whereby a problem is identified, a hypothesis (or hypothetical explanation) is stated, and that hypothesis is tested through the collection and analysis of data. If the hypothesis is verified, it becomes a theory.

Scientific testing The precise repetition of an experiment or expansion of observed data to provide verification; the procedure by which hypotheses and theories are verified, modified, or discarded.

Scurvy Disease resulting from a dietary deficiency of vitamin C. It may result in anemia, poor bone growth, abnormal bleeding and bruising, and muscle pain.

Sectorial Adapted for cutting or shearing; among primates, refers to the compressed (side-to-side) first lower premolar, which functions as a shearing surface with the upper canine.

Selective pressures Forces in the environment that influence reproductive success in individuals. In the example of the peppered moth, birds applied the selective pressure.

Senescence The process of physiological decline in body function that occurs with aging.

Sex chromosomes In mammals, the X and Y chromosomes.

Sexual dimorphism Differences in physical characteristics between males and females of the same species. For example, humans are slightly sexually dimorphic for body size, with males being taller, on average, than females of the same population.

Sexual selection A type of natural selection that operates on only one sex within a species. It is the result of competition for mates and it can lead to sexual dimorphism with regard to one or more traits.

Sickle-cell anemia A severe inherited hemoglobin disorder that results from inheriting two copies of a mutant allele. This allele results from a single base substitution at the DNA level.

Slash-and-burn agriculture A traditional land-clearing practice whereby trees and vegetation are cut and burned. In many areas, fields are abandoned after a few years and clearing occurs elsewhere.

Social structure The composition, size, and sex ratio of a group of animals. Social structures, in part, are the result of natural selection in specific habitats, and they function to guide individual interactions and social relationships.

Sociobiology The study of the relationship between behavior and natural selection. Sociobiological theory states that certain behaviors or behavioral patterns have been selected for because they increase reproductive fitness in individuals. Many researchers now prefer the term *evolutionary ecology*.

Socioecology The study of animals and their habitats; specifically, attempts to find patterns of relationship between the environment and social behavior.

Somatic cells Basically, all the cells in the body except those involved with reproduction.

Specialized Evolved for a particular function; usually refers to a specific trait (e.g., incisor teeth), but may also refer to the whole way of life of an organism.

Speciation The process by which new species are produced from earlier ones; the most important mechanism of macroevolutionary change.

Species A group of organisms that can interbreed to produce fertile offspring. Members of one species are reproductively isolated from members of all other species (i.e., they cannot mate with them to produce fertile offspring).

Stable carbon isotopes Isotopes of carbon that are produced in plants in differing proportions, depending on environmental conditions. Through analyzing the proportions of the isotopes contained in fossil remains of animals (who ate the plants), it is possible to reconstruct aspects of ancient environments (particularly temperature and aridity).

Stereoscopic vision The condition whereby visual images are, to varying degrees, superimposed on one another. This provides for depth perception, or the perception of the external environment in three dimensions. Stereoscopic vision is partly a function of structures in the brain.

Stratigraphy Study of the sequential layering of deposits.

Stress In a physiological context, any factor that acts to disrupt homeostasis; more precisely, the body's response to any factor that threatens its ability to maintain homeostasis.

Sympatric Living in the same area; pertaining to two or more species whose habitats partly or largely overlap.

Taphonomy (*taphos,* meaning "dead") The study of how bones and other materials came to be buried in the earth and preserved as fossils. A taphonomist studies the processes of sedimentation, the action of streams, preservation properties of bone, and carnivore disturbance factors.

Taxonomy The branch of science concerned with the rules of classifying organisms on the basis of evolutionary relationships.

Territories Portions of an individual's or group's home range actively defended against intrusion, particularly by conspecifics.

Theory A broad statement of scientific relationships or underlying principles that has been at least partially verified.

Theropods Small- to medium-sized ground-living dinosaurs, dated to approximately 150 million years ago and thought to be related to birds.

Transfer RNA (tRNA) The type of RNA that binds to specific amino acids and transports them to the ribosome during protein synthesis.

Transmutation The change of one species to another. The term *evolution* did not assume its current meaning until the late nineteenth century.

Undernutrition A diet insufficient in quantity (calories) to support normal health.

Uniformitarianism The theory that the earth's features are the result of long-term processes that continue to operate in the present as they did in the past. Elaborated on by Lyell, this theory opposed catastrophism and provided for immense geological time.

Upper Paleolithic A cultural period associated with early modern humans and distinguished by technological innovation in various stone tool industries. Best known from western Europe, similar industries are also known from central and eastern Europe and Africa.

Variation (genetic) Inherited differences between individuals; the basis of all evolutionary change.

Vasoconstriction Narrowing of blood vessels to reduce blood flow to the skin. Vasoconstriction is an involuntary response to cold and reduces heat loss at the skin's surface.

Vasodilation Expansion of blood vessels, permitting increased blood flow to the skin. Vasodilation permits warming of the skin and also facilitates radiation of warmth as a means of cooling. Vasodilation is an involuntary response to warm temperatures, various drugs, and even emotional states (blushing).

Vectors Agents that serve to transmit disease from one carrier to another. Mosquitoes are vectors for malaria, just as fleas are vectors for bubonic plague.

Vertebrates Animals with bony backbones; includes fishes, amphibians, reptiles, birds, and mammals.

Viviparous Giving birth to live young.

World view General cultural orientation or perspective shared by members of a society.

Zygote A cell formed by the union of an egg and a sperm cell. It contains the full complement of chromosomes (in humans, 46) and has the potential of developing into an entire organism.

Bibliography

Aiello, L. C.
1992 "Body Size and Energy Requirements." *In: The Cambridge Encyclopedia of Human Evolution,* J. Jones, R. Martin, and D. Pilbeam (eds.), Cambridge, England: Cambridge University Press, pp. 41–45.

Aiello, L. C. and B. A. Wood
1994 Cranial Variables as Predictors of Hominine Body Mass. *American Journal of Physical Anthropology,* **95**:409–426.

Aitken, M. J., C. B. Stringer, and P. A. Mellars (eds.)
1993 *The Origin of Modern Humans and the Impact of Chronometric Dating.* Princeton, N.J.: Princeton University Press.

Alland Jr., Alexander
1971 *Human Diversity.* New York: Anchor Press/ Doubleday.

Altmann, Jeanne
1981 *Baboon Mothers and Infants.* Cambridge: Harvard University Press.

Altmann, Stuart A. and Jeanne Altmann
1970 *Baboon Ecology.* Chicago: University of Chicago Press.

Anderson, J. Gunnar
1934 *Children of the Yellow Earth.* New York: Macmillan.

Andrews, Peter
1985 "Family Group Systematics and Evolution among Catarrhine Primates." *In: Ancestors: The Hard Evidence,* E. Delson (ed.), New York: Alan R. Liss, pp. 14–22.

_____
1992 "Evolution and Environment in Miocene Hominoids." *Nature,* **360**:641–646.

Andrews, Peter and Jens Lorenz Franzen (eds.)
1984 *The Early Evolution of Man.* Frankfurt: Cour. Forsch.-Inst. Seckenberg.

Andrews, Peter and David Pilbeam
1996 "The Nature of the Evidence," News and Views. *Nature,* **379**:123–124.

Ardrey, Robert
1976 *The Hunting Hypothesis.* New York: Atheneum.

Arensburg, B., L. A. Schepartz, et al.
1990 "A Reappraisal of the Anatomical Basis for Speech in Middle Paleolithic Hominids." *American Journal of Physical Anthropology,* **83**(2):137–146.

Arensburg, B., A. M. Tillier, et al.
1989 "A Middle Paleolithic Human Hyoid Bone." *Nature,* **338**:758–760.

Aronson, J. L., R. C. Walter, and M. Taieb
1983 "Correlation of Tulu Bor Tuff at Koobi Fora with the Sidi Hakoma Tuff at Hadar." *Nature,* **306**:209–210.

Arsuaga, Juan-Luis et al.
1993 "Three New Human Skulls from the Sima de los Huesos Middle Pleistocene Site in Sierra de Atapuerca, Spain." *Nature,* **362**:534–537.

Arsuaga, J. L., I. Martinez, A. Garcia, et al.
1997 "Sima de los Huesos (Sierra de Atapuerca, Spain). The Site." *Journal of Human Evolution,* **33**:109–127.

Ascenzi, A. I. Bidditu, P. F. Cassoli, et al.
1996 "A Calvarium of Late *Homo erectus* from Ceprano, Italy." *Journal of Human Evolution,* **31**:409–423.

Asfaw, Berhane
1992 "New Fossil Hominids from the Ethiopian Rift Valley and the Afar." Paper presented at the Annual Meeting, American Association of Physical Anthropologists.

Asfaw, Berhane et al.
1992 "The Earliest Acheulian from Konso-Gardula." *Nature,* **360**:732–735.

_____
1995 Three Seasons of Hominid Paleontology at Aramis, Ethiopia. Paper presented at Paleoanthropology Society meetings, Oakland, Ca., March 1995.

Asfaw, Berhane, Tim White, Owen Lovejoy, et al.
1999 "*Australopithecus garhi:* A New Species of Early Hominid from Ethiopia." *Science,* **284**: 629–635.

Avery, O. T., C. M. MacLeod, and M. McCarty
1944 "Studies on the Chemical Nature of the Substances Inducing Transformation in Pneumoccal Types." *Journal of Experimental Medicine,* **79**:137–158.

Ayala, Francisco
1995 "The Myth of Eve: Molecular Biology and Human Origins." *Science,* **270**:1930–1936.

Badrian, Alison and Noel Badrian
1984 "Social Organization of *Pan paniscus* in the Lomako Forest, Zaire." *In: The Pygmy Chimpanzee,* Randall L. Susman (ed.), New York: Plenum Press, pp. 325–346.

Badrian, Noel and Richard K. Malenky
1984 "Feeding Ecology of *Pan paniscus* in the Lomako Forest, Zaire." *In: The Pygmy Chimpanzee,* Randall L. Susman (ed.), New York: Plenum Press, pp. 275–299.

Baker, Paul T. and Michael A. Little
1976 "The Environmental Adaptations and Perspectives." *In: Man in the Andes,* P. T. Baker and M. A. Little (eds.), Stroudsburg, Penn.: Dowden, Hutchinson, and Ross, pp. 405–428.

Barash, David
1982 *Sociobiology and Behavior.* (2nd Ed.) New York: Elsevier.

Bartholomew, C. A. and J. B. Birdsell
1953   "Ecology and the Protohominids." *American Anthropologist,* **55:**481–498.

Bartstra, Gert-Jan
1982   *"Homo erectus erectus:* The Search for Artifacts." *Current Anthropology,* **23**(3):318–320.

Bar-Yosef, Ofer
1993   "The Role of Western Asia in Modern Human Origins." *In:* M. J. Aitken et al. (eds.), q.v., pp. 132–147.

_____
1994   "The Contributions of Southwest Asia to the Study of the Origin of Modern Humans." *In: Origins of Anatomically Modern Humans,* M. H. Nitecki and D. V. Nitecki (eds.), New York: Plenum Press, pp. 23–66.

Barzun, Jacques
1965   *Race: A Study in Superstition.* New York: Harper & Row.

Bass, W. M.
1987   *Human Osteology: A Laboratory and Field Manual* (3rd Ed.). Columbia, Mo.: Missouri Archaeological Society Special Publication No. 2.

Beard, K. Christopher, Yong Shenj Tong, Mary R. Dawson, Jingwen Wang, and Xueshi Huang
1996   "Earliest Complete Dentition of an Anthropoid Primate from the Late Middle Eocene of Shanxi Province, China." *Science,* **272:**82–85.

Bearder, Simon K.
1987   "Lorises, Bushbabies and Tarsiers: Diverse Societies in Solitary Foragers." *In:* Smuts et al., q.v., pp. 11–24.

Begun, David R.
1992   "Phyletic Diversity and Locomotion in Primitive European Hominoids." *American Journal of Physical Anthropology,* **87:**311–340.

_____
1994   "Relations Among the Great Apes and Humans: New Interpretations Based on the Fossil Great Ape *Dryopithecus.*" *Yearbook of Physical Anthropology,* **37:**11–63.

Begun, D. and A. Walker
1993   "The Endocast." *In:* A. Walker and R. E. Leakey (eds.), q.v., pp. 326–358.

Behrensmeyer, Anna K. and Andrew P. Hill
1980   *Fossils in the Making: Vertebrate Taphonomy and Paleoecology.* Chicago: University of Chicago Press.

Berger, Thomas and Erik Trinkaus
1995   "Patterns of Trauma Among the Neandertals." *Journal of Archaeological Science,* **22:**841–852.

Bermudez de Castro, J. M., J. L. Arsuaga, E. Carbonell et al.
1997   "A Hominid from the Lower Pleistocene of Atapuerca, Spain. Possible Ancestor to Neandertals and Modern Humans." *Science,* **276:**1392–1395.

Bernor, R. L.
1983   "Geochronology and Zoogeographic Relationships of Miocene Hominoidea." *In:* R. L. Ciochon and R. S. Corruccini (eds.), q.v., pp. 21–66.

Binford, Lewis R.
1981   *Bones. Ancient Men and Modern Myths.* New York: Academic Press.

_____
1983   *In Pursuit of the Past.* New York: Thames and Hudson.

_____
1985   "Ancestral Lifeways: The Faunal Record." AnthroQuest, **32,** Summer 1985.

Binford, Lewis R. and Chuan Kun Ho
1985   "Taphonomy at a Distance: Zhoukoudian, 'The Cave Home of Beijing Man'?" *Current Anthropology,* **26:**413–442.

Binford, Lewis R. and Nancy M. Stone
1986a   "The Chinese Paleolithic: An Outsider's View." *AnthroQuest,* Fall 1986(1):14–20.

_____
1986b   "Zhoukoudian: A Closer Look." *Current Anthropology,* **27**(5):453–475.

Birdsell, Joseph B.
1981   *Human Evolution.* (3rd Ed.). Boston: Houghton Mifflin.

Boas, F.
1910   "Changes in the Bodily Form of Descendants of Immigrants." *American Anthropologist,* **14:**530–562.

Boaz, N. T., F. C. Howell, and M. L. McCrossin
1982   "Faunal Age of the Usno, Shungura B and Hadar Formation, Ethiopia." *Nature,* **300:**633–635.

Bodmer, W. F.
1995   "Evolution and Function of the HLA Region." *Cancer Surveys,* **22:**5–16.

Bodmer, W. F. and L. L. Cavalli-Sforza
1976   *Genetics, Evolution, and Man.* San Francisco: W. H. Freeman and Company.

Boesch, C.
1994   "Hunting Strategies of Gombe and Tai Chimpanzees." *In: Chimpanzee Cultures,* R. W. Wrangham et al. (eds). Cambridge: Harvard University Press, pp. 77–91.

Boesch, Christophe and H. Boesch
1989   "Hunting Behavior of Wild Chimpanzees in the Tai National Park." *American Journal of Physical Anthropology,* **78:**547–573.

_____
1990   "Tool Use and Tool Making in Wild Chimpanzees." *Folia Primatologica,* **54:**86–99.

Boesch, Christophe, Paul Marchesi, Nathalie Marchesi, Barbara Fruth, and Frédéric Joulian
1994   "Is Nut Cracking in Wild Chimpanzees a Cultural Behaviour?" *Journal of Human Evolution,* **26:**325–338.

Boggess, Jane
1984   "Infant Killing and Male Reproductive Strategies in Langurs (*Presbytis entellus*)." *In:* G. Hausfater and S. B. Hrdy (eds.), q.v., pp. 280–310.

Bogin, Barry
1988   *Patterns of Human Growth.* Cambridge: Cambridge University Press.

_____
1998   "Social and Economic Class." *In: The Cambridge Encyclopedia of Human Growth and Development,* S. J. Ulijaszek, F. E. Johnston, and M. A. Preece (eds.). Cambridge, UK: Cambridge University Press, pp. 399–401.

Bongaarts, John
1980   Does Malnutrition Affect Fecundity? A Summary of Evidence. *Science,* **208**:564–569.
Bordes, François
1968   *The Old Stone Age.* New York: McGraw-Hill Book Co.
Bowler, Peter J.
1983, 1989   *Evolution: The History of an Idea.* Berkeley: University of California Press.

_____
1988   The *Non-Darwinian Evolution: Reinterpreting a Historical Myth.* Baltimore: Johns Hopkins University Press.
Brace, C. L. and Ashley Montagu
1977   *Human Evolution* (2nd Ed.). New York: Macmillan.
Brace, C. Loring, H. Nelson, and N. Korn
1979   *Atlas of Human Evolution* (2nd Ed.). New York: Holt, Rinehart & Winston.
Brain, C. K.
1970   "New Finds at the Swartkrans Australopithecine Site." *Nature,* **225**:1112–1119.

_____
1981   *The Hunters or the Hunted? An Introduction to African Cave Taphonomy.* Chicago: University of Chicago Press.
Bramblett, Claud A.
1994   *Patterns of Primate Behavior* (2nd Ed.). Prospect Heights, Ill.: Waveland Press.
Bräuer, Günter
1984   "A Craniological Approach to the Origin of Anatomically Modern *Homo sapiens* in Africa and Implications for the Appearance of Modern Europeans." *In:* F. H. Smith and F. Spencer (eds.), q.v., pp. 327–410.

_____
1989   "The Evolution of Modern Humans: A Comparison of the African and Non-African Evidence." *In:* Mellars and Stringer (eds.), q.v.
Brock, A., P. L. McFadden, and T. C. Partridge
1977   "Preliminary Paleomagnetic Results from Makapansgat and Swartkrans." *Nature,* **266**:249–250.
Bromage, Timothy G. and Christopher Dean
1985   "Re-evaluation of the Age at Death of Immature Fossil Hominids." *Nature,* **317**:525–527.
Brooks, Alison et al.
1995   "Dating and Context of Three Middle Stone Age Sites with Bone Points in the Upper Semliki Valley, Zaire." *Science,* **268**:548–553.
Brose, David and Milford H. Wolpoff
1971   "Early Upper Paleolithic Man and Late Middle Paleolithic Tools." *American Anthropologist,* **73**:1156–1194.
Brown, B, A. Walker, C. V. Ward, and R. E. Leakey
1993   "New *Australopithecus boisei*: Calvaria from East Lake Turkana, Kenya." *American Journal of Physical Anthropology,* **91**:137–159.
Brown, F. H.
1982   "Tulu Bor Tuff at Koobi Fora Correlated with the Sidi Hakoma Tuff at Hadar." *Nature,* **300**:631–632.

Brown, T. M. and K. D. Rose
1987   "Patterns of Dental Evolution in Early Eocene Anaptomorphine Primates Comomyidael from the Bighorn Basin, Wyoming." *Journal of Paleontology,* **61**:1–62.
Brues, Alice M.
1959   "The Spearman and the Archer." *American Anthropologist,* **61**:457–469.

_____
1990   *People and Races* (2nd Ed.). Prospect Heights, Ill.: Waveland Press.

_____
1991   "The Objective View of Race." Paper presented at American Anthropological Association 90th Annual Meeting, Chicago, Nov.
Brunet, Michel et al.
1995   "The First Australopithecine 2,500 Kilometers West of the Rift Valley (Chad)." *Nature,* **378**:273–274.
Buffon, George Louis Leclerc, Compte de
1860   *"Histoire Naturelle Generale et Particuliere."* Translated by Wm. Smellie. *In: The Idea of Racism,* Louis L. Snyder, New York: Van Nostrand Reinhold, 1962.
Bunn, Henry T.
1981   "Archaeological Evidence for Meat-eating by Plio-Pleistocene Hominids from Koobi Fora and Olduvai Gorge." *Nature,* **291**:574–577.
Burkhardt, Richard W., Jr.
1984   "The Zoological Philosophy of J. B. Lamarck." (Introduction) *In:* Lamarck, q.v.
Butzer, Karl W.
1974   "Paleoecology of South African Australopithecines: Taung Revisited." *Current Anthropology,* **15**:367–382.
Cann, R. L., M. Stoneking, and A. C. Wilson
1987   "Mitochondrial DNA and Human Evolution." *Nature,* **325**:31–36.
Cann, Rebecca L., Olga Rickards, and J. Koji Lum
1994   "Mitochondrial DNA and Human Evolution: Our One Lucky Mother." *In:* M H. Nitecki and D. V. Nitecki (eds.), q.v., pp. 135–148.
Carbonell, E. et al.
1995   Lower Pleistocene Hominids and Artifacts from Atapuerca-TDG (Spain)." *Science,* **269**:826–830.
Carrol, Robert L.
1988   *Vertebrate Paleontology and Evolution.* New York: W. H. Freeman and Co.
Cartmill, Matt
1972   "Arboreal Adaptations and the Origin of the Order Primates." *In: The Functional and Evolutionary Biology of Primates,* R. H. Tuttle (ed.), Chicago: Aldine-Atherton, pp. 97–122.

_____
1990   "Human Uniqueness and Theoretical Content in Paleoanthropology." *International Journal of Primatology,* **11**(3):173–192.

_____
1992   "New Views on Primate Origins." *Evolutionary Anthropology,* **1**:105–111.

Cavalli-Sforza, L. L., A. Piazza, P. Menozzi, and J. Mountain
  1988   "Reconstruction of Human Evolution: Bringing Together Genetic, Archaeological, and Linguistic Data." *Proceedings of the National Academy of Sciences,* 85:6002–6006.

Censky, E. J., K. Hodge and J. Dudley
  1998   "Over-Water Dispersal of Lizards Due to Hurricanes." *Nature,* 395 (6702):556.

Chagnon, N. A.
  1979   "Mate Competition Favoring Close Kin and Village Fissioning among the Yanomamo Indians." *In: Evolutionary Biology and Human Social Behavior: An Anthropological Perspective,* N. Chagnon and W. Irons (eds.), North Scituak, Mass.: Duxbury Press, pp. 86–132.

  1988   "Life Histories, Blood Revenge, and Warfare in a Tribal Population." *Science,* 239:985–992.

Chard, Chester S.
  1975   *Man in Prehistory.* New York: McGraw-Hill.

Charteris, J., J. C. Wali, and J. W. Nottrodt
  1981   "Functional Reconstruction of Gait from Pliocene Hominid Footprints at Laetoli, Northern Tanzania." *Nature,* 290:496–498.

Cheney, Dorothy L.
  1987   "Interaction and Relationships between Groups." *In:* B. Smuts et al. (eds.), q.v., pp. 267–281.

Cheney, D. L. and R. M. Seyfarth
  1990   *How Monkeys See the World.* Chicago: Chicago University Press.

Ciochon, R. L. and A. B. Chiarelli (eds.)
  1980   *Evolutionary Biology of the New World Monkeys and Continental Drift.* New York: Plenum Press.

Ciochon, Russel L. and Robert S. Corruccini (eds.)
  1983   *New Interpretations of Ape and Human Ancestry.* New York: Plenum Press.

Clark, W. E. LeGros
  1967   *Man-apes or Ape-men?* New York: Holt, Rinehart & Winston.
  1971   New York Times Books (3rd Ed.).

Clarke, R. J.
  1985   "*Australopithecus* and Early *Homo* in Southern Africa." *In: Ancestors: The Hard Evidence,* E. Delson (ed.), New York: Alan R. Liss, pp. 171–177.

Clarke, Ronald J. and Phillip V. Tobias
  1995   "Sterkfontein Member 2 Foot Bones of the Oldest South African Hominid." *Science,* 269:521–524.

Cleveland, J. and C. T. Snowdon
  1982   "The Complex Vocal Repertoire of the Adult Cotton-top Tamarin (*Saguinus oedipus oedipus*)." *Zeitschrift Tierpsychologie,* 58:231–270.

Clutton-Brock, T. H. and Paul H. Harvey
  1977   "Primate Ecology and Social Organization." *Journal of Zoological Society of London,* 183:1–39.

Colwell, Rita R.
  1996   Global Climate and Infectious Disease: The Cholera Paradigm. *Science,* 274 (5295): 2025–2031.

Conkey, M.
  1987   New Approaches in the Search for Meaning? A Review of the Research in "Paleolithic Art." *Journal of Field Archaeology,* 14:413–430.

Conroy, G., C. J. Jolly, D. Cramer, and J. E. Kalb
  1978   "Newly Discovered Fossil Hominid Skull from the Afar Depression." *Nature,* 272:67–70.

Conroy, G. C., M. Pickford, B. Senut, J. van Couvering, and P. Mein
  1992   "*Otavipithecus namibiensis,* First Miocene Hominoid from Southern Africa." *Nature,* 356:144–148.

Conroy, Glenn C., Jeff W. Lichtman, and Lawrence B. Martin
  1995   "Brief Communication: Some Observations on Enamel Thickness and Enamel Prism Packing in Miocene Hominoid *Otavipithecus namibiensis.*" *American Journal of Physical Anthropology,* 98:595–600.

Conroy, Glenn C., G. W. Weber, H. Seidler, et al.
  1998   "Endocranial Capacity in an Early Hominid Cranium from Sterkfontein, South Africa." *Science,* 280:1730–1731.

Coon, C. S., S. M. Garn, and J. B. Birdsell
  1950   *Races—A Study of the Problems of Race Formation in Man.* Springfield, Ill.: Charles C. Thomas.

Corruccini, R. S., M. Baba, M. Goodman, et al.
  1980   "Non-Linear Macromolecular Evolution and the Moleculer Clock." *Evolution,* 34:1216–1219.

Corruccini, R. S. and H. M. McHenry
  1980   "Cladometric Analysis of Pliocene Hominids." *Journal of Human Evolution,* 9:209–221.

Corruccini, Robert S.
  1994   "Reaganomics and the Fate of the Progressive Neandertals." *In:* R. S. Corruccini and R. I. Ciochon (eds.), q.v., pp. 697–708.

Crapo, Lawrence
  1985   *Hormones: The Messengers of Life.* New York: W. H. Freeman and Company.

Crews, D. E. and G. J. Harper
  1998   "Ageing as Part of the Developmental Process." *In: The Cambridge Encyclopedia of Human Growth and Development,* S. J. Ulijaszek, F. E. Johnston, and M. A. Preece (eds.). Cambridge, UK: Cambridge University Press, pp. 425–427.

Cronin, J. E.
  1983   "Apes, Humans, and Molecular Clocks. A Reappraisal." *In:* R. L. Ciochon and R. S. Corruccini (eds.), q.v., pp. 115–150.

Crook, J. H.
  1970   "Social Organization and Environment: Aspects of Contemporary Social Ethology." *Animal Behavior,* 18:197–209.

Crook, J. H. and J. S. Gartlan
  1966   "Evolution of Primate Societies." *Nature,* 210:1200–1203.

Culotta, Elizabeth
  1995   "Asian Anthropoids Strike Back." *Science,* 270:918.

Cummings, Michael
  2000   *Human Heredity. Principles and Issues* (5th Ed.). Pacific Grove: Brooks/Cole.

1997   *Human Heredity. Principles and Issues.* 4th ed. Belmont, CA: West/Wadsworth.

Curtin, R. and P. Dolhinow
1978   "Primate Social Behavior in a Changing World." *American Scientist,* **66**:468–475.

Curtis, Garniss
1981   "A Matter of Time: Dating Techniques and Geology of Hominid Sites." Symposium Paper, Davis, Ca., May 10, 1981.

Dalrymple, G. B.
1972   "Geomagnetic Reversals and North American Glaciations." *In: Calibration of Hominoid Evolution,* W. W. Bishop and J. A. Miller (eds.), Edinburgh: Scottish Academic Press, pp. 303–329.

Dart, Raymond
1959   *Adventures with the Missing Link.* New York: Harper & Brothers.

Darwin, Charles
1859   *On the Origin of Species.* A Facsimile of the First Edition, Cambridge, Mass.: Harvard University Press (1964).

Darwin, Francis (ed.)
1950   *The Life and Letters of Charles Darwin.* New York: Henry Schuman.

Day, M. H. and E. H. Wickens
1980   "Laetoli Pliocene Hominid Footprints and Bipedalism." *Nature,* **286**:385–387.

Day, Michael
1986   *Guide to Fossil Man* (4th Ed.), Chicago: University of Chicago Press.

Deacon, T. W.
1992   "The Human Brain." *In: The Cambridge Encyclopedia of Human Evolution,* S. Jones, R. Martin, and D. Pilbeam (eds.), Cambridge, England: Cambridge University Press, pp. 115–123.

Dean, M., M. Carring, C. Winkler, et al.
1996   "Genetic Restriction of HIV-1 Infection and Progression to AIDS by a Deletion Allele of the CKR5 Structural Gene." *Science,* **273**:1856–1862.

de Bonis, Louis and George D. Koufos
1994   "Our Ancestors' Ancestor: *Ouranopithecus* Is a Greek Link in Human Ancestry." *Evolutionary Anthropology,***3**:75–83.

DeGusta, D., W. H. Gilbert, and S. P. Turner
1999   "Hypoglossal Canal Size and Hominid Speech." *Proceedings of the National Academy of Sciences,* **96**:1800–1804.

de Heinzelin, Jean, J. Desmond Clark, Tim White, et al.
1999   "Environment and Behavior of 2.5-Million-Year-Old Bouri Hominids." *Science,* **284**:625–629.

Deino, Alan L., Paul R. Renne, and Carl C. Swisher
1998   "^{40}Ar/^{39}Ar Dating in Paleoanthropology and Archeology." *Evolutionary Anthropology,* **6**:63–75.

de Lumley, Henry and M. de Lumley
1973   "Pre-Neanderthal Human Remains from Arago Cave in Southeastern France." *Yearbook of Physical Anthropology,* **16**:162–168.

Delson, Eric (ed.)
1985   *Ancestors: The Hard Evidence.* New York: Alan R. Liss.

1987   "Evolution and Paleobiology of Robust Australopithecus." *Nature,* **327**:654–655.

Dene, H. T., M. Goodman, and W. Prychodko
1976   "Immunodiffusion Evidence on the Phylogeny of the Primates." *In: Molecular Anthropology,* M. Goodman, R. E. Tashian, and J. H. Tashian (eds.), New York: Plenum Press, pp. 171–195.

Desmond, Adrian and James Moore
1991   *Darwin.* New York: Warner Books.

Dettwyler, K. A.
1991   "Can Paleopathology Provide Evidence for Compassion?" *American Journal of Physical Anthropology,* **84**:375–384.

DeVore, I. and S. L. Washburn
1963   "Baboon Ecology and Human Evolution." *In: African Ecology and Human Evolution,* F. C. Howell and F. Bourliére (eds.), New York: Viking Fund Publication, No. 36, pp. 335–367.

De Vos, J.
1985   "Faunal Stratigraphy and Correlation of the Indonesian Hominid Sites." *In: Ancestors: The Hard Evidence,* E. Delson (ed.), New York: Alan R. Liss, pp. 215–220.

de Waal, Frans
1982   *Chimpanzee Politics.* London: Jonathan Cape.

1987   "Tension Regulation and Nonreproductive Functions of Sex in Captive Bonobos (*Pan paniscus*)." *National Geographic Research,* **3**:318–335.

1989   *Peacemaking among Primates.* Cambridge: Harvard University Press.

1996   *Good Natured. The Origins of Right and Wrong in Humans and Other Animals,* Cambridge, Mass.: Harvard University Press.

Dolhinow, P.
1978   "A Behavior Repertoire for the Indian Langur Monkey (*Presbytis entellus*)." *Primates,* **19**:449–472.

Doran, M. D. and A. McNeilage
1998   "Gorilla ecology and behavior." *Evolutionary Anthropology,* **6**:120–131.

Dorit, R. L., H. Akashi, and W. Gilbert
1995   Absence of Polymorphism at the Zfy Locus on the Human Y Chromosome. *Science,* **268**:1183–1185.

Duchin, Linda E.
1990   "The Evolution of Articulate Speech." *Journal of Human Evolution,* **19**:687–697.

Dumont, R. and B. Rosier
1969   *The Hungry Future.* New York: Praeger.

Dunbar, I. M.
1988   *Primate Social Systems.* Ithaca: Cornell University Press.

Durham, William
 1981 Paper presented to the Annual Meeting of the American Anthropological Association, Washington, D.C., Dec. 1980. Reported in *Science,* **211**:40.

Eaton, S. Boyd, Marjorie Shostak, and Melvin Konner.
 1988 *The Paleolithic Prescription.* New York: Harper and Row.

Eaton, S. Boyd and Melvin Konner
 1985 Paleolithic Nutrition: A Consideration of Its Nature and Current Implications. *New England Journal of Medicine,* **312**:283–289.

Eaton, S. Boyd, Malcolm C. Pike, Roger V. Short, et al.
 1994 Women's Reproductive Cancers in Evolutionary Context. *The Quarterly Review of Biology,* **69**:353–367.

Eiseley, Loren
 1961 *Darwin's Century.* New York: Anchor Books.

Eisenberg, J. F., N. A. Muckenhirn, and R. Rudran
 1972 "The Relation Between Ecology and Social Structure in Primates." *Science,* **176**:863–874.

Eldredge, Niles and Joel Cracraft
 1980 *Phylogenetic Patterns and the Evolutionary Process.* New York: Columbia University Press.

Etler, Denis
 1992 Personal communication.

Etler, Dennis A. and Li-Tianyuan
 1994 "New Archaic Human Fossil Discoveries in China and Their Bearing on Hominid Species Definition During the Middle Pleistocene." *In:* R. Corruccini and R. Ciochon (eds.), q.v., pp. 639–675.

Falk, Dean
 1980 "A Reanalysis of the South African Australopithecine Natural Endocasts." *American Journal of Physical Anthropology,* **53**:525–539.

 ———
 1983 "The Taung Endocast: A Reply to Holloway." *American Journal of Physical Anthropology,* **60**:479–489.

 ———
 1987 "Brain Lateralization in Primates and Its Evolution in Hominids." *Yearbook of Physical Anthropology,* **30**:107–125.

 ———
 1989 "Comments." *Current Anthropology,* **30**:141.

Fedigan, Linda M.
 1982 *Primate Paradigms.* Montreal: Eden Press.

 ———
 1983 "Dominance and Reproductive Success in Primates." *Yearbook of Physical Anthropology,* **26**:91–129.

 ———
 1986 "The Changing Role of Women in Models of Human Evolution." *Annual Review of Anthropology,* **15**:25–66.

Fisher, R. A.
 1930 *The Genetical Theory of Natural Selection.* Oxford: Clarendon.

Fleagle, J. G.
 1983 "Locomotor Adaptations of Oligocene and Miocene Hominoids and Their Phyletic Implications." *In:* R. L. Ciochon and R. S. Corruccini (eds.), q.v., pp. 301–324.

 ———
 1988 *Primate Adaptation and Evolution.* New York: Academic Press. 2nd ed., 1999.

Fleagle, J. G. and R. F. Kay
 1983 "New Interpretations of the Phyletic Position of Oligocene Hominoids." *In:* R. L. Ciochon and R. S. Corruccini (eds.), q.v., pp. 181–210.

Foley, R. A.
 1991 "How Many Species of Hominid Should There Be?" *Journal of Human Evolution,* **30**:413–427.

Foley, R. A. and M. M. Lahr
 1992 "Beyond 'Out of Africa.'" *Journal of Human Evolution,* **22**:523–529.

Fossey, Dian
 1983 *Gorillas in the Mist.* Boston: Houghton Mifflin.

Fouts, Roger S., D. H. Fouts, and T. T. van Cantfort
 1989 "The Infant Loulis Learns Signs from Cross-Fostered Chimpanzees." *In:* R. A. Gardner et al., q.v., pp. 280–292.

Francoeuer, Robert T.
 1965 *Perspectives in Evolution.* Baltimore: Helicon.

Frayer, David
 1980 "Sexual Dimorphism and Cultural Evolution in the Late Pleistocene and Holocene of Europe." *Journal of Human Evolution,* **9**:399–415.

 ———
 1992 "Evolution at the European Edge: Neanderthal and Upper Paleolithic Relationships." *Préhistoire Européenne,* **2**:9–69.

 ———
 n.d. "Language Capacity in European Neanderthals."

Friedman, Milton J. and William Trager
 1981 "The Biochemistry of Resistance to Malaria." *Scientific American,* **244**:154–164.

Frisancho, A. Roberto
 1978 "Nutritional Influences on Human Growth and Maturation." *Yearbook of Physical Anthropology,* **21**:174–191.

 ———
 1993 *Human Adaptation and Accommodation.* Ann Arbor: University of Michigan Press.

Frisch, Rose E.
 1988 Fatness and Fertility. *Scientific American,* **258**:88–95.

Froelich, J. W.
 1970 "Migration and Plasticity Physique in the Japanese-Americans of Hawaii." *American Journal of Physical Anthropology,* **32**:429.

Galdikas, Biruté M.
 1979 "Orangutan Adaptation at Tanjung Puting Reserve: Mating and Ecology." *In: The Great Apes,* D. A. Hamburg and E. R. McCown (eds.), Menlo Park, Ca.: Benjamin/Cummings Publishing Co., pp. 195–233.

Gambier, Dominique
 1989 "Fossil Hominids from the Early Upper Palaeolithic (Aurignacian) of France." *In:* Mellars and Stringer (eds.), q.v., pp. 194–211.

Gamble, C.
 1991 "The Social Context for European Palaeolithic Art." *Proceedings of the Prehistoric Society,* **57**:3–15.

Gao, Feng, Elizabeth Bailes, David L. Robertson, et al.
 1999 "Origin of HIV-1 in the Chimpanzee *Pan troglodytes troglodytes.*" *Nature,* **397**:436–441.

Gardner, R. Allen, B. T. Gardner, and
T. T. van Cantfort (eds.)
1989   *Teaching Sign Language to Chimpanzees.* Albany: State
        University of New York Press.
Garn, Stanley M.
1965, 1969   *Human Races.* Springfield, Ill.: Charles C. Thomas.
Garner, K. J. and O. A. Ryder
1996   "Mitochondrial DNA diversity in gorillas."*Mol.
        Phylogenet. Evol.,* **6**:39–48.
Gates, R. R.
1948   *Human Ancestry.* Cambridge: Harvard University Press.
Gavan, James
1977   *Paleoanthropology and Primate Evolution.* Dubuque, Ia.:
        Wm. C. Brown Co.
Gee, Henry
1996   "Box of Bones 'Clinches' Identity of Piltdown
        Paleontology Hoaxer." *Nature,* **381**:261–262.
Ghiselin, Michael T.
1969   *The Triumph of the Darwinian Method.* Chicago:
        University of Chicago Press.
Gibbons, Anne
1992   "Mitochondrial Eve, Wounded but Not Dead Yet."
        Science, **257**:873–875.

_____
1998   "Ancient Tools Suggest *Homo erectus* was a Seafarer."
        Research News, *Science,* **279**:1635–1637.
Gighlieri, Michael P.
1984   *The Chimpanzees of Kibale Forest.* New York: Columbia
        University Press.
Gingerich, Phillip D.
1985   "Species in the Fossil Record: Concepts, Trends, and
        Transitions." *Paleobiology,* **11**:27–41.
Goldizen, Anne Wilson
1987   "Tamarins and Marmosets: Communal Care of
        Offspring." *In:* Smuts et al. (eds.), q.v., pp. 34–43.
Goldstein, M., P. Tsarong, and C. M. Beall
1983   "High Altitude Hypoxia, Culture, and Human
        Fecundity/Fertility: A Comparative Study." *American
        Anthropologist,* **85**:28–49.
Goodall, A. G.
1977   "Feeding and Ranging Behaviour of a Mountain
        Gorilla Group, *Gorilla gorilla beringei* in the Tshibinda-
        Kahuze Region (Zaire)." *In: Primate Ecology.* T. H.
        Clutton-Brock (ed.). London: Academic Press, pp.
        450–479.
Goodall, Jane
1968   "The Behavior of Free Living Chimpanzees in the
        Gombe Stream Reserve." *Animal Behavior Monographs,*
        1:(3).

_____
1986   *The Chimpanzees of Gombe.* Cambridge, Mass.: Harvard
        University Press.

_____
1990   *Through a Window.* Boston: Houghton Mifflin.
Goodman, M., M. L. Baba, and L. L. Darga
1983   "The Bearing of Molecular Data on the Cladogenesis
        and Times of Divergence of Hominoid Lineages." *In:* R.
        L. Ciochon and R. S. Corruccini (eds.), q.v., pp. 67–86.

Gossett, Thomas F.
1963   *Race, the History of an Idea in America.* Dallas: Southern
        Methodist University Press.
Gould, Stephen Jay
1977   *Ontogeny and Phylogeny.* Cambridge, Mass.: Harvard
        University Press.

_____
1981   *The Mismeasures of Man.* New York: W. W. Norton.

_____
1985   "Darwin at Sea—and the Virtues of Port." *In:* Stephen
        Jay Gould, *The Flamingo's Smile. Reflections in Natural
        History.* New York: W. W. Norton, pp. 347–359.

_____
1987   *Time's Arrow Time's Cycle.* Cambridge: Harvard
        University Press.
Gould, S. J. and N. Eldedge
1977   "Punctuated Equilibria: The Tempo and Mode of
        Evolution Reconsidered." *Paleobiology,* **3**:115–151.
Gould, S. J. and R. Lewontin
1979   "The Spandrels of San Marco and the Panglossian
        Paradigm: A Critique of the Adaptionist Programme."
        Proceedings of the Royal Society of London, **205**:581–598.
Gowlett, John
1984   *Ascent to Civilization.* New York: Alfred A. Knopf.
Greenberg, Joel
1977   "Who Loves You?" *Science News,* **112** (August
        27):139–141.
Greene, John C.
1981   *Science, Ideology, and World View.* Berkeley: University of
        California Press.
Greenfield, L. O.
1979   "On the Adaptive Pattern of *Ramapithecus." American
        Journal of Physical Anthropology,* **50**:527–548.
Grine, F. E.
1993   "Australopithecine Taxonomy and Phylogeny:
        Historical Background and Recent Interpretation." *In:
        The Human Evolution Source Book,* R. L. Ciochon and J.
        G. Fleagle (eds.), Englewood Cliffs, N.J.: Prentice Hall,
        pp. 198–210.
Grine, Frederick E. (ed.)
1988a *Evolutionary History of the "Robust" Australopithecines.*
        New York: Aldine de Gruyter.
1988b "New Craniodental Fossils of *Paranthropus* from the
        Swartkrans Formation and Their Significance in
        "Robust" Australopithecine Evolution." *In:* F. E. Grine
        (ed.), q.v., pp. 223–243.
Haldane, J.B.S.
1932   *The Causes of Evolution.* London: Longmans, Green
        (reprinted as paperback, Cornell University Press,
        1966).
Hamilton, W. D.
1964   "The Genetical Theory of Social Behavior. I and II."
        Journal of Theoretical Biology, **7**:1–52.
Hanna, Joel M. and Daniel A. Brown
1979   "Human Heat Tolerance: Biological and Cultural
        Adaptations." *Yearbook of Physical Anthropology,* 1979,
        22:163–186.

Harlow, Harry F.
1959   "Love in Infant Monkeys." *Scientific American,*
           200:68–74.

Harlow, Harry F. and Margaret K. Harlow
1961   "A Study of Animal Affection." *Natural History,*
           70:48–55.

Harrold, Francis R.
1989   "Mousterian, Chatelperronian and Early Aurignacian
           in Western Europe: Continuity or Discontinuity." *In:*
           The Human Revolution, P. Mellars and C. Stringer (eds.),
           Princeton, N.J.: Princeton University Press,
           pp. 212–231.

Hartl, Daniel
1983   *Human Genetics.* New York: Harper & Row.

Harvey, Paul H., R. D. Martin, and T. H. Clutton-Brock
1987   "Life Histories in Comparative Perspective." *In:* Smuts
           et al. (eds.), q.v., pp. 181–196.

Hass, J. D., E. A. Frongillo, Jr., C. D. Stepick, J. L. Beard, and G. Hurtado
1980   Altitude, Ethnic and Sex Difference in Birth Weight
           and Length in Bolivia. *Human Biology,* **52**:459–477.

Hausfater, Glenn
1984   "Infanticide in Langurs: Strategies, Counter Strategies,
           and Parameter Values." *In:* G. Hausfater and S. B. Hrdy,
           (eds.), q.v., pp. 257–281.

Hausfater, Glenn and Sarah Blaffer Hrdy (eds.)
1984   *Infanticide. Comparative and Evolutionary Perspec-tives.*
           Hawthorne, New York: Aldine de Gruyter.

Hayden, Brian
1993   "The Cultural Capacities of Neandertals: A Review and
           Reevaluation." *Journal of Human Evolution,* **24**:113–146.

Henahan, Sean
1995   Men haven't changed in 270,000 years. Access
           Excellence, Genentech Inc., Worldwide Web Source.

Hiernaux, Jean
1968   *La Diversité Humaine en Afrique subsahariénne.* Bruxelles:
           L'Institut de Sociologie, Université Libre de Bruxelles.

Hill, A., S. Ward, A. Deino, G. Curtis, and R. Drake
1992   "Earliest *Homo.*" *Nature,* **355**:719–722.

Hill, Andrew and Steven Ward
1988   "Origin of the Hominidae: The Record of African Large
           Hominoid Evolution Between 14 my and 4 my."
           Yearbook of Physical Anthropology, 1988, **31**:49–83.

Hinde, Robert A.
1987   "Can Nonhuman Primates Help Us Understand
           Human Behavior?" *In:* B. Smuts et al. (eds.), q.v., pp.
           413–420.

Hirsch, V. M., R. A. Olmsted, M. Murphey-Corb, et al.
1989   "An African Primate Lentivirus (SIVsm) Closely Related
           to HIV-2." *Nature,* **339**: 389–392.

Hoffstetter, R.
1972   "Relationships, Origins, and History of the Ceboid
           Monkeys and the Caviomorph Rodents: A Modern
           Reinterpretation." *In: Evolutionary Biology* (Vol. 6), T.
           Dobzhansky, T. M. K. Hecht, and W. C. Steere (eds.),
           New York: Appleton-Century-Crofts, pp. 323–347.

Holloway, Ralph L.
1969   "Culture: A Human Domain." *Current Anthropology,*
           10:395–407.

——
1981   "Revisiting the South African Taung Australo-pithecine
           Endocast: The Position of the Lunate Sulcus as
           Determined by the Stereoplotting Technique."
           American Journal of Physical Anthropology, **56**:43–58.

——
1983   "Cerebral Brain Endocast Pattern of *Australopithecus
           afarensis* Hominid." *Nature,* **303**:420–422.

——
1985   "The Poor Brain of *Homo sapiens neanderthalensis.*" *In:
           Ancestors, The Hard Evidence,* E. Delson (ed.). New York:
           Alan R. Liss, pp. 319–324.

Horr, D. A.
1975   "The Bornean Orangutan: Population Structure and
           Dynamics in Relationship to Ecology and Reproductive
           Strategy." *In: Primate Behavior: Developments in Field and
           Laboratory Research,* vol. 4, L. A. Rosenblum (ed.), New
           York: Academic Press.

Howell, F. Clark
1978   "Hominidae." *In: Evolution of African Mammals,* V. J.
           Maglio and H.B.S. Cooke (eds.), Cambridge: Harvard
           University Press, pp. 154–248.

——
1988   "Foreword." *In:* Grine (ed.), q.v., pp. xi–xv.

Howells, W. W.
1973   *Evolution of the Genus* Homo. Reading, Mass.: Addison-
           Wesley.

——
1980   "*Homo erectus*—Who, When, Where: A Survey. *Yearbook
           of Physical Anthropology,* **23**:1–23.

Hrdy, Sarah Blaffer
1977   *The Langurs of Abu.* Cambridge, Mass.: Harvard
           University Press.

——
1984a   "Assumptions and Evidence Regarding the Sexual
           Selection Hypothesis: A Reply to Boggess." *In:*
           G. Hausfater and S. B. Hrdy (eds.), q.v., pp. 315–319.

——
1984b   "Female Reproductive Strategies." *In:* M. Small (ed.),
           q.v., pp. 103–109.

——
1995   "Infanticide: Let's Not Throw Out the Baby with the
           Bath Water." *Evolutionary Anthropology,* **3**(5):151–154.

Hu, Dale J., Timothy J. Dondero, Mark A. Rayfield, et al.
1996   "The Emerging Genetic Diversity of HIV. The
           Importance of Global Surveillance, for Diagnostics,
           Research, and Prevention." *Journal of the American
           Medical Association,* **275**(3):210–216.

Hublin, Jean-Jacques, F. Spoor, M. Braun, F. Zonneveld, and S. Condemi
1996   A Late Neanderthal Associated with Upper Palaeolithic
           Artifacts. *Nature,* **38**:224–226.

Hull, David L.
1973   *Darwin and His Critics.* Chicago: University of Chicago
           Press.

The Institute of Vertebrate Paleontology and Paleoanthropology, Chinese Academy of Sciences
1980   *Atlas of Primitive Man in China.* Beijing: Science Press
           (Distributed by Van Nostrand, New York).

Isaac, G. L.
1971   "The Diet of Early Man." *World Archaeology,* **2**:278–299.

────
1975   "Stratigraphy and Cultural Patterns in East Africa During the Middle Ranges of Pleistocene Time." *In: After the Australopithecines,* K. W. Butzer and G. L. Isaac (eds.), Chicago: Aldine Publishing Co., pp. 495–542.

────
1976   "Early Hominids in Action: A Commentary on the Contribution of Archeology to Understanding the Fossil Record in East Africa." *Yearbook of Physical Anthropology,* 1975, **19**:19–35.

Izawa, K. and A. Mizuno
1977   "Palm-Fruit Cracking Behaviour of Wild Black-Capped Capuchin (*Cebus apella*)." *Primates,* **18**:773–793.

Jensen, Arthur
1969   *Environment, Heredity, and Intelligence.* Cambridge, Mass.: Harvard Educational Review.

Jerison, H. J.
1973   *Evolution of the Brain and Behavior.* New York: Academic Press.

Jia, L. and Huang Weiwen
1990   *The Story of Peking Man.* New York: Oxford University Press.

Jia, Lan-po
1975   *The Cave Home of Peking Man.* Peking: Foreign Language Press.

Johanson, D. C. and T. D. White
1979   "A Systematic Assessment of Early African Hominids." *Science,* **203**:321–330.

Johanson, Donald and Maitland Edey
1981   *Lucy: The Beginnings of Humankind.* New York: Simon & Schuster.

Johanson, Donald, F. T. Masao, et al.
1987   "New Partial Skeleton of *Homo habilis* from Olduvai Gorge, Tanzania." *Nature,* **327**:205–209.

Johanson, Donald C. and Maurice Taieb
1976   "Plio-Pleistocene Hominad Discoveries in Hadar, Ethiopia." *Nature,* **260**:293–297.

────
1980   "New Discoveries of Pliocene Hominids and Artifacts in Hadar." International Afar Research Expedition to Ethiopia (Fourth and Fifth Field Seasons, 1975–77). *Journal of Human Evolution,* **9**:582.

Jolly, Alison
1984   "The Puzzle of Female Feeding Priority." *In:* M. F. Small (ed.), q.v., pp. 197–215.

────
1985   *The Evolution of Primate Behavior* (2nd Ed.), New York: Macmillan.

Jones, Rhys
1990   East of Wallace's Line: Issues and Problems in the Colonization of the Australian Continent." *In: The Human Revolution,* P. Mellars and C. Stringer (eds.), Princeton, N.J.: Princeton University Press, pp. 743–782.

Jungers, W. L.
1982   "Lucy's Limbs: Skeletal Allometry and Locomotion in *Australopithecus afarensis*." *Nature,* **297**:676–678.

1988   "New Estimates of Body Size in Australopithecines." *In:* F. E. Grine (ed.), q.v., pp. 115–125.

Kano, T.
1980   The Social Behavior of Wild Pygmy Chimpanzees (*Pan Paniscus*) of Wamba: A Preliminary Report. *Journal of Human Evolution,* **9**:243–260.

────
1992   *The Last Ape. Pygmy Chimpanzee Behavior and Ecology.* Stanford: Stanford University Press.

Kappleman, John
1996   The Evolution of Body Mass and Relative Brain Size in Fossil Hominids. *Journal of Human Evolution,* **30**:243–276.

Katz, S. H., M. L. Hediger, and L. A. Valleroy
1974   Traditional Maize Processing Techniques in the New World. *Science,* **184**:765–773.

Kay, R. F., M. Cartmill, and M. Balow
1998   "The Hypoglossal Canal and the Origins of Human Vocal Behavior (abstract)." *American Journal of Physical Anthropology, Supplement,* **26**:137.

Kay, R. F., J. G. Fleagle, and E. L. Simons
1981   "A Revision of the Oligocene Apes of the Fayum Province, Egypt." *American Journal of Physical Anthropology,* **55**:293–322.

Kay, Richard and Frederick E. Grine
1988   "Tooth Morphology, Wear and Diet in *Australopithecus* and *Paranthropus, In:* F. Grine (ed.), q.v., pp. 427–447.

Kelly, Mark and David Pilbeam
1986   "The Dryopithecines: Taxonomy, Comparative Anatomy, and Phylogeny of Miocene Large Hominoids." *In: Comparative Primate Biology.* Vol. 1, *Systematics, Evolution, and Anatomy,* D. R. Swindler and J. Erwin (eds.), New York: Alan R. Liss, pp. 361–411.

Kennedy, G. E.
1983   "A Morphometric and Taxonomic Assessment of a Hominid Femur from the Lower Member, Koobi Fora, Lake Turkana." *American Journal of Physical Anthropology,* **61**:429–436.

Kennedy, K. A. R.
1991   "Is the Narmada Hominid an Indian *Homo erectus?*" *American Journal of Physical Anthropology,* **86**:475–496.

Kennedy, Kenneth A. R. and S. U. Deraniyagala
1989   "Fossil Remains of 28,000-Year-Old Hominids from Sri Lanka." *Current Anthropology,* **30**:397–399.

Kimbel, William H.
1988   "Identification of a Partial Cranium of *Australopithecus afarensis* from the Koobi Fora Formation, Kenya." *Journal of Human Evolution,* **17**:647–656.

Kimbel, William H., Donald C. Johanson, and Yoel Rak
1994   "The First Skull and Other New Discoveries of *Australopithecus afarensis* at Hadar, Ethiopia." *Nature,* **368**:449–451.

Kimbel, W. H., R. C. Walter, D. C. Johanson, et al.
1996   Late Pliocene *Homo* and Oldowan Tools from the Hadar Formation (Kada Hadar Member), Ethiopia. *Journal of Human Evolution,* **31**:549–561.

Kimbel, William H., Tim D. White, and Donald C. Johanson
1988   "Implications of KNM-WT-17000 for the Evolution of 'Robust' *Australopithecus.*" *In:* F. E. Grine (ed.), q.v., pp. 259–268.

King, Barbara J.
1994   *The Information Continuum.* Santa Fe: School of American Research Press.

Kirkwood, T. B. L.
1997   "The Origins of Human Ageing." *Philosophical Transactions of the Royal Society of London B,* **352**:1765–1772.

Klein, R. G.
1989   *The Human Career. Human Biological and Cultural Origins.* Chicago: University of Chicago Press.

————
1992   "The Archeology of Modern Human Origins." *Evolutionary Anthropology,* **1**:5–14.

Konner, Melvin and Carol Worthman
1980   Nursing Frequency, Gonadal Function, and Birth Spacing among !Kung Hunter-Gatherers. *Science,* **207**:788–791.

Kramer, Andrew
1986   "Hominid-Pongid Distinctiveness in the Miocene-Pliocene Fossil Record: The Lothagam Mandible." *American Journal of Physical Anthropology,* **70**:457–473.

————
1993   "Human Taxonomic Diversity in the Pleistocene: Does *Homo erectus* Represent Multiple Hominid Species?" *American Journal of Physical Anthropology,* **91**:161–171.

Krings, Matthias, Anne Stone, Ralf W. Schmitz, et al.
1997   "Neandertal DNA Sequences and the Origin of Modern Humans." *Cell,* **90**:19–30.

Kroeber, A. L.
1928   "Sub-human Cultural Beginning." *Quarterly Review of Biology,* **3**:325–342.

Krogman, W. M.
1962   *The Human Skeleton in Forensic Medicine.* Springfield: C. C. Thomas.

Krummer, Hans
1971   *Primate Societies.* Chicago: Aldine-Atherton, Inc.

Kunzig, Robert
1997   "Atapuerca. The Face of an Ancestral Child." *Discover,* **18**:88–101.

Lack, David
1966   *Population Studies of Birds.* Oxford: Clarendon.

Lamarck, Jean Baptiste
1809, 1984   *Zoological Philosophy.* Chicago: University of Chicago Press.

Lamberts, S. W. J., A. W. van den Beld, and A-J van der Lely
1997   "The Endocrinology of Aging." *Science,* **278**:419–424.

Lancaster, Jane B.
1975   *Primate Behavior and the Emergence of Human Culture.* New York: Holt, Rinehart & Winston.

Lancaster, Jane B. and C. S. Lancaster
1983   Parental Investment: The Hominid Adaptation. *In: How Humans Adapt: A Biocultural Odyssey,* D. J. Ortner (ed.), Washington, D.C.: Smithsonian Institution Press.

Landau, M.
1984   "Human Evolution as Narrative." *American Scientist,* **72**:262–268.

Larick, Roy and Russell L. Ciochon
1996   "The African Emergence and Early Asian Dispersals of the Genus, *Homo.*" *American Scientist,* **84**:538–551.

Lasker, Gabriel W.
1969   "Human Biological Adaptability: The Ecological Approach in Physical Anthropology." *Science,* **166**:1480–1486.

Latimer, Bruce
1984   "The Pedal Skeleton of *Australopithecus afarensis.*" *American Journal of Physical Anthropology,* **63**:182.

Leakey, L. S. B., J. F. Everden, and G. H. Curtis
1961   "Age of Bed I, Olduvai Gorge, Tanganyika." *Nature,* **191**:478–479.

Leakey, L. S. B., P. V. Tobias, and J. R. Napier
1964   "A New Species of the Genus *Homo* from Olduvai Gorge." *Nature,* **202**:7–10.

Leakey, M. D.
1971   "Remains of *Homo erectus* and Associated Artifacts in Bed IV at Olduvai Gorge, Tanzania." *Nature,* **232**:380–383.

Leakey, M. D. and R. L. Hay
1979   "Pliocene Footprints in Laetoli Beds at Laetoli, Northern Tanzania." *Nature,* **278**:317–323.

Leakey, Meave G. et al.
1995   "New Four-Million-Year-Old Hominid Species from Kanapoi: and Allia Bay, Kenya." *Nature,* **376**:565–571.

Leakey, R. E. F. and M. D. Leakey
1986   "A New Miocene Hominoid from Kenya." *Nature,* **324**:143–146.

Lederberg, J.
1996   "Infection Emergent" (editorial). *Journal of the American Medical Association,* **275**(3):243–245.

Lerner, I. M. and W. J. Libby
1976   *Heredity, Evolution, and Society.* San Francisco: W. H. Freeman and Company.

Leroi-Gourhan, André
1986   "The Hands of Gargas." *October* **37**:18–34.

Lewontin, R. C.
1972   "The Apportionment of Human Diversity." *In: Evolutionary Biology* (Vol. 6), T. Dobzhansky et al. (eds.), New York: Plenum, pp. 381–398.

Li, Wen-Hsiung and Masako Tanimura
1987   "The Molecular Clock Runs More Slowly in Man than in Apes and Monkeys." *Nature,* **326**:93–96.

Lieberman, Daniel, David R. Pilbeam, and Bernard A. Wood
1988   "A Probalistic Approach to the Problem of Sexual Dimorphism in *Homo habilis*: A Comparison of KNM-ER-1470 and KNM-ER-1813." *Journal of Human Evolution,* **17**:503–511.

Linnaeus, C.
1758   *Systema Naturae.*

Lisowski, F. P.
1984   "Introduction." *In: The Evolution of the East African Environment.* Centre of Asian Studies Occasional Papers and Monographs, No. 59, R. O. Whyte (ed.), Hong Kong: University of Hong Kong, pp. 777–786.

Livingstone, Frank B.

1964   "On the Nonexistence of Human Races." *In: Concept of Race,* A. Montagu (ed.), New York: The Free Press, pp. 46–60.

_____   1969   "Polygenic Models for the Evolution of Human Skin Color Differences." *Human Biology,* **41**:480–493.

_____   1980   "Natural Selection and the Origin and Maintenance of Standard Genetic Marker Systems." *Yearbook of Physical Anthropology,* 1980, **23**:25–42.

Lovejoy, C. O.

1988   "Evolution of Human Walking." *Scientific American,* **259**(Nov.):118–125.

Lovejoy, C. O., G. Kingsbury, G. Heiple, and A. H. Burstein

1973   "The Gait of *Australopithecus.*" *American Journal of Physical Anthropology,* **38**:757–780.

Lovejoy, Thomas E.

1982   "The Tropical Forest—Greatest Expression of Life on Earth." *In: Primates and the Tropical Forest,* Proceedings, California Institute of Technology and World Wildlife Fund—U.S., pp. 45–48.

MacKinnon, J. and K. MacKinnon

1980   "The Behavior of Wild Spectral Tarsiers." *International Journal of Primatology,* **1**:361–379.

MacLarnon, Ann

1993   "The Vertebral Canal of KNM-WT 1500 and the Evolution of the Spinal Cord and Other Canal Contents." *In:* A. Walker and R. E. Leakey (eds.), q.v., pp. 359–390.

Mai, L. L.

1983   "A Model of Chromosome Evolution and Its Bearing on Cladogenesis in the Hominoidea." *In:* R. Ciochon and R. Corruccini (eds.), q.v., pp. 87–114.

Manson, J. H. and R. Wrangham

1991   "Intergroup Aggression in Chimpanzees and Humans." *Current Anthropology,* **32**:369–390.

Marshack, A.

1972   *The Roots of Civilization.* New York: McGraw-Hill Publishing Co.

_____   1989   "Evolution of the Human Capacity: The Symbolic Evidence." *Yearbook of Physical Anthropology,* 1989, **32**:1–34.

Masserman, J., S. Wechkin, and W. Terris

1964   "'Altruistic' Behavior in Rhesus Monkeys." *American Journal of Physical Anthropology,* **121**:584–585.

Mayer, Peter J.

1982   Evolutionary Advantages of Menopause. *Human Ecology,* **10**:477–494.

Mayr, Ernst

1962   "Taxonomic Categories in Fossil Hominids." *In: Ideas on Human Evolution,* W. W. Howells (ed.), New York: Atheneum, pp. 242–256.

_____   1970   *Population, Species, and Evolution.* Cambridge: Harvard University Press.

_____   1991   *One Long Argument.* Cambridge: Harvard University Press.

McGrew, W. C.

1992   *Chimpanzee Material Culture. Implications for Human Evolution.* Cambridge: Cambridge University Press.

McGrew, W. C. and E. G. Tutin

1978   "Evidence for a Social Custom in Wild Chimpanzees?" *Man,* **13**:234–251.

McHenry, Henry

1983   "The Capitate of *Australopithecus afarensis* and *A. africanus.*" *American Journal of Physical Anthropology,* **62**:187–198.

_____   1988   "New Estimates of Body Weight in Early Hominids and Their Significance to Encephalization and Megadontia in 'Robust' Australopithecines." *In:* F. E. Grine (ed.), q.v., pp. 133–148.

_____   1992   "Body Size and Proportions in Early Hominids." *American Journal of Physical Anthropology,* **87**:407–431.

McKenna, James J.

1982a   "Primate Field Studies: The Evolution of Behavior and Its Socioecology." *In: Primate Behavior.* James L. Fobes and James E. King (eds.). New York: Academic Press, pp. 53–83.

_____   1982b   "The Evolution of Primate Societies, Reproduction, and Parenting." *In: Primate Behavior.* James L. Fobes and James E. King (eds.). New York: Academic Press, pp. 87–133.

McKusick, Victor

1990   *Mendelian Inheritance in Man.* (9th Ed.) Baltimore: Johns Hopkins Press.

Mellars, P. and C. Stringer (eds.)

1989   *The Human Revolution.* Princeton, N.J.: Princeton University Press.

Mittermeir, R. A.

1982   "The World's Endangered Primates: An Introduction and a Case Study—The Monkeys of Brazil's Atlantic Forests." *In: Primates and the Tropical Rain Forest,* Proceedings, California Institute of Technology, and World Wildlife Fund—U.S., pp. 11–22.

Mittermeir, R. A. and D. Cheney

1987   "Conservation of Primates in Their Habitats." *In:* B. B. Smuts et al., q.v., pp. 477–496.

Montagu, A.

1961   Neonatal and Infant Immaturity in Man. *Journal of the American Medical Association,* **178**:56–57.

Molnar, Stephen

1983   *Human Variation. Races, Types, and Ethnic Groups* (2nd Ed.). Englewood Cliffs: Prentice Hall.

Moore, Lorna G. et al.

1994   Genetic Adaptation to High Altitude. *In: Sports and Exercise Medicine,* Stephen C. Wood and Robert C. Roach (eds.), New York: Marcel Dekker, Inc., pp. 225–262.

Moore, Lorna G. and Judith G. Regensteiner
  1983   "Adaptation to High Altitude." *Annual Reviews of Anthropology,* 12:285–304.
Morbeck, M. E.
  1975   *"Dryopithecus africanus* Forelimb." *Journal of Human Evolution,* 4:39–46.

  _____

  1983   "Miocene Hominoid Discoveries from Rudabánya. Implications from the Postcranial Skeleton." *In:* R. L. Ciochon and R. S. Corruccini (eds.), q.v., pp. 369–404.
Morgan, Elaine
  1972   *The Descent of Women.* New York: Stein and Day.
Morris, Desmond
  1967   *The Naked Ape.* New York: McGraw-Hill.
Mountain, Joanna L., Alice A. Lin, Anne M. Bowcock, and L. L. Cavalli-Sforza
  1993   "Evolution of Modern Humans: Evidence from Nuclear DNA Polymorphisms." *In:* M. J. Aitken et al. (eds.), q.v., pp. 69–83.
Mourant, A. E., A. C. Kopec, and K. Sobczak
  1976   *The Distribution of the Human Blood Groups.* Oxford: Oxford University Press.
Moyá-Solà, Salvador and Meike Köhler
  1996   "A *Dryopithecus* Skelton and the Origins of Great-ape Locomotion. *Nature,* 379:156–159.
Mueller, William H. et al.
  1979   "A Multinational Andean Genetic and Health Program. VIII. Lung Function Changes with Migration between Altitudes." *American Journal of Physical Anthropology,* 51:183–196.
Murray, R. D.
  1980   "The Evolution and Functional Significance of Incest Avoidance." *Journal of Human Evolution,* 9:173–178.
Nabhan, G. P.
  1991   Desert Legumes as a Nutritional Intervention for Diabetic Indigenous Dwellers of Arid Lands. *Arid Lands Newsletter,* 31:11–13.
Napier, J. R. and P. H. Napier
  1967   *A Handbook of Living Primates.* New York: Academic Press.

  _____

  1985   *The Natural History of the Primates.* Cambridge, Mass.: The MIT Press.
Napier, John
  1967   "The Antiquity of Human Walking." *Scientific American,* 216:56–66.
Nature
  1986   "Chernobyl Report." *Nature,* 323:26–30.
Neel, J. V.
  1962   Diabetes Mellitus: A "Thrifty" Genotype Rendered Detrimental by "Progress"? *American Journal of Human Genetics,* 61:1099–1102.
Nesse, R. M., and G. C. Williams
  1994   "Why We Get Sick." New York: Times Books.
Neu, H. C.
  1992   "The Crisis in Antibiotic Resistance." *Science,* 257:1064–1073.

Newman, Marshall T.
  1975   "Nutritional Adaptation in Man." *In: Physiological Anthropology,* Albert Damon (ed.), New York: Oxford University Press, pp. 210–259.
Newman, Russell W.
  1970   "Why Man Is Such a Sweaty and Thirsty Naked Animal: A Speculative Review." *Human Biology,* 42:12–27.
Newman, Russell W. and Ella H. Munro
  1955   "The Relation of Climate and Body Size in U.S. Males." *American Journal of Physical Anthropology,* 13:1–17.
Nishida, T.
  1968   "The Social Group of Wild Chimpanzees in the Mahale Mountains." *Primates,* 9:167–224.

  _____

  1979   "The Social Structure of Chimpanzees of the Mahale Mountains." *In: The Great Apes,* D. A. Hamburg and E. R. McCown (eds.), Menlo Park: Benjamin Cummings, pp. 73–122.

  _____

  1991   Comments. *In:* J. H. Manson and R. Wrangham, q.v., pp. 381–382.
Nishida, T., M. Hiraiwa-Hasegawa, T. Hasegawa, and Y. Takahata
  1985   "Group Extinction and Female Transfer in Wild Chimpanzees in the Mahale National Park, Tanzania." *Zeitschrift Tierpsychologie,* 67:284–301.
Nishida, T., H. Takasaki, and Y. Takahata
  1990   "Demography and Reproductive Profiles." *In: The Chimpanzees of the Mahale Mountains,* T. Nishida (ed.), Tokyo: University of Tokyo Press, pp. 63–97.
Nishida, T., R. W. Wrangham, J. Goodall, and S. Uehara
  1983   "Local Differences in Plant-feeding Habits of Chimpanzees between the Mahale Mountains and Gombe National Park, Tanzania." *Journal of Human Evolution,* 12:467–480.
Noe, R. and R. Bshary
  1997   "The Formation of Red Colobus-Diana Monkey Associations Under Predation Pressure from Chimpanzees. *Proceedings of the Royal Society of London, (B) Biological Science,* 264(1379). pp. 253–259.
Novitski, Edward
  1977   *Human Genetics.* New York: Macmillan.
Oakley, Kenneth
  1963   "Analytical Methods of Dating Bones." *In: Science in Archaelogy,* D. Brothwell and E. Higgs (eds.), New York: Basic Books, Inc.
Olliaro, Piero, Jackqueline Cattani, and Dyann Wirth
  1996   "Malaria, the Submerged Disease." *In: Journal of the American Medical Association,* 275(3):230–233.
Olson, John W. and R. Ciochon
  1990   "A Review of the Evidence for Postulated Middle Pleistocene Occupation in Viet Nam." *Journal of Human Evolution,* 19:761–788.
Ortner, Donald J.
  1981   "Biocultural Interaction in Human Adaptation." *In: How Humans Adapt.* Donald J. Ortner (ed.), Washington, D.C.: Smithsonian Institution Press.

Padian, Kevin and Luis M. Chiappe
   1998   "The Origin of Birds and Their Flight." *Scientific American,* **278**:38–47.

Parés, Josef M. and Alfredo Pérez-González
   1995   "Paleomagnetic Age for Hominid Fossils at Atapuerca Archaeological Site, Spain." *Science,* **269**:830–832.

Parker, Seymour
   1976   "The Precultural Basis of the Incest Taboo: Toward a Biosocial Theory." *American Anthropologist,* **78**:285–305.

Phillips, K.A.
   1998   "Tool Use in Wild Capuchin Monkeys." *American Journal of Primatology,* **46**(3):259–261.

Pickford, M.
   1983   "Sequence and Environments of the Lower and Middle Miocene Hominoids of Western Kenya." *In:* R. L. Ciochon and R. S. Corruccini (eds.), q.v., pp. 421–439.

Pilbeam, David
   1972   *The Ascent of Man.* New York: Macmillan.

   _____

   1977   "Beyond the Apes: Pre-*Homo* Hominids: The Ramapithecines of Africa, Asia, and Europe." Symposium Lecture, March 5, 1977, Davis, Ca.

   _____

   1982   "New Hominoid Skull Material from the Miocene of Pakistan." *Nature,* **295**:232–234.

   _____

   1986   "Distinguished Lecture: Hominoid Evolution and Hominoid Origins." *American Anthropologist,* **88**:295–312.

   _____

   1988   "Primate Evolution." *In: Human Biology,* G. A. Harrison et al., (eds.), New York: Oxford University Press, pp. 76–103.

Pinner, Robert W., Steven M. Teutsch, Lone Simonson, et al.
   1996   "Trends in Infectious Diseases Mortality in the United States." *Journal of the American Medical Association,* **275**(3):189–193.

Pope, G. G.
   1984   "The Antiquity and Paleoenvironment of the Asian Hominidae." *In: The Evolution of the East Asian Environment.* Center of Asian Studies Occasional Papers and Monographs, No. 59, R. O. Whyte (ed.), Hong Kong: University of Hong Kong, pp. 822–847.

   _____

   1992   "Craniofacial Evidence for the Origin of Modern Humans in China." *Yearbook of Physical Anthropology,* 1992, **35**:243–298.

Popp, Joseph L. and Irven DeVore
   1979   "Aggressive Competition and Social Dominance Theory." *In: The Great Apes,* D. A. Hamburg and E. R. McCown (eds.), Menlo Park, Ca.: Benjamin/Cummings Publishing Co., pp. 317–318.

Post, Peter W., Farrington Daniels, Jr., and Robert T. Binford, Jr.
   1975   "Cold Injury and the Evolution of 'White' Skin." *Human Biology,* **47**:65–80.

Potts, R.
   1984   "Home Bases and Early Hominids." *American Scientist,* **72**:338–347.

Potts, Richard
   1991   "Why the Oldowan? Plio-Pleistocene Toolmaking and the Transport of Resources." *Journal of Anthropological Research,* **47**:153–176.

   _____

   1993   "Archeological Interpretations of Early Hominid Behavior and Ecology." *In:* D. T. Rasmussen (ed.), q.v., pp. 49–74.

Potts, Richard and Pat Shipman
   1981   Cutmarks Made by Stone Tools from Olduvai Gorge, Tanzania." *Nature,* **291**:577–580.

Proctor, Robert
   1988   "From Anthropologie to Rassenkunde." *In: Bones, Bodies, Behavior. History of Anthropology* (Vol. 5), 6. W. Stocking, Jr. (ed.), Madison: University of Wisconsin Press, pp. 138–179.

Profet, M.
   1988   The Evolution of Pregnancy Sickness as a Protection to the Embryo Against Pleistocene Teratogens. *Evolutionary Theory,* **8**:177–190.

Pulliam, H. R. and T. Caraco
   1984   "Living in groups: Is There an Optimal Size?" *In: Behavioral Ecology: An Evolutionary Approach* (2nd ed.), J. R. Krebs and N. B. Davies (eds.), Sunderland, Mass.: Sinauer Associates.

Pusey, Anne E. and Craig Packer
   1987   "Dispersal and Philopatry." *In:* B. B. Smuts et al. (eds.), q.v., pp. 250–266.

Radinsky, Leonard
   1973   "*Aegyptopithecus* Endocasts: Oldest Record of a Pongid Brain." *American Journal of Physical Anthropology,* **39**:239–248.

Rafferty, Katherine L. et al.
   1995   "Postcranial Estimates of Body Weight, with a note on a Distal Tibia of *P. major* from Napak, Uganda. *American Journal of Physical Anthropology,* **97**:391–402.

Rak, Y.
   1983   *The Australopithecine Face.* New York: Academic Press.

Relethford, John H. and Henry C. Harpending
   1994   "Craniometric Variation, Genetic Theory, and Modern Human Origins." *American Journal of Physical Anthropology,* **95**:249–270.

Richard, A. F.
   1985   *Primates in Nature.* New York: W. H. Freeman and Co.

Richard, A. F. and S. R. Schulman
   1982   "Sociobiology: Primate Field Studies." *Annual Reviews of Anthropology,* **11**:231–255.

Rightmire, G. P.
   1981   "Patterns in the Evolution of *Homo erectus.*" *Paleobiology,* **7**:241–246.

   _____

   1990   *The Evolution of* Homo erectus. New York: Cambridge University Press.

   _____

   1998   "Human Evolution in the Middle Pleistocene: The Role of *Homo heidelbergensis.*" *Evolutionary Anthropology,* **6**:218–227.

Roberts, D. F.
1973 *Climate and Human Variability.* An Addison-Wesley Module in Anthropology, No. 34. Reading, Mass.: Addison-Wesley.

Roberts, Richard, Rhys Jones, and M. A. Smith
1990 "Thermoluminescence Dating of a 50,000-Year-Old Human Occupation Site in Northern Australia," *Nature,* **345**:153–156.

Robinson, J. T.
1972 *Early Hominid Posture and Locomotion.* Chicago: University of Chicago Press.

Rodman, P. S.
1973 "Population Composition and Adaptive Organisation among Orangutans of the Kutai Reserve." *In: Comparative Ecology and Behaviour of Primates,* R. P. Michael and J. H. Crook (eds.), London: Academic Press, pp. 171–209.

Romer, Alfred S.
1959 *The Vertebrate Story.* Chicago: University of Chicago Press.

Rose, M. D.
1991 "Species Recognition in Eocene Primates." *American Journal of Physical Anthropology,* Supplement 12, p. 153.

Ross, Caroline
1998 "Primate Life Histories." *Evolutionary Anthropology,* **6**:54–63.

Rovner, Irwin
1983 "Plant Opal Pytolith Analysis." *Advances in Archaeological Method and Theory,* **6**:225–266.

Ruben, John A., Christiano Dal Sasso, Nicholas Geist, et al.
1999 "Pulmonary Function and Metabolic Physiology of Theropod Dinosaurs." *Science,* **283**:514–516.

Rudran, R.
1973 Adult Male Replacement in One-Male Troops of Purple-Faced Langurs (*Presbytis senex senex*) and its Effect on Population Structure. *Folia Primatologica,* **19**:166–192.

Ruff, C. B. and Alan Walker
1993 "The Body Size and Shape of KNM-WT 15000." *In:* A. Walker and R. Leakey (eds.), q.v., pp. 234–265.

Rumbaugh, D. M.
1977 *Language Learning by a Chimpanzee: The Lana Project.* New York: Academic Press.

Ruvolo, M., D. Pan, S. Zehr, T. Goldberg, T. R. Disotell and M. von Dornum
1994 "Gene trees and hominoid phylogeny." *Proc. Natl. Acad. Sci.,* **91**:8900–8904.

Sachick, Kathy B. and Dong Zhuan
1991 "Early Paleolithic of China and Eastern Asia." *Evolutionary Anthropology,* **2**(1):22–35.

Samson, M., F. Libert, B. J. Doranz, et al.
1996 Resistance to HIV-1 Infection in Caucasian Individuals Bearing Mutant Alleles of the CCR-5 Chemokine Receptor Gene. *Nature* **382**(22): 722–725.

Sarich, V. M. and A. C. Wilson
1967 "Rules of Albumen Evolution in Primates." *Proceedings, National Academy of Science,* **58**:142–148.

Sarich, Vincent
1971 "A Molecular Approach to the Question of Human Origins." *In: Background for Man,* P. Dolhinow and V. Sarich (eds.), Boston: Little, Brown & Co., pp. 60–81.

Savage-Rumbaugh, E. S.
1986 *Ape Language: From Conditioned Responses to Symbols.* New York: Columbia University Press.

Savage-Rumbaugh, S., K. McDonald, R. A. Sevic, W. D. Hopkins, and E. Rupert
1986 "Spontaneous Symbol Acquisition and Communicative Use by Pygmy Chimpanzees (*Pan paniscus*)." *Journal of Experimental Psychology: General,* **115**(3):211–235.

Savage-Rumbaugh, S. and R. Lewin
1994 *Kanzi. The Ape at the Brink of the Human Mind.* New York: John Wiley and Sons.

Schaller, George B.
1963 *The Mountain Gorilla.* Chicago: University of Chicago Press.

Scheller, Richard H. and Richard Axel
1984 "How Genes Control Innate Behavior." *Scientific American,* **250**:54–63.

Scott, K.
1980 "Two Hunting Episodes of Middle Paleolithic Age at La Cotte Sainte-Brelade, Jersey (Channel Islands)." *World Archaeology,* **12**:137–152.

Semaw, S., P. Renne, W. K. Harris, et al.
1997 2.5-million-year-old Stone Tools from Gona, Ethiopia. *Nature,* **385**:333–336

Senut, Brigette and Christine Tardieu
1985 "Functional Aspects of Plio-Pleistocene Hominid Limb Bones: Implications for Taxonomy and Phylogeny." *In: Ancestors: The Hard Evidence,* E. Delson (ed.), New York: Alan R. Liss, pp. 193–201.

Seyfarth, Robert M.
1987 "Vocal Communication and its Relation to Language." *In:* Smuts et al., *Primate Societies.* Chicago: University of Chicago Press, pp. 440–451.

Seyfarth, Robert M., Dorothy L. Cheney, and Peter Marler
1980a "Monkey Responses to Three Different Alarm Calls." *Science,* **210**:801–803.

——— 1980b "Ververt Monkey Alarm Calls." *Animal Behavior,* **28**:1070–1094.

Shipman, P. L.
1983 "Early Hominid Lifestyle. Hunting and Gathering or Foraging and Scavenging?" Paper presented at 52nd Annual Meeting, American Association of Physical Anthropologists, Indianapolis, April.

——— 1987 "An Age-Old Question: Why Did the Human Lineage Survive?" *Discover,* **8**:60–64.

Sibley, Charles and Jon E. Ahlquist
1984 "The Phylogeny of the Hominoid Primates as Indicated by DNA-DNA Hybridization." *Journal of Molecular Evolution,* **20**:2–15.

Simons, E. L.
1969 "The Origin and Radiation of the Primates." *Annals of the New York Academy of Sciences,* **167**:319–331.

_____
1972   *Primate Evolution.* New York: Macmillan.

_____
1985   "African Origin, Characteristics and Context of Earliest Higher Primates." *In: Hominid Evolution: Past, Present, and Future.* P. Tobias (ed.), New York: Alan R. Liss, pp. 101–106.

_____
1995   "Egyptian Oligocene Primates: A Review." *Yearbook of Physical Anthropology,* **38**:199–238.

Simons, Elwyn L. and Tab Rasmussen
1994   "A Whole New World of Ancestors: Eocene Anthropoideans from Africa." *Evolutionary Anthropology,* **3**:128–139.

Simpson, G. G.
1945   "The Principles of Classification and a Classification of Mammals." *Bulletin of the American Museum of Natural History,* **85**:1–350.

Simpson, G. G., C. S. Pittendright, and L H. Tiffany
1957   *Life.* New York: Harcourt, Brace and Co., Inc.

Skelton, R. R., H. M. McHenry, and G. M. Drawhorn
1986   "Phylogenetic Analysis of Early Hominids." *Current Anthropology,* **27**:1–43; 361–365.

Skelton, Randall R. and Henry M. McHenry
1992   "Evolutionary Relationships among Early Hominids." *Journal of Human Evolution,* **23**:309–349.

Small, Meredith F. (ed.)
1984   *Female Primates. Studies by Women Primatologists.* Monographs in Primatology, Vol. 4. New York: Alan R. Liss.

Smith, Fred H.
1984   "Fossil Hominids from the Upper Pleistocene of Central Europe and the Origin of Modern Europeans." *In:* F. H. Smith and F. Spencer (eds.), q.v., pp. 187–209.

Smith, Fred H., A. B. Falsetti, and S. M. Donnelly
1989   "Modern Human Origins." *Yearbook of Physical Anthropology,* **32**:35–68.

Smith, Fred H. and Frank, Spencer (eds.)
1984   *The Origins of Modern Humans.* New York: Alan R. Liss, Inc.

Smuts, Barbara
1985   *Sex and Friendship in Baboons.* Hawthorne, N.Y.: Aldine de Gruyter.

Smuts, Barbara B. et al. (eds.)
1987   *Primate Societies.* Chicago: University of Chicago Press.

Snowdon, Charles T.
1990   "Language Capacities of 'Nonhuman Animals.'" *Yearbook of Physical Anthropology,* **33**:215–243.

Soffer, Olga
1985   *The Upper Paleolithic of the Central Russian Plain.* New York: Academic Press.

Solecki, Ralph
1971   *Shanidar, The First Flower People.* New York: Alfred A. Knopf.

Sponheimer, Matt and Julia A. Lee-Thorp
1999   "Isotopic Evidence for the Diet of an Early Hominid, *Australopithecus africanus.*" *Science,* **283**:368–370.

Stanford, C. B., J. Wallis, H. Matama, and J. Goodall
1994   "Patterns of Predation by Chimpanzees on Red Colobus Monkeys in Gombe National Park." *American Journal of Physical Anthropology,* **94**(2):213–228.

Stanyon, Roscoe and Brunetto Chiarelli
1982   "Phylogeny of the Hominoidea: The Chromosome Evidence." *Journal of Human Evolution,* **11**:493–504.

Steegman, A. T., Jr.
1970   "Cold Adaptation and the Human Face." *American Journal of Physical Anthropology,* **32**:243–250.

_____
1975   "Human Adaptation to Cold." *In: Physiological Anthropology,* A. Damon (ed.), New York: Oxford University Press, pp. 130–166.

Steklis, Horst D.
1985   "Primate Communicatioan, Comparative Neurology, and the Origin of Language Re-examined." *Journal of Human Evolution,* **14**:157–173.

Stern, Curt
1973   *Principles of Human Genetics,* 3rd ed. San Francisco: W. H. Freeman.

Stern, Jack T. and Randall L. Susman
1983   "The Locomotor Anatomy of *Australopithecus afarensis.*" *American Journal of Physical Anthropology,* **60**:279–317.

Stewart, T. D.
1979   *Essentials of Forensic Anthropology: Especially as Developed in the United States.* Springfield: C. C. Thomas.

Stiner, Mary C.
1991   "The Faunal Remains from Grotta Guatari." *Current Anthropology,* **32**(2)April:103–117.

Stoneking, Mark
1993   "DNA and Recent Human Evolution." *Evolutionary Anthropology,* **2**:60–73.

Straus, Lawrence Guy
1993   "Southwestern Europe at the Last Glacial Maximum." *Current Anthropology,* **32**:189–199.

_____
1995   "The Upper Paleolithic of Europe: An Overview." *Evolutionary Anthropology,* **4**:4–16.

Stringer, C. B. (ed.).
1985   "Middle Pleistocene Hominid Variability and the Origin of Late Pleistocene Humans." *In: Ancestors: The Hard Evidence,* E. Delson (ed.), New York: Alan R. Liss, pp. 289–295.

_____
1993   "Secrets of the Pit of the Bones." *Nature,* **362**:501–502.

_____
1995   "The Evolution and Distribution of Later Pleistocene Human Populations." *In:* E. Vrba et al. (eds.), op cit., pp. 524–531.

Stringer, C. B. and P. Andrews
1988   "Genetic and Fossil Evidence for the Origin of Modern Humans." *Science,* **239**:1263–1268.

Struhsaker, T. T.
1967   "Auditory Communication among Vervet Monkeys
(*Cercopithecus aethiops*)." *In: Social Communication
Among Primates*, S. A. Altmann (ed.), Chicago:
University of Chicago Press.

_____
1975   *The Red Colobus Monkey*. Chicago: University of
Chicago Press.

Struhsaker, Thomas T. and Lysa Leland
1979   "Socioecology of Five Sympatric Monkey Species in the
Kibale Forest, Uganda." *Advances in the Study of
Behavior*, Vol. 9, New York: Academic Press, pp.
159–229.

_____
1987   "Colobines: Infanticide by Adult Males." *In:* B. B.
Smuts et al. (eds.), q.v., pp. 83–97.

Strum, S. C.
1987   *Almost Human. A Journey into the World of Baboons*. New
York: W. W. Norton.

Sugiyama, Y.
1965   "Short History of the Ecological and Sociological
Studies on Non-Human Primates in Japan." *Primates*,
6:457–460.

Sugiyama, Y. and J. Koman
1979   "Tool-using and -making Behavior in Wild
Chimpanzees at Bossou, Guinea." *Primates*,
20:513–524.

Sumner, D. R., M. E. Morbeck, and J. Lobick
1989   "Age-Related Bone Loss in Female Gombe
Chimpanzees." *American Journal of Physical
Anthropology*, 72:259.

Suomi, Stephen J., Susan Mineka, and Roberta D. DeLizio
1983   "Short- and Long-Term Effects of Repetitive Mother-
Infant Separation on Social Development in Rhesus
Monkeys." *Developmental Psychology*, 19(5):710–786.

Susman, Randall L. (ed.)
1984   *The Pygmy Chimpanzee: Evolutionary Biology and
Behavior*. New York: Plenum Press.

Susman, Randall L.
1988   "New Postcranial Remains from Swartkrans and Their
Bearing on the Functional Morphology and Behavior
of *Paranthropus robustus*." *In:* F. E. Grine (ed.), q.v., pp.
149–172.

Susman, Randall L., Jack T. Stern, and William L. Jungers
1985   "Locomotor Adaptations in the Hadar Hominids." *In:
Ancestors: The Hard Evidence*, E. Delson (ed.), New York:
Alan R. Liss, pp. 184–192.

Sussman, Robert W., James M. Cheverud and Thad Q. Bartlett
1995   Infant Killing as an Evolutionary Strategy: Reality or
Myth? *Evolutionary Anthropology*, 3(5):149–151.

Suzman, I. M.
1982   "A Comparative Study of the Hadar and Sterkfontein
Australopithecine Innominates." *American Journal of
Physical Anthropology*, 57:235.

Swisher, C. C. III, G. H. Curtis, T. Jacob, et al.
1994   "Age of the Earliest Known Hominids in Java,
Indonesia." *Science*, 263:1118–1121.

Swisher, C. C., W. J. Rink, S. C. Anton, et al.
1996   Latest *Homo erectus* of Java: Potential Contemporaneity
with *Homo sapiens* in Southwest Java. *Science*,
274:1870–1874.

Szalay, Frederick S. and Eric Delson
1979   *Evolutionary History of the Primates*. New York:
Academic Press.

Tattersal, Ian, Eric Delson, and John Van Couvering
1988   *Encyclopedia of Human Evolution and Prehistory*. New
York: Garland Publishing.

Teleki, G.
1986   "Chimpanzee Conservation in Sierra Leone—A Case
Study of a Continent-wide Problem." Paper presented
at Understanding Chimpanzees Symposium, Chicago
Academy of Sciences, Chicago, Nov. 7–10, 1987.

Templeton, Alan R.
1996   "Gene Lineages and Human Evolution." *Science*,
272:1363–1364.

Tenaza, R. and R. Tilson
1977   "Evolution of Long-Distance Alarm Calls in Kloss'
Gibbon." *Nature*, 268:233–235.

Thieme, Hartmut
1997   Lower Paleolithic Hunting Spears from Germany.
Nature, 385:807–810.

Thorne, A. G. and M. H. Wolpoff
1992   "The Multiregional Evolution of Humans." *Scientific
American*, 266:76–83.

Thorsby, Erik
1997   "Invited Anniversary Review: HLA Associated
Diseases." *Human Immunology*, 53:1–11.

Tiemel, Chen, Yang Quan, and Wu En
1994   "Antiquity of *Homo sapiens* in China." *Nature*,
368:55–56.

Tishkoff, S. A., E. Dietzsch, W. Speed, et al.
1996   "Global Patterns of Linkage Disequilibrium at the CD4
Locus and Modern Human Origins." *Science*,
271:1380–1387.

Tobias, Phillip
1971   *The Brain in Hominid Evolution*. New York: Columbia
University Press.

_____
1983   "Recent Advances in the Evolution of the Hominids
with Especial Reference to Brain and Speech."
Pontifical Academy of Sciences, *Scrita Varia*, 50:85–140.

_____
1991   *Olduvai Gorge, Volume IV. The Skulls, Endocasts and Teeth
of* Homo habilis. Cambridge: Cambridge University
Press.

Trevathan, Wenda R.
1987   *Human Birth: An Evolutionary Perspective*. Hawthorne,
NY: Aldine de Gruyter.

Trinkaus, E.
1983   *The Shanidar Neandertals*. New York: Academic Press.

_____
1984   "Western Asia." *In:* F. H. Smith and F. Spencer (eds.),
q.v., pp. 251–293.

Trinkaus, E. and W. W. Howells
1979   "The Neandertals." *Scientific American*, 241(6):118–133.

Trinkaus, Erik and Pat Shipman
1992   *The Neandertals.* New York: Alfred A. Knopf.
Trivers, R. L.
1971   "The Evolution of Reciprocal Altruism." *Quarterly Review of Biology,* **46**:35–57.

——
1972   "Parental Investment and Sexual Selection." *In: Sexual Selection and the Descent of Man,* B. Campbell (ed.), Chicago: Aldine, pp. 136–179.
Tuttle, Russell H.
1990   "Apes of the World." *American Scientist,* **78**:115–125.
Ulijaszek, S.
1998   "The Genetics of Growth." *In: The Cambridge Encyclopedia of Human Growth and Development,* S. J. Ulijaszek, F. E. Johnston, and M. A. Preece (eds.). Cambridge, UK: Cambridge University Press, pp. 121–123.
Van Couvering, A. H. and J. A. Van Covering
1976   "Early Miocene Mammal Fossils From East Africa." *In: Human Origins,* G. Isaac and E. R. McCown (eds.), Menlo Park, CA.: Benjamin/Cummings, pp. 155–207.
Villa, Paola
1983   *Terra Amata and the Middle Pleistocene Archaeological Record of Southern France.* University of California Publications in Anthropology, Vol. 13. Berkeley: University of California Press.
Visalberghi, E.
1990   "Tool Use in Cebus." *Folia Primatologica,* **54**:146–154.
Vogel, F.
1970   "ABO Blood Groups and Disease." *American Journal of Human Genetics,* **22**:464–475.
Vogel, F., M. Kopun, and R. Rathenberg
1976   "Mutation and Molecular Evolution." *In: Molecular Anthropology,* M. Goodman et al. (eds.), New York: Plenum Press, pp. 13–33.
Von Koenigswald, G. H. R.
1956   *Meeting Prehistoric Man.* New York: Harper & Brothers.
Vrba, E. S.
1985   "Ecological and Adaptive Changes Associated with Early Hominid Evolution." *In: Ancestors: The Hard Evidence,* E. Delson (ed.), New York: Alan R. Liss, pp. 63–71.

——
1988   "Late Pliocene Climatic Events and Hominid Evolution." *In:* F. Grine (ed.), q.v., pp. 405–426.

——
1995   "The Fossil Record of African Antelopes (Mammalia, Bovidae) in Relation to Human Evolution and Paleoclimate." *In: Paleoclimate and Evolution with Emphasis on Human Origins,* E. Vrba et al. (eds.). New Haven: Yale University Press, pp. 385–424.
Wagner, Gunter A.
1996   "Fission-Track Dating in Paleoanthropology." *Evolutionary Anthropology,* **5**:165–171.
Wakayama, T., A. C. F. Perry, M. Zucotti, K. R. Johnson, and R. Yanagimachi
1998   "Full-term Development of Mice from Enucleated Oocytes Injected with Cumulus Cell Nuclei. *Nature,* **394**:369–374.

Walker, A.
1976   "Remains Attributable to *Australopithecus* from East Rudolf." *In: Earliest Man and Environments in the Lake Rudolf Basin,* Y. Coppens et al. (eds.), Chicago: University of Chicago Press, pp. 484–489.

——
1991   "The Origin of the Genus *Homo.*" *In:* S. Osawa and T. Honjo (eds.), *Evolution of Life.* Tokyo: Springer-Verlag, pp. 379–389.

——
1993   "The Origin of the Genus *Homo*" *In:* D. T. Rasmussen (ed.), *The Origin and Evolution of Humans and Humanness.* Boston: Jones and Bartlett, pp. 29–47.
Walker, A., D. Pilbeam, and M. Cartmill
1981   "Changing Views and Interpretations of Primate Evolution." Paper presented to the Annual Meetings, American Association of Physical Anthropologists. Detroit, Mich.
Walker, Alan and R. E. Leakey (eds.)
1993   *The Nariokotome* Homo erectus *Skeleton.* Cambridge: Harvard University Press.
Walker, Alan and Mark Teaford
1989   "The Hunt for *Proconsul.*" *Scientific American,* **260**(Jan):76–82.
Walters, Jeffrey and Robert Seyfarth
1987   "Conflict and Cooperation." *In:* B. B. Smuts et al. (eds.), q.v., pp. 306–317.
Wanpo, Huang, Russell Ciochon, et al.
1995   "Early *Homo* and Associated Artifacts from Asia." *Nature,* **378**:275–278.
Ward, S. C. and D. R. Pilbeam
1983   Maxillofacial Morphology of Miocene Hominoids from Africa and Indo-Pakistan." *In:* R. L. Ciochon and R. S. Corruccini (eds.), q.v., pp. 211–238.
Ward, Steven and William H. Kimbel
1983   "Subnasal Alveolar Morphology and the Systematic Position of *Sivapithecus.*" *American Journal of Physical Anthropology,* **61**:157–171.
Waser, Peter M.
1987   "Interactions among Primate Species." *In:* B. B. Smuts et al. (eds.), q.v., pp. 210–226.
Washburn, S. L.
1963   "The Study of Race." *American Anthropologist,* **65**:521–531.

——
1971   "The Study of Human Evolution." *In:* P. Dolhinow and V. Sarich (eds.), *Background for Man: Readings in Physical Anthropology,* Boston: Little, Brown, pp. 82–121.
Watson, J. B. and F. H. C. Crick
1953a   "Genetical Implications of the Structure of the Deoxyribonucleic Acid." *Nature,* **171**:964–967.

——
1953b   "A Structure for Deoxyribonucleic Acid." *Nature,* **171**:737–738.
Weiner, J. S.
1955   *The Piltdown Forgery.* London: Oxford University Press.
Weiss, K. M., K. K. Kidd, and J. R. Kidd
1992   "A Human Genome Diversity Project." *Evolutionary Anthropology,* **1**:80–82.

Weiss, Mark L. and Alan E. Mann
1981   *Human Biology and Behavior*, 3rd ed. Boston: Little Brown.

Weiss, K. M., D. W. Stock, and Z. Zhao
1998   "Homeobox Genes." *In: The Cambridge Encyclopedia of Human Growth and Development*, S. J. Ulijaszek, F. E. Johnston, and M. A. Preece (eds.). Cambridge, UK: Cambridge University Press, pp. 137–139.

Weiss, Robin A. and Richard W. Wrangham
1999   "From *Pan* to Pandemic." *Nature*, 397:385–386.

White, T. D.
1980   "Evolutionary Implications of Pliocene Hominid Footprints." *Science*, 208:175–176.

_____
1983   Comment Made at Institute of Human Origins Conference on the Evolution of Human Locomotion (Berkeley, Ca.).

White, T. D. and J. M. Harris
1977   "Suid Evolution and Correlation of African Hominid Localities." *Science*, 198:13–21.

White, T. D., G. Suwa, and B. Asfaw
1995   Corrigendum (White et al., 1994). *Nature*, 375:88.

White, T. D., D. C. Johanson, and W. H. Kimbel
1981   "*Australopithecus africanus:* Its Phyletic Position Reconsidered." *South African Journal of Science*, 77:445–470.

White, Tim D. and Donald C. Johanson
1989   "The Hominid Composition of Afar Locality 333: Some Preliminary Observations." *Hominidae*, Proceedings of the 2nd International Congress of Human Paleontology, Milan: Editoriale Jaca Book, pp. 97–101.

White, Tim D., Gen Suwa, and Berhane Asfaw
1994   *Australopithecus ramidus*, A New Species of Early Hominid from Aramis, Ethiopia. *Nature*, 371:306–312.

Whyte, Robert Orr (ed.)
1984   "The Evolution of the East Asian Environment." Centre of Asian Studies Occasional Papers and Monographs, No. 59. Hong Kong: University of Hong Kong.

Williams, George C.
1957   "Pleiotropy, Natural Selection and the Evolution of Senescence." *Evolution*, 11:398–411.

_____
1966   *Adaptation and Natural Selection: A Critique of Some Current Evolutionary Thought.* Princeton: Princeton University Press.

Williams, George C. and Randolph M. Nesse
1991   The Dawn of Darwinian Medicine. *The Quarterly Review of Biology*, 66:1–22.

Williams, Robert C.
1985   "HLA II: The Emergence of the Molecular Model for the Major Histocompatibility Complex." *Yearbook of Physical Anthropology*, 1985, 28:79–95.

Wilson, E. O.
1975   *Sociobiology. The New Synthesis.* Cambridge: Harvard University Press.

Wolf, Katherine and Steven Robert Schulman
1984   "Male Response to 'Stranger' Females as a Function of Female Reproduction Value among Chimpanzees." *The American Naturalist*, 123:163–174.

Wolpoff, Milford H.
1983a   "Lucy's Little Legs." *Journal of Human Evolution*, 12:443–453.

_____
1983b   "*Ramapithecus* and Human Origins. An Anthropologist's Perspective of Changing Interpretations." *In:* R. L. Ciochon and R. S. Corruccini (eds.), q.v., pp. 651–676.

_____
1984   "Evolution in *Homo erectus:* The Question of Stasis." *Paleobiology*, 10:389–406.

_____
1989   "Multiregional Evolution: The Fossil Alternative to Eden." *In:* P. Mellars and C. Stringer, q.v., pp. 62–108.

_____
1995   *Human Evolution* 1996 Edition. New York: McGraw-Hill Inc, College Custom Series.

_____
1999   *Paleoanthropology.* 2nd ed. New York: McGraw-Hill.

Wolpoff, Milford H. et al.
1981   "Upper Pleistocene Human Remains from Vindija Cave, Croatia, Yugoslavia." *American Journal of Physical Anthropology*, 54:499–545.

_____
1994   "Multiregional Evolutions: A World-Wide Source for Modern Human Population." *In:* M. H. Nitecki and D. V. Nitecki (eds.), q.v., pp. 175–199.

Wolpoff, M., Wu Xin Chi, and Alan G. Thorne
1984   "Modern *Homo sapiens* Origins." *In:* Smith and Spencer (eds.), q.v., pp. 411–483.

Wood, Bernard
1991   *Koobi Fora Research Project IV: Hominid Cranial Remains from Koobi Fora.* Oxford: Clarendon Press.

_____
1992a   "Origin and Evolution of the Genus *Homo*." *Nature*, 355:783–790.

_____
1992b   "A Remote Sense for Fossils." *Nature*, 355:397–398.

Wood, B. C. Wood, and L. Konigsberg
1994   "*Paranthropus boisei:* An Example of Evolutionary Stasis?" *American Journal of Physical Anthropology*, 95:117–136.

Wood, C. S., G. A. Harrison, C. Dove, and J. S. Weiner
1972   "Selection Feeding of *Anopheles gambiae* According to ABO Blood Group Status." *Nature*, 239:165.

Wrangham, R. W.
1977   "Feeding Behaviour of Chimpanzees in Gombe National Park, Tanzania." *In: Primate Ecology*, T. H. Clutton-Brock (ed.). New York: Academic Press, pp. 503–538.

_____
1980   "An Ecological Model of Female-Bonded Primate Groups." *Behavior*, 75:262–300.

1986   "Ecology and Social Relationships in Two Species of Chimpanzees." *In: Ecology and Social Evolution: Birds and Mammals,* D. I. Rubenstein and R. W. Wrangham (eds.), Princeton: Princeton University Press, pp. 352–378.

Wu, Rukang and S. Lin
1983   "Peking Man." *Scientific American,* **248**(6):86–94.

Wu, Rukang and C. E. Oxnard
1983   "Ramapithecines from China: Evidence from Tooth Dimensions." *Nature,* **306**:258–260.

Wu, Rukang and John W. Olsen (eds.)
1985   *Palaeoanthropology and Palaeolithic Archaeology in the People's Republic of China.* New York: Academic Press.

Wu, Rukang and Xingren Dong
1985   "*Homo erectus* in China." *In: Palaeoanthropology and Palaeolithic Archaeology in the People's Republic of China,* R. Wu and J. W. Olsen (eds.), New York: Academic Press, pp. 79–89.

Yellen, John E. et al.
1995   "A Middle Stone Age Worked Bone Industry from Katanda, Upper Semliki Valley, Zaire." *Science,* **268**:553–556.

Yi, Seonbok and G. A. Clark
1983   "Observations on the Lower Palaeolithic of Northeast Asia." *Current Anthropology,* **24**:181–202.

Young, David.
1992   *The Discovery of Evolution.* Cambridge: Natural History Museum Publications, Cambridge University Press.

Yunis, Jorge J. and Om Prakesh
1982   "The Origin of Man: A Chromosomal Pictorial Legacy." *Science,* **215**:1525–1530.

Zhou Min Zhen and Wang Yuan Quing
1989   "Paleoenvironmental Contexts of Hominid Evolution in China." *Circum-Pacific Prehistory Conference,* Seattle: University of Washington Press.

Zubrow, Ezra
1989   "The Demographic Modeling of Neanderthal Extinction." *In: The Human Revolution,* P. Mellars and C. Stringer, Princeton, N.J.: Princeton University Press, pp. 212–231.

Index

Page numbers in bold indicate marginal definitions. Page numbers in italics indicate illustrations or boxed material.

A

Photo Credits

Fig. 1–1, 2, Courtesy, Peter Jones; Fig. 1,.2, 3, Bettmann Archive; Fig. 1–3a, 5, Institute of Human Origins; Fig. 1–3b, 5, Lynn Kilgore; Fig. 1–3c, 5, Lynn Kilgore; Fig. 1–3d, 5, Robert Jurmain; Fig. 1–4, 11, Institute of Human Origins; Fig. 1–5, 11, Robert Jurmain; Fig. 1–6, 12, Courtesy, Judith Regensteiner; Fig. 1–7a, 12, Bonnie Pedersen/Arlene Kruse; Fig. 1–7b, 12, Robert Jurmain; Fig. 1–8a, 14, Lynn Kilgore; Fig. 1–8b, 14, Robert Jurmain; Fig. 1–9, 14, Courtesy, Lorna Pierce/Judy Suchey; Fig. 2–1, 26, Bancroft Library, University of California; Fig. 2–2, 27, Special Collections, American Museum of Natural History #318607; Fig. 2–3, 27, Special Collections, American Museum of Natural History #326703; Fig. 2–4, 28, Bettmann Archive; Fig. 2–5, 28, Bettmann Archive; Fig. 2–6, 29, Reprinted by permission from p. 115, 118 of *Historical Geology: Evolution of the Earth and Life Through Time,* by Reed Wicander and James S. Monroe, copyright © 1989 by West Publishing Company. All rights reserved; Fig. 2–7, 29, Special Collections, American Museum of Natural History #28000; Fig. 2–8, 30, Special Collections, American Museum of Natural History #326671; Fig. 2–9, 30, Special Collections, American Museum of Natural History #326701; Fig. 2–10, 31, Special Collections, American Museum of Natural History 326672; Fig. 2–13, 33, Lynn Kilgore; Fig. 2–14, 34, Special Collections, American Museum of Natural History #326696; Fig. 2–15a, 35, Michael Tweedie/Photo Researchers #4Q3468; Fig. 2–15b, 35, Breck P. Kent/Animals Animals #AA-124378; Fig. 3–7, 55, From: Harrison, C. et al.

1983. Cytogenics. Cell Genetics 35: 21–27, 1983. S. Karger, A. G., Basel; Fig. 3–9, 58, University of California Medical Center; Fig. 4–1, 74, Special Collections, American Museum of Natural History #328141; Fig. 5–1 box, 110, Lynn Kilgore; Fig. 5–2 box, 111, Lynn Kilgore; Fig. 5–3 box, 111, Lynn Kilgore; Fig. 5–10, 121, Courtesy, Fred Jacobs; Fig. 5–11, 121, Courtesy, Fred Jacobs; Fig. 5–12, 121, Courtesy, San Francisco Zoo; Fig. 5–13, 121, Courtesy, Bonnie Pedersen/Arlene Kruse; Fig. 5–15, 122, David Haring, Duke University Primate Zoo; Fig. 5–17, 123, © Zoological Society of San Diego, photo by Ron Garrison; 5.18, 123, Raymond Mendez/Animals Animals #AA-656863; Fig. 5–20, 124, Robert L. Lubeck/Animals Animals #AA626167; Fig. 5–22, 125, Robert Jurmain; Fig. 5–23a, 125, Courtesy, Bonnie Pedersen/Arlene Kruse; Fig. 5–23b, 125, Courtesy, Bonnie Pedersen/Arlene Kruse; Fig. 5–24, 126, Robert Jurmain; Fig. 5–26, 128, Lynn Kilgore; Fig. 5–27, 128, Robert Jurmain, Photo by Jill Matsumoto/Jim Anderson; Fig. 5–29a, 129, Lynn Kilgore; Fig. 5–29b, 129, Lynn Kilgore; Fig. 5–30a, 130, Robert Jurmain, Photo by Jill Matsumoto/Jim Anderson; Fig. 5–30b, 130, Robert Jurmain, Photo by Jill Matsumoto/Jim Anderson; Fig. 5–31, 131, Courtesy, Ellen Ingmanson; Fig. 5–2 box, 143, Lynn Kilgore; Fig. 5–3 box, 144, Robert Jurmain; Fig. 6–1, 147, Courtesy, John Oates; Fig. 6–2, 147, Courtesy, Jean De Rousseau; Fig. 6–3, 150, Courtesy, John Oates; Fig. 6–4, 153, Joe MacDonald/Animals Animals #AA527231; Fig. 6–5, 157, Lynn Kilgore; Fig. 6–6, 158, Lynn Kilgore; Fig. 6–7, 158, Adapted with permission of the publishers from *The*

Chimpanzees of Gombe by Jane Goodall, Cambridge, Mass.: Harvard University Press, Copyright 1986 by the President and Fellows of Harvard College; Fig. 6–8a, 161, Robert Jurmain; Fig. 6–8b, 161, Meredith Small; Fig. 6–8c, 161, Lynn Kilgore; Fig. 6–8d, 161, Arlene Kruse/Bonnie Pedersen; Fig. 6–9, 162, Lynn Kilgore; Fig. 6–10a, 165, David Haring, Duke University Primate Center; Fig. 6–10b, 165, Arlene Kruse/Bonnie Pedersen; Fig. 6–10c, 165, Robert Jurmain; Fig. 6–10d, 165, © Tom McHugh/Photo Researchers, Inc. #7U5895; Fig. 6–10e, 165, Robert Jurmain; Fig. 6–11, 166, Harlow Primate Laboratory, University of Wisconsin; Fig. 6–12, 166, Lynn Kilgore; Fig. 7–1, 176, Lynn Kilgore; Fig. 7–2, 179, Rose A. Sevcik, Language Research Center, Georgia State University; Fig. 7–4a, 182, Courtesy, The Jane Goodall Institute; Fig. 7–4b, 182, Courtesy, Carol Lofton/Distinctive Images; Fig. 7–5, 190, Lynn Kilgore; Fig. 8–12, 210, Hansejudy Beste/Animals Animals; Fig. 8–13, 210, J. C. Stevenson/Animals Animals; Fig. 8–14, 211, Doug Wechsler/Animals Animals #AA-656863; Fig. 8–18, 214, Robert Jurmain; Fig. 8–19, 215, Courtesy, David Pilbeam; Fig. 9–3, 232, Robert Jurmain; Fig. 9–1 box, 233, L.S.B. Leakey Foundation, San Francisco, CA; Fig. 9–4, 234, Harry Nelson; Fig. 9–5, 239, Robert Jurmain; Fig. 9–6, 240, Robert Jurmain; Fig. 9–10, 243, Courtesy, Larry Keeley; Fig. 10–5, 261, Harry Nelson; Fig. 10–7, 264, Tim D. White/Brill, Atlanta; Fig. 10–9, 265, Lynn Kilgore; Fig. 10–10, 266, Courtesy, Peter Jones; Fig. 10–11, 267, Institute of Human Origins; Fig. 10–12a,b, 268, Institute of Human Origins; Fig. 10–13,